SLAVE
AGAINST
SLAVE

SLAVE AGAINST SLAVE

Plantation Violence
in the Old South

JEFF FORRET

Winner of the
FREDERICK DOUGLASS
BOOK PRIZE

LOUISIANA STATE UNIVERSITY PRESS
BATON ROUGE

Published by Louisiana State University Press
www.lsupress.org

Copyright © 2015 by Louisiana State University Press
All rights reserved. Except in the case of brief quotations used in articles or reviews, no part of this publication may be reproduced or transmitted in any format or by any means without written permission of Louisiana State University Press.

Louisiana Paperback Edition, 2020

Designer: Mandy McDonald Scallan
Typeface: Sentinel

Portions of this text first appeared in "Conflict and the 'Slave Community': Violence among Slaves in Upcountry South Carolina," *Journal of Southern History* 74 (August 2008): 551–588; "'He Was No Man Attall'?: Slave Men, Honor, Violence, and Masculinity in the Antebellum South," in *Fathers, Preachers, Rebels, Men: Black Masculinity in U.S. History and Literature, 1820–1945*, ed. Timothy R. Buckner and Peter Caster (Columbus: Ohio State University Press, 2011), 23–40; "Slaves, Sex, and Sin: Adultery, Forced Separation, and Baptist Church Discipline in Middle Georgia," *Slavery & Abolition* 33 (September 2012): 337–358; "Before Angola: Enslaved Prisoners in the Louisiana State Penitentiary," *Louisiana History* 54 (Spring 2013): 133–171; and "'A Slave That Will Steal from a Slave, Is Called *Mean* as *Master*': Thefts and Violence inside Southern Slave Quarters," in *New Directions in Slavery Studies: Commodification, Community, and Comparison*, ed. Jeff Forret and Christine E. Sears (Baton Rouge: Louisiana State University Press, 2015), and are reproduced with permission.

Library of Congress Cataloging-in-Publication Data

Names: Forret, Jeff, 1972– author.
Title: Slave against slave : plantation violence in the Old South / Jeff Forret.
Description: Baton Rouge : Louisiana State University Press, 2020. | Includes bibliographical references and index.
Identifiers: LCCN 2020012439 (print) | LCCN 2020012440 (ebook) | ISBN 978-0-8071-7431-9 (paperback) | ISBN 978-0-8071-6112-8 (pdf) | ISBN 978-0-8071-6113-5 (epub)
Subjects: LCSH: Slaves—Violence against—Southern States—History. | Slaves—Southern States—Social conditions—History. | Slavery—Social aspects—Southern States—History. | Plantation life—Southern States—History.
Classification: LCC E443 .F67 2020 (print) | LCC E443 (ebook) | DDC 303.6086/250975—dc23
LC record available at https://lccn.loc.gov/2020012439
LC ebook record available at https://lccn.loc.gov/2020012440

CONTENTS

Acknowledgments   ix

Introduction: Violence, Community, and Agency in the Slave South   1

Chapter 1.
   Origins, Prevalence, and Patterns   28

Chapter 2.
   Slaves, Masters, Church, and the Civil Law of Slavery   71

Chapter 3.
   Intraracial Slave Homicide and the Criminal Law of Slavery   109

Chapter 4.
   Violence at Work and Play   166

Chapter 5.
   Violence and the Slave Economy   200

Chapter 6.
   Violence in the Creation, Maintenance, and Destruction of Slave Unions   236

Chapter 7.
   Honor, Violence, and Enslaved Masculinity   287

Chapter 8.
   Honor, Violence, and Enslaved Femininity   332

Epilogue: "Black-on-Black Violence" in Historical Perspective   384

Appendix: Intraracial Slave Homicides in Virginia, 1777–1864   397
Notes   405
Bibliography   489
Index   521

TABLES

I.1. Slave Population and Slaves as a Percentage of the Total Population, Upcountry South Carolina, 1830–1860 11
I.2. Slaves and Slaveholders in the South Carolina Upcountry, 1860 12
I.3. Slave Population of Selected Middle Georgia Counties, 1790–1860 13
I.4. Slave Population of the Northern Territories and States, 1790–1840 14

1.1. Slave-Slave Crimes as a Percentage of Total Slave Crimes in Six Georgia Counties 48
1.2. Homicide Rates for African American Victims in Virginia, 1790–1863 49
1.3. Homicide Inquest Rates for African American Victims in Edgefield and Horry Districts, South Carolina 51
1.4. Slave-Slave Murder-Victim Combinations in Virginia, 1777–1864 53
1.5. Slave-Slave Murder-Victim Combinations in Virginia, 1777–1864, Less Infanticides and Child Murders 53
1.6. Murderers and Victims of Intraracial Slave Homicides by Sex and Age, Virginia, 1777–1864 56
1.7. Intraracial Slave Homicides by Sex of the Assailant, Virginia, 1777–1864 57
1.8. Intraracial Slave Homicides by Year and by Decade, Virginia, 1777–1864 58
1.9. Intraracial Slave Homicide Convictions by Month of Trial, Virginia, 1777–1864 59
1.10. Intraracial Slave Homicide Convictions by County, Region, and Percentage of Total Slave Population, Virginia, 1777–1864 62–63

2.1. Slave Membership in Baptist Churches as a Percentage of the Population in Two Georgia Counties, 1860 96

3.1. Dispensations of Slave-Slave Violence Cases in Three Locations 119
3.2. Number of Lashes Inflicted as Punishment for Intraracial Slave Violence in Antebellum South Carolina 124
3.3. Selected List of Georgia Slaves Charged with the Murder of Other Slaves, 1813–1849 128
3.4. Age of Convicted Slave-Slave Murderers Awaiting Sale and Transportation in the Virginia State Penitentiary 139

TABLES

3.5. Duration of Convicted Slave-Slave Murderers' Stays in the Virginia State Penitentiary 140

3.6. Selected Slaves Sold and Transported Out of the Virginia State Penitentiary for Killing Other Slaves 142

3.7. Sample Transactions between the Commonwealth of Virginia and Slave Traders for Slaves Sold and Transported Out of the State Penitentiary 143

3.8. Virginia Courts of Oyer and Terminer Valuations of Slaves Convicted of Killing Other Slaves, 1777–1864 145

3.9. Enslaved Prisoners in the Louisiana State Penitentiary Convicted of Killing Other Slaves, 1835–1862 149

8.1. Sentences and Punishments of Convicted Female Murderers in Virginia, 1796–1864 339

8.2. Virginia Infanticide and Child Murder Victims by Sex, 1799–1860 375

8.3. Ages of Female Slaves in Virginia Convicted of Murder 379

E.1. Racial Distribution of Selected Violent Crimes in Texas, 1865–1868 388

ACKNOWLEDGMENTS

NINE YEARS ELAPSED from the time I began researching this book intensively in 2005 until the completion of the manuscript. Over the better part of a decade, I incurred a number of intellectual debts to an army of scholars and colleagues, librarians and archivists, many of whom I am fortunate enough to count not merely as professional acquaintances but also as friends. I am pleased to acknowledge here what I sincerely hope is a complete accounting of those individuals.

The first note of thanks goes to Peter Kolchin, who immediately recognized the value of this project after I stumbled upon the idea while researching court records for a previous book. From the beginning, Peter has always stood at the ready to read drafts of conference papers. As the manuscript took shape, he shouldered the added burden of becoming the first person to read the work in its entirety. John Boles, former editor of the *Journal of Southern History*, became an early champion of my research when some were not so willing. Also valuable in this project's infancy was Dylan Penningroth, who generously offered to sacrifice his anonymity as a reader for the manuscript I submitted to the *Journal of Southern History*. His true identity exposed, his correspondence with me proved fruitful in the formative stages of the project. Peter, John, and Vernon Burton regularly wrote letters on my behalf as I pursued monies to conduct research, and I apologize to them publicly for abusing their kind natures. Encyclopedia articles written at the invitation of Vernon, Ed Baptist, and Charles Reagan Wilson gave shape to my thoughts on slave violence and forced me to commit ideas to paper. Prior to beginning my labors at the Library of Virginia, Philip J. Schwarz offered useful advice on where to begin the herculean task of researching a topic that is not indexed. And almost from the inception of the book, I have benefited from lively and substantive conversations with Larry McDonnell and Kathy Hilliard, whom I always look forward to seeing.

Several scholars generously provided thoughtful commentary, conversation, and questions to ponder as I presented various portions of this book in embryonic form at conferences in the United States and in England. John Boles, Randal Hall, graduate students at Rice University, and others who attended the January 2007 meeting of the Houston Area Southern Historians (HASH) participated in the first public discussion of this work and prodded me to consider aspects

ACKNOWLEDGMENTS

of slave violence that took me years to answer with any degree of precision or coherence. Ed Balleisen and Christine Sears offered helpful remarks on my work regarding the slave economy; Brenda Stevenson, James Sidbury, Christine Heyrman, Dylan Penningroth, John Storey, Eric Kimball, Calvin Schermerhorn, and Ben Schiller on various aspects of the enslaved family. During two trips to present my work in England, Bob Elder, Tim Lockley, Lydia Plath, Sergio Lussana, and Becky Fraser aided my thinking about honor, masculinity, and femininity. Todd Hagstette and John Mayfield offered useful remarks as I wrote an article for their edited anthology on southern honor. Tim, Lydia, and Marianne Fisher-Giorlando shared fruits of their own research beneficial to my project. Paul Finkelman's keen observations spared me at least two embarrassing errors in my research on female slave murderers and gender identity. I also greatly appreciate the input from all audience members at the conferences I attended and Alecia Long's prompt replies to all questions New Orleans. Last but certainly not least, Ed Baptist twice gave a critical reading to the entire manuscript. Although I could not follow through on all of his recommendations, the manuscript still improved substantially as a result of his input, and I am grateful for his investment in the project.

An array of librarians and archivists helped me track down the elusive materials exploited for this study. Although it is impossible to name them all, I do wish to highlight some by name. Minor Weisiger got my research at the Library of Virginia off to a good start, and the entire staff there fielded my onslaught of questions and handled requests for governors' papers and other manuscript materials with grace and ease. Steve Tuttle and Marion C. Chandler at the South Carolina Department of Archives and History, Graham Duncan at the South Caroliniana Library, Dale Couch and John Harvey at the Georgia Archives, and Ed Esau at the Historic Natchez Foundation all deserve special mention. Thanks as well go to Mimi Miller in Natchez, Clinton Bagley at the Mississippi Department of Archives and History, Irene Wainwright at the New Orleans Public Library, Linda McCurdy at Duke University's Perkins Library, Taffey Hall at the Southern Baptist Historical Library and Archives, and Dave Nelson at the State Library and Archives of Florida. Theresa Hefner-Babb, government documents librarian at Lamar University, relentlessly pursued answers to arcane legal questions of mine, and Lamar's interlibrary loan staff filled an enormous number of requests for materials not present in the university's holdings. The staff members on weekend duty in the basement of Rice University's Fondren Library helped me locate some of the more obscure published sources used herein.

ACKNOWLEDGMENTS

Fortuitous encounters in the archives made friends out of strangers. I give a particular nod to Bob Elder and Erica Bruchko. Upon first meeting Todd Hagstette, he immediately shared with me an image of black violence that, through sheer coincidence, he just happened to be carrying with him at the time. The kindness and generosity of us southern historians sequestered together in the archives is really quite special.

My travels to archives and conferences would not have been possible without the financial support of others. Two travel grants from the Institute for Southern Studies permitted journeys to Columbia, South Carolina, for research at the state archives and on the campus of the University of South Carolina. I thank Thomas J. Brown and Bob Ellis for viewing my project favorably. Between 2006 and 2009, Lamar University awarded me a pair of Research Enhancement Grants and Faculty Development Leaves that liberated me to complete my research in Virginia, Georgia, Mississippi, Louisiana, and Texas. Under the leadership, first, of chairs John Storey and, later, Mary Scheer, departmental monies secured for me several reels of microfilm from the Georgia Archives and made conference travel possible, even after economic times were no longer so flush. Dean Brenda Nichols and Lamar's Office of Sponsored Programs were always ready to lend their support when unexpected invitations to speak at conferences arose. They underwrote my journeys to conferences in England that were valuable in the shaping of the book. I also owe a note of gratitude to Mimi Tangum for her valiant efforts in helping me secure outside funding for this book. Despite her labors, our efforts were technically unsuccessful; however, with some irony, I am compelled to thank all of those anonymous individuals whose comments accompanied their rejections of my fellowship applications. Whether they deemed the project wrongheaded, inappropriate, or foolhardy even to attempt given the evidentiary base, their hostility toward the undertaking only made the final product stronger than it would have been without their criticisms, as they exposed the idiosyncratic ways in which the literate public might misread, misunderstand, or misconstrue my actual meaning.

Within the Lamar University history department, Jimmy L. Bryan Jr. organized a brown bag lunch series through which faculty members share their research with colleagues. Though their fields lie outside my area of expertise, Jimmy, Rebecca Boone, Mark Mengerink, and Yasuko Sato attended these events when schedules permitted and shared their reactions to my work. Early on in my research, I talked much about slave violence with Tom Reid, who had the misfortune of occupying the office directly across the hall from mine.

ACKNOWLEDGMENTS

Robert Robertson read the HASH paper I first prepared on the topic of slave violence and, furthermore, chauffered Nancy Zey and me to Houston while battling both traffic and poor visibility on a particularly soggy January night.

Several Lamar students aided me at different points in my research. Leah Sims, an obsessive hoarder of primary source documents, shared all the examples of slave violence she had encountered while perusing eighteenth- and nineteenth-century newspapers, and Melanie Almufti helped with the statistical analysis of Georgia Baptist church records, offering independent verification of my number crunching. Students Misty Bernal, Danny Young, the late Paul Reid, and the late Tom Caraway performed other worthwhile chores for this work's benefit. Patty Renfro, administrative associate in the history department, did her usual stellar job in keeping me well supplied with all the materials needed for writing, storing, and printing off the book as it progressed.

Rand Dotson, my editor at LSU Press, lent immediate support to this project when it was only a vague idea confined to the nether reaches of my cranium. For his faith in me and patience I am grateful.

Saving the best for last, my family. My wife Sharon made the mistake of marrying a man whose job has no set hours and who is pathologically addicted to undertaking multiple and simultaneous academic endeavors. Because research and especially writing are such inherently insular activities, the one person who, for whatever constellation of unfathomable reasons, willingly chose to spend her life with me was book-widowed for some time. We spent weeks apart as I conducted research and, in the eighteen months that it took to write and revise the manuscript, lived our lives in isolation even when we occupied the same room. This great test of her patience and endurance has mercifully drawn to a close.

The most welcome diversion throughout the entire process has been our son Gabriel. From his first appearance into this world, Gabe's schedule determined mine. Fortunately for the book, by the time I began writing, he had developed good sleeping habits. Jamie Hudson, Kati Hicks, Debbie Mikulencak, and Jo Brewster of the Woodcrest Mother's Day Out program, as well as Nikki Bland, gave this father several hours on the laptop with full confidence that Gabe was in good hands. Ultimately, Gabe's arrival instilled in me the rigid discipline necessary to bring this project to completion, and I thank him for that. Although the book might have been finished somewhat sooner without him, my life would be infinitely emptier absent the daily, unanticipated joys of fatherhood. To him I dedicate this work, eagerly awaiting the day when he will be capable of reading the words himself.

SLAVE AGAINST SLAVE

INTRODUCTION
Violence, Community, and Agency in the Slave South

TRAGEDY AND DEATH befell the Warren County, Mississippi, plantation of Lawrence Clark in 1846. One July night, Clark "was roused from his sleep by a cry of distress." Clark hastened through the darkness to the origin of the commotion, some "half of a mile from his house." There, "he found his slave" David "injured badly," the victim of a stabbing perpetrated by Lewis, another of Clark's bondmen. "O my people," David uttered in his last moments. David's master interpreted the slave's dying words as a simple request to see those who meant most to him. Although David "said nothing else which indicated his apprehension of immediate death," he was quite possibly convinced of his imminent demise. But whom, precisely, did David consider his "people"? Was he referring only to the closest of loved ones? To immediate or extended family? Or possibly to fellow residents and fictive kin in the slave quarters? Perhaps to friends and relatives on nearby holdings throughout the local neighborhood? Or to a broader community of black people similarly held in bondage? And how did Lewis slot into David's understanding of humanity? Did David's enslaved murderer qualify as one of his "people"? Answers to these questions, impossible to ascertain from extant evidence, would prove meaningful. As David slipped out of this life, was he, as his master believed, summoning "my people" so that he might gaze upon them one last time? Or was he instead anticipating spiritual reunion with a religious community in the afterlife? Or offering social commentary, a final lament for the counterparts in bondage whom he was leaving behind? Drawing upon hundreds of similar incidents of intraracial violence, this book uses episodes of conflict between and among slaves as a window into slave life and culture in the American South.[1]

The slaveholding South was synonymous with violence. Historians have long confirmed that the physical violence permeating southern society was a distinguishing feature of the region. Scholarship shows that whites of all socioeconomic stripes engaged in violent acts. Southern gentlemen participated in honorific duels; lower-class whites fought rough-and-tumble brawls and eye-gouging matches; and masters wielded the whip to "correct" their slaves, exert dominion over their chattel, and perpetuate the institution of bondage.[2] But whites held no monopoly on the exercise of violence in the American South. Slaves engaged in violent, aggressive behaviors as well. Given the broad framework of violence in which they lived, it could hardly have been otherwise. When subjected by whites to excessive punishment or arbitrary, capricious treatment, they occasionally struck back in individual acts of violent confrontation, and on very rare occasion, they rose up in concerted, coordinated rebellions against white authority.[3] Whereas these episodes have gained scholarly notice, historians have granted scant attention to the frequent physical confrontations internal to the slave quarters. A book-length investigation of the violence that erupted between and among bondpeople themselves is long overdue.

For decades, the trajectory of slave scholarship militated against any such study. More than any other single work of its time, Stanley M. Elkins's seminal *Slavery: A Problem in American Institutional and Intellectual Life* (1959) determined the course in which slave studies headed, primarily by serving as the analytical punching bag for an entire generation of historians. Drawing upon an analogy to Nazi concentration camps, Elkins argued that the institution of bondage created in the American South a uniquely oppressive, "closed" system of slavery. A major consequence was the imposition upon slaves of a distinct, uniform personality type: the docile, harmless, and childlike Sambo. According to the Elkins thesis, the infantilized Sambo happily submitted to the absolute power of the master and molded to the owner's will. The controversy that Elkins ignited triggered a fierce and overwhelming backlash that shaped the contours of historical inquiry. Subsequent scholars refuted the notion that slavery reduced African Americans held in bondage to Sambos. Foremost among Elkins's critics was John W. Blassingame, who argued that the Sambo stereotype was not the dominant personality type among slaves but, rather, merely one in an entire "range of personality types." Moreover, Blassingame demonstrated that Sambo was a mask—a role that slaves performed for masters' edification—and that slaves could *play* Sambo without *being* Sambo. The submissive Sambo, Blassingame clarified, was indeed real in that slaves ritually expressed deference to their owners, but Sambo-like behavior did not signal any genuine psychic damage inflicted by the institution of slavery. For slaves, acting like Sambo served as a defense mechanism, allowing them to cope with the oppression of bondage.[4]

Although *The Slave Community* did not generate an immediate sensation when first published in 1972, it soon emerged as one of the classic works in the

INTRODUCTION

historiography of American slavery. In his rejection of the Sambo thesis, Blassingame not only provided a necessary corrective but also contributed to a fundamental reorientation of slave scholarship. Increasingly, historians in the early 1970s and beyond looked at slavery from the perspective of the bondpeople themselves. They recognized slaves not as passive objects of white treatment but as active agents in shaping their own lives. An entire generation of scholars demonstrated its intellectual debt to Blassingame as it emphasized in increasingly sophisticated studies the ways in which slaves' close familial networks, religious beliefs and gatherings, and rich culture insulated those in bondage from the brutal excesses of enslavement and helped them resist dehumanization.[5]

Nearly lost in the new historiographical thrust, however, were the stresses and strains inherent in the enslaved condition. By the early 1980s, historian Peter Kolchin observed that the conceptual misuse and abuse of Blassingame's work had produced a developing portrait of antebellum slavery that "present[ed] an exaggerated picture of the strength and cohesion of the slave community." The scholarship's "celebratory tone" and emphasis on the positive steps slaves took to cope with bondage often overlooked the harsh realities of their condition. Conceptually, the "slave community" had come to convey an artificial sense of solidarity and lack of division in the quarters. Kolchin cautioned students of slavery against the glorification of a harmonious, idyllic slave community virtually devoid of conflict, but it would still be some time before most academics heeded his advice.[6]

Ample evidence abounds challenging the overstated emphasis on communal solidarity among slaves. There was nothing easy or automatic about the formation of a slave community. Communities of any sort are necessarily the products of creative processes, and a number of factors posed obstacles to the construction of a viable slave community. In the colonial era, sex ratios heavily skewed in favor of slave men stymied the formation of slave families. Bondpeople's physical alienation from Africa, the disruption of their established kin networks, and the influx of Africans of varying ethnicities and rival tribes prevented any smooth transfer of culture, preserved fully intact, from one continent to another. Throughout the age of slavery, the spatial distribution of slaves and the density of the slave population also militated against the forging of a slave community. It proved particularly difficult to establish communal solidarity on small plantations of fewer than twenty slaves, where bondpeople faced virtually constant supervision by whites and labored under the watchful eyes of resident masters who routinely interfered with life in the quarters. Under such conditions, slaves lacked the independence to create an autonomous community of their own making. And some slaves were simply loners who rejected community membership altogether.[7]

Cleavages among bondpeople themselves only magnified the fragility of the slave community. Even as the "slave community" became entrenched in the literature, historians—including, ironically, John W. Blassingame himself—recognized an undercurrent of division among slaves. The slave community was in fact riven with strife, and slaves admitted as much in their narratives and autobiographies. Whether for reasons of "character, color, condition, or the superior importance of the respective masters," wrote successful runaway Henry Bibb, "[t]he distinction among slaves is as marked, as the classes of society are in any aristocratic community." Slaves sought to fill deep, emotional longings when they scrounged for scraps of status and distinction however they might. Some satisfied cravings for superiority over neighboring bondpeople on the basis of their masters' wealth and prestige relative to less affluent slaveholders. Even within the confines of a single plantation, a few bragged over the elevated purchase price the owner sacrificed to acquire them or the generous offers for them that the master rejected. Anytime a slave owner inequitably distributed rewards or provided opportunities to some slaves but not others, the beneficiaries might lord their preferential treatment over fellow bondpeople. "[S]ometimes," explained an exasperated Alabama planter, slaves even killed one another after "being supplanted by a rival in the confidence of the master or overseer."[8]

On large holdings of more than fifty slaves, the occupational distinction between house servants and field hands bred resentment and conflict. Domestic servants considered themselves the "slave aristocracy" and often adopted an attitude of superiority toward their lowly, hardworking counterparts laboring in the fields. Their lofty position in the plantation hierarchy often informed courtship decisions. According to former slave Rosa Starke of South Carolina, "A house nigger man might swoop down and mate wid a field hand's good lookin' daughter, now and then, for pure love of her, but you never see a house gal lower herself by marryin' and matin' wid a common field-hand nigger." Field slaves reciprocated by regarding house servants with resentment, suspicion, and mistrust for appearing too closely allied with and loyal to the master.[9] Likewise, the occupational hierarchy slaves constructed held black drivers in low esteem. Appointed by some slaveholders, especially in the lowcountry, slave drivers found themselves in the psychologically stressful position of having to enforce the master's dictates by directing the labor of their fellow bondpeople and punishing them as required.

INTRODUCTION

Drivers who did the master's bidding too eagerly or too aggressively risked alienation in the quarters.[10] At the opposite end of the hierarchy, slaves conferred status on skilled craftsmen, preachers, healers, and benevolent, well-intentioned conjurors, all of whom demonstrated their usefulness to fellow slaves in one form or another. Rosa Starke outlined the many "classes 'mongst de slaves," as she remembered them, to her Works Progress Administration (WPA) interviewer:

> De fust class was de house servants. Dese was de butler, de maids, de nurses, chambermaids, and de cooks. De nex' class was de carriage drivers and de gardeners, de carpenters, de barber, and the stable men. Then come de nex' class de wheelwright, wagoners, blacksmiths and slave foremen. De nex' class I 'members was de cow men and de niggers dat have care of de dogs. All dese have good houses and never have to work hard or git a beatin'. Then come de cradlers of de wheat, de threshers, and de millers of de corn and de wheat, and de feeders of de cotton gin. De lowest class was de common field niggers.

The occupational stratification evident on larger plantations was often correlated with skin color. Lighter-complected slaves, who were also more likely to serve as house servants, sometimes took pride in their white ancestry. Possibly the offspring or other blood relation of the master, they sometimes internalized white standards and ranked themselves superior to darker-skinned slaves.[11]

The possible sources of social distance between slaves were many. In his examination of runaway advertisements in South Carolina, Michael P. Johnson detected "two distinct slave communities," one urban and one rural. In the city, he argued, slaves' closer proximity to whites and their regular contact with them during normal work routines meant that white culture exerted a greater influence on the urban slave community, whereas in the countryside, an African American creole culture more openly hostile toward whites flourished.[12] Other historians have taken slaves' lack of collective resistance in the American South and their willingness to betray runaways to white authorities as reliable indicators of "the relative weakness of the slaves' collective mentality."[13] Several scholars, in short, have recognized multiple rifts and sources of conflict among slaves. As Bertram Wyatt-Brown summarized, "Deep mistrust and rivalry rent the harmony of the slave quarters."[14]

Nevertheless, the powerful "slave community" paradigm had taken on a life of its own. Assessing the state of the field, Peter Kolchin explained that the literature on slavery had veered "dangerously close to replacing a mythical world in which slaves were objects of total control with an equally mythical world in which slaves were hardly slaves at all." By the mid-1980s, one observer lamented that "[t]he dark side of community remains unexplored by historians of the slave community." A couple of years later, Wyatt-Brown noted that scholars had rediscovered "the darker side . . . but generally . . . place the emphasis on the remarkable endurance and even joyousness that slaves extracted from harsh conditions." By 1993, Kolchin could still write accurately that "the grubby reality of day-to-day social relations in the quarters—with all the conflicts and jealousies that inevitably exist in human relations even under the best of circumstances—has been almost totally unexplored by historians interested in demonstrating the vitality of the slave community."[15]

Beginning in the 1990s, historians finally began to investigate the fissures within the slave community with an unprecedented level of sophistication. Brenda E. Stevenson and, later, Christopher Morris explored unrest within slave families, Dylan C. Penningroth the conflicts engendered by the slave economy. As Penningroth pointedly observed, "There is no reason to think that the black community in the 1800s was any more harmonious than the white community." With the sanitized "slave community" becoming more and more anachronistic by the first decade of the twenty-first century, Anthony E. Kaye proposed an alternative analytical framework. Based on his examination of Southern Claims Commission records, Kaye discovered that slaves spoke in terms of "neighborhood" rather than "community" when describing their landscape of solidarity. For slaves, the concept of neighborhood embraced both social and geographic components. A neighborhood consisted of adjoining plantations in which groups of slaves lived, worked, traded, and forged social networks of kinship and friendship. The boundaries of neighborhood generally conformed to masters' plantation boundaries but remained continually in flux as slaves negotiated relationships and collective identities among themselves. In contrast to the universal solidarity implicit in the idea of a "slave community," the concept of neighborhood Kaye described was infused with a "sense of place." Through the process of neighborhood formation, Kaye explained, slaves "laid a groundwork for solidarity" among a selected group of bondpeople. Hence, slaves cultivated not a single, unified slave "community" but a multiplicity of neighborhoods. Consequently, when they viewed runaways with suspicion and refused to aid them, it was not because they shunned some nebulous "slave community" but because the fugitive was a stranger and not a member of their particular neighborhood.[16]

INTRODUCTION

This book contributes to the ongoing redefinition and refinement of the southern slave community by building on the work of Stevenson, Morris, Penningroth, Kaye, and others and taking it to its logical conclusion. Episodes of physical violence afford the most overt evidence of the divisions and disputes that wracked the quarters. Yet no comprehensive investigation of these incidents exists to parallel the thorough examinations of violence committed by southern whites or the interracial conflicts symptomatic of slaveholding southern society. To be sure, slaves did love, cooperate, and combat oppression. The point is not to deny any sense of communal solidarity among bondpeople but to probe the limits of that cohesion in an effort to remedy a distorted, incomplete view of the slave past. Slaves sometimes did lash out at friends and family members, beat or kill one another, or commit sexual assaults. Acknowledging as much is not to impugn the offender or levy moral judgment. Nor is it to imply anything innately racial, pathological, or dysfunctional, as a previous generation of scholars might have suggested. What it instead offers is an opportunity to unlock a neglected aspect of the slave experience and to plumb the ways in which the condition of slavery itself bred violence. As Ned Blackhawk's work on Native Americans in the Great Basin has shown, violence functions as a useful category of analysis or interpretive lens for understanding the "historical landscapes" of subaltern peoples. In the context of the slaveholding South, an examination of the violence committed by and exacted upon bondpeople promises to recover the misery and "tragedy of slavery" missing from so much of the post–*Slave Community* scholarship.[17]

If this book further complicates discussions of the "slave community," it also has bearing on questions of slave agency. Walter Johnson levied a brief but devastating critique of scholars who take evidence of slaves' agency in their own lives, "indexed by the presence of acts of self-determination," as a sign of bondpeople's fundamental humanity. Admittedly, on one level, the study of intraracial violence does precisely that. To overlook the presence of violent conflicts in the quarters is not only misleading historically but also wrongly elevates all slaves to virtual sainthood. This study asks readers to accept, if not necessarily embrace, the totality of bondpeople's humanity, replete with an entire spectrum of emotions and a range of responses to the circumstances they confronted in bondage. As Peter Kolchin observed, slaves were indeed "human beings" who "exhibited the full panoply of human failings, including their share of theft, violence, jealousy, deceit, wife beating, and child abuse." These are precisely the facets of slave life that this book examines. Johnson, however, challenges historians to go still deeper. It is no great feat, he wrote, to discover the obvious point that slaves were human; the more difficult task is to uncover the lived experiences and "condition of enslaved humanity," "to imagine a history of slavery which sees the lives of enslaved people as powerfully conditioned by, though not reducible to, their slavery." The chapters that follow attempt to fulfill this ambitious vision, illustrating the ways in which the law's failure to recognize slave marriages, the domestic slave trade, and other external forces help explain a substantial portion of the conflicts that erupted among bondpeople. Johnson furthermore cautions scholars to avoid equating agency with resistance to the institution of slavery. In the coming pages, slaves contend not with masters, overseers, and whites generally but with other slaves. They betray, fight with, murder, and cheat on one another, and they express agency with knives, fists, and fence rails. Choosing one's victim and committing violent acts upon other slaves mark, from a historiographical perspective, unflattering and unconventional forms of agency. Nevertheless, through the prism of violence we may successfully, as Johnson urges, "re-immerse ourselves in the nightmare of History."[18]

The project of deromanticization necessarily involves delving as deeply into slaves' private lives as possible, to peer, almost voyeuristically, into the hostilities, disagreements, and physical confrontations endemic to the slave quarters. Spying through cracks in slave cabin walls, prying into slaves' most intimate and vulnerable moments, and eavesdropping to gather shards of illicit conversation combine to capture the emotional intensity and complexity of life under bondage. Sparing no topic as taboo, this study exposes slave life marred by fragmentation, dissent, and turmoil; at times, it even provides a glimpse of the sordid and depraved. With only a careless, superficial glance, a few readers may leap to the conclusion that this work must be a conservative or, more accurately, reactionary diatribe chronicling black foibles and criminality from centuries past to resuscitate discredited scholarship antedating *The Slave Community*. Those anticipating racist polemics will be sorely disappointed, however. At the very least, the book may be misconstrued as grossly impolitic, but scholars ought not permit the expectation of political correctness to become burdensome by obstructing scholarly inquiry. However uncomfortable or politically charged the subject matter, cowing to societal pressure or fears of academic censure and rebuke accomplishes nothing but the perpetuation of a warped and incomplete understanding of the past. Historians, of all people, cannot allow themselves to revel in blissful ignorance. Walter Johnson wrote a stinging condemnation of academics content merely "to make [them]selves feel better and more righteous rather than to make the world better or more righteous." Genuine justice for bondpeople demands the

INTRODUCTION

fullest possible accounting of slaves' lives, warts and all. Only then do the true costs of bondage come into clearest possible focus.[19]

Recovering incidents of violence among slaves is a laborious task. Such episodes are elusive: no doubt the vast majority of them went unrecorded. If slaves belonging to the same master attacked one another, that master rarely had any legal recourse or justification for hauling the slave aggressor to court. Slaves, however, sometimes fought with bondpeople from nearby plantations. Masters might ignore such conflicts if any wounds inflicted were minor, and if they intervened at all, owners of the participants involved often handled such matters privately, without resorting to the court system. For trivial offenses, only the most litigious of masters utilized the courts for purposes of slave discipline. When slaves held by different masters severely injured or maimed one another, though, or in any case of homicide, slaveholders often pursued redress through formal legal channels, leaving a paper trail for scholars to follow. But because most violent confrontations between slaves never became a matter of public record, the total number of intraracial violence cases in the slaveholding South is certainly drastically underreported. Slaves surface in southern court records far more often for assaulting or murdering not fellow bondpeople but rather neighborhood whites. This is not surprising since slave codes across the South demonstrated a much stronger interest in prosecuting bondpeople for transgressions committed against white persons and property than upon others in bondage. A far greater proportion of all slaves who physically assaulted a white person would therefore face legal action, compared to only a small fraction who attacked another slave. Given the nature of the cases that appeared before southern courts of law, the sheer numbers hardly prove conclusively that slaves did, in fact, assault whites more frequently than other bondpeople.

The major advantage of court cases is that they enable us to hear not only from masters and other white witnesses to intraracial violence but also from the slaves themselves. Court transcripts give voice to slaves. Their depositions and testimony, recorded verbatim or nearly so, speak to the circumstances surrounding violence inside the slave quarters and supply insight into the motivations driving those assaults. By definition, slave violence cases that appeared in court were exceptional, usually the consequence of a fatality. Murder cases expose in starkest relief the fissures concealed inside the slave community. The emphasis on intraracial slave homicides is unproblematic for our purposes, however, because the motivations for the violence were consistent—indeed, identical—

whether or not the conflict turned deadly. All that differed was the magnitude and severity of the attack. This study therefore exploits a wide range of court records to gain access to slaves' violent encounters with one another.

The most accessible records, those of the state Supreme Courts, are an adequate place to begin, but a vastly richer trove of cases may be found at the county level. Slave violence cases only made it to the state Supreme Courts when they raised a pressing, substantive legal question. Most did not and were easily dispensed with by the various local courts summoned to administer justice in such cases. Slaves appeared before these lower courts routinely throughout the South, but some former slaveholding states better lend themselves to study. Virginia easily contains the most thorough, best preserved, and centralized collection of lower court records available in a former slaveholding state. Slaves charged with crimes, violent or nonviolent, against persons or property, appeared before county Courts of Oyer and Terminer convened on an ad hoc basis. These slave court records were neither preserved nor indexed separately but, rather, are buried within the regular county court proceedings. The Library of Virginia houses an embarrassment of judicial riches: to investigate each county's court records would take a team of historians a lifetime. To make the task more manageable, I first turned to the state auditor's records of slaves condemned to execution or transportation out of the United States in order to identify the slave-slave violence cases that resulted in fatalities and which ended in convictions of the accused. Backtracking through the legal process, I next consulted the county court order books and governors' papers in search of transcripts of the cases. By a Virginia law of 1801, county courts were required to submit the testimony from capital cases to the governor and council of the Commonwealth for a possible commutation of sentence or outright pardon. Only on rare occasion did courts not follow this process as prescribed by law. In 1860, the clerk of the Madison County court neglected to transmit a record of the trial of Philip for the death of Alfred, citing the large number of witnesses and the time and expense involved in committing the copious testimony to paper. A small number of other transcripts appear not to have survived. Testimony from most cases, however, may be found in either the county court order books, the governors' papers, or both. Using this information, I have assembled a database of 145 slaves from across the Commonwealth who murdered 142 fellow bondpeople from 1777 to 1864. (See the appendix.) Although not a complete catalogue of all slave-slave murders during the period, it is the most thorough database of cases from Virginia assembled to date.[20]

In South Carolina, slaves formally accused of crimes appeared before the local Courts of Magistrates and Freeholders. Trial papers survive from fourteen

INTRODUCTION

Table I.1. Slave Population and Slaves as a Percentage of the Total Population, Upcountry South Carolina, 1830–1860

	1830	1840	1850	1860
Anderson	4,427 (26%)	5,683 (31%)	7,514 (35%)	8,425 (37%)
Laurens	7,243 (35%)	8,911 (41%)	11,953 (51%)	13,200 (55%)
Pickens	2,866 (20%)	2,715 (19%)	3,679 (22%)	4,195 (21%)
Spartanburg	4,927 (23%)	5,687 (24%)	8,039 (30%)	8,240 (31%)
Total	19,463 (26%)	22,996 (29%)	31,185 (35%)	34,060 (37%)
Statewide	315,401 (54%)	327,038 (55%)	384,984 (58%)	402,406 (57%)

Source: Historical Census Browser, University of Virginia, Geospatial and Statistical Data Center (2004): http://fisher.lib.virginia.edu/collections/stats/histcensus/index.html.

antebellum South Carolina districts, with the bulk of the evidence on slave-slave violence found in the four upcountry districts of Anderson (including the former district of Pendleton), Laurens, Pickens, and Spartanburg. Upcountry South Carolina was different from other regions within the state. Whereas the coastal lowcountry had long maintained a "black majority," in the remote northwestern corner of the state, slaves comprised an unusually distinct minority of the population in all districts except Laurens; slaveholding was not widespread; the typical master owned few slaves; and, notwithstanding those in Laurens, farms were generally modest in size, tending to produce grains rather than cotton. (See tables I.1 and I.2.) Even in an upcountry setting characterized by a white majority, small holdings, and a diversified agricultural economy, Court of Magistrates and Freeholders records document no fewer than seventy-five incidents of violence among slaves in antebellum South Carolina serious enough to warrant litigation.[21]

Compared to the South Carolina upcountry, Middle Georgia was a region more thoroughly committed to slavery, as shown in table I.3. Between 1790 and 1860, Middle Georgia transitioned from a slave-importing region to a slave-exporting one. The number of slaves in a sample of seven Middle Georgia counties, settled in the late eighteenth and early nineteenth centuries, increased reliably up to 1820. Beginning in the 1820s, however, the domestic slave trade carried substantial numbers of Middle Georgia bondpeople to other parts of the state as well as to the burgeoning cotton frontier of the Old Southwest. The 1860 census revealed that the slave population of the seven selected counties had increased by only 2,600 bondpeople during the preceding 4 decades, while their percentage of the state's total slave population declined from 27 percent to 9. Inferior court

Table I.2. Slaves and Slaveholders in the South Carolina Upcountry, 1860

No. Slaves	No. Slaveholders			
	Anderson	Laurens	Pickens	Spartanburg
1	180	144	109	199
2	144	100	58	110
3	92	80	38	94
4	101	68	52	65
5	82	61	34	62
% 5 or fewer	54%	41%	55%	53%
6	64	56	37	45
7	71	46	25	54
8	58	46	25	45
9	37	53	25	36
% 9 or fewer	75%	60%	76%	71%
10–19	189	266	88	198
% less than 20	92%	84%	93%	90%
100+	0	5	0	2
No. slaveholders	1,103	1,093	529	1,007
No. slaves	8,425	13,200	4,195	8,240
Avg. slaves/master	7.6	12.1	7.9	8.2

Source: Joseph C. G. Kennedy, *Agriculture of the United States in 1860; Compiled from the Original Returns of the Eighth Census, Under the Direction of the Secretary of the Interior,* vol. 2 Agriculture (Washington: Government Printing Office, 1864), 237.

records from the five counties of Baldwin, Hancock, Jones, Lincoln, and Putnam provide a glimpse of slave criminality in a region known for plantation agriculture and where, after 1830, slaves comprised a majority of the total population.

On the cotton frontier of Mississippi, slaves toiling on sprawling plantations comprised an even greater proportion of the total population. By the 1840 census, slaves made up a slight majority of all people living in the Magnolia State. This study examines cases from several scattered Mississippi counties but focuses most intensely on that of Adams, nestled in the southwestern corner of the state, along the banks of the Mississippi River. Founded in 1799, Adams County was the oldest in Mississippi and already by 1840 the home of long-established, prosper-

INTRODUCTION

Table I.3. Slave Population of Selected Middle Georgia Counties, 1790–1860

County	1790	1800	1810	1820
Baldwin	—	—	2,550 (40%)	4,238 (55%)
Hancock	—	4,835 (33%)	6,456 (48%)	6,863 (54%)
Jones	—	—	2,587 (30%)	6,886 (42%)
Lincoln	—	1,433 (30%)	2,212 (49%)	3,063 (47%)
Putnam	—	—	3,220 (32%)	7,241 (47%)
Screven	—	766 (25%)	1,816 (41%)	1,833 (47%)
Wilkes	7,268 (23%)	5,008 (38%)	7,284 (49%)	9,705 (55%)
Total, 7 counties	7,268 (23%)	12,042 (34%)	26,125 (42%)	39,829 (49%)
Total, Georgia	29,264 (35%)	59,699 (37%)	105,218 (42%)	149,656 (44%)
7 counties' % of total	25	20	25	27

County	1830	1840	1850	1860
Baldwin	4,542 (62%)	4,107 (57%)	4,602 (56%)	4,929 (54%)
Hancock	7,180 (61%)	5,915 (61%)	7,306 (63%)	8,137 (68%)
Jones	6,829 (51%)	5,619 (56%)	6,279 (61%)	5,989 (66%)
Lincoln	3,276 (53%)	3,339 (57%)	3,780 (63%)	3,768 (69%)
Putnam	7,707 (58%)	6,482 (63%)	7,468 (69%)	7,138 (70%)
Screven	2,366 (50%)	2,623 (55%)	3,673 (54%)	4,530 (55%)
Wilkes	8,960 (63%)	6,501 (64%)	8,281 (68%)	7,953 (70%)
Total, 7 counties	40,860 (58%)	34,586 (60%)	41,389 (63%)	42,444 (65%)
Total, Georgia	217,531 (42%)	280,944 (41%)	381,682 (42%)	462,198 (44%)
7 counties' % of total	19	12	11	9

Source: Historical Census Browser, University of Virginia, Geospatial and Statistical Data Center (2004): http://fisher.lib.virginia.edu/collections/stats/histcensus/index.html.

ous, old-money slaveholding families. Slaves comprised roughly three-fourths of all residents by 1830 and, for a time in the antebellum decades, helped make Adams the single wealthiest county in the nation. Perhaps nowhere else in the Old South was cotton any more crucial to the local economy, and the Historic Natchez Foundation has labored strenuously to preserve the records that, for our purposes, supply clues to the violence that broke out among Adams County's bondpeople.[22]

The overwhelming majority of all slaves lived and labored in the rural South,

Table I.4. Slave Population of the Northern Territories and States, 1790–1840

Territory/State	1790	1800	1810	1820	1830	1840
Connecticut	2,648	951	310	97	25	54
Illinois	—	—	—	917	747	331
Indiana	—	—	—	190	3	3
Iowa	—	—	—	—	—	16
Maine	0	0	0	0	2	0
Massachusetts	0	0	0	0	1	0
Michigan	—	—	—	—	32	0
New Hampshire	157	8	0	0	3	1
New Jersey	11,423	12,422	10,851	7,557	2,254	674
New York	21,193	20,613	15,017	10,088	75	4
Ohio	—	—	0	0	6	3
Pennsylvania	3,707	1,706	795	211	403	64
Rhode Island	958	380	108	48	17	5
Vermont	0	0	0	0	0	0
Wisconsin	—	—	—	—	—	11
Total	40,086	36,080	27,081	19,108	3,568	1,166

Source: Historical Census Browser, University of Virginia, Geospatial and Statistical Data Center (2004): http://fisher.lib.virginia.edu/collections/stats/histcensus/index.html.

but the regions under scrutiny here offer some sense of the intraracial violence in a sample of urban areas as well. This study employs records of the Hustings Court of Richmond, Virginia, and other, smaller incorporated areas of that Commonwealth; the Chatham County, Georgia, inferior court, which encompassed within its jurisdiction the town of Savannah and its coastal environs; and the Adams County Courthouse Collection, which includes within its holdings cases from the boisterous river town of Natchez. Natchez-under-the-Hill was a notoriously lawless river port below the high bluffs overlooking the Mississippi River, where the more genteel and sophisticated set resided in graceful and opulent homes. That fugitives from justice from New Orleans sought temporary refuge in Natchez only bolstered the town's unseemly reputation. New Orleans marked the one significant city of the Deep South, so this study also examines, finally, the records of its First District Court, covering the sixteen years from 1846 to 1861.

I have neglected altogether one slaveholding region within the United States: the North. Slavery was a colony-wide institution during the colonial era, and northern bondpeople, like their southern counterparts, occasionally fought or

INTRODUCTION

killed one another. For example, two Massachusetts bondmen, Poro and Gambo, fought in 1750. Gambo delivered his adversary a blow to the head with a stick, inflicting injuries that resulted in his death the following day. Similar cases are difficult to locate among surviving records, however. In the wake of the American Revolution, all northern states outlawed slavery either via their constitutions or through legislation. Although a couple of New England states abolished slavery immediately, most northern legislatures passed gradual emancipation measures instead. As a result, small numbers of slaves could still be found in many northern states as late as the 1840s and later still in New Jersey, the last of the northern states to pass a gradual abolition law. (See table I.4.) While northern slaves certainly battled one another now and then, the time and expense involved in tracking down what is assuredly a small number of cases militated against the inclusion of the northern slaveholding colonies and states.[23]

The North notwithstanding, the broad cross-section of court records employed in this study, cutting across geopolitical boundaries and embracing regions as diverse as the tobacco-producing Virginia Piedmont, the generally small holdings of the South Carolina upcountry, the mature cotton-growing counties of Middle Georgia, the cotton frontier of the Old Southwest, and a variety of urban settings, was intended to permit fruitful comparisons internal to the South. Was intraracial violence among slaves more pronounced in cotton, tobacco, or nonplantation regions of the South? Did the contrasting economies and cultures of Virginia, upcountry South Carolina, Middle Georgia, and the Lower Mississippi River Valley produce different rates of violence? Did it become more or less frequent over time? How did the reasons for conflict differ from one area to the next? Ultimately, the available records do not allow us the confidence to posit answers to the first three questions with any degree of certainty. What may appear in the text as an appalling insensitivity to sense of place is actually the product of scarce, incomplete resources and perhaps an overabundance of caution. Regarding the last question, however, the motivations for intraracial slave violence proved remarkably similar in all regions, despite the social, cultural, and economic differences that characterized them. Distinctions are most readily apparent with regard to the respective legal systems that adjudicated slave crimes in the disparate locations under examination. But whereas laws and procedures differed from one state to the next, each southern state unfailingly developed ways to avoid infringing on masters' property rights.

For all of their benefits, court records also have their limitations. They privilege the sensational over the mundane as well as the violent conflicts that crossed plantation boundaries over those occurring within the confines of a single landholding. Documented cases are also partial to the violence perpetrated by enslaved men rather than by enslaved women, even though female slaves also engaged in violent quarrels. To compensate for these shortcomings, I pored over the records of nine Baptist churches from the Virginia Piedmont, fifteen from upcountry South Carolina, twenty-three from six counties in Middle Georgia, and another eighteen from Texas. Betty Wood, Emily West, Rebecca Fraser, and other historians have employed church minutes fruitfully in their studies, but such records remain regrettably underutilized in recovering the history of slavery. By the early nineteenth century, the Baptist Church was gaining increasing numbers of converts in the South, becoming the predominant religious faith in Virginia and other states by the onset of the Civil War. Slaves began flocking to evangelical churches in the late eighteenth century, attracted by their welcome embrace of enslaved congregants as the spiritual equals of whites and the enthusiasm of early evangelical worship. Evangelical churches' drive for respectability in southern slaveholding circles soon necessitated certain accommodations to bondage. They tamed their initial antislavery impulses and tempered some of the emotionalism of their services to make evangelical religion safe for slavery. Nevertheless, a portion of all slaves continued to find a spiritual home in these reinvented and sanitized evangelical churches. The Baptists gained more slave adherents than any other individual denomination. By 1860, half of the 100,000 worshipers in Virginia's Baptist churches were slaves or free blacks. The popularity of the Baptist Church among those in bondage makes that denomination the logical choice for analysis here.[24]

Moreover, the Baptists attached great importance to the maintenance of religious discipline, imbuing it with the regenerative power to spiritually purify the church.[25] Congregations routinely monitored the behavior of both black and white brethren, and when alerted to any of a pantheon of moral missteps committed by members, they initiated disciplinary proceedings. Clerks recorded accusations of congregants' wayward conduct, reported the findings of the church committee dispatched to investigate the charges, and noted the outcomes of the cases. Although useful as a catalogue of members' alleged moral infractions irrespective of race or status, church records do have their frustrations. Entries in church books lack detail. Cloaked behind a veil of propriety, they share no sustained stories of human weakness. They instead tease and suggest, only to dispense with congregational business in a brief remark or two. They are also remarkably inconsistent in their coverage. Some records of churches with biracial membership rolls document almost exclusively the infractions of whites, while others chronicle the moral failings of only the enslaved congregants. Often sloppy if not wholly indecipherable, depending upon the handwriting of the clerk, church records frequently identified members excluded for the vague rationale of "immoral" or "unchristianlike conduct," if they provide any justification at all. At other times, minutes state the allegations against members without supplying the resolution. No *precise* statistical breakdown of church infractions is therefore truly possible, but taken as a whole, patterns emerge from the records. Church minutes allow access to information almost completely unavailable elsewhere in more conventional sources. Most significantly, they document hostile encounters that did not turn fatal or violate the law per se, such as arguments that erupted between slave spouses or the sexual conflicts that disrupted slave families. In this manner, church proceedings nicely complement court records as a source.

Locating episodes of intraracial violence among slaves necessarily requires casting a wide net in search of sources. In addition to court and church records, this study makes extensive use of Loren Schweninger's Race and Slavery Petitions Project. His searchable Digital Library on American Slavery, available online at http://library.uncg.edu/slavery/, directs researchers to legislative and gubernatorial petitions relevant to their topics. I also scoured the records of the Louisiana State Penitentiary in Baton Rouge, the one state prison in the antebellum era most likely to incarcerate bondpeople convicted of crimes. Annual reports of the Board of Control listed all inmates by name imprisoned at the end of the year as well as the crime for which they were convicted, the sentence, and the date the prisoner entered the facility. The records do not list the victim of the crime and usually neglect to include the names of enslaved inmates' masters, but some identify the parish in which the crime was committed. With further research, a small number of intraracial slave homicides emerged from the penitentiary records. More conventionally, slave narratives and autobiographies, travelers' accounts, newspapers, and slaveholder diaries and journals, both published and unpublished, occasionally commented upon violent outbreaks within the quarters. Combined, the assembled evidence plucks hundreds of slaves from obscurity and exposes their darkest, most emotionally intense moments to scholarly scrutiny and public view. All direct quotations used in the text retain the original, at times erroneous, spellings and grammar found in the sources.

Because the documentary record is much richer for the post-revolutionary period than for the colonial era, the bulk of the book examines violence among southern slaves in roughly the last seven decades prior to emancipation. An exploration of colonial slaves' hostilities appears in chapter 1, which briefly traces the battles that took place in Africa and aboard the slave ships that conveyed captives through the Middle Passage. The ethnic clashes that fueled some violence yielded with the emergence of a hybrid African American culture, but by the early nineteenth century, the rise of the internal, domestic slave trade ushered in a new source of conflict. Other divisions between slaves were consistent over time. After chronicling some of the forces that lent motive to intraracial slave violence, chapter 1 engages in an extensive discussion of its prevalence, based on both the qualitative judgments of contemporary observers as well as some admittedly imperfect quantitative data culled from court records. Mining the database of 142 slave-slave homicides in Virginia between 1777 and 1864, I examine these fatal encounters through the lenses of gender, time, and geography. The chapter concludes with a look at the weapons slaves utilized in dispatching their victims.

Chapters 2 and 3 are related in that they document societal reactions to the violence that erupted in the quarters. Masters intervened as necessary in the quarrels of their bondpeople, and evangelical congregations in the South subjected slave churchgoers to an additional layer of white scrutiny and possible censure. Ultimately, however, slaves served as their own best police force, stepping in to defuse tense situations and prevent them from attracting the unwanted attention of the master. When all of these checks failed, and slaves were severely injured or killed, only slaveholders in Louisiana could seek redress through the civil law. In contrast, all of the slaveholding states granted owners access to the criminal courts. Chapter 3 examines the significant ways that court systems differed from state to state in the adjudication of intraracial slave homicides.

Having examined slave-slave violence from statistical and legal perspectives, the remaining chapters are dedicated to the most significant motives lurking behind bondpeople's conflicts, particularly those that culminated in death. The Alabama-born lawyer Daniel R. Hundley dismissed as "trivial" the causes for which "they will take the life of a fellow-slave." But what were they? One recent study described "[t]he circumstances of homicides among African American adults" as "largely unknown in the South before the Civil War." But a thorough examination of court records proves otherwise. In his monumental *Roll, Jordan, Roll,* Eugene D. Genovese briefly identified family, theft, and gambling as the major causes of violent outbreaks in the quarters. Philip J. Schwarz attributed a portion of intraracial slave homicides "to the circumstances of slavery" themselves. Glenn M. McNair's study of race and crime in antebellum Georgia mentioned in

INTRODUCTION

passing that "black Georgians . . . kill[ed] each other as a result of the frustrations and stresses engendered by slavery, out of jealousy, and over money." These brief comments, though not off the mark, deserve more intensive exploration. One scholar of slave law has called for "an exhaustive study of the causes of violence among slaves" to "capture the full texture" of bondpeople's lived experience. This book intends to do precisely that. The court records inspected here confirm and elaborate upon the observations of Genovese, McNair, and others. Chapter 4 examines disagreements born out of slaves' routine work and leisure-time activities, while chapters 5 through 8 analyze matters of property, family, and honor as motivations for slaves' disputes. The causes of violence were sometimes multiple, overlapping, and difficult to disentangle, and for that reason the same violent episode may merit analysis in more than one location throughout the text.[26]

Intraracial slave violence affords an unconventional avenue through which to approach tricky questions of black consciousness and identity between the American Revolution and the Civil War. The lens of violence is particularly useful in clarifying slaves' conceptions of gender and gender roles in the quarters. For decades prior to the 1980s, scholars accepted the experiences of male slaves as normative and therefore functionally genderless. Historians such as Deborah Gray White, Stephanie M. H. Camp, and others have since called attention to the gendered lives of enslaved women. Their work on female African Americans was crucial in showing that sex as well as race uniquely sculpted the contours of their lives. The experiences of female slaves differed in significant ways from those of their male counterparts.[27] Relatively little work has been done, however, to view slave men from the same gendered perspective. Several chapters herein examine enslaved men as husbands, fathers, and lovers, and chapter 7 places their violent conflicts within a distinctly gendered framework, mining the relationship between violence, honor, and masculinity within the quarters. Male slaves were routinely dishonored by masters and other whites in their daily lives, but in hostile exchanges with other bondmen, their words and actions betrayed a glimpse into the ethic of honor they boldly claimed and which bore striking similarities to that of the Old South's lower-class white men. Violence presented not the only but certainly one important route to the construction of a masculine identity for men residing in the quarters.

If violent, aggressive behaviors inside the slave community were crucial to the negotiation of enslaved masculinity, they also provide clues for understanding more deeply bondwomen's conceptions of enslaved femininity. To be sure, much of this book focuses on the violent deeds committed by bond*men* because they were more likely than female slaves to lash out physically and kill an adversary. Evidence of their affrays is therefore more abundant. Bondwomen nonetheless figure prominently herein, sometimes as the objectified possessions that male slaves either coveted or defended, but at many other times as volitional actors fighting over goods, men, or the power dynamics within the slave household. Chapter 8 turns exclusively to violence involving female slaves as either victim or perpetrator, devoting most attention to the topics of rape and infanticide. In county courts, on exceptionally rare occasions, bondmen were tried for the violation of female slaves' bodies. More frequently, enslaved women were charged with committing infanticide or child murder. From the courtroom testimony in these scattered cases emerges a portrait of enslaved femininity that prioritized bondwomen's sexual honor in spite of the routine degradations inflicted on their bodies by masters, overseers, and other white men.

A couple of remarks about what this book does not do. First, it does not systematically seek to explore conflicts between exclusively free black participants. It occasionally mentions bloody encounters between slave and free black combatants, but the focus remains on intraracial violence among only slaves, and only conflicts between bondpeople are included in the quantitative data. I consciously made this choice so that the book would enter into direct conversation with the scholarship surrounding the slave community. A by-product of that decision was the simplification of my task somewhat, providing an easy means of limiting the scope of my research. Moreover, the demographic realities of the South dictated that disputes between slaves and free blacks were far fewer in number than those involving only individuals held in bondage. By 1860, the slave population of Virginia outpaced that of free blacks by a ratio of better than 8 to 1. On the eve of the Civil War, slaves heavily outnumbered free blacks in each slaveholding state except Maryland, where their respective populations were very nearly equal, and Delaware, where the number of free blacks exceeded that of slaves by a factor of 11. A cursory glance at county court records from Virginia suggests that slaves and free blacks fought for many of the very same reasons that enemy slaves did: over disagreements during work and play, property, family, and honor. Additional research would be required, however, to explore the dynamics of slave-free black conflict more fully.

Second, this book concentrates on interpersonal conflict and does not examine incidents of self-inflicted violence, whether self-sabotage or suicide. Most accounts of slaves' self-mutilations involved the severing of one's own hands or fingers. Slaves who took such drastic action usually intended either to render themselves unfit for sale in the domestic slave trade or to avenge themselves upon the master financially by inflicting a bodily injury serious enough to depress their monetary value as human capital at market. On other occasions, maimings were intended to evade work, to register slaves' objections to an unfavorable hiring arrangement, or simply to spite a despised owner. Slaves pursuing only a brief respite from their labors might deliberately subject their bodies to minor injuries that temporarily disabled them. One bondwoman, for instance, secretly stuck her arm in a beehive occasionally to avoid work. The swelling from multiple stings incapacitated her for a time as her body flushed the toxins out of her system. Similarly, one Arkansas slave successfully shirked his labors by exercising his unique talent to dislocate his left shoulder at will.[28]

More seriously, some slaves took their own lives. On the African continent, as John Iliffe has shown, various honor-bound peoples committed ritual suicides out of a sense of shame. Men seized or defeated in warfare, for example, might sacrifice their lives as an alternative to living in disgrace. With the rise of the transatlantic slave trade, Africans taken captive by their enemies commonly killed themselves rather than submit to enslavement overseas. Those purchased by slavers for labor in the New World sometimes ended their lives before ever setting sail across the Atlantic. Others committed the deed during the Middle Passage, some by refusing food and starving to death. Olaudah Equiano described "poor African prisoners ... hourly whipped for not eating." He also witnessed captives drown themselves by jumping overboard. "[T]wo of my wearied countrymen" and "another quite dejected fellow," he related, leaped over the side of the slave ship and into the sea, "preferring death to such a life of misery." Occasionally reports filtered in of much larger, mass suicides aboard slaving vessels. One slave ship captain recalled an instance when "an hundred Men Slaves jump'd over board."[29]

Suicides were most prevalent among first-generation slaves stolen from Africa. Although most African cultures abhorred suicide, the circumstances of enslavement an ocean away compelled them to rethink their objections. A widespread folk belief among many African peoples maintained that, pending one's death, the individual returns to his or her native land to congregate with family and friends. Many Africans who terminated their own lives did so under the assumption that, in death, they would be reunited with ancestors in familiar surroundings. Certain rituals must be observed, however, to cross over to the ancestral realm. Slaves needed to effect their suicides at carefully chosen sites in or near the water. If successful, deceased individuals would then take flight across the water back to the land of their birth. The supernatural belief in suicide as a route to reincarnation in Africa proved most common among Calabar slaves and the neighboring Igbo people. Among New World masters in lowcountry South Carolina and Georgia, enslaved Igbo and others conveyed out of the Niger delta region gained a reputation for self-destruction. In one famous episode of collective suicide, a group of Igbo enslaved in the lowcountry marched into a river and drowned, surely anticipating that they would escape bondage by flying home.[30]

Compared to their African ancestors, American-born slaves proved less likely to commit suicide. Nineteenth-century travelers such as Harriet Martineau and politically motivated abolitionist ministers and writers such as Theodore Dwight Weld noted slaves' penchant for destroying themselves, but other contemporary observers bore witness to a noticeable reduction in the number of self-inflicted deaths. "However frequent suicide may have been among those brought from Africa," declared South Carolina planter James Henry Hammond, "I can say that in my time I cannot remember to have known or heard of a single instance of deliberate self-destruction, and but one suicide at all." The real decline in suicides by the nineteenth century correlated in part with slaves' understanding that American-born slaves could not fly back to Africa; that supernatural power was restricted exclusively to the African born. Eugene D. Genovese attributed the low rates of suicide among antebellum-era slaves to a "strong sense of stewardship in the quarters—of collective responsibility for each other." The growing power of the African American slave community, in other words, buoyed bondpeople's spirits, plucked them from the depths of despair, and deterred them from the commission of such a final and irrevocable act.[31]

Despite the downward trend in slave suicides over time, masters' denials of—and even concerted efforts to conceal—them were self-serving, a means of perpetuating the paternalistic myth. The closure of the transatlantic slave trade from Africa and the rise of an African American slave community did nothing to exterminate the conditions that bred self-destructive behaviors. A minute fraction of slaves continued to engage in willful self-annihilation to evade masters' chronic mistreatment or physical abuse. Virginia bondman James L. Smith seriously contemplated killing himself as he was being whipped with a cat-o'-nine tails. He had been punished so frequently, he explained, "that I was tired of life, for it became a burden to me." Others killed themselves to avoid lawfully mandated punishments. A Georgia bondman hanged himself while in jail in 1860 awaiting an impending branding. In Tennessee, a slave sentenced to die for the

INTRODUCTION

murder of another bondperson "anticipated the law" by hanging himself one month prior to his scheduled execution. Jacob, a virtually free enslaved waterman in Virginia who was implicated in Gabriel's conspiracy, committed suicide to avoid either capital punishment or sale and transportation out of the country and a lifetime condemned to the horrors of the canefields. Still other bondpeople killed themselves only after failing in their attempts to run away.[32]

The fates most nineteenth-century slaves sought to avoid through suicide were sale and separation from family. The breakup of the family, confirmed the Kentucky-born slave William Wells Brown, was "a frequent cause of suicide." Some slaves slated for sale opted instead for death. Stories of slave mothers extinguishing their own lives and those of their children rather than accepting life apart testified to the emotional devastation wrought by the domestic slave trade. Slaves committed suicide not only because they objected to permanent separation from family but also because they loathed or dreaded a new owner.[33] Still other bondmen and bondwomen killed themselves after the loss of a loved one to the internal traffic. One ex-slave from North Carolina remembered that her maternal grandmother "killed herself 'cause dey sold her husban'." Stripped of the emotional attachments that united them with others and fortified them to persevere in the face of hardships, either the commodified individual carried to a new plantation home on the cotton or sugar frontiers or the victimized spouse, parent, or child left behind might choose to end prematurely a life suddenly devoid of love and support. Severed from his wife and children and with "no hope of ever again seeing" them, one disconsolate Maryland slave sold to the Deep South pondered suicide to alleviate his emotional "anguish." Only the lack of an available rope prevented him from hanging at the end of it.[34]

Although never ubiquitous or routine, bondpeople's suicides were common enough in the nineteenth century to keep whites on notice. When one master in Mississippi planned to sell a slave away from his wife, the slaveholder's agent predicted that the bondman "will kill himself" rather than accept separation. Southern evangelical churches occasionally charged enslaved members with the moral offense of "attempting to commit suicide." Allegations proven true were enough to merit expulsion from the church.[35]

A sufficient number of slaves, Genovese concluded, "committed suicide to constitute an indictment of the regime." Any assessment of bondpeople's suicides, however, must wrestle with the complicated matrix of circumstances that prompted self-annihilation. Perhaps an exception or two notwithstanding, slaves did not leave suicide notes, so interpreting their final act is fraught with difficulty.

Certainly a tiny minority of all bondpeople suffered from mental illnesses that enslavement would only have exacerbated, and not all others were equipped genetically to cope equally well with the stresses of their condition. Scholars have suggested, on the one hand, that suicide may have signaled slaves' abject despondence, depression, and despair. According to this reading, suicide resulted from the cruelty and barbarity of the institution of slavery—the maltreatment, brutal punishments, separations from family, and so on. The sufferings that slaves endured broke them mentally and cast them into psychological depths from which they could not clamber out. Death thus marked the only possible escape from earthly torment, suicide the last tragic consequence of degrading bondage. On the other hand, slaves' self-destruction may be viewed as the ultimate form of resistance to an oppressive institution. However final its consequences, suicide represented an autonomous decision to determine one's fate, a mode of protest, and defiance of the master's authority. Self-destruction afforded the opportunity to seize control of one's own body, exhibit courage or manhood, and achieve a perverse form of liberation—spiritual only—through self-destruction. The difference between these two portrayals of slave suicide is profound and likely not as dichotomous in reality as presented here, but because suicide holds such important implications for our understanding of slavery more broadly, it deserves its own study elsewhere.[36]

Just as this book neglects suicides, it also eschews murder-suicides, a symptom of the records that I employ. Murder-suicides among slaves did occur. One bondwoman in 1736, for example, took her own life after killing her children and three of the master's other slaves. In 1755, a bondman murdered another slave before hanging himself. But successfully executed murder-suicides left no offender at all to prosecute in court or to censure in church. In exceptionally rare cases, however, slaves charged with homicide had attempted but failed to end their own life as well. In an unusual case from Powhatan County, Virginia, the bondwoman Jenny held her three children's heads under water until life departed their little bodies. She then attempted to drown herself but was prevented from doing so by the timely arrival of her master, Peter Stratton, at the creek. Trial papers naturally focused on the three murders rather than on the suicide attempt. In another case, a bondman in Covington, Kentucky, faced with looming separation from his wife and child through sale, killed his family in 1848 but botched the task of self-destruction. Placed on trial for murder, the slave received an unexpectedly generous outcome. A jury acquitted him of his crime, and a sympathetic community purchased his freedom.[37] But this case was an oddity. Any

INTRODUCTION

future, concerted study of slaves' murder-suicides must necessarily be based on plantation records, newspaper accounts, and the politically motivated writings of the abolitionist press rather than court or church records.

Proceeding from the premise that people fight over precisely what they value most, an examination of interpersonal, intraracial slave violence seems a worthwhile endeavor for gleaning insights into the culture of those held in bondage. Any final assessment of those quarrels and physical confrontations demands caution, however, for violence played an ambiguous role inside the slave quarters. Conflicts between bondpeople potentially signaled something quite negative, disconcerting, and troublesome about slave life. By nature, some slaves were mean, foul-tempered, and hostile to others in bondage. Statistically, a few surely were mentally imbalanced or psychologically unstable. A far greater number were normally level-headed and peaceable but could be driven to violence either by discrete incidents emanating from within the quarters or by circumstances engendered by the system of slavery itself. It does not diminish bondpeople in any way to acknowledge that any single one of them was capable of hatred, resentment, envy, and similarly dangerous emotions. When passions were aroused, slaves' fighting could have a devastating affect on slave life. Violence shattered whatever peace, harmony, and unity was present in the quarters and inflicted pain and suffering on enslaved victims, their families, and other loved ones. It produced schisms among slaves within a single holding or across plantation boundaries; divided bondpeople into hostile camps; damaged plantation morale; and, from the master's perspective, undermined the overall discipline and productivity of the estate. By any measure, the wanton abuse of a spouse or the murder of a fellow bondperson represented fundamentally antisocial behaviors. Yet, however destructive, violence could play a constructive role in the quarters as well. Under circumstances when it seemed "useful or necessary," violence assumed a different aspect. Violence afforded slaves an avenue through which to uphold cultural expectations, police themselves internally without interference from whites, and impose a moral and ethical code of their own creation. It could be used to delineate differences among the occupants of the quarters, establish rank, and clarify hierarchies. It also provided an outlet for the expression of masculine and feminine priorities, a display of bondmen's and bondwomen's gendered identities.[38]

The phenomenon of slave-slave violence belies the portrait of near-universal harmony and solidarity long implicit in the notion of a "slave community" but is not entirely incompatible with the larger concept. The intent here is not to deny any sense of community among bondpeople but to challenge any simplistic understanding of it. As Dylan C. Penningroth proposed, "we need not think of conflict among slaves . . . as something inimical to the making and survival of black communities." Although violence did erupt within and mar the purportedly idyllic slave community, its ambivalence was clear. Because it simultaneously embraced both destructive and constructive tendencies, violence occupied a complicated place in the quarters, as a force that both corroded and constituted community. Slaves chose community and determined its membership, and sometimes it was violence that physically demarcated those boundaries. As slaves' relationships of work, leisure, and love developed and dissipated, the perimeters of community correspondingly shifted, occasionally cleaving a single plantation in two. The study of trial papers, church records, and other sources suggests that we must accept violence as an organic part of southern society, for blacks as well as whites, a force that both stabilized and destabilized. If we do so, the "slave community" emerges as a contested arena of negotiation where slaves employed violence to create, maintain, or dissolve social ties. The resulting portrait is not a single, static "slave community" but a vibrant collection of multiple slave communities continually in flux and inhabited by complex, real people.[39]

Looking at intraracial slave violence, finally, informs and frames current-day discussions of violence among African Americans. The epilogue directly addresses the phenomenon of "black-on-black violence," a phrase I conscientiously avoid throughout the chapters to escape, at least temporarily, the cultural baggage associated with it. The pervasive devaluation of African American life in the U.S. legal system today and in much of the media's portrayal of racially charged events is indisputable. Despite civil rights advances over the past several decades, collectively our culture's obsession with race and with seeing race and even with attributing causation to race remains disturbingly strong, the conversations about racial issues, whether public or private, intense. In this context, stepping back to examine "black-on-black violence" through a wide historical lens is revealing. Slaves did fight, and they did not direct all of their aggression toward the master or other whites in acts of resistance. They lashed out at one another as well. But that historical fact need not burden the present. It would be a mistake to assume that slaves always fought *against;* they also fought *for.* Enslaved people, as the following chapters show, valued one another. As is so often the case, they hurt most and deepest the ones they loved, but also others who would hurt the ones they loved. Residents of the quarters very much understood that violent acts were meaningful ones with moral consequences. The socially constructed notion of "black-on-black violence" suggests something else, however, and by making the phenomenon appear timeless overlooks a much more complicated historical process. Avoiding stereotyped, caricatured portrayals of black life, the analysis of violent, intraracial encounters presented here seeks to elucidate slaves' cultural values on their own terms.

Chapter 1

ORIGINS, PREVALENCE, AND PATTERNS

IN APRIL 1821, a Georgia bondman named Peter killed "a certain negro man slave Abram belonging to John King" of Wilkinson County. Trial papers reveal little about assailant or victim and disclose no motivation for the attack, recording only that Peter "did violently beat & mortally wound" Abram "with a pestle of the value of one dollar."[1] A number of court records are equally uninformative, yet even unremarkable cases such as Peter's murder of Abram become valuable when viewed in the aggregate. This chapter pursues three distinct goals intended to lay the foundation for the study of intraracial slave violence. First, it chronicles the presence of violence among bondpeople intrinsic to the system of slavery, from the African roots of the transatlantic traffic, through the Middle Passage, to the sale and forced migrations of human cargoes on American shores. Second, it attempts to approximate the prevalence of intraracial slave murders, the specific type of violence best documented in extant sources. Third, through a database compiled of intraracial slave homicides in Virginia from 1777 to 1864, it seeks to discern broad patterns of violence between and among slaves. Specifically, the chapter investigates whether or not enslaved combatants belonged to the same owner, the sex of assailants and their victims, the distribution of intraracial slave homicides over time and across space, and the weapons slaves employed to attack fellow bondpeople. The resulting portrait cannot truly pinpoint overall levels of violence within the slave quarters of the American South, but on the basis of homicide cases alone, intraracial violence played a notable role in shaping life in the slave quarters.

Absent violence, the institution of slavery could have neither originated nor lasted a day. Mutually reinforcing, violence made slavery and slavery violence. From the inception of the commerce in African laborers destined for the Western Hemisphere, internecine tribal warfare supplied many of the captives for the slave trade. Having succumbed to the lure of European goods, the kings and chieftains of West and Central Africa engaged in ethnic combat designed to secure the prisoners to exchange for desired commodities. Inevitably, some foes were also killed in battle, but the preference was to capture enemies for trade. Kidnapping marked the other major means of acquiring African slaves. Frequently, observed slave ship physician Alexander Falconbridge, "those who kidnap others, are themselves, in their turns, seized and sold . . . Continual enmity is thus fostered among the negroes of Africa." According to Falconbridge, European traders rejected certain African captives "on account of age, illness, deformity," or other reasons. African captors might also kill those unpurchased. African peoples sometimes murdered enslaved captives in ritualistic homicides, to cement diplomatic or economic relationships, to attend to deceased owners in the afterlife, to honor ancestors, or simply to demonstrate wealth. Slavery produced high rates of homicide on Africans' native continent.[2]

Conveyed to slave fortresses along the African coast and sold to European slavers, captives were escorted to ships anchored offshore that became sites for further conflict among the diverse peoples of the continent. Throughout their confinement shipboard and for the duration of the Middle Passage, they suffered unspeakably brutal conditions, most notably the heat, stench, and overcrowding below deck, the by-products of the tight packing slavers practiced to maximize profits. Under such horrific and stressful conditions, tempers grew short, sparking fights among slaves. According to one report, Igbo captives were "always quarreling, biting and fighting, and sometimes choking and murdering one another, without any mercy." Atrocious shipboard conditions did not limit violent behaviors to any one ethnic group, however. Aboard vessels insufficiently provisioned or those unexpectedly delayed by unfavorable winds from arriving in New World ports as anticipated, desperate disputes broke out over scarce foodstuffs and other precious supplies. Most slaves felt "such an aversion to the horse-beans" they were customarily fed that, rather than consuming them, they often preferred employing them as projectiles. They "throw them . . . in each other's faces when they quarrel," noted Falconbridge. Disagreements were also rife between pairs of slaves shackled together. Even the basic act of relieving oneself necessitated the cooperation and forbearance of others. To make it to one of the buckets provided for that purpose, one captive might need to wake or otherwise disturb a reluctant partner. If that did not cause a fight, the journey to the tubs might. Together, the chained captives had to navigate the intertwined knot of bodies, all the while coordinating their movements to offset the undulating motion of the vessel on the high seas. Moreover, the wooden floor had likely been rendered slippery, a veritable sea of noisome filth. A noxious slurry composed of sweat having dripped from overheated skin, the vomit of seasick captives, the blood- and mucus-infused diarrhea from victims of the flux, and the urine and excrement of those unable to reach the offal buckets in time made upright movement treacherous. Probabilities were high that one or both shackled partners slipped, fell, or stepped on another prisoner. "These accidents, although unavoidable," Falconbridge wrote, "are productive of continual quarrels, in which some of them are always bruised." Other captives who witnessed a fight, perhaps outraged by the treatment of a fellow countryman, might then join the fray. As sailor William Butterworth noted, before long, the trading of jabs could escalate into a regular "battle."[3]

The general confusion and disorientation wrought by their enslavement further exacerbated the likelihood of violence among captives. Ripped from all that was familiar, they were often chained to strangers whose language, dialect, appearance, markings, and habits clearly identified them as foreigners, sometimes even as rivals or outright enemies. Held aboard one ship, Olaudah Equiano witnessed "a multitude of black people of every description chained together." Only when he "found some of my own nation" did he take some small solace. The fighting that erupted among slave ship captives sometimes inflicted serious or permanent injuries upon African bodies. In 1686, one violent outbreak among the human cargo aboard the *Lady Mary* culminated in "severall" slaves' deaths. Although such incidents were detrimental to slavers' bottom line, some captains of slaving vessels, fearful of shipboard conspiracies to rebel, nevertheless conscientiously bound together Africans of different cultural backgrounds as a means of reducing the prospect of revolt. Ethnic differences diminished the chances that Africans might foment a successful shipboard rebellion. According to Captain James Bowen, "Men of different Nations" thrust together in chains would often "quarrel and fight" one another rather than attack their European slavers. In 1682, one African conveyed to Nevis aboard the *Eglet* "cut another Negroe mans Throate & Stabd him in the Brest" before ending his own life at the end of a rope. Although "for what reason noe body knows," the cause may have originated in the audible and visible divisions among the human cargo. Animosities between such peoples as the Chamba and the Fante of the Gold Coast sometimes manifested themselves in violent conflicts when both occupied the same slave ship. The Chamba, who blamed the Fante for collaborating with the British to enslave them, aided slave ship crews in suppressing Fante shipboard uprisings. In another case, "The captain of the *Brome* survived a revolt in the Gambia in 1693 largely because of differences among his slaves." Bambara captives sided with the slavers against the hated Jollofes. A variation of the divide-and-conquer method, the strategy of coupling African captives of different tribal identities brought captains and crews diminishing returns as the slave trade progressed through the centuries. Slavers more successfully exploited cultural divisions early in the transatlantic traffic. With time, captives of different tribal affiliations came to understand that, in their European slavers, they shared a common enemy. In his database of almost four hundred slave-ship revolts, David Eltis uncovered no cases of African slaves "dying as a result of internecine onboard strife after 1750" despite the better preserved historical record documenting later transatlantic voyages.[4]

The ethnic antagonisms evident among African peoples when first taken captive and during the Middle Passage did not immediately disappear upon debarkation in the Americas. The constellation of volatile emotions—confusion, desperation, fear, shock, and anger among them—lingered, fueling continued conflicts among African-born slaves transported overseas and deposited on New World soil. Throughout Great Britain's North American mainland colonies, African ethnic groups quarreled in the late seventeenth and early eighteenth centuries over either the "remnants of ancient enmities" or hostilities originating more recently, with the advent of the African slave trade itself. On the whole, tensions between rival African tribes were less pronounced in the Chesapeake region than in the lowcountry. African imports to the Chesapeake declined after 1740, and the relatively few new arrivals from abroad were widely dispersed across the landscape, reducing the likelihood of ongoing interethnic conflicts with African roots. In contrast, the continued influx of African imports into the lowcountry permitted rivalries born in Africa to persist in the region late into the eighteenth century and even into the early nineteenth, thanks to Georgia's tardy closure of the transatlantic slave trade in 1798 and South Carolina's reopening of the traffic between 1803 and 1807. Mounting evidence suggests that captives stolen from Africa were not distributed at random on American shores. Some planters demonstrated clear preferences for slaves of a certain African ethnocultural heritage, based on either the perceived collective personality traits of the group or the very real skills and knowledge of crop cultivation its members possessed. Although slaveholder predilections resulted in pluralities of Angolans in South Carolina, Biafrans in Virginia, and Senegambians in Louisiana, the distribution of African ethnic groups in the colonial population was never as tidy or as rigidly segmented as that. Members of rival tribes were to some extent intermingled in the same colonies and on the same holdings, and African men, in particular, readily employed in physical combat the peculiar "martial traditions" they carried through the Middle Passage.[5]

However robust the initial willingness to defend one's people, with time the specific tribal identities that figured prominently in the early colonial era receded in significance and transformed. The pace of change differed from one region, one plantation, and even one individual to the next. Some captives, freshly arrived from Africa, strategically cast aside their differences quickly to forge alliances with shipmates. The shared experience of enduring the Middle Passage trumped those ethnocultural forces that divided them. Other slaves conformed to and claimed the identity of the predominant ethnic group in their immediate vicinity, regardless of their true birthplace or cultural origin. In time, the different peoples thrust together on the American continent forged a hybrid African American culture that reflected the influences of many tribes as well as varying degrees of contact with whites. Enslaved Africans' cultural flexibility—their willingness to jettison one identity and to assume another or to create one altogether new—thwarted some masters' conscious efforts to purchase slaves of diverse geographic origins, languages, and customs for the sake of inhibiting communication and decreasing the chances of revolt. Masters proved powerless to arrest the cultural process responsible for the construction of an African American identity.[6]

The formation of a distinct African American identity generated its own set of conflicts between creolized slaves and more recent arrivals from abroad. Born in the colonies, African American slaves often mocked unacculturated—or, in the language of their owners, "outlandish"—newcomers from Africa conspicuous in their speech, habits, and markings and ignorant of slave life on American shores. But the reverse might also be true. One-time African princes and others of high rank ensnared by the slave trade looked contemptuously upon other bondpeople of lesser stock—even the native-born—and dismissed them as inferior. Trial records documenting intraracial violence virtually never identified the ethnic origins of either victims or the accused, but in colonial Cumberland County, Virginia, on the basis of names alone, Cudjo's double murder of fellow slaves Iris and Beck "with a Hominy Pestle" and Mustapha's homicide of the bondman Bob may have been motivated, at least in part, by a rift between Africans and creoles. Compared to those in the Chesapeake, creole/African, acculturated/unacculturated divisions ran deeper and longer in the lowcountry. The slave population of the Chesapeake reproduced naturally a full generation earlier than that of the lowcountry, precluding the demand for significant African imports and hastening the creation of a relatively unified African American culture. In contrast, the high mortality rates present in lowcountry rice swamps demanded fresh bodies from Africa to perform the strenuous labor characteristic of rice culture. Newcomers thus continued to clash with more established resident slaves of the lowcountry as well as with other African-born adversaries.[7]

More subtle than the stark acculturated/unacculturated dichotomy were the varying shades of acculturation that also had the potential to set slaves at odds. Some bondpeople more than others, for example, readily incorporated the teachings of Christianity into their personal belief systems. A rare case of intraracial black violence from colonial New England proves instructive. In 1720, Joseph Hanno, a native African, one-time slave, and proud Christian who spent the last of his life as a free man, confessed to slaughtering his wife Nanny in Boston. After he "knock'd her down" with an axe, he delivered a "second Blow" so "that she might not recover." Nanny did not share her husband's faith and rejected attempts at conversion. Explaining the rage that led to the homicide of his wife, Hanno reported to the Puritan minister Cotton Mather, "she told me, that she had as liev talk with the Devil, as talk with any of GODS Ministers." The devout Hanno could not tolerate that level of blasphemy from his wife's mouth and promptly dispatched her. Almost a century later, on a plantation in Rockbridge County, Virginia, religion played a role in another murderous encounter. While chopping wood in 1817, the bondman Julius confronted a fellow slave. "Ned," he said, "you called me an ungodly man." The pair already had a contentious history, and after Ned questioned his adversary's religiosity, or perhaps his general lack of moral character, the offended Julius buried his axe in Ned's neck. The possibility exists that this was a dispute between converted and unconverted slaves. At the very least, Julius resented the challenge to his level of conviction.[8]

As conflicts rooted in the African slave trade diminished, the domestic slave trade gave rise to new hostilities. In 1798, Georgia became the last of the original thirteen states to prohibit the transatlantic traffic. Although South Carolina later reopened the trade, ensnaring another 40,000 bound laborers, on January 1, 1808, at the earliest moment permitted by the U.S. Constitution, Congress outlawed the United States' commerce in slaves from abroad. At the time, slaveholders in Virginia and other Upper South states held more slaves than required to complete the available tasks. In contrast, settlers in the Deep South states of South Carolina and Georgia and the Orleans and Mississippi territories hungered for additional laborers. The appetite for slaves on the rapidly expanding plantation frontier provided a ready market for the Upper South's surplus bondpeople. A thriving internal slave trade effected the redistribution of slaves within the South to those areas most in need. Especially in the Upper South, the domestic traffic devastated slave families and disrupted existing neighborhoods and communities. For masters, however, it provided an opportunity not only to profit from their excess bondpeople but also to expel undesirable, troublesome slaves from their midst. An indeterminable number sent to auction or sold to passing traders, Eugene D. Genovese notes, "had killed or dangerously quarreled with fellow slaves." Owners soon added threats of sale to the Old Southwest, and to the cane fields of Louisiana in particular, to their arsenal of weapons employed in the discipline of their chattel.[9]

Slaves forcibly conveyed from family and friends occasionally committed violent acts in transit to their new residences. In shock, angry, and resentful of the separations they suffered, some were primed to vent their frustrations on others in the coffle, most of whom they would never see again. Those who were smaller, younger, or weaker served as easy targets. Although chained to a kind, elderly bondman when marched from Norfolk to Richmond for resale, the eight-year-old John Parker did not initially absorb the lesson in magnanimity the senior slave exhibited. On the next part of his journey, en route from Richmond to Alabama, Parker was chained to another slave youngster, named Jeff. "He was smaller than I was," Parker recalled, and "had never been away from his mother" before. He "blubbered and cried, until I kicked him to make him keep still." Parker soon felt remorse for his actions, however; "took pity" on his frightened, overwhelmed companion; and later defended him from "another boy larger than either Jeff or myself" who "took Jeff's dinner, just because he was bigger and stronger." Parker attacked the bully until the latter was "glad" to surrender Jeff's meal.[10] Fights among domestically traded slaves of all ages, strangers to one another, were common enough, and traders needed to maintain vigilance to prevent damage to their human commodities. But not all conflicts were what they seemed. In 1829, sixteen bondpeople forcibly marched in a large coffle westward from Maryland mysteriously secured a file and secretly weakened their restraints. They then staged a fight as a diversion. When the traders approached to restore order, the enslaved conspirators attacked. Although they killed two whites before fleeing the scene, the slave plotters were later captured and four of them executed.[11]

In the quarters, slaves freshly delivered to new plantation homes via the domestic slave trade were often greeted with suspicion or hostility. The new arrivals were outsiders not automatically accepted as members of the existing slave community. For slaves who had clashed with other bondpeople and alienated themselves on a former holding, it was possible that being traded was a relief and provided an opportunity for a fresh start with a different set of enslaved peers. Bondpeople traded or forcibly relocated could of course initiate warm relationships and forge communities with other slaves they had never before met. In Washington County, Virginia, for example, Sam became fast friends with Green, who "had not been long in this place," having recently "come from the state of Tennessee with his former master." Yet slaves often struggled to adjust to alien surroundings and to navigate relationships with unfamiliar peers. In Elbert County, Georgia, "Marse Tom" Heard purchased one slave boy who "was mighty little" without acquiring either of his parents or any other kin. Essentially alone on a plantation of well more than one hundred slaves, "it was right hard for de little boy all by hisself, 'cause de other slaves on de plantation was awful mean to him. Dey wouldn't let him sleep in deir quarters." Only as the boy matured, performed more work on the plantation, and better pulled his own weight did the other bondpeople slowly warm to him.[12]

Other newcomers, by contrast, especially adults, had a more difficult time overcoming initial antipathies. Time and again, the internal slave trade disrupted plantation status quos and restructured hierarchies among resident bondpeople. In the states of the Old Southwest, where the frenzied pursuit of great riches enticed masters to maximize the sizes of their enslaved labor forces, slaves' places in the quarters were continually in flux. Slaves on one plantation signaled their ostracism of a newly acquired bondwoman who had immediately "quarreled with the other Negroes"—possibly in an attempt to establish an elevated position among the ranks of her peers—by refusing to "wash her clothes." The rejected, isolated slave was required to tend to that chore herself. Near Vicksburg, Mississippi, the slave cook Josephine "often quarreled with the other slaves." Because she was newly arrived from the New Orleans slave market, her mere presence invited the special resentment of Elsey, the displaced former cook. Presumably acquired to remedy Elsey's incompetence in the kitchen, Josephine daily reminded Elsey of her apparent failures in her former position. To make matters worse, the master may have banished the demoted Elsey to the hard labor of field work under the beating sun. It would take Josephine and other slaves in similar situations an extensive period of time to smooth over such ready-made antagonisms engendered by the domestic slave trade.[13]

Precise motivations for violent outbreaks among slaves are often impossible to discern. Neither plantation diaries, church minutes, nor court records that mentioned intraracial slave violence consistently identified likely motives. South Carolina slaveholder David Gavin remembered a time when his bondman Big Jim fought "another boy, Mike," and Tippah County, Mississippi, cotton planter

Francis Terry Leak observed in 1852 that a "negro fellow belonging to old Mr Wofford, killed another, belonging to Mrs Davis, last evening in a fight." As slave owners, however, they were not privy to the inner turmoil of the quarters and were in no position to speculate upon the circumstances that sparked the dispute. Church minutes, too, often recorded only the fact of conflict rather than its origin. Trial papers from the colonial era rarely provided verbatim testimony and are at best suggestive of possible causes. We may speculate, for example, that the Louisa County, Virginia, bondman Boatswain's double murder of Rachel and Will in 1745 was inspired by a jilted lover's jealousy, but we cannot know for certain. Many nineteenth-century court records are more complete but still overlook the question of motive. Two Spartanburg District slaves named Bob and Harry were charged with making "an affray"—"in a tumultuous manner"—with some neighborhood slaves, yet the court either did not care to find out, or at least record, why. Yet surely Anderson District court records were incorrect to report in 1846 that Nero drew a knife and repeatedly stabbed Sam "for no Reson or caus what ever."[14]

Largely on the basis of nineteenth-century court records, subsequent chapters zero in on the four most common causes of conflicts in the quarters: disputes resulting from slaves' leisure and work-time activities, disagreements over property, the defense or dissolution of family, and gendered performances of honor. Any one or some combination of these factors might drive slaves to violence, quite intentionally or in spite of themselves. Russell County, Virginia, bondman Richard "had once sworn he never would strike another d——d negro with his fist," but in an 1840 affray with a fellow slave named Cupe, he could not abide by his personal pledge. Under the circumstances, he believed violence culturally obligatory. Whether employed as a means to avenge a long-simmering feud or as an immediate response to insult, violence remained an essential device in many slaves' toolbox for conflict resolution.[15]

A number of slaves' disputes that emerge from available records suggest the sort of conflicts that occur quite naturally among those who live in close quarters. Rockbridge County, Virginia, bondmen Matt and Mike "lived at the same house" and "were often quarreling." Perhaps their personalities did not mesh well, but whatever the source of their hostility, Matt declared of his roommate "that he would rather fight him than . . . talk with him." He further predicted—prophetically, as it turned out—"that if he ever did fight with him he would almost kill him for he would not know when to stop beating him." Other cases smack of neighborly spats that crossed plantation lines. Household pets, for instance, generated a couple of known disturbances. In Kershaw District, South Carolina, one female slaveholder complained in 1811 "that a certain negro man named Eben the property [of] Robert Coalman... cause[d] his dog to bite a small negro of hers." Elsewhere, in Lunenburg County, Virginia, the bondman Bob complained of Nelson's throwing rocks at Bob's canine companion. Even if pets on rare occasion ignited conflicts, these disputes were fundamentally and deeply interpersonal. Pendleton District, South Carolina, slaveholder William Hamilton reported to the authorities in 1826 "that his Negro Fellow Dave was violently Beat & abused" by "two Negro Fellows by the Name of Ben & Aleck Belonging to John Adams & a Negro Boy Named Allen belonging to Arch[d] Keaton." Dave's three attackers did not care for his company. Through force of personality, temperament, or demeanor, some slaves were not as well liked as others. As a white man in Virginia observed of one family bondwoman, "Betsey has always been unpopular with the negroes on the place." It was similarly suggested at a slave trial in antebellum Georgia that the defendant "was without friends amongst the negroes at the stable, and that ... the balance of the negroes were associated to oppress and harass him."[16]

Among the circumstances that increased the likelihood of conflict among slaves was a differential in age. As a general rule, slaves showed respect for the elderly among them, but generational divisions did exist. From the moment Africans were first swept up in the transatlantic trade, historian Marcus Rediker notes, younger captives occasionally taunted older ones. Enslaved youngsters hustled onto slave ships were often unchained, while older, more physically threatening slave men were shackled. Some youth took advantage of the inversion of customary social hierarchies to mock their superiors. As explained in one report, "it is not unusual for the Boy Slaves, who are brought on Board, to insult the Men, who, being in Irons, cannot easily pursue and punish them for it." In the more mature slave society of antebellum Petersburg, Virginia, the bondman Billy called his opponent an "old man" before striking him on the head. Billy was reportedly "much younger" than his fifty-year-old adversary, but he could not escape the rebuke of fellow slaves for the abuse of his geriatric victim. A third bondman who interceded, pulling Billy off of his adversary, observed that "it was a damned shame to strike such an old man."[17]

Often correlated with age was size. The few cases that mention slaves' relative stature note the substantial disparity between the combatants. Occasionally, smaller, weaker slaves ended up in court because they resorted to the use of deadly weapons to compensate for a mismatch in strength or physicality. In Washington, D.C., John Clark, "a slave about thirteen years old, was indicted for the murder of another slave, named Burdet, about fifteen years old." Although

Burdet "was larger and stronger" than Clark, Clark, after absorbing several blows, "drew a knife" and stabbed the bully. In some instances, however, the smaller bondman appeared the aggressor. Muscogee County, Georgia, bondman "Bill was just grown and smaller than [his opponent] Caesar, who weighted 188 pounds." Despite their size differential, the comparatively diminutive Bill "devilled" Caesar and bantered him to fight, but his goading did not achieve the desired result. Giving up, he simply stabbed Caesar to death. "The disparity in the age, size and manhood of the parties," declared Judge Joseph Henry Lumpkin of the Georgia Supreme Court, "make it unlikely that the younger and weaker should have commenced the assault" without "some lurking cause." Nonetheless, "the only teasing" shown in court to have taken place was uttered by Bill. Because the youthful, pugnacious "Bill... was the aggressor," the Court upheld the verdict against him.[18]

Conflicts among slaves sometimes resulted from disloyalty to one's fellow bondpeople. As a rule, the emergence of an African American identity in the colonial era, first in the Chesapeake and a generation later in the lowcountry, subsumed tribal differences and prioritized the allegiances of bondpeople to one another. By the nineteenth century, the vast majority of slaves greatly prized the trust they shared. One of the greatest tests of their commitment to one another came when a bondperson spontaneously attacked the master or overseer. Assaulted whites frequently summoned nearby slaves for assistance. A small number of bondpeople sustained serious injuries or were killed as they intervened in defense of the master, the collateral damage in an enraged slave's frenzied assault upon a despised owner. But aid was often delayed, if it came at all. As Daniel was murdering his Halifax County, Virginia, overseer William Allen, for example, Allen "repeatedly" cried out to "big John" for help. Legally, slaves were insulated from the harshest of penalties—or any penalty at all, in some cases—if they harmed another bondperson while protecting their owner or the owner's agent. Article 51 of the Louisiana Black Code, for instance, mandated death for "every slave who shall kill any person, unless by accident, or in the act of defending his master." Even with assurances of lawful protection, of which bondpeople may or may not have been aware, slaves may have felt little compulsion to aid their oppressors. Big John did indeed approach the site of the attack upon his overseer, but how promptly did he respond? Did he instantaneously abandon his labors and rush to save him from imminent death? It seems not, as Allen called out "repeatedly." Big John may have mulled over his options, tarrying for a time. The risk of refusing to go to a white person's aid altogether was great. If later pressed to account for their absence, slaves might explain to inquisitive authorities that they failed to hear the cries of distress, but in many workday situations, that would not have been a plausible excuse. So slaves may have instead dallied before hastening to the overseer or master under attack. When Big John neared the battle between Daniel and Allen, "the murderer ran off into the woods," but he likely granted Daniel a few extra, gratifying moments in which to inflict injury upon the master's representative. Curiously, after his apprehension, Daniel informed a white man that "he hoped no body would be blamed for the murder but himself." "[A]ll the rest of the negroes were innocent," the bondman insisted. "[H]e committed the murder himself" because Allen "had whipped him... without cause." Daniel may have spoken the truth, but he may also have taken the opportunity after his arrest to spare from harm fellow slaves tangentially complicit in the assault.[19]

Slaves occasionally took steps to enforce the allegiance of bondpeople thought to be wavering in their loyalties to fellow residents of the quarters. A pair of cases from antebellum Mississippi illustrate the point. When slaves on one DeSoto County plantation conspired to murder their owner in 1852, the bondwoman Milly refrained from divulging the plot to "her master or the family... because Bill [a slave] threatened to kill her if she did tell," and "she was afraid of him." Five years later, in Issaquena County, Jack felt the same sense of fear and intimidation. After the bondman Sam took the life of his master, he threatened to kill Jack if he refused to help dispose of the corpse in the Mississippi River or if he revealed anything about the murder to white authorities. Compelled to extract coerced loyalty out of Milly and Jack, both enslaved murderers acknowledged the strains their violent actions imposed upon their relationships with fellow bondpeople. It stretched the bounds of reason to assume that their comrades would voluntarily keep a homicide secret.[20]

Although slaves usually supported and protected one another willingly, various factors tested their loyalty to fellow bondpeople. Some slaveholders granted special privileges and material rewards to bondmen who functioned as slave drivers on their estates. Black drivers served as masters' agents, supervising the fellow slaves under their watch and punishing them as they deemed appropriate. Bondpeople often reviled drivers who carried out masters' orders with excessive enthusiasm or aggression and sought revenge upon them. In French Louisiana, one black "Commander of... slaves... was so brutally treated by another negro that his teeth were loosened" and his life imperiled. Decades later, in Spanish Louisiana, the Guinea-born bondman Pedro fatally poisoned the black "overseer Gonzalo" because the driver had frequently punished Pedro, sometimes "by order of the master and sometimes through caprice." When crimes or lesser misdeeds occurred on plantations, slaves sometimes incriminated others to deflect suspicion and save themselves. Accused of poisoning her owner's family, one enslaved cook near Vicksburg, Mississippi, immediately fingered a field hand named George, who was known to have "a small vial of rat poison." In a similar case, a number of Virginia slaves pilfered and ate a sheep to fill their empty bellies. Afterward, one bondwoman who had partaken of the clandestine feast "went and told their master," and her compatriots "all received a severe whipping." Her loose tongue made her fellow slaves understandably "very cross" with her. Seeking retribution for perceived wrongs, a few black informants desired that their owners punish enemy slaves. One bondwoman who blamed a fellow female slave for the beating she suffered tattled to the master that her foe had weighed down a cotton bag with rocks. The attempted deception presumably earned the second bondwoman a whipping as well.[21]

Some of the slaves who betrayed their own anticipated some form of recompense for their allegiance to the master. Exposing runaways or their hideouts was one possible way to curry the owner's favor or to accrue material benefits. For six months, a bondman known as "Old Charlie" remained on the lam from a "vicious cruel" master. Although a number of neighborhood slaves "used to help feed him, ... one day a nigger 'trayed him," likely for personal gain, and Old Charlie was caught. When slaves engaged in activities beneficial to white society at large, whites other than the master sometimes took an interest in remunerating them. A number of "citizens of Georgetown district," South Carolina, petitioned the state's House of Representatives in pursuit of "a suitable & proper reward" for the bondmen Jack and Tom, who in 1822, "at every hazzard" seized one of "a gang of lawless ... runaways" responsible for the murder of planter George Ford. Another eighty petitioners across three South Carolina districts sought "compensation" from the state Senate for Royal, a slave whose "good faith" inspired him to lead a sufficient force of whites to the encampment of "the outlaw Joe," alias Forest, who had purportedly murdered a white man. Joe had long proven "so cunning and artful as to elude pursuit and so daring and bold" as to avoid apprehension. For four years, he led a gang of fugitive slaves, a nagging source of "insubordination and insurrection," across a wide swath of the state. Petitioners believed "the State generally ... deeply indebted to ... Royal for his fidelity and good conduct" in locating Joe. Thankful for his "rendered services," they requested "compensation as may be fully adequate and as your honourable and enlightened Body may think most Compatible with the best interests of the State."[22]

As far as southern whites were concerned, bondpeople could offer no greater possible service than exposing the intrigues of other slaves against their masters and the white population generally. Through this form of disloyalty to those in the quarters, slaves were complicit in preemptively suppressing revolts. Black informants appear in accounts of every major slave rebellion or conspiracy in the American South. Their allegiance to whites sometimes reaped for them the ultimate reward: freedom. One Virginia master emancipated his bondman Will in 1710 for revealing a plot brewing among his fellow slaves in Surry County. More famously, the Virginia legislature liberated Tom and Pharaoh from bondage for betraying the Gabriel conspiracy of 1800. The colony of Georgia codified rewards for certain slave informants into law. Its slave code of 1765 encouraged bondpeople to "inform on their fellows who were involved in or contemplated committing" the offense of poisoning. The law did not promise freedom to the bondperson but did hold forth an enticing financial incentive, pledging an annual stipend of "twenty shillings per year as long as he or she resided in the colony."[23]

Although such rewards from white society were possible, more often slaves' disloyalty to their fellow bondpeople earned them the wrath of those in the quarters. Slaves knew that the risks of betrayal might outweigh the rewards. When the Virginia bondman Lewis ratted out several slaves involved in a conspiracy in 1802, he suspected it "would cause his death, for he spoke against his color, and the blacks would kill him." A pair of Spotsylvania County whites expressed concern over one female informant who might suffer "the rage of the people of her own colour." Captain John Marshall, a Virginia planter, returned from church one Sabbath in 1856 to find that "some of my negroe men had taken Billy [a slave] and stripped and whipt him," probably for betraying them. Pittsylvania County bondman Shadrack took umbrage with George because "George had caused his master to whip him." After Shadrack fatally fractured George's skull with a shovel, he delighted that "he had given George his death blow," for "he would be damned if he would not kill any negro that would make his master take his shirt off." Slaveholders' faithful, devoted, and trustworthy bondpeople were, to the residents of the quarters, traitors who deserved to be dealt with harshly, possibly even killed.[24]

Pesky questions of prevalence dog any study of violence among blacks. In the context of the pre–Civil War South, the central dilemma facing scholars is methodological: because episodes of intraracial slave violence did not necessarily enter the court system, it is impossible to know the precise frequency of such confrontations. Historians have largely offered only speculation and vague assessments. Kenneth M. Stampp, whose 1956 interpretation of slavery emphasized the harshness, severity, and exploitation inherent in the institution, maintained that because slaves had "to submit to the superior power of their masters," many deflected their anger and frustration onto their own and "were extremely aggressive toward each other." Writing during an era when the scholarship had turned to the ways in which slaves successfully resisted the terms and conditions of bondage, Eugene D. Genovese downplayed the magnitude of violence among bondpeople. He noted that violent affrays most often erupted when slaves were inebriated and their inhibitions loosened. Some scholars continue to marvel that, "despite the considerable pressures facing slaves, instances of black-on-black antagonisms were rare." Increasingly, however, historians have grown more comfortable acknowledging that slaves "did not hesitate to fight each other when the occasion warranted." Bondpeople, observed Glenn M. McNair in a study of slaves in Georgia, "committed few serious crimes relative to their numbers in the population," but they nevertheless "engaged in a wide range of violent behaviors with . . . fellow blacks," the product of "a violent American culture, an especially violent southern culture, and in response to the unique circumstances of their enslavement and social degradation." McNair noted that black Georgians "killed each other from time to time," most often over matters of "money, women or honor," three of the major motivations for intraracial slave killings to be explored in depth in later chapters.[25]

The slave quarters did bear witness to a spectrum of violent affrays. Conflicts among slaves ran the gamut from minor to major. At one end of the scale were routine disputes and disagreements. These shaded into casual forms of violence, such as the play or roughhousing of children and young adults, usually men. More serious were spontaneous acts of violence committed in immediate response to a specific word or deed. Farther along the continuum and still more serious in nature were premeditated acts of violence and, in the most extreme cases, homicides. Not all violent behavior was thus created equal, and the broad range of possible violent acts complicates any attempt to assess just how violent the slave quarters were.

The evidence is indeed conflicting. One respondent to a white Works Progress Administration interviewer denigrated her fellow former bondpeople as unconscionably violent. According to the Georgian, "slaves warn't civilized folks den—all dey knowed was to fuss and fight and kill one 'nother." The effects of white interviewers on black interviewees in the racial climate of the 1930s produced a number of such denunciations of fellow blacks by former slaves. The recollections of other ex-bondpeople were not similarly influenced by their interviewers' race. Another woman enslaved in Georgia observed "very little killing among the slaves," and a former Alabama bondwoman concurred: "Niggers didn't kill one 'nudder much in dem days." They "jes' had fights 'mong de'selves, [and] ef day got too bad white fo'ks whup 'em." Qualitatively, the striking lack of physical confrontations in the quarters impressed several antebellum planters and white travelers. "[W]ith truth it may be said," declared Liberty County, Georgia, planter and clergyman Charles Colcock Jones, "there are fewer personal injuries, and manslaughters, and murders among the Negroes in the South, than among the same amount of population in any part of the United States; or, perhaps, in the world." Because he was a slaveholder, Jones's hyperbole might be quickly dismissed were it not verified by other sources. According to British geologist Charles Lyell, then visiting coastal Georgia, "There were more serious quarrels, and more broken heads, among the Irish in a few years, when they came to dig the Brunswick Canal, than had been known among the negroes in all the surrounding plantations for half a century." While in Glynn County, Lyell recorded that "[t]he murder of a husband by a black woman, whom he had beaten very violently, is the greatest crime in this part of Georgia for a great length of time."[26]

As part of a broader project documenting historical violence in the United States, Randolph Roth has undertaken the most diligent efforts to quantify murders among blacks in early America. Homicides represent just one, exceptional form of violence but the type that best lends itself to quantitative analysis. In the colonial era, reliable data even for murders are scarce. Roth's figures nevertheless suggest that, at least in Virginia by the middle decades of the eighteenth century, intraracial slave homicides had already passed a peak apparent upon the arrival of Africans on American shores. By the 1730s Roth detects a "decline in homicides of blacks by blacks in the Chesapeake and the Shenandoah Valley" of Virginia, the likely result of a maturing slave society, the rising numbers of native-born creole slaves, the development of family and kinship networks, and the elaboration of an emerging African American identity that subsumed formerly pronounced ethnic antagonisms. Discerning a rising sense of racial solidarity among colonial-era slaves, Roth places black homicide rates at "probably no more than 2 per 100,000 adults per year" from the 1730s to the end of the colonial period. The rate never increased until after the American Revolution, when it grew "to 3 per 100,000 adults per year" in Virginia and "to 4 per 100,000" in both Edgefield District, South Carolina, and Florida. Roth attributes the rising tide of intraracial homicides following the revolution to black frustrations that the War for Independence had not produced more substantive change for those held in slavery. The failure of the infant United States to live up to the promise of the Revolutionary-era rhetoric of liberty, freedom, and equality dashed the collective hopes of those of African ancestry. Disappointed by unmet expectations, Roth contends, blacks increasingly turned on one another by the early nineteenth century. Through a growing number of murders, lesser forms of violence, and threats of physical harm, they extracted from other African Americans the respect denied them in white society.[27]

If Roth's statistical analysis, as well as some contemporary observers, may be believed, intraracial murder rates among southern slaves compared favorably to those of antebellum blacks living in the urban North. Eric H. Monkkonen's research shows that whites, including European immigrants, committed the vast majority of violent crimes in nineteenth-century New York City, where "years often elapsed" between the murder of one black resident by another. Altogether, "less than 4 percent of all offenders or victims" of homicide in New York City were African American. Monkkonen estimates that, "for the decade centered on 1860," the black homicide rate stood at 32 per 100,000 adult men, a figure approximately double the 15.7 rate for German immigrants but lower than the rate of 37.5 among the Irish. Philadelphia also witnessed relatively low rates of black homicide. There, African Americans perpetrated just 25 of the 190 total homicides (13 percent)—including 3 upon white victims—committed between 1839 and 1859. Over the course of those 2 decades, the number of black Philadelphians hovered consistently around 20,000 even as the total population more than doubled from roughly 258,000 to 566,000. Blacks' share of the overall population thus dwindled from less than 8 percent in 1840 to less than 4 percent in 1860. Although the percentage of all homicides blacks committed exceeded their percentage of the city's population, the absolute number of murders remained small: little more than one per year, on average. As in New York City, the homicide rate for Philadelphia's Irish population exceeded that of slaves.[28]

The difficulty in attempting any statistically precise comparison of black homicide rates in the North and in the South resides in the nature of the sources used to derive the numbers. In the North, the vast majority of black intraracial killings would have placed the defendant in the courtroom. In contrast, trial papers from the South certainly underreport intraracial slave violence because masters so often handled such incidents privately, on the plantation. McNair's examination of black crime in Georgia yielded only 30 intraracial homicides involving slaves. Georgia bondpeople killed 26 enslaved men and 2 enslaved women, plus an additional 2 free blacks. Surely, in a state with more than 460,000 resident slaves on the cusp of the Civil War, these figures are artificially low. But just how much higher they actually were remains the stuff of speculation.[29]

Whether or not homicide rates among slaves were higher than those among their racial counterparts in the North, they were without question low compared to rates among southern whites. Chief Justice Thomas Ruffin of North Carolina declared it "an incontestable fact, that the great mass of slaves—nearly all of them—are the least turbulent of all men." "They sometimes kill each other in heat of blood," he acknowledged, but such occurrences were "much less frequent than among whites." Ruffin attributed the disparity to blacks' innately "duller sensibility to degradation." Although we may easily dismiss the eminent jurist's racial assumptions, scholars, too, have long noted the pervasive violence committed by southern white men of all socioeconomic classes. In his study of Middle Florida, Edward E. Baptist observes that "[b]oth in absolute and in relative terms, whites committed far more murders . . . than did blacks." In Leon County, whites committed an "incredible" number of homicides. From December 1841 to May 1847, somewhere between 17 and 22 white men were indicted for murder, compared to only 3 blacks, even though blacks outnumbered whites in the overall population. Averaging at least 3 indictments for homicide per year in a county of roughly 4,500 white residents, Leon County's murder rate among whites was between 55 and 60 per 100,000. As Baptist explains, "compared to the bloody record of local white-on-white violence, the almost complete silence of court, newspaper, and plantation records on the subject of black-on-black violent crime is stunning . . . [T]he virtual absence from extant documents of serious slave-on-slave crimes like murder speaks volumes, especially in a region rife with white lawlessness. The facts argue that the level of violence between slaves must have been far lower than that between whites."[30]

The higher murder rate among whites in Middle Florida compared to that among blacks was no aberration. In one study of Richmond, Virginia, from 1784 to 1820, "white males committed substantially more murders than black males." The same can be said of rural as well as urban Virginia. In Mecklenburg County, for example, whites were charged with attacking other whites eight times between 1853 and 1858. During the same period, only two slaves assaulted other bondpeople. In South Carolina, all of the Courts of Magistrates and Freeholders records employed for this study yielded some seventy-five cases in which slaves inflicted violence, both lethal and nonlethal, upon an enslaved opponent. By comparison, the state's Courts of General Sessions, which adjudicated white crimes, documented more than 1,800 violent encounters—assaults and batteries, murders, manslaughters, and the like—between whites in antebellum Laurens and Spartanburg Districts alone. According to Randolph Roth, the rate at which nineteenth-century blacks "killed each other remained at less than half the rates at which . . . whites murdered each other."[31]

Yet homicide was only one, extraordinary form of violence. The vast majority of violent encounters were less exceptional and not productive of courtroom proceedings. Church records serve as an alternate gauge of the levels of black violence vis-à-vis white, one not so fixated specifically on murder. Southern whites who attended the evangelical churches that faithfully reported their members' misdeeds were a self-selecting segment of the overall population. Some black congregants may have gone of their own accord as well, although the master may have made attendance for them compulsory. If churchgoers took seriously the biblical injunction to turn the other cheek, they would not—or, for fallible sinners, at least rarely—have entered into violent scrapes. Indeed, fighting was not the foremost offense that evangelical churches disciplined. White churchgoers were most commonly charged with drinking; fighting usually ranked a distant second or lower in the list of moral infractions that garnered congregational attention. Among enslaved members, fighting rarely appeared in the top five. Churches more diligently inquired into slaves' alleged sexual offenses, violations of white property, careless use of language, and morally objectionable leisure-time pursuits. Slaves' purported adultery, fornication, theft, lying, and drinking all earned more frequent scrutiny than bondpeople's fighting. Nevertheless, the pattern from court records, in which whites attacked whites more frequently than blacks attacked blacks, holds. In a sample of nine Southside Virginia Baptist churches, accusations of fighting or quarreling among white members were, collectively, four times more common than those among black churchgoers, both slave and free. Similarly, in the South Carolina upcountry, whites were charged with fighting 3.5 times as often as blacks. A lack of reliable congregational membership data prohibits the extraction of additional meaning from these numbers, but in Georgia, membership figures broken down by race are available for a subset of twelve of the twenty-three sample churches examined for this study. Those dozen churches investigated twice the number of allegations of white-white violence than black-black, even though the average number of white and black congregants was nearly equal, at sixty-eight and fifty-nine, respectively. White members only slightly outnumbered black, but they were subjected to double the number of church investigations for fighting.[32]

As might be expected, individual congregations sometimes defied the broader patterns outlined here. An atypical congregation might accuse black members of fighting more frequently than whites. Or, even if blacks were charged with fighting less frequently, allegations against them exceeded those of whites on a per capita basis. Between 1834 and 1856, for example, Brushy Creek Baptist Church in Greenville County, South Carolina, charged 5 whites and 3 slaves with fighting. But because, over that span of years, an average of 112 whites and just 28 blacks attended Brushy Creek, 1 in 9 slave members was so charged, compared to 1 in 22 whites. Per capita calculations notwithstanding, church minutes verify the findings based on court records: by no quantifiable measure were slaves any more violent to each other than southern whites were to other whites. Certainly the antebellum southern slave community was decidedly less violent than the region's whites when gauged by the numbers of intraracial homicides, but using church records as a guide, the same may be said of nonlethal forms of violence as well. As Eugene D. Genovese suspected, "The violence that slaves inflicted on each other fell far short of the appalling southern norm."[33]

Southern law was structured for the benefit of whites, and on the basis of extant records, the victims of the vast majority of slave crimes, whether crimes against property or people, were white. Restricting ourselves to crimes against persons, court records suggest that slaves were more likely to physically attack whites rather than fellow blacks, most often either in retaliation for poor treatment, to defend the "rights" slaves claimed for themselves, or when confronted with threats of impending sale. Investigating colonial South Carolina, Robert Olwell found that thirty South Carolina slaves were executed for violent crimes in the decade of the 1750s, but only six of those crimes, or 20 percent of the total, were committed against other bondpeople. The same basic pattern held in nineteenth-century South Carolina as well. If anything, the proportion of slaves' intraracial violent crimes dwindled over time. The seventy-five incidents of slave-slave violence recovered in the state's Courts of Magistrates and Freeholders records comprise but a small fraction of all slave crimes, ranging from 3 to 8 percent in Laurens, Spartanburg, Anderson, and Pickens Districts. In Laurens District, slaves were six times more likely to appear in court for inflicting violence, lethal and nonlethal, upon a white victim than upon another black. At least 18 of 302 cases in Spartanburg District (6 percent) and 31 of 429 cases in Anderson District (7 percent) involved slaves who had inflicted violence upon a counterpart in bondage. These percentages were somewhat higher elsewhere in South Carolina, up to 14 percent in Clarendon District. But the Clarendon figure is based on a total of only seven cases of slave crime. Among districts with a sig-

Table 1.1. Slave-Slave Crimes as a Percentage of Total Slave Crimes in Six Georgia Counties

County	Years	Total Slave Crimes	Slave-Slave Crimes	Slave-Slave Crimes as % of Total Crimes	Frequency
Baldwin	1812–1838	17	3	18	1/8.67 years
Chatham	1813–1827	20	4	20	1/3.5 years
Hancock	1843–1850	4	1	25	1/7 years
Jones	1818–1846	6	2	33	1/14 years
Lincoln	1814–1838	6	1	17	1/24 years
Putnam	1813–1843	12	1	8	1/30 years
Totals		65	12	18	1/10.75 years

Source: Inferior Court Records, GA.

nificant number of slave criminal cases, Kershaw District had the highest rate of intraracial slave violence, at 12 percent of all alleged slave crimes. At the other extreme, none of the thirty-four cases in Greenville District recorded instances of violence among slaves. Most slaves who stood before the Courts of Magistrates and Freeholders instead appeared charged with theft or retailing liquor, among a plethora of other offenses.[34]

Statistics from Georgia mirror those of South Carolina. In inferior court records from six sample Georgia counties, documenting slaves' lawful offenses between roughly the 1810s and 1850, crimes committed against fellow slaves—all of which were violent, interpersonal incidents since slaves laid no legal claim to property—comprised between 8 and 33 percent of all infractions for which bondpeople were charged. On average, less than one in five cases that appeared before the inferior courts resulted from one slave assaulting or killing another. Eighty-two percent of slave offenses were directed instead against white people or property. The typical Georgia inferior county court heard a case of intraracial slave violence on average once every eleven years. (See table 1.1.)

Virginia legal records echo the story common to South Carolina and Georgia. Of the 216 Virginia slaves Philip J. Schwarz discovered "executed or transported for murder between 1785 and 1834 and whose victims are known, only 57, or 26.4 percent, had killed slaves." Indeed, slaves in the Commonwealth were more than twice as likely to be convicted of murdering a white as a fellow slave. The state auditor's records of bondpeople sold or transported for their crimes reveal that

Table 1.2. Homicide Rates for African American Victims in Virginia, 1790–1863 (per 100,000 adults per year)

Years	Blacks Murdered by Blacks	Blacks Murdered by Whites	Blacks Murdered by Unknown Assailants
1790–1800	0.0	1.0	0.0
1801–1831	2.9	4.8	2.1
1832–1839	1.4	2.5	0.0
1840–1863	3.9	2.9	1.4

Source: Randolph Roth, American Homicide Supplemental Volume, Historical Violence Database, American Homicides (revised May 2010) (AH); http://cjrc.osu.edu/sites/cjrc.osu.edu/files/AHSV-American-Homicides-5-2010.pdf. Accessed January 23, 2015.

slaves killed at least 142 other bondpeople but nearly 300 whites. Surely homicides within the slave quarters occasionally went unreported, which, given the racialized social order of the South, would not have been the case when a white person was the victim. It is unlikely, however, that more than half of all intraracial slave killings escaped the notice of the law. Even making some allowance for unreported incidents confined to the quarters, slaves almost certainly killed whites more frequently than other bondpeople. And as would be expected, they were more likely to be executed for violent crimes committed upon whites than blacks.[35]

Slaves faced a much greater danger of physical assault or death at the hands of whites than from their fellow inhabitants of the quarters. Every slave was the potential victim of a whipping as part of routine plantation discipline, and occasionally overaggressive masters or overseers let their passions overwhelm them during "correction." Non-slaveholding and poor whites also sometimes assaulted or killed slaves when the time they spent convivially drinking, gambling, and carousing across the color line went awry. Regardless of the precise circumstances surrounding white attacks upon bondpeople, the first slaves to colonial British mainland North America killed one another, according to Randolph Roth, "at only half the rate at which they were murdered by European colonists." As intraracial slave homicide rates in the Chesapeake and Shenandoah Valley declined after 1730, whites proved three times more likely than slaves to murder a bondperson. A variety of measures show similar patterns for the nineteenth century. Court of General Sessions records from Laurens and Spartanburg Districts in South Carolina reveal that sixteen whites were charged with murdering slaves or "negroes" (possibly free) between 1800 and 1865. Another fourteen were accused of assaulting, beating, or cruelly punishing a bondperson. The thirty combined attacks dwarfed the number of violent intraracial encounters among blacks in those districts. In Adams County, Mississippi, slaves were 4.5 times more likely to be killed or non-fatally assaulted by whites than by other slaves, while those in Albemarle County, Virginia, were 18 times more likely to be murdered by a white than by another bondperson. From 1853 to 1858, whites in Mecklenburg County, Virginia, appeared in court only twice for attacking slaves, but during that same stretch, no slaves showed up on the docket for assaulting a white. Altogether, Roth estimates the average rate at which whites killed nineteenth-century African Americans at more than twice that at which blacks died at the hands of each other.[36] (See tables 1.2 and 1.3.)

The extant historical record, in short, documents no epidemic of murder internal to the slave quarters. But while intraracial slave homicide was far from routine, precision is elusive. Evidence is particularly sparse for the colonial period. Even in Virginia, the state with the richest set of available source material, court order books or minute books chronicling slaves' homicides do not survive for every county, and those that do are not terribly informative, rarely delving into motivations and other pertinent details of the assaults. For all crimes combined, Philip J. Schwarz uncovered a total of only forty-one slave trials in all of the Old Dominion between 1706 and 1719, and fewer than one hundred from 1725 to 1739. In only nine of the trials from 1706 to 1739 were slaves convicted of killing fellow bondpeople. According to Schwarz, another seventeen cases of intraracial slave homicide appeared before Virginia courts from 1740 to 1785, raising the total to twenty-six for the 1706 to 1785 time period. "Slaves killed other blacks ...," Schwarz concluded, "but not to a degree that seriously threatened the stability of the slave communities of eighteenth-century Virginia." Shifting the time frame slightly, historian Philip D. Morgan agreed: "Thirty murder cases involving only slaves—the total for twenty-four Virginia counties between 1710 and 1790—does not seem, in and of itself, to betoken serious internal conflict within the slave community."[37]

The most readily identifiable cases of intraracial slave violence in Virginia are located via the state auditor's records, which, beginning in the early 1780s, chronicle those criminal convictions that ended with a sentence of death or sale and transportation out of the United States or, later, transferals to the public works. They direct the researcher to county court records, which themselves are an imperfect source. Within those records, some of the victims of slave hom-

Table 1.3. Homicide Inquest Rates for African American Victims in Edgefield and Horry Districts, South Carolina (per 100,000 persons ages sixteen and older per year)

County	Date Range	Blacks Murdered by Blacks	Blacks Murdered by Whites
Edgefield	1844–1863	4.1	6.7
Horry	1849–1863	0.0	22.7

Source: Randolph Roth, American Homicide Supplemental Volume, Historical Violence Database, American Homicides (revised May 2010) (AH); http://cjrc.osu.edu/researchprojects/hvd. Accessed March 17, 2013.

icides are never identified, so their race or status cannot be determined. In a few cases, the handwriting of county court clerks is so illegible as to render the trial papers indecipherable. No doubt, with time, the present figure of 142 intraracial slave homicides included in the appendix for the years 1777 to 1864 will rise. Indeed, the number is already artificially small because it does not include either enslaved murderers of slaves who were punished without recourse to law or, with only two exceptions, those who appeared in court but escaped a capital sentence, either because they were not convicted of the charge against them or because they were found guilty of a lesser offense that did not mandate the severest possible punishments. To illustrate the point, look more minutely at any Virginia county. The courts of Thomas Jefferson's Albemarle County, for example, tried slave defendants for ten murders of other slaves, only two of which appear in the database. Five accused bondpeople were judged not guilty and discharged, while another three were convicted but not punished capitally. Only the two who were eventually sold and transported appear in the state auditor's records. The total number of intraracial slave homicide victims from Albemarle County that appeared in court, then, is five times greater than the number indicated by the database. If Albemarle County was typical (and further, tedious research at the county level will be required to determine that), the real number of slave-slave murders tried before Virginia courts from 1777 to 1864 may be more than seven hundred, or, on average, approximately eight per year during that span of time. Another three Albemarle County slaves were tried for violent but nonlethal assaults upon fellow bondpeople. The database overlooks these cases as well.[38]

As more sources have been uncovered, the number of intraracial slave homicides in the Old Dominion has already been upwardly revised through time. A century ago, Ulrich B. Phillips documented only 85 murders of Virginia slaves by other slaves. In the 1980s, Daniel Flanigan elaborated upon Phillips's findings, noting that, from 1790 to 1855 and from 1859 to 1864, Virginia bondpeople were convicted of killing 59 male slaves, 14 female slaves, and a dozen slave children. Adding in 7 free black victims, Flanigan upped the total figure of blacks murdered by slaves to 92. Philip J. Schwarz's thorough examination of slave crime in Virginia revealed that, from 1785 to 1864, slaves killed 121 fellow bondpeople as well as 14 free blacks. This study adds another 21 slave-slave homicides to Schwarz's tally, and future scholars will surely recover additional cases not included in the statistics here. Adding in approximately another 30 known intraracial slave murders from the colonial era produces a grand total of 172 Virginia bondmen murdered by slaves from 1706 to 1864, not counting those punished privately or who did not receive a capital sentence in a court of law.[39]

However incomplete the Virginia murder database for 1777 to 1864, it proves nonetheless informative, suggestive of broader patterns of violence within the slave community. More often than not, assailant and victim belonged to different masters. Philip J. Schwarz discovered that, in a sample of nine intraracial homicides in early colonial Virginia, between 1706 and 1739, two-thirds of all slaves convicted of attacking other bondpeople belonged to different owners, a fraction that would prove remarkably consistent over time. Of the known murders of slaves by slaves in Virginia from 1777 to 1864, the parties involved belonged to different masters half the time, and in 10 percent of the cases, ownership cannot be determined from surviving records. Subtract out the cases of infanticide and child murder, however, in which enslaved women purportedly destroyed the master's property to which they had given birth, and the slaves involved in fatal encounters belonged to different owners in almost two-thirds of the cases. Among intraracial slave homicides involving only adults, killer and victim were more than twice as likely to be owned by different masters as by the same master. This finding is not surprising for two reasons. First, cross-plantation murders were less likely than intraplantation killings to evade notice of the law. Second, as Anthony E. Kaye has explained, conflict and violence were, paradoxically, crucial in the forging of slave solidarity, delineating the boundaries of neighborhood that knit some slaves together to the exclusion of others. Thus, when one white man in the South Carolina upcountry witnessed some "pretty violent quarreling" in Laurens District between "Bullocks Dave & Motes negroes," he got an intimate glimpse at Bullock and Motes bondmen determining who counted as friends within the neighborhood and who would be regarded as strangers, at least for

ORIGINS, PREVALENCE, AND PATTERNS

Table 1.4. Slave-Slave Murder-Victim Combinations in Virginia, 1777–1864 (N = 153)

Same master:	61 (40%)
Different masters:	77 (50%)
Unknown:	15 (10%)

Source: Appendix.

Table 1.5. Slave-Slave Murder-Victim Combinations in Virginia, 1777–1864, Less Infanticides and Child Murders (N = 119)

Same master:	36 (30%)
Different masters:	76 (64%)
Unknown:	7 (6%)

Source: Appendix.

the time being. Creating solidarity among one set of slaves necessarily generated conflict with other bondpeople standing outside that communal, neighborhood unit. In regions with larger, more sprawling plantations than in the Old Dominion, geographic realities and limitations on slaves' mobility may have conspired to confine quarrels more frequently to the same plantation. Records from the cotton-producing Black Belt are more scarce and less accessible, however, than those in the older slaveholding states to the east.[40] (See tables 1.4 and 1.5.)

Even if a majority of enslaved murderers and their enslaved victims belonged to different masters, odds were nearly certain that they were at least acquainted with one another, if not family or erstwhile friends. Although court records do not always permit us to tease out the precise nature of the murderer-victim relationship, a significant number of intraracial slave homicides produced the deaths of spouses or lovers, infants or children, or, much less frequently, siblings. More often still, murderer and victim were neighbors or lived in close proximity and had become familiar with one another as they co-labored in the fields or gathered together to socialize. Almost never did bondmen or bondwomen end the life of an anonymous stranger. In rural, agricultural settings and the small, close-knit communities of the slave South, it could hardly have been any other way. The overwhelming majority of intraracial slave homicides represented spontaneous acts involving bondpeople who knew one another. Court records suggest premeditation in only a distinct minority of all cases.[41]

In at least 12 of the 142 cases (8.45 percent) of intraracial slave homicide in Virginia, the convicted slave murder belonged to the estate of a master who had died. The assailant and victim were the property of different slaveholders in only a slight majority of these cases. In almost 42 percent of the cases, the slaves involved in murderous affrays belonged to the same owner and presumably, in most instances, would have lived and worked together on the same plantation. Dinwiddie County court records listed Peter as "the property of the estate of William P. Claiborne" when it was alleged in 1800 that the bondman did "plot & conspire with other slaves unknown [in] the murder of Matt," likewise another slave of the deceased. It cannot be certain, but perhaps slaves seized the opportunity presented by the master's demise to act out the murderous impulses they held in check during the lifetime of the owner. Masters' deaths generated uncertainty and anxiety within their slaves, who knew quite well that their lives might be cast into turmoil. Slaves remained in limbo until the provisions of the master's will were executed, and for those who anticipated being forcibly relocated, either bequeathed to another family member or sold to cover the deceased master's debts, they may have felt themselves at liberty to unleash their hatred upon a fellow bondperson. With the prospect of removal or sale looming anyway, they had less to lose.[42]

Almost all slave-slave homicides in the Old Dominion began as confrontations between individuals. When slaves acted in concert in the commission of crimes against persons or property, the victim was almost invariably white. From 1740 to 1785, slaves conspired in the death of but one Virginia bondman. Only 6 of the 142 victims included in the database (4.2 percent) from 1777 to 1864 were murdered by multiple assailants, and 2 of those deaths were entirely accidental. Slaves Hainey, Dick, and Daniel, all three the property of the estate of Mecklenburg County master Francis W. Boyd, plotted with Amanda Dedman's bondman Nelson to poison the reputedly troublesome "rascal" Henry Baptist, another of Boyd's slaves. Inadvertently, Baptist's children Tucker and Amy drank the adulterated water intended for him. The day the youngsters died, Daniel told Nelson that their scheme had gone awry. Baptist lived, Daniel informed his co-conspirator, "but dam him, I wish it had been him instead of the children." Baptist was one of but a handful of slaves who possessed the unique ability to ruffle sufficient feathers to inspire a murder plot. Female slaves were complicit in two-thirds of the deaths for which more than one bondperson was convicted. The Hainey who colluded in the unintentional poisoning of Henry Baptist's son and daughter was a woman, and the mother-daughter team of Rinah and Fanny collaborated to poison Prince Edward County bondman Oxford with "highland hemlock." Sally and Lizzy were also mother and daughter, but they took a bloodier approach, fatally assaulting the bondwoman Amey with knives. The greatest number of slaves known to have collaborated in the murder of an individual bondperson was seven. In Benton County, Alabama, Frank, Jerry, Trussvan, and four other slaves were indicted for the stabbing death of LaFayette, or Fayette, in 1855. As the Alabama Supreme Court explained, "If several persons conspire to do an unlawful act ... all the members of such illegal combination are responsible for the acts of each, done, in prosecution of their common purpose."[43]

Just as few slaves were victimized by multiple assailants, few slaves were ever held responsible for the deaths of more than one bondperson. In two cases from the colonial period, a bondman killed one enslaved man and one enslaved woman, suggesting possible lovers' triangles. Louisa County's Boatswain hanged for the murders of Will and Rachel in 1745; eight years later Cudjo of Cumberland County met the same fate for ending the lives of Iris and Beck. In post-revolutionary Virginia, the multiple victims were almost always children. King and Queen County bondwoman Amey was convicted of killing her daughter Isbell and son Harrison in 1799 with an axe and a knife, respectively. The pregnant slave woman Jenny of Powhatan County was also found guilty of child murder, the triple drowning in 1815 of her offspring Anderson, Julius, and Violett. The only enslaved man found solely responsible for murdering a child was the Spotsylvania County bondman Jarret, who also killed Rose, the youngster's mother, in 1831. Otherwise, bondwomen committed, or at the very least collaborated in, the murders of twenty-seven of the twenty-eight infants and children included in the database.[44]

One-hundred and forty-five slaves were held responsible for the 142 murders included in our tally for Virginia. Of the enslaved assailants, 106 (73 percent) were male, 39 (27 percent) female. Victims included 91 bondmen (64 percent of all bondpeople killed by other slaves), 22 bondwomen (15 percent), 28 infants or children (20 percent), and 1 individual whose sex was never specified in court records (1 percent). (See table 1.6.) If we exclude infanticides and child murders from the total number of homicides, enslaved men constituted 80 percent of all adult slaves killed by other residents of the quarters, enslaved women 20 percent. These findings for the last quarter of the eighteenth century and the slaveholding portion of the nineteenth approximate Philip J. Schwarz's figures for the early colonial period. Of the 9 enslaved victims attacked by other bondpeople between 1706 and 1739, 6 were male (67 percent), 2 female (22 percent). In the one re-

Table 1.6. Murderers and Victims of Intraracial Slave Homicides by Sex and Age, Virginia, 1777–1864

	No. Males	No. Females	No. Infants/Children	No. Unknown	Total
Murderers	106 (73%)	39 (27%)	0 (0%)	0 (0%)	145
Victims	91 (64%)	22 (15%)	28 (20%)	1 (1%)	142

Source: Appendix.

maining case, the sex of the deceased was not listed (11 percent). Assuming the unknown slave was likely male, the percentages of adult male and adult female slave victims for 1706 to 1739 and for 1777 to 1864 were virtually identical.[45]

We may identify additional trends in intraracial slave homicides by further breaking down the data by the sex of the assailants. This process is complicated somewhat by the occasional collaboration of accomplices to effect a slave's demise. In cases where two slaves conspired to kill a third, I have credited each slave with half of a death. In two different cases, children were killed by a combination of four total people: three bondmen and a bondwoman. I have therefore held the male slaves responsible for three-fourths of each of the two deaths and the female slave for the balance, leading to the seemingly odd fractions of a death that appear in table 1.7. Enslaved men tended to murder other bond*men* rather than bondwomen or enslaved infants or children. Eighty-two percent of men's victims were the same sex as themselves. Their victims were adult slave women in only 15 percent of the murders bondmen committed. From the 1600s to the early 1800s, Randolph Roth estimates that black men in the Chesapeake murdered female blacks at a rate of only 0.3 or 0.4 per 100,000 women. For their part, female slaves were equally likely to murder bondmen and bondwomen, but their most likely victims were infants and children, who comprised 65 percent of all slaves killed by bondwomen. Put differently, enslaved women killed only 8 percent of all male slave victims, 32 percent of all female slave victims, and a substantial 91 percent of all victims who were infants or children; enslaved men killed 92 percent of all male slave victims and 68 percent of all female slave victims but just 9 percent of all victims who were infants or children. Concerning enslaved men, the numbers here generally mirror Schwarz's figures for 1740 to 1785. During that period, Schwarz found just 17 total slave-slave murders in which the sex of the victim was known. Male slaves perpetrated 15 (88 percent) of them. Twelve of enslaved men's 15 victims (80 percent) were other bondmen,

Table 1.7. Intraracial Slave Homicides by Sex of the Assailant, Virginia, 1777–1864

	No. Victims of Male Murderers	No. Victims of Female Murderers	No. Total Victims
Male	84 (82%)	7 (18%)	91 (64%)
Female	15 (15%)	7 (18%)	22 (15%)
Infant/Child	2.5 (2%)	25.5 (65%)	28 (20%)
Unknown	1 (1%)	0 (0%)	1 (0%)
Totals	102.5 (100%)	39.5 (101%)	142

Source: Appendix.

essentially the same percentage of bondmen's male victims from 1777 to 1864. Enslaved men were convicted for 12 of the 13 murders of bondmen (92 percent) in the 1740 to 1785 timeframe, a figure identical to that for 1777 to 1864. Schwarz uncovered only 2 cases from 1740 to 1785 in which enslaved women were convicted for murder. In one the victim was male; in the other, female. This sample is too small to permit meaningful comparisons over time.[46]

The documented intraracial slave homicides included in the database were not distributed equally over time. (See table 1.8.) With 142 murders spanning 88 years, the Old Dominion averaged just 1.6 slave-slave homicides per year in which a convicted bondperson was condemned either to death or to sale and transportation, an arrestingly low figure in a Commonwealth where the total slave population climbed from 293,000 in 1790 to 491,000 by 1860. The average disguises annual variations, however. Twenty-five separate years, including 21 from 1778 to 1812, witnessed no murders of slaves that resulted in capital punishment for the convict. Long periods without evidence of slave-slave homicides, including 1787 to 1791 and 1804 to 1810, likely indicate unnatural gaps in the extant sources. The years 1813 to 1834 and 1848 to 1864 all witnessed at least 1 intraracial slave homicide somewhere in Virginia. Six years—1824, 1840, 1851, 1852, 1858, and 1861—proved the most deadly, with 5 documented intraracial slave killings in each. A typical full decade saw 16 slave-slave homicides. The 1850s was easily the most tumultuous decade for such crimes, with more than twice the number of slaves than in the preceding 20 years combined convicted of murdering other bondpeople. Even taking into account the growth of Virginia's slave population, the per capita rate of intraracial slave homicides climbed noticeably in the 1850s, reflecting perhaps greater white skittishness about any signs

Table 1.8. Intraracial Slave Homicides by Year and by Decade, Virginia, 1777–1864 (N = 142)

		1790	0	1810	0	1830	2	1850	1		
		1791	0	1811	1	1831	2	1851	5		
		1792	2	1812	0	1832	2	1852	5		
		1793	1	1813	2	1833	3	1853	2		
		1794	2	1814	2	1834	2	1854	4		
Unk.	1	1795	1	1815	3	1835	0	1855	4		
		1796	4	1816	3	1836	0	1856	4		
1777	2	1797	0	1817	3	1837	3	1857	3		
1778	0	1798	1	1818	2	1838	1	1858	5		
1779	0	1799	3	1819	2	1839	1	1859	2		
	2		14		18		16		35		
1780	0	1800	1	1820	4	1840	5	1860	3		
1781	0	1801	1	1821	1	1841	0	1861	5		
1782	1	1802	2	1822	2	1842	2	1862	1		
1783	0	1803	1	1823	2	1843	1	1863	1		
1784	0	1804	0	1824	5	1844	1	1864	1		
1785	0	1805	0	1825	1	1845	2				11
1786	1	1806	0	1826	3	1846	1				
1787	0	1807	0	1827	2	1847	0				
1788	0	1808	0	1828	1	1848	3				
1789	0	1809	0	1829	1	1849	1				
	2		5		22		16				

Source: Appendix.

of slave aggression or simply better recordkeeping. At the opposite extreme, the 1780s and the first decade of the nineteenth century witnessed, respectively, only 2 and 5 intraracial slave homicide cases, again the likely consequence of limited surviving records.

The occurrence of slave-slave murders varied not only from one year to the next but also within the calendar year. Table 1.9 lists the months in which bondpeople were tried and convicted in Virginia courts for intraracial slave homicides from 1777 to 1864. Trials took place usually the same month as the crime or occasionally the month following, and in an average month, there were about a dozen such trials. The highest percentage of cases appeared in court in Novem-

Table 1.9. Intraracial Slave Homicide Convictions by Month of Trial, Virginia, 1777–1864 (N = 142)

Month	No.
January	15 (11%)
February	13 (9%)
March	11 (8%)
April	6 (4%)
May	16 (11%)
June	11 (8%)
July	7 (5%)
August	10 (7%)
September	15 (11%)
October	9 (6%)
November	19 (13%)
December	9 (6%)
Unknown	1 (1%)
Total	142 (100%)
Average	11.8

Source: Appendix.

ber, followed by May, January, and September. In contrast, April and July were markedly less likely to witness the convictions of slaves for murdering another slave. In each of those two months, convictions were less than half of what they were in any one of the four busiest months. The distribution of cases appears quite random and betrays no seasonal pattern tied to the agricultural cycle of Virginia tobacco production. The more intensive labor involved in tobacco cultivation picked up in April as weeding and transplanting began. Because few murder trials were held in April, it might be tempting to assume that slaves were too busy or too exhausted to kill. The same steps in raising tobacco were still being performed in May, however, one of the months with an unusually high number of convictions. Similarly, of the two months dedicated to harvest, August and September, one was below average and the other above average in the number of convictions. Late in the year, with the worst of slaves' labor complete, convictions stood at only nine in both October and December. Strangely, November saw more convictions than both the preceding and succeeding months combined. An inordinate number of homicides did take place late in the year, during the Christmas holiday season, which explains the high number of cases tried in January.[47]

Temporal patterns are much more evident when looking at the week as the unit of measure. In Virginia and throughout the remainder of the South, the overwhelming preponderance of intraracial slave killings took place during slaves' time off, late on Saturdays and Sundays. "The Sabbath is considered a very suitable day for the settlement of their difficulties," observed the white Georgian Charles Colcock Jones. According to the former slave Henry Bibb, "Those who make no profession of religion, resort to the woods in large numbers on that day to gamble, fight, get drunk, and break the Sabbath." Ironically, Sunday violence often broke out at or near a church. As the holy attended services, the profane, it seemed to critical whites, ran amok just outside. Anne Newport Royall, traveling in Huntsville, Alabama, recorded that "[t]here were seven fights here, between negroes, near the doors of their churches." Slaveholder Maria Wofford of Spartanburg District, South Carolina, groused that Joe, "a servant of D W Moores was engaged in a riotous way on the second Sabbath in February 1851 exciting her Boy Bassett to a breach of the peace by following him on his way home and committing an assault on his person all of which was a disturbance of the good order of the Town." Sabbath-day violence also erupted in Raleigh, North Carolina, in 1825. A local newspaper alerted its readers to a quarrel between "[t]wo negro boys" that culminated in "[a] murder ... committed in our streets on Sunday evening last, about eight o'clock."[48]

As the previous two examples demonstrate, a portion of all intraracial slave violence took place in the South's small towns and cities. Writing of slaves, Charles Colcock Jones explained, "They come to open breaches ... with their neighbors on adjoining plantations, or lots, if they live in towns." Historian Edward L. Ayers describes antebellum southern cities as generally violent places. As Eugene D. Genovese explains it, slaves who lived in towns "resorted to violence more frequently than did those in the more disciplined countryside" because judgment-impairing liquor was more readily accessible in urban locales. In my database for Virginia, however, documenting murders as the most extreme form of violence, urban homicides accounted for only 11 of the 142 convictions for intraracial slave killings. At 7.7 percent, this figure was more or less consistent with the proportion of urban slaves in the Commonwealth over time. Richmond led the way with seven intraracial slave murders, followed by Petersburg's two and Lynchburg and Norfolk, with one apiece. The data for incorporated Virginia indicate no epidemic of urban slave-slave homicide. Evidence from the larger city of New Orleans tells a similar story. There, writes Judith Kelleher Schafer,

"Slaves and free people of color ... committed crimes ... far below their proportion in the city's population." In the sixteen years from 1846 to 1861, the First District Court of New Orleans heard only a dozen cases in which slaves were charged with murder or other violent assaults upon fellow bondpeople. Henry, for one, publicly and fatally stabbed a twenty-one-year-old native South Carolinian named John in the middle of Camp Street in 1853. But even in the largest city of the Lower South, such attacks were not common occurrences. Throughout the prewar South, slave-slave murder was an overwhelmingly rural phenomenon, a consequence of the vast majority of all slaves' employment at various agricultural pursuits.[49]

The likelihood of intraracial slave homicide was not equitably distributed within the borders of individual states. In Virginia, the 142 murder convictions were scattered across 68 (46 percent) of the Commonwealth's 148 different counties. (See table 1.10, which lists the city of Richmond independently from Henrico County.) Forty-seven of them witnessed only 1 or 2 intraracial killings from 1777 to 1864. The city of Richmond served as the backdrop to the greatest number of slave-slave murders, with 7, or 4.9 percent of the total. Together, Richmond combined with half a dozen Virginia counties—Chesterfield, Mecklenburg, Pittsylvania, Powhatan, Prince Edward, and Spotsylvania—to account for 26 percent of all the Commonwealth's intraracial slave homicide convictions even though they comprised just 10 percent of the 68 counties where such conflicts occurred. Eleven of the 68 counties (16 percent)—those with 4 or more murders—accounted for 37 percent of the convictions, and 21 of the 68 (31 percent)—those with 3 or more—58 percent. Spatially, a majority of the intraracial slave homicide convictions—85 of the 142, or 60 percent—were handed down in the Virginia Piedmont. The top 7 Virginia counties for intraracial slave homicides, 9 of the top 11, and 17 of the top 21 were all located in the Piedmont region. Eight counties of the Central Piedmont alone accounted for 36, or one-quarter, of all such killings. On the whole, the Piedmont was overrepresented in its number of intraracial slave murders compared to the region's proportion of Virginia's total slave population. The Central Piedmont subregion, including the city of Richmond, was primarily responsible for the statistical aberration. Outside the Piedmont, 2 counties of the Central Blue Ridge, Amherst and Rockbridge, ranked highest in the number of slave-slave murders, with 4 each. The oldest slaveholding region of Virginia, the Tidewater, contained only 1 county with 3 or more cases of intraracial slave killings. Indeed, the Tidewater was as underrepresented in the spatial distribution of slave-slave homicides as the Piedmont

Table 1.10. Intraracial Slave Homicide Convictions by County, Region, and Percentage of Total Slave Population, Virginia, 1777–1864

Region	No. Murders	Slave Pop., 1860
Piedmont	**85 (60%)**	**249,748 (51%)**
Northern Piedmont	15 (11%)	47,919 (10%)
Caroline (2), Hanover (2), King George (1), Louisa (3), Orange (2), Spotsylvania (5)		
Central Piedmont	37 (26%)	75,049 (15%)
Appomattox (3), Buckingham (3), Chesterfield (5), Cumberland (4), Fluvanna (1), Henrico (4), Powhatan (5), Prince Edward (5), Richmond (city) (7)		
Southeastern Piedmont	19 (13%)	62,348 (13%)
Brunswick (1), Charlotte (3), Dinwiddie (1), Lunenburg (3), Mecklenburg (5), Nottoway (3), Petersburg (2), Prince George (1)		
Southwestern Piedmont	14 (10%)	64,432 (13%)
Bedford (3), Halifax (3), Henry (1), Lynchburg (1), Patrick (1), Pittsylvania (5)		
Tidewater	**19 (13%)**	**104,319 (21%)**
Urban Tidewater	1 (1%)	12,190 (2%)
Norfolk (1)		
Southern Tidewater	6 (4%)	27,525 (6%)
Greensville (2), Nansemond (1), Southampton (2), Surry (1)		
Northern Tidewater	12 (8%)	64,604 (13%)
Accomack (1), Essex (1), Gloucester (1), James City (1), King and Queen (3), Middlesex (2), New Kent (1), Northampton (2)		
Blue Ridge	**15 (11%)**	**61,600 (13%)**
Northern Blue Ridge	4 (3%)	
Albemarle (2), Nelson (1), Rockingham (1)		
Central Blue Ridge	9 (6%)	
Amherst (4), Botetourt (1), Rockbridge (4)		
Southern Blue Ridge	2 (1%)	
Giles (1), Pulaski (1)		
Northwest	**9 (6%)**	**33,859 (7%)**
Culpeper (1), Fauquier (3), Madison (2), Rappahannock (2), Shenandoah (1)		
West Virginia	**9 (6%)**	**18,371 (4%)**
Brooke (1), Greenbrier (1), Hardy (1), Harrison (1), Kanawha (2), Lewis (1), Monroe (1), Pendleton (1)		

Table 1.10. (cont.)

Region	No. Murders	Slave Pop., 1860
Potomac	3 (2%)	15,673 (3%)
Fairfax (1), Loudoun (1), Stafford (1)		
Appalachian Plateau	2 (1%)	7,295 (1%)
Russell (1), Washington (1)		
Total	142 (99%*)	490,865 (100%)

* Due to rounding, figure does not equal 100 percent.

Source: Historical Census Browser, University of Virginia, Geospatial and Statistical Data Center (2004): http://fisher.lib.virginia.edu/collections/stats/histcensus/index.html.

was overrepresented. The reasons are not entirely clear, although the locus of tobacco cultivation and the strains it engendered had shifted to the west by the nineteenth century. With the exceptions of the Piedmont and the Tidewater, the geography of intraracial slave homicides in the other regions of Virginia accurately reflected those regions' percentages of the Commonwealth's total slave population.[50]

Throughout the antebellum South, bondpeople usually harmed their enslaved adversaries with one of two categories of weapons: those used to beat and those used to cut. Although court records did not always indicate the precise vehicle for inflicting injury or death, in upcountry South Carolina, Georgia, and Adams County, Mississippi, slave aggressors most commonly struck, beat, or bludgeoned their victims with such weapons as sticks, clubs, hickory switches, fence rails, billets of wood, poles, brickbats, rocks, pestles, or iron rods. Of these, sticks were by far the most common. Collectively, blunt instruments were overwhelmingly opportunistic weapons not suggestive of premeditation. Many were normally the tools slaves wielded in service to the master. In Virginia, where such weapons ranked second to those that were sharp, enslaved murderers beat their enemies with agricultural implements, including hoes, shovels, mattocks, and adzes. Others employed hammers, pestles, and other tools or, less conventionally, oars, bed posts, iron pots, and even a flaming log. In the Old Dominion, however, the weapons slaves most commonly used to dispatch their enemies were knives or, to a far lesser extent, dirks, axes, hatchets, razors, or similar stabbing or cutting instruments. One Virginia slave died after being slashed in the throat "with a piece of glass bottle," another from a vicious assault with a table fork. But knives were easily slaves' most frequently brandished weapon in the Commonwealth (sticks were a distant second and axes third), probably a reflection of their centrality to the cultivation of tobacco. Bondpeople in other states frequently used knives as well, more often, in fact, than did antebellum white assailants. In one unusual case, a Georgia bondman used a sword to chop and almost sever an enemy slave's hand from his wrist. But in Georgia, the South Carolina upcounty, and Adams County, sharp objects were narrowly edged out by blunt instruments as slaves' weapons of choice.[51]

Only rarely did other media for inflicting pain or death defy the system of categorization presented here. The New Orleans bondwoman Sanite offered one peculiar example. She "severely scalded" the "negro boy" Auguste, "aged about fourteen," by throwing a pot of boiling water in his face. More common were cases of poisoning. Despite sporadic reports of poisonings in the nineteenth century, the preponderance of such allegations occurred during the colonial era and late in the eighteenth century, likely fueled by masters' anxieties over enslaved conjurors' esoteric powers transported directly or indirectly from Africa. The powers of conjuration might be used for good or ill. The aged bondman Old Matt of Cumberland County, Virginia, for example, claimed to have "given Negroes roots and medicine three or four times to make their masters & mistresses love them," but he had also "threatened to fix three of Capt Bookers negroes and . . . lay them upon their death beds." According to Philip J. Schwarz, "Slaves were regularly prosecuted for poisoning other slaves." He uncovered the cases of forty-six Virginia slaves placed on trial for poisoning other bondpeople from 1706 to 1784. During the same time period, slaves purportedly poisoned almost twice the number of white people. Of the ninety accused of poisoning whites, sixty-two (69 percent) were found guilty, but when poisoning victims were other slaves, the conviction rate fell to 50 percent. Sixteen of the twenty-three slaves convicted of poisoning other bondpeople (70 percent) escaped the death penalty for their crime. Cumberland County bondman Quash administered medicine in 1759 to Peter and another slave named Quash. Because Quash showed no malicious intent in dispensing his concoction, he "received benefit of clergy and thirty-nine lashes rather than the death sentence." Similarly, after the slave Toby "feloniously did prepare & exhibit sundry Medicines" in 1764 and give them to Tom, Phillis, and Jenny, a Cumberland County court convicted him and ordered that he be given thirty-nine stripes and burned in the hand. Slaves' likelihood of escaping capital punishment only increased with time. From 1785 to 1831, only two of the thirty-five slaves (5.7 percent) convicted of poisoning other slaves were sentenced to death.[52]

From 1706 to 1784, only seven slaves in the Old Dominion were sentenced to the gallows for poisoning fellow slaves. That number included Caroline County's Peter and Cupid, slated to hang in 1762 for "administering Poyson or medicine," respectively, to "Jeffry a negro man Slave" and to "Frank a negro woman slave."[53] But because poisoning charges were so difficult to prove, half of the slaves accused of poisoning other bondpeople were found not guilty and had their cases discharged. The bondwoman Letty of Middlesex County, Virginia, purportedly gave contaminated "Cyder Water Bread & Meat . . . to one Simon a Negro Man Slave," who suffered more than half a year before dying on April 1, 1748. The protracted duration of his illness cast some doubt upon Letty's culpability for the crime, and she was found not guilty. In Powhatan County, Thomas Harris's slave Frank supposedly poisoned the bondwoman Susannah, owned by the same master, in 1782. Although "Susannah was deprived of her life," Frank was found innocent. The bondman Harvey of Nansemond County, "charged with preparing and furnishing Frank . . . with [the] poison," likewise escaped punishment. A few years later, another Powhatan County slave named Frank (or possibly the same bondman, now belonging to a different owner) was "charged with administering Poison to a Negroe woman named Anakey," but no evidence was produced against him, and he was discharged. In Powhatan and Cumberland Counties combined, a total of six slaves were suspected of poisoning other bondpeople in 1773, 1780, 1782, and 1785. None were found guilty.[54]

Occasionally Virginia courts found slaves not guilty of poisoning but punished the accused anyway because they threatened the security of slave property or, more broadly, the peace and stability of colonial society. "Tom a negro man Slave" of Caroline County allegedly administered "Several Poysonous Powders Roots Herbs and Simples" into "the drink of Joe" in 1744. The unsuspecting Joe drank "the mixture" and "grievously Languish[ed]" for two weeks before his death. Tom was judged not guilty of murder, but the Caroline County court that heard his case transported him out of Virginia nonetheless because it was believed he had given poisonous substances to other slaves as well. That "Caesar a negro man slave belonging to Nathaniel Carrington" prepared "poisonous medicine" and exhibited it "to Jenny a negro woman slave" was of little concern to the Cumberland County court that heard his case in 1773. The justices became convinced, however, that the bondman was "plotting the murder of the said Nathaniel Carrington" and ordered him hanged. Caesar may have miscalculated in divulging his plans to Jenny, whose loyalties in this circumstance lay with the white Carrington family.[55]

Writing shortly before the Civil War, Alabama planter and lawyer Daniel R. Hundley complained that "the negroes nearly always poison one another." The malevolent slave, he explained, "proceeds under cover of night to the cabin of the most famous witch or conjurer in the neighborhood" in a quest for the proper "medication" to administer to a despised enemy. Court records from Virginia indicate no epidemic of slave-slave poisonings in the mid-nineteenth century, however. As Philip J. Schwarz observed, poisonings of fellow slaves did increase after 1830 compared to previous decades. From their colonial-era highs, convictions for poisoning other slaves dwindled to just two from 1785 to 1829 before rising to eleven after 1830. But those eleven bondpeople included several who collaborated in the deaths of fellow slaves. Altogether, they were found guilty of administering toxic substances to a total of only half a dozen enslaved victims. Outside Virginia, other southern states witnessed similarly small numbers of prosecutions in the nineteenth century for poisoning slaves. In Natchez, Mississippi, one grand jury presented "Peter a negro man slave" in 1812 for "maliciously and feloniously plotting and intending to poison one Martin a negro man the fellow slave of him the said Peter." The bondman purportedly "put a large quantity of white essence, being a deadly poison, into a cup of milk," which he "set out for ... Martin to drink." Although Peter was found guilty, poisonings of fellow slaves were no easier to prove in the nineteenth century than in the eighteenth. Many slaves evaded convictions for poisoning other bondpeople because medical professionals could not provide the incontrovertible proof required by law.[56]

Poisoning cases notwithstanding, court records regularly assessed the value of the weapons used to produce death. At the end of the eighteenth century, King and Queen County, Virginia, bondwoman Amy slay her daughter Isbell "with a certain ax made of iron & steel of the value of five shillings" and her son Harrison with a knife valued at "six pence." In the slaveholding South, murder weapons often cost no money at all. Anyone with ill intentions might find at any time a wide assortment of sticks and stones, capable of causing death, strewn randomly on the ground. In late 1813, while Mississippi was still a territory, the "Negro man Milo" mortally assaulted "Leah a woman of colour ... with a certain stick of cypress wood of no value."[57] Many other weapons were worth but a pittance, including a "billet of wood, of the value of six cents" that Adams County slave Anthony used to kill Harry. The relatively more expensive agricultural implements and tools used to harm or kill fellow slaves—a hoe "of the value of twenty five cents," knives costing "fifty cents" or a dollar, "a shovel of the value of one dollar," or a two-dollar "mattock made of Iron & steel with a wooden handle"—would in almost all cases have been purchased by the master and made available to bondpeople for the completion of their labors without the slightest thought that they might someday be used for more sinister purposes.[58]

In only a small number of homicide cases across the South did slave attackers use nothing but their bare hands. In 1795, a Middlesex County, Virginia, court convicted the bondman Peter of choking "a certain negro woman slave, named Alice," with a linen handkerchief. Most strangulations and suffocations were committed by female slaves, however, in the deaths of infants or children. One enslaved mother in the Old Dominion drowned her offspring in a creek. More often, bondmen utilized their own bodies plus an array of weapons. Spotsylvania County's Harry and Ned assaulted their fellow slave James not only with "hands & feet" and "fists" but also with "sticks, whips, switches and clubs," and in Shenandoah County, Fortune attacked "Sukey a negroe Woman" "with axes fists hand and feet" before throwing her "with great force and violence" down a set of stairs, killing her. Sometimes in murder cases, what began as a simple fistfight escalated into something more. On Washington Street in Natchez, Mississippi, "Stuart, a negro man," landed a punch on the slave Horace, who returned "a backhanded blow with his right hand." Unfortunately for Stuart, Horace's hand also clutched a knife. Stuart immediately felt the blade, crying out, "d——d if I am stabbed."[59]

Whereas slaves routinely wielded knives, sticks, and the like in the infliction of violence, they rarely used guns. Bondpeople lived within a gun culture but were not fully incorporated into it. They were sometimes threatened by masters or overseers with gun violence or even shot at, but normally the whip sufficed. And lack of opportunity meant that the overwhelming majority of all slaves never clutched a firearm. Southern whites feared armed bondmen and began passing legislation prohibiting slaves' access to guns as early as the colonial era. Cyclically, however, whites grew complacent over slaves' use of firearms and ignored the law, only to have the rare slave rebellion or a rumored conspiracy periodically jolt them into a renewed recognition of the dangers of gun-toting bondmen. The sudden resurfacing of latent anxieties unleashed fresh hysteria and resulted in new rounds of restrictive legislation reinforcing and elaborating upon existing statutes. Whereas colonial-era laws authorized slaves' access to firearms under certain exceptional circumstances, those rights gradually eroded with time, replaced by complete bans. Legally, by the antebellum decades, slaves could neither purchase, own, possess, nor—except by order of the master—carry firearms. Were the law fully abided by or enforced, virtually no slaves would ever have committed any sort of crime with a gun. Yet they did. In his study of Georgia before the end of the Civil War, Glenn M. McNair found that, combined, black and white Georgians charged with murder or attempted murder employed firearms in almost 17 percent of the cases.[60]

Although slaves rarely committed acts of gun violence upon one another, there are scattered examples from across the South. Many cases involved some variety of love triangle or the interference of one slave in an enslaved couple's martial union. All of the gun-wielding offenders uncovered in this study were male. Gun possession bestowed upon enslaved men a sense of power denied them in southern society and enhanced their self-esteem. A deadly weapon at the ready sent an unmistakable message to rival bondmen. In antebellum Louisa County, Virginia, John "was in the habit of carrying a pistol for Tom," "which on two occasions he exhibited" to another slave. Anderson District, South Carolina, bondman George threatened to kill his adversary, also named Tom, and on one occasion pistol-whipped him, striking "a severe blow or two." For the attack, he was charged with assault and battery. George was unique among slaves in using a gun during a violent encounter to bludgeon his victim rather than shoot him. Armed slaves embroiled in heated conflicts almost always pulled the trigger and fired the weapon, precisely as it was designed to do, at their enslaved opponent. But shooting at and hitting a particular target were at times two very different matters. In Delaware, the enslaved Bill Jefferson "shot at a negro girl" named Alice James "with a gun loaded with shot, and within shooting distance." Since "[n]one of the shot hit her" and his intended victim lived, Jefferson was indicted for assault with intent to commit murder. In Georgia, the bondwoman Fanny was not so fortunate. Another of her Jones County master's slaves, Adam, "did kill & Murder" Fanny in 1835 "by shooting her with the contents of a loaden Musket in and upon the head." An expensive weapon valued at "eight dollars," the musket had been "charged with gunpowder and four leaden bullets and two slugs." Adam hit his mark, striking Fanny "near her right temple" and inflicting a "mortal wound of the depth of five inches and of the breadth of three inches." The bondwoman "instantly died."[61] In cases fairly evenly distributed over the first six decades of the nineteenth century, bondmen's usual victims of gun violence were other male slaves. In 1858, Gloucester County, Virginia, slave Augustine Read "with a Pistol ... loaded with gun Powder and a leaden bullet" brought the bondman Frank to a grisly end, discharging the weapon into "the right side of the face."[62]

ORIGINS, PREVALENCE, AND PATTERNS

Although gun violence was never pervasive in the quarters, that any slaves were shot by fellow bondmen at all suggests a degree of systemic failure. Always at least subconsciously aware of the dangers of firearms in the hands of slaves, southern whites often neglected to exercise due vigilance, growing lax in the enforcement of legal prohibitions against slaves' possession of firearms. Despite the law, slaves found any number of ways to procure such weapons. Some masters casually flouted slave codes whenever convenience suited them and permitted trusted bondmen to hunt with guns. One purportedly "indulgent master" in Stafford County, Virginia, allowed "[a]ny of the servants ... the privilege of using [his] gun to shoot a beef or a fox or a halk [hawk]." His bondpeople "had free access to the gun," as it was kept in the owner's room, "not locked up." The enslaved Jeff Brooker, who "frequently had the gun" and "killed squirrels" with it, in February 1861 used the weapon to shoot his brother John, who succumbed to his wounds some hours later. Just "a day or two before," no doubt with at least the master's tacit permission, Jeff had shot a fox with the same gun. Other violations of the lawful restrictions against slaves' access to firearms were less deliberate and more the product of slave owner carelessness. At the corner of Seventh Street and St. Charles in New Orleans, master A. H. Justamond "always" kept "a single barreled shot gun" in his home, propped up "in the corner" near "the head of the bed." His bondman Cornelius used the unguarded weapon to shoot Justamond's bondwoman Sally "in the left side of the face[,]" according to a coroner's graphic report, "carrying away [a] portion of the upper and lower jaw bone, cutting ... the carotid arteries and jugular vein, passing into the brain [and] causing immediate death." Other firearms were furtively borrowed from the master, if not outright stolen. When possible, fugitive slaves commandeered their owners' guns prior to taking flight. The weapons offered them a means of securing food, protecting themselves, and fending off pursuers. Moses, a North Carolina runaway, shot the slave Gabriel in 1829 for fear he might betray him. Similarly, fugitives Jim and George were "lurking" in one DeKalb County, Tennessee, neighborhood in 1843, "both armed" and prepared to kill Isaac, a slave "who[m] they suspected of being employed to arrest them." To preserve their liberty, Jim tracked down Isaac and fatally shot him. All of these cases suggest that guns were more readily available to slaves than they should have been according to law.[63]

Despite the pressures and strains inherent in bondage, slaves cannot be demonstrably shown to have exhibited any abnormally high propensity for homicide upon their own. To the contrary, available evidence suggests significantly lower rates of intraracial murder among slaves than among antebellum southern whites. Moreover, whites more often than fellow bondpeople were the targets of lethal slave assaults. But the particular numbers are less important than what the known cases tell us about the enslaved condition and slaves' values. Even if no epidemic of homicide plagued southern slave quarters, intraracial slave murders as well as other, vastly more common but less well documented, nonfatal violent encounters prove instructive in delineating the fault lines present within the "slave community" and the meanings that slaves attached to them.[64] An exploration of the violence bondpeople did commit upon one another promises to help complicate our understanding of black life under slavery.

Chapter 2

SLAVES, MASTERS, CHURCH, AND THE CIVIL LAW OF SLAVERY

A WAKE COUNTY, North Carolina, bondman named Nelson placed his owner, Susannah Wilkins, in a difficult economic position. In 1839, Nelson murdered Gabriel, the property of Benjamin Ward, and was slated for execution in retribution for his crime. The impending loss of Nelson would deal a crushing blow to Wilkins, a widow reputed to live in "poverty." Although Wilkins counted among the ranks of southern slaveholders, Nelson was "one of two only that she possesses," and his "services are indispensable to her." Ultimately, a gubernatorial pardon of Nelson spared Wilkins the prospect of financial devastation that had loomed menacingly on the horizon. The anxious weeks Wilkins endured, contemplating fiscal ruin, underscored slaveholders' dependency on their chattel. Although masters across the South prided themselves on their independence, it was an independence predicated paradoxically upon their reliance on enslaved labor. When slaves attacked, wounded, maimed, or killed one another, they compromised the economic position—even the very security—of the victim's master and, quite possibly, as in the case of Susannah Wilkins, the assailant's owner as well. Slaveholders therefore mobilized and coordinated an array of strategies and institutions intended to keep violence among slaves in check.[1]

Although masters inevitably found it impossible to cleanse the quarters of violent conflict, multiple strata of authority in place across the South worked to reduce the damage wrought when slaves unleashed aggression against their counterparts in bondage. This chapter begins the excavation of those layers. Masters' own vigilance, combined with careful monitoring by their representatives in the fields, afforded one important line of defense of slaveholders' property interests. For that fraction of slaves who attended religious services in the slave South, church oversight assisted in the project of slave discipline. Only the most serious incidents of intraracial slave violence—ones that resulted in serious injuries or death—invited the intervention of southern law. As the next chapter will show, masters throughout the South might file suit in criminal court, especially when one slave grievously wounded or killed a bondperson belonging to a different owner. In contrast, as we will see in this chapter, only in Louisiana could victimized masters seek recourse through civil litigation. To focus only on masters, overseers, church disciplinary proceedings, and the civil and criminal law—all individuals or institutions representing white authority—would be a mistake, however, for such an approach would overlook the first deterrent to violence in the slave community: the slaves themselves who labored to keep the peace. Enslaved peacemakers frequently interceded in the internecine struggles of the quarters to prevent slaves' conflicts from escalating and inviting the interference of white folks in bondpeople's affairs.

Southern masters frequently expressed their disapproval of slaves' violent conflicts at work or in the quarters. "Negroes should not be allowed to ... do whatever they please to each other," wrote one Georgian, or "to impose one upon another." An Alabama planter agreed, stating simply: "They are forbidden to quarrel or fight." "No Negro will be suffered under any pretense whatever to strike another," declared slaveholder W. P. Bocock, notwithstanding enslaved parents' "moderate correction" of their children. Only a minority of slaveholders proved more lenient toward violence among slaves. A Georgia master who witnessed one of his bondmen "beat another slave" at a frolic expressed atypical approval of his slave's violent act. That the enslaved adversary he pummeled had drawn a pistol, posing a threat to all the slaves gathered for the festivities, may have shaped the owner's opinion, but the master's own notions of southern honor also contributed to his unusually liberal attitude toward his bondman's behavior. As the slaveholder informed his enslaved man, "he had better always fight back when anyone struck him, whether the person was white or black," and if he failed to do so and the master heard of it, "a whipping would be in store for him." Among slaveholders, such a cavalier acceptance of slave violence was truly aberrant. The overwhelming majority loathed news of violent outbreaks involving their bondpeople. Many owners of larger holdings instructed overseers to remain constantly vigilant against the possibility of violence among the slaves. "In the intercourse of negroes among themselves," advised one planter, "no quarreling ... should ever be allowed." However unrealistic the expectation to purge the slave quarters of arguments and disputes, it remained the ideal for most planters.[2]

Planter antipathy toward slave conflicts stemmed from largely practical concerns. Masters preferred their slaves not engage in violent scrapes and suffer harm. Worst-case scenario, slaves injured as a result of violence might die, in which case owners were deprived of their investment in human property and of the profits reaped through a lifetime of bound service. Slaves who survived but were severely wounded or maimed lost monetary value. Depreciation at the slave market extended not only to bondpeople who sustained violence but also to those who inflicted the damage. Like victims of severe assaults, slaves with a reputation for violence commanded lower prices. The most common detriment that masters suffered as a result of intraracial violence in the quarters was the loss of slaves' labor. Slaves beaten and bruised from fighting each other might require a short time off work, not labor as quickly or efficiently, and be less productive than if completely healthy. More serious injuries might necessitate the loss of days' or weeks' worth of labor as they recuperated, defeating their economic function. As former slave Henry Gladney of South Carolina explained, "My old marster no lak dat way one of his slaves was crippled up" by fighting on the plantation. Two Mississippi bondmen recalled that "the owner would get riled up if one ob his slaves got hurt or crippled up" because they "wouldn't be worth nothing to wuk." Less serious but nonetheless frustrating to slaveholders, fighting also sometimes distracted slaves' full attention from their labors. While embroiled in a fight with another "hand," the enslaved Lewis Evans "let de cows git away," much to the chagrin of his owner.[3]

Severe and potentially fatal injuries required the additional expense of summoning the local physician. In coastal North Carolina, "a negro named Hammond" stabbed the bondman John one Sunday evening in 1828. The doctor called to examine the wound thought it "very dangerous" and considered John's chances of survival "extremely dubious." In 1855, eight or ten days after a South Carolina slave "was struck on the head ... by another negro, ... his skull ... fractured by the blow," three area physicians performed a trepanation to relieve pressure on the brain. For each of these slaves, the prognosis was grim. But whether they lived or died, the enslaved victims of the assaults incurred for their master the costs for medical care and treatment.[4]

Slaveholders' opposition to unruliness in the quarters was not entirely economic, however. Some masters viewed the maintenance of peace and quietude on the plantation as a paternalistic obligation to their slaves. According to one student of slave management in late antebellum Tennessee, "Oppression and even violence will run riot there [in the quarters], unless the master is what his providential situation requires him to be—the protector, the arbiter, the friend of his servants. He must protect them, not only from those without, but within." Good masters properly exercised "magisterial power" to promote "the repression of vice and open sin of all kinds," including "quarreling." Slaves "should feel secure in this confidence" that the owner fulfill his masterly duty. "Where no decisive measures are taken to suppress" misbehavior in the quarters, cautioned Georgia planter and Presbyterian minister Charles Colcock Jones, "plantations sometimes become intolerable." Lax discipline encouraged fighting, and fighting reflected poorly on the master of the plantation.[5]

On the eve of the Civil War, South Carolina plantation mistress Keziah Brevard expressed an additional concern about violent conflicts among her slaves. "I have heard of fighting on my place," she complained in March 1861, "& I am not satisfied that some negroes should be punished every time they fight & others go unpunished." For Brevard, the issue was one of fairness. She believed all slaves guilty of fighting should be punished equitably, but because slaveholders did not directly witness most clashes among their bondpeople, they were rarely able to reconstruct a comprehensive portrait of whatever violence had transpired. The result was a dangerously arbitrary imposition of punishment upon the presumed guilty parties, any misapplication of which bred needless resentment among the slaves.[6]

Slaves understood that their masters loathed fighting in the quarters. "We were not... allowed to quarrel among ourselves," remembered one former Walton County, Georgia, bondman decades after emancipation. The story was the same in Louisiana, where, according to one ex-slave, "White folks wouldn't let us fuss, ... Dey don low us to fight." "[O]ld Missis sho' didn't 'low dat," another recalled. Cognizant of masters' almost certain wrath should they learn of violence having erupted in the quarters, slaves constituted the first line of defense against conflicts getting out of hand. Time and again, they endeavored to quell unrest in the quarters before it garnered the unwanted attention of the master or overseer. Steven Hahn has suggested the significance of enslaved elders and, on larger plantations, slave councils in holding "personal and familial altercations in check." Court records are not useful in recovering the roles of these enslaved sages or deliberative institutions, but they offer ample indications of slaves—usually but not always men—stepping up to prevent violent conflict. Some even held leadership positions on the plantation. As a slave foreman in Chesterfield County, Virginia, Sam "interfered & prevented" a quarrel between master Henry T. Drewry's bondmen Fleming and John in 1842. Some slave drivers were themselves renowned for their fighting abilities. "In the field," remembered one former slave, "was always a big strong nigger to keep peace among the hands... He had to be good with his fists to make the boys who got bad in the field walk in line." On one Kentucky plantation, that man was "Jim Hayden, a Guiana negro," described superlatively by an ex-slave as "the most powerful man, either white or black, that ever was known in the State of Kentucky." Jim "was very useful on the plantation. When a number of negroes would get to fighting, Jim was called, and quickly dispersed the mob."[7]

More often than not, however, slaves who rose to the occasion to defuse a tense standoff between slaves or to break up a fight had no special authority on the plantation. Rather, the opportunity presented itself, and they acted spontaneously to preserve peace in the quarters. In Virginia, bondmen Peter, John, and Tom all had "their coats off" in 1826, "preparing to fight," when fellow slave Jessie "interposed" in an effort "to keep them apart." When "Andrew and Jim quarreled" in the spring of 1862, "Other servants interfered and they did not fight."[8] Occasionally bondwomen interceded and took command of a dicey situation. To avoid an early-morning "fuss" between slaves George and Shadrack, "aunt Philis the Cook ... gave George his breakfast and told him to go away."[9]

If enslaved women sometimes intervened verbally or physically to prevent conflict from escalating, they frequently summoned male slaves to help them avert dangerous confrontations. In late 1863, Sally of Pittsylvania County "was sleeping in the bed" when she awoke to find her husband Henry and another slave named Kit fighting. "[S]he begged me to part them," explained the bondman Nathan, also present in the room. Nathan dutifully complied with Sally's request. In another case, upon hearing "a noise in an adjoining house," the enslaved woman Betty, or Betsy, of Nottoway County awakened her husband Paschal from his slumbers and "told him to go and see what was the matter." Roused from bed, Paschal went next door and found bondmen Ben and Lewis locked in battle. A pair of enslaved women had already rushed in to quell the violence bodily. "Biddy and Lerina had hold of Lewis" and "together pushed Lewis to the other end of the house," putting distance between him and Ben. Paschal took charge, told the assembled slaves "it was no place for fighting," and "shoved Ben out of the house." As the incident demonstrated, though, enslaved women took direct, forceful action when necessary. When Nelson menaced fellow bondman Bob with a hoe in Lunenburg County, Judy "took [the implement] from him, and threw it about twelve yards off."[10]

Despite their best efforts, slaves were not always successful in cooling tempers and neutralizing conflict. At a Kanawha County, Virginia, frolic in early 1834, the bondman Dennis took umbrage when Harry whipped out a switchblade knife. After Dennis threatened to knock Harry down, Sam "went to where Dennis was and put his right arm on his shoulder," saying to him, "hush it up and say no more about it." Before long, Harry and Dennis began fighting anyway, at which point "Morris' Jim[,] another negro man, then parted them, by taking Dennis away." But meaningful intervention sometimes came too late. The night of the frolic, slaves concerned about the hostility between Harry and Dennis had taken the initiative by summoning a well-respected slave known as Isaac Frazier or, more descriptively, as Big Isaac, "to make peace, with a parcel of black people who were quarreling." Although Isaac "begged for peace," Harry eventually did stab Dennis with the knife. Big Isaac wrested the weapon from Harry as he scolded him, "damn it what made you act so." Some slaves were determined to inflict harm in spite of fellow slaves' pleas for peace. In Chatham County, Georgia, bondmen Frank and Sandy begged Prince to desist from his attack upon the bondman July, but Prince declared that even "if his master came he would chop him or any Damd son of a Bitch."[11]

In their self-regulation of the quarters, some slaves went to truly heroic lengths to subdue the violent passions of fellow bondpeople. Buckingham County, Virginia, slaves Bob Winston and Davy were "in their house" preparing a meal in 1839 when Tom, from nearby Louisa County, entered and "called for" food. Affronted, Davy "replied that he did not cook supper for Company." Tom took offense at the inhospitality and reached for a series of different weapons with which to attack Davy. Winston bravely divested Tom, sequentially, of "a piece of timber" and "a large piece of white oak." Then, when Tom "took up a broad axe with which he made two passes" at Davy, Bob "stepp[ed] in between and ward[ed] off the blows." But when Tom next "took up a piece of broken iron pot" weighing some nine or ten pounds and hurled it at Davy's head, he hit his mark. "Tom you have mighty nigh killed me for nothing," Davy uttered as he bled from the nose, mouth, and ears. Still with fight in them, Tom and Davy pulled knives on each other, but Bob ordered Davy "to go and lie down." The injured slave complied. Despite returning to his normal work routine, Davy later fell into "a state of delirium" and died. A physician's postmortem examination found a fractured skull "and inflammation of the membrane of the brain."[12]

Slaves' internal conflicts could have a truly divisive impact on the plantation and on neighboring estates. Many bondpeople were disinclined to believe that their fellow slaves with whom they lived and worked were capable of violent crimes. When the New Orleans bondman Cornelius confessed to Nancy, another of his master's slaves, that he had killed "one Sally a slave woman," Nancy initially dismissed his remarks as absurd, perhaps even a tasteless joke. She called Cornelius a "fool" and demanded that he not frighten her. After he convinced

Nancy of his heinous deed, the bondwoman replied, aghast, "oh Cornelius you have done murder." Although we do not know how Nancy's newfound knowledge altered her existing relationship with Cornelius, fatal assaults sometimes split a slave community into hostile camps. The enslaved Moses Wilson of Kanawha County, Virginia, took umbrage with his fellow bondman John for killing a third slave, named Yamma. Fueled by a simmering cauldron of emotion that included anger and possibly betrayal and grief, Wilson explained to several other slaves that "John had killed a man for nothing, and ... he would dig coal all night to go and see him hung." He told another that, were it not for the deterrent of lawful consequences, he would "tie ... [John] to a stake[,] take a rifle or pistol[,] and blow his heart out for what he had done." Slaves' assaults upon one another sometimes did generate such social friction that bondpeople were motivated to commit acts of violence in retribution for the suffering of loved ones. After James Madison's slave James Huston "had a fight with Isaac," a slave on the nearby Smith estate, three Smith family slaves accosted Huston in his home, dragged him off, "tied him to a tree and beat him for three hours" with sticks. Ties of camaraderie, friendship, and loyalty sometimes demanded retaliatory violence to redress a wrong.[13]

Especially when they might sufficiently punish enslaved wrongdoers themselves, slaves maintained a general reluctance to invite white intervention into conflicts internal to the quarters. When questioned by a white person the day after the incident in which Tom threw the iron pot at him, Davy, whose head injuries would eventually claim his life, denied that any fight had taken place and explained that he and Tom merely "had been playing." As Virginia slaves "Julius & Dick were quarrelling" indoors on Christmas 1855, the bondman Tom recommended they "go out," or "they would disturb mistress," call attention to themselves, and possibly elicit a whipping. A former Mississippi bondman observed that slaves suffered "little punishment" for fighting only because the master "didn't always know when they fought." Masters were aware of slaves' reticence to reveal disturbances in the quarters. As one perceptive southern white observed, "the Negroes are scrupulous on one point; they make common cause, as servants, in *concealing* their faults from their owners. Inquiry elicits no information; no one feels at liberty to disclose the transgressor; all are profoundly ignorant; the matter assumes the sacredness of a 'professional secret.'" Slaves, in short, were not to snitch. In Pittsylvania County, Virginia, Primus counted upon slaves' conspiracy of silence to shield his guilt in the stabbing death of the bondman Abram. As the realization that he had just committed murder dawned upon him, Primus plotted "to straighten out his [victim's] damned leggs and bend his Damned arms" and drag his corpse "to the big Road" so "that if none of the other negroes would say any thing about it[,] it would not be known who killed him." The desire to suppress and withhold information from the master was so great that in one known case a slave apparently bribed a fellow bondman to remain quiet. Davy had previously refused to divulge the incident with Tom, he explained the day before his death, because "he was paid not [to] tell." Uncertain of Davy's allegiance, Tom, seemingly, had sought additional guarantees of his victim's silence.[14]

Slaves generally did keep mum without special incentives. Squealing on fellow bondpeople was socially proscribed. According to some masters, slaves who might otherwise faithfully report misdeeds in the quarters refused to do so because they "may hereafter require the same concealment of their own transgressions." Moreover, were they to expose fellow bondpeople, "their names [would be] cast out as evil from among their brethren." Fears of rebuke and ostracism were powerful forces in the quarters. In a society in which whites regarded slaves as inferiors, no bondpeople wished to become pariahs among their own. Violating their implied oaths to remain loyal to each other might even provoke "personal violence or pecuniary injury" at the hands of disgruntled slaves. After suffering a beating at the hands of other slaves in 1828, James Huston of Madison County, Virginia, refused to identify his attackers "for fear [they] would kill him."[15]

For slaves to violate the mutually understood code of silence and to report wrongdoing to the master or overseer voluntarily was unquestionably serious stuff. Nevertheless, conflicts in the quarters sometimes merited the threat of exposure to whites. The bondman John of Charlotte County, Virginia, warned bondwomen Harriett and Matilda, then arguing over a male slave, to stop bickering, or "I would go and tell Mass. Buck Harrell." When another slave named John, in Kanawha County, muttered that he "intend[ed] to kill" his fellow bondman Yamma "at the risk of my life before Saturday night," the enslaved Moses replied, "I will go and tell Master John." John, Yamma, and Moses were all the property of John D. Lewis, and although John and Moses were usually on "friendly" terms, Moses suspected John might cut him if he reported to their owner. John, after all, cautioned Moses in no uncertain terms, "look out the Jack of Clubs will catch you." Ultimately, Moses did not tattle to the master, not out of fear, if we can trust his own words, but "because he forgot it" as "John's threat passed out of his mind." In Essex County, the bondmen John and Peter began arguing about John's wife Celia. When Celia heard Peter say that either he or John "will die tonight," the bondwoman "got alarmed and sent a boy for Mr. Alexander the overseer." Perhaps as a woman, she did not believe it within her power or place to intervene directly in the quarrel and therefore promptly resorted to the overseer. As Thornton Alexander reported, he received the message from Celia "requesting [him] to come and interfere to prevent mischief" between John and Peter, "which he did." As a third-party observer to their conflict, Celia summoned the overseer preemptively. Oftentimes, however, a vow to inform the master or overseer was a defensive strategy slaves employed in the heat of conflict. In 1827, Lunenburg County, Virginia, bondman Nelson "cursed" the slave Bob and "said he would whip him." In response, Bob called him "a damned rascal" and "said that if he did not let him alone, he would make his master whip him." Such threats may have been enough to prevent some fights, but not the one between Nelson and Bob. Bob retrieved a stick with which he planned to "cane" Nelson. Nelson, however, grabbed a hoe and used it to kill his adversary.[16]

Usually slaves did not consult masters or overseers unless or until a dispute resulted in grave injury or death. After the Prince George County, Virginia, bondwoman Betsey stabbed another of her master's female slaves, her victim, Patty, assessed her injury and declared, "I am going to white folks." On May 15, 1832, Northampton County overseer William S. Smith "was roused from his bed at about 8 or 9 oclock at night by the information that one of the negroes in the kitchen was killed." Smith raced to the scene to find a bondman named Ben "stabbed about the left breast." The slave expired moments later. In Brunswick County, the bondwoman Jinny "went into the apple orchard to get some apples" in 1824, only to discover Cary moaning in pain as he bled upon the ground from a stab wound to the chest. Only hours before, Cary and the bondman Stephen had quarreled "in her house," and Jinny quickly pieced together what had transpired. Jinny summoned "master Frederick" Lucy to the orchard. When Lucy arrived, the slaveholder found Stephen "trying to get Cary up" as Cary clung to life. "[Y]ou Grand Rascal," Lucy roared at Stephen. "[Y]ou have killed him."[17]

Masters labored not to allow conflicts to escalate to that stage. As patriarchs of the plantation, ideally their mere presence deterred conflict. In Pittsylvania County, Virginia, Shadrack and George ceased fighting one morning precisely because they saw their master approaching from a distance. Fleeing from a hostile gang of other slaves in Henrico County, a desperate Martin counted on the protection of his wife's master, Christian Seber, on whose plantation he often stayed. After Martin related his fear that his enslaved pursuers were going to kill him, Seber retrieved "an Old French Musket" and fired a warning shot to scare away the intruders. More often, masters had no advance knowledge of slaves' disputes and could therefore take no preemptive action. Owner intervention was usually reactive. Marion County, Mississippi, master James Duncan recounted an incident in which his bondman Green and the enslaved Harry Faulk "fell out with each other at a log rolling at his [Duncan's] house and were threatening each other with their handspikes when he interfered and stopped the quarrel." Verbal warnings and threats of whippings were standard, but a Saluda District, South Carolina, slaveholder instead offered his bondpeople a constructive alternative to fighting. "If he ever heard any of them quarrelin' wid each other," recalled one bondman, "he would holler at them and say: 'Sing! Us ain't got no time to fuss on dis place!'" In the absence of the master, overseers or even whites with no particular authority other than the prerogatives of race intervened. In Charleston District, a Mrs. Church, upon hearing "quarrelling" one Sunday morning between an enslaved couple, informed the husband that "if he did not hush his noise I would have him taken up." The man turned and conveyed the message to his wife, telling her: "that Lady says we make too much noise." Through various means, many conflicts between slaves were co-opted in their early stages.[18]

Slaves who committed violent acts upon other residents of the quarters reacted differently when they realized the severe—and sometimes fatal—injuries they inflicted. Some intraracial deaths, though probably a minority, were entirely accidental. Slaves who never intended to kill their victims expressed shock at what they had done. The trio of Madison County, Virginia, bondpeople who beat the enslaved James Huston for several hours with sticks were incredulous when informed that the target of their hostility had actually died. Huston's assailants "fell upon the ground," "astonished," and cried, "have we come to this[?]" Enslaved murderers' expressions ran a whole gamut of emotions, however. At one end of the spectrum, some displayed immediate regret for their behavior. In Rockbridge County, Virginia, Julius fatally hacked at Ned with an axe, nearly severing Ned's head. According to a white witness to the aftermath, Julius "seemed sorry & penitent, crying verry much." After King George County bondman Hubard killed the slave man Tom, the murderer displayed "deep regret" and expressed "extreme sorrow for what had happened." Most did not show remorse so quickly, if at all. To the contrary, many more bondmen who had killed another slave proved utterly unapologetic, even defiant. Pittsylvania County, Virginia, slave Shadrack blamed George for getting him in trouble with the owner they shared, prompting the master's lashing of Shadrack. After delivering George "his death blow," Shadrack declared "that he would be damned if he would not kill any negro that would make his master take his shirt off." The Henrico County bondman Martin, whose assault led to the 1837 death of Lewis, said that he "did not care if he had stabbed him to his damned heart." Susannah Wilkins's slave Nelson went even further, reportedly saying "after he had killed Gabriel that he would kill him if it was to do again." After Cupe, a Russell County, Virginia, bondman, stabbed the enslaved Richard in 1840, he divulged his murderous plans for the future to a white shoemaker, revealing that "if he got clear of this affair he would [also] kill Mr. Alexanders Pat, Ferguson's Smith, and Mr Garretts Prior."[19]

Other slaves denied the horrible consequences of their violent acts. The enslaved Charles Loadnum of Delaware was uniquely distraught after striking Jacob dead with a stick in 1798: Jacob was his brother. Although the pair had a long history of conflict and had immediately prior to the assault exchanged "high words," Charles did not intend to kill his sibling. Possibly in shock, "Charles kept saying he is not dead," explained one witness, "... [and] seemed to be much alarmed." Primus, enslaved in Pittsylvania County, Virginia, fatally stabbed Abram but also refused to accept that his victim had perished. The murderer frantically sought "a needle & thread" from the slave kitchen "to sew up the wounds" but was unsuccessful in locating any, foiling his plan to play amateur physician and patch up his victim. The Botetourt County slave Ralph eventually admitted tearfully that he had "struck" the bondwoman Fan "with his Fist, choked her & threw her into the creek." When she recovered from the initial assault and sloshed toward the opposite bank, Ralph pursued, "struck her on the head" with a stick, "& finished her." But when several slaves first discovered Fan's body in the water, he attempted to conceal his crime by claiming that she had drowned. Ralph's reluctance to pluck Fan, still evincing "some slight appearance of life," from the creek ("he was afraid to touch her"); a half-hearted attempt to pull her out, in which he let Fan's body fall unceremoniously into the stream; the shallow depth of the water, insufficient for drowning; and Ralph's suspicious absence from the quarters with "the rest of the negroes" at the time of the assault all pointed toward the bondman's guilt.[20]

Another common response to an assault upon or murder of a slave was the flight of the enslaved assailant. Slaves naturally feared the punishments that awaited them for their crimes. In Virginia, Essex County bondman Peter went missing for "several days" after he stabbed the slave John to death in 1826. The next decade, Sam told Harry, who had just fatally knifed Dennis in Kanawha County, "that he would tie him and take him to the white people." While Sam searched for a rope, however, "Harry ... ran out at the door, and made his escape."

In 1827, Nelson likewise "absented himself" after he murdered Bob in Lunenburg County. Nelson remained on the lam until his master "made it generally known in the neighbourhood that he wished" his slave "to surrender," which he did "voluntarily." Other runaways had no intention of offering themselves up. Solomon stabbed Ben "about the left breast" in their master's Northampton County kitchen in 1832. The enslaved killer "went off" to hide "& was not afterwards seen ... until ... his apprehension." In 1840, Nottoway County bondman Lewis absconded to Petersburg after he murdered Ben but was successfully taken up one month later. Some slaves who took flight ventured far and wide to evade the consequences of their action. A "negro man named Henry" of Covington County, Mississippi, fled after murdering Jacob Duckworth's bondman Peter the day after Christmas 1830. Determined to locate, seize, and discipline the absconded slave, Duckworth "pursued him ... at great expense and trouble, having traveled through the State of Alabama, and through the Choctaw nation and a part of the State of Louisiana, and at length found ... Henry at the town of Baton Rouge," where the slave was finally apprehended. Adam, of Jones County, Georgia, was not nearly as successful at eluding his pursuer. After shooting his spouse in the head in 1835, Adam took flight, driving his master's cart down the road toward Milledgeville. He was soon overtaken, however, and escorted back to gaze upon his wife's lifeless body. Resigned to his presumed fate, Adam sighed, "take me out and hang me." The Georgia criminal justice system happily obliged.[21]

In the overwhelming majority of cases in which masters and overseers failed to thwart slaves' violence, they administered justice without resort to the southern court system. Most incidents of intraracial slave violence were never formally prosecuted but were instead handled privately, on the plantation. As South Carolina planter James Henry Hammond explained, "on our estates we dispense with the whole machinery of public police and public courts of justice. Thus we try, decide, and execute the sentences, in thousands of cases, which in other countries would go into the courts." In as much as was possible, no masters wished to surrender authority over their slaves to the legal apparatus of the state. Slaveholders preferred to dispense their own forms of plantation justice. According to one Louisiana planter, a host of slaves' offenses, including "fighting, and quarreling[,] must be invariably punished," but the punishments to be meted out were properly determined by the master. Certainly masters adjudicated cases of slaves' minor infractions, including fights between slaves belonging to the same owner, but even for serious crimes, such as murder, some masters were loath to employ the formal judicial system. Pursuing proper legal channels was time-consuming and interfered with the productivity of the plantation. As Gus Clark, who toiled as a water boy in the Louisiana cane fields, remembered, "Dem niggers quar'l an' fight an' kills one 'nother. Big Boss, he rich, an' doan 'low no sheriff ter come on his place. He hol' cou't an' settle all 'sputes hisself. He done bury de dead niggers an' put de one what killed him back to work." Regular court action was also costly and, depending upon the verdict, potentially devastating to masters' economic interests. One Texas master, owner of a homicidal slave, "was unwilling to incur the additional loss of punishing the murderer by law" and so took "the punishment into his own hands." He was not alone.[22]

Masters investigated slaves' infractions, procured evidence, and questioned witnesses to reconstruct the events that culminated in violence. When he learned of Stephen stabbing a fellow bondman, Brunswick County, Virginia, slaveholder Frederick Lucy "seized him by the collar and led him to the house." There, he bound Stephen and interrogated him. When the slave denied having a knife, Lucy said, "I will make you produce it" and "gave him four or five licks." Torture extracted the information Lucy sought. A "few stripes" persuaded Stephen to strike a bargain. "[I]f you wont whip me any more," he volunteered, "I will get the knife." He then retrieved the secreted murder weapon from its hiding place in "a barrel of lime" in "the kitchen or cookhouse." With the "necessary information" gathered, masters, as judges and juries on their own estates, rendered verdicts and passed sentence upon the enslaved parties to the conflict.[23]

Almost universally, masters' punishment of choice for slaves who had committed violence upon one another (or who were believed guilty of any other misdeed, for that matter) was whipping. Slaveholder Alexander Telfair of Georgia cared little for the peculiar circumstances surrounding a fight between bondpeople. Rather than delve into the minutiae of the affair, he prescribed a blanket course of action. "If there is any fighting on the plantation," he advised his overseer, "whip all engaged in it, for no matter what the cause may have been, all are in the wrong." Several ex-slave respondents in the Federal Writers' Project narratives indicated that conflicts in the quarters were not tolerated by masters. After one slave "beat up my uncle," recollected ex-bondman Jake McLeod of South Carolina, "my old boss put it on him." Even masters whom slaves claimed were otherwise disinclined to use the whip made exceptions when bondpeople clashed. As a former slave in Texas belonging to Watt Rosborough remembered, "The niggers wasn't whipped much 'cept for fightin' 'mongst themselves." "Marse' Ben nebber low' much whippin'," recalled a former bondman held by

Ben Brandon of South Carolina. "But one day us nigger' boys hopped into a fight," and "Marse' Ben done his own whippin' den.'" On large holdings, masters often entrusted overseers to administer the punishment. In Harrison County, Texas, where Simp Campbell was born into slavery, "the overseer had order to whip us for fightin'." Former slave Nathan Best related how his overseer whipped him after a bondwoman "got mad at me an' slapped me in de mouf" and "I stuck a knife . . . in her arm." Virginia slaveholder Richard Eppes adopted a different strategy, compelling slaves who had been caught fighting and quarreling with one another "to whip each other."[24]

Female slaves involved in ruckuses on the plantation were not immune to the crack of the whip. Occasionally they were punished for conflicts with enslaved men. Henry Baker, born a slave in Virginia but conveyed to Washington County, Texas, recalled a "whippin'" his mother received "becuze her an' a nigger dat dey called Uncle Dick, had a fight. De marster, he cum up while dey waz fightin' an' whipped my mother wib a cowhide whip . . . till de blood jus' streamed from her." Some bondwomen developed reputations for being quarrelsome and belligerent. Former Texas slave Richard Jackson's "mammy . . . was bad 'bout fightin' and the overseer allus tended to her." Particularly noteworthy to others, whether free or slave, were bondwomen's conflicts with other female slaves. Perhaps because it seemed so unbecoming for women to engage in physical confrontations, rice planter P. C. Weston observed that "[f]ighting, particularly amongst women, . . . is to be always rigorously punished." Accordingly, when one enslaved Alabama "woman cussed my mother" and "had a fight," explained ex-slave Eliza Evans, "Old Master had them both whipped. My mother got ten licks and de other woman got twenty-five." Oftentimes, though, slaveholders seemed to show confrontational bondwomen somewhat more leniency than they granted bondmen. On one Greene County, Georgia, plantation, "Sometimes de women uster git whuppins for fightin'," but the master never fully fulfilled his threats. "Ol' marster uster tell my mother all de time dat he wus goin' to give her one-hundred lashes if she didn't stop fightin'," recalled former slave Isaiah Green, "but he never did do it though." Some recognition of bondwomen's femininity may have stayed masters' hands and restrained their wrath. Economically savvy slaveholders also would not have wanted their punishments to affect adversely the ability of female slaves to bear children. For whatever reason or combination of reasons, when "some niggah womens got to fightin in de cotton fiel'" on one South Carolina plantation, "Boss bring em all to de gallery of de big house, and giv em all a lick or two with a whip, then sent back to the fiel' en tole em to 'have deir selfs." Just "a lick or two" was all he deemed necessary to restore order. A certain kind of white male condescension toward female slaves is evident in the recollections of one Attala County, Mississippi, bondman: "One time his mother and another woman were fighting over their children, and his master 'just sort of spanked her' and put an end to the fight." Although it is possible that the former slave who shared this story felt pressure to modify it to accommodate a white interviewer and used "spanking" as a euphemism for "whipping," if it was an actual spanking, the episode suggests the master's regard toward female slave conflict as childish—and therefore relatively harmless—by nature.[25]

For their conflicts in the quarters, some unfortunate slaves suffered the fury of the whip and then some. The Reverend W. B. Allen, born a slave in South Carolina but carried to Alabama at the age of five, recalled, "I have personally known a few slaves that were beaten to death for ... Hitting another Negro, Fussing, fighting, and rukkussing in the quarters." In Georgia, William Ward's master whipped slaves "for infractions ... such as fighting." He "handled" "[s]erious offense[s] like killing another person" by "hang[ing] him to a tree by the feet or by the neck, as he saw fit." Former slave Sarah Wilson's master once "whipped a whole bunch of the men on account of a fight in the quarters, and then," to scare them into submission, "took them all to Fort Smith to see a hanging." Spear Pitman, enslaved in Edgecombe County, North Carolina, was forced to witness the sadistic torture of Alex Hunter, a bondman who "got into a fight" with the enslaved Noah Billamy. For reasons never identified, "Alex cut Noah in the belly so bad that his insides came out." Alerted to the attack, overseer John Savage "came running up and whipped Alex until they quit fighting." Alex was bound as his master was informed of the stabbing. As Pitman recalled, the master "sent word back to pretty near kill Alex, but not quite. So they whipped him, and then turned the dogs loose on him." Alex tried to get away from the ferocious canines, but "[t]hey tore him pretty near to pieces," Pitman recounted, and quite possibly "ate some of what they pulled off." After the dogs were ordered off, "raw alcohol" was poured over Alex's wounds. "He had been screaming all the time the dogs were tearing him," Pitman shuddered, "but it was worse than ever when they put the alcohol onto him." Pitman tried to turn away from the horrific scene, but the overseer "told me if I didn't stay and see it he would give me some of the same thing. So I had to stay." The savagery of Alex's punishment, contrary to the master's orders, culminated in the slave's death, costing his owner the $1,000 the deceased bondman was worth.[26]

If whipping was the standard plantation punishment for violent conflicts among slaves, confinement was also employed with regularity. "I'se seen one negro that got to fighting with another slave and broke his arm," reported one enslaved eyewitness in Red River County, Texas, "and Maser put him in chains." According to another Texas bondwoman, "I nebber seed no slaves in chains . . . , 'cept w'en dey git drunk, or fight." Chains were only the beginning. Some masters put enslaved combatants in the stocks. "The strictest rule" masters in Washington County, Mississippi, "had was about fighting," reported ex-slave Mark Oliver. "They wouldn't have none of that. If you do it anyway, and somebody gets bad hurt, you be put in the stocks for that." During the Christmas holiday especially, "Better not be no fighting 'cause that shore meant the stocks." Sometimes one "common white trash" overseer in Mississippi "punished the niggers for disobedience and for fighting mongst themselves" by depositing them in a makeshift plantation prison. As ex-slave Aaron Jones recalled, "they were locked in the gin house or some other farm house." "Niggers would git too rowdy-lak, drinkin' liquor and fightin'," an ex-slave from Hall County, Georgia, remembered, "and dat was when de white folks slapped 'em in de gyardhouse, widout a bite to eat." "Dere was a guard house" on Billy Neal's Georgia plantation as well, where "de wust Niggers was kept, and . . . fed but once a day."[27]

However terrible to endure, whipping and incarceration were ultimately fleeting; sale from family and friends was permanent. Some slaveholders disposed of troublesome, combative slaves by selling them to passing traders or unsuspecting buyers at auction. A Virginia master named Clark sold the bondwoman Salina to Mark Lowery of Sparta, Tennessee, "'cause she was a fighting, mule-headed woman." Former slave Emanuel Elmore related a story in which "a lot of the negroes in the quarter" of one upcountry South Carolina holding "got drunk[,] and ma got to fighting all of them." Once sober, she feared her master "was going to send her back to Alabama." She therefore "went and hid in the woods." In June 1803, as president and slaveholder Thomas Jefferson was in the midst of buying the Louisiana Purchase, he contemplated the sale of Cary, a Monticello bondman who had seriously bludgeoned another slave, named Brown, with a hammer. Were the enslaved victim to die, Cary would be punished through formal legal channels. But, Jefferson explained, "should Brown recover so that the law shall inflict no punishment on Cary, it will be necessary for me to make an example of him in terrorem to others, in order to maintain the police so rigorously necessary among the . . . boys." Jefferson well understood the power of the private sale as punishment. The prospect of permanent separation supplied a possible deterrent to slave misconduct and thereby contributed to plantation discipline. The president expressed his hope that "negro purchasers from Georgia passing about the state" would relieve him of Cary's presence. Barring that, sale "in any other quarter so distant as never more to be heard of among us" would suffice, as "it would to the others be as if he were put out of the way by death." To reap the disciplinary benefits of Cary's departure, Jefferson was even prepared to absorb a pecuniary loss on the bondman's sale. "I should regard price but little," wrote the master of Monticello, "in comparison with so distant an exile of him as to cut him off compleatly from ever again being heard of."[28]

As a slaveholder in Virginia, Jefferson possessed full legal authority privately to sell slaves out of state. That liberty was not readily available to all masters. Delaware slaveholders, for example, were subject to a law passed in February 1787 forbidding them from selling bondpeople outside the cozy confines of the geographically diminutive First State. The legal restriction dramatically narrowed the pool of possible buyers. Owners of violent or otherwise troublesome slaves in Delaware therefore petitioned county court justices for permission to transport belligerent bondpeople beyond state boundaries. In New Castle County, Isaac Stidham, "Owner and Possessor of a Negro Man, named Sam," pleaded in 1791 for "License for the Exportation of the said Negro ... to Some of the Neighboring States, or Elsewhere." Sam had proven "a wicked and ungovernable Servant." Among a plethora of misdeeds, he had "wickedly attempted to murder a Negro woman" and had threatened to kill the master as well. Stidham deemed Sam's deportation out of state essential "for the better, and more perfect Security of your Petitioner and Family." Farther south, in Sussex County, master Stephen Mitchell complained of his own "Negro Man Slave named Sam" in 1795. Purportedly a conjuror, Sam had "been guilty of many wicked and unsufferable actions." He not only kept a white woman as his wife but also poisoned another of Mitchell's slaves. In both cases, judges of the respective Courts of Quarter Sessions granted permission to transport the defiant Sams out of state. In reality, the additional layer of government involvement in Delaware did not necessarily prevent the sales of slaves across state lines; it only imposed an administrative impediment that could be hurdled with relative ease.[29]

Masters exercised most but not exclusive authority to punish slave-slave violence; those slaves who attended southern churches were additionally subject to church disciplinary action for a full panoply of moral transgressions. Some bondpeople across the South attended the same churches as their masters. Evangelical denominations—preeminently the Baptists—attracted enslaved members in the late eighteenth and early nineteenth centuries through their declarations of blacks' spiritual equality with whites and the emotional enthusiasm of their services. Baptists received enslaved congregants by baptism, by the relation of an experience of grace, or by letter from a slave's prior church home. Membership was contingent, however, upon the slave owner's consent. In 1832, the bondwoman Molly "related an experance" before Brushy Creek Baptist Church in Greenville District, South Carolina, "but her reception was defer[r]ed until she obtained permission from her master." The next month, Keziah also sought admission "but had not a permit" supplied by her owner. Thomas E. Watkins's bondman Nelson visited Mt. Tirzah Baptist Church in Charlotte County, Virginia, better prepared, armed "with a recommendation from his master as a faithful and orderly servant and as one who sustains a good Christian character." Nelson "related a work of grace in his heart, whereupon the church received him as a candidate for baptism." Requiring a letter of recommendation struck the leaders of nearby Mossingford Baptist Church as such a good idea that it began to "require servants applying for membership to bring a sertificate of character from their master or Overseer."[30]

For some enslaved churchgoers, attending services was compulsory, but many others embraced church membership for the range of possible rewards it offered—some spiritual, some social. The religious and sensory experiences of worship were attractions, but another was the fellowship derived from belonging to a Christian community. Slaves relished the togetherness they felt at church even as their hair, dress, and adornment at services sometimes emerged as sources of competition. Evangelical churches also functioned as social service agencies, with white congregants taking interest in aging and impoverished slaves. The congregation of Flint Hill Baptist Church in York District, South Carolina, took it upon itself to locate someone "to take charge of" Sucky, "an old colored member" apparently suffering from neglect. Powelton Baptist Church of Hancock County, Georgia, appointed four white men "to look into and inquire the wants of Violet a colored member" in 1849, but they were gratified to learn that she was not "in the immediate want of any thing and did not require any assistance from the church."[31]

Although routinely addressed as "brothers" and "sisters" by white churchgoers, enslaved congregants were hardly equal members of southern evangelical churches. Seating arrangements inside the physical space of the church betrayed the racial inequalities found throughout southern society. Already by the late eighteenth century, just as evangelical churches began drawing enslaved converts in numbers, congregations designated where black members were to sit. Enslaved churchgoers sat apart from their masters and their masters' families. In September 1791, Philips Mill Baptist Church of Wilkes County, Georgia, reserved "[t]he North West Side of the Meeting house ... for the use of the Black Brethren," "the two front seats" notwithstanding. In nearby Hancock County, Powelton Baptist Church agreed at the end of 1808 that "the Black Brethren ... be seated behind the whites." Segregated seating remained the custom across the South until black members were expelled or left voluntarily during and after the Civil War. In 1864, "the Negroes" at Lower Duncan's Creek Baptist Church in Laurens District, South Carolina, sat at "the West end" of the church, "up to a certain point." The white membership of Mt. Tirzah Baptist Church in Charlotte County, Virginia, authorized black congregants to occupy part of the main sanctuary only conditionally, when the number of white worshipers "should be small, and the gallerys [already] filled with Colored people." At Washington First Baptist Church in Wilkes County, Georgia, whites made greater accommodations for black churchgoers, who comprised three-quarters of the congregation's membership. Whereas segregated seating almost always signified blacks' subordination to whites, when the "colored church & congregation" of Washington First Baptist conducted its worship services "every alternate Sabbath afternoon," the whites agreed to "occupy the side seats."[32]

Despite the inequalities woven into the fabric of southern evangelical churches, many were so successful in recruiting black members that they were forced to enlarge their church structures. In 1850, a committee at Mt. Tirzah looked into "the propriety of making some alterations in the house of worship and of building a gallery for the black people." The committee believed that "building a gallery in the west end will add much to the comfort of both classes black and white." Construction expenses often prevented churches from expanding to accommodate their black members. Lower Banister Church in Pittsylvania County, Virginia, explored the costs of "building ... a shed to the east side of the meeting house for the accommodation of the Black people." Apparently the church was unable to raise the necessary funds, for the next year, it requested that "all black members living near other churches ... join them" to alleviate overcrowding. Eight years later, Lower Banister again appointed a committee "to draw up a plan of an addition to this meeting house for the accommodation of the Black people." Wilkes County's Sardis Baptist Church resolved in 1856 to build an addition on the north side of the meeting house "for the benefit of the black people," and in 1843, Rabun Creek Baptist Church of Laurens District,

South Carolina, "took into consideration the Expediency of Preparing a place at the side of the house for the Black People to go into in time of Worship." Rabun Creek's "Black Brethren and friends" were to "Prepare the Lumber" and carry it to the church, where the congregation's whites would "meet & Direct & help them" erect the structure.[33]

The behavior of both black and white members of southern evangelical churches was subject to the scrutiny of the wider congregation. All churchgoers were expected to comport themselves in accordance with the tenets of their faith, and the Baptists in particular invested extraordinary powers in the congregation to discipline those who strayed from the path of moral righteousness. Eschewing hierarchy, Baptist churches claimed "the sole right and privilege to govern themselves according to the Holy Scriptures." As with church governance generally, in matters of wayward members, they exercised congregational autonomy, each wielding the authority to "reprove for sin" and to exclude the "incorrigible . . . from their seats." In their church covenant, the founding members of Shiloh Baptist in Charlotte County, Virginia, declared that they would "endeavour to suppress every species of vice and immorality especially in our own families." Church pioneers of Poplar Springs Baptist in Laurens District, South Carolina, made a solemn pledge, "through . . . divine aid to watch over one another: to Reprove, Rebuke, and admonish Our Brother or Sister . . . and not to Suffer Evil in them." At its founding in the late antebellum years, the First Baptist Church of Hemphill, Texas, followed a long-established practice when its covenant directed members "having a knowledg[e] of public transgressions in another member . . . to make sutch offenses known to the church on the first opportunity." Informing on fellow congregants represented nothing less than a sacred duty, and members understood their responsibilities if accused of wrongdoing. As explained by the fifth rule that governed Flint Hill Baptist Church in York District, South Carolina, "We promise individually to pay a respectful regard to the advice and admonitions of the church and to be subject to its discipline as directed by the word of God and conducted in the Spirit of the Gospel." Slaves were not exempt from church oversight and possible censure. Indeed, Virginia's Roanoke District Association declared "it the Duty of Every Church to rule her Members . . . & Regulate all disorders that may be among the black Members."[34]

White congregants took acute interest in the real or perceived moral failings of their black brethren. Poplar Springs Baptist Church appointed a committee of seven white men in 1853 "to hear and Set[t]le and determine any matter [of] difficulty or immoral Conduct arising or growing out of the Coulerd Members of said Church." The church granted "full Power" to the committee "to exclude or retain and hear their Recantation and Restore to fellowship again or otherwise debar until we have some assureance of their Penetince And Repentance." Many Baptist churches established "colored committees" to aid in the regulation of black members' conduct. As early as 1790, Philips Mill Baptist Church of Wilkes County, Georgia, "Ordered that [a] conference be held . . . in order to Examine into the Disputes of the Negroes." By 1808, nearby Sardis Baptist Church established a colored conference "for the black Brethren" as well. Not until 1850 did Georgia's Horeb Baptist Church follow suit. There, a committee of three white men "draft[ed] rules to govern" such an assembly. Horeb's conference formed about the same time as that in the First Baptist Church of Houston, Texas, toward the western extremity of the slave South, where in May 1850 a "special conference was held for the purpose of attending to cases of discipline among the colored members."[35]

Colored conferences, or colored committees, met on schedules that varied by congregation. Some Baptist churches held meetings to discuss black churchgoers' behavior on an ad hoc basis. In 1830, Wilkes County's Rehoboth Baptist Church resolved to convene a "conference . . . for the benefit of the colored people" only "as occasion may require." Although Rehoboth had a sizeable black churchgoing population, colored conferences often met sporadically in those churches with few black members. Commonly, however, colored conferences convened with some regularity, usually quarterly. In 1803, Hancock County's Powelton Baptist Church "agreed to hold conference . . . on the Sunday before every quarterly meeting for the purpose of enquiring into the order of our black brethren." Decades later, Goshen Baptist in Lincoln County, Georgia, "[r]esolved that the third Sunday before communion day be the day set apart to settle any difficulties that may rise among the Black Members of this church." Sardis Baptist Church did not implement a regular schedule until 1860, when it "appoint[ed] the third Sabbath in February, May, August and November for a conference among the colored members." Washington First Baptist Church of Wilkes County formerly held "quarterly Conference[s] . . . for the Colored Members," but because blacks comprised roughly 75 percent of its membership, in 1848 it "[a]uthorized the Colored Conference to be held once a month" to devote sufficient time to black discipline.[36]

Although black members were present at colored conferences to air their grievances against one another, white churchgoers maintained authority by presiding over the meetings. At Fishing Creek Baptist Church in Wilkes County, at least six different white men—but usually Guy Smith, until his death in 1830—acted as moderator of the colored conference between August 1822 and January 1831. "Brother Stephen H. Willis Moderator" oversaw Beaverdam Baptist's "Collored Conference" of August 1844. To relieve any one white male church member of full responsibility over colored conferences, many congregations appointed a committee of several trusted leaders within the church who might rotate the duty among themselves. To preserve order, some congregations required a minimum white presence during colored conferences. The First Baptist Church of Houston required that no fewer than three whites "attend the meetings of the coloured members and assist in the business of their conferences." Back in Georgia, Sardis Baptist established an even stricter rule in 1860. Colored conferences at Sardis could only be held if "there be seven white male members present."[37]

The whites who moderated the proceedings at colored conferences were occasionally pleased to find that all was quiet among black churchgoers. "The black Brethren upon inquiry is found to be at peace among themselves," recorded the clerk of Sardis Baptist in 1808. Similar reports emanated from other congregations. At a Washington First Baptist Church "Conference for Blacks" in July 1838, "the time was spent in singing and prayer" since there was "no business before the Church." Inevitably, however, colored conferences often occasioned the public airing of discord among black congregants. Although Lower Banister Church of Pittsylvania County, Virginia, found its "Black members" "in good order" in November 1826, the same had not been true in July 1811 at a meeting called "to settle any matter of distress which may be amongst them." Brother John Stone's slave George had generated a kerfuffle by "his taking a wife secretly," and the church notified the clandestinely united couple to appear the following day.[38]

Either blacks or whites might lodge grievances against co-religionists, but regardless of who registered the initial complaint against a black member, typically one or more white male church members investigated it. Mt. Tirzah Baptist Church dispatched Brother James Morison to investigate, "and settle if possible, a dif[f]erence between two coloured members," Simon and Abram. By the following month, their conflict was resolved. In South Carolina, Padgett's Creek appointed a committee of five white men "to enquire into a report about sister Gibbs negroes and settle the matter." At Ash Camp, or Keysville, Baptist Church in Charlotte County, Virginia, an enslaved couple objected to a bondwoman they knew "who wished to join" the congregation. Two white men assigned to the issue discovered that the unnamed female slave "had not shown a christian spirit" toward the enslaved husband and wife. Deeming her unworthy of fellowship, they concluded that "we had better not receive her." In Laurens District, South Carolina, Poplar Springs Baptist Church named "A Comity of 7" in June 1853 "to attend to the present Case between the 2 coulerd Members and to all the difficultys that may here after take Place Amoung the Coulerd members."[39]

Even as whites investigated most matters pertaining to black members of evangelical churches, black brethren were not completely bereft of authority over themselves. In some churches, prominent whites empowered selected, trustworthy male slave members to leadership positions over other black congregants, as auxiliaries to white command. Careful monitoring of fellow black members represented an important component of their duties as agents of the church. In 1852, the First Baptist Church of Houston appointed "Brethren Simon, Ned and Jasper ... a committee of Watchmen, whose duty it is to keep an oversight of the coloured members ... and to report either to the Pastor or some of the leading white male members whenever any coloured members shall be guilty of immoral or unchristian conduct." Other churches made similar appointments. In 1857, Bethabara Baptist Church of Laurens District, South Carolina, "moved and agreed upon" the propriety of constituting "a committee of five Black Persons to look over the affairs of the Black congregation and to keep order amongst them." In Virginia, Mt. Tirzah Baptist named Dabney, Solomon, and Henry—three slaves, each belonging to a different master—to a committee in April 1853 "to attend to matters relative to the colored members of the church." Nearby Mossingford Baptist Church appointed six slaves the very next month "to superintend the interests and conduct of the coloured members of the church." Eight years later, Mossingford assigned A. V. Daniel's bondman George "to Overseer the coloured members in his neighbourhood."[40]

Some congregations sent black leaders to investigate allegations against members of color. Whites sometimes accompanied them in their ministry to errant black congregants but not necessarily. After "hear[ing] an evil report" about the bondman Julius in 1814, Flint Hill Baptist Church in York District, South Carolina, "direct[ed] Bro' Billy his fellow servant to labor with him, & if satisfaction is not obtained, to cite him to attend the Church ... tomorrow." Those churches comfortable enlisting the assistance of enslaved members in the disciplinary process often dispatched a "committee of three members of colour" to visit accused black congregants and cite them to appear at an upcoming colored conference. In 1845, Clarke's Station Baptist Church of Wilkes County, Georgia, sent black members Jefferson, Daniel, and Peter to investigate a charge against another slave; five years later, the slave Dick joined Jefferson and Daniel to labor with the same bondman. Washington First Baptist Church employed slaves Mingo, Lewis, and Dangerfield to cite Moses to appear at the next colored conference and answer to charges of "improper conduct" on his part. Virginia's Mossingford Baptist Church employed a "colored standing committee" to inquire into disputes among enslaved congregants. In 1859, "[s]ervants Danniel & Moses" investigated the "Sundrie charges made against" the enslaved member John, and the following year, "[t]he coloured members present" at the colored conference were asked to gather evidence about "the character" of six different slave members "and report at our next meeting."[41]

Black churchgoers were sometimes granted the ability to vote on disciplinary matters among black members. Metaphorically, the door to southern evangelical churches was a revolving one. Baptists across the South sometimes forgave members for their transgressions, but they also regularly expelled others, both black and white, and occasionally welcomed them back after a period of separation. Black congregants were permitted no input on the fate of white members charged with moral offenses, but they might be given a voice in the dispensation of accused black members' cases. Black brethren might vote to exclude their own from fellowship or to forgive co-religionists their sins and retain them. They might also vote to approve or reject former black congregants when they applied for restoration to the church. White leaders allowed these votes taken in colored conferences to stand, provided the outcomes coincided with prevailing white opinions. In 1835, former Fishing Creek Baptist Church member Herrod, excommunicated three years earlier "for quarreling" with and "parting" from his wife, "confessed his error" and sought readmission. "The colored brethren are willing to restore him to fellowship," the clerk reported, but the regular conference refused. Island Creek Baptist Church in Hancock County, Georgia, excluded the enslaved member Caroline in 1861. Two years later, she petitioned the colored conference to reinstate her. The colored conference was willing to restore her, but the white membership overruled it. White leaders at Island Creek, exasperated by their black co-religionists' spiritual generosity, "[o]rdered that the colored conference be discontinued on account of their failure to exercise discipline among their members." Having stripped members of color from weighing in on disciplinary matters, henceforth, whites alone would rule on black members' behavior.[42]

The clash between black and white congregants over discipline was open and hostile at Washington First Baptist Church. A conflict in 1862 centered on a cryptic affair between enslaved congregants Isaac and Spencer. Citing a lack of evidence, whites acquitted Isaac of wrongdoing, but the black members, siding with Spencer, refused to accept the judgment. The white minority within the church viewed black objections with indignation. "[T]he church," recorded the clerk, "is grieved at the persistence of certain colored brethren in expressing opposition to the action of the church in the case of Isaac." Characterizing the black dissenters as "unreasonable and unchristian," whites cautioned them that "further continuance on his cause, which is calculated to weaken the authority, and impair the harmony of the church, will certainly and speedily subject them to the discipline of the Church." To underscore their determination to impose order, the whites of Washington First Baptist launched an initiative "to give more definite form to the principles on which the colored portion of the Church is governed." Part of the overhaul mandated that the "old church business of the colored brethren be brought directly before the white male members," rather than to the intermediate step of the colored conference. At least three black congregants would be appointed "to report disorderly persons . . . and generally to represent the interest of the colored membership." The following month, six "colored brethren" were so chosen.[43]

Disciplinary mechanisms in place, southern evangelical churches afforded a portion of all slaves an institutional pathway through which to morally police themselves. Precisely how many bondpeople professed to be Christian is uncertain. However popularly ingrained the connection between slavery and Christianity, one recent study suggests that fewer than 40 percent of all slaves, and more likely between 25 and 30 percent, believed in Christianity. Of those, the percentage who formally belonged to a particular church or attended religious services regularly would have been even smaller. Baptist church records from a pair of the better documented counties in Georgia—Lincoln and Wilkes—show that the sample churches included only between 6 and 8 percent of the two counties' total slave populations in 1860. (See table 2.1.) These figures do not include non-Baptist denominations, however, or churches for which records have been lost or destroyed by the ravages of time.[44]

As a percentage of all slaves, the true tally of black evangelical churchgoers was probably small, but those enslaved congregants gained access to a forum for airing grievances within the quarters. A dispute between two slaves belonging to master Charles H. Gresham appeared before Wilkes County's Beaverdam Baptist Church in 1844. "Edmond a Collored Brother" charged "Clary a Collored Sister" with "unchristian conversation" for telling another bondwoman and church member "that if she had her just des[s]erts She would have bin in hell long ago."

Table 2.1. Slave Membership in Baptist Churches as a Percentage of the Population in Two Georgia Counties, 1860

County	Sets of Baptist Church Rcds. Examined	Total Black Congregants, 1860	Total Slave Pop. in County, 1860	% Total Slave Pop. in Sample Churches
Lincoln	5	229	3,768	6.1
Wilkes	7	603	7,953	7.6

Sources: Minutes of the Georgia Baptist Association, Held at New Providence, Warren County, Georgia, on the 12th, 13th, and 16th October, 1860 (Atlanta: Franklin Printing House, 1860), Drawer 21, Reel 67, GA; Historical Census Browser, University of Virginia, Geospatial and Statistical Data Center (2004): http://fisher.lib.virginia.edu/collections/stats/histcensus/index.html.

Upon reprimand, Clary defiantly proclaimed that she would be equally happy "out of the church as in it." She was consequently excluded from fellowship. Summoned to appear before Rabun Creek Baptist Church in 1835, bondwoman and church member Lorissa acknowledged "that she has had a fight or Difference with a black Woman" belonging to a master other than her own. The church condemned Lorissa's conduct in "Following... & striking" her female adversary, but she showed sufficient contrition that the church "Restored her to our fellowship again."[45]

Fighting was not a common charge levied against enslaved churchgoers. To be sure, white members—almost all men—were much more likely to be accused of violent offenses. In my sample of nine Southside Virginia Baptist churches as well as in the twenty-three sets of Middle Georgia Baptist churches under study, fighting was the second most common charge against whites, behind drinking. Among white congregants, drinking and fighting easily outpaced all other moral infractions. The sample Georgia churches charged whites with fighting 36 percent more frequently than they did blacks. Compared to blacks, whites in fifteen upcountry South Carolina churches were charged with fighting roughly six times more often. Among enslaved members in the sample churches from both Virginia and Georgia, fighting ranked as only the sixth most common offense, trailing behind accusations for such wrongs as theft and the related charge of lying, adultery, and fornication. Though charged with fighting less frequently than their white co-religionists, black churchgoers were more likely to be expelled from the congregation for the infraction. In Laurens District, South Carolina, for example, Warrior Creek Baptist Church in 1848 "[e]xcluded Richard a black Brother for fiting the property of Harmon Garrett." "We uster 'church' people for ... fightin'," acknowledged one former Mississippi slave in the 1930s, "but now," he added ruefully, "the preacher don't want to lose a member afraid he'll lose a dime, so we don't have no churchin."[46]

Usually it was slaves themselves or their masters who settled bondpeople's disputes on the plantation. Less often, churches intervened in conflicts among enslaved congregants. In some cases, southern courts got involved. Although a few slaveholders believed their plantations above the law, neither the overwhelming majority of masters nor southern churches functioned independently of the judicial system. Indeed, at Chestnut Ridge Baptist Church in Laurens District, "[d]eacons ... appointed to assist Masters in the investigations of misconduct occurring amongst the negroes" pledged to initiate "legal proceedings ... against said negroes" "should masters of negroes implicated refuse properly to correct such slaves." Just as evangelical churches exercised spiritual authority over masters' slaves, Chestnut Ridge's threat to bring the law to bear upon the chattel of obstinate masters recognized the earthly power of the courts.[47]

Despite the constant presence of southern law prepared to adjudicate cases involving slaves, few incidents of violence among bondpeople entered the legal record. Such confrontations were not fundamentally threatening to the broad social structure of the South. Masters felt no particular compulsion to surrender their authority over their bondpeople to the legal apparatus of the state and did not bother reporting incidents they could handle themselves. Slaves were much more likely to appear in court for those instances in which they posed a greater danger to the racial status quo, such as when they damaged white property through arson, assaulted whites physically or sexually, or conspired to rebel.[48] Violent slave behavior tended to enter the southern courtroom most often when the victim was white. Between 1777 and 1864, for example, enslaved Virginians were more than twice as likely to appear in court for the murder of whites as of other blacks. Enslaved violence upon other slaves entered formal legal channels infrequently, primarily when it resulted in a bondperson's death.

The violent, lethal acts slaves perpetrated upon one another raised a host of perplexing legal issues, including masters' responsibility for their bondpeople's behavior. The next chapter examines slave violence through the lens of criminal law, but violent conflicts between slaves raised questions in the realm of civil law as well. If one slave wounded, maimed, or killed another, was the master civilly liable? If so, on what grounds? As legal historian Thomas D. Morris plainly put the question, "Should a master pay?" On one hand, an aggrieved master might think recompense only fair for the diminished worth of a slave who was injured or, if murdered, for the loss of a slave's entire value as well as a lifetime of service. On the other hand, the owner of a slave who perpetrated a violent act—assuming the master did not command it—might not think it just to pay for the wrongdoing of someone else. The fault lay with the slave, not the owner. Moreover, holding masters accountable in civil court for their slaves' misconduct made slaveholders vulnerable: their own slaves could precipitate their financial demise. Argued one lawyer in Tennessee, such a policy "might prove unjustly ruinous to owners, as the slave has the physical ability to do mischief" that would "far exceed his whole value to his master." Slaveholders did not want to be fiscal hostages to their slaves' behavior and cringed at the prospect of allowing bondpeople such coercive power over them. Masters' degree of authority over and responsibility for their chattel thus stood at the crux of the matter. "Was a slave owner's power absolute," Morris asked, "and, if so, was liability absolute?" Individual slaveholding states decided the answers for themselves. The choices states made depended on whether they functioned according to the civil law, the common law, or the common law modified by statute.[49]

Louisiana was the only slaveholding state that followed the civil-law tradition and unequivocally maintained masters' civil liability for their slaves' misbehavior. The state proceeded under the premise that slaves committed wrongs when improperly supervised, when masters exerted lax control. Slaveholders' dereliction of duty—their failure to monitor their chattel properly—made them culpable for slaves' actions. Article 180 of the Louisiana Civil Code of 1838 held that "the master shall be answerable for all the damages occasioned by an offence or quasi-offence committed by his slave, independent of the punishment of the slave." Masters, Morris explains, were therefore "civilly liable under the Code for all criminal or civil wrongs of a slave." The Louisiana Supreme Court confirmed owners' liability for their slaves' misconduct in 1841. According to the verdict in the case of *Gaillardet v. Demaries,* "The liability of the masters of slaves is a consequence of their ownership. It is one of the burdens of this species of property; it is absolute and exists whether the slave is supposed to be acting under their authority or not."[50]

If Louisiana masters' liability was absolute, owners whose slaves were murdered or injured by other slaves could reasonably expect remuneration. Driven by a sense of decency and justice, some owners of offending slaves reached "an *amicable* arrangement" or gentlemanly agreement with the enslaved victim's master outside court, preempting the need for civil action. If reparations were not forthcoming, however, the owner of the dead or wounded slave could file suit against the master of the enslaved offender. With absolute liability fixed in law, the peculiar circumstances of the case were irrelevant. As the Supreme Court of Louisiana affirmed in the *Maille v. Blas* decision of 1860, "Where one slave kills another, the merits of the quarrel between them ... are immaterial ... The proof of the loss is sufficient to fix the liability." The *Maille v. Blas* case stemmed from a conflict in which B. Maille's bondman Joe chased A. Blas's Jack from a New Orleans coffeehouse and did battle with him in the street with a combination of fists, rocks, billets of wood, and knives. Jack got the better of the encounter, inflicting upon Joe a fatal stab wound. Joe's master sued Jack's for damages, and the Court verified that Blas was liable under the law.[51]

Rules unlike those found in any other southern state applied when Louisiana slaves' assaults permanently disabled other bondpersons. Louisiana law held that "[i]f the slave ... be *for ever rendered unable to work*, the offender shall be compelled to *pay the value of said slave*, according to the appraisement made" at law. More than that, "the slave thus disabled shall for ever be maintained at the expense of the person who shall have thus disabled him." These statutes imposed double monetary penalties upon masters of bondpersons whose violence irreparably impaired other slaves. Owners were responsible for paying not only the value of the injured slaves but the lifetime costs of upkeep as well. The law produced awkward situations that prioritized the reimbursement for masters' loss of useful property over the best interests of disabled slaves who survived an attack. The case of *Jourdan v. Patton* (1818), for example, centered around a slave whose one functioning eye was "put out" by another slave, rendering the victim totally blind. In accordance with the verdict of the Louisiana Supreme Court, the owner of the blinded slave was to receive $1,200 in compensation for the full value of the slave. Once indemnification had been paid in full, ownership of the blind bondman transferred to the master of the slave who had robbed him of his sight. The burden of the slave's continued maintenance fell to the maimed bondman's new owner, however potentially detrimental to the slave. Although the new master, resentful of the financial obligation thrust upon him, might treat the slave with "[c]ruelty and inhumanity," Louisiana justices did not feel that they could safely presume as much. "The principle of humanity," decreed the court, "cannot be taken into consideration" in the disposition of the case.[52]

Financial settlements were not the automatic result of civil litigation in Louisiana, however. Masters of slaves injured or killed were still obligated to supply sufficient evidence in their favor to earn payment. The plaintiff in *Sterling v. Luckett* (1828), who "claims the value of his slave, killed by a slave of the defendant," failed to reach that threshold. In 1820, the Louisiana Supreme Court reversed a civil judgment in favor of plaintiff Adam Steel. Steel, "a stranger" from Kentucky, had arrived in New Orleans "on a trading voyage" via "a keel boat with several slaves, as oarsmen." An unidentified slave boatman of his was severely beaten and wounded at a frolic by a slave named Burton, or Benton, property of the Frenchman Cazeaux. The enslaved victim died three days later, and Steel took Cazeaux to court, claiming "the sum of 1200 dollars, the value of said slave." The First District Court sided with Steel, but Cazeaux appealed. The Supreme Court of Louisiana found the evidence of Burton's guilt "too light" to merit the awarding of damages.[53]

To be sure, a civil suit that compelled one master to reimburse another could result in pecuniary hardship for the owner of the offending slave. Had the Supreme Court of Louisiana not overturned the judgment against him, Cazeaux would have felt the law's economic pinch. Although Cazeaux conceded that "he was satisfied his boy had killed Steel's" and acknowledged "that it was hard for the plaintiff to lose his slave," he also observed that it "would be equally so for him [Cazeaux] to lose his." Alarmed by the possible economic consequences of his slave's actions, the Frenchman deflected some of the blame onto his neighbor, Alexander Fortin, who hosted the frolic where Steel's slave received his mortal wound. Cazeaux believed Fortin "very wrong in allowing the frolic." Citing Fortin's negligence, Cazeaux wanted to "make him pay for the slave" or "remunerate him for the loss," minimizing the economic blow. Thankfully for the Frenchman's financial fortunes, the Supreme Court did not find him liable for the loss of Steel's slave.[54]

Louisiana masters unable to provide monetary compensation to an enslaved victim's owner had the legal alternative of surrendering the slave who committed the violent act. Article 181 of the Louisiana Civil Code of 1838 outlined the *actio-noxalis*, which supplied a method for limiting the economic impact on a master whose slave was convicted of a crime. Rather than pay damages in cash, under Article 181 of the Louisiana Civil Code, a master had the option to "abandon" the offending slave "to the person injured" "within three days after the judgment awarding such damages shall have been rendered." The recipient of the bondperson was then authorized to "sell such slave at public auction in the usual form, to obtain payment of the damages and costs." Any surplus, or "balance," was to "be returned to the master of the slave." If the price obtained at auction "should not be sufficient to pay the whole amount of the damages and costs," the slaveholder would nevertheless "be completely discharged" from further financial obligation. Although Article 181 disqualified masters who ordered "the crime or offence" in question, those owners eligible under its provisions did not necessarily have to bear the full costs derived from a bondperson's wrongdoing. Nevertheless, the *actio-noxalis* was small consolation for a slaveholder such as the Frenchman Cazeaux. Prior to winning his case against Steel, Cazeaux reportedly complained about the prospect of having "to give up his boy." "[I]t is hard for me, to abandon my boy," bemoaned the Frenchman. However difficult it would have been to surrender the slave, the *actio-noxalis* permitted the state of Louisiana to uphold the principle of masters' absolute liability for slaves' misdeeds while in fact reducing the pecuniary consequences for slaveholders.[55]

Given its distinctive legal system, Louisiana sometimes saw the exact same slave crime result in a criminal trial for the accused bondperson as well as a civil suit filed by the victimized master against the offending slave's owner. By the time Adam Steel sued Cazeaux for damages in civil court, Cazeaux's slave Burton had already been tried criminally. Although the Louisiana Supreme Court rejected the record from the criminal prosecution and refused to admit evidence from it in the civil suit, the dual layers of court action had the potential to work at cross-purposes. During civil litigation, for example, Cazeaux's attorney argued that a master could not be compelled to pay damages civilly if the offending slave had been criminally sentenced to capital punishment or long-term confinement in prison. His rationale was simple: owners cannot surrender slaves under the *actio-noxalis* who had already been put to death or who were no longer in their possession as they awaited execution or were incarcerated. However intriguing the point Cazeaux's lawyer raised, the Louisiana Supreme Court dismissed it as not germane to the case at hand. The high court addressed the issue directly almost three decades later in *Arnoult v. Deschapelles* (1849), a case from Jefferson Parish in which the owner of Lewis, a slave found guilty for the death of the bondman Henry, denied all civil liability and attempted to exempt himself from Article 181's abandonment provision. According to his master, since Lewis had been sentenced criminally to life in the state penitentiary, "he ... ceased to belong to the defendant," thereby absolving the owner of financial responsibility for him. The Court noted, however, that the state had paid Lewis's master $300 in compensation and that the "slave is represented by the sum received from the State." Therefore, "under the spirit and intent" of Article 181, the Court ordered Lewis's master to surrender the $300 to the owner of the deceased Henry "within three days after this decree becomes final. This appears to us a fair and legal inference," the Court concluded, "and a proper extension of the *actio noxalis*."[56]

Louisiana excepted, all slaveholding states of the American South followed the common-law tradition. Unlike the Bayou State, common-law states such as Missouri accepted the slave as a "responsible moral agent." In September 1848, a slave named Anderson was working on the public roads in Missouri's Clay County. One evening, he and the bondman Henry "engaged in a quarrel and fight" that culminated in Henry's death. Henry's owner, a man named Thompson, sued "for the recovery of damages," likening his situation "to actions brought against owners, for injuries done by their animals of a dangerous and mischievous disposition." Thompson claimed that Anderson's master was negligent in allowing his unruly slave—purportedly "in the habit of beating and wounding other slaves"—"to go at large without his possession and beyond his control." In *Ewing v. Thompson* (1850), the Missouri Supreme Court rejected the analogy to "the brute creation." In contrast to oxen, dogs, or other domesticated animals, slaves were "responsible moral agent[s]." The slave, "like his master," was accountable "for his own transgressions."[57]

Masters in Missouri and other common-law states could not be held liable for their slaves' actions, a small number of exceptions enacted into law notwithstanding. "Nothing is better settled in England," declared the Supreme Court of Tennessee in *Wright v. Weatherly* (1835), "than that the master is not liable for the wanton trespasses of his servants." Tennessee and all slaveholding states other than Louisiana merely "extend[ed] the English doctrine, in relation to master and servant, to the relation of master and slave." Missouri's "municipal laws," explained that state's high court, "have not given to the master that absolute dominion over his slave which would enable him absolutely to prevent the commission of crime ... This seems to be the view of the relation between master and slave, in all the States of the Union where slavery exists, excepting Louisiana, where the civil law on this subject has been adopted." Even in Louisiana, some lonely judicial voices betrayed sympathy with the common-law approach. In a dissent to the majority opinion in *Maille v. Blas*, Chief Justice E. T. Merrick of the Louisiana Supreme Court recognized, as did judges in common-law states, that slaves were not "devoid of reason," "inanimate thing[s]," or "inert matter" but willful, "intelligent beings ... responsible to the law for their unlawful acts." He opined that awards in Louisiana civil suits ought to take into consideration the specific circumstances of the case. "[A] party's right to recovery for the loss of his slave depends in many cases upon the question whether the slave, for which he [the master] claims recompense, has or has not acted lawfully and prudently, or whether he has not brought the injury upon himself by his negligence, his malice or felonious intent," Merrick explained. By Merrick's reasoning, "the master's right of recovery for an injury done to his slave" should have been more contingent upon the slave's "volition and intention." But in the civil-law state of Louisiana, Merrick was in a distinct legal minority.[58]

Just as the occasional judge in the civil-law state of Louisiana noted the advantages of operating according to the common law, judges in common-law states sometimes expressed support for the civil law. In Rutherford County, Tennessee, the slave Andrew mortally wounded the bondman Jerry with a knife, and Jerry's master, named Weatherly, sued "to recover damages for the loss of his slave." Initially, the circuit court jury that heard the case ruled in Weatherly's favor, but the case progressed its way to the Tennessee Supreme Court of Errors and Appeals in 1835. "Is a master liable, in any form of action, for a trespass wilfully committed by his slave when not in his employ, and without his knowledge or consent?" asked the Court in *Wright v. Weatherly.* "It is believed that he is not liable by the common law," answered the judges, nor can he "be liable according to the civil law, which we have not adopted" in Tennessee. Although the Tennessee Supreme Court remained firmly within common-law tradition and reversed the circuit court decision to award damages, in delivering the majority opinion, Judge Nathan Green expressed the Court's belief that "the injured party ought, in justice, to be entitled to damages." As it was not the Court's responsibility to legislate but to interpret state laws as they existed, however, Weatherly received no payment, nor was the bondman Andrew abandoned to him under the *actio-noxalis*.[59]

Some slave-state legislatures instituted minor deviations from the common law. Although a common-law state, Arkansas introduced civil liability for certain slave crimes delineated by statute. None were felony offenses, however, so masters of slaves murdered by slaves had no legal standing to sue in civil court. Missouri law was similar, allowing for civil suits in some specified instances. That state's Supreme Court explained its modification of the common law in *Ewing v. Thompson* (1850): "The power of the master being limited, his responsibility is proportioned accordingly. It does not extend to the willful and wanton aggressions of the slave *except where the statute has expressly provided.*" But Missouri law did not permit the master of an enslaved murder victim to seek damages from the offending slave's owner: "If a slave feloniously kill the slave of another master, his owner is not liable for the loss of the slave killed." As the Arkansas and Missouri examples suggest, newer, more westerly slaveholding states were more likely to tweak the common-law understanding of masters' liability than were the older slaveholding states of the Atlantic seaboard. Nevertheless, Mississippi and Alabama did not tamper with the common law and continued to spare masters from civil liability. Mississippi, Alabama, and other states with large slave populations, in which blacks outnumbered whites or where the proportion of blacks and whites in the population was more nearly equal, proved less likely than states with high ratios of whites to blacks to make such revisions.[60]

Where the common law held sway, masters need not expect remuneration for slaves injured or killed by other slaves, with but one exception. When slaveholders ordered a slave to commit the crime, they were no longer insulated from civil liability. A victimized master could lawfully seek damages if his bondperson was killed by another slave at the command of the owner. In these cases, verdicts hinged in large part on the conduct of the master. In 1843, Mississippi slaveholder William Simmons sought retribution from William P. Leggett in Pike County Circuit Court because Leggett's slave Moses had fatally stabbed Simmons's bondman Solomon with a pocketknife. Evidence revealed that the two slaves had been consuming alcohol supplied by Leggett at the time of the assault, so a Pike County jury found in favor of the plaintiff, awarding Simmons $1,180. The Mississippi High Court of Errors and Appeals overturned the judgment, however. Although Leggett, cognizant of the slaves' behavior, "was doubtless censurable" for his carelessness in failing to intercede "between the slaves at the outset of the fatal difficulty," Simmons could not recover the value of his deceased slave because Leggett had not actually commanded the slave to commit the crime. "The liability of a master in a civil action for the felonious killing by his slave of the slave of another," explained Justice Joseph Thacher, "seems to depend upon the criminal knowledge or agency of that master in the transaction." Masters were civilly liable only for slave criminal actions that they had explicitly ordered.[61]

Depending on the precise circumstances surrounding the injury or death of a slave, however, masters might escape civil liability even when they had authorized the violence. Two cases from Louisiana illustrate the point. In both instances, masters of slaves killed by other bondmen were denied restitution because their slaves had been shot to death while in the act of committing a crime. In 1837, East Baton Rouge Parish master Joseph Bernard alleged that a slave belonging to Louis Pyburn fatally shot Bernard's valuable, twenty-six-year-old bondman Peter "wantonly maliciously & unjustifiably." Alleging that Pyburn was present and had told his slave to pull the trigger, Bernard requested $1,500 in compensation for his deceased slave, plus another $1,000 because he had "sustained damage & injury" to that amount "in the loss of the [slave's] services," which Bernard valued at $25 per month. The $1,000 also included recompense for the "necessary expenses" Bernard had "incurred . . . to compel the said Pyburn to do him justice." Pyburn was unapologetic. Having suffered a mysterious loss of pigs, he had given one of his slaves a gun with instructions to shoot the culprit, which Pyburn claimed he thought was a dog. When his slave spied Bernard's slave Peter "in the woods in the act of killing hogs," "the negro acted under the orders of his master" and shot him. Later, Pyburn defiantly "observed that he would shoot any negro whom he found killing his hogs." After three separate trials, the Supreme Court of Louisiana ruled in 1840 that Pyburn was not obligated to pay Bernard for the loss of his slave. Under the circumstances, Peter's death was a justifiable homicide.[62]

Slaveholder Vincent Hebert of Lafourche Interior Parish made the same argument in July 1846 after his "negro slave Paul" shot Thomas Bibb's "negro Wilson" on Hebert's plantation. According to Bibb, Hebert had "instructed" Paul to "ambush" Wilson and "deliberately" shoot and "kill him." Bibb demanded $600 in damages, which he was willing to accept in $10 monthly installments representing the value of what Wilson's "services . . . were worth." For his part, Hebert rejected "all amicable adjustment." The slaveholder did not deny that Paul was following orders when he shot Wilson, but as he further explained, for the past three weeks the neighborhood had been plagued by a rash of thefts. Weary of the "depredations on their habitations," Hebert and a neighbor plotted to catch the offender "in the act of stealing." The "negro Wilson" was unquestionably the guilty party. Described as a white-haired and bearded "negro boy about fifty or sixty years old," the clever slave had devised a "snare . . . for catching hogs," a homemade contraption designed "with the intention of preventing the squealing or noise of the hog." This incriminating device as well as "baite"—"a bag containing several ears of corn"—were found on Wilson's body the night of the shooting. Taking the evidence under consideration, a Louisiana court absolved Hebert of financial responsibility despite having ordered the killing.[63]

Under most circumstances, slaveholders in common-law states enjoyed little or no genuine opportunity to recover damages for injured or murdered slaves in civil court. They therefore had to pursue other avenues of redress. Some petitioned state legislatures hoping to gain a sympathetic ear. Ambrose Hundley, the one-time owner of Robert, "a valuable negro man slave" trained as a house joiner, requested the Virginia General Assembly in 1808 to "grant him such relief... as may appear just & Equitable." Robert had been murdered eleven years earlier "in a most cruel manner by a Negro man slave belonging to Thomas Roane," named Willoughby. The accused slave was tried and found guilty of manslaughter in King and Queen County, but more than a decade after Robert's death, Hundley still felt "severely the loss of his... negro," "valued at 140 pounds." Hundley gathered more than ninety signatures in his favor, requesting "relief" from the Virginia legislature. It is not certain whether lawmakers responded affirmatively, but often they did not. The North Carolina legislature replied in the negative to nineteen petitioners on behalf of Bertie County slaveholder Andrew Northcoatt. In 1846, a slave of Northcoatt's "was waylaid and attacked" by two bondmen, Harry and Isaac. Northcoatt's "badly wounded" slave suffered for five days before succumbing to his injuries. One of the assailants, Harry, "was arrested and given bail for his appearance to the next superior court," but he "failed to appear," having fled to "parts unknown." As a result, Harry's master forfeited a $250 bond to the Bertie County sheriff. Northcoatt's petitioners thought it only fair to redirect the funds retained by the sheriff to Northcoatt "to indemnify him for the loss he has sustained in the death of his negro." The North Carolina legislature disagreed and rejected the proposal. As with its northern neighbor, no pity moved the state of South Carolina in 1824 to compensate Union District slaveholder Ellis Palmer. Palmer's enslaved woman Anaca was executed for the murder of her two children. Palmer thus suffered the loss of three of the five slaves he owned, "and they the most valuable." He received $122.45 in compensation for Anaca, but his plea for additional relief went unheeded.[64]

Some aggrieved slaveholders resented the stinginess of state assemblies. It seemed appallingly unfair to them that state governments lawfully compensated masters of slaves convicted of capital offenses (as will be discussed in detail in the next chapter) but had no established policy for reimbursing masters whose bondpeople were victimized by enslaved criminals. Pittsylvania County slaveholder Pleasant Waller highlighted this incongruity in an 1820 petition to the Virginia General Assembly. Waller's slave Abraham had been murdered by the bondman Primus, who was convicted of the crime. The state paid Primus's master $700—"adequate compensation," in Waller's opinion—for the loss of his slave, despite the "flagrant outrage" he had committed. Meanwhile, Waller complained, "your Petitioner[']s slave, no way guilty, of any violation of the laws has been taken from him, and he excluded from indemnification." According to Waller, "the great principles of Public justice" demanded compensation, and "sound policy would not forbid it." Furthermore, he claimed, "his own poverty"—no doubt exacerbated by the loss of Abraham—"induces him to ask" for the state's largess. Virginia lawmakers, unmoved, rejected Waller's petition.[65]

The reluctance in common-law states to raid the public treasury to reimburse masters for slaves' criminal actions upon fellow slaves was pervasive. Their parsimony was felt most acutely when enslaved murderer and enslaved victim belonged to the same owner. Under these circumstances, there was no other master involved with whom to strike a mutually agreeable private settlement. The owner could be lawfully reimbursed for the enslaved killer but not for the deceased. The master was therefore entirely at the mercy of the legislature he petitioned. In December 1810, Israel Mathis of Kershaw District, South Carolina, purchased three adult slaves—Sawney, Sarah, and Annaky—from Virginia's Matthew Sims. Just two months later, "the Negro Sawney did Feloniously Kill and Murder the said Annaky." Mathis knew he had no grounds to sue Sims for damages, but having lost one of his recently acquired slaves to homicide, he asked the South Carolina state Senate "to Grant him such Relief or Aid as in your Wisdom you may think most proper." South Carolina legislators' collective wisdom told them it was most proper to reject the petition and provide no relief whatsoever to the unfortunate Mathis. Another slaveholder, Dr. Samuel Fairchild of Charleston District, attempted to bolster his chances for compensation by citing the expert opinions of "three honest and worthy Citizens of Edisto Island." Fairchild's slave Solomon had been "convicted and executed for the atrocious crime of murder... of his Wife, Dorcas, a wench," property of the same master. Fairchild requested the South Carolina state Senate to "grant him such compensation" for "his great loss" "as you may in your wisdom and justice deem proper." To nudge them in the right direction, he observed that the "worthy Citizens of Edisto Island" appraised Dorcas at £125. Any sum approximating that amount, he implied, would be "proper." Based on the case from Kershaw District, there is no reason to think that Fairchild was any more successful in his quest for compensation than was Mathis.[66]

Slaves often resolved disagreements and disputes in the quarters among themselves. Any slave might remind or caution a fellow bondperson to comport himself or herself according to the social conventions that governed the slave community. Slaves' self-policing mitigated an untold number of conflicts that never entered the historical record. Despite slaves' best efforts, however, some bondpeople failed to act with propriety and earned other slaves' rebuke, censure, and alienation. Depending on the severity of the differences that arose, inappropriate behavior sometimes attracted the unwanted intervention of masters or overseers, every one of whom claimed the right to intercede in slaves' internal affairs. With a vested economic interest in their enslaved property, masters *were* the law on their holdings, but they were not the only disciplinary force to act upon slaves from outside the quarters. That fraction of slaves who attended southern evangelical churches was subject to religious discipline as well. The most egregious conflicts between slaves—those that resulted in debilitating injury or death—moreover invited legal repercussions. Slaves' violent acts did not expose their owners to civil liability, unless bondpeople had acted upon their masters' direct order or belonged to Louisiana slaveholders. But as volitional beings, slaves were directly accountable for their violent behaviors primarily in the realm of criminal law, as detailed in the following chapter.

Chapter 3

INTRARACIAL SLAVE HOMICIDE AND THE CRIMINAL LAW OF SLAVERY

"ALBERT IS A NEGRO of no ordinary character," observed Winslow Robinson, the clerk of the Charlotte County, Virginia, court. Over the course of his lifetime, Albert betrayed a pattern of violence toward other slaves. He holds the ignominious distinction as the only known bondperson in the Old Dominion to kill more than one enslaved adult in the years after the American Revolution. Remarkably, the two murderous incidents attributed to him were separated by thirty years. In 1822, Albert, then owned by Joanna Bouldin, was tried in Charlotte County court, "charged with having feloniously and willfully murdered Dick a negro man slave the property of Thomas Read." The justices who heard the case found Albert "not guilty of murder but of voluntary manslaughter" and ordered that he "be burnt in the hand in open court and receive thirty lashes on his bare back well laid on at the Common Whipping post." Albert either never absorbed the lesson his punishment was designed to impart or forgot it as the decades passed, for in 1852, the same bondman, still in the possession of the Bouldin family (Mary, Nancy, and Francinia), stood accused of making a malicious assault with a hammer "upon the body of Mike, a slave the property of Abram H. Roberts," killing him. The Charlotte County justices found Albert guilty of the fatal attack, assessed his value at $580, and sentenced him to sale and transportation outside the United States. Governor Joseph Johnson confirmed the punishment, refusing to grant any pardon or reprieve to the repeat offender. Like all Virginia slaves slated for deportation, Albert would await his sale to lands unknown at the state penitentiary in Richmond. Clerk Robertson wisely recommended that "the person to take him" from Charlotte County to the state capital "should be attended by at least one Guard."[1]

The troublesome Albert, who as recently as 1851 had also earned thirty-nine lashes for forging free papers for another slave, was one of hundreds of slaves who went to trial in the Old South, charged with the deaths of fellow bondpeople. Filing suit in criminal court when one slave killed another replaced civil litigation for masters in almost all slaveholding states. In states such as Virginia, where the civil law did not apply, criminal actions often served as the best available substitute for civil suits. Since Louisiana was unique in permitting owners of murdered slaves to sue the killer's master for damages, in all other southern states the criminal law filled the void. It afforded masters murderously deprived of a bondperson their only path to any semblance of justice within the judicial system. A master would not be financially reimbursed for his deceased slave, but the enslaved assailant's possible punishment at law might rid the neighborhood of enslaved troublemakers like Albert and prevent any similar incident from happening again. It might also provide the aggrieved owner a sense of vengeful satisfaction, knowing that the master of a convicted bondperson also might suffer the loss of a slave, through the punishment lawfully meted out. Public courts were thus sometimes utilized for private purposes, to bring resolution to neighborhood tensions and simmering feuds between planters.[2]

This chapter examines the adjudication of intraracial murder cases among blacks in the slave South. Trial procedures varied by state and over time, but throughout the South slaves accused of killing other bondpeople were not automatically convicted, and for those who were, executions did not follow as a matter of course. Hanging was one of a range of possible punishments that included whipping, branding, or a combination of both, sale and transportation, condemnation to the public works, and imprisonment. In most states, masters could expect compensation for slaves executed, lawfully sold off, or sentenced to hard labor. Intraracial slave homicide cases imposed unforeseen legal dilemmas upon southern courts forced to grapple with a host of perplexing issues originating in slaves' violent acts. Masters who disputed verdicts against their bondpeople had different options available to them through which to register their complaints. Further court action and, in an age of small state governments intimately connected to the citizenry, personal correspondence and petitions to governors or state legislators provided possible recourse. An analysis of intraracial slave homicides from Virginia and other southern states reveals significant variations among southern slave codes and underscores the point that the foundations of slave law were poured at the state level.

Slave-slave homicides that crossed plantation boundaries landed in criminal court more frequently than those that took place within the confines of a single plantation.[3] But as noted in chapter 1, counting infanticides, some 40 percent of the documented intraracial slave killings in Virginia from 1777 to 1864 involved bondpeople belonging to the same master. Separating out infanticides reduces the figure to 30 percent, still a significant proportion of all cases. At first glance, it may seem odd for slaveholders to prosecute their own bondpeople for murder, but there were valid reasons for doing so. Murder was a capital offense for which slaves were lawfully accountable, and owners had a legal obligation to report the crime. Murder and manslaughter were not only criminal offenses but also, as moral transgressions, intrinsically repugnant to the consciences of many slaveholders. Unlike cows, pigs, or other farm animals, slaves constituted a unique form of property morally culpable for the crimes they committed. As Judge Joseph Henry Lumpkin of Georgia explained, "slaves are property," but "still they are rational and intelligent beings" accountable for their actions. When perpetrator and victim belonged to the same owner, masters understood that reporting homicides between their bondmen could actually serve their best economic interests as well. They could use the legal system to dispose of an unwanted, murderous slave and, in almost all southern states, receive monetary compensation for any convicted bondperson who was executed or sold as punishment. Masters across the South could be reasonably confident that the court system would not trample their rights as slaveholders, so the prosecution of their own slaves for murder was not as fraught with danger as it first appeared.[4]

By their very nature, however, murder trials did interfere in the relationship between master and slave and limited the authority of the owner to dispense with the matter at his own discretion. Some masters were unwilling to surrender control of their slaves to the court system and refused to relinquish their private right to punish wayward bondpeople. One former slave woman born in Floyd County, Georgia, recalled that master Billy Neal meted out his own macabre punishment for murder. "If one slave kilt another, Marse Billy made de overseer tie dat dead Nigger to de one what kilt him, and de killer had to drag de corpse 'round 'til he died too." Although we may greet with skepticism the recollection that the enslaved murderer "never lived long a-draggin' dem daid ones 'round," the morbid practice must have indeed "skeered 'em to death" metaphorically. Some masters refused to punish homicidal slaves at all. One bondman in Georgia escaped rebuke altogether despite killing his enslaved cousin. A few belligerent masters flagrantly flouted the law when it intruded into their affairs and actively labored to circumvent it. The bondwoman Harriet of Lowndes County, Mississippi, was indicted for infanticide in 1848, purportedly having beaten her infant mortally with a stick. Over a period of four years, her owner helped her evade arrest on five different occasions, either by secreting her in a favorite hideout or sending her out of the county. After one North Carolina slave fatally stabbed a "negro" on election day 1857, his master "sold him to a speculator" in an apparent attempt to skirt prosecution. By eluding justice, the owner no doubt planned to dispose of the homicidal slave at an economic advantage. The enslaved "murderer . . . was caught," however, and lodged in the Hillsboro jail to await trial. These sorts of exceptions notwithstanding, a substantial portion of masters did report intraracial slave homicides to the lawful authorities.[5]

Sometimes when masters proved hesitant to subject their violent slaves to the legal process, white neighbors intervened and exposed bondpeople's wrongdoing to the authorities. News of murders and other violent acts—even those confined to a single plantation—surely became fodder for conversation among local slaves and eventually attracted the attention of area whites. Whites may have overheard slaves' discussions or been confided in by a loyal bondperson. A few intraracial slave homicides garnered the immediate attention of everyone in the vicinity of the crime. Screams or, more rarely, gunshots alerted those nearby to the violence. At the end of August 1835, Joseph Lester, a white man living in Jones County, Georgia, "heard a very loud report of a Gun," the weapon that the bondman Adam, the property of neighborhood slaveholder Jeremiah Mullens, discharged into the skull of his wife, likewise Mullens's property. Whether it was because Mullens was delinquent in reporting the murder or because Lester possessed an acute sense of justice, maintained an ongoing rivalry with Mullens, or harbored a personal grudge against him, Lester took it upon himself to file the charge of murder against Adam with the Jones County court.[6]

Certainly intraracial slave murders and lesser forms of violence had the potential to incite the animosity and competitive instincts of neighborhood slaveholders. In Spartanburg District, South Carolina, master David W. Moore swore before the court that Bassett, "a Negro slave the property of Mariah J. Wofford did commit an assault & Battery on Joseph a negro slave his property," one Sunday in February 1851 "by striking him with a stick." Found guilty as charged, Bassett was sentenced to "receive on his bare back forty four Lashes well laid on." But Bassett's owner, Mariah (or Maria) J. Wofford, was no wilting southern belle. She filed a countersuit, alleging that Joe, "a servant of D W Moores was engaged in a riotous way[,] . . . exciting her Boy Bassett to a breach of the peace by . . . committing an assault on his person." Convicted, just as Bassett was, Joe was dispensed twenty-three lashes, little more than half the punishment meted out to his adversary. Each master in this case took steps to make sure the other's slave was lawfully punished.[7]

Not all slaveholders were similarly hostile toward one another in the aftermath of their slaves' violent acts. South Carolina lowcountry rice planter John Berkley Grimball recorded an incident in 1840 in which his bondman Moses, wielding a stick, fought "Col. Jenkins's man Will." Although Will defended himself with a knife, and "[t]he other hands, working near by, ran to part them," Will sustained injuries from which he subsequently died. "Moses," Grimball related, "has in consequence been taken up and is now in stocks at my place." Grimball further reported that, as he visited Moses on his Slann's Island plantation, "Col. Jenkins rode up . . . to see me." Whereas Jenkins might have been livid at the loss of his bondman, he stoically accepted it as one of the perils of slave ownership. Grimball appeared impressed and possibly even surprised by Jenkins's magnanimity. "He behaves very well," Grimball wrote of his planter colleague. "[He] says he feels more for me than for himself," for while "his man is dead," "he has made up his mind to the loss," and "my trials are still to be gone through." Jenkins anticipated that Moses would hang.[8]

Criminal trials of slaves charged with murdering other bondpeople were conducted just like trials of slaves accused of other crimes, but the process differed from one state to the next. By the antebellum decades, only a minority of southern states denied accused slaves access to a jury trial. In Virginia, ad hoc county Courts of Oyer and Terminer, summoned as necessary, adjudicated slaves' capital crimes from 1692 to 1785 and all slave felony trials from 1786 to 1865. Courts of Oyer and Terminer consisted of at least five justices of the peace empowered "to try, condemn, and execute, or otherwise punish or acquit, all slaves committing capital crimes within their county." Beginning by law in 1690, South Carolina slaves formally charged with the commission of crimes, violent and otherwise, appeared before the state's Courts of Magistrates and Freeholders. Two magistrates and from three to five freeholders determined the fate of accused slaves. Louisiana likewise employed special tribunals to hear cases of slaves charged with capital crimes. By a law of 1806, its slave courts were composed of a parish judge or two parish justices of the peace and three to five freeholders. As of 1846, the state's revised black code required that a tribunal of two justices of the peace and ten slave owners try capital cases. The new law did not entrust justice to mere freeholders but rather specified slaveholders' participation. Accordingly, tribunals of two justices and ten masters decided the cases of Isaac and Hannah when they allegedly killed fellow slaves in West Feliciana and Lafourche Parishes, respectively.[9]

Unlike Virginia, South Carolina, and Louisiana, other states transitioned away from special slave tribunals to jury trials. Maryland granted slaves jury trials from the early eighteenth century; Delaware followed suit in 1789, and North Carolina made the change in 1793. During the colonial era and the first years of statehood, Tar Heelers tried slaves before a panel of at least three justices of the peace and four slaveholders. After 1793, slaves were awarded jury trials at county court. Beginning in 1816, slaves' capital cases went to the superior court but were still heard by a jury of twelve. Georgia abandoned special slave tribunals in 1811. Modeled upon the 1740 slave code from neighboring South Carolina, Georgia slave law in 1755 directed that slave crimes be tried by two justices of the peace and three to five freeholders. Colonial Georgia law neglected to prohibit blacks from killing one another, however, other than by poisoning. A revised slave code of 1770 closed that loophole by making it a capital offense to "maliciously kill any slave or other person." It also upped the number of freeholders that heard slaves' cases to a minimum of seven. Under a new state constitution implemented in 1798, Georgia established superior courts in each county and granted the legislature the flexibility to create as many inferior courts as needed. In 1811, jurisdiction over slaves' capital crimes transferred from the justices and freeholders to the inferior court system. Henceforth, at least three judges from the inferior court and a twelve-man jury, rather than the seven freeholders, presided over slaves' trials, and the jury determined the enslaved defendant's guilt or innocence. In 1850, jurisdiction over the capital cases of slaves shifted to the superior courts, but the role of jury remained paramount. Following Georgia's lead, Alabama converted to jury trials for slaves accused of capital crimes by 1812. Tennessee followed suit by 1819.[10]

Although a twelve-man jury trial became the standard for slaves charged with capital crimes in the nineteenth century, the jury did not consist of a bondperson's peers. Only white men could serve as jurors, and in North Carolina, they were furthermore required to own slaves so that they would be sympathetic to other masters embroiled in litigation. Tennessee, which modeled its slave code on that implemented in North Carolina, similarly required slaveholding jurors, but only until 1825. After that date, freeholders were deemed suitable substitutes as jurors if an insufficient quantity of slaveholders was available, although, to protect masters' interests, the non-slaveholders pressed into service were forbidden from dividing the jury. Georgia did not exhibit the same insecurity or anxiety over non-slaveholder loyalty to the slave regime. Confident of non-slaveholding Georgians' investment in the system, there, slaveholding was not a prerequisite for jury service. Some slaveholding states split the difference between these extremes, mandating that slaveholders comprise a fraction of each jury. Starting in 1822, Alabama required that half the juror pool own slaves. In 1841, that portion increased to two-thirds. Mississippi followed a similar strategy for populating the jury box. By the Civil War, slaves accused of capital crimes—and in some states, of other felonies as well—appeared before a jury throughout most of the South. Virginia, South Carolina, and Louisiana remained the exceptions, standing pat with the justice-freeholder system.[11]

Shrewd defense lawyers for some slaves questioned whether statutes that outlawed murder applied to intraracial slave homicides. Indeed, some laws punishing homicidal acts made no explicit distinction between the enslaved or free status of the victim. Counsel for the enslaved Seaborn and Jim of Macon County, Alabama, contended that in Alabama "a slave cannot be convicted of murder for killing a slave." More than a decade later, attorneys for the Alabama bondman Crockett of Pike County likewise argued that "the murder of a slave by a slave was not punishable under the laws of the State." In both cases, the Supreme Court of Alabama held that statutes against murder applied to slave-slave homicides. "[T]he general term, 'murder,'" explained the Court in 1852, "is used without regard to whether the person murdered was a freeman or slave." Citing the precedent of *Seaborn and Jim v. State,* the Court verified ten years later that the Alabama penal code "includes the offense of murder of a slave by a slave." The Supreme Court of Louisiana considered the identical legal question in two cases decided in March 1849. The bondmen Dick of St. Tammany Parish and Jerry of Madison Parish were both tried for the deaths of other slaves. Independently, their respective counsels made the argument that no statutes "declare the killing of one slave by another to be murder." The high court disagreed. As it opined in *State v. Dick,* "A slave may be punished for the murder of another slave." The verdict in the case of Jerry promptly affirmed that decision. The Supreme Court of Georgia likewise maintained in 1855 that the state penal code's definition of murder applied equally to trials of whites as well as of slaves.[12]

Whereas slaveholding states ultimately agreed that slaves could be held legally responsible for murdering their own, they divided on the question of whether degrees of homicide existed. Arkansas, for example, recognized "only a single degree of murder ... for slaves," punishable by death. In Alabama, Crockett attempted to evade his conviction for murder by indicating the jury's failure "to specify in their verdict the degree of the offense." The Alabama Supreme Court was unpersuaded, ruling in 1862 that "[m]urder committed by a slave is not divided into degrees." Other states made finer distinctions. A Delaware court, for instance, found the bondman Anderson guilty of the second-degree murder of a slave. Virginia law recognized degrees of murder for slaves only after 1848. The common law acknowledged no degrees of murder, and when the Virginia assembly initially graded the offense in 1796, the distinction applied only to whites. After 1848, Virginia slaves charged with murder were often found guilty of the reduced charge of murder in the second degree.[13]

By 1859, slaveholding states unanimously agreed that slaves could be found guilty of manslaughter in the deaths of other bondpeople. In 1855, the Georgia Supreme Court clarified in the case of *William (a slave) v. the State* that laws against manslaughter covered the enslaved as well as the free. In Louisiana, the Black Code did not explicitly allow a slave to be charged with manslaughter, but it happened nevertheless. No fewer than seven Louisiana slaves were convicted of manslaughter in the 1850s, at least two of whom killed another bondperson. Although Jack appeared before the First District Court of New Orleans in 1858 on a charge of murdering a fellow slave named Joe, the court found "the accused guilty of Manslaughter" instead. The district judge arrested judgment, in part "on the ground that a slave cannot under our laws be found guilty of the crime of Manslaughter." Jack's case coursed its way to the Louisiana Supreme Court, which ruled that, despite the applicable statute of 1857 outlawing only murder by name, "a slave may be found guilty of man slaughter."[14]

Unlike murder, manslaughter required no malicious intent or deliberation, such as when one slave killed another inadvertently in a fight. As one Mississippi judge instructed a jury impaneled to hear the case of Horace for killing a fellow slave, "Malice is essential to constitute the crime of murder, and unless the jury believe" Horace acted "from a malicious purpose to destroy human life, they cannot find [him] guilty of murder, but may find him guilty of manslaughter." In 1827, Lunenburg County, Virginia, master Reuben Vaughn pushed for a conviction for manslaughter rather than murder for his enslaved man Nelson. Nelson, Vaughn deposed, had explained to him that "he had killed Bob without any intention of doing so" after "Bob had knocked out two of his foreteeth." Parties interested in the fate of Richmond, Virginia, slave Scott, found guilty of killing his ex-wife, argued that there was "grave doubt . . . whether the killing was wilful, deliberate and premeditated." To the contrary, they explained, "The assault grew out of a sudden and unexpected quarrel" and turned deadly only when Scott was "provoked."[15]

One good indicator of the presence or absence of malice was the alleged instrument used to produce death. As one Mississippi court explained, "malice is implied by law from the nature of the weapon" and its usage "in a fight," self-defense notwithstanding. Satisfactory proof of deadly intent demanded a conviction for murder; otherwise, it was manslaughter. Thus, in North Carolina, it seemed to many contemporary observers that "the death of Gabriel was sudden and entirely unpremeditated, ... provoked by a gross insult immediately resented by a blow stricken with a large piece of fence rail which happened to be at hand." In seizing the fence rail, Gabriel's assailant, an enraged bondman named Nelson, grabbed, unthinkingly, the most convenient weapon available. The Virginia bondman Scott had an even stronger case for a reduction of charges to manslaughter. Relying on only his bare hands to beat his victim, he "used none of the ordinary weapons calculated to produce death—no knife, no pistol[,] no bludgeon." In the case of Horace, from Mississippi, the judge reminded the jury that even a slave's possession of a knife did not necessarily signify "any preparation for a murderous purpose" or "a malicious intention to take human life" because many slaves routinely carried knives on their person for work.[16]

Slaves could escape criminal responsibility for the death of another bondperson altogether if the master had ordered the fatal attack. Southern law did not view slaves as mere extensions of the owner's will, but neither did courts expect bondpeople to abide by the dictates of their own consciences if it meant disobedience to the master. As a result, when "Richard, a slave of Robert Rowand, was tried" in Charleston, South Carolina, "for the murder of Maria, another slave of the same person," the Court of Magistrates and Freeholders acquitted him. To be sure, "the blows were struck by Richard," but "in the presence of his mistress, and by her order." Therefore, ruled the court, "his mistress was legally the murderer." Rowand was later tried for Maria's murder but found not guilty because "the woman so beaten, was in bad health" prior to the attack. An identical assault, it was reported, "would not have killed a robust woman!" In Hanover County, Virginia, master Simeon Souther was vigorously lashing the bondman Sam when he "became fatigued with the labour of whipping." To help him administer punishment, he enlisted "two of his slaves, a man and a woman, to cob" Sam with a "shingle" and then "wash him" in a "preparation of warm water and red pepper." Finally, Souther commanded them to "confine" Sam's "feet in stocks, by making his legs fast to a piece of timber, and to tie a rope about the neck ... , and fasten it to a bed post in the room, thereby strangling, choking and suffocating" the unfortunate slave. While Sam was restrained, Souther also "compelled his two slaves to apply fire to the body." Commenced in the morning, Sam's painful ordeal continued throughout the day until he at last expired. But having acted under the master's orders, neither of the slaves who participated in the protracted torture and murder of Sam was prosecuted. It was, rather, Souther who was found guilty of the crime and sentenced to five years in the penitentiary for his "atrocious and wicked cruelty." On an Alabama plantation, Cato Carter's master (and uncle) placed a gun in his bondman's hand and ordered him to kill another of his slaves who had been abusing the mules. Carter expressed his reluctance to comply, but his owner insisted he complete the deed. The slave located his quarry, but rather than shoot him, he divulged the instructions he had been given. To escape the dilemma in which they had been placed, the pair of bondmen ran away. Through flight, Carter neither committed the murder nor suffered the master's wrath for disobeying him.[17]

An analysis of the verdicts of cases in which slaves were charged with killing or assaulting other bondpeople shows that the accused were not presumed guilty of the crime. In a sample of intraracial slave violence cases from Southampton County, Virginia, Philip J. Schwarz found that all six bondpeople charged with attacking other slaves were convicted. The 100 percent conviction rate was not indicative of any uniform pattern throughout the South, however, or even within the Old Dominion. A minority of slaves escaped conviction altogether; many others were found guilty of a reduced charge. A sample case from colonial Virginia illustrates the possibilities. In Elizabeth City County, "Frank a Negro" was placed on trial in 1741 "for the Murder of Chelsea a negroe." Although exonerated of the murder, Frank was nevertheless ordered to receive "Thirty lashes" because he had absented himself "from his Masters service on his plantation and . . . was fighting with the Deceased Negro." Slaves in the nineteenth century could also avoid guilty verdicts and the harshest of penalties. The Spartanburg District, South Carolina, bondman Fed, for example, was not convicted of Sam's murder because he acted in self-defense. Sam had "struck [Fed] across the back with a piece of fence rail twice" and was about to land a third blow when Fed grabbed a fence rail of his own and "struck Sam on the head." Fed "had no intention of killing him": "his sole object was to keep Sam from hurting him." Immediately upon realizing the severity of Sam's injury, Fed "got Sam water" from the creek, washed his victim's face, moved him to a shaded location, and ran to retrieve the master. Although found not guilty of murder, Fed was sentenced to one hundred lashes in punishment.[18]

Seeking out conviction rates for violent acts between slaves requires investigations at the local level. The following figures are based on a dozen cases each of intraracial slave violence, including murders and lesser charges, from the city

THE CRIMINAL LAW OF SLAVERY

Table 3.1. Dispensations of Slave-Slave Violence Cases in Three Locations

	New Orleans	Albemarle County, Va.	Six Georgia Counties
Not prosecuted/discharged	1	1	1
Not guilty	1	6	2
Guilty	10	4	8
Unknown	0	1	1
Total	12	12	12

Sources: First District Court of New Orleans, 1846–1854, NOPL; Albemarle County Court Records, Commonwealth Causes, LVA; Baldwin County, Georgia, Inferior Court Minutes, Trial of Slaves, 1812–1828; Chatham County, Georgia, Inferior Court Trial Docket, 1813–1827, Drawer 90, Reel 33, GA; Hancock County, Georgia, Inferior Court Minutes, County Purposes & Lunacy, 1843–1850; Jones County, Georgia, Inferior Court Minutes, 1818–1846; Lincoln County, Georgia, Inferior Court, Docket of Slaves indicted for capital crimes, 1814–1838; Putnam County, Georgia, Inferior Court Records, 1813–1843, Record of the Proceeds of the Court for Trial of Slaves.

of New Orleans; Albemarle County in rural Virginia; and the six Georgia counties of Baldwin, Chatham, Hancock, Jones, Lincoln, and Putnam, counted collectively. As table 3.1 shows, in the twelve cases tried before the First District Court of New Orleans between 1846 and 1861, slaves were found guilty in ten of them (83 percent). The figures were similar in Georgia, where between 1813 and 1849 slaves were convicted at least two-thirds of the time. Albemarle County proved the outlier, finding the accused guilty in only one-third of the cases from 1802 to 1845. Subtracting out the three slave-slave assault cases from the Albemarle County total still results in a conviction for only four of the nine slaves taken up for murder (44 percent).

One case in each of the three sample locations was tossed out. Two were discharged for reasons not specified in the court records. In a case from New Orleans, A. H. Justamond's slave Cornelius was not prosecuted for the fatal shooting in June 1861 of Justamond's bondwoman Sally, probably due to lack of evidence. Nancy, a third Justamond family slave, testified to the coroner that, immediately after Sally's death, Cornelius confessed his crime to her. Cornelius then went outside and retrieved the watchman, but when Nancy informed the watchman of Cornelius's confession, Cornelius denied it. On cross-examination, Nancy conceded, "I have often had quarrels with Cornelius because he always wanted to have his own way." That Nancy may have harbored resentment toward Cornelius or had a vendetta against him undermined the veracity of her statements.[19]

Only nine slaves in my sample of thirty-six cases across the three locations (25 percent) were found not guilty. Six of the nine verdicts came from Albemarle County, where Harry was exonerated of the charge of attempted murder in 1826 and Armstead of maiming the bondman Satchell with a scythe in 1841. The remaining slaves were found not guilty of murder. One was acquitted of the poisoning deaths of three different bondpeople. Bartlett had purportedly administered "a great quantity of white arsenic" to "Celia a negro woman slave" and to two other slaves in the 1820s. It was notoriously difficult to secure a conviction for poisoning, however. Elsewhere in Virginia, the Hustings Court of Richmond absolved "James a slave" of the attempted poisoning of Scilla in 1842. In Halifax County, the Court of Oyer and Terminer acquitted three slaves of poisoning charges in October 1796 alone. Albemarle County's Bartlett was similarly discharged in 1826. Acquittals were also possible in cases of more violent deaths. In 1824, Isaac, the property of an aging Thomas Jefferson, was found not guilty of "having feloniously given a Negro Woman Slave by the name of Suckey a Mortal Wound on the head with the eye of a hoe." Suckey, another of the former president's slaves, lingered a month before she died of her injuries. Of the four slaves charged with the beating death of bondman James Huston in Madison County, the Court of Oyer and Terminer found Hilliard alone not guilty. To spare their friend, the other three slaves explained "that Hilliard knew nothing of their intention to beat" Huston and had attempted to prevent them from committing the deed. That Hilliard further pulled off one of the assailants during the fray earned him a discharge.[20]

In twenty-two of my thirty-six sample cases (61 percent), courts found the enslaved defendants responsible for the deaths of fellow bondmen. Of those, however, not all were found guilty of murder. Six of the eight guilty verdicts in the Georgia counties and three of the four in Albemarle County, Virginia (75 percent in each location) and three of the nine guilty verdicts in New Orleans (33 percent) were for manslaughter. Of these figures, only the data from Georgia conform to the broader pattern typical of the South. Slaves were far more likely to be found guilty for manslaughter than for murder in every slaveholding state except Virginia. (Albemarle County defied the statewide trend.) Convicting a bondperson of manslaughter rather than murder made abundant sense in the slaveholding South. As Glenn M. McNair observed in his study of Georgia, whites presumed blacks to be naturally passionate, frequently acting without giving forethought to the consequences. In the absence of premeditation, manslaughter was a more appropriate charge than murder. Manslaughter was a uniquely fitting charge when slaves killed other bondpeople for other reasons as well. As potentially devastating financially as the death of a slave was to a master, such a homicide was not fundamentally threatening to the social order. The southern legal system took greater interest in murders committed by slaves when the victim was white rather than black. Many whites dismissed disagreements internal to the quarters—even those that turned deadly—as trivial. Murder was a capital offense, but many southern whites believed that the death of one valuable slave hardly warranted the possible lawful execution of a second. Although manslaughter, like murder, was a capital crime in Kentucky, in most southern states, such as Georgia, it was not. Nevertheless, McNair's study uncovered only six enslaved men in Georgia *charged* with manslaughter in the deaths of half a dozen black victims. What happened more frequently was that slaves in Georgia were charged with murder but convicted of the lesser offense of manslaughter. The overall conviction rate in Georgia was actually higher when slaves killed other blacks than when the victim was white. Although this may seem counterintuitive, the difference was that slaves who killed whites would hang if convicted. Since Georgia did not compensate masters for executed slaves, juries betrayed a reluctance to condemn a master's property to death. By contrast, juries hearing the cases of slaves charged with killing other bondpeople often convicted them of the reduced charge of manslaughter, which in Georgia was not a capital crime. In half of the cases when the victim was black, convicted slaves escaped the gallows. Punishments less than death satisfied the demand for justice and served as a possible deterrent to future violence in the quarters but preserved slaveholders' rights to their property's value and labor.[21]

Regardless of the original charge in the indictment, if convicted of manslaughter, slaves in most states were not sentenced to death. With few exceptions, whipping, branding, or a combination of both was the standard punishment across the South for crimes less than murder. In Texas, slaves convicted of manslaughter were "subject to a public whipping by the sheriff." In antebellum Florida, no black person found responsible for the death of another black was found guilty of murder and executed, as was the case when the victim was white. Instead, they were all found guilty of manslaughter, whipped, and returned to work. Virginia counties also sometimes prescribed whipping alone as an appropriate punishment for manslaughter or similar violent crimes against fellow slaves. Mecklenburg County bondman Lovelace "receive[d] 39 lashes on his bare back" in 1860, "well laid on," for the manslaughter death of Robert, and Halifax County's Davy twenty for attempting "to maim disfigure & kill" the "negro slave Tom" the previous year. An Albemarle County court ordered Reuben, "guilty of manslaughter only" in the stabbing death of Ellick, to "receive on his bare back at the public whipping post twenty lashes." But beginning in the colonial era and extending into the nineteenth century, slaves convicted of manslaughter might suffer branding as an alternative to lashes. In 1725 and 1785, respectively, Lancaster County's George and York County's Daniel were ordered "burnt in the hand" for killing other bondmen. Lashings or brandings alone were insufficient to punish Albemarle County bondmen Isaac and Archer; they got both. Each judged guilty of manslaughter, Isaac was "burnt in the hand in open court by the Jailor and receive[d] thirty nine lashes"; Archer was also branded but given a relatively more merciful "twenty lashes."[22]

Even as punishments of mutilation disappeared from northern law and were less frequently employed against southern whites, they remained likely for slaves. One study of the Richmond, Virginia, Hustings Court showed that more than 80 percent of the enslaved men and 63 percent of the enslaved women convicted of all crimes by that body were branded "in the palm of the left hand with a hot poker." Some brandings in Virginia were administered upon slaves who successfully invoked the benefit of clergy after a first conviction for a clergyable felony charge. Beginning in 1765, Virginia law allowed slaves convicted of manslaughter to claim the benefit of clergy when the victim was another slave. If the court approved the motion, the slave avoided the gallows and was instead branded in the hand. The indelible mark left behind was intended as a deterrent to misbehavior, for a convicted slave could only claim the benefit of clergy once. Virginia was not alone in specifying clergyable offenses for slaves. North Carolina and Kentucky, for example, did as well. In contrast, other states such as South Carolina deemed blacks ineligible to receive the benefit of clergy for any crime. Kentucky eventually abolished the practice in 1847; Virginia followed suit the next year, but not before the enslaved Charles of Henrico County, "charged with stabbing Lewis a slave," acknowledged his guilt but "craved the benefit of Clergy."[23]

Branding served as a lawful and routine punishment across much of the South for an array of slave crimes. Chances were high that slaves who killed or seriously injured other bondpeople might be branded. A Delaware Court of Oyer and Terminer found Charles Loadnum guilty of manslaughter and ordered that he "be burnt in the brawn of the left thumb with the letter M." Found guilty of manslaughter in 1855, Little Jorden of Adams County, Mississippi, was also "[s]entenced to be branded in the hand." The telltale M white authorities seared into the skin not only served as a painful punishment but also cautioned potential future buyers of the dangers of purchasing a slave so marked.[24]

Southern states often employed branding in conjunction with whipping as punishment for many slave crimes, including violent offenses within the quarters. The Supreme Court of Alabama maintained in 1827 that "[w]here a slave is indicted for the murder of another slave, and found guilty of manslaughter only, he may be punished by whipping and branding." Alabama law limited the maximum number of stripes that a jury might impose to one hundred. Other states implemented no such restriction. In Georgia, taking all crimes into account, 38 enslaved convicts received more than 117 lashes; 17, exactly 117; and 25, less than 117; with a range from 25 to as many as an astounding 1,200. For killing fellow bondpeople, Simon of Greene County, Osborne of Wilkes County, and George of Hancock County were sentenced to 39, 50, and 200 lashes, respectively, in addition to branding. In my sample of 6 Georgia slaves charged with murder but convicted of manslaughter, all were branded with the letter M and whipped. In 5 cases, the brand was on the cheek; the sixth was "on the fleshy part of the Thumb of the right hand." Four of the 6 bondmen suffered 117 lashes. One got 100, and the last 500. To administer such tortuous punishments without jeopardizing the slave's life or excessively depreciating his value in the field or at market, white authorities distributed the lashes over time, often on 3 consecutive days or every other day. The customary sentence of 117 lashes was administered in 3 increments of 39 lashes each. The unfortunate Hancock County slave Warren received his 500 lashes over the course of 20 days from June 28 to July 17, 1850. Every Monday, Wednesday, and Friday, plus one Saturday, during that agonizing stretch of time, he endured 50 stripes "executed with regard to Humanity."[25]

The typical number of lashes inflicted upon slaves was higher in Georgia than in neighboring South Carolina. For all slave crimes in Anderson District from 1819 to 1865, bondpeople punished by whipping suffered from 5 to 39 stripes. Thirty-nine represented the norm throughout most of the antebellum era, rising to 56 in the 1850s. Intraracial slave violence invited somewhat harsher punishments. A sample of 63 cases from the antebellum decades shows that the most common punishment inflicted upon South Carolina bondpeople for killing or otherwise physically harming fellow slaves was 100 stripes, followed by 75, but the average number of licks was 67. (See table 3.2.) Some slaves suffered substantially more than that, however. Convictions for manslaughter garnered the

Table 3.2. Number of Lashes Inflicted as Punishment for Intraracial Slave Violence in Antebellum South Carolina (N = 63)

No. Lashes	10	12	15	19	20	23	25	30	32	35	37	39	40	42	44	45	47	50	60	75	100	150	200	300	500
																					X				
																				X	X				
																			X	X	X				
	X																	X	X	X	X				
	X		X		X		X											X	X	X	X				
	X		X		X		X	X				X				X		X	X	X	X	X		X	
	X	X	X	X	X	X	X	X	X	X	X	X	X	X	X	X	X	X	X	X	X	X	X	X	X

Note: Each X represents one convicted slave.

Sources: Court of Magistrates and Freeholders records for Anderson, Clarendon, Fairfield, Kershaw, Laurens, Pendleton, Pickens, and Spartanburg Districts, South Carolina, SCDAH.

greatest number of lashes. Kershaw District bondman Titus was sentenced to 500 as punishment for the death of a slave named Frank. The Court of Magistrates and Freeholders ruling on his case ordered that Titus receive 150 stripes the night of the verdict, plus 25 each day until the additional 350 had been inflicted. Titus was to be held in jail throughout the 15 days necessary to complete the terms of his sentence. For the Civil War–era deaths of bondmen Bill and Sam, respectively, Lank of Laurens District and George of Spartanburg District were each sentenced to 300 lashes and 2 months in jail. Lank was to receive 100 licks on 3 different days, each 1 month apart; George's were distributed in 6 weekly increments of 50. Other bondmen convicted of manslaughter earned as many as 150 stripes. The greatest number of lashes earned by a convicted female slave in my sample was 200. Found guilty of infanticide, the Fairfield District bondwoman Polly was slated to have her punishment administered in increments of 75, 75, and 50. Lesser offenses, such as assault and battery upon a fellow slave, earned the guilty party as many as 100 stripes. At the low end of the spectrum, South Carolina slaves escaped with as few as 10 lawfully administered licks for the minor roles they played in various fights, affrays, and riots.[26]

However excruciating the whippings bondpeople received, they paled in comparison to some of the more gruesome forms of legal retribution slaves suffered in the colonial era and during the first years of the new republic. Mutilation was more common in the eighteenth century than in the nineteenth. In early Richmond County, Virginia, Harry had his ears cut off for stabbing another slave. Hannah, "a Negro wench" tried and convicted in 1799 for the poisoning death of her master's "Negro fellow" Brandon, earned the same fate. She was to "receive thirty nine Lashes on her bare back well Laid on" at "the public whipping post," "and then have her ears nailed to the pillory and cut off." In Amelia County, the enslaved Will was lawfully beheaded in 1747 in retribution for the murder of Jack. The court that heard his case ordered that, after Will's hanging, "the Sheriff sever his head from his Body and fix it on a pole at the fork of the road near Southalls ordinary"; the decapitated corpse was to be buried. As punishment for the homicide of a fellow bondman, a Rockbridge County slave in 1786 likewise had his head cut off and "stuck on a pole at the forks of the road" for public display.[27]

Yet eighteenth-century Virginia could not match the elaborately ghastly punishments possible in Louisiana during the same era. With its 1724 slave code grounded in France's draconian *Code Noir*, Louisiana could dispense severe justice to convicted slaves. When the Louisiana bondman Clement was found guilty of killing his brother Pierre in 1778, he was sentenced to death via the ancient Roman punishment for parricide. The court ordered that Clement's feet and hands be bound. He was then to "be mounted on a beast of burden with a halter around his neck" and paraded publicly as "the voice of the town crier ... will make known his crime." After the humiliating and terrifying course to the gallows, Clement was to "be whipped and afterwards hanged" by "Miguel, the negro executioner." Clement's punishment would then take its most creatively bizarre turn. As the court explained, "his body will be put into a leather sack with a dog, a viper, a monkey and a cock, the mouth of the sack sewed up, ... [and] pitched into the river." The corpse would surely have been mutilated by the four panicked, desperate creatures stitched into the bag with the body, struggling with each other and to avoid suffocation and drowning. Before long, Clement and his unconsenting animal companions all would sink to the murky depths of the Mississippi and rot with the passage of time.[28]

Compared to the eighteenth century, the use of branding, ear cropping, and other punishments of mutilation for convicted slaves declined in the nineteenth-century South but did not altogether disappear. Sentences tempered even in Louisiana. Slaves found guilty of killing or wounding other bondpeople in the late antebellum era were sometimes merely shackled and put back to work. In 1853, the First District Court of New Orleans sentenced one homicidal bondman "to work in iron for one year in the service of his master." Other slaves, including James, convicted of killing Victor with a broken bottle, first endured a mandated number of lashes before being placed in irons. After submitting to the last of his stripes, James was "to wear an iron collar with three branches during five years at the service of his" owner. A Rapides Parish court sentenced one bondman who had killed another "to receive one hundred lashes on four successive days and to wear a ball and chain for three months." Gruesome, tortuous punishments, though no longer as common as they had been, continued. In 1836, an unidentified "negro man" in New Orleans engaged in the "horrid butchery" of a female slave with "a large Bowie knife." The assailant "was immediately arrested, and condemned to be burned to death over a slow fire, which was put into execution." That he had inflicted "no less than 17 dreadful wounds" upon the bondwoman's master as he attempted to interfere in the assault surely earned him the harsher penalty. The same year, in Hot Springs County, Arkansas, a slave named William, distraught with his forced migration from Tennessee to Texas, slaughtered his master and a second white man en route, with an axe. For reasons that are less clear, he also butchered five other slaves. He then returned to the Memphis area, but his claim that the others of his party had been killed by Indians was met with disbelief.

William was tied to a tree and burned alive. As in Louisiana, the deaths of whites magnified the ruthlessness of the punishment.[29]

As one scholar has argued of the slave South, "punishments for black-on-black crime were much less severe than slave crimes against whites." Legal historians have debated for decades the degree of procedural fairness accorded slaves in southern courtrooms. When enslaved defendants were tried for violent acts against other bondpeople, the racial dynamics inherent in trials of slaves accused of crimes—especially violent ones—against whites evaporated, and verdicts stood a better chance of being decided on the merits of the case. Moreover, courts showed greater leniency toward slaves convicted of violent offenses against other slaves than against whites. This is not to argue that slaves never faced the ultimate penalty—execution—when judged accountable for the death of a fellow bondman, but the certainty of death was relatively higher when the victim was white. In an analysis of Essex, Henry, Southampton, and Spotsylvania Counties in Virginia between 1785 and 1829, Philip J. Schwarz discovered that all eighteen slaves found guilty of killing a white person were ordered capitally punished, whereas only half of the fourteen slaves convicted of murdering other slaves were slated to hang. Glenn M. McNair's results from Georgia were similar. Less than half of those convicted of the deaths of blacks were put to death. Southern slave codes did not mandate differential penalties for those bondpeople who killed whites and those who killed blacks; theoretically, the crime of murder carried equal weight under the law, regardless of the victim's race or complexion. The difference was that slaves who physically attacked whites threatened the South's racial hierarchy. Those whose victims were also enslaved did not, so justice did not demand the destruction of valuable slave property. In at least the most egregious cases of intraracial slave homicide, however, courts overcame their reluctance to impose the death penalty. Even as whipping, branding, or a combination thereof were the more common punishments for slaves' violent acts upon one another, some were hanged.[30]

Of more than four hundred cases of slave crime from antebellum Georgia, McNair unearthed twenty-eight enslaved murderers of other bondpeople, a partial list of which is given in table 3.3. Of the twenty-eight, thirteen hanged, representing fewer than 14 percent of all executions in the state. Another thirteen were whipped and branded and two only whipped. Neither of the two slaves convicted in the murders of free blacks was executed: valuable slave lives took priority over justice for free black victims. One bondwoman named Fanny, enslaved in Hancock County, was put to death in 1833 for poisoning two other slaves, Martha

Table 3.3. Selected List of Georgia Slaves Charged with the Murder of Other Slaves, 1813–1849

Date	County	Alleged Murderer	Verdict	Punishment
1813	Chatham	Carter	guilty of murder	hanging
1815	Baldwin	Tom	guilty of manslaughter	117 lashes; branding
1819	Chatham	Adam	guilty of manslaughter	117 lashes; branding
1820	Chatham	Titus	not guilty	none
1821	Baldwin	Peter	guilty of manslaughter	117 lashes; branding
1821	Baldwin	Edmond	discharged	none
1827	Chatham	Prince	unknown	unknown
1831	Putnam	Dick	guilty of manslaughter	117 lashes; branding
1835	Jones	Adam	guilty of murder	hanging
1838	Lincoln	Elick	not guilty	none
1846	Jones	Thomas	guilty of manslaughter	100 lashes; branding
1849	Hancock	Warren	guilty of manslaughter	500 lashes; branding

Sources: Baldwin County, Georgia, Inferior Court Minutes, Trial of Slaves, 1812–1828; Chatham County, Georgia, Inferior Court Trial Docket, 1813–1827, Drawer 90, Reel 33, GA; Hancock County, Georgia, Inferior Court Minutes, County Purposes & Lunacy, 1843–1850; Jones County, Georgia, Inferior Court Minutes, 1818–1846; Lincoln County, Georgia, Inferior Court, Docket of Slaves indicted for capital crimes, 1814–1838; Putnam County, Georgia, Inferior Court Records, 1813–1843, Record of the Proceeds of the Court for Trial of Slaves.

and Peter, who belonged to her master. Two other slaves who hanged were Carter of Chatham County and Adam of Jones County, both of whom used firearms to commit murder. Committing their crimes with weapons lawfully forbidden to slaves invited the harshest of punishments. Adam was ordered to be taken to the "place of public execution" on Friday, October 2, between 10:00 a.m. and 2:00 p.m. "and publicly hung upon a Gallows for that purpose by the neck until he be dead." Georgia law specified that slaves sentenced to death be executed from five to thirty days after the courtroom verdict. Willis Cofer, once enslaved in Wilkes County, remembered the process. "If one Nigger did kill another Nigger," he reminisced, "dey tuk him and locked him in de jailhouse for 30 days to make his peace wid God. Evvy day de preacher would come read de Bible to him, and when de 30 days wuz up, den dey would hang him by de neck 'til he died."[31]

No state capitally punished more slaves than Virginia, a function of both the Commonwealth's large enslaved population and, as will be discussed below, its comparatively generous policy of compensating masters for executed slaves. From 1785 to 1865, the Old Dominion put more than six hundred slaves to death for a range of crimes, well more than double the number that South Carolina executed between 1800 and 1855. A law of 1786 required that Virginia Courts of Oyer and Terminer be unanimous in condemning a slave to death, but that proved no impediment. In a sample of 145 slaves charged with the murder of other slaves from 1777 to 1864, 109 (75 percent) were sentenced to death, including almost all enslaved defendants prior to 1849. Thereafter, revisions to the law permitted Courts of Oyer and Terminer to sentence slaves found guilty of killing another bondman to punishments less than death, including sale and transportation. From 1849 to the end of the Civil War, only fifteen of the fifty slaves found guilty of murdering another slave (30 percent) confronted the prospect of execution. Altogether, approximately 9 percent of all slaves hanged in Virginia between independence and the end of the Civil War died for the murder of other bondpeople, but no Virginia slaves were ever executed for simple assaults or attempted murders of other slaves.[32]

The Old Dominion was exceptional in the numbers of slaves it charged with, convicted of, and executed for the murder of other slaves. As in Georgia and other states, Virginia slaves charged in such homicides virtually always pleaded not guilty of the charges. An unknown fraction of accused slaves were surely innocent; others who were guilty may have instinctively thought it imprudent to admit blame to white authorities, and many masters probably insisted upon a not guilty plea in an effort to preserve the lives of their chattel. Spotsylvania County bondman Jarret defied the customary pattern by pleading guilty in the August 1829 deaths of the bondwoman Rose and her child. But it did not matter. The Court of Oyer and Terminer likely recognized that Jarret had abused his physical superiority over victims smaller and weaker than himself, and the justices were not inclined to show mercy. They found Jarret guilty and sentenced him to "be hanged by the neck until he be dead." Slaves condemned to death were confined in the local jail until the day of execution arrived. Court clerks documented the date and time set for the impending execution, typically within a matter of a few weeks of the verdict, along with any special instructions given by the justices. In the case of Henrico County's King, the court specified that the condemned slave be taken "to the gallows to be erected for the purpose near the grave yard of coloured persons in the vicinity of the City Poor House." When the appointed day for execution arrived, county sheriffs carried out the deed. Upon hearing the case of Monroe County bondman Moses, accused of the murder of Will, six justices found the defendant guilty and ruled that he shall "suffer death by Hanging by the neck till he is Dead Dead Dead," on Tuesday, March 19, 1811. Sheriff Tristan Patton "duly carried" the sentence "into Effect" per the court's instructions. In 1814, a Botetourt County Court of Oyer and Terminer directed that Ralph, found guilty in the death of "Fan a negroe Woman slave," be hanged on August 20 between the hours of 10:00 a.m. and 3:00 p.m. As Deputy Sheriff William Rowland informed the court, "Decree was Carried into effect by Me."[33]

In most southern states, masters received compensation for slaves who were lawfully executed. As Maryland legislators recognized early in the eighteenth century, "it too often happens that Negro Slaves . . . commit many Heinous and Capital Crimes, which are endeavoured to be smothered, and concealed, or else such Negroes . . . are conveyed to some other Province, and Sold by their Owners, who for the sake of the Interest they have in their Lives and Services, suffer them to escape Justice." In the wake of the Stono Rebellion of 1739, South Carolina similarly acknowledged that "owners of slaves may . . . be tempted to conceal the crimes of their slaves, to the prejudice of the public." Lawmakers' solution to masters' concealment and evasion was compensation. Beginning with Virginia, which adopted the first compensation statute in 1705, reimbursement provided an inducement for slaveholders to bring slaves suspected of capital crimes to justice before the law. Owners who summarily executed slaves on the plantation, without recourse to the courts, earned no recompense whatsoever; those whose slaves were hanged by order of a jury, did. To a degree, then, compensation programs relieved masters from the quandary of deciding between the implementation of justice and their personal economic interests.[34]

Compensation laws disseminated the costs of reimbursement across a wide swath of southern society. The precise process for underwriting compensation expenses differed from one location to the next. In colonial South Carolina, beginning in 1717, the money came from a tax on all slaveholders of the parish in which the slave was executed. By 1722, however, lawmakers ordered that monies be gathered from a tax on both land and slaves, compelling even non-slaveholders to contribute to the fund. Likewise in colonial North Carolina, funds derived from colony-wide taxes levied even on those with few or no slaves minimized the financial burden on slaveholders. Lawmakers could rationalize non-slaveholding taxpayers' subsidizing of slaveholding by noting that a dangerous slave's execution benefited the safety and security of all society. In 1796, North Carolina did shift the pecuniary responsibility somewhat back upon masters. That year, seven slave-rich counties in the eastern part of the state imposed a tax to pay for the compensations of executed slaves. Counties with comparatively fewer slaves were relieved of the fiscal load. But many southern slaveholders resisted shouldering the burden exclusively. In 1830, Kentucky considered a proposed tax of one-fourth of 1 percent to "be levied upon the value of all slaves in the State for the creation of a fund out of which to make ... disbursements." The bill did not pass. To acquire sufficient funds for disbursement, taxes to compensate masters of slaves executed in Alabama and North Carolina applied not only to whites but also to free blacks, further diluting the costs to slaveholders. Alabama's law imposed a tax of "one cent on all negroes under ten years, and two cents on all negroes over ten and under sixty." Through various means, then, the public coffers were filled for the distribution of compensation monies. In spreading out the costs to the public, slaveholders as well as non-slaveholders, lawmakers struck a balance between masters' property rights in slaves and the security of society as a whole.[35]

In deferring to the legal system, the vast majority of all southern masters did not have to absorb the economic loss of a slave in full. But the narrow question of precisely how much to compensate masters was fraught with difficulty. One observer wrote in 1737 about executed slaves in North Carolina that "the Planters suffer little or nothing by it, for the Province is obliged to pay the full value they judge them worth to the Owner ... to prevent the Planters being ruined by the loss of their slaves, whom they have purchased at so dear a rate." In actuality, most colonies and, later, states did not authorize payment of the full value of condemned slaves. Individual states implemented various measures. Alabama, Mississippi, and Texas reimbursed masters one-half of the assessed value of a slave, as determined by the jury. In consequence, when Patsy was executed in June 1825 for cutting the throat of a "Negro boy named Prior" in Perry County, Alabama, master Elijah Gorman received $132.50 of Patsy's $265 valuation. The states of Delaware and North Carolina permitted the compensation of as much as two-thirds the value of the slave. Other states imposed a maximum dollar figure that valuations could not exceed. For most of the antebellum period, the Louisiana slave tribunals that appraised condemned slaves could not legally reimburse masters more than $300, regardless of the realistic market price a slave might fetch. A Louisiana law of 1854 declared that valuations shall "not exceed the sum of $750," of which the state would reimburse masters no more than a maximum of two-thirds, or $500. South Carolina proved even more parsimonious, forbidding in 1843 any compensation greater than $200. The state's compensation provisions, complained one resident, "furnish so poor a relief for the abuse to which they apply, that they will rarely be resorted to." By 1858, the state upped the amount of reimbursement to as much as one-half the slave's appraised value. The uniform trend across the South of valuing enslaved criminals at less—and sometimes substantially less—than their market price reflected, to some degree, the understanding that the slaves diminished their value when they demonstrated their capacity to commit crime. Stingy compensation policies also spared strain on state budgets and reduced the temptation for masters to exploit the legal system by falsely claiming that a sick, diseased, elderly, disabled, frustratingly troublesome, or otherwise unwanted slave had committed a capital crime. Slaveholders' economic interests would be better served by selling them at public auction.[36]

Some colonies and states pondered full compensation but decided against it. Colonial South Carolina, which experimented with restoring the full value of an executed slave to the master from 1712 to 1714, quickly deemed the practice prohibitively costly. Thus, in 1714, South Carolina imposed a limit of £50 on slave valuations. After another flirtation with full compensation, the colony limited the maximum outlay to £80 in 1722. By the 1740 slave code, South Carolina raised the assessment cap to £200, to be divided between the owner of the executed slave and the white person victimized by the convict's actions. Next door in North Carolina, reimbursement maximums established in the colonial era were periodically adjusted to conform to fluctuations in slave prices at market. In 1758, lawmakers set the compensation limit at £60, upping it to £80 in 1764 to protect the master's ability to purchase an adequate replacement for the executed slave. After it achieved statehood, North Carolina restricted reimbursements in 1779 to £700 in continental money. In 1786, the state terminated all compensation for executed slaves, only for it to return a decade later. In the nineteenth century, states continued to toy with the idea of full compensation for condemned slaves. In Alabama, Governor Benjamin Fitzpatrick vetoed such a bill in December 1842, arguing that masters, confident of reimbursement in full, would take little interest in the trial of a bondperson accused of a capital crime. When James Henry Hammond suggested in 1855 that South Carolina revive the policy of full compensation, lawmakers objected to the proposal because they suspected that negligent masters were at least partially responsible for slave criminality.[37]

States carefully crafted compensation statutes to preclude the overly rapid draining of the public treasury. The limited funds available for disbursement in state coffers required proper safeguarding. Blaming masters for failing to prevent serious slave crimes, lawmakers established various exclusions—as do modern-day insurance policies—under which the state refused to compensate slaveholders for executed bondpeople. Nineteenth-century South Carolina disallowed reimbursement for enslaved murderers and insurrectionists prior to 1843. Alabama and Louisiana also denied compensation to masters of slave rebels. States adopted various other restrictions and exemptions as well. Concerned about masters' manipulation and exploitation of the law, several statutes refused all compensation if the owner had ordered the crime for which the slave was put to death. After 1796, North Carolina masters were compensated conditionally, pending proof that they had treated their slaves well. Lawmakers in the Tar Heel State understood that insufficient food or clothing or inhumane treatment sometimes drove slaves to crime, and they did not want a master to profit by creating the conditions that bred slaves' felonious behavior. Alabama restricted compensations only to masters resident in the state. Thus, a slave from neighboring Mississippi, for example, executed for a crime in Alabama did not cost the state anything. Despite these efforts to minimize costs, the capital outlays for compensations were substantial. By 1830, the Commonwealth of Kentucky had already indemnified slaveholders some $68,000 for executed bondpeople.[38]

Georgia found the simplest, easiest way to avoid such expenses: after 1793, it offered masters of executed bondpeople no compensation whatsoever. Georgia's colonial-era slave code of 1770 had authorized payment of as much as £40, but lawmakers repealed the policy twenty-three years later. Instantly, the execution of slaves in Georgia became a more serious matter for masters. Absent the safety net of financial compensation, Georgia found alternative punishments to hanging. Depending upon the crime, Georgia slaves received ever more lashes or a combination of whipping and mutilation. The change in sentencing marked a compromise between the twin desires to punish unruly slaves and to protect masters' enslaved property. Execution was reserved only for those slaves found guilty of the most heinous of crimes.[39]

Maryland and Virginia adopted a starkly different reimbursement policy than that of Georgia. Both Maryland, from 1751 to emancipation, and Virginia, after 1786, authorized payment for the full value of slaves put to death by the criminal justice system. "Full value" was in reality a misnomer, however. Whether truly guilty or not, slaves convicted of capital crimes diminished their market value by suggesting to hypothetical buyers the felonious behaviors of which they were capable. A Virginia law of March 1840 mandated that "the justices who shall condemn ... [a] slave shall value him or her at the cash price for which he or she would, in their opinion, sell at public sale under a knowledge of his or her guilt." Payment to the slave's owner was determined by taking an average of the judges' five appraisals. After a Nottoway County Court of Oyer and Terminer convicted Lewis for the murder of Ben in 1840 and sentenced him to die, the five "Gentleman Justices" valued Lewis from $500 to $650, and the state compensated Lewis's master the "average sum [of] $575."[40]

Valuations hinged on an array of factors, including a convicted slave's age, sex, general character, and overall health. When an Appomattox County court condemned Reuben to death in 1837 for killing Tom, the justices took into account Reuben's "diseased bodily condition" when it assessed him "at the cash price of Four Hundred Dollars." Unusually frightening or horrifying crimes that offended the sensibilities of the judges also diminished their appraisals. In 1832, a Prince Edward County court valued the bondwoman Rinah, found guilty of poisoning Oxford, at the measly "sum of Fifty dollars," and justices in Spotsylvania County assessed Jarret, convicted of killing an enslaved mother and her baby, at the even more paltry "sum of Twenty five dollars" in September 1831.[41]

The variable most commonly cited explicitly for increasing a condemned slave's value was his or her occupation or skill set. In Greenville County in 1798, "Abram being a Blacksmith by Trade was by the Court valued at Seven Hundred and Eighty Three Dollars and Thirty-four Cents," two and three times the price of other slaves executed for the murder of other bondpeople at about the same time. Norfolk's "Bill Williams a slave" was found guilty of slitting the throat of "Henry a black man" in 1807. He was nevertheless valued at an above-average "five hundred dollars, he being by trade a valuable Black worker." In 1827, during a period when most condemned slaves were assessed at between $300 and $400, Lunenburg County justices valued Nelson, convicted of the murder of the bondman Bob, at $540, "it being proved to the Court that the said Nelson is a good carpenter." As "a good Blacksmith and miller," Spotsylvania County bondman Beverley was appraised in 1854 at $1,350, $500 to $1,000 higher than any other slave condemned from 1853 to 1855. Condemned female slaves also sometimes reaped higher payments for their masters on the basis of recognized skills. Although "Jenny a negro woman slave ... was found guilty and sentenced to be hanged by the neck until she be dead" for murdering "three of her own children" in 1815, a Powhatan County Court of Oyer and Terminer valued her "to the sum of Four hundred dollars, considering her more valuable than other women slaves in consequence of her having been an excellent weaver." (The court postponed her execution on account of her pregnancy.)[42]

Fluctuating market prices for slaves, which typically moved in tandem with cotton prices, also account for variations in compensation amounts. Nothing sent the dollar value of assessments higher, however, than the formation of the Confederacy and the onset of the Civil War. Depreciating Confederate currency inflated the market prices for all manner of goods during wartime, including slaves. As a result, masters of Virginia slaves condemned as the Civil War raged received astronomical disbursements of increasingly worthless Confederate bills. To illustrate the dramatic change, in 1860, the year before secession and war, a Prince George County court appraised the bondwoman Betsey at a mere $200 upon a conviction for second-degree murder. The same year, Madison County's Philip, guilty of the identical crime, was assessed at a much higher $1,200, "such value being in the opinion of the Court the cash price for which he would sell at public auction with a Knowledge of his condemnation." Superficially, wartime compensations appeared comparatively generous, even to Philip's lofty price. Henry, convicted of the death of the bondman Kit in Pittsylvania County, and Harriett, found guilty in Charlotte County of "choking" Matilda, "compressing her windpipe," "suffocating and strangling" her, and beating her with a hoe, were each valued "at Three Thousand dollars" in spite of the verdicts against them. Unfortunately for their owners, payments in Confederate currency were not remotely as impressive as they appeared.[43]

Of the 109 Virginia slaves known to have been sentenced to death for the murder of another bondperson between 1777 and 1864, slightly more than half actually swung from the gallows. No fewer than three dozen bondpeople slated for execution for killing a fellow slave were reprieved by Virginia governors for sale and transportation. The Old Dominion occasionally transported condemned slaves in the last quarter of the eighteenth century, but a law passed in January 1801 transformed sale and transportation into a normative practice. Timing of the law was not accidental, passing mere months after the Gabriel conspiracy had been unearthed in the environs of Richmond. Sale and transportation afforded several advantages. Virginia whites recognized the possibility that slaves might be wrongfully executed. They also proved reluctant to capitally punish slaves for certain crimes less threatening to the social order, such as the homicides of other slaves. For these reasons, many prominent whites in the Commonwealth, including Thomas Jefferson, accepted the sale and transportation of enslaved convicts as a reasonable, humane, and merciful alternative to hanging. In 1801, Virginia institutionalized a procedure for disposing of dangerous slaves without sending them to the gallows. It fell to the governor to make the final determination to spare the lives of enslaved convicts and send them out of the country. Two years later, in 1803, Nottoway County bondman Tom became the first known slave condemned to death for the murder of a fellow slave to be reprieved by the governor for sale and transportation under the 1801 law. One master in 1824 expressed his desire that transportation might give his young bondman, convicted of killing another slave, "an opportunity" to atone "for his past errors, become a useful servant, and finally leave this life reconciled both to God and man."[44]

With a revamping of the Virginia slave code in the late 1840s, sale and transportation became an increasingly common outcome for slaves convicted of murdering other bondpeople. No longer a fate determined strictly by the governor, Courts of Oyer and Terminer might lawfully sentence a convicted slave to sale and transportation. From 1850 to 1864, they ordered sold and transported no fewer than thirty-five slaves found guilty of the death of another slave. Prince Edward County bondman Ned, who had taken the life of Stephen, became the first to receive such a sentence in lieu of the standard hanging. Many of the thirty-five slaves sentenced to sale and transportation for killing a fellow bondperson were convicted of second-degree murder, and Ned was one of them. According to the justices who heard his case, "it is the opinion of the Court that . . . Ned is not guilty of murder in the first degree but that he is guilty of murder in the second degree and that for the said offence he be transported beyond the limits of the United States." The onset of the Civil War did not alter the possibility of transportation but required that a slave such as James, found guilty of the second-degree murder of Andrew by the Hustings Court of Richmond during the war, be sent "beyond the limits of the Confederate States for the term of his natural life." Theoretically, then, he might have been carried to Maryland, Kentucky, or Missouri, none of which had seceded and therefore qualified as part of a foreign country. Virginia slaves were more likely to be transported if they had killed other slaves than if their victims were white, in which case hanging was the more common punishment. Among slaves convicted in the deaths of other bondpeople, those sold and transported outnumbered those who were executed. Altogether, from 1777 to 1864, they were almost 27 percent more likely to be transported than hanged. Philip J. Schwarz places the total tally of Virginia slaves sold and transported for all criminal offenses between 1785 and the end of the Civil War at almost one thousand. Of these, at least seventy-one, or approximately 7 percent, were sold and transported from 1803 to 1864 for killing another slave. Twenty-three of the seventy-one had been sentenced directly by Courts of Oyer and Terminer to sale and transportation; governors reprieved the other forty-eight. Some free black criminals were also subject to transportation. Hilliard Johnson of Amelia County, convicted in the voluntary manslaughter case of a slave named Phil in 1825, was robbed of his free status, "sold into perpetual Slavery," and "transported and banished beyond the limits of the United States."[45]

The deportation of enslaved convicts was not unique to Virginia. Other southern states also employed transportation as a substitute for the execution of slaves and free blacks who committed homicide upon black victims. Georgia did not allow the practice, but states such as Missouri and South Carolina did. For killing another slave, one Clay County, Missouri, bondman suffered thirty-nine stripes and sale out of state. Following a two-hour deliberation, one South Carolina Court of Magistrates and Freeholders made banishment from the state an optional part of a convicted slave murderer's sentence. John Berkley Grimball's Moses, found guilty of the second-degree murder or manslaughter of the bondman Will, was ordered to "solitary confinement for six months," where he would "receive 50 lashes per month, unless at the end of 3 months his owner shall send him out of the State never to return." Grimball thought the penalty "a very severe one," but resolved to "ship" Moses away after the first three months of incarceration "to save him the balance of his whipping—and also because he is now exceedingly obnoxious to the neighborhood." Courts of Magistrates and Freeholders typically did not leave transportation to the discretion of the master. Enslaved in Union District, South Carolina, Clarissa "was tried in 1838 . . . for killing her child Rachel & . . . was sentenced to be removed from the State & sold," which she was. In 1846, it was the governor who ordered the Charleston District bondman Henry "banished from the State" following a conviction for "manslaughter on a slave of Mack Williams." No state better documented its sales and transportations of slave convicts than Virginia, however.[46]

By law, Virginia's slave convicts ordered sold and transported had to be carried not only out of the state but out of the United States altogether. They were typically conveyed to the West Indies; to New Orleans, prior to its acquisition by the United States in 1803; or to Spanish Florida, up until the signing of the Adams-Onís Treaty of 1819 that secured the region for the United States. Slaves were boarded on ships to reach new homes in the Caribbean; those destined for locations on the North American mainland might be carried overland in a coffle. The system was not without its flaws. Foreign governments did not always welcome the influx of enslaved criminals and their potential to foment unrest. At other times, there was no need for their labor. One correspondent informed Governor James Barbour in 1813 that "Florida and the Spanish Provinces, the places to which People of this description were formerly carried, afford now no demand for such property." Those enslaved convicts deposited in Spanish Florida were often illegally resold to buyers in the United States along the burgeoning cotton frontier of the Old Southwest and to the sugar cane plantations of Louisiana. In many cases, slave traders casually disregarded Virginia law and unlawfully resold convicted slaves in the Deep South, a fact commonly understood by state governments. Aware of the dangers posed by slave convicts unlawfully conveyed within or smuggled back into the country, Louisiana passed a measure in 1817 to prevent their sale in the Bayou State. Mississippi followed suit in 1822. Despite such laws, convicted slave criminals, including the two dozen "Williams Negroes" carried illegally from Virginia into Louisiana in 1840, did reappear on American soil. For its part, Virginia declared that any condemned and transported slave who returned to the Old Dominion would be executed.[47]

Enslaved Virginians sentenced to or reprieved for sale and transportation out of the United States were deposited in the state penitentiary in Richmond to await their fate. The transfer from the county court to the capital provided the rare enslaved prisoner an opportunity to flee. On his way to Richmond from Pittsylvania County, where he had been convicted in early 1820 of the death of the bondman Abraham, Primus was lodged at a tavern in Scottsville, Powhatan County. There, despite being "handcuffed and chained" and "tied to a heavy bedstead," Primus effected his escape. His liberation was but fleeting, however. Penitentiary rolls document that Primus entered the institution in June.[48]

Penitentiary records show that the slaves convicted for murdering other bondpeople were generally not a youthful cohort. Oftentimes, neither master nor slave knew a bondperson's precise age, but even the approximations provided in the records are informative. Of the eighteen male prisoners for whom an estimated age is given, the average was a little more than thirty-one years. Half were in their twenties, four in their thirties, three in their forties, and one in his fifties. Only one was a teenager. Deadly violent acts committed by male slaves thus peaked during bondmen's twenties and declined thereafter.[49] The statistics trended younger for enslaved women. Half of the sample of ten bondwomen in the penitentiary were teens, all convicted of infanticide. Another three were in their twenties; two were thirty. In none of the sample cases were they older than that. (See table 3.4.)

Virginia slaves confined to the penitentiary to await sale and transportation for killing other bondpeople usually did not remain there for long. A sample of

Table 3.4. Age of Convicted Slave-Slave Murderers Awaiting Sale and Transportation in the Virginia State Penitentiary

Name	County	Date Received	Age
Men (18)			
Hubbard	Southampton	Feb. 17, 1817	25
Julius	Rockbridge	Mar. 20, 1817	55
Primus	Pittsylvania	June 8, 1820	26
Jim/James	Cumberland	June 12, 1820	26
Henry	Chesterfield	Mar. 29, 1824	26
Sam/Samuel	Greenbrier	Jan. 3, 1825	23
Nelson	Lunenburg	June 7, 1827	34
Jerry/Jere	Madison	Apr. 19, 1828	30
Tom	Madison	Apr. 19, 1828	46
Sawney	Madison	Apr. 19, 1828	45
Hubard/Herbut	King George	May 29, 1830	33
Solomon Stevens	Northampton	July 19, 1832	18
Israel Jones	Buckingham	Oct. 24, 1833	25
Harry Burns	Kanawha	Mar. 13, 1834	27
Martin Price	Henrico	Mar. 16, 1837	30
Tom/Thomas	Buckingham	June 12, 1839	23
Joe Wills/Willis	Nelson	Dec. 20, 1840	29
Cupe	Russell	Jan. 21, 1841	45
Women (10)			
Polly	Buckingham	Not given	18
Liza	Surry	Dec. 16, 1819	17
Letty/Letitia	Wheeling (city)	Oct. 3, 1822	28
Milly/Mildred	Louisa	Oct. 11, 1824	30
Martha	Prince Edward	Oct. 31, 1827	18
Ally/Alley	Fairfax	Mar. 14, 1833	19
Clary/Clara	Greensville	Jan. 4, 1834	30
Kesiah	Richmond City	May 17, 1834	18
Viney/Lavinia	Bedford	Jan. 23, 1838	25
Malinda	Southampton	Mar. 5, 1840	20

Source: Auditor of Public Accounts, Condemned Blacks Executed or Transported, Records—Condemned Slaves, Court Orders, and Valuations, 1858–1865, Misc. Reel 2555, Frames 988–997, LVA.

Table 3.5. Duration of Convicted Slave-Slave Murderers' Stays in the Virginia State Penitentiary

Name	County or City	Date Received	Date Sold	Duration
Men (14)				
Henry	Chesterfield	Mar. 29, 1824	Mar. 25, 1825	1 year
Sam/Samuel	Greenbrier	Jan. 3, 1825	Apr. 30, 1825	4 mos.
Jerry/Jere	Madison	Apr. 19, 1828	Feb. 3, 1829	9.5 mos.
Tom	Madison	Apr. 19, 1828	Feb. 3, 1829	9.5 mos.
Sawney	Madison	Apr. 19, 1828	Feb. 3, 1829	9.5 mos.
Hubard/Herbut	King George	May 29, 1830	May 3, 1831	1 year
Solomon Stevens	Northampton	July 19, 1832	Mar. 19, 1833	8 mos.
Israel Jones	Buckingham	Oct. 24, 1833	Jan. 28, 1834	3 mos.
Harry Burns	Kanawha	Mar. 13, 1834	July 7, 1834	4 mos.
Martin Price	Henrico	Mar. 16, 1837	Aug. 30, 1837	5.5 mos.
Tom/Thomas	Buckingham	June 12, 1839	Sept. 16, 1840	15 mos.
Beverley	Spotsylvania	Mar. 14, 1854	Aug. 20, 1854	5 mos.
Edward	Richmond (city)	Nov. 23, 1854	June 30, 1855	7 mos.
Johnson Archer	Chesterfield	Apr. 19, 1855	June 30, 1855	2.5 mos.
Women (11)				
Milly/Mildred	Louisa	Oct. 11, 1824	Mar. 3, 1826	17 mos.
Martha	Prince Edward	Oct. 31, 1827	Feb. 3, 1829	16 mos.
Ally/Alley	Fairfax	Mar. 14, 1833	July 17, 1833	4 mos.
Clary/Clara	Greensville	Jan. 4, 1834	Jan. 28, 1834	3 wks.
Kesiah	Richmond City	May 17, 1834	July 7, 1834	2 mos.
Viney/Lavinia	Bedford	Jan. 23, 1838	Aug. 1, 1838	6 mos.
Malinda	Southampton	Mar. 5, 1840	Sept. 16, 1840	6 mos.
Lucy Frances	Richmond (city)	Nov. 11, 1852	Dec. 20, 1852	5 wks.
Lizzie	Halifax	Mar. 16, 1854	Aug. 20, 1854	5 mos.
Lucy	Richmond (city)	June 15, 1855	June 30, 1855	2 wks.
Louisa	Fauquier	July 10, 1855	Sept. 11, 1855	2 mos.

Source: Auditor of Public Accounts, Condemned Blacks Executed or Transported, Records—Condemned Slaves, Court Orders, and Valuations, 1858–1865, Misc. Reel 2555, Frames 988–997, 1035, 1037, 1038, LVA.

twenty-five cases in which we know the dates when individual slaves entered and were sold out of the penitentiary (see table 3.5) shows that they typically spent about six months imprisoned. The fourteen male slaves spent an average of seven and one-half months incarcerated, two months longer than the average for the eleven female slaves for whom we have data. Bondmen languished in the penitentiary from two and one-half months to as long as a year. The range for bondwomen was wider. Some—especially fecund young women found guilty of infanticide—might be sold within two or three weeks. At the opposite extreme, two female slaves spent close to a year and a half in confinement. Compared to slaves, free blacks spent longer stretches of time in the penitentiary for various assaults upon other blacks, free or enslaved. "Matilda Finney, a free negro," for example, charged by the Richmond Hustings Court with an 1854 attempt to "feloniously, unlawfully and maliciously stab, cut, and wound Elizabeth Southard, a negro, with intent . . . to maim, disfigure, disable and kill," was sentenced to "be imprisoned in the public jail and penitentiary house of this Commonwealth for the space of two years." The identical judgment befell "Lavinia Martin, a free negro," for assaulting "Lewis Scott, a free negro."[50]

Slave traders interested in purchasing convicted slaves housed in the Virginia penitentiary for transport and resale elsewhere submitted bids to the governor of the Commonwealth. Trader John T. Lewis wrote Governor Henry A. Wise in May 1856, in care of auctioneer N. B. Hill of Richmond. Lewis enclosed a list of slaves then occupying the penitentiary, along "with [the] prices I am prepared to pay for them, should it be your pleasure to sell them at this time." Among the slaves on the list was "1 woman Opha Jane age 20," who had been found guilty in Powhatan County of infanticide. Although she had been sentenced to hang, the governor had reprieved her sentence to sale and transportation. Lewis was willing to pay $500 for her, an amount Governor Wise deemed insufficient. Lewis's offer was "not accepted." Several other slaves, however, including—as table 3.6 shows—those imprisoned for perpetrating violent acts upon one another, were sold to slave traders in accordance with this procedure.[51]

The goal of the governor was to sell convicted slaves at the highest possible price to help defray the costs of compensation to the master. The Virginia law of 1801 that routinized the sale and transportation of condemned slaves also granted owners of transported slaves the same sort of compensation allotted masters of slaves lawfully executed. Ideally, proceeds from the sale of a slave out of the penitentiary would offset the state's outlays in reimbursing the owner. As one contemporary Virginian understood, "a slave can be sold to advantage, and . . . a sale can be made to save the Treasury from expense." Occasionally, all went according to plan, and traders paid the state exactly what the Courts of Oyer and Terminer determined the slaves to be worth. In 1844, for example, A. R. Givens

Table 3.6. Selected Slaves Sold and Transported Out of the Virginia State Penitentiary for Killing Other Slaves

Date of Sale	Slave	County or City	Purchaser
Jan. 1834	Israel	Buckingham	Robert Currin
Jan. 1834	Clary	Greensville	Robert Currin
July 1834	Harry	Kanawha	George W. Harris
July 1834	Kesiah	Henrico	George W. Harris
Aug. 1837	Martin	Henrico	Robert Lumpkin
Aug. 1838	Viney	Bedford	N. Matthews
Sept. 1840	Tom/Thomas	Buckingham	R. Littlejohn
Sept. 1840	Malinda	Southampton	R. Littlejohn
Sept. 1842	Joe Wills	Nelson	J. D. James
Sept. 1842	Cupe	Russell	J. D. James
1844	Emanuel	Richmond (city)	A. R. Givens
June 1845	Gustavus	Lynchburg (city)	Grimm
June 1846	Washington	Albemarle	J. W. Coleman
Apr. 1848	Bob	Mecklenburg	J. W. Coleman
June 1852	Green	Washington	G. P. Ware
1852–1853	Fanny	Albemarle	Z. T. Ross
1852–1853	Lucy	Richmond	Z. T. Ross
1853–1854	Lizzy	Halifax	R. Davis
1853–1854	Beverley	Spotsylvania	R. Davis

Source: Auditor of Public Accounts, Condemned Blacks Executed or Transported, Records—Condemned Slaves, Court Orders, and Valuations, 1858–1865, Misc. Reel 2555, Frames 1003, 1009, 1011, 1013, 1017, 1019, 1021, 1026, 1028, 1041, 1065, 1067, 1071, LVA.

purchased Emanuel, a Richmond slave sentenced to hang for the death of Isaac but reprieved for sale and transportation, as well as nine other slaves confined in the penitentiary, for a total of $4,150, precisely the cumulative sum of disbursements paid to their masters. In a sample of nine transactions between slave traders and the government shown in table 3.7, however, the deal with Givens was the only one in which the state broke even.[52]

Usually the state coffers incurred a deficit. When one trader purchased a lot of ten slaves in 1838 that included the bondwoman Viney of Bedford County, convicted of killing another female slave, he paid $5,800. The state had compensated masters of these slaves $6,080 and therefore suffered only a modest loss of $280. In many other cases the state fared significantly worse. Trader J. D. James

Table 3.7. Sample Transactions between the Commonwealth of Virginia and Slave Traders for Slaves Sold and Transported Out of the State Penitentiary

Slave Trader	Year	No. Slaves Purchased	Compensation Cost to State	Sale Price	Loss to State	% Loss
Robert Currin	1834	9	$4,925	$3,200	$1,725	35
George W. Harris	1834	12	$6,190	$5,000	$1,190	19
Robert Lumpkin	1837	17	$15,340	$7,750	$7,590	49
N. Matthews	1838	10	$6,080	$5,800	$280	5
R. Littlejohn	1840	27	$20,485	$12,500	$7,985	39
J. D. James	1842	30	$15,890.33	$7,100	$8,790.33	55
A. R. Givens	1844	10	$4,150	$4,150	$0	0
Grimm	1845	12	$6,317.08	$5,600	$717.08	11
J. W. Coleman	1846	15	$6,688.33	$4,825	$1,863.33	28
Totals		142	$86,065.74	$55,925	$30,140.74	35

Source: Auditor of Public Accounts, Condemned Blacks Executed or Transported, Records—Condemned Slaves, Court Orders, and Valuations, 1858–1865, Misc. Reel 2555, Frames 1003, 1005, 1011, 1017, 1019, 1021, 1026, 1028, LVA.

acquired a parcel of thirty convicted slaves in September 1842, paying $7,100. Unfortunately for the state, the masters of those slaves had been reimbursed almost $16,000. With apparently no better offer, Virginia absorbed a nearly $9,000 shortfall, equivalent to 55 percent of the collective value assessed by the courts. When trader Robert Lumpkin purchased seventeen slaves out of the penitentiary in 1837 for $7,750, he, too, struck a substantial bargain. A Henrico County court had valued just one of the slaves in his lot, the bondman Martin, convicted of killing Lewis, at $2,000. The notable disparity between slaves' valuations by the Courts of Oyer and Terminer and the actual sale prices paid by slave traders prompted the Virginia legislature to pass the law of 1840 that required justices to appraise enslaved convicts under the premise that buyers possessed knowledge of a slave's guilt. But legislation did not resolve the state's dilemma. The economic cost to the Commonwealth convinced some Virginia whites that "it would be better to pass a law making the loss fall upon the master who is so unfortunate as to own a felon."[53]

Presumably, amid the rampant dishonesty and deception in the world of the slave marketplace, traders stood to reap immense profits through the resale of slaves salvaged from the penitentiary. All traders wanted to buy low and sell high.

Only the most scrupulous and morally upright would have disclosed convicted slaves' criminal pasts to unwitting potential buyers, and the sordid business of trafficking in human flesh did not much lend itself to those of such saintly character. Trader schemes to willfully conceal bondpeople's tangles with the law were complicated, however, by the need for slaves' complicity. Bondpeople might well leverage a sale by withholding knowledge of their personal history from a potential buyer or squelch a deal by divulging it, contrary to traders' instructions.[54]

Although traders' bids for slaves in confinement rarely equaled Virginia's outlays for compensation, the state was nevertheless able to recoup a portion of its expenses. Looked at positively, *any* money that accumulated to the state for a bondperson sold and transported was money that the state would not have received had the convicted slave been put to death. Historian James A. Campbell observed that each gubernatorial commutation of the twenty-six death sentences handed down by the Richmond Hustings Court from 1830 to 1860 saved state coffers more than $600. The public treasury needed all the infusions of cash it could get. Irrespective of specific crimes for which slaves were convicted, Philip J. Schwarz found that, by 1820, Virginia had already distributed more than $150,000 in compensation to masters of slaves sold and transported. By 1850, that tally stood closer to $476,000. And neither of these figures included reimbursements for slaves who had been put to death. For slaves found guilty of killing other slaves and for whom disbursement data are available, Virginia compensated masters roughly $79,000 between 1777 and 1864, as illustrated in table 3.8. The nearly $60,000 reimbursed for convicted bondmen was almost triple that awarded for condemned bondwomen, but the sample includes three times as many enslaved male than female convicts. Over the course of almost nine decades, the average per capita cost of compensation differed little between male and female slaves, although the value of the average bondman per decade exceeded that of the average bondwoman in every decade before the Civil War. More than half of the $79,000 in compensation money for slaves found guilty of killing other bondpeople went to masters whose slaves who were sold and transported. Only about half as much was distributed for slaves put to death. The remainder was awarded to masters for slaves transferred to the public works.[55]

With the support of Governor Henry A. Wise, the Virginia legislature in 1858 instituted the practice of sentencing slaves to labor on the public works as an alternative to sale and transportation. The "employment of negro convicts on the public works" was not terribly popular among Virginia citizens, who felt uncomfortable with convict laborers in their midst. By 1858, the punishment be-

Table 3.8. Virginia Courts of Oyer and Terminer Valuations of Slaves Convicted of Killing Other Slaves, 1777–1864

Years	No. Male Slaves/Dollar Value*	Avg. Dollar Value, Males*	No. Female Slaves/Dollar Value*	Avg. Dollar Value, Females*	Total No. Slaves/Dollar Value*	Avg. Dollar Value, All*
1777–1799**	16/$4,493	$281	2/$433	$216	18/$4,926	$274
1800–1809**	5/$1,826	$365	0/$0	n/a	5/$1,826	$365
1810–1819	11/$5,750	$523	5/$2,300	$460	16/$8,050	$503
1820–1829	20/$8,605	$430	4/$1,250	$313	24/$9,855	$411
1830–1839	10/$5,975	$598	6/$1,895	$316	16/$7,870	$492
1840–1849	14/$7,548	$539	1/$450	$450	15/$7,998	$533
1850–1859	22/$16,310	$741	13/$9,265	$713	35/$25,575	$731
1860–1864	7/$7,826	$1,118	4/$5,020	$1,255	11/$12,846	$1,168
Total	105/$58,334	$556	35/$20,612	$589	140/$78,947	$564

* Figures rounded to the nearest whole dollar.
** Some figures converted from British pounds to U.S. dollars using a conversion factor of 3.33.

came increasingly attractive to government officials, however, as the number of locations outside the United States lawfully eligible and willing to receive transported slave convicts had dwindled over the decades. All other political entities in the Western Hemisphere except Puerto Rico, Cuba, and Brazil had outlawed the institution of slavery before the United States completed the work of emancipation in 1865. The perpetuation of the American South's increasingly anomalous labor system complicated enforcement of Virginia's laws regarding the sale and transportation of slave convicts. As a result, Virginia governors from 1858 to 1864 commuted the punishments of at least thirteen slaves convicted of the deaths of other bondpeople "to labor on the public works for life." Nine bondmen and four bondwomen received such a reprieve. After Jeff Brooker, enslaved in Stafford County, murdered his brother in the early 1860s, he was sentenced "to banishment beyond the confines of the United States," but the governor intervened and directed him to the public works instead. Virginia laborers on the public works included slaves and free blacks, men and women. Contractors Robert F. and David G. Bibb of the Covington and Ohio Railroad used convict labor by October 1859 at the latest and by June 1860 employed eighty-two slave and free black prisoners. Rather than foisting enslaved felons upon foreign lands or unsuspecting masters in the Deep South, convicted slaves "would be made useful, and yet kept from mischief and crime."[56]

Virginia was not alone in dispatching convicted slaves to the public works. Louisiana conducted a similar experiment in the early 1840s. In 1843, for example, enslaved and free black prisoners toiled under the state engineer's supervision to build "the road from Baton Rouge to Clinton," in East Feliciana Parish.[57] Louisiana officials pondered putting convicts of color to work at internal improvements other than road-building, such as draining swamps or clearing bayous, but no legislative enactment can confirm that they performed these dangerous and unhealthy labors. Likewise, there is no evidence to suggest that they worked on levee construction along the Mississippi River and its tributaries, as so many postbellum black convicts did.[58] The expense of employing enslaved convicts on infrastructure projects as well as popular resistance to it combined to convince the state legislature to terminate the practice in 1845. Calls in the 1850s to revisit the idea of employing them on the public works fell on deaf ears. From 1845 to the Civil War, convicted slaves instead labored within the confines of the Louisiana State Penitentiary.[59]

No other state incarcerated slaves convicted of crimes to the extent Louisiana did. The bondwoman Sanite, for example, was sentenced in 1855 to six months in the parish prison (and twenty-five lashes) for throwing boiling water in the face of "Auguste a negro Boy aged about fourteen years." Although she scalded her victim and "probably... maimed" him, she did not cause his death. Auguste's injuries did not warrant more severe punishment than whipping and half a year in confinement. Across the South, however, courts of law rarely condemned African Americans in bondage to time in prison. At most, slaves might be detained briefly in local public jails or workhouses, either to await trial or execution, as punishment for minor crimes, or until sale at auction. Slaves sometimes occupied jails only as long as required to administer the number of lashes mandated by the court that convicted them, with the period of confinement proportional to the quantity of stripes to be administered. In South Carolina, for example, slaves sentenced to fifty or sixty lashes for assaulting another bondperson remained in jail for two weeks, those given one hundred lashes sat in their cells for a month, and those slated to receive three hundred stripes were confined for two months. Henry, enslaved in Clarendon District, defied the overall pattern by receiving 150 licks during a brief, 2-week stint in jail. In almost all cases across the South, prison was a site of fleeting, temporary detention, and slaveholders preferred it that way. Slaves sitting in jail were not working. Moreover, jails had gained a well-deserved reputation as crowded, dangerous, disease-prone places where valuable bondpeople might contract frostbite or a deadly illness. One desperate Charleston District, South Carolina, master implored Governor Whitemarsh B. Seabrook to "pardon... his slave Peter Blacklock, who accidentally struck and killed another slave with a board." Peter had been found guilty of manslaughter and, atypically, was "sentenced to two years in jail," where, his master believed, he "will most likely die." Surely aware of the conditions in public jails, the governor complied with the request and had the bondman transported out of state instead. Local incarceration facilities in early America were also notoriously insecure. In August 1777, the bondman Sambo was committed to jail in Goochland County, Virginia, "on suspicion of preparing poisonous medicine" and administering it "to a Negroe Man Slave," but as the date of his scheduled trial loomed, Sambo made his escape.[60]

If few slaves spent even a brief stint in a local jail for any wrongdoing, they almost never languished in an antebellum southern penitentiary. By the outbreak of the Civil War, in keeping with a reformist impulse that began in the North, all southern states except the two Carolinas and Florida had erected a penitentiary for the incarceration of criminals, beginning with Kentucky in 1794. But as one Mississippi bondman explained, "you niver heard tell uf a slave bein' sent ter de pen" during slavery. In many ways, it made little sense to imprison slaves in the penitentiary. Slavery itself already represented an institution of social control that denied people rights and freedom. Depositing bondpeople in prison was therefore redundant. Many southern whites hardly considered incarceration an appropriate punishment anyway, as it provided slaves a reprieve from the fields and plantation labor. One committee of Louisiana lawmakers opined that "confinement is to [slaves] no adequate punishment, but in many cases is actually preferred to their former condition." More important still, for masters, slaves represented an investment in human property. A bondperson serving time in the state prison was neither productive nor profitable for the owner.[61]

Despite the illogic of incarcerating slaves and the reservations some southern whites expressed, a small number of slaves were nevertheless confined in state penitentiaries. For a brief period, Maryland and Arkansas both accepted slave prisoners.[62] Maryland sentenced slaves to the penitentiary from its opening in 1812 until 1819, receiving some sixty slaves during those years. A revised state law thereafter required the transportation out of state of any slave convicted of a serious crime and not sentenced to hang.[63] Arkansas authorized the incarceration in the state penitentiary of slaves convicted of manslaughter for as long as seven years, but few slaves actually served time before the legislature eliminated the penalty in 1858.[64] Virginia did not sentence slaves to imprisonment in the penitentiary, but the state prison did house on a temporary basis both male and female slave convicts awaiting sale and transportation out of the United States. After 1818, only Louisiana regularly incarcerated slaves as an alternative to execution. And whereas Virginia slaves usually lingered in the penitentiary for only weeks or months until a trader arrived to convey them away, enslaved prisoners in Louisiana measured their terms of imprisonment in years, decades, and lifetimes.[65]

Louisiana courts sentenced roughly two hundred slaves to hard labor in the state penitentiary in Baton Rouge between its opening in 1835 and its seizure by Union troops in 1862. No fewer than forty-seven of them, or approximately one-quarter of all enslaved inmates whose crime is known, were imprisoned for murder. At least nine (and perhaps several more) had been found guilty of killing other slaves, all between 1848 and 1859, as seen in table 3.9. Eight of the nine slaves were men, including all four convicted of murder rather than manslaughter. The standard sentence for the murder of another slave was life imprisonment at hard labor for the state. Accordingly, the bondman Fleming was committed to the penitentiary upon his conviction for fatally knifing Casimire Lacoste's slave Jose. The four bondmen convicted of manslaughter were sentenced to

Table 3.9. Enslaved Prisoners in the Louisiana State Penitentiary Convicted of Killing Other Slaves, 1835–1862

Date Admitted	Name	Crime	Term of Sentence	Parish of Sentence	Birthplace
Mar. 1848	Fleming	Murder	Life	New Orleans	Virginia
May 1848	Lewis	Murder	Life	Jefferson	Virginia
Dec. 1848	Cuffy	Manslaughter	10 years	New Orleans	Virginia
Dec. 1854	Stephen	Manslaughter	3 years	n/a	n/a
Feb. 1855	Hannah	Manslaughter	Life	Lafourche	North Carolina
July 1855	Tom Evans	Manslaughter	15 years	New Orleans	Virginia
Jan. 1857	George	Murder	Life	New Orleans	Louisiana
Mar. 1858	Henry Hoops	Murder	Life	Madison	Virginia
June 1859	Jack	Manslaughter	5 years	New Orleans	South Carolina

Sources: State v. Fleming, slave of Casimire Lacoste (1848), First District Court of New Orleans, 1945, NOPL; *Arnoult v. Deschapelles* (1849), 4 La. An. 41, in *Judicial Cases Concerning American Slavery and the Negro*, vol. 3, ed. Helen Tunnicliff Catterall (Washington, D.C.: Carnegie Institution of Washington, 1932), 594–595; *State v. Cuffy, property of the New Orleans and Carrollton Railroad* (1848), First District Court of New Orleans, 3016, NOPL; *Annual Report of the Board of Directors of the Louisiana Penitentiary, to the Governor of the State of Louisiana. January, 1856* (New Orleans: John Claiborne, 1856), 20; *State v. Hannah (a slave)* (1855), 10 La. An. 131, in *Judicial Cases Concerning American Slavery and the Negro*, vol. 3, ed. Helen Tunnicliff Catterall (Washington, D.C.: Carnegie Institution of Washington, 1932), 634; *State v. Tom Evans (slave)* (1855), First District Court of New Orleans, 10487, NOPL; *State v. George, slave of James Hopkins, Jr.* (1856), First District Court of New Orleans, 12584, NOPL; *Report of the Board of Control of the Louisiana Penitentiary* (Baton Rouge: J. M. Taylor, 1859); *State v. Jack (slave)* (1858), First District Court of New Orleans, 13653, NOPL.

varying terms of three, five, ten, or fifteen years. Cuffy, the property of the New Orleans and Carrollton Railroad, received a ten-year sentence to "hard Labour in the Penitentiary" for stabbing Miles, another enslaved railroad worker, in the abdomen. The "slave boy" Tom Evans got the lengthiest of the terms for manslaughter after using "a large Butcher knife" to stick the sixty-year-old St. Louis, Missouri, bondman Edmond, off Terpsichore Street in New Orleans. The First District Court of New Orleans ordered the bondman Jack punished by a comparatively light "five years imprisonment at hard labor in the State Penitentiary" but additionally specified that he "receive ten lashes every sixty days" throughout his confinement. Hannah, the lone bondwoman in my sample, earned the longest sentence—life—for a manslaughter conviction. A majority of all slaves found responsible for the deaths of other bondpeople were not Louisiana natives but had been carried via the domestic slave trade from Virginia. One of the native Virginians, Cuffy, served out his ten years in the penitentiary and was discharged in December 1858. Another enslaved prisoner, Stephen, died only two months into his period of confinement. All other slaves in the table vanished from the record after Union soldiers invaded Baton Rouge and commandeered the penitentiary.[66]

Through its peculiar administration of justice for slaves found guilty of crimes, the state of Louisiana appropriated for itself the role of the enslaved convict's new master. Whenever bondpeople were sentenced to life imprisonment, owners surrendered the title of convicted slaves to the state, which put them to work. The vast majority of enslaved inmates in the Louisiana State Penitentiary labored in either the prison brickyard or cotton factory, the latter of which engaged "chiefly in the manufacture of coarse cotton and woolen cloths, of negro shoes, and of cotton bagging and rope from hemp." In no other slaveholding state did the penitentiary become a more or less permanent repository for enslaved criminals.[67]

Masters who contested the convictions or punishments of their bondpeople for killing other slaves had different options at their disposal. Over the course of the antebellum decades, the ability of slaveholders to file an appeal to a higher court on behalf of a condemned slave expanded. Appeals processes were first introduced in Georgia in 1829, in South Carolina in 1833, and in Virginia in 1848. Not all states that recognized the master's right to appeal, including Maryland, South Carolina, and Virginia, allowed slaveholders to take a case to the state Supreme Court. Studying slaves' cases that did appear before state Supreme Courts, legal scholar A. E. Kier Nash emphasized the procedural fairness of their trials. One piece of evidence in his favor is that slaves convicted of murdering other bondpeople might have convictions overturned on the basis of legal technicalities. Sloppily written indictments were sometimes the basis for an appeal. In Texas, Calvin was sentenced to hang for the 1858 killing of Vina, but his case made it all the way to the state Supreme Court on the grounds that the indictment listed different masters for Vina, gave conflicting causes of death, and neglected to use the legally meaningful word "feloniously." Enough was amiss that the Court set aside the verdict and returned the case to the Rusk County grand jury. The Hinds County, Mississippi, case of John, the property of a North Carolina slaveholder named Baxter and the alleged killer of a "very stout" slave named Austin, made its way to the Mississippi Supreme Court in 1852 because the indictment misidentified John's owner as John D. Cook. Mississippi judges did not find the error sufficiently problematic to reverse judgment. Citing an 1850 statute stating that it was unnecessary to "name ... the owner of any slave guilty of any crime punishable ... with death," the Court held that the specific owner was irrelevant to the crime. In 1851, the Supreme Court of Georgia reversed a judgment from Bibb County against the bondman Allen for the murder of Sam. Names on the bill of indictment had been flip-flopped, but more important, inadmissible evidence had been used to secure Allen's conviction. The Supreme Court of Tennessee in 1858 granted the slave John, convicted in the homicide of his wife in Grainger County, a new trial. According to the justices, the lower court had improperly refused a continuance to the next term that John's counsel had sought "on the ground of the great excitement in the public mind to his prejudice."[68]

Several appeals in intraracial slave homicide cases stemmed from concerns about individual jurors or the jury collectively. Counsel for the slave Jack, tried in Texas "for the murder of his wife, a negro woman named Nicey," contended that the judgment against the slave was invalid because the Guadalupe County jury convicted him despite one juror's comment that "he did not think the negro ought to be hanged or punished with death," an opinion incompatible with a guilty verdict. Another juror in the same case had been drinking. Nevertheless, the state Supreme Court affirmed the judgment against Jack. In Hancock County, Georgia, lawyers for the bondman Warren moved for a new trial in part because the inferior court that sentenced him to death for murdering George in 1849 included "an impartial Juror": "Redding Blount—who served on the trial, was determined to hang him before the trial was gone into." At his retrial, Warren was found guilty of manslaughter only and ordered branded and whipped. On other occasions, slaves' lawyers challenged jurors' competency. At the trial of the Georgia bondman Henry, juror James Hamlin was unable to answer whether "his mind was perfectly impartial between the State and the accused" because he did not know the definition of "impartial" and therefore did not understand the question. Another of the jurors in the case had admitted a "bias or prejudice" toward Henry. In 1843, the Supreme Court of Tennessee ruled that the jury in the case of Jim did an incompetent job. "Instead of weighing the credibility of ... witnesses by the legitimate mode of general weight of character and probability of their statements," criticized the Court, the jury evaluated the veracity of testimony by conducting experiments to see if they could overhear a conversation through a wall, as a witness claimed: "This mode of arriving at the truth of testimony cannot be permitted ... [W]e cannot permit verdicts which have been obtained like this, upon uncertain and dangerous experiments, instead of a calm, deliberate and philosophical examination of the proof, to stand where the lives of individuals are at stake."[69]

Among the more vexing questions raised as a result of intraracial slave homicide trials was the admissibility of slaves' confessions to their masters, jailers, or other white authorities. Few slaves acknowledged their guilt in murdering a fellow bondperson. Those who made such admissions, however, made the prosecution of their cases no more clear-cut. Slave tribunals and juries needed to weigh carefully the circumstances under which the confession was made. Was it motivated by fear of the consequences should a slave not admit his guilt, or by the anticipation of the master's protection? Was it coerced or voluntary? Was it even theoretically possible for a slave to make a confession to a white person voluntarily? Georgia attorney Thomas R. R. Cobb observed in 1858 that slave confessions "should be received with great caution, and allowed but little weight." Bondpeople, he insisted, were pathological liars, suffering from a "mendacious disposition." The veracity of their reports was therefore unworthy of belief. Because "the slave is always ready to mould his answers so as to please the master," Cobb explained, "no confidence can be placed in the truth of his statements." In addition, slaves' "habit of obedience" compelled slaves "to answer all questions" without thinking of the consequences of their words to themselves. In particular, slaves were trained "to obey every command and wish" of the master and lacked the "will to refuse obedience," even when slaves' own lives were at stake. Bondpeople freely divulged incriminating information to their master because the slave owner was trusted as "protector," "counsel," and "confidant." Slaves sometimes confided in good faith to their masters and made them privy to the details of a crime.[70]

The North Carolina Supreme Court ruled in the 1830 infanticide case of the enslaved woman Charity that, just as the state's masters could not testify on behalf of their slaves, neither could they be compelled to give evidence against them. Charity's case originated in Orange County, where the bondwoman was indicted for murdering her own child. At her trial, prosecutors placed her master on the stand to divulge the confession that Charity had made to him. On the strength of his testimony, the Orange County Superior Court found Charity guilty and sentenced her to hang. Charity's master filed an appeal to the state Supreme Court because he had been forced to testify over his objections and against his will. The Court accepted his argument. As Justice Thomas Ruffin explained, "a party to a suit, or one directly interested in the result, is not competent to testify" either for or against "his interest." The North Carolina Supreme Court granted Charity a new trial, and in 1831 she was found not guilty of the crime.[71]

To be lawful and credible, slaves' confessions needed to be voluntary. As it handed down its verdict in the case of Simon, a Copiah County bondman charged with the murder of Norvall, the Supreme Court of Mississippi declared in 1858, "A confession is not admissible unless it is made freely and voluntarily without any restraint, and without any hope of reward, or fear of punishment." Simon had fled after Norvall's death and "was pursued with dogs, as a runaway," for miles. At the time, he was not a suspect in the murder, but when captured, he was "bitten by the dogs," given a blow to the head "with the butt of a negro whip," and interrogated about Norvall's demise. When reminded "that it would be better for you to tell the whole truth about the matter," Simon—to the surprise of his captors—confessed to the homicide. These circumstances did not meet the Court's standard of a "free and voluntary" confession, so it was ruled inadmissible. Simon, however, had difficulty keeping his mouth shut. While Simon was confined awaiting trial, jailers Moses H. Curtis and W. H. Bondurant each overheard the slave tell his visitors, on several different occasions, that he had killed Norvall. In 1859, Simon again appeared before the Mississippi Supreme Court, which ruled that these jailhouse "confessions were perfectly voluntary." Simon's conviction was upheld.[72]

One Virginia bondman's statement met the standard for a voluntary confession. When Botetourt County slaveholder Barclay Kyle approached his slave Ralph in 1814 and implored him to tell the truth surrounding the death of a bondwoman, Ralph "shed tears" and asked his master, "if he told him the truth would he . . . whip him?" Kyle assured him that he would not. When Ralph confessed to the crime, an angry Kyle seized his bondman and exclaimed, "you Rascal you have murdered the woman & must be hung for it." The master's testimony—permitted in slave trials in the Commonwealth of Virginia—helped secure Ralph's conviction, and the slave was executed just as his owner had predicted.[73]

An Alabama Supreme Court decision of 1852 stretched the definition of what qualified as voluntary. The bondmen Seaborn and Jim, suspected in the murder of a third slave, were under duress during an examination by a magistrate and "several gentlemen" of Macon County. In the presence of their masters, "a gun and a stick" visible to them, the two slaves, "each chained with a padlock around his neck," were told, "it was a bad business, or a bad situation, they were in." Seaborn concurred, "Yes, it was; but that it was too late," and "shook his head" in despair. Interrogated separately, Seaborn confessed his guilt, and Jim corroborated his story. Despite the efforts of the slaves' legal counsel to exclude the confessions, the Court allowed them, affirming the guilty verdict of the Macon County Circuit Court. As the Supreme Court indicated, "A slave's voluntary confessions of guilt are admissible evidence against him." Although it conceded that the magistrate present during questioning ought to have cautioned the slaves about the import of their words, the Court maintained that his failure to do so could not justify the exclusion of the confessions: "The facts that he is a slave, and ignorant, and to some extent unacquainted with the consequences which may attend the making of such confessions, do not affect the admissibility of the evidence."[74]

Partial confessions were another matter. During the waning months of the Civil War, the Supreme Court of Alabama ruled on the case of William, found guilty of killing the bondwoman Clarissa in the autumn of 1863. William awakened his master, J. L. Bozeman, early one morning with the intention of confessing his crime. Bozeman "got up, dressed himself hastily, caught up a loaded whip, with which he usually whipped his slaves, went out into the yard where [William] was, and, in an angry and excited manner said to him, 'What in the hell do you want with me?'" William replied, "Master, I have killed Clarissa." "What!" cried the master in disbelief, "where did you kill her?" "At the gin-house," William answered. "How did you kill her?" Bozeman inquired. "I cut her throat," admitted the bondman. Bozeman then interrupted William's confession to locate Clarissa's body. William's lawyer argued that the confession was inadmissible because it was "made through the hope of reward, or fear of punishment," and was "only partial." William was not granted the opportunity to make "a full and fair statement of the facts in relation to the killing." Whereas the lower court nevertheless allowed the confession as evidence, the state Supreme Court reversed the judgment. "Partial confessions [are] not admissible," declared the highest court in Alabama. "A slave's confession to his master, though voluntary, is not admissible evidence against him, when it is shown that his master interrupted him, and would not let him finish his statement." Because William "was prevented from finishing his statement, or making his confession full, by the command of some one having lawful authority over him," the Court asked, "how can it be known that he was not about to add, if he had been permitted," "some explanation or exculpation of his conduct," such as self-defense? The slave must not be denied the opportunity to provide a full and complete statement; if interrupted, the enslaved suspect must be presumed innocent. The Supreme Court of Louisiana had reached the same conclusion in 1848. West Feliciana Parish bondman Isaac confessed to his master that "he had killed the slave Jim." When the slave "commenced justifying the act," however, his owner cut him off and informed him that he would be taken in to the authorities. The Louisiana Supreme Court overturned the guilty verdict against Isaac. "The confession appears to have been voluntary," acknowledged the Court, "but should have been excluded on the ground that it was interrupted and never completed. When confessions of guilt are given in evidence, the whole must be taken together."[75]

The professions of guilt easiest to dismiss were those extracted through threats or violence. In DeSoto County, Mississippi, the fugitive slave Jordan killed the bondman Aaron, who was attempting to arrest the runaway. Once Jordan was captured, two white men labored to extract a confession from him. When Jordan refused to talk, his interrogators—one wielding a cocked pistol, the other a stick—threatened to kill him. Only when one of the white men struck Jordan with the stick did Jordan confess. The verdict of the Mississippi Supreme Court held that Jordan's admission of guilt was "extorted by violence" and therefore involuntary. The accused had the right "not only ... to preserve his entire silence in regard to the killing, but to resist force by force, to compel him to act otherwise." The judgment against Jordan was thus reversed on the inadmissibility of the confession.[76]

Whenever masters believed the southern criminal court system failed them, they might exercise their right to petition the state legislature or governor. A range of grievances inspired masters of convicted bondpeople to take up the pen. Fair and just compensation for deceased slaves was one of slaveholders' greatest concerns. Cumberland County, Virginia, master William Anderson challenged the £95 valuation of his slave John, put to death in 1777 for the murder of Buckner, another of Anderson's bondmen. As Anderson explained to the general assembly, John was an exceptional, "valuable young fellow brought up to the Business of shoemaking & coopering," and £95 was "a Sum which y[ou]r petitioner think insufficient to purchase another [slave] of equal value." He urged the legislature to "make such farther allowance as will be adequate to the loss he has sustained." Lawmakers, hypersensitive to the fledgling state's budget woes during the American Revolution, rejected Anderson's plea.[77]

Masters who owned both the assailant and the victim felt the economic loss of slave violence twofold and therefore took acute interest in their reimbursement. William Royall petitioned the South Carolina House of Representatives in 1804 because he "owned a valuable Negro fellow [Jack] about 30 Years of Age who was lately prosecuted convicted & executed for the Murder of a Negro woman [Beck] also belonging to Your Petitioner." For a man of Royall's "pecuniary Circumstances," "the loss of two such Prime Hands is Particularly hard and unfortunate." In Royall's estimation, the magistrates' and freeholders' $200 appraisal low-balled the value of his bondman. The anxious owner implored the South Carolina House "not to make any deduction from the inconsiderable sum of two Hundred Dollars but Grant him the full amount thereof." In South Carolina, compensation could be lawfully divvied up between the master of the convicted slave and the white person injured by the slave's misconduct. Masters who owned both enslaved perpetrator and enslaved victim feared that the state might be tempted to slight slaveholders' financial interests and so sought assurances that they would be granted the assessed amount in full. From at least 1822 (the year of the alleged Denmark Vesey conspiracy), until increased by law in 1843 to $200, the standard compensation for a slave lawfully put to death in South Carolina was a paltry $122.44 or $122.45, hardly a sufficient sum to purchase a substitute bondperson. Magistrates and freeholders appraised Abbeville District bondman Umphrey at $122.45 when he was convicted and hanged in 1842 for the murder of Sampson. Preemptively, Samuel Jordan, master of both slaves, sent a petition to the South Carolina legislature requesting "that he may be paid the Sum allowed by law in such cases." Members of the court "agree[d] that the said Samuel Jordan is Entitled to the whole amount as both Umphrey and Sampson was his slaves."[78]

Some masters' petitions suggested that they were less concerned with the amount of compensation than the timely receipt of it. Slaveholders sometimes experienced what seemed like excruciating delays in the distribution of reimbursements. Dr. Samuel Fairchild of Charleston District, South Carolina, was owed £65 for his slave Solomon, executed for the murder of Dorcas, Solomon's wife and Fairchild's bondwoman. Believing his disbursement tardy, Fairchild petitioned the South Carolina legislature, observing that he had "not received any part of the said appraisement" from the Charleston District treasurer. The situation was similar but more complicated for Virginian William Baker, administrator for the estate of the deceased Benjamin Warden. Warden's "Negro Girl named Mary"—Mary Jane Willis—was sold and transported upon an infanticide conviction in 1856. As administrator, Baker was responsible for collecting the compensation awarded, but attempts to contact Virginia's auditor of public accounts in Richmond, who coordinated disbursements, proved fruitless. Unsure "how to proceed," Baker wrote Governor Henry A. Wise for instructions "to obtain the Money" for the Warden estate. "I would prefer a check on the Farmers Bank or the Valley Bank in Winchester," Baker added in a postscript, "if such arrangement can be [made]."[79]

Legal hassles complicated the process of reimbursement for Hubbard, a

Southampton County, Virginia, bondman convicted in 1817 of killing another slave. Hubbard was scheduled to "be hanged by the neck" on February 21 "till he is dead dead dead," but the governor reprieved him for sale and transportation. Like Mary Jane Willis's, Hubbard's master had died. Hubbard belonged to the estate of James Blow, who, in a will executed in 1814, had bequeathed the now convicted killer as well as two other slaves, land, a feather bed, other assorted furniture, and almost all of his worldly possessions to "Fanny alias Fanny Blow" and any descendants born unto her. Fanny was "a mulatto girl born the property of Major Thomas Vaughan," but Vaughan had emancipated her from slavery. The precise nature of her relationship to the deceased James Blow is unclear, although it is tempting to speculate that she was Blow's mixed-race daughter. As his primary heir, Fanny surely meant a great deal to Blow. The youthful, formerly enslaved girl stood to receive the $780 in compensation for Hubbard, but, explained John Thomas, sole executor of James Blow's estate, she "is not of lawfull age and has no guardian." Legally, Thomas was "the only person authorized to receive the amount of the valuation." Given her dilemma, "Fanny Blow a free girl of Colour" named Thomas her guardian in March 1817 to expedite the receipt of the money due her.[80]

If the subject of compensation inspired petitions, so did the punishments meted out to enslaved convicts. Occasionally, neighborhood whites welcomed the pending demise of a troublesome local bondman. After Job, held as a slave in Maryland in 1770, had thrown him "into a Bunch of Briers," an enraged Tom, "much Intoxicated with Liquor," killed him. Dozens of whites acquainted with Tom eagerly awaited his death because "it is Notorious his Character has always been that of a Villain of the blackest dye." As the eighteenth century surrendered to the nineteenth, the emergence of the cotton economy, the entrenchment and expansion of slavery in the Deep South, and the rising prices for slaves at market made such expressions of enthusiasm for a slave convict's death increasingly rare. Instead, masters' petitions frequently sought to mitigate the punishments of convicted bondpeople.[81]

Whereas state legislatures fielded petitions for compensation, masters pleading for a commutation of sentence directed their communications to state governors. Out of respect for the legal system, most memorials did not request full pardons of enslaved convicts. Many petitioners may have realized the futility of seeking full pardons: governors rarely negated courtroom proceedings by granting them. In Virginia, very few slaves found guilty of killing another bondperson and sentenced to capital punishment were absolved of their crime. Gubernatorial clemency spared Matthew of Northampton County the gallows in 1816, and in 1843, Maria McCoy of Pendleton County was pardoned for killing Wash after new evidence surfaced post-trial showing that she had acted in self-defense. But these were exceptional cases.[82]

In Louisiana, issuing outright pardons generated unique administrative nightmares for the state auditor. The Bayou State compensated masters not only for slaves who were executed but also for those condemned to the penitentiary for life. (Masters received no recompense for convicted bondpeople imprisoned for terms less than life because the enslaved convict would eventually be returned.) When masters surrendered enslaved convicts to the penitentiary, they also "relinquished their title to the State." In the event Louisiana's governor pardoned a slave incarcerated for life, the owner was required to refund the compensation previously received from the state, but until 1860, there was no provision codified into law for restoring the title to the master. Post-imprisonment, the slave's legal status remained technically ambiguous, a troublesome point should the slaveholder subsequently wish to sell the formerly incarcerated bondperson. The Louisiana legislature only remedied the oversight in a March 1860 law stating that "owners shall be reinvested with the title and possession of such pardoned slaves on reimbursing to the State the amount originally received as compensation." A dearth of full pardons kept these bureaucratic complications to a minimum. More frequently, slaveholders sought merely a reduction of punishment for their bondpeople. Governors represented their last avenue of appeal.[83]

Even in non-capital cases, some masters and their allies questioned the severity of punishments courts handed out to slaves. Petitioners from Grant County, Kentucky, appealed to Governor Charles S. Morehead on behalf of the slave John, who had been convicted of manslaughter in the death of George, another bondman. Concerned citizens regarded the 175 lashes to which John had been sentenced as "excessive and inhuman," utterly disproportional to the crime. Morehead rejected the petition, citing a lack of sufficient information to render an informed judgment. In South Carolina, petitioners complained not only about the number of lashes but also about the confinement ordered for slaves found guilty in the manslaughter deaths of other slaves. Charleston District bondman Henry was "to receive One Hundred fifty lashes and Six months solitary confinement." On appeal, South Carolina's governor cut the sentence in half, to seventy-five lashes and three months in solitary, but simultaneously mandated Henry's banishment from the state. The original sentence was even harsher for Isaac, who beat his enslaved wife Katura to death in 1834. The Charleston District freeholders who heard his case ordered him "to receive twenty five lashes on the bare back at the public whipping post at the market place on the first Monday in each month for twelve months, and kept in solitary confinement for that time." Isaac's master, Edward Carew, complained to Governor Robert Y. Hayne "that the sentence ... is severe almost beyond precedent, and exceeds the extent of merited punishment for his offence, alone." Carew denied any "desire to screen his slave from a just and adequate penalty for his offence," but he did seek "a mitigation of its severity." Although Isaac was not sickly, neither was he robust and healthy. Carew doubted "[t]he physical ability of the Slave to endure twelve months solitary confinement and three hundred lashes." The concerned master pleaded for leniency, fearing that his bondman would not survive an unduly harsh sentence.[84]

In capital cases, a slave's life always hung in the balance. Courts of law understood the serious consequences for both slave and master when a bondperson was condemned to death. Pursuant to the law as written, prior to the 1850s, Virginia Courts of Oyer and Terminer regularly sentenced slaves found guilty of killing other slaves to die at the gallows but, tempering the finality of the mandated punishment, often invited the intervention of the governor to prevent their destruction. After the five justices on a Chesterfield County Court of Oyer and Terminer in 1824 found the bondman Henry responsible for John's death, they ordered him hanged but "recommended him to the Executive of the Commonwealth as a fit object of mercy." In 1842, the Richmond Hustings Court "unanimously recommend[ed] the ... slave Emanuel to the clemency of the Executive, Because of circumstances of mitigation attending the ... murder" of the enslaved Isaac. Taking their cues from the Courts of Oyer and Terminer, the respective governors during the ordeals of Henry and Emanuel reprieved each to sale and transportation. At times, however, the gentleman justices of the courts were disinclined to encourage commutation. In the 1826 trial of Peter, convicted in Essex County of the murder of John, the court "unanimously overruled" the enslaved convict's "motion ... to be recommended to the mercy of the Executive." The governor commuted his sentence to sale and transportation anyway.[85]

In remarkably few memorials to state governors did petitioners delve into legal issues that would warrant a reduction of sentence. Questions of law more appropriately coursed their way through state court systems, with but few exceptions. In Virginia, five justices of a New Kent County Court of Oyer and Terminer petitioned Governor James Barbour in 1814 because the court had been negligent in recording the testimony, as required by law, taken at the slave Jim's trial for the murder of Claiborne. Jim was found guilty and sentenced to hang, but given the court's oversight, there was no transcript to submit to the governor for review and upon which to base a decision whether to reprieve the convicted slave. Realizing the mistake, the judges from the trial appealed to the governor and his council. "[S]olely for the benefit of the criminal," they presumed "that the sentence of the law cannot be executed upon him." They instead urged Governor Barbour to transport Jim out of the country, which was done. Legally more substantive, petitioners to Governor John Floyd in 1834 challenged the conviction of Kanawha County bondman Harry in the death of fellow slave Dennis because it was "not warranted by the laws of the land." The county Court of Oyer and Terminer had found Harry guilty of second-degree murder, but Virginia law would not recognize degrees of murder committed by slaves for another fourteen years. Petitioners acknowledged "that the Executive is not to be regarded as an appellate tribunal, authorised to review and correct the proceedings of the Court of Oyer and Terminor, and to grant new trials upon erroneous convictions," but, considering "the illegality of the conviction," they prayed for either a "pardon, or commutation of punishment." Dennis was accordingly sold and transported.[86]

The same petitioners to Governor Floyd also criticized the death penalty as generally inappropriate for bondpeople. They opined that "capital punishment, is not at all necessary to the good government and regulation of the slave property of this county." It was reportedly "the almost unanimous wish [of] our citizens" that Jim not be put to death. Opposition to the executions of bondpeople was widespread enough that, in Madison County, Virginia, nine white men signed a petition on behalf of slaves condemned to die for killing a fellow slave even though the petitioners admitted that they "did not hear the evidence in the case" and did not "know anything of the circumstances connected with" it. They nevertheless felt "no doubt that public Justice would be amply fulfilled by transportation instead of... Execution."[87]

Many petitions to the governor invoked in support of a condemned slave the erstwhile good character of the individual bondperson. The effusive praise heaped upon enslaved suspects often began during the trial. In Madison County, the white William Smith testified that Sawney, one of the three slaves charged with the death of the enslaved James Huston, had displayed "so good a charracter, that he frequently spoke of him to other slaves as an example." Tom, enslaved in Louisa County, seemed an unlikely candidate to have murdered the bondman John in 1849. As Robert J. Bibb, son of the slave's deceased master observed, "Tom had no scars or bruises on him." His consistently good behavior had kept him out of fights and spared him the lash. Captain Charles Barrett testified further that, while on patrol, he had "never caught Tom in any improper conduct, & never saw him [at] a grog shop nor at negro frolics." In Fauquier County, several white witnesses testified on behalf of the slave Dick, or Dick Gray, charged with the death of Simeon D. Armstrong's bondman Edmond. They variously described Dick as a "quiet & orderly boy," a "peacible ... negro," and "a no[.] 1 hand." One witness could not recall "his doing any thing amiss" throughout their entire decade of acquaintance. He "is not bad tempered" or "quarrelsome, generally good humored and good natured—always politic." "I think Dick an elegant servant," the witness concluded. "[H]e has won the respect of all who know him." Signs of his trustworthiness as a servant abounded. Dick "commanded" such "confidence" that he "carried the keys" for his master and, when employed on the road, was sent to retrieve whiskey. His owner, Alexander Campbell, admitted that he and his family were "very partial to him." The only smudge against Dick's character came from a fellow slave named Sage, who described Dick as "quarrelsome at shuckings." Upon Dick's unexpected conviction for Edmond's murder, individuals familiar with him sent missives to the governor to prevent his sale and transportation. At master Alexander Campbell's request, G. H. Norton, rector of St. James Church, wrote in Dick's defense, and the clerk of the court informed the governor that "[t]he boy[']s character was unimpeached, for obedience docility and good temper." Their efforts came to naught, however, as the governor refused to interfere.[88]

One strategy at trial and in subsequent petitions was to draw the contrast between the slaves involved in a deadly encounter. In Richmond, Emanuel was placed on trial for killing Isaac in 1842. An enslaved witness described the victim as "a very quarrelsome man," and Isaac's employer at a tobacco factory agreed that he was "ill tempered." Emanuel, the accused, could not have been more different: "he is an excellent servant; very peaceable and orderly." When the Hustings Court convicted Emanuel and scheduled him for execution, his lawyers were shocked. James A. Sedden and Herbert A. Claiborne Jr. fired off a letter to the governor and executive council begging for clemency. The victim, they said, was "a quarrelsome, drunken vicious negro" who had used "language of the most savage character," had repeatedly threatened to murder Emanuel, and had even once "attempted to kill one of the overseers in the factory with an adze." To Emanuel's credit, the convicted bondman had taken "no notice of the rancorous enmity" Isaac had shown. Indeed, Emanuel "manifest[ed] a self control ... which is seldom exhibited by those of a better class." The pleas on Emanuel's behalf saved him from the gallows and earned a reprieve for sale and transportation.[89]

To spare their slaves, some masters adopted the strategy of overwhelming the governor with the sheer numbers of petitions and signatures requesting clemency for a convicted slave. Wake County, North Carolina, superior court found the slave Nelson guilty in 1839 of murdering Gabriel and sentenced him to death. Purportedly, "all his life," the enslaved convict had been "a negro of good, quiet & peacable character—altogether superior to what belongs to his class in society and quite remarkable in any slave." Governor Edward B. Dudley received no fewer than five petitions on Nelson's behalf, totaling more than three hundred signatures. That the governor's house was located in Raleigh, in close proximity to the site of the murder, surely expedited the flow of petitions to the governor's desk. Dudley must have been impressed by the outpouring of support for Nelson. The slave, slated to die in November, first received a respite until January 1840, but prior to the New Year, the governor issued a rare pardon.[90]

Whereas the petitions for Nelson and many other convicted bondpeople often cited slaves' good character, only a few memorials made the case for slaves' temporary insanity. Claiming insanity during courtroom proceedings was not a common defense in cases of intraracial slave homicide. "Will a Negroe man Slave" in Henrico County, Virginia, proved an exception to the rule. In 1785, the Court of Oyer and Terminer ruled that Will was guilty of "Murdering a negro woman Slave, Nan," but at the time, "he was a Lunatic & not in his proper senses." The court therefore acquitted him, and he was discharged. Decades later, "William Dillahunt, negro," appeared before the Delaware Court of General Sessions, charged with the murder of another black man, William Frisby Green. Dillahunt pleaded insanity and put Dr. L. P. Bush of Wilmington on the stand as an expert medical witness. Bush diagnosed that Dillahunt suffered from a medical condition known as *"mania a potu*, brought on by abstaining from liquor, after free indulgence." Going off the bottle cold turkey, Bush explained, invited *mania a potu*, a variety of "temporary insanity" resembling monomania. The "peculiar characteristic" of the disease, he continued, was "that it invests the imagination with full power over the judgment." In such an altered mental state, "the distinction between right and wrong and the responsibility of the individual is ... destroyed." The physician's explanation convinced the court that the murder did not result from "the frenzy of drunkenness" but from the sudden cessation of "habitual intoxication." This was an important distinction. "Drunkenness is no excuse for crime," explained the court, but *"mania a potu* is a disease" tantamount to insanity. It therefore acquitted Dillahunt.[91]

Petitions invoking insanity and made on behalf of slaves convicted of killing other bondpeople usually sought to spare enslaved women condemned to death for infanticide or child murder. With no medical understanding of mothers' bodily chemistry or the hormonal changes accompanying pregnancy and the imbalances that cause postpartum depression, nineteenth-century Americans presumed that one must be insane to terminate the life of one's own child. In 1815, Powhatan County, Virginia, master Peter Stratton's bondwoman Jenny, herself again pregnant, drowned her three children—Anderson, Julius, and Violett—in a creek. Jenny may also have successfully committed suicide were it not for a second enslaved woman who alerted the master in time to prevent Jenny from taking her own life as well. The Court of Oyer and Terminer that heard Jenny's case sentenced her to hang for the triple homicide, but the execution was postponed until after she delivered her baby, who, by law, was her master's property. The delay provided residents of Powhatan County the opportunity to gather signatures for petitions begging mercy on the grounds of Jenny's alleged insanity. Although public opinion was not unanimous in Jenny's favor, the petitions raised enough doubt that the governor reprieved her sentence in March 1816 to sale and transportation. In another case from Virginia, thirty-seven petitioners claimed that the Louisa County bondwoman Milly was temporarily insane at the time she killed her four-year-old daughter Nancy. There could be no doubt that Milly was not in her right mind, one correspondent begging for clemency informed the governor, because "the Deed itself is contrary to the laws of nature." Moreover, Milly also "attempted to commit suicide by hanging herself." In this case, too, the governor saw the bondwoman as a fit subject for mercy and commuted her sentence from death to sale and transportation.[92]

Straddling the divide between slaves of good character and those who were purportedly insane were those who acted out of "passion." Many petitions invoked the idea of passion in their pleas either to pardon or to reprieve slaves condemned for killing their own. Two lawyers for Kanawha County bondman Harry wrote Virginia's governor in 1834 "suggesting the propriety and expediency of commuting" the condemned slave's punishment for killing the slave Dennis to sale and transportation. Harry, they explained, had acted "under the influence of his passion, upon reasonable provocation." Harry "had been violently ... assaulted and beaten." He responded "instantly" to the provocation by stabbing his assailant: "No time had intervened for the passion to subside or reason to resume its controul." Harry did not deserve to be punished capitally, argued his attorneys, because "[t]he case presents nothing of the malignant purpose, and previous preparation, which marks the conduct of a murderer." Dennis's death instead resulted from "the fury and passion of the moment." The sort of passion that seized Harry overwhelmed reason and, according to his counsel, rendered him less culpable for his actions. Drunkenness unleashed and magnified passion. Master Charles McClung petitioned Virginia's governor in 1824 after his slave was convicted of killing another slave at a "corn Husking" where liquor flowed freely. The unfortunate incident, McClung explained, was "purely the effect of passion and excitement of intoxication." The master also implied that his slave's youth may have constrained his capacity to control his passions. Sam, he reported, "is . . . not more than Eighteen or nineteen years of age." McClung was not the first to make the link between a convicted slave's age and an inability to regulate heated emotions. "[S]undry inhabitants" from Louisa County petitioned Virginia's governor in 1793 because George, who had been sentenced to death for murdering a female slave in an "impulse of passion," was "very young not exceeding 16 years of age." Moreover, "in his Intel[l]ect" George was reportedly "but little removed from an ideott." The eight individuals who "solicit[ed] a pardon" for the slave were unsuccessful, and he was executed for his crime.[93]

The emphasis on "passion" was legally meaningful. If one slave killed another in an "impulse of passion," that indicated an absence of premeditation, downgrading the homicide from murder to manslaughter at the most. Petitioners for North Carolina slave Nelson noted that "the act of violence which occasioned the death of Gabriel was sudden and entirely unpremeditated, . . . provoked by a gross insult [and] immediately resented by a blow"—a blow "given in the heat of blood." The governor pardoned Nelson precisely because "the homicide was committed in the heat of momentary excitement and not premeditated." Seeking transportation for three slaves charged with murder and slated to hang, petitioners from Madison County to Virginia's governor observed that "it was not the intention to kill." Seven signers pursued a pardon for Henrico County bondman Martin, condemned for the murder of Lewis, on similar grounds. Lewis's death, they contended, did "not amount to any thing more than Manslaughter" because Martin and Lewis were "strangers" who "had met for the first time only a few minutes previous to the quarrel." Murder required "willful deliberate & premeditated design."[94]

Slaves who assaulted, maimed, or killed one another caused tremendous problems for their masters. They disrupted plantation discipline, interfered with the rhythms of ordinary work routines, and sometimes immersed owners in the hassles of unwanted legal proceedings. Slaves' violence internal to the quarters demands a fresh look at the nature of slave "agency." Whereas the scholarship on slavery conventionally discusses agency in overwhelmingly positive terms, with slaves seizing an array of opportunities to shape and control their lives, murder and other forms of violence within the slave community are no less a form of volition, however physically destructive. Agency expressed in this way not only frustrated masters but also confounded southern lawmakers compelled to pass statutes, revise slave criminal codes, and amend them again to meet the challenge of balancing masters' interests in wayward enslaved property with the more abstract demands of justice. State criminal court systems were repeatedly called upon to resolve the vexing issues that intraracial slave violence brought to the fore. State by state, courts cobbled together legal guidelines for the adjudication of slaves' violent crimes upon one another. The slaveholding states agreed upon no uniform set of responses to the fact of slave-slave violence.

Chapter 4

VIOLENCE AT WORK AND PLAY

ON THE EVENING of Monday, December 3, 1860, Britton, an enslaved man living in Appomattox County, Virginia, struck "John Robert a negro man slave ... upon the head with a large hickory stick." The assault, which produced John Robert's death four days later, took the three other slaves in the room by surprise. According to Britton's half-brother, the bondman Peter Womack, "I never knew of any falling out between these persons." Moses, another slave present at the time of the attack, likewise "knew of no quarrel between them." In fact, he added, "they were often boxing and playing with each other." That very night, confirmed the enslaved man George LeGrand, "The boys had been Joking and playing." They "seemed to be in a good humor with each other," Moses remarked, "running on" lightheartedly with one another. It was with virtually no warning, then, that Britton approached John from behind and delivered a blow to the side of his head, knocking him to the floor and spilling blood from his nose and ears. "[T]here now," an alarmed George cried out to Britton, "you have killed John Robert." Upon realizing what had just transpired, Moses declared that he would retrieve "the white folks." Britton, the aggressor, still probably holding the stick, initially said, "no don[']t go yet." But almost immediately remorseful for his actions, he quickly changed his mind and urged Moses to "make haste and go on," for "they may save him."[1]

What had prompted Britton to bludgeon his erstwhile compatriot? Shortly before the assault, Moses reported, "John Robert had just eaten his supper and ... drop[p]ed off to sleep," likely exhausted after completing his first day of labor in the new work week. Standing by the hearth, however, Britton refused to let John Robert drift off. He instead poked and prodded the drowsy slave and ordered him "to get up and bring in some wood" for the fire. As Moses related, "John Robert told Britton to go away and let him alone" so that he might sleep. He also "drew his knife" and halfheartedly threatened to cut Britton if he did not desist. Denied the rest his body craved, John Robert arose and, despite his irritation, closed his knife without making any menacing move toward Britton. He instead got a drink of water from a bucket and stood with his hands in his pockets, gazing out the open cabin door, his back to Britton. At that point, Britton came from behind and struck him, first with his fist, instructing "John Robert not to talk about cutting him with his knife." Britton then administered the ultimately fatal blow with the stick.[2]

On one level, John Robert and Britton's quarrel over gathering firewood appears shockingly petty. The nature of their dispute hardly merited John Robert's death, even if Britton took less offense at John Robert's refusal than at the suggestion that he might cut his friend. John Robert may even have retrieved firewood on similar occasions in the past, but on this particular Monday night, he was extraordinarily tired. The tragic fate of John Robert offers a stark reminder that slavery was ultimately a form of forced labor. The outpouring of slave scholarship in the 1970s and 1980s, with its emphases on a vibrant slave culture and ubiquitous slave resistance, often overlooked this basic fact. The lacuna in the literature prompted historians Ira Berlin and Philip D. Morgan to issue a corrective, a 1993 anthology dedicated exclusively to slaves' working lives. Like practically any other slave across the South, John Robert had labored a good share of the day for the benefit of someone else. By the evening, he was exhausted and grew so frustrated with his comrade's pestering him and interrupting his rest that he unthinkingly uttered the offending words.[3]

Yet John Robert and Britton also socialized, frequently in a rowdy, boisterous, masculine fashion. Many older slave boys and enslaved men fought, wrestled, and boxed, in contests either orchestrated by the master or arranged by the slaves themselves for sport and amusement. John Robert and Britton participated in recreational fighting. Physically, they "boxed"; verbally, they "ran on" each other. Moreover, added Peter Womack, "The boys had been in the practice of Swearing" at one another in games of linguistic dexterity. Such behavior was so commonplace that Peter failed to gauge accurately the genuineness and intensity of Britton's anger. "I did not know that he was mad," he admitted. The two slaves' customary roughhousing and ribbing had imperceptibly taken a sinister turn.[4]

Slaves' work and play typically proceeded without such drama. To prevent unwanted turmoil, masters and overseers usually kept close eyes on bondpeople's labors as well as many of their leisure-time activities. To be sure, more often than not both work and play had the effect of building community. Slaves helped sick or lagging bondpeople complete their tasks to avoid the lash and frequently distributed the fruits of their independent economic activities to those in need. Similarly, recreational pursuits afforded slaves the opportunity to unwind and to bond with friends and family. Simultaneously, however, work served as both a site and a cause for disputes among slaves, and slaves' most popular pastimes occasionally descended into chaos. Violence had the potential to mar slaves' time at work and play.

Work intruded early into the lives of the enslaved. Even before masters dispatched them to the fields around the age of ten or twelve, youngsters began performing chores commensurate with their abilities. As a boy, Madison Bruin of Fayette County, Kentucky, went with another slave "to cut de weeds w'at grow up 'roun' de place," but the kinds of roughhousing typical of young boys quickly interfered with their work. "We ain't hardly git started befo' we stop and go to fightin'," Bruin recalled. The youngsters surely had no malicious intent as they sparred but rather engaged in the sort of aggressive play common to childhood. Yet their antics were unproductive, and the potential to damage the master's human property loomed. The owner therefore ordered the pair to gather the willow switches he wielded to punish them for their misbehavior and lack of focus. In Mississippi, John Matthews's master tasked him and "a black gal by de name uf Sally" with sweeping a yard filled with cedar trees. Both just children, Matthews and Sally turned their chore into a competition, "quarrel[ing] an' sometimes fight[ing] 'bout who had de most to do." The harmless scrapping and petty rivalries of childhood grew more serious as slaves matured and became full "hands."[5]

Work bred disagreements within the slave community. Scholars have long debated the significance of occupational cleavages on holdings sufficiently large to allow for a division of labor among the slave workforce. They have directed most of their attention to the categories of house servants and field hands. Eugene D. Genovese downplayed the mutual hostilities and animosities between the two groups, arguing that their shared experiences as slaves did more to bind them together than to drive them apart. Although house servants did not labor under a brutal, beating sun out in the fields, they, too, were subject to abuse, not only during working, daylight hours but around the clock. Not all historians stress the unity of the slave population, however. Michael P. Johnson's investigation of slave narratives revealed field hands' widespread suspicions of house servants as agents of the master and house servants' condescending attitudes toward lowly field hands. "Dere was no good feelin's 'twixt field hands and house servants," confirmed John Collins, born a slave in Chester District, South Carolina. His master owned "about twenty men, women, and chillum to work in de field and five house slaves." Why the chasm between the two categories of servant? On the Collins plantation, "De house servants put on more airs than de white folks. They got better things to eat . . . than de field hands and wore better and cleaner clothes." Other slaves echoed Collins's recollections. Owners may have recognized the elevated status of house servants, but at the very least they wanted them to reflect well on the master's household. The material benefits house servants received as a result sometimes encouraged them to identify with the master's interests, whereas the masses of enslaved field workers did not. These occupational divisions applied to only a fraction of all slaveholdings across the South, however. Most simply were not large enough to accommodate this form of social stratification.[6]

Even on smaller holdings, work still had the power to set slaves at odds. Various forms of slave resistance involved shirking labor. The slave who feigned illness to avoid work thrust the burden of that individual's labor onto other bondpeople. Any slave might play sick occasionally, but to make it a habit risked generating friction in the quarters. Likewise, bondpeople might also resent the additional work foisted upon them by slave truants who absconded from their labors temporarily, for a few days or weeks at a time. One slave's break from plantation routine forced other slaves to take up the slack in addition to fulfilling their normal duties.[7]

Work frequently provided the setting for violent and nonviolent disputes among slaves. As Georgia minister Charles Colcock Jones recognized, "Living so near each other, and every day working together, causes of difference must necessarily arise." Slaves very rarely had any choice with whom they worked, and individual personalities sometimes clashed. When South Carolina plantation mistress Keziah Brevard sent her bondman John with instructions for her slave driver Jim to work John and the slave Sam together, Jim resented it. Perhaps as driver, Jim knew that the pair did not get along, or he viewed the order as undermining his own authority over his fellow slaves. Regardless, grumbled Brevard, "instead of coming to me & asking me not to let Sam & John be together," Jim delivered a "severe" kick to John's stomach in retribution for his conveying their mistress's message. John returned "crying" to Brevard, who felt insulted by her driver's insolence.[8]

Enslaved men more frequently came to blows than did enslaved women, but female slaves were no less immune to work-related disagreements than bondmen. On the Sea Islands of South Carolina, the Boston missionary Charles P. Ware predicted that field work would progress more smoothly if only enslaved women's disputes could be held in check. While chopping cotton in Louisiana, the bondwoman Betty quarreled with the slave Molly and filleted the flesh off her face with a hoe. Female arguments turned deadly far less frequently than those of their male cohorts. In Robeson County, North Carolina, a fifteen-year-old male slave fatally shot a free black man employed by the bondman's master. Harrison County, Virginia, slaves David and Isaac "were at work together" in 1817 when "David complained of Isaac" shortly before killing him. According to one enslaved eyewitness, David and Isaac "disputed about their work," and "Isaac called David a mean Negro several times." A slave named Squire ordered the two to desist, when out of the corner of his eye he saw David "throw a Mattock" that struck Isaac in the forehead and penetrated the skull, leading to the latter's death an agonizing eight days later.[9]

Because enslaved men engaged in a wider range of work than enslaved women, their conflicts at work took place not just in the fields or about the plantation but in any number of settings. When Bill murdered fellow Georgia bondman Caesar in late 1854, for example, "both... were employed about a livery stable in Columbus." Slaves Elbert and Mat, involved in a homicidal fray in 1862, both belonged to the Georgia Railroad Company. A panicked Henrico County, Virginia, bondman named Martin complained of "damned factory sons of bitches" who "wanted to kill him." The normally "peaceable and quiet" slave Emanuel beat Isaac to death when both were working in a Richmond tobacco factory in 1842. The slave Horace, alias Forest, of Adams County, Mississippi, stabbed the bondman Stuart on the streets of Natchez one Monday evening in 1859. According to trial testimony, "The boys work at Mr. Field's brick yard." The quarrel that prompted the homicide began with the rehashing of "a fuss they had" two days earlier, either while laboring together on Saturday or partying that night. Horace and Stuart, Elbert and Mat, Emanuel and Isaac, and Bill and Caesar: each pair was acquainted through the work they performed either alongside or in close proximity to one another.[10]

Hired slaves were involved in some of the most serious work-related skirmishes. As explained in the first chapter, most slave-slave murders involved perpetrators and victims who either belonged to the same owner or at least knew one another. Although the bonds of community might foster friendship and cooperation, familiarity also sometimes bred contempt and hostility. Enslaved newcomers hired to work in alien surroundings would have been in many instances complete strangers who lacked any sense of community with the potential to reduce the likelihood of violent encounters, and working together did not necessarily help forge bonds between enslaved laborers. In Middlesex County, Virginia, the slave Levi stabbed Mortimer in the neck. Daniel Ellison had hired three bondmen, including Levi and Mortimer, "and had them oystering together" in the waters of the Chesapeake. Before he succumbed to his injuries, "Mortimer said to Levi that they were partners and he did not think that he would have served him so." In presuming an amicable, mutual understanding of their relationship, Mortimer made a fatal miscalculation. Some hired slaves surely resented the terms of the arrangements that dislodged them from family and friends and therefore began their labors with a grudge, primed to lash out. Their personalities also sometimes clashed with their new enslaved co-workers. A Mr. VanBokkelen hired "a colored man named Hamilton" to work at his North Carolina turpentine distillery in 1853. Hamilton "got into a difficulty with a negro of Mr VanBokkelen's, whom he stabbed."[11]

Some slaves hired to labor together already knew one another, but familiarity failed to stem the violence between them. A Georgia bondman named Nelson Young, hired to work at a Habersham County gold pit, was found dead in the late 1840s, partially submerged in the pit, the victim of a blow to the head. Another slave with whom he had had an antagonistic history incriminated himself in the murder through a series of careless statements.[12] Colleton District, South Carolina, master John Inabinet hired his bondman Caesar to the superintendent of public works Colonel B. F. Whitner in 1829, with the explicit instruction not to employ him on the state road north of Providence Swamp. In violation of their agreement, Whitner worked Caesar "on the upper section of the road," where "another negro slave named Jesse" killed Inabinet's bondman. Perhaps Inabinet had imposed the geographic restriction on the use of Caesar because he wanted to keep his slave close by. But maybe he was aware of some antagonism between his bondman and a slave or slaves in the vicinity of the murder.[13]

Bondmen who labored on roads or railroads or aboard steamboats seemed particularly prone to deadly, violent encounters. The "transportation revolution" that began in the early nineteenth century put countless slaves to work on various internal improvement projects, such as the construction of railroads. The New Orleans and Carrollton Railroad owned both Cuffy and his victim Miles, whom he killed in July 1848. Miles had struck the first blow "with an Iron hoop." Cuffy retaliated, knocking Miles down. As Miles rose to his feet, Cuffy said, "stand again You damn (Son of a Bitch)." Miles inflicted another blow with the hoop, at which point Cuffy stabbed him in the abdomen. A special tribunal found Cuffy guilty of manslaughter and sentenced him "to hard Labour in the Penitentiary of this State for the Term of Ten Years."[14]

Whereas Cuffy and Miles had been acquainted for some time, many enslaved laborers responsible for building the antebellum southern infrastructure worked far from home among unfamiliar slaves. In Hinds County, Mississippi, the slave John, property of a master back in North Carolina who had hired him "to work on the railroad," was charged with strangling a "very stout" bondman named Austin, whose work had frequently taken him "to the depot ever since the railroad was built, hauling cotton and other freight." What transpired between Austin and John is not clear, but shortly before Austin was "found dead near a wagon on the road," John had told the slave Davy "while at work together, that he thought he ought to kill somebody." At the time, Davy dismissed the comment as "a mere foolish remark." John's carelessness, combined with a fresh head wound, a missing tooth, and a bloody shirt, cast suspicion upon him for Austin's death.[15] Another deadly encounter involving "some negroes" took place aboard the steamer *Vicksburg*, docked in New Orleans in 1858. The bondman Dick, "a large powerful looking negro, with a fine face," belonging to the prosperous druggist and Spanish native J. Llado of Conde Street, "was employed on board" the vessel "as an engineer's assistant . . . working at a gauge cock when Edward and the others got into the fuss with him." The property of Thomas Pipkin of New Orleans's Second Ward, Edward "was one of his master's gang of levee laborers, who were unloading the Vicksburg." He and his accomplices administered a severe beating to Dick before Dick, in defense, "gave a desperate blow" with "a long-bladed pocketknife," fatally stabbing Edward in the chest and "cleaving his heart." Edward died "instantly."[16]

Records typically do not reveal the precise causes of most disputes in the workplace setting, but slaves did sometimes clash over the tools available to complete their assigned tasks. Any slave could become upset if denied access to the best implement for the job. Without the proper tool, a given chore might not be completed as easily or as efficiently, increasing the burden of labor falling to the slave. Some slaves also claimed possession of particular tools and objected to another bondperson using it. In Edgecombe County, North Carolina, a dispute arose between Will and Allen, two bondmen of master James S. Battle, over "a hoe which the former [Will] claimed to use exclusively on the farm on account of his having helved it in his own time." When Allen, the slave foreman on the estate, "directed another slave to use [the hoe] on that day," he denied Will the sweat equity he had invested in crafting the implement, and "angry words" passed between them.[17]

Slaves also sometimes argued over how best to complete a particular task. Sam and Fed, two bondmen belonging to Spartanburg District, South Carolina, master Henry Fergerson, came to blows in 1864 in a dispute over how properly to construct a fence. Sam insisted that Fed "had not built it right," declared "that he intended to have his own way," and struck Fed with a fence rail. It was in the best interests of both slaves to erect the fence correctly, for an enclosure that failed to meet the master's satisfaction might prompt a whipping, but they still had their differences. In Delaware, the perceived mismanagement of oxen led to a cursing match between two enslaved brothers, Charles and Jacob Loadnum. Charles ended their dispute by killing Jacob with the stick he had been using to drive the oxen. Many slaves expected work to proceed in a certain way and took offense when another slave deviated from the plan. David and Isaac of Harrison County, Virginia, quarreled over the digging of iron ore. David objected when Isaac broke off a piece of ore to ascertain its quality because David thought it easier to work if intact. Their argument escalated to the point that David threw a mattock that killed his co-worker.[18]

The slave Ben described another incident in which slaves disputed over their work. In Fluvanna County, Virginia, Ben and three other bondmen were unloading bags of meal from a wagon. The fifty-five-year-old George climbed into the wagon and handed a bag first to Ben, then to Jim. Jim, however, "would not take the bag set for him but reached around and got a bag from the top," perhaps to find a lighter one. Jim's behavior tested George's patience, maybe because it minimized the role that George, the elder of the two slaves, played in unloading the wagon. George told Ben that if Jim "done the like again he would knock him down," and Ben relayed the message to Jim as they passed. When Ben returned for the next sack, he saw Jim and George "Pitching at one another." According to another slave unloading the wagon, Jim had again attempted to reach around George to get a bag of his own choosing, but "George clamped Jim" to stop him. Jim picked up a stick from the ground "and struck George twice in the wagon." George climbed out to return the attack but died in the ensuing fray.[19]

Slaves such as George were prepared to punish the incompetence they encountered on the job. Several slaves in Bibb County, Georgia, were using a block and tackle to hoist hay into a loft in 1851 when the rope snapped. From his perch in the loft, the frustrated bondman Jim shimmied down the rope to yell at the slave Johnson for pulling on the rope, causing it to break. The two slaves fought. Jim overpowered his smaller adversary, repeatedly throwing him to the ground. After Jim let him up, Johnson left and retrieved a pistol, with the intention of killing Jim for having "imposed upon" him. He instead shot an enslaved friend by mistake.[20]

Some slaves took tremendous pride in the performance of their labors. They could do so for intrinsic reasons, entirely independent of any desire to please the master and without internalizing the master's values. Those who took personal satisfaction in their work sometimes gained the respect of the owner and renown in the broader white community for their ability to excel at certain jobs. The field hand who plowed exceptionally straight furrows or picked cotton with uncanny dexterity, the slave carpenter whose woodworking showed remarkable craftsmanship, or the slave cook who prepared consistently delicious meals all distinguished themselves from other bondpeople. Inside the quarters, the slave who labored well for the master risked resentment but, especially if generous with her or his time and talent, might also earn the acknowledgment and accolades of other slaves. Conversely, those who failed to meet minimum standards of respectable workmanship were subject to ridicule. A week before Copiah County, Mississippi, slave Simon dispatched the thirteen-year-old Norvall with an axe helve, Norvall laughed at Simon "for his awkward plowing." A seething Simon, humiliated by Norvall's "laughing," had warned the youngster that, if he did not cease his teasing or "pestering," "he would be damned if he didn't put his head under the dirt."[21]

The enslaved carpenter Daniel of Goochland County, Virginia, observed that fellow bondman and carpenter "Jim was the damedest fool he ever worked with." Daniel had been hired for a five-year term to William Gaulding (or Gauldin), an undertaker, presumably to build caskets. Jim was also in Gaulding's employ, working under Daniel's direction. In the spring of 1820, Daniel and Jim had completed their labors for Gaulding, so he sent them to Hugh Rains's to complete "some small specified piece of work" one Saturday morning. Once that was finished, Gaulding would not require their services again until Monday, intending for the two slaves to have the balance of the day Saturday and all of Sunday for themselves. Mid-morning, after making short work of Rains's job, "Daniel asked Jim . . . to assist him in sawing some Timber" for Daniel's "own benefit." Jim no doubt thought Daniel bossy and overbearing. Although Daniel was Gaulding's "head man," he had no formal authority over the underling Jim once the work for Rains was finished. Seemingly offended by the request, Jim refused to help, eager for his weekend to begin. Daniel then offered to pay Jim for his time, threatening that, "if he was so contrary and muleish they would get their tools" and return to Gaulding's place immediately. "Jim told Daniel to go on," Rains recalled. "[H]e would go when he pleased." At that point, "a quarrel commenced & each cursed & abused the other very much." Jim whacked Daniel in the side of the head with a piece of lumber, knocking him to the ground. Daniel rose, apparently unhurt, but later in the day began to "puke blood." He was dead within seven hours.[22]

As the account of Daniel and Jim suggests, slaves occasionally hired one another for wages. A small number of exceptional slaves—typically men—who received cash payments for extra work in industry, through self-hire, or by special agreements with their owners notwithstanding, most slaves did not earn money in return for their labor for the master. Cash was more commonly injected into the slave quarters through both the workings of the informal slave economy and thefts from whites. But because cash did circulate in the quarters, when slaves employed each other, they expected monetary or other compensation. Scholars know much more about slaves hired by whites or those given the opportunity to hire out their own time, and for good reason: accounts of slaves' hiring among themselves, much less the details of their arrangements, are elusive. Yet it happened. In one Georgia village, the enslaved carpenter George Cary needed an assistant for a project he was completing. On his own initiative, he "hired a slave named Gains from Travis Weaver." To compensate his help, he "charged the cost to a customer's account with Weaver."[23]

Dylan Penningroth has observed that many slaves who hired other slaves were themselves hired out or self-hired slaves. This may have been true of the enslaved Charles Johnson, who in Richmond, Virginia, "hired a negro woman named Maria to stem tobacco at Sizer & Dickinson's factory" in the 1850s. On one occasion, Johnson had "to get change for a five dollar note to pay her." Among many other questions, we do not know why Johnson hired Maria, how he learned she was available for hire, why she agreed to work for him, how long she was in his employ, or how he acquired the money to compensate her for her labors. But Johnson's hiring of a fellow slave was not unique. Amherst County, Virginia, slave Henry hired his friend and fellow bondman Jefferson "to work for me" for "the balance of the day" sometime around Christmas 1858. In Virginia's tobacco fields and on cotton plantations across the South, where the gang system of slave labor predominated, much of the internal hiring within the quarters likely took place during slaves' customary holiday break between Christmas and the New Year. Only then, during the brief respite from their labors for the master, did they get the opportunity to pursue projects of their own, such as improving a slave cabin. The day he employed Jefferson, Henry was playing cards with several slaves and "winning at bluff." As Jefferson explained, Henry interrupted his game "& got a hoe for me to work with." Jefferson set off with the hoe before noon to begin the task he took on voluntarily.[24]

In more sinister dealings, slaves hired other bondpeople to kill for them. In Greene County, Georgia, the bondman Thornton was charged in 1858 with arranging for another slave to kill a white man. Hired slave assassins might target their own as well. According to several slaves on the Mecklenburg County, Virginia, estate of Francis W. Boyd, bondman and conjuror Henry Baptist was "a dam[ned] rascal" widely despised throughout the plantation. As the enslaved woman Ann, in whom he may have taken some unwanted sexual interest, explained, Baptist had "got this plantation in such a twist that she did not want to stay." Baptist's fellow slaves were somehow convinced that he was the cause of the bondwoman Hainey's "being broken up and hired out" against her preference, separating her from her husband Grief. Upon hearing the news of his wife's imminent departure, Grief flew into a rage. After he demolished the inside of the slave cabin, he "came out in the yard, and said, dam[n] Henry Baptist['s] soul, he was the occasion of his wife being hired out." Grief pledged "to get revenge out of him or kill him," but, describing her husband coldly as of "no account to her," Hainey placed little faith in Grief's ability to seek retribution upon Baptist for her relocation. She instead spent New Year's Day 1851 plotting with three enslaved men to "send him to Hell." The bondman Dick, one of the slaves equally eager to see Baptist dead, had the expertise to concoct a deadly poison but pledged he "would not budge a peg except they paid him"; his fellow slaves must first "show the money." Hainey promptly retrieved "four Dollars" from her chest to underwrite the contract killing of Henry Baptist.[25]

Far less dramatic than paid assassination but vastly more common was workplace aggression involving slave drivers and those under their charge. Several white observers criticized the conduct of drivers. When British actress Fanny Kemble married a slaveholder and moved to coastal Georgia in the 1830s, she was taken aback by "the unbounded insolence and tyranny . . . of the slaves towards each other": "This is almost a universal characteristic of the manner of the Negroes among themselves." South Carolina plantation mistress Keziah Brevard registered frequent complaints against her "impudent" and "self willed negro," the slave driver Jim. He expected "every servant on the place to look to him as a superior," she lamented, and exerted "great influence over my negroes": "[E]very servant knuckles to him—if they do not—his family will put them down." Self-servingly, whites commonly alleged that slave drivers or slave foremen proved harsh taskmasters—harsher than even white owners or overseers. The recent deaths of "two Negroes . . . killed . . . by two other Negroes who were acting in the capacity of *Drivers!*" proved conclusively to the editor of the Abbeville, South Carolina, *Banner* "what has often been asserted before[,] that Negroes are more cruel to their fellow slaves, where they are entrusted with power over them, than white men are." Whites were oblivious to black overseers such as Gabe, who only lashed fellow slaves when compelled to do so in the presence of the master. Otherwise, when the owner was inattentive or out of sight, Gabe cracked the whip on a post while the slave suffering "punishment" screamed in feigned pain for the master's aural edification.[26]

Though invested with authority by the master, slave drivers often found themselves in an unenviable and ungratifying position. That slaveholders bestowed special responsibilities upon them, in one regard, marked a form of flattery. The master trusted the driver's knowledge and abilities enough to place him in charge and serve as the owner's representative among the other slaves. Simultaneously, however, in enforcing the master's rules and in pushing his fellow bondpeople to meet set production goals, drivers also clashed with them. For the enslaved masses, drivers were often resented as darker-skinned extensions of the master's authority, regardless of the driver's shared slave status. According to the report in the Abbeville *Banner*, the deaths of the two slaves at the hands of their drivers "were caused by severe chastisement for inattention to business." The deceased slaves may have attempted to relax and shirk their labors, thinking that one of their own would refrain from punishing them. But with slaveholder pressure on drivers to perform, they were dreadfully mistaken. Slave driver George Skipwith, who managed his absentee master's Alabama plantation, offered a general defense of driver behavior. A literate slave, he wrote in 1847 that "I have whiped none without a caus." "Suky" received "som four or five licks over her clothes" for not tending to her work, while "I gave isham too licks over his clothes for covering up cotton with the plow." After "frank, isham, violly, Dinah Jinny eveline and Charlott" underperformed in plowing the cotton fields, "I gave them ten licks a peace upon thir skins." In addition, "I gave Julyann eight or ten licks for misplacing her hoe." Held accountable for the misdeeds and failures of other slaves, Skipwith felt amply justified in administering the punishments he did.[27]

Many slaves failed to recognize the balance drivers attempted to achieve, and former slaves' resentment of the slave driver was palpable decades after bondage. As one recalled, her driver "was called by the other slaves 'nigger traitor' behin' his back." A Union District, South Carolina, bondman complained of his "nigger driver" waking the slaves under his charge "at break of day" for work: "He was a sorry nigger dat never had no quality in him a'tall, no sir-ee." Bondpeople also took exception to drivers' verbal criticisms of slaves who allegedly underperformed at their labors. That "straw-boss slave . . . call us lazy," groused one. Disparaging remarks about slaves' efforts in the fields seemed particularly unwarranted if the driver labored under inflated and unrealistic expectations of productivity. Slaves on one lowcountry South Carolina plantation where work was organized according to the task system despised "the colored oberseer," a native of Africa, because "he lay task on 'em tey ain't able to do," and those who failed to complete the impossible tasks assigned them were punished.[28]

Without question, slaves hated drivers primarily because they had the authority to whip them in the master's name. Ex-slave Madison Griffin observed matter-of-factly that the "nigger foremen" on master Billy Scott's South Carolina plantation "sometimes whipped de niggers." But most WPA respondents' recollections were infused with more passion and emotion when the subject turned to slave drivers. Merciless lashings inspired ex-slaves' vehement denunciations of drivers, characterized as "de meanest man, white or black, I ever see," or "de meanest devil dat ever lived on de Lord's green earth." Former bondpeople who expressed such visceral hatred for slave drivers related personal stories in which loved ones were severely beaten, while the masters' representatives relished, almost perversely, the power they wielded over their charges. Decades after slavery, visions of Henry Cheatam's mother and his pregnant aunt being beaten by the driver remained fresh, indelibly imprinted on his memory. South Carolina bondman Ben Horry recalled that his despised driver took his mother, who "won't do all he say," to the barn, strapped her to a device known as "the Pony," and administered "twenty five to fifty lashes till the blood flow," all in the presence of Horry's helpless father.[29]

Many slaves resisted the driver's authority and frustrated his attempts to control them. One Alabama slaveholder placed a driver "in charge of a bunch of niggers," but the "seven or eight young, well muscled bucks . . . wouldn't do anything he told them to do . . . because any one of them could whip him in a fight." They acquiesced to whippings by the master, "but they wouldn't let another nigger whip them because he was a nigger the same as they were." Concordia Parish, Louisiana, bondman Samuel refused to submit to a lashing by the slave driver Bill and threatened "to cut him to pieces with his hoe." When an "old negro driver" near Savannah, Georgia, summoned some twenty other slaves to assist him in subduing an intractable William Grimes, Grimes head-butted "one of the stoutest of them" so severely that the others dared not touch him.[30]

So hated were some slave drivers that bondpeople at times dreamed of violent revenge. While still a boy, emotionally traumatized from witnessing the driver's abuse of close family, Henry Cheatam "promise[d] myself when I growed up dat I was a-goin' to kill dat nigger if it was de last thing I ever done." Some slaves did indeed plot to kill these internal enemies. While at work in a field, the Mississippi bondwoman Ursula urged two other female slaves to unite with her in killing their slave driver by beating him with hoes. They refused. Ursula proposed that night that they kill him with axes instead, but again, her potential accomplices declined to be a part of the scheme. Other slaves mustered the courage to go through with it. Cases in which slaves murdered their black drivers date back to the colonial era. In Spanish Louisiana, the slave Pedro poisoned the black "overseer Gonzalo," who had punished him "by order of the master and sometimes through caprice." Decades later, a slave in West Feliciana Parish cut his driver "to pieces." Bondmen Ned and Taylor, enslaved in Yazoo County, Mississippi, ambushed and murdered their slave driver Ely one Sunday in 1856. After bludgeoning Ely to death with the eye of an axe, Ned and Taylor rowed with the corpse into the middle of a lake and dumped the body overboard.[31]

Stafford County, Virginia, slave Jeff Brooker's resentment of his driver took a more personal turn; his driver was also his brother John. An enslaved woman named Jane Parker described the dynamic between them: "John was the head man of the plantation... and took authority over all the servants." As his brother, "Jeff was restive under the authority of John," and they "fell out sometimes. John wanted [to] give orders to Jeff which he did not like." Jeff served as a personal attendant to a Captain Dade Hooe, "an old and afflicted man" and "cripple" who "had to be lifted about." Jeff also tended the horses. On February 6, 1861, however, he made a trip to market and neglected to return home, remaining in town all night, drinking. Captain Hooe dispatched John to retrieve the errant brother. John scolded Jeff and threatened to carry him home by force, but Jeff shot him in the side. According to one white observer who had previously broken up the "frequent quarrels and disputes" between the siblings, "Jeff was always a peaceable & quiet fellow" and "a tip top servant," "very attentive to his master," but "when Jeff had been drinking he was inclined to get in a fuss." And there was no love lost between him and his brother, the "head man."[32]

Bondmen serving in the capacity of drivers were the most visible enslaved agents of their masters, but slaves sometimes aided owners in other ways as well. Although the vast majority of bondpeople usually remained loyal to the residents of the quarters, some were forced or coerced into acting against their will. After a Virginia bondwoman assaulted her owner, the master commanded a slave named Big Jim to restrain the attacker for her lashing. Similarly, Lucretia Alexander's owner made "two girls"—Angeline and Nancy—hold her for a whipping. Alexander might have been angry at them for the bondwomen's complicity in her lashing, but as she understood, "They didn't much want to hold me anyhow." One Virginia slaveholder "directed" a bondman named Jacob "to go into the garden and get some switches to whip Bartlett," Jacob's own brother. It was not uncommon for masters to delegate the punishment of slaves to other bondpeople. Female slaveholder Frances Miller appointed two enslaved men to punish refractory slaves. A slave named William was compelled to administer the stripes due the bondwoman Rose for attending an illicit party. Enslaved in Louisiana, Solomon Northup was forced to lash a slave girl who had been stripped naked and tied to stakes driven into the ground.[33]

Slaves usually could not object and refuse to mete out the ordered whipping. Under certain circumstances, however, disobedience was more likely. When the mistress of one Texas plantation ordered "Mammy Lize" to "whip Oscar and Hagar," two children, for fighting, the bondwoman declined, preferring to punish them without resort to violence. Mammy Lize was emboldened to propose an alternative punishment either because the command came from the mistress rather than the master or because at least one of the children was her own, and she had no intention of surrendering disciplinary authority over them. In a different case, a protective slave mother in Mississippi countermanded an order from the master's daughter. J. T. Tims recalled that, as a young enslaved boy, he had bitten the white girl, who in response "called for William"—another slave—"to come and beat me." William dutifully approached as instructed, Tims reminisced, but "Ma had been peeping out from the kitchen watchin' the whole thing." In defiance of the directive of the master's daughter, "she come out with a big carving knife and told [William], 'That's my child and if you hit him, I'll kill you.'" Age, experience, and maternal love combined to trump the young white girl's command, despite her race and class standing. Surely Tims's mother would not have been so bold had the master's daughter summoned her father or an overseer.[34]

Some slaveholders counted on their bondpeople not only to administer punishment but also to assist in the recovery of those who absented themselves from the plantation. In Baldwin County, Alabama, one slave chanced upon a truant named Ben. He urged Ben to return home and threatened to "tell his master if he did not." After Ben promised to surrender himself the following day, he reconsidered and decided instead to preserve his freedom by murdering the potential slave snitch. Slaveholders used enslaved men to capture fugitives more often than one might logically expect. Should a slave encounter a runaway when no whites were present, a shared identity based on color or status might dictate that the hunter ignore or even aid the hunted, barring some inducement that might entice a slave to turn in another bondperson. Many of those slaves willing to betray fellow bondpeople or volunteer their services to the master likely anticipated some sort of reward for their allegiance. But there may have been other reasons as well. Slaves might aid a master or overseer in corralling a disobedient slave out of fear, either of punishment if they failed to comply or of what might happen to absconded friends or family members if a white authority found them first. Alternatively, slaves may have loathed the troublesome bondperson or held that individual in the wrong. Whatever his motivation, "Tom a negroe man slave" of Pittsylvania County, Virginia, apprehended another bondman. "I caught him & we had a scuffle," Tom explained, but "he could not get away. I threw him down, tied him & carried him" to his employers.[35]

Sometimes whites out to capture a fugitive slave thought it wise to track with a companion—even one held in bondage—because they would potentially need the strength of numbers. In Yalobusha County, Mississippi, the white Daniel Martin teamed up with the slave Henry in 1855 to capture a "negro runaway" named Prince, known to be "a powerful negro." Martin and Henry hatched a plot whereby Henry, upon learning of Prince's whereabouts, would borrow Prince's knife, "ostensibly to mend ... Henry's shoes." Once Prince was unarmed, Martin and Richard Boles, the man to whom Henry was hired, would ambush the runaway. Slaves such as Henry likely lacked the ability to decline participating in the slave hunt for fear of the repercussions, but on this occasion, as a bonus for his role in this intrigue, Henry was to earn "one dollar" for his trouble. When Prince was discovered, however, all did not go according to plan. Wielding an iron rod in one hand and a knife in the other, Prince scuffled with Martin, inflicting two blows to the white man's shoulder. Martin "cursed ... Henry" and ordered him to "seize Prince" before he landed a third blow with the iron bar. Following Martin's instructions, "Henry clasped Prince about the body and arms." Though constricted by the bear hug, Prince slashed at Henry with the knife, and Henry loosened his grip. Prince made his escape for only a few moments before he was dragged down by slave-catching dogs. Henry, whose physical effort may have saved Martin's life, then helped tie up the apprehended runaway. He certainly earned the dollar Martin had promised him and presumably received it. No evidence survives to chronicle how Henry, now a dollar richer, was treated back in the quarters, but it is easy to imagine that other slaves, especially any of Prince's friends or relatives, may have been quite hostile.[36]

For bondmen like Henry, willing to betray fellow slaves, cooperation with whites might end quite badly. In DeKalb County, Tennessee, whites "employed

Isaac to catch George," a slave who had run away in concert with Jim, the enslaved cousin of George's wife. George and Jim had been at large together in the neighborhood woods for some time and, through their connections with unidentified "persons" sympathetic to them, were aware "that Isaac had engaged to betray them." Armed with pistols, the pair of runaways was well prepared for a dangerous game of cat and mouse. Both slaves made "frequent threats" to take Isaac's life in defense of their freedom, and they evinced no scruples against attacking a fellow slave allied with white authorities. A slave named Sam heard Jim declare that he intended to kill Isaac; he also recalled George saying, "If Isaac was one of the sort that would betray black people, he would be none too good to hurt him." On a Saturday night early in 1843, it was Jim—at George's urging—who made good on his threat. As Isaac lay on a kitchen floor in front of a fire, Jim inserted the barrel of his gun through a crack in the wall near the door and fired. Isaac died soon thereafter of the wounds he received. After the murder, Jim went to his cousin's house and told her "that he had shot the damned rascal." The next morning, he was found "in a cave about half a mile" from the site of the crime. Indicted for Isaac's murder, Jim was convicted at trial and sentenced to death. As explained by the court that sealed his fate, "Isaac had not only excited the enmity of George and Jim, but he seems to have lost caste with the other negroes in the neighborhood" because "[h]e had combined with the white folks to betray" fellow slaves: "This was no slight offence in their eyes: that one of their own color, subject to a like servitude, should abandon the interests of his caste, and, for hire, betray black folks to the white people, rendered him an object of general aversion." One slave admitted to withholding information from the authorities because "she did not want to destroy Jim for such a fellow as Isaac was." Her loyalty lay with the slave who had not betrayed the trust of the quarters. One bondwoman succinctly captured the complexity of slaves' potentially conflicting allegiances to master or fellow bondperson: "Some niggers would catch you and kill you for the white folks; and then there was some that wouldn't."[37]

Slaves killed in the act of trying to arrest fugitives raised significant legal questions. In DeSoto County, Mississippi, the runaway Jordan fatally stabbed the slave Aaron as the latter attempted to apprehend him in May 1856. Aaron had been hired to a John Urie but was assisting a white man named Jim Mallory in apprehending Jordan, who, when not sold from his present owner as he wished, had absconded two days earlier. Following up on a rumor, Mallory, Aaron, and Mallory's dogs went to Urie's cabins one evening in search of Jordan, then on to Urie's mill, "where there was a fire light . . . very dim." Glimpsing a shadow flee ahead of them, Mallory, Aaron, and the dogs took pursuit. The canines cornered their quarry "in a pond." Mallory ordered Aaron "to knock down" Jordan, and when Aaron made the attempt, Jordan thrust a knife, stolen from Urie's kitchen, into Aaron's neck, severing the "carotid artery or jugular vein." "[O]h Mass Jim!" gurgled a dying Aaron as Jordan escaped his grasp. Jordan was recaptured, tried, found guilty of murder, and sentenced to hang, but his counsel secured a new trial, making the clever argument that, legally, slaves could not arrest one another; therefore, Aaron lacked the authority to seize Jordan, and Jordan, "in resisting the arrest, was not guilty of murder." Moreover, Mallory was not Aaron's master. Mallory did not have the right to compel Aaron to service, and Aaron, as "a volunteer," was "not . . . bound to obey" his orders. Aaron, rather, "acted at his peril," as Jordan's equal, with no special protection under the law. The Supreme Court of Mississippi agreed with Jordan's counsel. A slave's right to arrest a fugitive, the Court ruled, was restricted to "the premises of his master." Among whites, only "the owner, master, or overseer" could rightfully compel a slave to arrest a runaway. Since Mallory bore none of these relationships to Aaron, the highest court in Mississippi reversed the judgment against Jordan.[38]

As a rule, the laws of Mississippi and other southern states refrained from infringing upon the rights of masters over their chattel. Masters were empowered to command their slaves to capture or to aid in the apprehension of fugitives, forcing selected bondmen to choose between obedience to the master, on the one hand, and cohesion of the quarters on the other, or, more broadly, the principle of racial unity. Refusal risked punishment and personal safety; compliance offered possible rewards but risked social ostracism among one's peers or, potentially, death. A "Valuable Negro Man" named Jim, belonging to Abbeville District, South Carolina, slaveholder William Ware, "was barb[ar]ously stabed & killed" in 1814 while "attempting to apprehend 2 Negro fellows who . . . had been plundering & stealing through the neighbourhood." Suspecting one of the fugitives, Sam, of "Sculking about my house" or lurking about "at my Kitchen," Ware "ordered my Negro fellows to take him" or at least to "give me some intelligence . . . so that I could Get hold of him." In July, Jim "came across" Sam, but "Unfortunately for him & Me," wrote the economically damaged Ware, Jim "was stabed to the Heart" and "died the Same day." "My fellow" Jim "was amongst the first class of Negros," his master eulogized, "a likely Negro Man about thirty years old," valuable as both a field hand and a smith. Pleading to the South Carolina legislature for $500 in compensation for his deceased slave, Ware observed that Jim "was doing a Laudable Act"—a public service—"by apprehending [the] said Villain" and was merely "obeying my lawful orders" when murdered. It is not known whether the state responded to Ware's petition favorably.[39]

Masters placed a premium on slaves they believed reliable and loyal to their white families. Ascertaining any individual bondperson's true allegiance was difficult for masters to gauge. Enslaved in Alabama, Anna Baker was bribed by her owner to eavesdrop on other slaves' conversations and report back to him, promising "dey'll be somp'n' good in it for you." Unbeknownst to the master, however, she also reported back to the slaves what she heard discussed among whites. Despite the obvious risks of placing faith in their bondpeople, masters' self-perceptions bred artificial confidence in their chattel. Stories of loyal slaves widely reported in the southern press assured them that their faith was not misplaced. Slaveholder Richard Johnson of St. Matthew's Parish in Orangeburg District, South Carolina, considered "a Negro man named Jim . . . of much value, on account of his fidelity & usefulness & the general correctness of his deportment." As proof of Jim's loyalty, in August 1838, the slave killed another of Johnson's bondmen "who was in the act of committing depredations" upon unspecified property of Johnson's that "had been placed under [Jim's] charge." Jim took his responsibilities seriously. Whether motivated by fear of punishment or by genuine identification with the master's interests, Jim murdered another slave he did not necessarily like but at least must have known well.[40]

After Jim's arrest on homicide charges, however, his story took a tragic turn. Normally a "sound, healthy, and intelligent man," Jim crumbled both physically and mentally. He exhibited "in his language & conduct, strong Evidence of bodily indisposition & severe mental agitation, which increased . . . as the Constables were conveying him to the Court." When Jim died suddenly the night before his trial, his master—having now lost not one but two valuable slaves—attributed his slave's demise to "his arrest & confinement in gaol under the authority of the state." Since Johnson viewed Jim's death as a "consequence of the operation of a State Process," he petitioned the South Carolina House of Representatives for compensation. A helpful neighbor confirmed that Johnson would have difficulty replacing Jim with a slave "equally trust worthy and useful."[41]

Across the South, trusted slaves defended their owners' economic interests, by violence if necessary. Deep Creek, Virginia, merchant James Seguine left his "trusty man servant Charles, (an elderly negro,) to occupy the room adjoining his store during the night" when Seguine was away on business in Portsmouth. In Seguine's absence, "two stout negro fellows" "armed with bowie knives and bludgeons" broke into his store to rob it. Still awake, Charles "seized his master's double barrelled gun," made available for the slave's use despite laws against slaves bearing firearms, and, in Charles's words, "shot a nigger and killed him." The other he missed. The burglars "would undoubtedly have murdered the faithful fellow," predicted the appreciative Norfolk *Herald,* "if he had not been provided with [t]he means of defence." More frequently, given the agricultural orientation of most slaves' working lives, masters placed bondmen in charge of stock or animals. Along the Georgia coast, for example, two slaves seized the runaway bondman Lewis as he attempted to steal a calf. In Civil War–era Warren County, Mississippi, master N. G. Flowers put "the Negro Boy Aleck" "in charge of the Hog Pen." Flowers supplied Aleck "a Double barrel Shot Gun" and instructed him to protect the pigs from thieves. When "the Negro Boy Dick" attempted to pilfer some pork on the first day of April 1863, Aleck shot him to death.[42]

Although slaves escaped legal repercussions for violence upon their own committed by order of the owner, slaves' aggressive defense of the master's property could stir ample resentment in the quarters. In South Carolina, the enslaved "cattle-minder, James, an exceedingly vigilant and faithful negro," occupied a house inside his master's cattle pen and twice foiled the efforts of slaves Winningham and Sancho to steal livestock. Because "the negro was too watchful," Winningham, Sancho, and four others joined forces and cooperated in James's murder, afterward stealing "thirteen oxen."[43]

If slaves' labors for the master bred violence among themselves, so did their leisure-time pursuits. Many men formerly held in bondage observed in the WPA narratives that fighting was a convivial sport among young male slaves in the quarters. "[W]e children . . . fight and frolic like youngsters will do when they get together," explained a former North Carolina slave. The "little Nigger chillum," reported another, "scrapped . . . bad as game chickens." Usually these engagements marked nothing more than a lighthearted pastime with no ill intent. "[S]ome times we would lie up and fight," acknowledged former Mississippi slave Dave Walker, but he dismissed such conflicts as harmless "devilment." Fighting, several formerly enslaved men declared, counted among "de mos' fun dat we had in dem days." Even if anger fueled a violent childhood quarrel, all was quickly forgiven. As one ex-bondman from Mississippi explained, in boyhood he would get mad with other slaves, enter into a fistfight, and then "git up an' shake hands." For the enslaved youngster who lost, the chance for redemption was only one spirited battle away. As boys grew into men, their leisure-time fights and wrestling matches took on greater social significance as they transformed into ritual performances designed to attract female slaves. For their part, enslaved girls were less likely than boys to tussle physically with one another but no less likely to engage in other forms of mischief. Mississippi's Emily Dixon, for example, threw hickory nuts at other slaves. Proud of her accuracy, she admitted she had "hit many a little nigger on de head wid 'em."[44]

Innocent childhood play or good-spirited fighting among youthful slaves occasionally turned serious. In 1825, the Hanover County, Virginia, bondman Armistead, his brother Elic, and the slave John were "talking about fighting," probably for recreational purposes, when they were joined by a fourth bondman, named Moses. Moses "step[p]ed between them" so that he might participate in the impending wrangle as well. His motives were less innocent, however, in that he apparently had some unidentified "old grudge" against Armistead. Elsewhere, near Alto, Texas, Preely Coleman won all the footraces on his master's plantation. On one occasion, a frustrated competitor showed remarkably poor sportsmanship by throwing a rope over Coleman's head and dragging him by the neck, with the intention of throwing him into a nearby spring. Coleman's friend Billy fought to free him, but the horror concluded only through the intervention of a white man.[45]

Some slaveholders actually promoted fighting among enslaved children, adolescents, or young men. The master of Mississippi bondman Isaac Wilson, for one, had the grown children not only run footraces but also wrestle and box. These structured, organized sports channeled violence in sanitized ways for the benefit of white observers. Such leisure-time contests, typically held on Sundays, provided amusement for slaveholding families and, at least according to Wilson's recollection, enjoyment for the slaves as well. Masters staged fights not only among their own bondpeople but also across plantation boundaries. Competitions between slaves from different plantations provided an entertaining diversion for whites but took on a more serious cast in that they afforded neighboring masters an opportunity to gamble. Masters arranged bouts between male slaves equally matched by size and weight from the different plantations and placed, at times, substantial wagers on the outcome. These "nigger fights," as former slave John Finnely of Alabama termed them, were "more for de white folks' joyment," although slaves got to watch, too. Masters of the two contestants set the rules governing the match and, according to former Alabama slave Carter J. Jackson, "managed the fight to see it was fair." Slaveholders imposed limits to minimize any damage to valuable slave property. In Mississippi, Tom Floyd's master restricted the available weapons to fists: "Wont no sticks 'lowed." With so much at stake for betting whites, some slaveholders groomed their contestants into finely honed fighting machines, providing them extra rations and breaks from routine labor. Expert fighters earned a reputation for their physical prowess as well as respect in the quarters.[46]

In the slaveholding South and throughout the preindustrial world, work and play were not necessarily discrete activities. Laboring and socializing overlapped at such events as log rollings, house raisings, and harvest. In the fall, slaves from neighboring plantations frequently gathered at corn shuckings, or corn huskings. Competing teams made their way through piles of corn at a furious pace, earning rewards such as a swig of alcohol for finding red ears and for finishing first. Losers might charge their opponents with cheating, perhaps by having furtively tossed some ears of corn onto their rivals' pile, yet when the work was completed, bondpeople feasted and danced well into the night. Daina Ramey Berry describes these "working socials" in overwhelmingly positive terms, as sites for "courtship, counsel, and camaraderie." Their most distinguishing feature, she argues, was their sense of community. "We had a big time at cornshuckings," confirmed a former slave in Moore County, North Carolina. "We had plenty of good things to eat, and plenty of whiskey and brandy to drink... We had a good time, and I never saw a fight at a cornshucking in my life."[47]

Many other slaves, however, remembered corn shuckings as virtually synonymous with violence. As Sergio Lussana has shown, fights at corn shuckings were commonplace, intended for sport and amusement. Former slave Jasper Battle of Taliaferro County, Georgia, recalled how "wrastlin' matches started" at corn shuckings, and "marster allus give prizes to de best wrestlers." As a rule, Battle's owner did not encourage "fussin' and fightin'" on the plantation, but "dem wrastlin' matches was all in good humor and was kept orderly." Slaves on an Alabama plantation remembered that corn shuckings boasted "some good fights, but no one was killed." The loser "took it" and gracefully accepted his defeat. But because liquor often flowed freely at corn shuckings and other work frolics as a reward for completing onerous, grueling, and time-sensitive tasks, tempers were easily aroused at "working socials," and organized fighting contests sometimes went awry. In Floyd County, Georgia, Callie Elder's master gave the slaves "coffee and whiskey all night." The "shucks did fly," but the combination of caffeine and alcohol "made 'em git rough and rowdy." With "so much... liquor drinkin'" from master's "little brown jug," reported an ex-slave from Georgia's Oglethorpe County, "lots of fightin' took place. It was awful. Dey cut one another wid razors and knives." Sparked by alcohol and impaired judgment, the fights at corn shuckings were not willful, premeditated attempts to harm, but they could quickly turn dangerous nontheless.[48]

Occasionally a night of hard work and festive revelry ended tragically, in death. After an 1824 "corn Husking" in Greenbrier County, Virginia, two slaves, both named Sam, "were familiarly jesting and joking with each other" at supper—"apparently in a good humour & in a lively mood"—when one of them, only eighteen or nineteen years old, "became ir[r]itated" and stabbed the other. As Charles McClung, master of the homicidal Sam, explained, "as is customary, much spirituous liquor was used" at the corn shucking, and his slave "became intoxicated." Thus, the murder was "purely the effect of passion and excitement of intoxication"; his bondman Sam lacked "the proper use of his judgment and the exe[r]cise of his reason." The same may have been true of Nelson County, Virginia, slave Big Joe Wills, who killed Little Joe with a "bed stead post" after shucking corn in November 1840. The night of the murder, the neighborhood slaves had finished their work and were retiring "to the house to get supper." On the steps into the dwelling, a dispute broke out between the differently sized Joes. According to a white witness, "the negroes had drank spirits." Although he did not believe the Joes were drunk, tensions quickly escalated between them. After Little Joe drew a knife and threatened his physically larger namesake, Big Joe retreated, grabbed the post, and knocked his adversary in the head.[49]

Despite a host of state laws intended to restrict slaves' access to alcohol, many bondpeople were no strangers to the allure of the bottle. Liquor uplifted slaves' spirits and momentarily ameliorated the degradation of their condition. Whether used as a temporary psychological escape, medicinally, to fortify oneself against a winter chill, in cooking, or in celebration and fellowship, alcohol was frequently uncorked in the slave quarters. Although slaves might procure alcohol through their own covert efforts, often by trading illicitly with poor whites, masters directly supplied slaves a portion of the liquor they consumed. Most often, owners lubricated slaves' throats with alcohol during holiday festivities or as an extra incentive at harvest. The Bedford County, Virginia, bondman Plato, who murdered his one-time wife Edy, was reportedly "addicted to intoxication." His master believed him sober at the time of the crime but admitted that Plato nevertheless "had free access to a hogshead of New Cider." Slaveholders' willingness to dispense liquor did not mean they were oblivious to the inherent dangers and potentially subversive effects of alcohol upon their slaves. In Adams County, Mississippi, an enslaved woman named Charity was known to be "greatly addicted to intemperance and the use of spirituous liquors," rendering herself "almost useless by the too great indulgence in drink." But slaves need not be notorious drunkards like Charity to produce shoddy work or to miss work altogether. Bondpeople also undermined plantation discipline when they stole alcohol from their masters or pilfered goods from them to exchange clandestinely with "unscrupulous" whites for ardent spirits.[50]

And when slaves overimbibed, they were also more likely to assault one another. When he had been drinking, Missouri bondman Anderson "was in the habit of beating and wounding other slaves." When Jacob, of Spartanburg District, South Carolina, "commit[ted] a violent assault & Battery by stab[b]ing" Asa in 1848, both slaves had partaken of the bottle. In Hall County, Georgia, Anderson Furr's master distributed spirits at Christmas, "and atter us drunk a lot of liquor it warn't long 'fore dere was a Nigger fight goin' on." Once cotton picking concluded on one Elbert County, Georgia, plantation, "dancin' and all sorts of frolickin'" commenced. According to one former slave, "Plenty of liquor in dem little brown jugs" occasionally made the evening "too lively," but, he quickly added, "De few fights dey had when dey was drinkin' heavy didn't 'mount to much."[51]

One Georgia physician and careful observer of slaves acknowledged in 1860 the "controlling power" of festive occasions and alcohol "in the management of negroes" as inducements to be dangled in front of the slaves and withdrawn at the master's discretion. For such purportedly "childish and sensual creatures," he remarked, the prospect of a "big dinner" at a corn shucking "greatly animated and encouraged ... their labours," and threat of its cancellation proved more effective in maintaining discipline "than the terrors of the rod itself." Masters "should allow their servants to eat freely of the fruits of their labor, and to enjoy all the pleasure of which their ... carnal nature is susceptible," he advised, but to avoid "injury to health," "whiskey should be dealt out very sparingly at these gatherings" if permitted at all: "Negroes will take too much of this if they have an opportunity, and the custom of handling the bottle around for all hands to drink at pleasure is highly injurious both to health and morals," even among the relatively "torpid and unexcitable systems of negroes." The dangers were real. Amid "scenes of overflowing joy and outrageous merry-making" at corn shuckings, "it has sometimes happened that a valuable negro has been killed in the drunken frays that are very likely to arise from the too free use of such drinks." As long as alcohol consumption was carefully monitored by whites and spirits doled out only in "small measure," however, corn shuckings "will have a most happy influence" over the slaves and be "conducive to health, cheerfulness and contentment."[52]

However much masters wanted to regulate their slaves' intake of alcohol and evade the deleterious effects of the bottle, bondpeople frequently drank on their own terms—when and where they pleased, for reasons and in quantities they chose. As the collective regulators of much of their own alcohol consumption, slaves tolerated drinking—and drinking to excess—on some occasions but hardly allowed the quarters to become sites of uninhibited bacchanal. At a quilting in an Oglethorpe County, Georgia, slave quarter, a drunken bondman jumped on a quilt some enslaved women had hung on a frame, bringing the apparatus crashing to the floor. Singing religious hymns as they labored together, the hard-working bondwomen suddenly changed their tune. They "all got fightin' mad at 'im," locking the intoxicated slave in the smokehouse until the next morning in retribution for his drunken foolishness. Yet despite slaves' vigilance over family, friends, and acquaintances, inebriated bondpeople sometimes harmed one another, just as masters feared.[53]

Alcohol was featured at many impromptu gatherings of slaves. One night in January 1811, "the negro boys and men" owned by Monroe County, Virginia, master Oliver Ewing drank "some spirits made of the Pumice of Apples" with slaves belonging to owner Lane Paterson. Assembled in the kitchen, the slaves invited Ewing "to Drink of the Liquor," but he declined and went to bed. When a noise jolted him awake, he proceeded to the kitchen and discovered that Moses had stabbed his slaves Jerry and Will, the latter mortally. Moses, "when intoxicated with Liquor," was reportedly "quarrelsome and apt to give bad language," having previously threatened to kill Will, others of Ewing's slaves, and "the Black family Generally." That night, according to one slave present when the drinking commenced, "Moses appeared to be angry" and, wielding "a large pen knife," warned Will, "I will rip you." Will replied, "you are a small man[.] I won't strike or trouble you." Raising his hand, he told Moses, probably with a nod toward his fist, "if I was to throw this at you, I would not Value your Knife." Philles, a female slave busy "Spinning" during the dispute, "did not Observe [what] began the affray" but believed Moses and Will had a falling out "about grain."[54]

Many former slaves fondly recalled Saturday or Sunday night parties, or frolics, where they danced and ate, courted and commiserated, in the precious few hours between the end of work on Saturday and the beginning of the new work week early Monday morning. Male and female slaves took the opportunity to escape the stresses of work, have fun, and perhaps pursue a sweetheart. Some, including an ex-slave in Texas, denied that any "fightin'" took place at the parties; others conceded that fighting for entertainment broke out, but the participants "didn't do no killin'." "Some times at de dance, dere was a fight," acknowledged a Tennessee-born slave removed to Texas. "'Twas always a fair fight," however, "'cause we uns not 'lows tudder kind. W'en one nigger gits down, an' hollers, 'Calf Rope,' den we uns makes de udder fellah quit." The self-imposed rules of slaves' carousing typically kept dangerously violent behaviors in check. But, remembered one slave, "[d]e good times wuz mixed at times wid a little truble or 'citement." An ex-slave from Simpson County, Mississippi recalled how, at square dances, slaves "would git to fightin' . . . [and] tie up and fight lack mad dogs." Aware of masters' disapprobation, they knew to wage their battles in secret.[55]

At some frolics, however, alcohol impaired slaves' judgment, prompting violent quarrels that dampened the festivities. One fight led to the premature breaking up of some Anderson District, South Carolina, slaves' Christmas dance in 1855. A sizeable crowd of enslaved revelers dispersed, heading toward their respective homes. Most of the partygoers had likely been drinking at the ball, causing tempers to flare, and "several fracuses" erupted on the road that night.[56]

One frolic at the Fauquier County, Virginia, dwelling of the free mulatto woman Maria Brown turned deadly in 1857. The bondman Richard, also identified as Dick, or Dick Gray, the property of wealthy planter Alexander S. Campbell, allegedly struck Simeon D. Armstrong's slave Edmond on the head with a stick, inflicting a mortal wound. Although their masters lived in the same vicinity, the two slaves were reportedly "not acquainted," and Brown had "heard of no quarrel before that night." Rather, the dance at Brown's set the stage for the deadly encounter. News of the murder rippled through the crowd, immediately spoiled the evening's festivities, and sent the enslaved partygoers scattering. For her part, Brown had been "raised in Salem," Virginia, but "was under bad character and had to leave" under pressure of the community. Based on census records from 1860, Brown was about twenty-seven years old in 1857, an impoverished, illiterate mother of three young girls, roughly the ages of five, three, and one. She eked out a living washing and ironing the clothes of paying customers. As court records revealed, Brown also hosted "negro dances" in her home, a possible factor in her ouster from Salem. One white Virginian complained that area blacks were there "dancing all the time." Brown claimed that she did not intend to hold a party the evening of the murder, but when two local slave fiddlers and others "asked me to let them have a little fun," she consented to their use of her dwelling. One slave attendee contradicted his mulatto host, however, when he stated that he had "heard on the street that there was to be a party or dancing" at Brown's that night. Word must have spread quickly, for "the house was full." The presence of "some girls" surely helped draw a crowd.[57]

Brown did not allow simply any passerby to attend her parties. When two whites, Jonathan Dillard Baker and his one-eyed brother William Baker, requested entry the evening of the murder, Brown informed them, "it was no place for white men." Even when Jonathan "offered her a quarter to let him in," the mulatto woman refused, recommending him "to go among his own color." "[W]hite people & colored must not mix," Jonathan recollected Maria saying. He denied in court having ever been to "a negro dance before," stating "it was whiskey that carried me there . . . Whiskey was bigger than I was, was stronger than I was, [and I] felt . . . devilish and rich." Humbled by a free mulatto woman, Jonathan "[c]omplained of Maria not letting us in," finding it "hard for negroes to be let in & we kept out," but the Baker brothers were not alone in their exclusion. Brown refused entry to the youthful William S. Melton as well. Like the Bakers, Melton—also white—insisted in court, "It is not my habit to go to these negro dances." He claimed never to have attended one before and denied any interest in the frolic at Brown's. He merely happened upon the party, "heard the music & stopped." He did admit, however, that the night of the murder he "was pretty tolerable drunk" and "hot & stupid," but, he clarified, "not too stupid to know what was going on." He "was not so drunk that I could not stand up. I could walk" and "get on without help," he further specified, "but it was pretty much of a bargain." According to Maria Brown, "Mr. Melton cracked at the door & asked me to let him in" for twenty-five cents. "I would not let him or the Bakers in," she explained, reiterating her belief that "white & black must not mix." "I did not want any of the white people in the house," she admitted frankly.[58]

During Dick's trial for the murder of Edmond, Melton, who so meticulously described his degree of inebriation, emerged as the most important witness for the prosecution, despite being a "boy, drunk & the associate of negroes." Loitering near the entrance to Maria Brown's home, he "heard Edmund say if any one pestered him he would run a knife in him" "to his heart." In Melton's telling, Dick seemingly took Edmond's pronouncement as a dare. The slave "said he would knock him in the head," picked up a stick, whacked Edmond on the skull, and ran away. "I am positive that Dick was the man who struck the blow," Melton declared. Two white men, both prominent local physicians, challenged Melton's courtroom recollections. They had each heard him say that "he was drunk and asleep sitting on the bank" when "people rushing out [of] the house hollowing waked him up." "I was not asleep but . . . most miserably sick," Melton averred. "I was sitting down with my head down."[59]

Maria Brown shed greater light on the events that transpired. A number of people "were knocking at the door," she explained, "and I said to Edmond, I wish to the Lord you would not let them Knock the door down." Edmond pledged not to let that happen, agreeing to serve as a bouncer of sorts. "I will stop them," he vowed, "let them be white or black." Stationing himself in the doorway as gatekeeper to the party, Edmond offended Dick. As Brown explained, "Dick did not try to get in"; rather, he waited outdoors for his enslaved friend Bob, who was inside at the frolic. Patiently biding his time, Dick planned to travel the road home in company with Bob since their masters' plantations lay less than a mile apart. Edmond may have misconstrued Dick's lingering presence near the entrance to Maria Brown's, thinking he was one of the culprits banging on Brown's door. "By God did you say that I knocked at the door," Dick asked. Replied Edmond, "not no more than any body else." "By God," Dick responded, "I have as much right to take it up as any body else." These shreds of conversation provide the only clues to the motivation behind the murder of Edmond. If Dick was actually guilty (and there was some dispute over the color of the perpetrator's "pantaloons"), court records hint that he resented an insinuation by another slave that he demanded entrance to Maria Brown's party.[60]

As their frolics suggest, slaves' favorite pastimes often provided fertile ground in which violence took root. Gambling ranked among the more popular leisure-time pursuits of enslaved men across the South. Bondmen usually wagered their money and property in contests held on Saturday nights or Sundays. Mississippi's Primous Magee recalled going "deep in de woods many a time" to shoot craps "all night" with fellow bondmen. A fellow Mississippi slave "obtained ... Jewelry from a negro man by gambling one night ... west of Aberdeen." As with corn shuckings and frolics, violence was often the natural by-product of such gambling and nocturnal carousing. Occasionally, Magee confessed, there "would be a disagreement wid a few fights." One Saturday night in 1843, a number of slaves had been quaffing spirituous liquor and gambling in a Mississippi "negro-house" when the festivities raged out of control. Solomon and Moses ran in circles around an oak tree as Solomon slashed at his opponent with a knife and swore "he would kill Moses, if he was the last negro in the world." By morning, however, it was Solomon whose corpse was found, "a knife lying by his hands." A "majority" of slaves on one Trimble County, Kentucky, plantation went to local towns on the weekends to "drink, gamble and fight." Slaves' fleeting taste of liberty at the conclusion of the work week, their ability to travel and pursue leisurely pastimes, and a relative lack of physical exhaustion on Sundays meant that the Sabbath more than any other day played host to gaming contests among slaves that culminated in violence. In the South Carolina upcountry, Spartanburg District slaves "Will & Charles was Gamling and Bet money on cards on the sabbath" when a fight broke out between them over the "50 cts down."[61]

Some disputes at the gaming table merely provided the pretense for settling long-simmering feuds. One winter Saturday in 1834, "about 20 Colored people" (but "only two or three women") congregated at a "negro dance" in Kanawha County, Virginia. Armed with a deck of cards, the bondman Harry "proposed to play a game ... called 'spots'" with the slave Sam Hancock. As they played on a barrel, a dispute erupted between them, and Harry brandished a knife. A third bondman, Dennis, quickly interceded. Dennis may have appeared to want to keep tempers in check, but he had ulterior motives for stepping in. As one slave reported, an "old grudge" between Dennis and Harry dated back to the previous Christmas, and the original minor disagreement between Sam and Harry morphed into a major conflict between Harry and Dennis. Complaining to Sam that Harry "ought not to have" drawn the knife, Dennis ordered Harry to close it, or "I'll knock you down." Sam then adopted the role of peacemaker, telling Dennis to "hush it up and say no more about it" and advising Harry to go home, since "he had transgressed in drawing his knife." Against Sam's counsel, Harry stayed and was sitting before the fire when Dennis came up from behind and delivered an unexpected blow to the head or neck. Despite the intervention of a white man, Harry drew his blade and sliced Dennis's "belly," spilling his intestines. In this case, the original dispute over the game had virtually nothing to do with the murder; it merely unleashed long simmering, pent-up rage unrelated to the cards or the bets.[62]

More commonly, gaming violence had everything to do with the cards on the table or the roll of the dice. Whether because they were bad sports or because they made injudicious wagers and lacked the means to settle up, slaves sometimes refused to pay when they lost. In Spartanburg District, South Carolina, bondmen Martin and Jim "were playing for Pocket Book & cards" in 1857: "Jim won the pile & Martin kept the cards & Jim collard Martin," prompting a brawl that concluded with Jim's death. Nearby, another affray broke out among several slaves gaming in the proximity of Anderson District's First Creek Meeting House in 1858. Probably because the slave Berry lost it in a wager, bondmen Jink and Joseph seized Berry's coat. A "scuffle" ensued in which Jink struck Berry "three licks." The "quarrel about a coat" earned Jink fifteen lashes and Joe twenty-five for "Riotous & Disorderly conduct." The "free negro" Powhatan Scott of Rockbridge County, Virginia, recounted that one Tuesday night in October 1853 he had boarded a boat in which the slaves Jim Gooch and Sam "were sitting under the tent playing cards." After playing two or three games of seven up, Sam had won "ninepence" and "a quarter of a shoat" from Gooch, who failed to surrender the property he had wagered. Fully expecting to receive the tangible rewards for his victories, Sam announced, "I am done playing without you put up the money." For Sam, triumph seemed less sweet if he had to keep a mental tally of what the luckless Gooch owed him. Gooch "would not pay him," he later told a white man, because he disputed the outcome of the hand. In actuality, the slave had risked property not in his possession. He and Sam "went round the tent," when Gooch, desperately hoping to recoup his losses, offered to play for an unidentified "something in his chest." Sam's good fortune continued, however, and he won the mystery good as well. Gooch invited Sam to "come round here and I give you the thing out of the chest." When Sam approached the chest, Gooch explained that "the thing was not in the chest" or that *"that something* was gone." (He later admitted that he was trying to cheat Sam.) Growing increasingly impatient, Sam replied, "if the thing is not here I will get the chest." Gooch objected: "you can't carry that chest out from here." But Sam insisted, "I will take it out." In the ensuing fray over the chest, Gooch stabbed Sam with a knife that he carried to defend himself from attacks by "wild varmints." Despite the efforts to save Sam's life, the slave's run of good luck at last came to an end. "[D]amn it," Gooch said prophetically, "I will be hung for him." The court that convicted him of Sam's murder refused to recommend him to the mercy of the governor, and he was executed as he predicted.[63]

Although they belonged to different masters, Jim Gooch and Sam were acquainted through the rough and masculine world of riverine commerce. Gooch had plied Virginia's inland waterways for some time. Thomas Smith, a manager on the North River Canal, had known the bondman for fifteen years. Gooch's master routinely hired him out, and several of the bondman's former and current employers spoke highly of him. Gooch had worked for Aaron D. Rhodes since 1848, during which time, Rhodes explained, he was "the easiest managed negro he ever had anything to do with." Hudson Marks, a manager of boats on the James River & Kanawha Canal, had only known Gooch since Christmas 1852 but nevertheless concurred. John R. Buchanan, who directed Gooch the year of the murder, called him "one of the most humble & biddable negroes that he ever had." Another white riverman added that, in his five or six years' acquaintance, Gooch had proven a "peaceable negro." Several of Gooch's employers admitted, however, that the slave "would drink sometimes, and gamble sometimes . . .

[and] sometimes quarrel with the other hands in the boats." Much the same could be said of Sam. He, too, enjoyed drinking and gambling. His master "never saw him drunk" and thought "his general character was good" but once whipped him when he caught him gambling. One white riverman reported that his slaves believed Sam "overbearing," and he had once "driven him off from his boat." The only possible indication of any preexisting hostility between Sam and Gooch took place on a Saturday two or three weeks prior to Sam's death. According to a free black cooper named Edward Nash, Gooch was quarreling with the enslaved Harry Hunt during a meeting of the presbytery at Falling Spring Church. Sam injected himself into their dispute, telling Gooch to "go sit down and behave yourself." Sam had no direct interest in the matter, but as he explained to Gooch, "I don't like to see an old man like you going about and meddling with things of the account." Flashing an open switchblade knife before tucking it in his pocket, Gooch informed Sam that "if he meddled with him, he would kill him." Harry Hunt recalled that Gooch told Sam that he "was a better man than he was," "that he intended to kill him," "and that seven years was not too long in time to do it in"—incriminating evidence suggesting premeditation.[64]

A majority of all slaves possessed little money and owned precious few material goods, so to lose them gambling could be a devastating blow. Some even wagered more than they had to lose. As a result, some slaves were unprepared to accept the verdict of the cards on the table. Alabama planter Daniel R. Hundley marveled at how readily slaves killed one another over a simple "dispute about a game at cards or marbles." But for slaves, the matter was not always as "trivial" as Hundley claimed. To be sure, most bondpeople took defeat in stride. In the spring of 1859, for example, Amherst County, Virginia, slaves Jefferson and Alfred "commenced playing cards in the wood lot." Jefferson quickly reconciled himself to the fact that Alfred "won 10 cents from me." But not all slaves were such gracious losers. The same day Jefferson gambled away his dime, he and Alfred joined with three other slaves—Norvell, Henry, and Jefferson's co-worker on the railroad John Red—to play cards in a stable, or "cow house." Jefferson departed to complete some wage work for Henry, but the remaining four bondmen "played 3 or 4 hours." As their game progressed, John Red and Alfred "had a scuffle" or "little quarrel," seemingly resolved when Red produced "a tickler of liquor" he had recently purchased. As Henry reported, the slaves "took a drink & made friends & continued playing cards." At some point, however, Alfred won Red's hat. Red pledged to "retake it." Until then, "Alfred put it back on his head" and the game resumed. Presumably the combination of liquor, resentment over losing his treasured hat, and failing to reacquire it prompted Red to violently and fatally assault the new owner of his headwear.[65]

Dancing, drinking, and gambling: the most significant leisure-time pursuits correlated with violent conflicts among slaves all fell under the scrutiny of southern evangelical churches. More than any other religious faith in the antebellum South, Baptists imposed strictures against a range of earthly pleasures and demanded the vigilant monitoring of churchgoers' private lives. The behavioral restrictions implemented by southern Baptist churches, although enforced inequitably, applied to all members and did not target black congregants specifically. Beaverdam Baptist Church in Wilkes County, Georgia, condemned all "card playing for amusement" as "an eavel." In nearby Hancock County, Powelton Baptist Church determined that "purchasing... Lottery Tickets" qualified "as a Species of Gambling not to be authorized or encouraged by us." Various Baptist churches also condemned keeping racehorses, betting on horse races, attending the theater or circus, playing billiards or backgammon, and bowling. Prohibitions against a full spectrum of worldly entertainments asked much of Baptist congregants, and the level of asceticism demanded of them took its toll on some. When "Sister Fanny Cook," a white woman in Virginia, severed her ties to the Baptist Church in 1842, she explained that, by departing, "she thought she could enjoy herself better."[66]

Baptist churches disciplined spiritually wayward whites more often than blacks for violating theological directives against behaviors that much of society accepted as normative and regarded as fun. In the slave South, white members of Baptist churches were charged with drinking or intoxication more frequently than any other offense. Fewer bondpeople were excluded on grounds of alcohol consumption. Church disciplinary committees also penalized whites far more frequently than blacks for violating prohibitions against gaming.[67] Black and white congregants alike were subject to disciplinary action for failing to abide by musical taboos. Churches most commonly censured slave members for the sin of playing the violin. In 1861, York District, South Carolina, slave Jefferson was restored to Flint Hill Baptist Church only after "[h]e promised to lay aside his fiddle."[68] Black churchgoers were sometimes excluded for "singing corn songs" as well, but more often, with a sincere acknowledgment of wrongdoing, congregations forgave that musical infraction.[69]

Countless Baptist churches throughout the South also issued harsh resolutions denouncing dancing as a sin of the flesh and threatened the expulsion of members who either engaged in that worldly pastime or held dances in their homes.[70] Strictures against dancing disproportionately targeted widows and other poor white female churchgoers who, struggling economically, often fell under suspicion for operating "disorderly houses" where drinking, dancing, and illicit sexual activity took place.[71] But they also led to investigations of black churchgoers. In November 1813, Darien Baptist Church in Hancock County, Georgia, expelled a black member for boldly proclaiming that "he me[a]nt to go to all the frolicks he could hear of and do worse." He fully intended "to play the devil." Powelton Baptist dispatched three white men in July 1841 "to investigate a report of our coloured Sister Battle's Edith having had a dance at her house, and Bledsoe's Mourning for attending the same." Both were apparently excluded but restored to membership the following September. Occasionally slaves exposed their own to public view. At Rehoboth Baptist Church in Wilkes County, Georgia, B. A. Arnett's bondman Peter charged Rebecca and Peggy, two other Arnett slaves, "with dancing and other sins." Both were expelled in 1855. In the end, church oversight did little to quell slaves' interests in drinking, gambling, and dancing or the violence that sometimes marred those normally convivial pastimes.[72]

In the Old South, masters exercised ultimate authority over slaves' time. The hours devoted to labor vastly outnumbered those dedicated to recreation, but whether at work, play, or an event such as a corn shucking that fused elements of both, the possibility of violence loomed. In the precious time they made their own, late at night and on weekends, many slaves danced and frolicked, gambled and drank. The prevalence of alcohol fueled violence as it loosened slaves' inhibitions and invited them to vent frustrations upon one another. Although much of the violence that erupted was not premeditated or malicious in its intent, it was nonetheless damaging to enslaved bodies. Many masters who abhorred violence among their bondpeople ironically promoted physical aggression, especially among male slaves, from an early age. Whether arranging fights on the plantation or wrestling matches with neighbors' slaves, masters were complicit in encouraging violent behaviors. Knowingly or not, owners also set bondpeople to work with other slaves whose personalities clashed, and the practice of hiring out in some cases landed slaves among strangers with no emotional bonds or connections to them at all. When one slave cared more deeply about and took pride in the work in which a number of bondpeople were engaged, it was only natural that disputes erupted over how best to finish the job assigned. And when owners relied upon slaves to monitor and govern their own or to serve as auxiliaries of masterly authority, restraining fellow bondpeople for a whipping, apprehending fugitives, or protecting slaveholder property, conflicts were unavoidable. Slaves grappled with tremendous internal tensions when ordered to collaborate in the oppression of a friend, family member, or other enslaved acquaintance. Slaves were not merely malleable property of the master's will but people filled with a constellation of conflicting emotions. Just as one slave struggled between obedience to the master and betrayal of a fellow slave, another vacillated between running to freedom and inflicting harm on a slave loyal to the master. The institution of bondage itself bred the conditions that gave rise to violence in the quarters.

Chapter 5

VIOLENCE AND THE SLAVE ECONOMY

DURING THE CIVIL WAR, Henry, an enslaved blacksmith in Albany, Georgia, killed "his striker or apprentice," a bondman named Gilbert, who had worked at the shop for two years. Henry thought himself "foreman of the shop" and believed Gilbert "under his control." When the keys to the shop and stable went missing, Henry accused Gilbert of stealing them. To force Gilbert to surrender the keys, Henry employed a ruse. He asked Gilbert "if he had change for five dollars." Uncertain whether he did, Gilbert "pulled out his money to look." Henry quickly "snatched three dollars from him," promising to return Gilbert's money when the keys resurfaced. That the clever attempt to extort the keys from Gilbert failed bolstered the striker's claim that he had not taken them. Nevertheless, Henry continued to insist upon Gilbert's guilt. The evening of their deadly encounter, Henry and Gilbert quarreled so loudly that their argument could be heard from across the street. Henry, who had been drinking and was seen staggering about, resolved to whip Gilbert "for stealing the shop keys." To administer the punishment, Henry employed an unconventional choice for correction: an axe helve. The one or two blows that he delivered to Gilbert's head were sufficient to render Gilbert mute and kill him a little more than a day later. Henry fled but soon returned voluntarily. Dougherty County Superior Court found him guilty of murder.[1]

The Georgia homicide of the slave Gilbert raises several related questions. Among them, how had the slave Henry come to think of a shop and a set of keys as his, rather than as the property of his master? By what process had a fellow slave been transformed into an employee Henry felt at liberty to reprimand? How had Gilbert accumulated a wad of cash to thumb through to see if he could make change? How had Henry secured alcohol sufficient to cause inebriation? And where was the master throughout this ordeal? Extant sources permit an answer to at least the last question. Henry and Gilbert both belonged to the estate of Davis Pace, a prominent planter and one-time mayor of Albany who had died in 1861. Gilbert had only made John A. Davis, supervisor of the deceased's estate, aware "that Henry had three dollars of his money" earlier in the evening of their fatal affray. Davis assured Gilbert that "he would see that he got his money, and

... whip Henry besides." Pace may have invested Henry with sufficient latitude to run the blacksmith shop that the slave imagined himself its owner and proprietor, which in turn would help explain his rage over the keys. But on the night of the murder, Henry was on the cusp of receiving his comeuppance via Davis's lash. Lurking behind Gilbert's demise, then, were bondmen's unconventional working lives, the significance they attached to theft, and, more broadly still, the functioning of the slave economy.[2]

Although bondpeople did not reap the just rewards from their labor, many navigated their working lives in ways that allowed them to accumulate property. Slaves were prohibited from property ownership by law, but despite formal restrictions, many masters permitted them to acquire goods of their own. Although virtually all slaves remained poor, property ownership was widespread among the enslaved population. Across the South, an extensive informal slave economy allowed slaves opportunities to work for themselves. Especially in the Carolina and Georgia lowcountry, masters gave bondpeople access to land upon which they planted gardens to feed their families and grow surplus produce for sale at market. Even under gang labor regimes in tobacco and cotton fields, where work from sunup to sundown was customary, slaves used part of Saturday, Sundays, and holidays to work for the benefit of themselves and their families. Skilled slaves accepted side jobs or took advantage of opportunities for overwork in the evenings and on weekends. Slaves who were hired out or the exclusive few who hired out their own time enjoyed the flexibility to earn money, as did industrial slaves who performed extra work, such as sweeping a floor, at the end of the day. Enterprising slaves throughout the South either earned a modest wage or committed their time, at the sacrifice of rest, sleep, and recreation, to produce various goods and wares that they sold or exchanged on the home plantation, in the local neighborhood, along southern roads and waterways, or in urban markets. Fellow bondpeople, masters, and non-slaveholding whites all participated in the trading networks of southern slaves. Southern Claims Commission records attest to the quantities of property slaves were successfully able to accumulate.[3]

Scholarship on slaves' internal economy blossomed in the 1980s and 1990s, beginning with a pioneering pair of articles from Philip D. Morgan. Most historians who studied the economic activities of those in bondage and the property they accumulated through their own efforts emphasized overwhelmingly the independence, autonomy, and empowerment engendered by the slave economy. Lawrence T. McDonnell was the first scholar to caution against thinking about slaves' economic activities in unabashedly positive terms. Dylan Penningroth and Kathleen Hilliard have also recognized the ambivalence inherent in the slave economy.[4] For all of its material benefits, property ownership among bondpeople led to the stratification of slave society and contributed to divisions within the slave community. Some masters more than others granted bondpeople the latitude to pursue independent or semi-independent economic activities. As such, slaves on neighboring plantations might live at noticeably different levels of material comfort. Moreover, the initiative and energy of individual slaves and the collective efforts of enslaved families or households produced disparate degrees of wealth within a single plantation. Bondpeople readily recognized the inequitable distribution of wealth among their number. Money and possessions might confer status and buy the respect of fellow slaves, but they also could also generate envy and antipathy. Those bondpeople who were less economically successful sometimes resented those who had accumulated more or better consumer goods. By creating "haves" and "have-nots" within the quarters, slaves' participation in market activities as both producers and consumers exposed the boundaries and limitations of the slave community. As white observer and Presbyterian minister Charles Colcock Jones of Georgia recognized, "Families grow jealous and envious of their neighbors" as "some essay to be *leading* families."[5]

Dylan Penningroth has offered the most sophisticated portrait of the ways in which disputes over property and property ownership undermined slaves' sense of community. Because slaves' ownership of property lacked legal standing, their claims to property remained tenuous and subject to challenge. Ownership required the validation of other bondpeople. Slaves often displayed their property not simply out of pride (although they may have been justifiably proud of their economic accomplishments) but to gain public acknowledgment from whites and other blacks that their property belonged to them. Publicly showcasing one's possessions created a mutual understanding of who owned what. The need for public affirmation underscored the social relations inherent in slaves' claims to property. To claim livestock or hogs as their own, slaves might brand them or engage in acts of public enumeration, counting them out loud in the presence of others who might dare contend with them for ownership. Slaves' disputes over property, Penningroth observed, sometimes prompted verbal disagreements and "loud talk" in defense of their possessions. Curiously, Penningroth's work stopped short of discussing the physically violent acts those same arguments inspired. Yet property disputes engendered tremendous passions within slaves, whose own initiative and hard work helped them achieve ownership of consumer goods in spite of their own status as property and the lawful neglect of their claims. Justifiably proud of their economic accomplishments yet legally insecure about their possessions, slaves used violence against other bondpeople in the quarters to enforce their asserted rights to property.[6]

A sizeable portion of the violent encounters among bondpeople originated in property disputes and the workings of the informal slave economy. Slaves came to blows over the possession of property, the issue of theft in the quarters, the repayment of debts they owed to one another, and the breakdown of functional economic relationships. That many violent confrontations among bondpeople had their source in disagreements over property holds implications for historians' understanding of both the slave economy and the slave community. Although positive in many respects, the internal economy also prompted conflicts disruptive to the harmony and solidarity of the slave quarters. But for most slaves, whatever commodities they claimed as their own were precious indeed and very much worth defending.

Slaves highly prized the property they claimed. Although many bondpeople owned property, the vast majority owned very little, making it that much more significant to them. Conflicts over property began as early as the Middle Passage itself. Aboard westbound slaving vessels traversing the Atlantic from Africa, recorded ship surgeon Alexander Falconbridge in the late eighteenth century, the captive "women are furnished with beads for the purpose of affording them some diversion. But this end is generally defeated by the squabbles which are occasioned, in consequence of their stealing them from each other." Property was no less important to slaves in the mature slave society of the mid-nineteenth century. When fatally attacked by a fellow bondman in Baldwin County, Alabama, one slave, aware of his imminent death, with his last breaths "directed his fellow-servants what to do with the little effects he had." In his dying moments he thought about his property, the few belongings that he had accumulated over the course of a lifetime. In the absence of a lawful will—something unavailable to slaves—he expended his last ounce of energy verbally distributing his hard-earned possessions. He was not alone. Many slaves bequeathed property to friends and family. The material goods an enslaved parent struggled to amass, perhaps over a span of decades, might well be passed down as an inheritance to the next generation of enslaved laborer, assuming the slave community acknowledged the deceased's right to dispense with the property in question.[7]

The single commodity over which slaves most frequently came to blows was clothing, and the usual combatants over apparel were enslaved women. Several scholars have noted the social and cultural significance of bondpeople's raiment, especially to female slaves. The workaday attire of enslaved women, sewn of drab, coarse "negro cloth," generated virtually no conflicts among them. Disputes erupted, rather, over fancier attire, possibly passed down secondhand or bought for them new by the plantation mistress, or purchased or traded for through their own efforts or those of an enslaved husband or sweetheart. Young bondwomen wanted to look and feel attractive for possible slave suitors. When they attended illicit dance parties deep in the woods, they wore fancy dresses, fixed their hair, and adorned their bodies with jewelry. For enslaved women, fashionable displays that incorporated their own aesthetic flourishes signified personal expressions of femininity and, by extension, humanity. The symbolic importance attached to material goods such as elaborate dresses and other relatively upscale garments, combined with their scarcity in the quarters, made these possessions all the more valuable to enslaved women and certainly worth fighting over. In Elbert County, Georgia, Adeline alleged that Zilla "took some of her under coats and things," a charge Zilla denied. Supporting her accusation, Adeline reclaimed a prized cape, "which she said was hers," from Zilla's house. Hoping to restore peace, Zilla's "husband promised to carry back the under coat." Copiah County, Mississippi, slave woman Lucretia Alexander treasured "a nice pair of stockings from the store" her mistress had bought her. After wearing them once, Alexander related, "I washed them and put them on the fence to dry." When another female slave, Martha, "stole them and put them on, "I beat her and took them off of her." Martha may have made an innocent mistake. On some plantations, masters thought of slave clothing as communally owned, and slaves shared a common wardrobe. Alexander and most other bondpeople, however, assigned possession to individual slaves, even when masters did not. Another Mississippi slave, a "spirited" girl named Emily Dixon, quarreled over the exclusive possession of her clothing. Just as she disliked having to don other slaves' outfits, she "did not want any ob de res' to wear my dresses." Those who did faced the wrath of the scrappy Dixon and her brother. During the Civil War, Charles Preston Ware, a Boston missionary to the Sea Islands of South Carolina, observed that female slaves sparred over the clothing left behind by plantation mistresses who had fled the advancing Union army. Ware heard them say as they quarreled, "I as much right to ole missus' things as you." Clothing itself sometimes fell victim to spats between enslaved women. In August 1863, Ware's kinswoman Harriet, a fellow missionary, reported with a tone of moral condemnation that female slaves "tore each other's clothes in a most disgraceful way, much to the mortification of the better part of the community." Tears and ripped stitching might damage a beloved dress beyond repair and diminish the carefully cultivated appearance of the enslaved woman who took pride in wearing it.[8]

Female raiment sometimes became a flashpoint for marital unrest in the quarters. Recalling her girlhood while enslaved in Mississippi, one woman remembered that her "mammy got mad 'caus'n pappy slipped her clo'es out'n her ches'." The mother's anger was only exacerbated when her husband delivered the garments "to de other gals fer to dance in." Upon his return, the spurned wife did "fight him." Issues of marital fidelity motivated a similar conflict on James Chesnut's plantation in South Carolina. Chesnut's cook, Molly, used a "red-hot poker" to attack "a negro woman her husband Lige had given *one of Molly's calico frocks.*" After knocking the woman down, Molly "proceeded to burn the frock off her back with the red-hot poker." A conflict between two female slaves over an enslaved man on the Charlotte County, Virginia, holding of George J. H. Roberts underscored apparel's significance in the world of enslaved women. Accused of an affair with the victim's husband, the bondwoman Harriett beat about the head with a hoe and strangled to death a hired slave named Matilda. The forty-five-year-old Matilda, well past her physical prime, no longer labored in the fields. She instead lived in the same dwelling as Roberts and engaged in spinning for him as she watched the younger Harriett's child during the workday. One Thursday in September 1864, Roberts left his plantation, and by Friday word had somehow reached him that "Matilda was missing." He returned home on Sunday and discovered Matilda's corpse lying facedown in the mud, almost completely naked. "She had no clothes on except a pair of stockings," Roberts recalled.[9]

Clothing was deeply entwined in the enslaved women's conflict. Tellingly, Roberts found Matilda's body in the nude, the "pair of stockings" notwithstanding. Still more incriminating, "some of Matilda's clothes . . . were found in Harriett's chest." The garments discovered there "were her Sunday clothes," including a "blue muslin dress" as well as "some under clothes, two pillow cases with buttons on them, and a pair of Sunday shoes." Matilda's son Henry, who searched Harriett's house, added that, among "a good many of Mother's clothes," he identified "two underskirts, two pair of stockings, . . . a chemise, two handkerchiefs, and some pins" that belonged to her. The "pair of Mother's shoes" was actually found "sewed up in Harriett's bed tick." Slaves also located in Harriett's home Matilda's knife, secreted "behind a cupboard" and lying on Matilda's new "pocket," a pouch that sported a recognizable "border . . . woven in the cloth." Like many slaves, Henry kept a meticulous mental tally of not only his own possessions but also those of other bondpeople. According to another slave, named John, "Harriett never helped Matilda to wash her clothes that I know of," so the accumulated material evidence against Harriett could not be casually dismissed as clean laundry. Perhaps, however, Matilda and Harriett shared various articles of clothing and exchanged them freely, a practice that would have effectively multiplied enslaved women's limited wardrobes. "Aunt Matilda was in the habit of trading Harriett's clothes," John conceded, but "Matilda never lent Harriett but one dress that I know of, . . . the same dress that was found in Harriett's chest." He knew, though, that "Harriett had carried it back to Matilda after she [last] borrowed it." Many of the other items discovered in Harriett's quarters had no business there. For example, John explained, "I never knew [Matilda] to lend her under clothes." However frequently enslaved women swapped items of clothing, they refrained from sharing underwear. All doubt about Harriett's guilt was erased when the slaves taking stock of her dwelling found the murder weapon, a hoe caked with "black mud." Homicide was not Harriett's only crime; the greed that compelled her to strip the deceased's body and rob Matilda of her property provided the evidence necessary to secure her conviction.[10]

Enslaved men fought over clothing much less frequently than did enslaved women. The intoxicated bondman Sam of Greenbrier County, Virginia, stabbed another slave who "tore his jacket" in 1824. In the absence of alcohol, however, the infraction probably would not have seemed worthy of death. Two Chesterfield County bondmen began quarreling in 1842 after "Fleming called John's handkerchief an old rag." John resented the seemingly petty slight, and since Fleming had a preexisting "old grudge" toward him, their hostile exchange sparked Fleming's fatal assault upon John "with a table fork." The accessory about which enslaved men appeared the most sensitive was their hats. In Richmond, the slave Charles Johnson took great offense when the free black Henry Thacker cut the bondman's hat "all to pieces" with a switchblade. A more serious, deadly encounter took place on the waters off Virginia's Eastern Shore in 1816. In late May, Northampton County slaves Matthew and Ben had a falling out over a hat that Matthew commandeered from Ben. After a brief fight, Matthew, still in possession of the hat, climbed into a canoe, accompanied by two other blacks. With a parting vow to make Ben "sip sorrow by ladles full," Matthew and his compatriots paddled well offshore and began fishing. Ben, with one other fellow slave, pursued "in another canoe & demanded his hat." Matthew "peremptorily refused to deliver up" the headwear. Using a fish gig—a long spear with multiple prongs on the end—Ben attempted to snag his hat out of Matthew's canoe, but Matthew repeatedly repelled him with a gaff hook, the pole with a hook on the end that fishermen use to hoist large fish out of the water. Still clutching the fish gig, Ben "declared that he would have his hat or die in the attempt," at which point Matthew clocked him with a "heavy oak paddle." The force of the blow propelled Ben into the deep water, and he drowned.[11]

Rather than hats or any other apparel, the form of property enslaved men most frequently fought over was various foodstuffs. Enslaved men often went to great lengths to contribute food to their family's diet. In some cases, especially where the task system predominated and slaves enjoyed access to garden plots, masters expected slaves to grow or secure the bulk of their own sustenance. More often, slaves' provisioning efforts supplemented the typically meager and monotonous rations allotted by masters. The initial dispute between Northampton County's Matthew and Ben concerned "some crabs" that Ben "had in his possession" but Matthew "claimed" as his. Each wanted the delectable crustaceans, either for food or as a market commodity to sell. When Matthew attempted to seize the crabs, Ben administered "several blows," which Matthew returned. Only after their terrestrial fray did they board their respective canoes to engage in their lethal maritime battle over the hat. In another case, two blacks, one free and one slave, hired in Warwick County, Virginia, got into a scrape over meat in 1860. For reasons that are not clear, the free black George Owens had possession of the slave Caesar Old's meat, and when the bondman asked for it, Owens refused. Owens believed of the meat that "somebody had cut it," suggesting that Caesar had already sliced a portion that did not belong to him. As for the rest, Owens "meant to keep it." The pair grappled with one another, rolling down a hill before being separated. Soon afterward, Caesar, described as about fifty years old, "a small & slender man," and "a quiet & timid negro," bested the much younger, larger, and stronger Owens by beating him to death with a stave billet. In West Florida's Escambia County, another conflict over meat resulted in the fatal 1821 shooting of Sarah McNeil's bondman Harry. McNeil had dispatched her slave on horseback "on some business." When Harry's pony frightened away a squirrel that Henry Wilson's slave Tom, then out hunting, was about to shoot, the irate hunter denied his prey put a bullet in each of Harry's knees. Tom reportedly muttered to Harry that "you scared my squirrel—if it had not been for you I would have killed it": "now I have shot you." Harry lingered long enough to share the story of his painful encounter with Tom before succumbing to his injuries.[12] Slaves clashed over not only protein sources but also carbohydrates. In Monroe County, Virginia, the enslaved men Moses and Will had a dispute "about grain" in 1811, during which "Will threw Moses... in the fire," and Copiah County, Mississippi, bondman Simon confessed that he killed the thirteen-year-old slave Norvall "about some misunderstanding about mollasses."[13]

Enslaved men sparred over possession of a range of commodities. "Jones, a colored man" from Delaware, stabbed a fellow black named Ralston in "a quarrel ... about a lamp." In Rutherford County, Tennessee, the bondman Nelson murdered Sam over a knife. After the slaves finished shucking corn on the property of William H. Blankenship, the company retired "into a shed room to supper." Nelson used "a large pocket knife" or "bailing knife" to carve meat for the assembled slaves, but, overcome by festive drinking, he began "swearing" and carelessly waving the dangerous instrument. Blankenship's son, present at the dinner, seized the knife from him, and Nelson blamed Sam for having it taken away. Nelson vowed "revenge out of him," telling one witness that "he intended to kill Sam if it took him twenty years." It did not take nearly that long for Nelson to avenge the loss of his knife.[14]

Slaves also fought over money. The internal economy did not function along an exclusively or even a predominantly cash nexus, yet cash was very much present in the quarters. In the early nineteenth century, a surprising number of slaves had the opportunity to earn money in payment for work they performed. Much of the initial scholarship on the slave economy described the feelings of independence cash in the hands of bondpeople engendered. More recently, Walter Johnson cautioned that slaves with money were not necessarily psychologically liberated from bondage. Closer investigations of the "meanings of money" in the quarters suggest a more ambivalent portrait of slaves' possession of cash. Slaves might use their money to contribute to local churches, buy goods to support the family, or forge a sense of camaraderie and belonging. In Mississippi, for example, three bondpeople who collaborated to kill their overseer divvied up their victim's money and distributed it to appreciative fellow slaves on the plantation. Yet money might just as easily generate pressures and tensions within the slave community. In Albemarle County, Virginia, William Crenshaw's slaves Moses and Phill begged the bondwoman Maria, a third Crenshaw slave, "for money, for the purpose as they said to buy medicine to poison their master." Maria's enslaved father, John, attempted to convince Crenshaw's bondwoman Betty to taint the master's brandy with the poison, promising her "a nice comb or a half dollar" if she complied. Crenshaw's enslaved men saw cash as a means to achieve a desired end, but not all slaves on the plantation may have been equally eager to participate in the master's demise. How willing was Maria to part with her funds to underwrite the larger project of murder, however despised Crenshaw was? Did Betty feel as though she had a choice whether or not to adulterate the master's liquor? To pursue their goal, a subset of Crenshaw's slaves coerced possibly unwilling bondwomen into spending money and accepting it as payment. Cash circulating in the quarters played an ambiguous role in slaves' interpersonal relationships.[15]

Money contained the very real potential to undermine communal solidarity. Larry E. Hudson Jr. has studied the significance of cash in the slave quarters and its propensity to produce divisions therein. Slaves who accumulated greater sums of cash could parley their money into material goods that other bondpeople lacked the resources to acquire. The infiltration of cash and market values into the quarters thus created visible distinctions of wealth between relatively "rich" and "poor" slaves. Successful slaves could gain status and prestige but also elicit the envy and hostility of other bondpeople. Slaves, observed northern missionary Charles Preston Ware, "will not sit quietly and see another earning all the money." Although neighborly covetousness might motivate slaves to emulate others' success, as an engine of social differentiation, cash had a negative effect on relations among slaves.[16]

Slave dances and frolics demonstrated the exclusionary power of cash. Discrepancies in wealth among slaves, Hudson observed, were especially evident in their personal appearance and during courtship. At parties, slaves showcased their finest clothing and wooed the objects of their desire. Poorer slaves were therefore at a disadvantage. Moreover, parties were not always free to whichever slaves showed. Hudson described one get-together held in April 1838 in which a slave and a free black "employed" the bondman Austin "to give the supper." Austin hosted the gathering at his home and supplied a fish dinner. To compensate him for his hospitality and effort, everyone who attended paid a twenty-five-cent admission fee. The story was similar in Fauquier County, Virginia, almost twenty years later. When two enslaved fiddlers asked the free mulatto woman Maria Brown to host a dance, Brown replied that "they must pay me some little for the house." Just as the poor but enterprising woman demanded payment from the musicians for the use of her domicile, she also charged admission to patrons of the party. As she herself confirmed, "They had to pay when they went in." The bondman Henry, for example, "paid $12\frac{1}{2}$ cents to go in." Brown charged only half what Austin did two decades before, but Austin served a full meal; there was "no meat & bread" at Brown's. Although Brown was unsure of her total take the night of the murder, "the house was full" despite the price of admission. Nevertheless, at

Brown's as at Austin's, only slaves who could afford the entry fee were able to partake in the revelry. Those excluded by their poverty may well have resented it.[17]

As Kathleen Hilliard has observed, historians have yet to examine slave numeracy, or numerical literacy. With cash common in the quarters, slaves needed to be able to count money, perform basic mathematical calculations such as addition and subtraction, and assess values and commodity prices. Masters sometimes relied on slaves with these abilities. As one white Virginian remembered, the Stafford County bondman "Jeff... carried some market stuff to town for my son & wife—he drew the money out of his pocket and counted it down in a chair rightly." Not all slaves possessed these skills. In 1821, the enslaved thief Sam "had some money which he wanted counted" and asked fellow bondman Peter "to get some person to count it." Peter located "a Negro man who could count money to go and count it." Perhaps Sam and Peter utterly lacked the capability to count money, but the complexity of the task may also have been a factor. In the antebellum decades, a confusing array of currencies and bank notes of various denominations, some from foreign countries, circulated in the United States. As late as 1841, a Richmond, Virginia, slave stole U.S. money as well as "four silver coins of the Kingdom of Spain, of the value of twelve and a half cents each." In 1853, a white man in Adams County, Mississippi, divested "a certain negro slave named Bill" of "one Gold Watch of the value of Fifteen Dollars, Two half Dollars, one twenty five cent piece and one five cent piece of the currency of the United States," along with "one five franc piece of the currency of France." Given the proximity of the port town of Natchez just upriver from the former French outpost of New Orleans, circulating francs may not have been an oddity in the Lower Mississippi River Valley even half a century after the United States acquired Louisiana. Despite the unique challenges posed by antebellum-era monetary exchange, most slaves commanded a sufficiently sophisticated understanding of money to engage in economic transactions without apprehension of being cheated. When the slave George arrived at Maria Brown's frolic in Fauquier County, Virginia, he was prepared to pay the admission fee, but he asked the bondwoman Sage, already present at the party, "for a quarter change." Sage, accordingly, "got from Buckham's Daniel two levirs [livres] in change."[18]

The flow of cash among bondpeople could ignite disagreements. Two slaves of master John D. Lewis in the mining region of Kanawha County, Virginia, "fell to fighting" over "something about money." The bondman John or John Bull was a confrontational slave. He frequently quarreled with Lewis's bondman Moses Wilson "about their coal picks." Wilson complained of John "taking his picks away from him" and would have fought him to "make him quit it" were it "not from fear of his master." Despite the persistent "ill will" between John and Wilson, they refrained from physical violence. Only a week after one quarrel over their picks, however, John killed Lewis's slave Yamma, stabbing him with a dirk in August 1848. Three weeks before the incident, John revealed to another of Lewis's slaves "that there was a man on our place . . . he was going to injure" because "he had his money." John "intended to cut" Yamma and "kill him" because Yamma "bothered him" and deserved to "feel the weight of that knife." Records do not explain precisely how Yamma came to possess John's money. One possibility is that Yamma had stolen it.[19]

Southern whites widely regarded slaves as thieves. "They are proverbially *thieves*," charged the Reverend Charles Colcock Jones of Georgia, perpetually ready to pilfer indiscriminately, "from each other; from their masters[;] from any body." Given the sheer availability of goods and the opportunities for theft, bondpeople probably stole from whites more often than from other blacks, with masters the most common victims. Alex Lichtenstein framed bondpeople's thefts from their owners as a vital part of an ongoing negotiation between master and slave over the moral economy of the plantation. The act of pilfering from the master could prove not only materially beneficial but also psychologically gratifying. Theft marked a mild form of day-to-day resistance to slaveholder authority and contained elements of risk and sport. Successful burglaries gave slaves a satisfying, momentary triumph over the master or other white victim. Although some enslaved parents, including Henry "Box" Brown's mother, instructed their children "not to steal," Eugene D. Genovese pointed out that the ethic of the quarters excused thefts from owners as mere "taking" rather than "stealing." If masters owned as property both slaves and commodities they filched, any of the goods bondpeople appropriated without permission to eat or use for themselves ultimately remained in the master's possession, so owners suffered no net loss. Sometimes, however, slaves sold or bartered pilfered goods in the marketplace or through underground economic networks that included blacks as well as poor whites—exchanges that posed a somewhat more direct challenge to the slave system.[20]

Slaves did not limit their thefts to white victims. They occasionally preyed upon free blacks. One Virginia bondman, for example, accosted the free black Isaac Brown "on the public road & robbed him of bacon, coffee & sugar" in 1819. Confrontations between slaves and free blacks were more likely in Upper South states such as Virginia, which alone contained 28 percent of all free people of color living in the South in 1820. Eight of every ten southern free blacks lived in Delaware, Maryland, Virginia, and North Carolina, so slave thefts from free blacks were most probable in those states. Even in the Upper South, however, demographics alone dictated that slaves who stole from blacks usually deprived fellow bondpeople of their property. In 1820, the slave population of the South was more than 11.5 times greater than its free black population; slaves outnumbered free people of color by almost 1.4 million. No wonder, then, that the light-fingered slave Bob of Frederick County, Virginia, stole "sundry . . . articles" belonging to three slaves owned by different masters.[21]

Certainly in their cramped slave cabins, most bondpeople lacked any truly safe repository for their possessions. They might conceal goods under a loose floorboard or other favorite hiding spot, but the quarters' dearth of privacy often made these presumptively secret locations virtually common knowledge among the slaves. Some slaves accumulated and saved cash or secured valuable possessions by depositing them with the master for safe keeping, but this required surrendering control of their goods and placing inordinate trust in the hands of their oppressors, who might easily and without fear of legal repercussions swindle them out of their belongings. Banks, rare in the Old South, were practically never an option; with only a few, isolated exceptions among industrial slaves, southern blacks would not gain experience with such institutions until the creation of the Freedman's Savings Bank at the end of the Civil War.[22]

Bondpeople who earned money, acquired consumer goods, or stole commodities other slaves envied therefore needed to exercise caution and vigilance. Employing creativity in secreting their possessions did not hurt. In Mississippi, an enslaved husband and wife buried stolen money in a tin box in a hen house, while other slaves stashed their loot in a trunk belonging to a lower-class white man whom they trusted. Similarly, one prolific enslaved thief in Southampton County, Virginia, knew he could not safely stow his bonanza in or near his dwelling; rather, he secreted his bounty "in a stump," in "a Hollow Tree," in "another Tree," and under a log. With no better alternative available, a different Virginia slave hid the small treasures he had robbed from a bondwoman in the woods.[23]

However isolated or remote, these sylvan locations were hardly secure. Slaves' cash and commodities were therefore perpetually at risk of plundering by fellow bondpeople. In upcountry South Carolina's Pickens District in 1853, mistress Sarah Burgess's bondman Wiley, "a man of coler, Did steele some Tobacco and half a dollar in mony . . . on the sabeth from Jesse a man of color the Property of Elizabeth Fields." As John Campbell has explained, slaveholders' efforts to rein in bondpeople's independent economic activities were making cash increasingly scarce among upcountry South Carolina slaves in the 1840s and 1850s. As a result, there would likely have been a concomitant escalation of temptation when slaves spied untended or irresponsibly guarded money.[24]

Some bondpeople went so far as to purchase locks to help secure valuables from the depredations of fellow slaves. "They have locks on their doors," observed traveler William Thomson, "which are necessary, for they steal like rats." Ubiquitous locks reinforced whites' perception that dishonesty plagued the quarters. "Locks, bolts, and bars secure articles desirable to them," wrote Charles Colcock Jones. Prudence dictated that "the *keys,* must always be carried." Travelers to the South frequently commented upon slaves' use of security devices and the motives behind their use. Visiting the slave huts of lowcountry South Carolina, one contemporary "observed that many of the doors were fastened by a padlock and chain outside." Upon inquiring into the matter, he learned that "honesty is not a virtue they have towards each other. They would find their things stolen if they did not lock their doors." On a plantation in the Georgia lowcountry, Charles Lyell noticed "a large wooden padlock" that slaves used "to guard their valuables from their neighbors when they are at work in the field, for there is much pilfering among them." Since "the slave quarters were generally deserted through the entire day," cautious slaves "closed and locked" the "Negro cabins" of Mississippi, too. According to Frederick Law Olmsted, along the James River in Virginia, some quarters boasted "lock-up closets" to secure slaves' belongings. In Charlotte County, the enslaved woman Matilda "had two chests that she kept her nice clothes in, and always kept them locked." "Mother always kept her clothes locked up," Matilda's son remembered. "She was very particular with her clothes." She "wouldn't trust [even] her husband to go to them."[25]

The prevalence of locks in the quarters meant that it would not have been unusual for slaves to keep keys on their person. Matilda routinely "carried her bunch of keys in her pocket." When she was found murdered, the keys that opened her trunks were missing. Whereas when slaved carried their own keys, they demonstrated their mistrust of other residents of the quarters, when masters deemed a slave sufficiently trustworthy to bestow upon him or her a set of keys, they implicitly testified to the confidence they placed in the bondperson. Keys, thus laden with symbolic, relational value, inspired passionate emotions. An enslaved blacksmith in Dougherty County, Georgia, mortally wounded another slave with an axe helve for "stealing shop keys and stable keys" that belonged to the master but which he guarded as though they were his own.[26]

Theft from fellow slaves met with widespread disapproval and rebuke in the quarters. Slave culture was firmly grounded in a highly localized sense of place. Those slaves who were not forcibly relocated with their masters or made victims of the domestic slave trade often never ventured far from the home plantation over the course of their lifetimes. Passes or tickets dispensed by the master were required for slaves to travel even short distances unmolested by patrollers or other whites they encountered along the road, any of whom might accost and interrogate an enslaved sojourner. Compared to enslaved women, enslaved men enjoyed somewhat greater freedom of movement, taking advantage of opportunities to leave the plantation either on business for the master, to court a sweetheart on a nearby holding, or to visit an abroad spouse. Yet even for enslaved men, the ability to travel was limited. A few trips to the mill notwithstanding, Virginia bondmen Henry "Box" Brown and his brother "would have known nothing whatever of what was going on anywhere in the world, excepting on our master's plantation."[27]

In slaves' circumscribed world, relationships with fellow bondpeople mattered greatly. Due to reasons of family, distance, and—considering the unreliable sources of food and water and the prospect of encountering patrols or other hostile whites—the sheer odds against success, most slaves could not realistically risk an attempted flight to freedom. Like it or not, they lived and worked with a given cohort, some larger than others, of fellow bondpeople on the home plantation and in the immediate vicinity. To be sure, membership in these enslaved peer groups was fluid, given the buying and selling of the internal slave trade and the compulsory migrations prompted by masters' often incessant search for more profitable lands, but in no case did a sense of camaraderie or belonging among a group of bondpeople come automatically. Slaves needed to create ties of trust to forge the bonds of neighborhood and community.[28]

When they stole from one another, they undermined that trust by violating the ethic that bound them together. "I am sure that, as a rule, any one of us who would have thought nothing of stealing a hog, or a sack of corn, from our master," declared successful fugitive John Brown, "would have allowed himself to be cut to pieces rather than betray the confidence of his fellow-slave." Thefts from masters could be justified; thefts from other slaves could not. Bondpeople denounced and condemned those among them whose demeanor and actions marked them as "mean." "[A] slave that will steal from a slave, is called *mean* as *master*," explained former bondman Lewis Clarke. "This is the lowest comparison slaves know how to use: 'just as mean as white folks.'" Masters were the ultimate thieves, stealing slaves' time, the products of their labor, their parents, their spouses, their children, and their lives. Nevertheless, Clarke insisted, the "nigger dat . . . steal from nigger, he meaner nor all." Such individuals unraveled the social fabric of the quarters.²⁹

Some enslaved thieves caught in their crimes committed violence upon the bondpeople who caught them in the act, to prevent them from revealing their treachery to the master or to other slaves. Traveling in the vicinity of Athens, Georgia, England's James Silk Buckingham heard stories of slaves "in which poisonings and secret murders had been committed by them on their own relatives, to prevent disclosures" of thefts. Dishonest bondpeople surely did want to conceal their crimes to avoid the master's discipline as well as the opprobrium of their fellow residents of the quarters. Slaves' widely held contempt for the thieves among them may have proven the most effective deterrent to misdeeds. In Kathleen Hilliard's analysis of 234 cases of property crimes committed in the upcountry South Carolina districts of Anderson and Spartanburg, only 14, or 6 percent, of the indictments "involved accusations of intra-plantation theft by slaves from slaves."³⁰

Bondmen and bondwomen highly valued their personal reputations for honesty inside the quarters. Their sense of honor will be discussed more explicitly in chapters 7 and 8, but it was keen enough that enslaved women and men took offense even when merely accused of theft. The bondwoman Milly in DeSoto County, Mississippi, acknowledged that she had a "quarrel with Laura . . . because Laura accused her of Stealing Some of her things." Near Montgomery, Alabama, a slave ferryman confronted a "d——d nigger" for stealing his gourd. The second slave resented the allegation and threatened to "smash your wool skull in if you call me tief." The ferryman replied with a violent threat of his own. Some slaves went beyond verbal attacks by committing physically violent assaults to avenge a charge of stealing.³¹

In fact, most property-related violence between slaves revolved around theft. Two cases from upcountry South Carolina illustrate how allegations of theft might trigger a violent response from the accused bondman. After the slave Dick of Anderson District declared that Toney "had stolen more leather than his back could pay for," Toney confronted Dick and assaulted him, "severely hurting him verry much." Toney announced that "he would whip Dick or any other negro that accused him of stealing" or "talked about him," because "he had as many we[a]pons as any one els[e]." Toney also fought the slave Sy for what "Sy had said about him in regard to some stolen leather." When Spartanburg District slave Sam accused George of stealing his hammer, George took umbrage and fatally smote

Sam on the head with an axe and a pole. Neither Toney nor George wanted to be diminished in the eyes of their fellow bondpeople, so they relied on violence to defend their reputations. It is also quite possible that they feared their accusers might inform the master on them, inviting punishment.[32]

Slaves occasionally employed violence to prevent theft of their valuable possessions. Solomon Northup, a northern free black kidnapped and sold into slavery in Louisiana, was walking a road late one night, "carrying a dressed pig in a bag swung over my shoulder." Probably ascertaining the contents of the sack, a pair of fugitive slaves attempted to waylay and rob him. They approached rapidly from behind, one bearing a club. Northup dodged them as they "snatched at the bag," grabbed a "pine knot," and hurled it at the head of one of his assailants, knocking him "apparently senseless to the ground." Northup staved off the attack and preserved possession of the pig. Similarly violent episodes unfolded when bondpeople caught other slaves in the act of thievery, whether on the public roads, in the woods, or in a slave cabin.[33]

Despite the social opprobrium bondpeople attached to theft within the quarters, stealing among slaves remained a persistent problem over time and, on certain plantations, reached epidemic proportions. Most frequently, the object of such thefts was food. Of all categories of nourishment, slaves most commonly stole meat from one another, perhaps a whole pig or a slab of bacon. Enslaved in Dougherty County, Georgia, Henry murdered Gilbert for "eating his chicken," a charge the victim denied to the end. Less commonly, bondpeople pilfered any number of commodities not included as a part of standard plantation fare: eggs, butter, sugar, coffee, or liquor. Although masters typically allotted their slaves rations of meal and molasses, some were compelled to augment their supply by filching from other bondpeople. That food was the most frequent target of enslaved thefts of other bondpeople's property suggests that they were driven to steal by necessity. Hungry slaves were desperate slaves, willing to violate social norms against thievery in the quarters and risk their reputations.[34]

Currency, including both cash and coin, marked the second most common item slaves stole from one another. Money was so insecure in the quarters that many slaves elected to spend whatever amounts came into their possession almost immediately at a local store or crossroads grogshop rather than risk losing it to another bondperson. That money was so frequently stolen suggests its pervasiveness as a medium of exchange among enslaved consumers. Most slaves lacked the opportunity to accumulate and save substantial sums, however, so the quantities stolen were generally small.

Slaves scored more impressive sums when they robbed whites or white-owned stores and shops. Enslaved thieves in Virginia divested white victims of "a quantity of Silver and Copper Money of the value of Fifty dollars" and "certain Bank notes of the value of fifty five dollars and certain silver coin current money of this Commonwealth to the amount of $12.65 cents." The efforts of another yielded a more modest "six half dollars, "forty six dimes," and "two half dimes current coins of the United States." Successful thefts from whites probably injected a good share of the cash that circulated within the slave economy. After food and money, slaves most commonly stole from other slaves tobacco and other commodities they could claim as theirs and sell at market. Practical items such as clothing also ranked high in desirability.[35]

Slaves typically stole from one another furtively, when their enslaved counterparts' backs were turned, but they also occasionally committed violent robberies. In Spanish Louisiana, the enslaved overseer Pierre returned from market laden with cash "because he sold some pigs in the city and had not spent all the money." Unlike the numbers of enslaved men, in particular, who promptly deposited the money that came to them with purveyors of alcohol, "Pierre did not drink." Those who knew the teetotaling Pierre would have had some idea of the sums in his possession despite the urban temptations presented him. Pierre's brother Clement was a notorious thief, and Pierre, in his capacity as overseer, "had told him that the first time he stole again he would be killed with the beating he would receive." Brotherly bonds strained, Clement reportedly "feared Pierre more than he did his master." When Pierre went missing on his way home, suspicion naturally fell to Clement. When Pierre's "blood-stained purse" was found in "Clement's sheaf of rice," Clement revealed the location of the gun he used to commit the robbery and fratricide and, under threat of punishment, led whites to his brother's body. Decades later, a "very stout" bondman named Austin was "found dead ... on the road" in Hinds County, Mississippi, the rope that strangled him still wrapped around his neck. Theft was a likely motive for the murder, for "[t]he dead negro's pocket had been rifled after death." In a similar case, "Scott a negro lad" of Lunenburg County, Virginia, viciously beat and robbed the bondman Bob one Sunday evening in March 1823. Bob had just purchased "a bottle of Rum & some Sugar" at Thomas A. Filbert's grocery store at Lunenburg Courthouse. Present at the store, Scott followed Bob home and waylaid him with a stick. Bob survived the attack long enough to share what had transpired, fingering Scott as his assailant. Scott had taken the rum, the sugar, and the "three quarters of a dollar in silver" that Bob had in his pocket when he left Filbert's store.

At trial, Filbert identified the unique bottle that "he had filled with rum" for Bob, which was found where Scott lived, spattered with "two spotts of blood." Scott had gone home the evening of the murder, "groggy" or "very drunk" from quaffing of a "tumbler" or "bottle of spirits" that he invited the slaves Sarah and Solomon to share with him. He also had "some sugar in his hands" and either one or two of the stolen silver quarters. Altogether, there was ample evidence to guarantee that Scott would hang for the murder.[36]

When slaves committed thefts inside the quarters, the victim might pursue different avenues for recourse. Some appealed to the master or overseer. Like many slaveholders, Virginia's Richard Eppes, who commanded his slaves not to steal from anyone, including "your . . . fellow servants," implored his bondpeople to alert the overseer "immediately" upon realizing any goods were missing so that he might root out "the rogue" and administer the proper punishment. Some slaves elected to follow this sort of direction. During the Civil War, Dougherty County, Georgia, slave Henry accused the bondman Gilbert of "eating his chicken," while Gilbert claimed "that Henry had taken two dollars from him." Seeking resolution, they started off together "to see Mas John about it." A pair of slaves in Isle of Wight County, Virginia, simultaneously protected their foodstuffs and performed loyal service to the master by trapping an enslaved thief they discovered sneaking about the plantation. A bondman named Nat "was going to see his wife" when he noticed the smokehouse door ajar. Upon hearing a noise inside, he went to the kitchen and informed "the old negro woman" Silvy. Together they crept up to investigate and spied an enslaved thief named Jordan lingering suspiciously among the cured meats. While Nat and a third slave detained the intruder inside the smokehouse, Silvy hastened to inform the master. Slaves on one Mississippi plantation persuaded their owner to sell a particularly aggravating, kleptomaniacal slave woman who chronically stole from them. Cognizant of thefts among his slaves, one planter in Georgia established a rule that, any time "one negro steals from another," the driver was required to seize the equivalent value "of the marauder's goods and chattels" to make restitution. If the enslaved thief proved unable to compensate the victim within a reasonable timeframe, punishment ensued. Most commonly, masters employed the whip in their futile efforts to cleanse the quarters of thievery.[37]

Reporting thefts to the master might backfire against the enslaved victim, however, by fueling the resentment of the bondperson who suffered "correction." On the Amherst County, Virginia, holding of Charles Taliaferro, a dispute erupted between slaves Isaac and Robin in November 1819. Isaac accused Robin of "stealing his clothes," prompting Addison Taliaferro to administer Robin a severe whipping. One bondman heard Robin blame Isaac for the lashing he received and threaten to kill him. Robin gained his vengeance by bludgeoning Isaac with a pestle, fracturing the slave's skull. When slaves such as Isaac sought the master's intervention, some bondpeople saw betrayal. Ultimate loyalty must reside with one's fellow slaves; consulting the master qualified as tattling, ratting out, or snitching, and enslaved snitches made themselves vulnerable to retribution in the quarters. When the Copiah County, Mississippi, bondman Simon murdered Norvall in a "misunderstanding about mollasses," the victim was not a suspected thief but rather a hapless witness to thievery: "Simon said he killed Norvall because Norvall had seen him stealing molasses & had told his master about it or ... would tell him & ... Simon was afraid his master would whip him."[38]

Because slaves did not legally own the property they possessed, they were unable to air their grievances in courts of law, with but rare exception. When enslaved thief and enslaved victim belonged to different masters, litigious slaveholders might guide a case of theft through the court system. In Chesterfield County, Virginia, Thomas Traylor's slave Peyton was "charged with Highway robbery," stealing "a bundle of clothes and [a]bout 5$ in cash" from Mrs. Cheatham's bondwoman Sarah. Sarah "was returning home from Market" shortly after Christmas 1817 when she overtook and passed Peyton "on the public road." Peyton then approached her from behind, "struck her with a stick and demanded her money, which he took, together with a bundle of clothes which she had in a basket."[39]

The imprudent use or display of purloined goods was often the undoing of slaves who stole from their peers. The slave Isham confirmed the identity of Sarah's assailant after spying Peyton "with one of his shirts on, of which Sarah had been robbed." Isham's testimony exposes one of the great difficulties inherent in thefts from other slaves. Bondpeople knew precisely what goods they owned, and they proved astute observers of the commodities others possessed as well. To evade detection and blame, the enslaved thief was best served by either consuming stolen property immediately or pawning it off to another individual, black or white, and taking other goods or cash in exchange. Attempting to wear, use, or display stolen merchandise was fraught with danger. In 1856, for example, the South Carolina bondman Dan gazed longingly at the shoes of fellow slave George. So covetous was Dan of the shoes that he offered to purchase them. George refused. The next morning, George awoke to find his window open and his shoes missing. He instantly thought of Dan, and the next week at church, Dan was wearing the filched footwear. Suspicion confirmed.[40]

The biracial evangelical churches of the slaveholding South occasionally intervened in the property disputes of enslaved congregants. Church disciplinary committees frequently investigated charges of theft lodged against their members. Sometimes white churchgoers levied accusations of theft against other white members as an alternative to court action. Very rarely, a white man might even be accused of stealing from a black. At Bethabara Baptist Church in Laurens District, South Carolina, "brother Samuel Jones" was excluded from fellowship in 1837 on charges of "drunkenness, and other gross offences," such as "taking some money from a colord man at a muster ground in the neighbourhood." Churches were vastly more interested in the depredations committed by enslaved members upon property owned by whites. They commonly charged slaves with theft and the concomitant charge of lying to mask the deed. In the gang labor regimes of the tobacco-producing Virginia Piedmont and cotton-growing Middle Georgia, churches most frequently accused slaves of stealing meat—the pork and poultry that filled slaves' bellies as a supplement to paltry rations. The congregation of Beaverdam Baptist Church in Wilkes County, Georgia, came to understand that some masters even encouraged their slaves' thievery. As John M. Strozier purportedly instructed his slave Willis, "if you did not get enough to eate to steal it." In South Carolina, where variations of the task system were more widely employed, a greater proportion of slaves were granted permission to raise stock or to grow their own fruits and vegetables in garden plots allotted by their masters. In consequence, South Carolina churches were more apt to charge slaves with the theft of cotton, tobacco, or wheat that they might sell at market, rather than consume as food. Churches also cited enslaved members as accessories to theft. Bethel Baptist Church of Hancock County, Georgia, charged the bondwoman Celia with "consealing stolen property for her children and telling lies" about it. In Wilkes County, Fishing Creek Baptist Church likewise condemned the enslaved woman Sarah as an "accomplice" in "the pilfering act of her Daughter." Their respective congregations excluded these protective slave mothers from fellowship. Evangelical churches monitored a whole array of dishonest behaviors.[41]

Although enslaved members of southern evangelical churches were subject to intense scrutiny and possible disciplinary action, they could also use those same religious institutions to mediate conflicts among black churchgoers over thefts in the quarters and other issues. In 1822, Philips Mill Baptist Church in Wilkes County, Georgia, received "[s]ome unfavorable reports" about the bondman Daniel for having stolen unspecified goods and gotten into "an affray with Major Terrels servants" as a result. Daniel gave satisfaction and remained within the fold. Another Wilkes County church forgave an enslaved man who confessed in May 1850 "that he took two dozen eggs of a woman of Color the property of Neal Meadows." In acknowledging "he had [done] rong," he expressed sufficient sorrow to retain fellowship. As these examples suggest, churches more willingly excused slave thefts when the victim was also enslaved rather than white. But forgiveness was not automatic in such cases. In July 1838, Horeb Baptist Church in Georgia's Hancock County heard a complaint against "brother Deedham, a man of colour, the property of brother Tucker," for "taking Bacon and Butter, from ... [a] negro woman and disposing of the same to his own benefit." Church testimony confirmed that "he had received both Bacon and Butter, at different times, which had been stolen." For his misdeeds, "he was excluded from the fellowship of the church."[42]

Rather than summoning the assistance of the master or invoking the disciplinary authority of the church, however, slaves usually handled cases of theft in quarters on their own, without external interference. Ex-slave Jacob Stroyer explained in elaborate detail the supernatural techniques (sometimes fused with Christian elements) through which bondpeople in his South Carolina neighborhood in the 1850s detected thieves among them. Sometimes they read the movement of either a Bible or a sieve suspended from a string. Another method, imported from West Africa and purportedly more reliable, employed graveyard dust. Slaves took dust from the grave of the most recently deceased slave, placed it in a bottle, and poured in water to dissolve the dust. If a suspected thief drank the mixture and was innocent, nothing happened. If guilty, it was said, the thief would die, go to hell, and burn in fire and brimstone. Because so many slaves believed in magic and conjuration, this ritual often elicited confessions. If none of these techniques rooted out the thief, the slaves chalked up the theft to strangers from outside the neighborhood.[43]

Slaves who ferreted out the thieves among them devised their own solutions to the crisis of community signified by theft. Some slaves mediated disputes or acted as agents on behalf others. When the Dougherty County, Georgia, bondman Gilbert complained to his enslaved friend John that Henry had taken Gilbert's two dollars, John labored with Henry—unsuccessfully—"to get the money for Gilbert." Social ostracism served as one potent weapon wielded by bondpeople to punish light-fingered slaves. To be made an outcast shunned by fellow bondpeople not only deterred some thefts from taking place but also spurred enslaved thieves to make amends. For restoration into a community of slaves, the robber must perform the appropriate penance. According to Jacob Stroyer, when slaves identified the individual who stole a chicken, "if he had any chickens he had to give four for one, and if he had none he made it good by promising that he would do so no more." Slaves without compensatory poultry thus escaped any retributive punishment; an apology and pledge to do better sufficed. The leniency slaves showed such persons may indicate their recognition that the guilty bondperson probably stole out of dire need. At the other end of the enslaved socioeconomic spectrum, a relatively prosperous slave who already owned ample fowl but nonetheless stole a chicken paid for the crime fourfold. In many other cases, slaves accepted recompense at the ratio of one to one. If the stolen property could not be returned or an identical commodity supplied to its enslaved owner, substitute goods were permitted at the discretion of the victim of theft. In Muscogee County, Georgia, the bondman Neil charged Phil in 1853 with stealing his money and using it to buy alcohol. Neil was willing to take the jug of liquor as his just compensation.[44]

Cunning slaves might also reestablish social harmony by framing an enslaved thief. Probably not done frequently, it was theoretically possible for them to steal goods themselves, plant them about the premises or on the person of the enslaved offender, and lead the master or other white authority to the evidence. According to British traveler James Silk Buckingham, slaves "revenged themselves" for a host of "offences committed by brothers and sisters, by stealing articles, and placing them secretly in the pockets of those they wished to injure, then accusing them, and becoming witnesses to convict them of the crime." Isaac, a slave with a reputation as "a quarrelsome, drunken vicious negro," devised such a strategy as a means to secure "recompense" from Emanuel, a fellow bondman with whom he worked at a Richmond, Virginia, tobacco factory. Laboring under the false impression that Emanuel informed their common employer that Isaac had stolen tobacco, Isaac vowed to "have his 'recompense' out of Emanuel, that night, if not before." According to one eyewitness to their quarrel, "Isaac . . . swore that if he could not be revenged in any other way, he would steal something and put it in Emanuel's house, and then inform the police of it and bring them to the place." Slaves who cleverly planted evidence to effect the punishment of an enslaved adversary, Buckingham related, "often subsequently [confess] their wickedness, and [boast] in the success of their plots."[45]

Many slaves directly confronted bondwomen and bondmen who violated their claims to property. Because most bondpeople owned very little and would have had difficulty replacing stolen goods, they placed a premium on what they did possess and rallied in defense of their goods against the incursion of thieves among them. A pair of cases from Anderson District, South Carolina, illustrates the ways in which slaves broached the subject of theft. In 1844, Louisa, Austin, and Yancy "had Lost some meat." Suspicion fell to the slaves of J. W. Norris, so they plotted to "Lay out J.W. Norris['s] Negroes on Sunday to make them confess about stealing the Bacon." Florilla, the property of Norris, was on her way to church when the aggrieved bondpeople accosted her and threatened to "kick her Durned Brains" out to elicit a confession. The trio of slaves "did assault beat & in a Riotous manner abuse Florilla." In another case, when one witness saw Mary D. Anderson's slave John "leaving Mrs. Guitans premises just before day break with a bout ½ B[ushel] of corn in a Bage" in November 1855, he assumed it was "stolen property." Margaret Guitan's bondman Dan also spotted John, approached the thief, and "put his hand on the corn," informing John, "you are two fat this morning." John instructed Dan to "say nothing A bout it," as "it did not come from here." Dan was apparently not convinced that the corn came from elsewhere, for a fight broke out. John and an enslaved friend attacked Dan "with a stick on the Arm and then the head." Outnumbered, Dan still managed to inflict some "wounds with an Ax" or stick, sending John away "with his head brused and Blody."[46]

In both of these instances, slaves relied on violence as a means of self-preservation. They had a vested interest in the crime that took place. The theft of bacon or corn meant less food in their own bellies. Therefore, slaves willingly fought to safeguard their provisions. Trespassers likely understood what was at stake; otherwise, John would not have emphasized that his bag of stolen corn "did not come from *here*." He implicitly assumed that if the theft did not reduce Dan's rations, Dan would permit John to slip off with the pilfered foodstuff. But John was wrong. Slaves protected the master's property even when it had no immediate value to them. In 1854, for example, William Duckworth's Ned, another Anderson District slave, crept "in to the Black Smith Shop" of Tom N. Smith, "pilfering and as tho he wished to Steal some of his Iron until his negros run him out of the shop." Five of Smith's slaves and one bondman of Mrs. Guitan ran off Ned, but not before Ned struck the slave "Bill 2 Blows with his fist," sparking a melee. The slaves who entered the fray likely did not do so out of simple allegiance to the master. Had they not prevented the theft, they may have taken the blame for the missing iron and suffered unwarranted punishment.[47]

Thefts in the quarters often provoked violent reactions among enslaved men eager to punish thieves and send a clear message to deter other, would-be criminals. When Pickens District, South Carolina, slave Jesse, peaceably playing marbles one Sunday with fellow bondman Wiley, suddenly whirled and identified Wiley as "the Negro that stole his tobac[c]o," the two slaves quarreled. Jesse informed Wiley that "he came there after his tobacco and if he could not get it he could whip him." True to his word, Jesse "struck the first lick." After the Muscogee County, Georgia, slave Phil failed to repay the money he had allegedly stolen from Neil or to surrender the jug of liquor he purportedly bought with it, the two bondmen faced off, one wielding a plow handle, the other a wooden club. After a third slave intervened and placed a momentary stop to their skirmish, their battle resumed. Neil then fatally stabbed Phil with a bowie knife.[48]

Slaves who pursued violent retribution upon other bondmen they accused of theft sometimes failed to exact the vengeance they sought. To the contrary, they became the victims of the encounters they had initiated. During the Civil War, Mat, an enslaved Georgian, lost some money. Rummaging through the pocketbook of the bondman Elbert, Mat discovered a three-cent piece he claimed as his. The pair argued a while before dispersing, but two nights later, still obsessed with his missing money, Mat seized a pickaxe to attack Elbert. On this occasion, violence afforded no satisfaction to the aggrieved slave. Mat's plan to harm Elbert physically backfired when his intended victim preemptively struck Mat on the head with an axe, killing him. The story was much the same in Charlotte County, Virginia, where the slave Dick complained that "his wife had stolen 7 dollars" from him. Dick reserved the greater share of his venom, however, for the bondman Julius, whom he described as a "D——d Rascal" who protected "his ... wife, in a wrong." Dick proclaimed his intention "to cut [Julius's] G—d d—d guts out of him" and "to see him in hell before day." Dick got the worse of their encounter, but as he lay dying, he still believed he had taken the proper course of action. "You all think I am a fool," he said as he breathed his last, "but thank God I am not a fool yet." Many enslaved men no doubt concurred with Dick that violence had its proper place inside the slave community.[49]

One overlooked motive for slaves' thefts was a need to repay debts owed to other slaves. Bondpeople with financial resources and property had the wherewithal to make various small loans to other slaves who were then beholden to them, and slaves lent to and borrowed from one another with striking frequency. "In every servants' quarter there are ... debtors and creditors," wrote a Tennessee minister and editor in 1859. Slaves were excluded from conventional white credit networks. On some plantations, they enjoyed the flexibility of individual accounts established by the master through which they might discharge their debts. If they had a credit with the master, for example, they might—with the slaveholder's permission—withdraw money from the account to give to a fellow bondperson, or ask the master to transfer that credit into another slave's account. With the possible exception of the master, however, whites did not lend money or goods to slaves or advance them any form of credit on their own account. Doing so would symbolically undermine masters' authority and acknowledge slaves' equality as *homo economicus*. Practically, potential white lenders thought it unwise to lend anything or extend credit to slaves because repayment was far from assured. Bondpeople might abscond, leaving their debts unpaid. Masters might hire them out outside the neighborhood, sell them to distant lands, or forcibly convey them away as owners searched for fresh, fertile soils. Slaves, in short, were a huge credit risk. Bondpeople therefore relied upon one another in times of need. In Elbert County, Georgia, Edmund borrowed $2 from Jack and $1.25—"one silver dollar and two 12 $^{1}/_{2}$ cent pieces"—from Nancy. When possible, some slaves preferred taking out loans from family members. One Fauquier County, Virginia, bondman went into debt by purchasing a horse with $50 borrowed from an enslaved cousin. He may have felt somewhat more comfortable entering into a business relationship with kin rather than an unrelated friend or acquaintance. Or, the cousin may have been the only slave he knew with the substantial sum of $50 available to lend. No less than whites, however, in spite of the risks involved, enslaved creditors expected repayment and sometimes pressured indebted slaves to settle up.[50]

Stealing from whites provided one quick way to expunge their debts to fellow slaves. In Loudoun County, Virginia, slave James Hogan purloined two loads of wood and sold them to two different white men in 1819 because "he owed Six Dollars to a black waggoner over the ridge belonging to Mr[.] Whiting." Another Virginia slave stole flour to pay back a debt. In 1839, the white Daniel Bond of Georgia accused a slave named Edmond of stealing seven dollars' worth of silver coins from him. Edmond aroused suspicion because he had not only purchased watermelon at a camp meeting with his spoils but also used a silver dollar to repay a debt to a fellow slave. When emancipated, many slaves were slow to abandon their established, extensive networks of credit. As Dylan Penningroth calculates, after the Civil War, 44 percent of the debt cases that appeared before Freedmen's Bureau courts in Kentucky, South Carolina, and Virginia involved blacks seeking repayment from other blacks.[51]

Most debts were probably repaid with little fuss. In 1852, without any trouble whatsoever, the South Carolina bondman Emory received the fifty cents Amos owed him. The next year, Isaiah, concerned for his economic reputation in the quarters and conscientious about repayment, sought out Leslie because "he was owing him and he wanted to pay him." Financially embarrassed slaves unable to pay back what they owed sometimes received aid from fellow blacks. At "a negro dance" in Kanawha County, Virginia, bondman Sam Hancock demanded that Harry pay him "what he owed him," a total of "four pence half penny." Harry lacked the means, but "Abigail Wilson a free woman of Color" offered to pay the debt for Harry "if Hancock would change nine pence," which he did. Whether out of courtesy, neighborliness, or friendship, slaves did sometimes forgive the debts owed them. James City County, Virginia, slave Abram tested the bondman Nat when he "asked Nat if he owed him any thing." Nat acknowledged he owed Abram "a small sum," but Abram shrugged it off. The grateful Nat replied that he owed Abram "good will, if nothing else." In Winston County, Mississippi, the "negro man" Tazwell "bought a piece of tobacco of [slave] Randall for the sum of 5 cents whi[ch] he promised to pay." According to Randall, Tazwell agreed to meet him at a spring "late at night" after "[t]he white people had all gone to bed," "to pay him" for the tobacco. Tazwell, however, denied that he ever "made any agreement with Randall to meet him ... at the spring or any where else" to repay his debt. Tazwell insisted that "Randall said he did not care whether [Tazwell] even paid him for the tobacco or not." Most slaves did not prove as nonchalant about reimbursement as Tazwell implied.[52]

Most slaves were assiduous custodians of their limited financial resources and engaged in very careful mental bookkeeping. Enslaved creditors knew who owed them and precisely how much. Despite the instability inherent in the enslaved condition that might permanently sever debtor from creditor, the vast majority of those slaves owed money expected due compensation. An important means of exerting pressure for prompt repayment was to make the debtor-creditor relationship widely known in the quarters and, more broadly, throughout the slave neighborhood. In Albemarle County, Virginia, Daniel Scott's bondman William owed a debt to Washington, the property of George Rives. Other slaves were aware of the economic tie between the men. The enslaved man Putney, for example, had knowledge of the debt even though he did not belong to either Scott or Rives but to John H. Coleman. As Dylan Penningroth argues, slaves employed public acknowledgment to affirm property ownership. Similarly, they did not keep debtor-creditor relationships private. A common understanding throughout the neighborhood of the slaves actively participating in enslaved networks of credit may have brought to bear the collective weight of the slave community.[53]

Still, slaves across the South sometimes felt compelled to engage in violent confrontations over the repayment of debts they owed one another. Anderson District, South Carolina, slaves Amos and Andrew, for example, "fell out about a debt contracted by Andrews having purchased some bread from him." In New Orleans, James demanded repayment from Victor in 1846. "James called Victor a son of a bitch," smashed a bottle over the debtor's head, and, still clutching the neck of the bottle in his hand, thrust its jagged edges into Victor's chest. Unlike James and Victor, both the property of the same owner, the vast majority of enslaved combatants who fought over debts belonged to different masters. Slave creditors and debtors living on separate plantations may have lacked at least some of the emotional bonds that cemented relationships among those who lived and worked together on the same holding. The physical distance separating them from those indebted to them may also have made slave creditors more nervous than if they lived in closer proximity. An enslaved debtor on another plantation might be sold or forcibly relocated without the creditor's advance knowledge. Without the ability to closely monitor those indebted to them, slave creditors' anxiety over repayment intensified proportionally as the miles widened.[54]

Slaves who fought and died over debts almost always fought and died over money rather than consumer goods. In most cases the amount was some unspecified, negligible sum. Slaves are known to have been murdered for debts of "fifty cents," "twenty five cents," and even less. The New Orleans slave James killed Victor over "Five Cents, which he owed him," the equivalent of a little more than a paltry $1.50 in 2013 dollars. However seemingly inconsequential the sum, for slaves, it mattered dearly. But the devaluation of enslaved life was stunning. A slave sometimes died in a dispute over less money than it cost to purchase the knife that killed him. Murderous affrays over such petty sums speak less to the worth slaves attached to human life, however, than to the continued significance of cash in the quarters. Southern white shopkeepers in the early nineteenth century, runaway slave Charles Ball observed, eagerly did business with slaves because they paid with cash, unlike many whites, who frequently purchased goods on credit. As the antebellum decades wore on, slaveholders clamped down on and attempted to extricate cash from the slave economy to reduce the autonomy slaves gained through the money in their pockets. But despite masters' best efforts, the power of slaves' internal economy could not be curtailed to planters' satisfaction. Slaves' disputes over debts underscore the degree to which market values had infiltrated the quarters and seeped into the slaves' consciousness. It is not abundantly clear the way in which Mississippi bondmen Tazwell and Randall determined how much tobacco "5 cents" purchased. Their agreement may have represented little more than a mutual understanding completely arbitrary in nature, but it seems more likely that both slaves recognized a five-cent plug of tobacco when they saw one because their transaction—and hence the repayment to the creditor—was ultimately pegged to the cash nexus of the antebellum marketplace.[55]

A full spectrum of disagreements ignited the violent conflicts over cash. Some disputes centered on what, if anything, one bondman owed another. Some slaves, such as Reubin of Henry County, Virginia, denied owing a debt at all. In 1830, he threatened to kill Frederick if he "ever asked him for [the] twenty five cents which he claimed." This proved no empty promise. Yet Frederick was not entirely without fault. When his request for repayment was rebuffed, he informed Reubin that "he would have to fight." Both slaves, then, entered their fatal affray of their own accord, under different motivations. Reubin knifed Frederick to death after a corn shucking, and Reubin himself later died at the gallows.[56]

Other slaves acknowledged the debt they owed but conscientiously avoided their creditors. Virginia slaves Washington and William lived on adjoining plantations in Albemarle County. William needed to repay Washington some money but reportedly "had given him . . . the dodge." Growing increasingly impatient with his enslaved neighbor, in October 1845 a knife-wielding Washington threatened to "cut William . . . unless William paid him what he owed him." Some slaves familiar with Washington gave his words little credence, dismissing them as harmless bluster. One bondman "thought he was projecting" or "fooling." Washington "was much in the habit of scuffling" with other slaves and often made idle threats that "I will cut you with my Knife," but he was actually well liked in the quarters. For that reason, William may not have realized how serious Washington was when he confronted him. Seeking recompense, Washington seized from William "a bundle" that contained "some sugar and Cotton." William promptly registered his objection. "It is not mine!" he exclaimed, but the property of the overseer's wife. Washington declared that William must surrender the bundle, or one of them would be killed. In the ensuing scuffle, Washington stabbed William to death.[57]

In another case, a South Carolina slave apparently gave his creditor the runaround. One Saturday night at William Duckworth's "negroe houses" in Anderson District, Micajah B. Williams's slave Baylis asked "Lazarus Tranums boy Jake" for the money he owed him. Jake explained that he had paid Daniel Owens's slave Lewis, who was then to convey the money to Baylis, but when Baylis approached Lewis in Duckworth's kitchen to demand repayment, Lewis "denied having [been] paid the mony for Baylis." Angry and frustrated at having been sent on a fool's errand, Baylis tracked down Jake. A fight ensued that concluded when Jake threw a rock that struck the slave creditor on the forehead and "nearly killed" him.[58]

Disagreements and misunderstandings over repayment frequently turned violent. Those who could not pay their debts in a timely manner because they were strapped for cash and could not afford to do so invited physical retribution. On Sunday, November 2, 1823, Accomack County, Virginia, slave Daniel went to the home of Henny Stockly, "a free woman of colour" and wife of the bondman Levi, and asked her "for money that she owed him." Stockly explained "that she had not the money but as soon as she got it she would pay him." She invited Daniel into her home, but Daniel declined, perhaps sensing an ambush awaiting him inside. Henny reassured him "that there was no person there to hurt him." When Levi appeared from the doorway, Daniel, perhaps out of deference to Stockly's gender or free status, launched into a tirade against her enslaved husband, "quarreling cursing and abusing . . . Levi . . . very much." Levi ordered Daniel to leave multiple times, but Daniel responded that "he would go when he pleased." The confrontation ended when the enslaved creditor stabbed Levi in the throat with a knife valued at "ten cents."[59]

Another episode in nearby Southampton County began similarly but ended with the death of the enslaved creditor. On Thursday, January 2, 1817, "Hubbard a negro man slave" and property of a free black woman murdered the bondman West. That day, West approached Hubbard and asked "for some money which he owed him." West had been attempting to track down Hubbard for at least two days. On Tuesday, he had inquired of Hubbard's whereabouts because Hubbard was beholden to West for "fifty cents," which West wanted by Thursday so that he might purchase "some Spirits." West tracked down Hubbard on Thursday, but Hubbard "told West he had not the money," provoking "a quarrel." Anticipating fisticuffs, Hubbard "stripped himself to fight and called West . . . a damd rascal." After West "collared" him, the debtor swiped at West's abdomen with a knife, spilling the creditor's intestines into his hands. West lived about a day before he died.[60]

Unlike Henny Stockly and Hubbard, each of whom admitted to their creditors that they lacked the funds to repay a debt, Anderson District, South Carolina, bondman Steve struck a more defiant tone. When master William Duckworth's slave Jess approached Steve for "what he owed him," Steve neither acknowledged a dearth of resources nor humbled himself before his creditor. Rather, he dismissed the demand, retorting that he would "pay when ready." Steve did not deny the debt outright but took issue with the timing of the repayment. Apparently disgusted that a debtor—the subordinate economic actor in a relationship with a creditor—had the audacity to declare unilaterally that he would determine on his own when to settle up, the cheated bondman Jess called Steve "a damned rogue," "damned [him,] and told him to keep it." Jess's reply touched another nerve altogether. Steve not only resented the obvious insult but also took offense at Jess's suggestion that Steve was the type to renege on a debt. Enraged, Steve stabbed Jess in the side with a knife and smote him on the head with a rock. Fear of gaining a reputation for failing to uphold economic bargains may have even coerced some slaves into paying up. When Hubbard neglected to discharge his debt promptly, West observed that he "took Hubbard to be more of a Gentleman than he found him to be." The implication was that a "Gentleman" acknowledged his obligations and settled them responsibly.[61]

On rare occasion, issues of slaves' indebtedness to other slaves surfaced in southern evangelical churches. Two incidents at Powelton Baptist Church in Hancock County, Georgia, separated by about a half century, show different ways in which church disciplinary committees engaged bondpeople's economic relationships as debtors and creditors. In July 1805, "Daniel Mitchell's negro Jack" filed "a complaint against one of our Black Members"—the bondman Ned—for "neglecting to pay his Just debts." Jack had experienced difficulty recovering what was owed him, and rather than resort to violence as other slaves did, he invoked the power of the church. An investigating committee consisting of four white brethren determined that "Pope's Ned" had indeed failed to pay Jack accordingly and had used "deception" in dealing with him. By November, with the aid of the church's intercession, Jack and Ned had settled their dispute.[62]

Churches were not only places for enslaved creditors to lodge allegations against bondpeople in default on their debts. Almost half a century later, an enslaved debtor used the church to help him discharge his obligation to another slave. The enslaved brother Abner needed "to pay a debt he owed Mr[.] Herbert['s] Paul." To do so, he placed a bill in the collection plate and made change for himself, part of which he intended to pass along to his creditor. But Abner's banking practices during services got him into trouble. In October 1854, the colored conference of Powelton Baptist charged him with placing "a two dollar bill of dead money" in the collection, taken for the purpose of compensating the preacher. With the death of the centralized Second Bank of the United States in 1836, a number of state-chartered local banks and privately owned banks began printing their own money. The plethora of bank notes in circulation created a chaotic monetary situation in the latter decades of the antebellum era. The currency Abner put in the collection plate had been printed at the defunct "old Macon bank" and by 1854 was utterly worthless. Abner nevertheless made change based on the face value of the bill he deposited in the plate and withdrew for himself "good money"—valid currency—to use in paying off his debt. The church detected something sinister in Abner's action. His purported plot foiled, Abner was promptly excluded from fellowship.[63]

Notwithstanding those few exceptional cases in which southern churches mediated slaves' disputes over debts, religious institutions tended to obstruct or stymie slaves' independent economic activities. Decade after decade, they railed against enterprising bondpeople who peddled the devil's wares, retailing "spirituous liquors" outside church or in close proximity to camp meetings. In August 1860, Padgett's Creek Baptist Church in Union District, South Carolina, cautioned "that all slaves bringing spiritous liquors watermelons & cakes on the grounds, & selling, or offering for sale the same, will be legally de[a]lt with." Nine months later, the same congregation directed that slaves engaged in those activities "receive 25 stripes" for the first offense, fifty for the second.[64]

Compared to the economic disagreements of black members, evangelical churches intervened in those of white members far more frequently. For white brethren, church disciplinary proceedings offered either a substitute for or an auxiliary to legal action. Churches heard complaint after complaint of whites swapping horses or otherwise trading on the Sabbath; stealing livestock; selling sick, unsound, or defective animals; slaughtering, shearing, or marking animals not their own; disposing of goods that belonged to others; marketing the same crop twice; migrating without alerting creditors or welshing on debts; forgery, fraud, swindling, or sharp dealing; and trading with slaves. Evangelical churches served as a moral buffer between aggrieved churchgoing consumers and the profane forces of the market that caused even good men to stray from the path of economic righteousness. Evangelical churches wielded powers to arbitrate economic conflicts and to censure those in the wrong, but slaves could not fully partake of the services offered to settle the fiscal conflicts of the quarters.

Slaves made a variety of business arrangements among themselves. Most were simple exchanges involving some combination of cash, commodities, or service and entirely free of drama. Periodically, however, the informal economy failed to function according to slaves' own expectations. In these cases of economic exchange gone awry, slaves sometimes resorted to violence. In 1826, Essex County, Virginia, slave Peter took "some chickens in the morning . . . to

Tappahannock to sell." That evening, Peter had an altercation with the bondmen Kingston and Henry, whom Peter claimed "had cheated him out of some money," possibly related to the day's sale of poultry. Peter and "one of the... slaves had a tussle," during which Peter threatened to "get his knife... and stick it in some negro before he slept that night."[65]

Many slaves proved savvy consumers, challenging even whites when circumstances warranted. In Spartanburg District, South Carolina, slaves knew that the white Robert Martin operated a dram shop and was "in the habit of keeping Liquor for sale." Martin participated in slaves' underground economy, dispensing spirits without scruple. In 1850, the bondman Larken visited Martin's establishment and "called for Liquor. Martin poured some out in a mug and set it on the counter and said there is your Liquor." Larken paid for the alcohol but expected change to complete the transaction. Martin refused, explaining "that he did not have his change." Martin may have been telling the truth, but he may also have been attempting to exercise his racial privilege and profit a few extra cents from his illicit commerce with a slave. Jason, a Martin family bondman, then intervened, informing Larken that "he never had that much" and directing the frustrated slave consumer to leave the premises. By this point, Larken determined that he was being cheated: the money he paid exceeded the value of the drink he received. Larken refused to go, "for he intended to have his change before he went." The dispute ultimately escalated to violence. Jason administered "two blows on the head with a stick," splintering the weapon and "knocking off Larkins cap." Larken, in turn, inflicted a mortal wound in Jason's right side with a knife. The confrontation, which earned Larken one hundred lashes for manslaughter, originated when the workings of the underground economy soured. Larken simply wanted a drink, and was willing to pay for it, but he also understood the economic value of his purchase and refused to be duped out of his money. When Jason challenged Larken's claim to his change, violence ensued. In a similar case from 1827, the bondman Charles threatened Robert Cobb's slave Dick at a store in Pendleton District, South Carolina, "because Dick would not draw him... whiskey." Charles assumed that Dick, perhaps left to tend the shop, would supply a fellow slave his alcohol. Denied, Charles later attacked him with a stick for refusing the liquor.[66]

The occasionally violent fallout from slaves' economic exchanges sometimes pivoted on the quality of the goods involved. Despite their meager to modest levels of material comfort, slaves remained discriminating consumers. Products needed to meet or exceed certain standards for bondpeople to be satisfied with them. Jim and Andrew, enslaved in Richmond, Virginia, "fell out about an exchange of caps" in 1862. Jim experienced the equivalent of buyer's remorse: "After the exchange," he "said he did not like the Trade, and took his cap back" to Andrew, presumably to get the respective hats returned to their original owners. Andrew was not amenable to the swap. Instead, for some inexplicable reason, he "cut up both caps." Jim vowed to "have satisfaction" for his shredded headwear. A week later, he stabbed Andrew to death. Also in Virginia, U.S. Senator Littleton W. Tazewell's bondman Solomon informed another of Tazewell's slaves, Ben, in 1832, "I will not pay you for the knife you sold me because it is not worth any thing." The substandard knife was already in Solomon's possession. Ben had given it to him without receiving payment at the time of the transaction, trusting that Solomon would compensate him soon. When Solomon withheld payment, without offering to return the knife, Ben replied with growing menace. "[Y]ou shall pay me," he informed Solomon. "I will not lose my twelve cents," the amount Solomon owed. Ben took a swing at Solomon with his fist, which Solomon returned threefold. Solomon also wielded a knife that he jammed into Ben's chest. Ben died over a matter of $3 and change in 2013 dollars.[67]

However small the amount owed, the failure to pay for goods or services rendered marked a serious breach of the unwritten code that governed the slave economy as well as the American economy generally. Yet bondpeople preferred not to invite the master into their private dealings. Only churchgoing slaves might invoke the power of disciplinary committees to resolve economic disputes, but only in a very limited range of cases. The courtroom was virtually off limits, notwithstanding the odd case of a master acting on the slave's behalf. The internal economy was an economy grounded in slaves' mutual trust. In Richmond, the routine functioning of the slave economy fell victim to a messy personal squabble. In the fall of 1859, the bondman Scott paid a visit to the bondwoman Priscilla at a house on Franklin Street to retrieve "his coat." Priscilla "was a middle aged woman, living to herself and washing for a livelihood." Scott and Priscilla "had previously lived together as man and wife," but the dynamic between them had changed after Scott left her only weeks earlier. Priscilla still laundered his clothes as she had when they were a couple but now expected payment for the service she provided. Priscilla refused to surrender Scott's coat until he "paid her for washing." (She also suggested Scott "go along and stay where you have been staying," suggesting the residual emotional baggage between the pair.) Perhaps realizing one of the lost benefits of his former union, Scott flew into a rage. "I will have my coat this night," Scott exclaimed. All reason then departed him.

"You damned bitch," he told Priscilla, "I mean to kill you." Scott launched into a vicious assault upon his ex-wife, "feloniously and maliciously striking, beating, kicking, choking and Stamping her." Priscilla lingered in pain for a month before she died.[68]

As the tragedy involving Scott and Priscilla suggests, matters of slaves' household economy could serve as a flashpoint for violence. By the very nature of their unions, enslaved husbands and wives were intimately bound to one another through economic as well as (ideally) affective ties. Scholars often neglect to think of slave households as the financial entities they were, probably because the cooperative efforts that enslaved spouses undertook on behalf of each other and their family's welfare was uncompensated labor. But when slave families failed to function as a cohesive unit, conflicts arose. Charleston District, South Carolina, bondman Isaac killed his wife Katura in 1834 in part because the bondwoman failed to fulfill Isaac's expectations of her as the female partner in their relationship. He entered their home one Sunday and "asked for something to eat," but Katura "had no bread" and refused to feed him. He then "ask[ed her] for his pantaloons, which caused some dispute" as well, presumably because Katura had not gotten them washed. Denied both sustenance and clean laundry, the cultural responsibilities of the woman, Isaac beat his wife with a hoe. A lack of economic teamwork also plagued the slave union of Hubard and Gracy in King George County, Virginia. Gracy had apparently neglected to consult her husband prior to making a significant purchase for their household from Tom, another slave. Hubard "objected to Tom's having any thing to do with his wife[,] as Tom had sold her a pig" without his authorization. Hubard may have believed it his responsibility rather than his wife's to transact that piece of household business.[69]

When slave unions collapsed, household commodities were at times the objects of misdirected physical aggression, ammunition in verbal jousts, and fodder for disputes over ownership. After the Prince George County, Virginia, bondwoman Betsey caught Patty, another female slave, with Betsey's husband John, Betsey stomped up to Patty's "room & broke her things up." Unapologetic, she then informed John "that if he paid Patty for the pitcher she broke that she would kill her or him." Once Betsey finally resolved to leave her adulterous husband, she berated his economic contributions to their household, noting dismissively, "all you have got here is a pale & a pot." The economic ramifications of broken slave unions and altered living arrangements generated some degree of confusion in the quarters. In 1827, the bondmen Nelson and Bob were heard "quarrelling about breaking up a small piece of ground" on the lands of William Bagley in Virginia's Lunenburg County. Bagley had hired Bob, and the slave's presence became the source of some unrest. Nelson feared that Bob and Plenny, presumably Bob's wife and quite possibly Nelson's former spouse, "were about to shut him out of his house." Bob contended that "the ground" Nelson wanted to work "belong[ed] to this house" that he and Plenny now occupied and from which Nelson may have been recently ejected. The displaced Nelson described Bob's claim to the land as "a damned lye" and vowed to "fight through Hell and damnation" before Bob and Plenny "should take away his ground from him." He proceeded to beat Bob to death with a hoe.[70]

Slaves participated in a dense web of economic relationships. Their efforts in the internal economy permitted some to acquire money and goods to improve materially their lives and those of their loved ones. Slaves' experiences in the market produced a profound ambivalence, however. Differing levels of material wealth generated social distinctions and status differentiation among slaves. The very success that might elicit the respect and admiration of fellow bondpeople might just as easily inspire jealousy and heated rivalries. The infiltration of cash and commodities into bondpeople's lives eroded the communal ethic of southern slave quarters. The values of "mutuality, reciprocity, and care for others"—all hallmarks of a cooperative ethos—withered in the face of the inequitable distribution of cash and property both within and across plantation boundaries. Among slaves, disputes over property were frequent and sometimes devolved into violent, even deadly, encounters. Without discounting the benefits that accrued to slaves via the slave economy, it is equally important to acknowledge its negative consequences, most evident in the violent confrontations that erupted over the possession of property and cash, theft in the quarters, indebtedness, and lapses in the smooth functioning of slaves' economic networks. The violence itself played an ambiguous role within the slave community.[71]

Chapter 6

VIOLENCE IN THE CREATION, MAINTENANCE, AND DESTRUCTION OF SLAVE UNIONS

FORMER SLAVE ERVIN E. SMITH of York District, South Carolina, was only about ten or eleven years old when he witnessed a murder. As the Civil War was drawing to a close, he saw Violet Harris fatally and publicly stab Warren Fewell in the heart with a butcher knife, "right at the fence at her gate." "[B]oth colored," clarified Smith to a Works Progress Administration interviewer in the 1930s, "They fell out over something." If Smith ever knew the precise motivation for the homicide, the decades that had elapsed since the incident in Ebenezer Township rendered his memory fuzzy. He nonetheless reported with confidence, "It come over a family quarrel some way."[1]

A significant portion of violent conflicts between slaves were products of such "family quarrel[s]."[2] Bondpeople's personal relationships were perpetually tenuous and fragile, subject to the master's will and sundering by the domestic slave trade. But despite the realities of their commodification, the vast majority of slaves found the courage to risk loving other bondpeople. Though aware that their interpersonal bonds might be cut on a whim, they could not deny the instinctive emotions that welled up from inside. Enslaved men courted women, and they joined together in matrimony for mutual support and companionship. Although slave marriages were unrecognized in law, they were widely acknowledged by custom among both blacks and whites. Acceptance of the marital union, however, did not imply inviolability, and the tenuousness of enslaved family structures, constantly vulnerable to division and destruction, only intensified slaves' efforts to exert control where they could, in contexts internal to the slave quarters. Most slaves regarded their loving unions as worthy of defense and prioritized specific families over a generalized sense of community among slaves. Enslaved men at times resorted to physical violence as they vied for bondwomen during courtship, protected their wives from the overtures of rival bondmen, or took vengeance upon enslaved interlopers who challenged or successfully violated male sexual claims to enslaved women. In a few cases, female slaves also clashed violently with other slaves—almost always bond*women*—in the competitive arena of courtship or to preserve existing relationships. Whenever slaves employed physical aggression to create, maintain, or defend family structures, they implicitly testified to the value they placed on the loving attachments and personal commitments between bondmen and bondwomen, despite the vulnerabilities of affective ties under bondage.[3]

Yet enslaved unions were no less impervious to marital strife and conflict than the marriages of any other group. As historian Deborah Gray White rightly observes, "Harmony did not always prevail in slave households." A portion of all bondmen had combative relationships with their spouses and physically abused them, and a few bondwomen gave as well as they got. Domestic quarrels compelled some enslaved partners to terminate their marital unions, but discarded husbands occasionally refused to accept their breakups, claimed continued possession of bondwomen who no longer loved them (if they ever had), and attacked ex-wives' subsequent suitors. Just as slaves' relationships were sometimes forged in violence, they sometimes ended in violence as well. Whether for good or ill, violence proved a distinguishing characteristic in the histories of many relationships between enslaved men and women.[4]

That slaves routinely came to blows over matters of love and intimacy contributes to our increasingly sophisticated understanding of enslaved families. In 1965, then Assistant Secretary of Labor Daniel Patrick Moynihan issued a controversial governmental report titled *The Negro Family: The Case for National Action*. Better known simply as the Moynihan Report, it attributed contemporary poverty and violence in the black community to a tradition of dysfunctional, matriarchal families that dated back to slavery. Rejecting Moynihan's findings, historian Herbert G. Gutman published in 1976 a seminal work celebrating the resilience of the slave family. He portrayed the typical enslaved family as stable and nuclear, with a male head of household present. For Gutman, the institution of family served as a source of strength for slaves resisting the oppression of bondage.[5] His interpretation dominated historical scholarship for two decades, and the thrust of the literature conveyed the impression that the black family was, in Nell Irvin Painter's words, "preternaturally immune to the brutality inherent in slavery."[6] More recent scholarship has challenged Gutman's thesis. Brenda Stevenson, Christopher Morris, and Emily West have all demonstrated that domestic violence marred slave families. They and others have suggested that Gutman's classic work overestimated the number of two-parent slave households and exaggerated the stability of the enslaved family. Historians have increasingly recognized that the institution of slavery undermined slave families and imposed incredible strains on husbands and wives in bondage. Without denying the centrality of the family to slaves' survival, the current generation of scholarship acknowledges the presence of stress, marital strife, and disharmony within it.[7]

This chapter investigates the ways in which bondpeople's violent acts touched enslaved families. A systematic study of court and church records captures evidence of the violence perpetrated upon enslaved husbands, wives, and lovers. Slaveholder and southern intellectual George Fitzhugh, surely no disinterested observer, was woefully off base when he declared that "we have never heard or read of a negro murdering his wife at the South."[8] Though murders were indeed exceptional, enough courtroom proceedings survive to document ample instances in which slaves' violence raged out of control. Deadly encounters exposed in starkest relief the sorts of familial crises that evoked such heated passions. The less sensational cases found in church records reveal patterns of behavior and assumptions that also shed light on the stresses and strains of bondage affecting enslaved suitors and spouses. Together, court and church records permit us to become voyeurs into slaves' most intimate moments and witness the commitment of some slaves—as well as the relative indifference of others—to their unions.

Courtship marked a significant source of conflict and competition among enslaved men. Contests over female companionship were common throughout the history of slavery in the American South but more intense in certain times and places. Disagreements between enslaved men over claims to enslaved women probably peaked during the early eighteenth century, a function of demographics. The recent influx of African imports skewed heavily toward male slaves. With relatively few enslaved women available, competition for their affection must have been fierce. In 1746, for example, the Louisa County, Virginia, bondman Boatswain was embroiled in one of the countless rivalries for the attention of a desirable bondwoman. By the nineteenth century, the gender imbalance of the South's slave population had largely corrected itself. In those locations where bondwomen still proved scarce, such as Louisiana's sugar parishes, sex ratios remained weighted toward enslaved men. The reality there of a predominantly male slave population prompted continued friction and violent clashes over the available women. Jealous rivalries were also more pronounced wherever slaveholdings were small, including the South Carolina upcountry. Whereas slaves on large plantations might select from a variety of possible mates, on small holdings, young, single slaves confronted a more limited—or even nonexistent—market of marriageable bondpeople. Enslaved men's quests for love and companionship necessarily guided them to neighboring or nearby farms and plantations, pitting them against enslaved rivals as they vied to capture female attention.[9]

According to social convention, male slaves took the lead during courtship, and in contests for female affection, rival slave suitors sometimes came to blows. As per a conjurer's instructions, one upcountry South Carolina slave man thrashed a competing admirer about the face with a swatch of grapevine to warn him away from his sweetheart. South Carolina's Anderson Bates challenged not one suitor but an alleged seven for the affections of "dat sugar lump of a gal" Carrie. "I knocks one down one night, kick another out de nex' night, and choke de stuffin' out of one de nex' night," he recalled proudly. "I landed de three-leg stool on de head of de fourth one," and "de others," now intimidated, opted to "carry deir 'fections to some other place than Carrie's house." Head over heels in love, the triumphant Bates eventually married the woman for whom he had fought. Formerly enslaved in Georgia, Sallie Blakely recollected one instance "when two slave cousins quarrelled over a girl." The "one became so infuriated he picked up a rock and hit the other in the head[,] killing him." Deaths that occurred during the courtship process could bring the law to bear on the enslaved murderer, but more commonly enslaved men's quarrels over bondwomen were not fatal and invited the intercession only of masters or their agents. Sarah Laws Hill's enslaved father once "became embroiled in a fight with another slave over the affection of her mother." After he "gave the other slave a beating," his punishment was "to do both men's work until the other slave recovered."[10]

Violence motivated by a jealous desire to subdue competition in the forging of relationships was not the unique preserve of male slaves. Although far less often than enslaved men, enslaved women occasionally committed violent acts during courtship. Their victims were the bondwomen with whom they contended for male attention. As my database of Virginia murders shows, sometimes their violence, too, proved fatal. Of the thirty-nine enslaved women convicted in the Old Dominion between 1796 and 1864 of murdering other slaves and punished capitally, only eight, or about one-fifth of the total, were found guilty of killing adult slave women, all between 1816 and 1864 inclusive. Since two women cooperated to produce the death of William Link's bondwoman Amey in 1853, there were actually only seven total adult female slave victims, a remarkably small figure. Between 1816 and 1864, an enslaved woman was convicted of the murder of another female slave roughly once every seven years. Calculating the average from 1796, the figure drops to basically one per decade.

In her pioneering study of enslaved women, Deborah Gray White acknowledges that, among female slaves, "sisterhood could coexist with discord." Living and working so closely together on a daily basis, enslaved women did fight one another, usually verbally but sometimes physically, far more frequently than the murder convictions from Virginia would suggest. Their disputes tended not to enter the historical record, however, because they so rarely turned lethal and were normally punished as part of routine plantation discipline. In the handful of cases in which it is known that enslaved women inflicted fatal injuries upon other female slaves, the deadly assaults usually had something to do with an enslaved man. In 1816, the Spotsylvania County, Virginia, slave Clara killed her master's enslaved woman Grace. According to the testimony of the slave Ben, Clara had repeatedly threatened to murder the female slave. After she carried out the deed, she took Ben "to the place where the bones were," unceremoniously chucked the remains "into the river," and confessed that "she had killed her" "on his ... account." Clara's obsession with Ben was so strong that she was willing to commit murder to secure his love.[11]

Slave courtship was necessarily a public process. Privacy was difficult to achieve in the quarters. Whether young male suitors pursued a woman on the home plantation or, as they often preferred, journeyed to a nearby holding in search of companionship, they labored under the watchful eyes and prying ears not only of masters but also of other slaves. Slaves, revealed the Reverend Charles Colcock Jones, "overhear conversations and domestic disagreements; become privy to improper conduct; [and] depredate upon each other." Much of slaves' wooing took place at bondpeople's dances, frolics, and secret parties. There slaves congregated, socialized, and charmed their way into another's heart. Such occasions were also competitive and conducive to violence. Held in bondage in Louisiana, Solomon Northup recalled how the bondman "Sam cherished an ardent passion for Lively," an aptly named female slave. Described as "a heartbreaking coquette," Lively was magnetic. She enchanted several enslaved "boys" present at a frolic, all of whom attempted to win her heart through a display of fancy footwork. Lively danced with Sam first, which her other suitors resented. They "intimated they would like to pitch into Mr. Sam and hurt him badly," Northup remembered. Sam tired, however, so Lively danced, in turn, with his enslaved rivals Pete Marshall and Harry Carey. The energetic Lively outlasted them all. The competition for Lively took place in full view of other slaves well aware of what was at stake. Matches enslaved men and women made at these dances fell under the scrutiny of peers. Sometimes a pairing made at a "drunk dance," reported one former bondwoman, fostered resentment as "de men and de women together ... wrassle and hug and carry on" and "sing about going to somebody elses house and sleeping wid dem." Such boisterous revelry made "de good people mad, and sometime dey have killings about it." An enslaved husband or father who discovered that "his wife or one of his daughters" had "been to de woods"—a polite euphemism for engaging in illicit sex—might "catch her and beat her and cut off de rim of her ears." Because for slaves, formal, lawful marriages would never legitimize their unions, as relationships formed and matured, enslaved couples required validation for their relationships from fellow bondpeople on the plantation and throughout the neighborhood.[12]

Enslaved parents sometimes objected to the matches their adolescent and young-adult children made. Many mothers and fathers, especially in the older slaveholding states of the Atlantic seaboard, were denied the opportunity ever to register complaints about their sons' and daughters' choice of partner because the domestic slave trade severed parent-child relationships. But in family units spared by the internal traffic and left intact, some enslaved parents protested young slaves' budding romances. As one overseer in Louisa County, Virginia, explained in 1849, the slaves "John & Abby wanted to marry each other a year or eighteen months ago, but her father & mother objected." Abby may have argued passionately in defense of John, but she ultimately proved an obedient daughter, submitted to her parents' wishes, and broke off her relationship. Denied approval for the match, Abby instead united with the bondman Tom, taking "him for her husband with the consent of her own parents, & of her mistress & of his master." As Abby's case makes clear, generational conflicts erupted between young slaves of marrying age and their parents over spousal choice.[13]

Fragmentary evidence suggests that, compared to enslaved fathers, enslaved mothers were more vociferous in objecting to their children's unions. Taking into account enslaved suitors' character, skills, and prospects as provider (despite the challenges of bondage), mature bondwomen readily judged potential sons-in-law unworthy of their daughters' hands. The bondman Edmund of Haywood County, North Carolina, counted among those who encountered resistance from a would-be mother-in-law. For about a year, Edmund had attempted to court the bondwoman Deely, but her mother Dicey refused him permission. As Deely recounted, Edmund "asked mother for me and ... she told him that she would not let him have me." Rage slowly welled up inside Edmund, simmering, until he at last felt compelled to lash out. Brandishing "a certain knife of the value of six pence," he slit Dicey's throat. If Edmund believed that eliminating Dicey would clear the path to her daughter, he was sorely mistaken. His conviction for murder eliminated whatever slim opportunity he might have had.[14]

A small number of other enslaved men resolved that, if they could not possess the objects of their desire, neither would anyone else. The frequently inebriated bondman Isaac paid unwelcome attention to the enslaved woman Charlotte in late antebellum Granville County, North Carolina. Upon her rejection of him, Isaac "threatened to murder" her. A few followed through on such threats. In Pittsylvania County, Virginia, Alfred, locked in competition with Robin for the female slave Rinah, informed Rinah's mother Aunt Kitty that Robin had come to visit her daughter. It was a strategic move. Alfred knew that Aunt Kitty despised Robin and therefore identified her as an ally. Upon hearing Alfred's report, Aunt Kitty dutifully marched to Rinah's house and "told Robin to go away from there, he shouldn't be with her daughter." What she found disagreeable or offensive about Robin is not known, but to reinforce her point, the protective mother threatened to "poison" Robin "and put him in the ground" if he persisted in his courting. After Aunt Kitty departed, Robin, freshly scolded, asked Rinah whether she would rather "dissatisfy her mother or him." Rinah replied that "she had given her word to her mother, she wouldn't be with him & she wouldn't falsify her word." Robin could not accept the reaffirmation of her pledge. Spurned, he murdered the very woman he coveted.[15]

Rather than kill the bondwomen they pursued so strenuously, other despondent slave men attacked the victorious husband who won a desirable female slave's hand. When the Henrico County bondman Stephen asked an unidentified "mulatto girl" in 1801 "if she would have him, she answered that she would not." Stephen replied, "then I am determined to commit murder this night." True to his word, sometime between midnight and 2:00 a.m., Stephen knocked at the mulatto girl's dwelling. Another bondman, his rival Aaron, opened the door. When Stephen asked to fight him, Aaron fled into the night, to the home of the mulatto girl's father, Davy. Stephen followed, uttering "many oaths" and clutching a "Chunk of fire" he had grabbed out of the mulatto girl's fireplace. Stephen hurled the flaming weapon at Aaron, which struck him and knocked him down. Stephen yanked Aaron up from the ground to berate his adversary, only to find that Aaron was dead, vanquished by his competition for the mulatto girl's love.[16]

Losers in contests for bondwomen's affections thus unleashed their rage and frustration upon different targets. Some who were denied the relationships they sought preferred to exact revenge indirectly by committing crimes against property. Nathan, a Buckingham County, Virginia, slave, complained that master James M. Johns "& his black folks was all against him." Nathan developed "the habit of coming to Mr. Johns'" plantation to court a bondwoman, but the master, his enslaved "head man" Albert, and other plantation slaves "objected altogether to Nathan's coming there." The source of their hostility is not clear. Perhaps a resident slave on the Johns plantation may have desired the same woman, or they simply disliked Nathan personally. Warned away, the bondman hatched a plot "to do white people harm" and "to injure black people too." He divulged to a neighboring slave (and brother of the woman he wanted for a wife) that "he intended to leave them all in trouble" at the Johns plantation and that all "the neighbourhood should see it." Days later, Johns' tobacco barn was set ablaze. The fire consumed an "abundance of tobacco" belonging to Johns as well as to Albert, the "head man" hostile to Nathan. The economic loss occasioned by the arson surely did affect the quality of life for both white and black on the Johns estate, precisely as Nathan intended. It is doubtful, however, that the blaze endeared the slave to anyone on the Johns estate.[17]

Slaves' desire to sustain loving relationships extended from courtship to marriage. Enslaved unions were subject to division not only upon the whim of the master but by the choices of slave partners themselves. For some bondmen and bondwomen, the pale semblance of marriage allotted them—legally meaningless, subject to permanent division—did not inspire faithfulness to one's spouse and instead promoted morally questionable choices. Slaves and ex-slaves at times condemned their own for engaging in promiscuous sexual practices. Successful fugitive slaves, encouraged by abolitionist allies, frequently lamented bondpeople's licentiousness. "Marriage," conceded the runaway Frederick Douglass, ". . . has no existence" under slavery, "except in such hearts as are purer and higher than the standard morality around them." For those still in bondage, complaints of infidelity were more personal. The bondwoman Lavinia pleaded to her mistress not to allow her husband Jimmy to take up with one enslaved woman she denounced as "worse than Mary Magdelene," a "devil" whose "sparkling black eye" ensnared "other wimmin's husbands." In Louisa County, Virginia, the bondman Tom grumbled "of the way his wife Abby carried on with men." Formerly upset with the bondmen attracted to Abby, by 1849 he had come to the realization "that it was she who ran after the men." Whereas slaves anxious over an errant spouse might beg for the master's intervention on their behalf, others were willing to shoulder their own burdens. One former Mississippi slave cautioned his wife, whom he suspected of cheating, "that if she didn't look out, some day, . . . I would find her in some of her rascality and would knock her brains out."[18]

By the antebellum decades, the overwhelming majority of all slaves, men as well as women, expected monogamy of their partners, and "as a general rule," remarked one North Carolina Supreme Court justice in 1853, bondpeople "respect the exclusive rights of fellow-slaves who are married." Polygamy was more common during the colonial era than in the late eighteenth or nineteenth century. Many of the slaves conveyed to the American South via the Middle Passage before the formal closing of the transatlantic slave trade in 1808 brought African traditions of polygamy with them. The practice of holding multiple wives survived for decades in the colonial Carolina lowcountry. There, the continued importation of slaves from abroad kept distinctly African cultures very much alive, and the minority white population of the region exerted less cultural sway upon the slaves. Outside the lowcountry, in places such as the colonial Chesapeake, a hybrid African American culture more rapidly emerged that accepted the standard of marriage as uniting one man, one woman. Although Solomon Northup, enslaved in antebellum Louisiana, observed that slaves "can have as many husbands or wives as the owner will permit," the vast majority of slaves by the nineteenth century expected exclusivity within their marital relations. Bondpeople who strayed faced the consequences. One former Clyde County, Georgia, slave remembered that "my pappy wus bad 'bout wimen. Sometimes he an' mammy wud fight bout his gwine out at night."[19]

Despite the established standard of monogamy by the antebellum decades, some bond*men* nevertheless maintained multiple relationships simultaneously on nearby holdings. Far more frequently than enslaved women, enslaved men received liberty from the master to leave the plantation on errands or social calls. Some took the opportunity to cultivate plural marriages. Ex-slave Annie Frazier remarked that planters in the vicinity of Georgetown, South Carolina, did not countenance slaves who led "double lives or have two wives or husbands." Other reports from locations not far away contradicted her, however. Along coastal Georgia, the enslaved carriage driver Hector explained to Frances Kemble "that a great number of the men on all the different plantations had *wives* on the neighboring estates as well as on that to which they properly belonged." Although masters and overseers were "perfectly" aware of "this extensive practice of bigamy," Kemble lamented, they "never in any way found fault with or interfered with" it. "Perhaps," she conjectured, "this promiscuous mode of keeping up the slave population finds favor with the owners of creatures who are valued in the market at so much per head." Scattered evidence from the antebellum decades confirms that some enslaved men continued to claim multiple wives into the nineteenth century and accept a range of different family structures. The bondman Abram of Pittsylvania County, Virginia, may have been attempting to secure a second wife when he tampered with Primus's marriage. Unwilling to share the bondwoman he loved, Primus killed Abram and scolded his deceased body, saying "I can do with one wife ... & you might have done the same." Like Abram, Middlesex County bondman Levi flouted the monogamistic principle. When, on one occasion, Mortimer "took hold of Margaret," a female slave, Levi objected, observing that "she was his wife." Mortimer "then took hold" of a second bondwoman, Jane. Levi again protested because Jane "was his wife also." "[W]hich do you love best[?]" Mortimer inquired. Levi replied, "both." Mortimer departed but soon "returned with a long knife," complaining that "Levi thought he was a fool." In the tussle that ensued, Levi fatally stabbed Mortimer in the neck.[20]

As Brenda Stevenson has explained, many slaves heralded "male sexual prowess." As disruptive to bondpeople's "sense of community" as they may have been, the "sexual conquests" of male slaves earned them respect among their fellow bondmen. Most notably, slave breeding men derived status from their sexual potency. Their virility became the stuff of legend in the quarters. One enslaved man reportedly possessed such stamina that the different bondwomen he had impregnated delivered "sebenteen little black babies" on the same momentous day. Paradoxically, however, bondmen praised values associated with behaviors that could just as easily strike back against them.[21]

Innumerable enslaved men confronted the anguish of white men sexually exploiting their female partners and the accompanying powerlessness to prevent it, but they also had to guard against the sexual incursion of other bondmen upon the women they claimed. Elizabeth Fox-Genovese notes that, without the legal sanction of marriage, bondmen routinely lost their wives to other enslaved men. It was when other slaves rather than white men seduced their wives, however, that bondmen were more apt to respond violently in bondwomen's defense. Whether or not bondwomen desired it, enslaved men took it upon themselves to protect them from the sexual depredations of other bondmen. In the South Carolina upcountry, Anderson District slaves Bas, the property of Charles Irby, and "Duckworth's Joe" fought because "they fell out about a woman." A Laurens District bondman died after "there was a fuss about Wills wife," and the murderous slave was warned "dont go there." Similarly, Sampson struck Manuel a fatal blow in 1857 over "some dificulty concerning a negro Girl his wife which arose from Jeolesy between him and the boy."[22]

Jealousy may have been particularly pronounced among enslaved men in the South Carolina upcountry because slaveholdings there were considerably smaller there than in other portions of the state. In such areas, slaves' marriage market proved more limited compared to other regions across the South where slaveholdings were larger. On small holdings, young, single slaves may have had no suitable mates, or at the very least, fewer potential spouses from which to choose. To avoid violating marriage taboos, slaves on small farms and plantations necessarily had to seek partners elsewhere. But they had to overcome the widespread objections of southern masters to abroad marriages. Virginia bondman Henry "Box" Brown encountered one forlorn group of slaves who "were obliged to marry persons who worked on the same plantation, as the master would not allow them to take wives from other plantations." Many slave owners resented the loss of control cross-plantation unions entailed. Appomattox County, Virginia, master Joel W. Coleman explained that, when he purchased the bondman Nelson, his newly acquired slave "had a wife" who "lived some 9 or 10 miles from my house. I allowed him to go see his wife once," over the weekend, but because Nelson was "late getting back on Monday morning, I told him he would have to get a wife nearer home or stop going to see the one he had." Moreover, owners of enslaved men who fathered children on neighboring plantations saw no economic benefit from the resulting offspring, who instead augmented the wealth of the enslaved mother's master. Slaveholder reservations, however, confronted the demographic realities of slavery in the South Carolina upcountry and similar regions where the preponderance of small holdings demanded that masters set aside any qualms against cross-plantation unions. Emily West estimates that abroad marriages accounted for 34 percent of slave households in antebellum South Carolina as a whole. Surely the proportion of abroad marriages in the upcountry exceeded that figure.[23]

Although disadvantageous in some ways, many enslaved men found abroad marriages appealing. Bondmen with spouses and children on nearby plantations avoided witnessing firsthand the heart-wrenching spectacle of family members being beaten, raped, or abused—horrors they were virtually powerless to prevent. In addition, gender conventions among bondpeople held not only that male slaves initiated courtships but also that husbands did the traveling to visit abroad spouses.[24] Cross-plantation marriages, then, not only gave enslaved men a sense of personal autonomy in making their own marital choices but also awarded them a degree of mobility and time away from the home plantation.[25] The relative freedom of movement helped enslaved men with abroad spouses create their own "social space" or "rival geography" distinct from that of their masters.[26] Slave owners abetted this process, typically granting bondmen a pass on the weekends to call upon a partner living abroad. Occasionally a master such as F. N. Fitzhugh of Caroline County, Virginia, sanctioned an additional midweek visit. Fitzhugh permitted his slave Jim to go "to his wife's house every other Wednesday night" as well as each Saturday. Far more often, bondmen's visits during the week were unauthorized, undertaken at the risk of encountering the patrol.[27]

Despite their bondage, Emily West concludes, enslaved men involved in cross-plantation unions "saw themselves as initiators, protectors, and providers." West provides an overwhelmingly positive assessment of cross-plantation marriages. Slave commitment to them, she insists, suggests the "strength of the slave family" and "the wider resilience of the slave community." Indeed, West contends, the maintenance of cross-plantation ties resisted threats to the slave family, for the vitality of abroad marriages permitted enslaved families and the slave community the strength to cope with and survive local separation or sale.[28]

Peter Kolchin acknowledges such advantages as mobility that abroad marriages held for slaves but describes cross-plantation unions on the whole as detrimental to "family stability or communal loyalty." Evidence from the South Carolina upcountry lends support to his contention. The relatively small holdings of the region narrowed the market of slaves available to wed. Realistically, the time available for travel on the weekends restricted slaves' options for cross-plantation mates to partners within a reasonable distance, usually less than a comfortable day's walk (longer if a slave was fortunate enough to have access to a horse). Aware of their circumscribed social geography and a rough estimate of marriageable women within it, enslaved men often resented it when other bondmen came onto their plantations wooing eligible female slaves or enslaved women already claimed by another bondman at home. Abroad marriages provided fertile breeding ground for jealousy.[29]

The cases of enslaved men jealously defending female slaves from the sexual advances of other black men vividly expose the fierce competition for mates in regions such as upcountry South Carolina with relatively few slaves. Antipathy toward slaves belonging to other masters was not automatic, however. Depending on the size of holding and the slaves' own relationships with bondmen on neighboring estates, enslaved men sometimes welcomed those bondmen with whom they were acquainted or had cultivated friendships. When relations with neighboring slaves were tense or outright hostile, hospitality was not so forthcoming. And sometimes bondmen's acceptance of enslaved outsiders was contingent, at times a matter of sheer numbers. A case from Spartanburg District illustrates the friction among enslaved men as they vied for bondwomen in the South Carolina upcountry. By September 1843, "two negro boys" belonging to William Waldrip had "wives at Sampson Bobo's," but apparently "another one of the Old Gentleman's boys was . . . trying to get a wife there, too." Bondmen on the Bobo and surrounding plantations, perhaps eyeing the remaining Bobo bondwomen, tallied up the eligible female slaves in the vicinity and calculated that a third marital union between Waldrip and Bobo slaves was too many. Mysteriously, the "negro man Allen," one of Waldrip's slaves who either had a wife or was trying to secure one on the Bobo estate, turned up dead. Allen left his master's plantation one Saturday to visit his sweetheart and was not seen again until Tuesday, when his "badly beaten" corpse was found near Bobo's, "covered up at the root of a tree which had been blown down." Allen's skull had been fractured by "some Clubbs" lying next to his body. Bobo swore before the magistrate that Waldrip's slave Dick had killed Allen. Waldrip implicated four other slaves as accomplices, including the bondman Aleck and Bobo's bondwomen Grace and Randy. Testimony did not disclose what role Grace and Randy supposedly played in the murder, and they and Aleck all earned a verdict of not guilty. Regrettably incomplete, the trial papers nevertheless reveal the tensions in the quarters and the seething passions sometimes unleashed over the relationships between enslaved men and enslaved women.[30]

Enslaved men in the South Carolina upcountry asserted their manhood when they protected and defended enslaved women from the sexual overtures of other bondmen. In Anderson District, George, a slave hired out to an H. Cobb, assaulted Elijah Wyatt's slave Len "with a heavy stick." "George," testimony revealed, "had complained of Len's talking & mischief making with a female slave in the employ of Mr. Cobb." Also in Anderson District, bondman Jeff ordered Emory "out of his house" for "running after Becky," his wife. Former slave Henry Gladney recalled that his father "didn't 'low other slave men to look at my mammy," once breaking an enslaved rival's leg. When asked "what would be the consequences if one man were to take another man's wife," one Spartanburg District slave replied that "it would be near about a death crime." Another area bondman concurred: "if any man was to take his wife he believes he should kill him." Or die in her defense. The slave John's efforts to safeguard his wife Lavinia, who reportedly had "the name of being a strumpet," cost him his own life. John fought with the slave Henry because the latter "would visit Johns house" and "trouble his wife." John got the worse of the struggle, however, when Henry beat his head with an iron rod, killing him. The "cause of [the] disturbance," confirmed a bondman at the coroner's inquest, was jealousy.[31]

Although jealousy over claims to other slaves was conspicuous in upcountry South Carolina, it was not unique to the region. A few married bondmen in Virginia were allegedly so overwhelmed and debilitated by jealousy over their cross-plantation wives that their masters committed them to the Eastern Lunatic Asylum in Williamsburg. Peter, enslaved in York County, suffered from "jealousy ... of his wife who lived on an adjacent farm" and who was apparently wooed by at least one other suitor. Caroline County bondman Stafford "got in a fight with another man about his wife, & was then driven off the plantation by her master." Although Stafford "continued ... to visit her by stealth," he purportedly "became deranged" from the mental stress of his predicament.[32]

Unlike in the cases of Peter and Stafford, jealousy tended to manifest itself externally rather than internally. Broaching the subject of intraracial slave homicide, Alabama planter and social commentator Daniel R. Hundley asserted that, most frequently, it was "jealousy [that] leads to the fatal deed, or a strong desire to get rid of a troublesome wife or husband in order to solace themselves with some new 'affinity.'" Even in places such as Alabama, where plantations were larger or slave populations denser than in the South Carolina upcountry, bondmen rallied in defense of wives and families. In cotton-intensive, slave-rich Adams County, Mississippi, Harry countenanced no interference from other bondmen in his relationship with Celeste, another of his master's slaves. In 1834, Harry cautioned the "negro man" Sam "to go away, and not meddle with his business." Sam may possibly have had a relationship with Celeste, past or present, and Harry did not want him around. Should Sam refuse to leave voluntarily, Harry threatened to "make him go away." As tensions escalated, Sam backed down, replying that "he was only funning." But for many enslaved men, "proprietary" claims to bondwomen were no laughing matter. Harrison, another Mississippi slave, murdered a fellow bondman who dared say that he "was inside of the House with his [Harrison's] wife and that he might help himself if he could." Merely to suggest cuckolding another bondman hazarded one's life.[33]

One plot to break up an existing slave couple backfired on a bondman in Georgia. William, or Bill, an enslaved foreman, complained of another of his master's slaves, George, because "George ... is working some prank to get me away from my wife." Their "fuss" actually dated back some "four or five years," but recently George had concocted a plan "to get Bill off the place" so that George might "cultivate his wife," Ann. William and Ann had been married "thirteen or fifteen years," and the enslaved husband resented George's attempt to insinuate himself into Ann's good favor. The stratagem to separate him from his wife was the last straw. When William killed George in 1863 with a hoe, neighborhood slaves were hardly surprised. One had predicted that either William or George would be "the cause of the death of the other," driven by the "bad feeling" between them. He strongly suspected that "the devil might get in" William, who "might kill George" in defense of his longstanding union.[34]

Despite the legal fiction of slave marriage, enslaved men guarded their wives in an ongoing struggle waged on two fronts. They carefully monitored the behavior not only of rival bondmen such as George but also of their own spouses. Constant vigilance was necessary to enforce claims to enslaved women. In tobacco-producing Mecklenburg County, Virginia, the bondman Daniel "seemed to be jealous of his wife" Ann and the enslaved "rascal" Henry Baptist, whom he suspected of sexual improprieties. Daniel was not alone in doubting the faithfulness of an enslaved spouse. Chesterfield County bondwoman Isabel explained that "Essex her husband was Jealous of her and quarreled with her" over his insecurities. That "she went away and slept from home one night" after a fight only exacerbated his suspicions.[35]

Enslaved men were often willing to employ violence in the defense of an existing union. By 1840, Nottoway County bondman Ransom had heard disconcerting news about Maria—the woman he had taken as a wife—and the enslaved man Tom. Both the property of Asa Oliver, Ransom and Tom had an antagonistic history, "frequently quarrelling." Described by his master as loyal but possessed of a "high temper," Ransom had once threatened violence upon Tom, telling him, "God damn him, if his knife would not do his axe should." Several months later, Ransom confronted Tom one morning and informed him that "I want to read salvation to you, God damn you." He stormed off, determined to ferret out the truth about Tom's relationship with his wife. Later that day, he interrogated the bondwoman Maria about what he had heard concerning Tom's "intimacy" with her. Afterward, to "settle accounts," Ransom "drew his knife and made at Tom," stabbing his foe in the chest. Ransom declared in triumph, "Ah! Have I staggered you." He was not the only bondman to crow about dispatching an enslaved rival. At a Pittsylvania County dance, the bondman Abram took the liberty of speaking to Primus's wife Dilsey. Primus objected and fatally stabbed Abram for interfering in his marriage. Standing over Abram's fresh corpse, Primus gloated, "now God Damn you you will not get between me & my wife any more."[36]

Enslaved women shared in the jealousy that sometimes gripped enslaved men. Generalizing about the opposite sex, Colleton District, South Carolina, planter David Gavin described jealousy as "common amongst women white and black." It was the origin of numerous "quarrels amongst my negro women," he complained. One Mississippi bondwoman explained how her fellow female slave "Laura had taken her husband, Bill, from her." Although she now conceded that Bill was together with Laura, "they had a great deal of quareling about it." On rare occasion, jealous slave women employed violence to maintain family structures in the face of challengers. Traveler Harriet Martineau recorded the story of one bondwoman who hurled an axe at her husband's head "in a fit of jealousy," narrowly missing him. The female slave had scrupulously "kept watch over her husband, declaring that she would be the death of any girl" her spouse might attempt to take as a wife. In Greensville County, Virginia, the enslaved woman Frankey and the young slave mother Clary vied for the affections of the slave Ben. Over the course of their heated, longstanding quarrel, "each threaten[ed] to take the life of the other." The stakes were high. As one bondman explained, "Ben was considered the husband of Frankey but... both claimed him." Clary was a nursing mother, and perhaps Ben was the father of her child. In late 1833, the dance floor became the bondwomen's theater of competition. Clary interrupted a dance between Ben and Frankey and "cut Frankey out." Frankey retorted snidely that "Clary had better go and nurse her child." Apparently weary of competing for Ben's affections, Clary called her nemesis "a damn bitch," "struck her ... with her fist," and stabbed her with a knife in a desperate bid to make Ben exclusively hers.[37]

Disparities in age supplied the fuel for some bondwomen's jealousy. In 1864, the forty-five-year-old Charlotte County, Virginia, slave woman Matilda accused Harriett, some fifteen or twenty years her junior, "of keeping her husband" Eckelbert. One recent rainy night, Matilda's "husband ... staid with Harriett without coming to Matilda's house," even though it was a matter of steps away "in the same yard." Eckelbert may only have wanted to stay dry, but Matilda suspected a less innocent motive for his absence. She was no doubt hurt by her husband's apparent betrayal and felt sexually threatened by her younger rival. For her part, Harriett once crept up to "the chimney corner of Matilda's house" and eavesdropped on Matilda's conversation with Eckelbert; they were talking about her. Whatever Harriett overheard upset her, and the next day she confronted Matilda "in a great rage." An enslaved man stepped in and, as he believed, they "made friends," but the bondwomen's quarrel renewed a few days afterward. Fed up with the more senior slave's constant tormenting of her, Harriett threatened to knock Matilda's "brains out." A week later, the elder bondwoman was strangled, struck by a hoe, and left for dead, lying face down in the mud. David Gavin's dismissal of jealousy as the source of endemic "quarrels amongst the low, narrow minded, and sensual" overlooked the genuine, passionate commitment present within many slave relationships despite the challenges bondage imposed upon enslaved couples.[38]

Inevitably, despite slaves' vigilant efforts to protect and preserve the integrity of their marital relationships, rivals for a spouse's affection sometimes bested them, and an enslaved partner slept with another bondperson. The magnitude of slave adultery has been difficult for scholars to determine. Eugene D. Genovese argues that "[e]xisting evidence cannot sustain the charge of widespread marital infidelity," and to be sure, whites' misunderstandings or sheer cluelessness often led them to perceive adultery and moral laxity in the quarters where none existed. Yet the very conditions of slavery oftentimes bred that infidelity. Masters who paired slaves with partners not of their own choosing, forbade slaves from visiting abroad spouses, sold away half an enslaved couple, or moved westward with a husband or wife involved in a cross-plantation union all inadvertently encouraged adulterous liaisons.[39] In contrast to Genovese, Brenda Stevenson describes adultery as an "internal problem" that "rocked slave families or communities," a phenomenon fostered by the tenuousness of a marital institution that was denied the force of law and existed only by the will of the owner. Despite bondpeople's general expectation of faithfulness, knowledge that enslaved families could be torn asunder with ease, Stevenson suggests, could have undermined at least some slaves' commitment to their marital unions and produced rates of infidelity higher than if slaveholding society had valued the enslaved family as an inviolable unit. This mindset may indeed have predisposed some slaves to cheat on their spouses, and certainly there were some bondpeople who casually disregarded their own marital obligations or dismissed the sanctity of others' commitments. In Pittsylvania County, Virginia, Abram brazenly informed fellow bondman Primus that Primus's wife "Dilsey was as much for him as she was for Primus." If court and church records are any indication, adultery was a common source of conflict in the quarters.[40]

Most masters understood the potential for slaves' adulterous relationships to fracture the plantation community. Southern whites recognized infidelity as a primary source of discord among slaves and often naturally assumed that disputes between bondmen were grounded in competition over female slaves. After the murder of a fellow bondman in Copiah County, Mississippi, Simon was asked "if there was no woman matter in it." Following Martin's murder of Lewis in Henrico County, Virginia, the bondwoman Harriet was questioned at the coroner's inquest over the deceased's body. Had "any feeling of jealousy" "prompted [Martin] to commit the crime"? No, responded Harriet, he and his victim "were entire strangers." Martin "could not have been influenced by jealousy."[41]

Condemnation or punishment of slave adultery devolved largely upon slaveholders as a matter of plantation management or, for that portion of slaves who belonged to evangelical congregations, church disciplinary committees. "There is no special disgrace nor punishment visited upon those [slaves] who criminally violate their marriage vows," declared the Reverend Charles Colcock Jones, "except what may be inflicted by owners, or . . . by the church in the way of suspension and excommunication." Southern evangelical churches resoundingly condemned adultery in the slave quarters. Along with fornication and theft, Jones described adultery as one of slaves' top three "most common vices." More commonly, however, as one observer explained, slaves' "sexual intercourse is left to be regulated by their owners." Yet slaveholders picked their battles carefully and did not uniformly denounce promiscuity. Individual plantation owners were not necessarily inclined to exert their influence in minimizing the magnitude of adultery that occurred. After all, adulterous relationships that resulted in pregnancy and childbirth only added to the wealth of bondwomen's owners. Other masters more actively interceded in the adulterous dramas of the slave quarters. Slaveholders such as James Henry Hammond of South Carolina convened and presided over informal family courts on the plantation, meting out punishments and closely managing enslaved husbands' and wives' living arrangements. Upon holding "a trial of Divorce & Adultery cases" in 1840, Hammond ordered two enslaved couples to reunite, separated a third, and flogged the bondman Tom Kollock thirty lashes for "interfering with Maggy Campbell, Sullivan's wife."[42] Some slaves welcomed and encouraged the mediation of their marital disputes. Probably many more resented the master's or the congregation's interference in their affairs and preferred to resolve disputes percolating inside the quarters on their own.[43]

Slaves' adulterous liaisons strained marital unions and sparked violence by the wronged spouses. In Spartanburg District, South Carolina, the bondwoman Betsey struck her enslaved husband William after learning of his "Adultery." Usually, however, enslaved men inflicted the retributory violence upon an unfaithful spouse, as they were, according to Elizabeth Fox-Genovese, "faced with the woman's more or less open infidelity" in the quarters.[44] Fueled by jealous rage, cuckolded slave husbands often punished the adulterous behavior of an enslaved wife. Occasionally the violence they inflicted upon the women who betrayed their trust turned deadly. In Pittsylvania County, Virginia, Robin went to visit his wife Rinah, enslaved on a nearby plantation, one Saturday night before Christmas 1843. As Robin related to another slave, "when he got there, some person was in the bed with Rinah." Assuming benignly it was the bondwoman Aunt Letty, Robin casually "made up a fire," and Rinah arose to join him. But when "Robin then went to the bedside," he discovered the other occupant of the bed to be "a man instead of aunt Letty." Robin administered three deadly blows with an axe to his erstwhile spouse and was executed for his crime. Another Pittsylvania County bondman, Jim Mays, murdered his free black wife Charity Stevens in 1849. Although Charity had "a parcel of children"—some "five or six" perhaps—by Mays, she had had other sexual partners as well. Driven by the impression that the slaves "John, Abram[,] Jim & Will [had all] kept her," Mays stabbed her with a dirk, tellingly, in the "groin." Despite Mays's enslaved status and his wife's freedom, he still claimed her as his and his alone.[45]

If some bondmen committed violence upon adulterous wives because their sense of ownership or possession had been violated, violence also helped them regain manhood stripped away through cuckolding. In the urban setting of New Orleans, a quarrel erupted in 1856 between the bondman George and his enslaved wife Josephine at 361 Royal Street. George "told her to go away" because "he did not want to have nothing to do with her." Defiantly, Josephine struck her husband and threatened to "have him whipped." Standing his ground, George "told her that he was not afraid of her." The couple exchanged blows before George grabbed a dagger from his bed and stabbed his wife nineteen times in the chest. When questioned about his motivation, he replied that, while "out of this city," Josephine "had slept with another man," and "he did not want no woman to conquer him."[46]

Although cuckolded slave men in some instances physically punished the unfaithful wife, the evidence more clearly demonstrates a craving for violent retribution against the enslaved interloper who disrupted an established marital union. Perry of Richmond, Virginia, fatally stabbed Abram, another slave, for "interfering between him and his wife," and in Alabama, the slave Sam reportedly followed through on his threats to kill the bondman Edmund for being "too intimate" with Sam's wife. Through the death of the "other man," enslaved husbands reasserted and reclaimed manhood lost through lapses in control over their wives' sexual behavior. Cuckolded slave men need not necessarily kill their competition to defend an existing union, though: displays of willingness to commit violence or violent assaults that stopped short of murder might suffice. An Anderson District, South Carolina, slave brandished a firearm in defense of his marriage. Denouncing George as "a damned rascal in beding with my wife every night," the bondman Ed drew a pistol and vowed to "blow out his damned brains."[47] Another Anderson District slave named George assaulted Tom in 1854, striking him "a severe blow or two with a pistol" and threatening to shoot him with it after Tom publicly "boasted of having separated . . . George & his wife." Trial papers make no specific indication of what Tom had done to break up George's marriage or why. It is not clear whether Tom had slept with George's wife, but he nevertheless claimed responsibility for "the wife of slave George driving him off." Resentful of Tom's interference in his marriage, George cocked a brass firearm "& several times presented it as if to shoot Tom but was prevented by . . . [the enslaved man] Isaac." At the conclusion of the neighborhood drama, George was avenged without loss of life.[48]

The vast majority of murderous encounters over enslaved adultery crossed plantation lines. For all of the advantages of abroad marriages, enslaved men with an abroad wife were more susceptible to cuckolding than were those who lived on the same plantation as their spouse. Local sales or hiring arrangements involving one half an enslaved couple also rendered bondmen vulnerable to infidelity. Under such circumstances, bondmen could not closely surveil the women they claimed or guard against the sexual attention of other male slaves. Baldwin County, Georgia, slave John "had done very well" with his wife Louisa, or Lou, when they both resided on the same holding, but when Louisa was transferred to Maria MacDonald's, their relationship suffered. There, the slave "Jackson . . . gained her affections [and] . . . undermined" John. "I have got no wife," wailed John to an enslaved acquaintance. The brokenhearted bondman attributed the loss of his spouse to conjure. Jackson, he claimed, "had been working some of his damned root works under the ground, and had cut him out." But John vowed "that Jackson would meet his des[s]erts." He explained to another slave "that Jackson was fooling about [with] his wife" and that he was prepared to "kill him" if Jackson did not desist. Driven by a yearning to destroy his rival and restore the living arrangements he had enjoyed with Louisa in the past, John bashed in Jackson's head with a rock, splattering his adversary's brain. Just as an acquaintance had predicted, if John and Jackson "would get to fighting, . . . one would murder the other."[49]

So sensitized were some bondmen to cuckolding by other slave men that they violently assaulted those merely suspected of sexual improprieties that violated slave unions. Yet by its very nature, infidelity could be difficult to prove. Pendleton District bondman Tom may not have been alerted to his partner's unfaithfulness until she contracted a venereal disease. Accused of beating the bondwoman Mariah in 1824, Tom had confided to a friend that "Mariah had the clap." Perhaps it was uncertain paternity that sparked a tumult "with sticks and Knives" between Anderson District slaves Simon and Sam "about a chile that Hetta had." Adulterous liaisons could come to light in any number of ways, and when they did, enslaved men were frequently driven to violence.[50]

Yet some bondmen acted prematurely, with no conclusive evidence of adulterous liaisons at all. In 1849, Louisa County, Virginia, bondman Tom killed his wife Abby's ex-boyfriend John, whom Tom believed guilty of continued intimacies with her over the course of the year the couple had been married. Convinced of his wife's infidelity, Tom resolved to dispatch his rival. If an enslaved acquaintance of John may be believed, John had never actually "had any thing improper to do with [Abby]," and Tom was simply "of a jealous disposition & crabbed." In the events that transpired, Tom was clearly the aggressor. Whether cuckolded or not, roughly half a year after first threatening to kill John, he found the opportune moment to exact revenge. Two hours before dawn one Saturday, Abby awoke and ventured to the saw mill "to get wood to make up a fire to do some washing." En route, either by coincidence or prearranged meeting, she encountered John. Unbeknownst to her, Tom was lurking about and "meant to kill" his foe. As John conversed with Abby, Tom spotted them, approached, and told John, "you have been running here all the year and I have caught you at last." Tom fractured John's skull with a stick of wood. After daybreak, Tom explained to another slave that "he had been following John & Abby," spied them "at the saw-mill, standing [and] talking together," and had "given John a good crack."[51]

False assumptions of infidelity, misunderstandings, and misinformation sometimes provoked tragic mistakes. Hubard, enslaved in King George County, Virginia, stands as one example of a slave who may have reacted violently without command of the facts. He was passing by the house of a bondman named Tom when he heard Tom and Hubard's wife Gracy "in conversation. He stopped & listened and thought he heard a conversation very like persons in sexual intercourse." Instantaneously outraged, Hubard hopped the fence, ordered Tom "not to meddle with his affairs," and killed him. Tom, described as "a very well disposed servant," was "between 50 and 60 years of age," approximately two decades older than Hubard. Gracy implied at Hubard's trial that he had acted presumptively. She had gone to Tom's, she explained, merely "to get medicine for her child that was sick."[52]

Absolute certainty of infidelity derived from catching a spouse actively engaged in the adulterous act. In Raleigh, North Carolina, William Lightfoot's slave Jacob, believing that the free black Trueman Goode was having an affair with his wife, arrived home unexpectedly, found him there, and beat him with a stick. The violence went further in Louisiana, where Lewis murdered Henry, another slave. When asked, "Why did you stab that boy?" Lewis replied, "Because I found him in my cabin, with my wife." The Virginia bondman John experienced the same shocking scene, catching Sam "in bed by his wife." Initially, John consulted the master to complain that Sam "was very intimate" with his spouse. But when Sam defied the white man's order commanding him never again to step onto the estate, John, eager to eliminate Sam's chronically disruptive presence, dispatched his foe by striking him with a stick several times in the head. In this case, their battle was prearranged. Sam, weary of sneaking around, had agreed to meet John "to fight him until one or the other should be killed."[53]

Unlike John, not all cuckolded slave men successfully achieved the retribution they sought from a wife's illicit lover. In some cases, the male interloper who violated the enslaved husband's sexual claims triumphed. "Eli, a slave" in Forsyth County, North Carolina, was married to Lucy Hine, "a free woman of color," but for four years the bondman Frank was nevertheless "intimate with Lucy." Frank and Lucy "endeavored to keep this intimacy a secret from Eli," but in 1858 Eli caught Frank "at her house," and a fight erupted between them. Eli's corpse, its head bruised, "was found in a mill-pond, about half a mile from the house of the woman Lucy." Blood trailed back to Lucy's house, and traces remained inside despite "recent attempts ... to wash them out." A set of footprints matching Frank's shoe size, along with incriminating "ashes of burnt clothes in the fire place" at Lucy's, sealed Frank's guilt for Eli's death.[54]

Accustomed to living by their quick wits in interactions with whites, a number of slaves possessed the skills to conceal extramarital affairs from an unsuspecting spouse, but even for those most practiced in deception, masquerades occasionally collapsed. Frank and Lucy must have been remarkably discreet—or accomplished fibbers—in managing to hide their liaison from Eli over a span of several years, but records do not divulge their techniques for maintaining secrecy. The Buckingham County, Virginia, case of the enslaved couple Joe and Betty and her lover Israel is more telling. By 1833, Joe had reason to doubt his wife's fidelity. Intentionally picking a time Betty would not be expecting him, he ventured over to the house where she lived one Monday night and knocked on the door, fully anticipating Israel would be there. Betty allowed Joe entry, but when he observed no "light wood" available for a fire, Betty recommended that he "look yonder near the lower corner of the garden" where wood had been piled. Upon departing, only to find "no lightwood at the place pointed out," Joe realized that his errand was a diversion: Betty had sent him there "to afford [Israel] an opportunity" to flee. Sure enough, after Joe had left to complete his brief chore, "Israel ... slipt out of the house in his shirt tail." Quickly scanning his surroundings, Joe spied "Israel making his escape" and dashed off in pursuit. He overtook his quarry, "concealed in some hop vines & Jamestown weeds," but Israel delivered three deadly cuts "with a scythe blade" upon the cuckolded husband's head.[55]

Israel was well prepared to protect himself in the event an irate husband discovered him. He "had been in the habit of visiting" Joe's wife "for a long time." Twice before, Joe had caught him and "whipped [him] away." Israel thus secured "an old cutting knife, for the purpose of defending himself in case Joe should be there." As part of his routine, he concealed the weapon "in the corner of the fence near Joe's wife's house" and carried it inside during his trysts with Betty. As Joe retrieved the fictitious lightwood, Israel "picked up his blade," fled the house, "& squatted in some weeds" in the garden. When Joe tracked him down, Israel was ready.[56]

Only on very rare occasion did enslaved women violently attack other bondwomen for dalliances with enslaved men. In some of these cases, the "other woman" committed the assault; in others, wives attacked female slaves who had either captured the eye of a philanderous slave husband or had taken a more aggressive role in stoking an adulterous, extramarital affair. In August 1860, the bondwoman Betsey became upset when she "caught her husband [John] up in Patsey's [Patty's] room" on the Prince George County, Virginia, plantation where all three resided. "Betsey & her husband had a fight," and over the next month their relationship deteriorated. The cuckquean did her best to make Patty's life miserable for having ruined her marriage. On one occasion, "Betsey had gone up to [Patty's] room & broke her things up." Patty implored the overseer to "make Betsey let her alone as she was always after her," and in the latter half of September, one attack turned physical. Betsey and Patty "had a fuss" in which the wronged wife cut Patty severely. Betsey had gone to retrieve "her husbands bucket" from Patty, and when Patty returned it, "Betsey knocked her." The two fought. Patty had a knife, but she tossed it to the side. The opportunistic Betsey scooped it up and stabbed her opponent "under he left arm." As Betsey was placed "in [the] smoke house" as punishment, she confessed, "I am a murderer. I have killed Patty but did not do it designedly." Betsey's case was exceptional. Compared to enslaved men, bondwomen did not often seek violent resolutions to their disputes. Rarer still did they ever kill an enslaved opponent.[57]

Domestic violence marked another significant category of violent behavior in slave households. Although the incidence of domestic abuse is impossible to quantify, it was not rare. Still, evidence is difficult to accumulate. Few cases of enslaved men abusing bondwomen surface in the entire collection of Works Progress Administration slave narratives, but most black respondents would not have volunteered such information to white interviewers, and domestic violence likely occurred far more frequently than the narratives indicate. Historians seeking to uncover familial violence inside the quarters have consulted a wide array of sources, including plantation records, personal reminiscences, and newspapers. Some enterprising researchers have even retrieved clues to slaves' marital discontent by reading backward in time from Freedmen's Bureau records. Formerly enslaved spouses, some of whom had taken the opportunity provided by emancipation to liberate themselves from unsatisfying unions, occasionally lodged marital complaints to Freedmen's Bureau agents about the husband or wife they suffered under bondage. All of these sources share a tendency to underestimate the degree of violence that occurred. Elizabeth Fox-Genovese suggests, in fact, that domestic abuse was rife among enslaved couples. The physical violence present within slave marriages, observes Brenda Stevenson, reflected the strains inherent in the system of slavery. Among other factors, stressors included the master's pairing of enslaved couples against their will, the sexual abuse or coercion of bondwomen by white men, and sheer physical exhaustion after a hard day's work.[58]

Without discounting the reality that slave families were a source of strength and support for those in bondage, evidence from court records and church minutes hints at the prevalence of domestic abuse within the slave cabin. Proslavery apologist George Fitzhugh no doubt exaggerated when he contended that masters "never permit the maltreatment by slaves of their wives and children." Bondpeople spent too many hours of their lives outside slaveholder surveillance to allow masters full knowledge of slaves' domestic relations. Fitzhugh notwithstanding, some slave owners admitted as much. One South Carolina slaveholder, seeking a mitigation of sentence for his bondman Isaac, convicted of uxoricide, or wife murder, described the case as "not distinguishable from many others of conflict between [enslaved couples]": "the evidence only shews a common instance of a quarrel between a negro and his wife which are of frequent occurrence and not deemed to merit more than moderate correction." The court that found Isaac guilty concurred that his spouse's death "grew out of such quarrels and altercations as frequently occur between people of their description": slaves.[59]

Evidence of domestic violence within slave marriages dates from the colonial period. The initial dearth of available bondwomen deposited on the colonial British North American mainland might have prompted enslaved men to value their wives greatly and militated against spousal abuse. Husbands may not have assaulted wives knowing that bondwomen might easily find another lover or be given by the master to someone else. Yet the scattered cases of domestic conflict that surface in the historical record surely disguise a larger number of incidents that went unreported. In June 1710, slaveholder William Byrd whipped one bondman "for beating his wife." (Simultaneously, "Jenny was whipped for being his whore.") The colonial-era balance of slave men to slave women soon achieved parity, so whatever effect the precious rarity of bondwomen may have exerted upon staying an enslaved husband's hand, if any, quickly dissipated. Colonel Landon Carter complained in 1770 that the "wench Nelly" was "far from being well" because "that rascal Pantico, her husband . . . gave her [a] beating." One scholar detects a seasonal pattern to abuse within the slave household. Because it was often drunken husbands who battered their family members, and because alcohol flowed more freely as an incentive during harvest, levels of household violence escalated when crops were being brought in from the fields.[60]

A number of impressionable young slaves witnessed domestic abuse in the quarters before they reached maturity, and their observations shaped and molded attitudes toward marriage. Domestic violence within enslaved families was prevalent enough that former Mississippi bondwoman Emily Dixon "wuz fraid ter git married." She traced her apprehensions about matrimony not only to fears of the possible forced separation from her spouse through sale but also because she "neber wanted no man a beatin' me up." Consequently, she continued, "I raised my six chillum wid out de fears and worries ob bein' married." Her solution for easing her anxieties—bearing children out of wedlock—proved no personal source of shame, even if neighborhood whites may have thought of her as a black woman of stereotypically loose morals. Her decision was, to her, a rational response to very real and legitimate concerns. Gabe Butler, born a slave in Amite County, Mississippi, understood that domestic abuse caused not merely physical pain but mental anguish as well. His father Aaron "wud fight my mammy" and "hit her ober de hed." According to some, her constant maltreatment at the hands of her husband "wus whut run her crazy." Having observed firsthand the fighting of her enslaved parents, Lula Jackson of Alabama resolved that there "[w]ouldn't be none of that with me. Honey, when you hit me once, I'm gone. Ain't no beatin' on me and then sleepin' in the same bed," as had been the case with her mother and father. For slaves, however, flight was not a readily available option for avoiding domestic conflict. Where was an abused spouse to go in search of safe haven? Former South Carolina bondwoman Annie Coley remembered her first husband as "the meanest niggah dat ever lived," beating her as she labored in the fields. Unwilling to endure further torment, she recollected, "I tuk my three chilluns en run off to my brother." But her solution—refuge with family—would not have been workable prior to emancipation absent the cooperation of the master.[61]

Male slaves across the South struggled to assert authority over their families. Their marital unions lacked legal recognition and existed only by the mercy of the master. Ultimately, slaveholders exercised more control over enslaved families than did bondmen themselves. Not only did the fate of the family reside with the master; bondage also constrained the ability of enslaved men to fulfill the conventionally masculine roles of provider and protector.[62] In the perverted context of bondage, violence readily functioned as an outlet for domination, the product of a bubbling emotional cauldron that included a volatile mix of rage, resentment, inadequacy, and frustration. Although the omnipresence of masters and other white authorities deterred some measure of violence, abuse of family permitted some enslaved men to display their manhood inside the slave cabin. There, male slaves could channel the anger and frustration they repressed when around the master and liberate themselves temporarily from their relative powerlessness.[63]

Enslaved men sometimes exerted control over their families through the abuse of their offspring. Indeed, slaveholders frequently complained of how bondpeople—women as well as men—treated their children. Bond*men* in particular were sensitive to the loss of authority over their children they suffered when whipped in their presence. When enslaved fathers and mothers physically punished their children, they not only corrected their sons and daughters for specific infractions but also instilled in them a respect for the parental authority undermined when masters disciplined enslaved parents within full view of their progeny. Violence served as a means to reestablish parental supremacy, but not without cost. Enslaved husbands and fathers, in particular, who beat their children were not recollected fondly. "I had de bad luck ter have a cruel pa," lamented one former slave from Mississippi. "He wuz mean to us chillun an' 'specially to ma."⁶⁴

Sources better document how enslaved men unleashed their pent-up rage and frustration not upon their children but rather upon their spouses. "Negroes are by nature tyrannical in their dispositions," declared one Georgia slaveholder, "and if allowed, the stronger will abuse the weaker; husbands will often abuse their wives." An indeterminable but not insignificant number of bondmen regarded their wives as their most prized possessions. A bondwoman highly sought after by other men in the quarters enhanced her husband's prestige, but she was also to be monitored and controlled. Many enslaved men took it as their husbandly prerogative to correct their wives with violence, maintain spousal relationships through force, and thereby stake a claim to patriarchal authority over the slave household. Some bondmen reportedly disciplined their wives more severely than masters for identical offenses.⁶⁵

A pair of cases from Adams County, Mississippi, illustrates a broader pattern of acceptance on the part of enslaved men to use violence to discipline errant spouses. Only one year after liberation, the "Colored" John Williams allegedly "committed an assault and Battery on his wife Molly." On an August evening in 1866, he "commenced cursing and abusing his wife as usual." Several whites testified to the long train of abuses Molly had suffered at the hands of her husband. "He beats his wife unmercifully & frequently," one reported. He "crippled her" on several occasions and constantly employed "abusive and insulting & indecent language." John Williams saw matters differently. "I never beat my wife," he objected. "All I did was to slap her." Williams casually accepted mild domestic violence as normative, and he was not alone. In 1866, Jane, John Harding's wife of four or five months, charged him with assault and battery for throwing a stick at her and threatening to "break my damned head" and "blow my d——d brains out." Harding defended himself, explaining matter-of-factly, "I think I have a right to correct my wife in any position in which she may be." Both of these cases appeared in court but one year removed from emancipation, and while they may reflect the altered family dynamics wrought by emancipation, they hint at sentiments harbored by men of color during bondage.⁶⁶

Under slavery, bondmen often distinguished between acceptable and unacceptable forms and degrees of domestic violence. A decade prior to the arrival of freedom, the bondman Frank of Prince Edward County, Virginia, struck his wife Violet twice in the head with an axe, killing her, apparently upset because he believed she had made an unsettling report to her master "about that Tobacco."

Whereas Frank sought confrontation with his wife, Violet was dismissive of her spouse. "[G]o about your business," she told her husband brusquely. Rebuffed, Frank retrieved his axe and dealt the deadly blows as Violet was "taking up dinner." Asked to explain his actions, he said "that he had not intended to hit her with the eye of the axe, but with the ax helve," the latter of which Frank implied would serve purposefully as an instrument of correction, inflicting but minor injury. Frank lost control of his senses, however, and disciplined his wife, as he admitted, "in a passion." Although uxoricide was not common, many enslaved husbands relied on moderate levels of spousal abuse to establish their primacy as the head of the household. In Louisiana, an enslaved man named "Demps gave his wife Hetty a light cut or two & then locked her up to prevent her going to the Frollick." In Demps's mind, as the man in the relationship, he had every right to discipline his wife and to control her movement.[67]

From its beginnings in the American South, the institution of slavery reconfigured family structures and redefined gender roles. For first-generation slaves, the transition could be jarring. Charles Ball, a slave in the early nineteenth century, recounted how the African-born husband of a bondwoman named Lydia supplied little for his family: "[A] native of a country far in the interior of Africa, he had been a priest in his own nation, and had never been taught to do any kind of labor." Although as a slave "[h]e was compelled by the overseer to work, with the other hands, in the field," at the end of the day "he . . . maintained, as far as he could, the same kind of lazy indignity, that he had enjoyed at home." Formerly the beneficiary of ten women's labor in Africa, he now had only one spouse, yet "as soon as he had come into his cabin, he took his seat, and refused to give his wife the least assistance in doing any thing." Unaccustomed and unreconciled to his reduced circumstances, Ball explained, "This man was very irritable, and often beat and otherwise maltreated his wife, on the slightest provocation." Slavery erased bondmen's former status in Africa, however exalted, and inherently fostered some confusion over the proper relationship between men and women within the slave household. Gender conventions in white society prescribed that men protect and provide for their families. As much as enslaved men aspired to fulfill this vision of masculinity, bondage circumscribed their ability to conform to that model of manhood. Violent behaviors at times filled the void. As Elizabeth Fox-Genovese explains, "a high level of violence resulted from slave men's inability to exercise the domination over women that most societies have awarded to men." Psychologically, perhaps this explains why the enraged Louisiana bondman Jim struck his wife Rachel on the head with a poker. For not only slaves who endured the horrors of the Middle Passage but for subsequent generations temporally removed from African tradition, gender roles remained in a constant state of flux as enslaved couples continually negotiated and renegotiated household relations of power.[68]

Bondwomen sometimes contested enslaved men's exercise of rank within the household. In Spartanburg District, South Carolina, slaves Asa and Peggy quarreled in 1849 over whether or not "to cut a Pound Cake." Such a seemingly trivial decision was laden with meaning inside the four walls of the slave cabin. Did Asa, as the man, make the determination to cut the cake, or did Peggy, as the woman customarily in charge of domestic responsibilities such as food preparation? For her part, Peggy, fuming, claimed that "if she was a man . . . she would whip Asa for the way that he had treated her." A few bondwomen followed through on what Peggy only threatened. Wife-beating certainly occurred in slave cabins, but there were also tough, courageous bondwomen who refused to submit to such treatment. An enslaved woman in Mississippi who fatally stabbed her husband, for example, was found not guilty in a court of law because she acted in self-defense. Female physical violence directed against a spouse was probably most often a reaction to male aggression, although a few bondwomen apparently took the offensive. In one possible case of husband abuse, a bondman named Mollo complained that his ill-tempered wife was "continually fighting and scratching him."[69]

However obscure the internal dynamics of slave households remain, sources provide tantalizing clues about how slaves understood the organization of the domestic realm. Bondmen and bondwomen alike shared certain expectations of their partners. A spouse's failure to meet minimal thresholds of gendered performance risked violent retribution. Male slaves, for instance, upheld standards of female domesticity within the slave cabin. At the conclusion of a long day in the fields, the domestic responsibilities of cleaning and cooking devolved upon bondwomen. Despite their exhaustion from the day's labors, enslaved wives who neglected to keep their dwellings tidy and presentable or who prepared unsatisfactory meals might suffer their husbands' ire. The bondman Jim abused his wife Maria unapologetically because, as he explained, she was lazy. Surely tired, perhaps unhappy with her marriage, or indifferent to her husband's wishes, Maria refused to clean house or wash or mend Jim's clothes. She also served meals on dirty plates "with peas all sticking to them." Her failure to perform her gendered chores did not sit well with her husband. Reduced to cleaning the cabin himself, Jim regretted their marriage and expressed his frustration and disappointment physically upon his wife. A North Carolina bondwoman also suffered for her failure to meet her husband's standards of domesticity. In Craven County, the "negro woman slave" Flora "had frequent quarrels" with John, her spouse of six years. Their disputes were sometimes serious enough that they "separated and came together again" once tensions between them subsided. On one occasion in 1848, John, "complaining that his dinner was not property prepared, got angry, and gave her a whipping, and turned her out of his house, saying that she should not live with him any longer." John enjoyed unusual leeway in being "permitted to keep house," and he exercised authority over his domain by expelling Flora from it. But because most bondmen lived in a dwelling supplied by the master, they would have been unable to banish an unwanted spouse as John had done. Despite these examples, many enslaved husbands thought of themselves and their wives as a team. For that reason, Henry Jones, a slave near Natchez, Mississippi, felt betrayed when his wife Diana refused to run away with him. Jones wanted to keep his family intact, so when she declined to abscond, he assaulted and fatally stabbed her for subverting his initiative.[70]

Enslaved women contributed equally to the construction of slaves' gendered household norms. Many bondwomen expected sweethearts and husbands to bestow upon them gifts or small tokens of affection despite the often formidable obstacles men faced in acquiring consumer goods via the slave economy. Female slaves nevertheless took seriously the social convention that men were to provide, and enslaved men customarily accepted the challenge. In Virginia, the bondman Peter was sure he could woo the bondwoman Anica by demonstrating his ability to supply her with niceties. Anica's "master had ordered Peter not to come to her home again," but the smitten Peter persisted. In 1819, he resolved "to get some dresses" for Anica and, with an enslaved accomplice named Merit, broke into the "Store house of Ludwell Gwaltney" in Isle of Wight County and pilfered four pieces of muslin fabric worth more than $30 as well as "8 yards waist coating of the value of Eight dollars and twenty five cents." Peter then delivered to Anica "five yards of . . . muslin," which she accepted, not knowing they were contraband. Upon later hearing that Peter was accused of the thefts from Gwaltney's store, the morally upright Anica returned the fabric "and told him to carry it away[,] that she would have nothing to do with it." Whereas Anica could not in good conscience keep her ill-gotten gains, other bondwomen may not have maintained such strict scruples about the provenance of the gifts they received. In Hancock County, Georgia, Lizza "turn[ed] off her husband for nothing more than because he wont get her any thing or do any thing for her." She adamantly refused "to take her husband again" and was therefore stripped of her membership at Island Creek Baptist Church. Some bondmen undoubtedly resented the imposition of having to secure and bear gifts to insistent, demanding, coercive, or ungrateful wives. The enslaved husband Sawny of Charlotte County, Virginia, allegedly attempted to poison his wife in 1860 "by placing quicksilver (gotten off a looking glass) in a bowl of soup." Sawny had reportedly said that, with his wife's anticipated demise, "she would be so low ... that she would not need a pair of shoes which she had asked of him."[71]

Fatherhood thrust even greater responsibilities upon enslaved men as providers. Although bondwomen bore the brunt of child-rearing duties, they nevertheless looked to enslaved fathers to supply those wants and needs overlooked or knowingly neglected by the master. While many enslaved men rose to the occasion, others cringed or recoiled from impending fatherhood. They may have dreaded the loss of the precious few hours they claimed as their own, shunned the added obligations—economic, emotional, and otherwise—of paternity, regretted enriching the master by fathering the next generation of enslaved laborer, or suspected that the child was not theirs at all. In Charleston District, South Carolina, Katura informed her husband Isaac in 1843 "that she was pregnant by him." For reasons only he knew, Isaac did not greet the news with enthusiasm and instead "tried to pass out of the Door" to the house. Katura denied him, declared "that he, a son of a bitch, should not go," and proceeded to block his alternate exit out of a window. Isaac, who "in the course of quarrelling" threatened to "beat her if she did not let him go out into the street," administered "four licks" upon his pregnant wife's head "with a hoe handle," inflicting injuries that culminated in her death. In another case, a bondwoman born in Mississippi and conveyed to Texas remembered a bondman who "begged" the master "to let him have" a particular female slave, but when she became pregnant contrary to the bondman's wishes, "he just choked her to death," killing her and her unborn child. He then committed suicide.[72]

Only in cases of death did the legal system intrude upon marital relations in the quarters; otherwise, the master was the law. Owners universally condemned the domestic conflicts in the slave cabins. They repeatedly entreated fellow slaveholders and instructed overseers to monitor carefully enslaved men's treatment of their spouses, singling out wife-beating for particular censure. "I never permit a husband to abuse, strike or whip his wife," declared one Georgia planter. Although the physical correction of women was common within the confines of nineteenth-century white marriages, masters frequently commented upon the "disgrace" of an enslaved man who struck his wife, who, steeled by hard labor, in reality would often not have been the delicate, fragile female specimen of slaveholders' imaginations. "[I]t is disgraceful for a man to raise his hand in violence against a feeble woman," a chivalrous Georgian proclaimed, "and that woman, too, the wife of his bosom, the mother of his children, and the companion of his leisure, his midnight hours." Another slave owner heartily agreed. "Men," he wrote, "should be taught that it is disgraceful to abuse or impose on the weaker sex."[73]

Whites' gendered expectations of proper comportment within the marital union ran both directions. Either enslaved spouse might shatter the tranquility of the household. Just as bondmen were implored not to abuse their wives, enslaved women were sometimes implicated for inciting disputes with their significant others. While no one sex exercised a monopoly on spousal abuse, as a general pattern, men were more likely to resort to physical aggression, women to verbal harassment. Masters unquestionably accepted the sharp-tongued scold as a female type present in the quarters and were prepared to identify with a relentlessly harangued enslaved husband. One York District, South Carolina, master attributed his slave Shadrock's suicide to the "merciless woman he had for a wife," a veritable shrew who tormented and maltreated him. "If the wife teases and provokes him by her nightly chatter or crabbed deportment," explained a Georgia slaveholder, and an investigation "establishes the fact, she is punished." The enslaved wife, insisted the planter, must learn "to use her tongue with less bitterness and be more conciliating in her behavior."[74]

In upcountry South Carolina, several apparent domestic quarrels involved an enslaved husband violently assaulting his wife for failing either to hold her tongue or to censor her speech accordingly. When female words touched a nerve, bondmen at times responded with violent force to women's perceived insolence. In Pendleton District, Lemuel Hall's bondman Tom "violently Beat and abused" John McPhail's slave woman Mariah after she "talked crossly" to him, calling him "a scape Gallow son of a Bitch." One witness claimed, however, that "Mariah in fact did not curse ... much untill she was ... abused." In 1843, Major P. L. Calhoun rushed to his slave quarters to investigate "an unusual uproar at one [of] the Negro houses." There he found William, the property of Elizabeth East, holding his bondwoman Ann "by the throat & beating her severely with a large hickory," "at least thirty lashes." Ordered to explain himself, William "replied she had used blackguard language to some of the other negroes & to him." Although it is not absolutely clear from the records that these were cross-plantation couples, both cases smack of marital discord and enslaved husbands exercising physical dominance over wives whose cutting words challenged male authority.[75]

Many masters believed enslaved wives imbued with the capacity to provoke the violence committed by their husbands and understood that reasonable correction might be justified. Early nineteenth-century society tolerated—without necessarily condoning—a degree of physical abuse within the confines of marriage. Georgia law explicitly sanctioned white husbands' discipline of wives from 1833 to 1857. The Supreme Court of North Carolina ruled in 1852 that "the husband had a right to give to the wife moderate chastisement" at his discretion. He was criminally liable only in the event that "permanent injury is inflicted" or threatened. For the most part, courts followed the "rule of thumb," through which a man might correct his wife with any stick not thicker than the said digit of the male hand, although as Stephanie Cole has shown, there were ample instances in the antebellum decades of prosecution for domestic assaults that imposed strict limits on the exercise of patriarchy through violence.[76]

That slave owners could not be confident that female slaves were necessarily the innocent victims of domestic conflict confounded the exercise of plantation discipline. In 1861, plantation mistress Keziah Goodwyn Hopkins Brevard of South Carolina knew that "Ben had [wrongly] beaten Louisa," but she expressed uncertainty how to proceed because "she may be as hard as he is." A frustrated Brevard concluded ruefully of the abuse, "I am sorry I noticed it." Whites in charge of one Alabama plantation absolved themselves of the responsibility to ferret out the truth behind enslaved couples' violent squabbles and simply punished the pair of participants equally. "[D]e overseer useta whip mammy an' pappy" both, Everett Ingram recalled, "'ca'se day fight so much."[77]

Despite the burdens of disciplining enslaved couples, most slaveholders proved willing to take action in cases of domestic violence. Runaway slave Charles Ball remembered one enslaved man who was inordinately cruel to his spouse. The overseer was unusual in that he "refused to protect her, on the ground, that he never interfered in the family quarrels of the black people." Few slaveholders were so lenient. With a vested economic interest in their female slave property as both producers and reproducers, owners almost always responded promptly to bondwomen's complaints and pleas about violent husbands, and most bondwomen could reasonably expect the master to act as a buffer against an abusive spouse. Pittsylvania County, Virginia, slave Rinah consulted her master and "spoke emphatically" to him that she no longer wished the bondman Robin "to visit her," as he "had always abused her very much." When asked about the matter, "Robin acknowledged he had . . . treated her badly." Rinah was by then "away from him" and "wished to remain so," separated, with the consent and aid of the master.[78]

Other bondwomen were reluctant to seek their owners' assistance in resolving domestic conflicts. Whether because they did not want to see their husbands punished or because they feared the violent retribution that might befall them after exposing an enslaved spouse with a known temper, a number of bondwomen refused to report instances of domestic abuse to their owners. After her husband Jim "hit her over the head with the poker," Rachel did not divulge the incident to the master. When he inquired about the "big knot" that "raise[d] up" noticeably on her skull, she replied dismissively that she had bumped her head. As a fellow bondwoman explained, "She dasn't tell on Uncle Jim or Marse sure beat him."[79]

Most masters or overseers took such keen interest in slaves' domestic relations that they need not be summoned to the slave cabin to respond to allegations of abuse: they proactively intervened without invitation. As one Deep South planter explained, enslaved "husbands are taught by sad experience to know that they shall not abuse their better halves." Masters dutifully whipped violent bondmen as they deemed necessary. One planter advised resisting the temptation to permit the victimized wife "to strike her husband" in retribution, however, "for fear of its unhappy influence over their future respect for and kindness to each other."[80]

Ironically, masters' own plantation management decisions at times directly provoked the very domestic quarrels they sought to quell. In their eagerness to unite bondmen and bondwomen for purposes of procreation, some owners demeaned what passed for marriage in the quarters. Slaveholders exercised ultimate authority to decide which slaves wed. Although they frequently acquiesced to bondpeople's own preferences and desires, other masters matched slave couples with gross disregard for their feelings, pairing individuals lacking mutual attraction, affection, or emotional attachment. Many enslaved spouses so callously thrust together did not learn to love or respect one another, creating a breeding ground for domestic abuse. As an enslaved girl in Texas, Rose Williams refused to submit to sex with Rufus, the bondman selected by the master to impregnate her. When Rufus tried to crawl into bed with her, Rose clubbed him over the head with "de poker." Despite Rufus's repeated attempts to consummate their union, Rose's defenses remained high. She continually warned her unwanted husband away "'fore I busts yous brains out and stomp on dem." By the same token, bondmen such as Rufus might resort to violence to subdue a reluctant spouse such as Rose, spirited in her defiance. Nourished by the tension and stress inherent within unions among enslaved couples forcibly joined, abuse by both husbands and wives was prevalent. Scattered voices of slaveholders acknowledged the desecration of marriage under slavery. "On account of the changes, interruptions and interferences in families," wrote the Reverend Charles Colcock Jones, "there are *quarrelings* and *fightings*." Jones's concern quickly turned practical, however, noting that "a considerable item in the management of plantations is the settlement of family troubles."[81]

For that minority of all slaves who were regular churchgoers, evangelical churches functioned as auxiliaries to masters' authority. Indeed, a thorough examination of slaves' marital lives was sometimes required to gain membership into a given congregation. When "Eliza a woman of colour" applied to Powelton Baptist in Hancock County, Georgia, the church first had to investigate the reported "difficulty ... existing between her & her husband." At their "interview," Eliza complained that "her husband is so bad that she cannot live with him." Despite the labors of the committee, the bondwoman remained resolute in her determination not to reconcile and thereby subject herself to continued abuse. To the church's displeasure, it was also discovered that she had recently "used violence" in retaliation against him. Although the committee concluded "that both are to be blamed for their unhappy disagreement and seperation" and that Eliza was not solely responsible for her marital distress, the church clerk recorded that "we do not deem it expedient to receive her."[82]

Churches might have constructively mediated domestic conflicts, but the minutes of their proceedings more clearly demonstrate how enslaved congregants' family quarrels, when aired in the public forum of the monthly meeting, earned black members' expulsion. In Wilkes County, Georgia, Philips Mill Baptist Church "[e]xcommunicated Gabriel a Man of Colour ... for [a] difference between him and his wife," while Rehoboth Baptist expelled both Joseph W. Cooper's slave Jack and "his wife Ann the property of Brother Huguley" for "fighting and lying." When only one half of an enslaved couple was clearly at fault, churches reprimanded the guilty party alone. In 1846, Philips Mill excluded "Ficklins Ralph ... for drunkenness and violently b[e]ating his Wife."[83]

Evangelical churches tackled a host of moral offenses rooted in the family. Among the truly aberrant were allegations of incest in slave households. No less than whites, slaves considered incestuous relationships taboo. Former slave Sally Brown of Georgia remembered that her owners, the Nashes, once sold a bondman "[be]cause the other slaves said they wuz gonna kill 'im 'cause he had a baby by his own daughter." We cannot be sure that the offenders' fellow slaves would have followed through on their threat, but the master's knowledge of the outrage in the quarters, combined with his own economic stake in the offending slave, was sufficient to compel him to sell the bondman who had violated commonly understood sexual mores.[84]

Infinitely more common than incest, the domestic troubles churches investigated stemmed from the ubiquitous charges of adultery levied against enslaved members and the threats or acts of violence unfaithfulness inspired. A love triangle involving one bondman and two bondwomen, all members of Island Creek Baptist Church in Hancock County, Georgia, provided ample fodder for discussion in conference. Sam was married to Phillis but was charged with "being too intimate" with Peggy, they "not being Man and wife." Discovery of the extramarital liaison inflamed passions among all participants. The church excluded Peggy for "quarrelling with Sister Phillis her fellow serv^t," "calling her a Liar," and "threatening to Murder her if she was turned out of the church on her account" (as she ultimately was). Sam, too, was expelled, for "threatening to smother his wife in her own blood and other abusive Language and ill Treatment." It charged his wife Phillis "with unchristian Like conduct in quarreling with . . . Bro Sam her own husband," but, unlike her philandering spouse, she "made satisfactory acknowledgements and was continued in fellowship."[85]

Slave marriages often lacked permanence. Although it was generally in masters' best interests economically to keep enslaved couples together, they might arbitrarily forbid a cross-plantation union, sell an enslaved spouse, or migrate with half an enslaved couple in tow, leaving a heartbroken husband or wife to grieve the loss. In Virginia, the Roanoke Association of Baptist Churches "agreed in 1788 that it was not allowable to separate a slave husband and wife unless one had used every endeavor to keep them together." But in their quest for respectability among slaveholding whites, religious injunctions that impinged upon owners' mastery over their chattel were often ignored. John Leland, a Baptist minister from New England who preached for fifteen years in the Old Dominion, acknowledged of slaves' unions that "masters may and do part them at pleasure." Although he characterized the wanton separation of enslaved spouses as sinful, he added that "it is not in the power of the masters to prevent their being forced apart, in numberless instances." In their effort to rationalize and excuse the destruction of enslaved unions, slaveholders often cited circumstances beyond their control—an unforeseen economic calamity, for example—that compelled them to sever slave couples in spite of themselves. A dismayed Leland departed Virginia in 1790, by then an ardent critic of slavery.[86]

Slaves were not merely the objects of masters' compulsory, de facto "divorces," however. Bondpeople party to unhappy marriages or heedless of their conjugal commitments sometimes effected their own separations. Lacking the benefit of lawful unions, slaves did not have access to the formal legislative or judicial divorces available to southern whites, which were rare and cumbersome to secure anyway. Instead, they at times consulted white authorities—the master or overseer—for permission to separate. In Prince George County, Virginia, bondwoman Betsey caught her husband John cheating on her with another female slave, sparking a series of fights. During one quarrel, Betsey threatened to leave him. John responded that "he dont care." The jilted bondwoman complained to the overseer "that John had been treating her unkindly" and sought assistance because "she wished to leave him." The overseer deferred to his employers, however, to make a decision of such import. The master and mistress, he explained, "are the proper ones to separate you."[87]

Slave owners greeted the subject of slave separations with a range of possible responses. According to one South Carolina lowcountry bondwoman, planters preferred that slaves not "leave one wife or a husband for another" at all. But sometimes the peace and quietude of the plantation demanded it. South Carolina slaveholder James Henry Hammond allowed for the annulment of slave marriages if either an aggrieved husband or wife could show "sufficient cause," but "the offending party," he added, "must be severely punished." "Where both are in the wrong," he continued, divorce came at a steep price for the unhappy couple, for "if they insist on separating [they] must have a hundred lashes apiece." Moreover, "neither can marry again for three years." Many other masters did not view the separation of enslaved spouses with such gravity. As Solomon Northup, illegally conveyed into bondage in Louisiana, observed of enslaved husbands and wives in his vicinity, "either is at liberty to discard the other at pleasure." A Yankee traveler in Virginia likewise noted that "[t]he negroes pretend to have wives and husbands," but without "ceremony in marriage" to validate their unions, they "lay side beside till they disagree, and then will part." Without necessarily seeking whites' authorization, they instead terminated their own unions, "parting with," "turning off," "putting away," or "quitting" an unwanted spouse in informal, extralegal acts of divorce.[88]

Gendered patterns emerge from the known cases of slaves who "put away" their partner. To be sure, some personalities simply did not mesh well. According to Mississippi bondman Nelson Dickerson, he and his wife "cudnt git er long—we fought so much; she wus unruly an' I cudnt do nuffin wid her so I jes' up an' left dat woman." Dickerson's recollection suggests some possible frustration with his inability to control his wife's conduct. A common motivation for enslaved men quitting a spouse was a wife's flirtatious behavior or adulterous liaisons with other bondmen. In Louisa County, Virginia, Tom wearied "of the way his wife Abby carried on with men." He confronted her and ordered her "to give him his key" so that he might "get his things" from their cabin and move out. Harry Pope, enslaved in Texas, terminated his union after his wife bore "a child by another negro." Elsewhere, the bondman Alex drove off his wife of eight or nine years because he was not convinced that he was the father of their newborn baby. Furious, Alex "broke up her bedstead, threw it out of doors, 'bundled up all her things [and] . . . threatened to kill the first man who interfered with him in his own house.'" Enslaved women sometimes complained of their husbands' philandering as well. One Florida bondwoman named Rose objected to her husband Renty "having so Many Children," implying either marital infidelity or promiscuous behavior prior to their marriage. More often, the physical abuse or other maltreatment enslaved women suffered at the hands of a husband convinced them to separate from their spouse. Domestic violence prompted one Mississippi bondwoman to leave her husband. "Jim Malone fight my ma so much," her son explained, "she wouldn't stay wid him." Different bondwomen tolerated varying levels of abuse, but that which was either chronic or extraordinarily brutal inspired some to abandon their partner.[89]

Baptist churches across the South frowned on the unforced breakups of slave unions. Only about 4 percent of first slave marriages in the Upper South were willfully terminated by an enslaved husband or wife. On those rare occasions "when they part voluntarily," declared preacher John Leland, "the slaves are guilty of adultery." Baptist church disciplinary committees paid little heed to the cause of slaves' marital problems. Evidence of emotionally or physically abusive slave relationships made little difference in their decisions. Deacon James Evans requested that the colored conference of Island Creek Baptist Church allow his bondwoman Hannah to remarry because her spouse "treated her badly and quit." The case was important enough to submit to the white conference, which denied the petition. The story was similar at Powelton Baptist Church. In 1826, "the black brethren . . . generally acquitted Isaac of blame in his taking a second wife while his first was living as she had treated him very shamefully," but the regular conference overruled them. As a rule, churches maintained that slaves united in matrimony should uphold the biblical imperative to remain so. The degree of misery wrought by the union did not matter.[90]

But the vast majority of enslaved couples' separations were involuntary. The sale or forcible removal of a spouse exacerbated levels of violence within the slave quarters. With little hope for reunion with the partner left behind, departed slaves in most instances attempted to build a new family in unfamiliar surroundings. In so doing, they sometimes threatened existing relationships that bondmen were willing to defend physically. Either ignorant of or, at times, willfully heedless of the enslaved couples present in their new location, enslaved outsiders—strangers—might clash with their more established neighbors as they staked a claim to rank in the local slave hierarchy and forged their own niche within the community. The bondman Green "had come from the state of Tennessee with his former master" to Washington County, Virginia, probably in the early 1850s and "had not been [there] long" when he had a scuffle with Tom over the affections of the bondwoman Hannah. By the same token, forcibly abandoned partners left behind typically looked for a new spouse on the home plantation or in their familiar neighborhood. That process, too, could breed violence. Thomas County, Georgia, bondman George was dismayed when his wife, owned by a different master, was carried away from him. Like her owner, it was reported, she "has moved and is gone now." With his wife presumably lost forever, George coveted the bondwoman Ann. Ann, however, had been joined for more than a decade to William, the slave foreman, who killed George for interfering in his marriage.[91]

Slaves were essentially helpless to prevent the dissolution of a marriage if one spouse was slated for sale or removal. In only a handful of extraordinary cases did slaves reverse an impending separation. Henry "Box" Brown, for example, paid $50 to a white man to purchase his wife and children locally to prevent their sale to some faraway place. Most slaves lacked the combination of resources, contacts, and cooperative masters all required to strike such a bargain. Without the benefit of formal matrimony, some presumptive slave couples did not even share a mutual understanding of the nature of their relationship. Charlotte County, Virginia, slaves "Julius & Dick were quarrelling" on Christmas 1855 over their respective connections to the bondwoman Nancy. Dick thought himself Nancy's husband and complained "that Julius carried his wife strolling about Drake's Branch." As Nancy explained, however, "I am not any body's wife." Dick was laboring only under the illusion that he was married to her. She actually "lived with Julius" as her "sweetheart" but did not think of herself as his wife, either. Apparently no informal ceremony or church proclamation had ever solemnified Nancy's bond to either man, and each could only assess his relationship to her on the basis of their shared moments together. The complicated situation was enough to enrage a "very drunk" Dick, who damned Julius and declared that "he meant to cut his guts out that night." Emboldened by liquor on the holiday, the unarmed Dick, barely able to stand, did not make a formidable foe. Julius slammed a rail into his head, inflicting injuries that led to Dick's death a few days later.[92]

Enslaved women sometimes resolved to terminate the unsatisfying marital unions to which they were party. Whereas enslaved husbands typically had no choice but to accept the loss of a spouse to sale or relocation prompted by the master, when wives instigated the separation, male slaves sometimes fought the end of relationships with the women they loved or desired to keep. In Buckingham County, Virginia, Joe's wife Betty had told her abroad spouse that "she cared nothing about him" and ordered him "not to come there again to see her." Joe was adamantly opposed to their breakup, however, and continued to frequent Betty's cabin. On his last, unannounced visit, he surprised Betty and her lover, the latter of whom killed him. Baldwin County, Georgia, bondman John blamed the slave Jackson for stealing his wife, but according to one slave observer, "His wife turned him off." Refusing to concede the loss of his spouse, John killed Jackson in retribution. The bondman Robin of Pittsylvania County, Virginia, also did not handle rejection well. In one confrontation with the woman of his desire, he "asked Rinah if she intended to love him. Rinah told him no . . . [H]e had given her more abuse than ever her mistress or master," so "she would not live with him." Immediately enraged, Robin declared, "by God if I dont enjoy you, no body else shall" and "the worst will become of you." Rinah detected the threat and "asked him what he meant by telling her that, do you mean to kill me[?]" Robin denied any intention "to strike you a lick," promised not "to pester you any more," and departed for home. Exercising caution, Rinah then "tied the door with a leather string around a nail," but her efforts afforded little security. At some point during the night, Robin returned to fatally injure the woman he wanted for himself.[93]

Male slaves' obsessions with the bondwomen they claimed at times did express themselves in violent, destructive ways. Whether enslaved men's passion arose because they were so deeply invested emotionally in the relationship or because they harbored an unhealthy psychological need to possess their spouses cannot be safely gleaned from extant records. Regardless, a small fraction of all bondmen could not let go of wives who had given their hearts to another. Bedford County, Virginia, bondman Plato, for instance, "had Kept Eadey," or Edy, "for 18 months" and was distraught to learn "that She Was about to take up With another Man," a slave named Sam. Plato had repeatedly threatened to "kill her if she had Sam" (or leave it to "God Almighty" to "Send a Thunder Clap, and take [her] both Soul and body"). Were Edy to marry Sam, one slave recollected, Plato proclaimed "that She Should do him no Good and . . . he Would murder her." His was no idle threat. Plato continued to think of Edy as his wife even if she did not, and in 1822 he delivered his one-time spouse two or three deadly blows to the head with an axe to prevent her union to another bondman.[94]

Sometimes enslaved husbands initiated the breakups with their wives. Often the split was symbolized by the retrieval of clothing or made public knowledge through the unceremonious dumping of an estranged spouse's material belongings outside the slave cabin. In August 1836, Samuel and Mima, an enslaved couple in North Carolina, quarreled. Samuel "took a bundle of clothes . . . to carry off, saying, he intended to part with his wife." In the absence of formal divorces, one reason the bondwoman Hannah of Washington County, Virginia, considered "herself and [her husband] Tom as parted" was that "Tom had sent for his clothes." Piles of consumer goods tossed into the yard also alerted other slaves that a marriage had dissolved. After Pittsylvania County, Virginia, slaves Robin and Rinah had their falling out in the autumn of 1843, slave witnesses "saw all Rinah's things thrown out of doors" in a public display of her ejection from Robin's abode as well as his heart. In the city of Richmond, slaves Scott and Priscilla, who "had previously lived together as man and wife," quarreled over access to Scott's clothing. Priscilla did "washing for a livelihood" but presumably had done Scott's laundry for free while they were married. Scott's abandonment of her changed the dynamic of their relationship. When he returned to demand his coat, she refused to surrender the cleaned garment until her ex-husband paid her for her labors. "I wont give you any coat," Priscilla retorted. "[G]o along and stay where you have been staying." Provoked, Scott called her a "damn bitch" and choked her to death.[95]

Although Scott seemingly had no regrets about leaving his enslaved wife, others did. With sufficient time to reflect, some bondmen realized, in hindsight, that they could not truly sever their emotional ties to a former spouse. Contrite slave husbands appealed to ex-wives to take them back. Some took the humbling, apologetic approach; others used threats of physical force to coerce a reluctant bondwoman to agree to a former husband's return. The enslaved woman Violet of Louisa County, Virginia, for example, separated from her husband, the bondman Barnett, in the early nineteenth century. After a period apart, Barnett "told her that if she did not commit to become his wife again he would destroy her, which induced her thru fear to consent." Spousal intimidation could produce the opposite effect, however. After having "quarrel[ed] and separated" from his wife, one enslaved man seeking reconciliation was rebuffed because, stupidly, "he drawed back to hit her with a chair" as he pleaded for her hand once again. Only the intervention of the bondwoman's brother prevented her from sustaining serious injury.[96]

In a number of instances, enslaved wives were violently assaulted after they refused to reconcile with the husbands who left them. Jones County, Georgia, bondman Adam broke up with his wife Fanny after he caught another slave "in bed together" with her. Some time after the couple "parted," Adam found it within himself to forgive Fanny and asked her "to live with him again." She declined, which likely inspired Adam to shoot her in the head "with a musket gun loaded with powder and balls." In a homicide case from Virginia, a rejected bondman murdered his ex-wife because she would not take him back. Pittsylvania County slaves Robin and Rinah, briefly mentioned above, "lived together as man & wife" but split in 1843 after a quarrel while "toating" tobacco. Having reached the limits of his toleration, "Robin struck ... Rinah and told her if she come to his house at night any more, he would kill her." He also informed another slave, "if Rinah did not do better or leave him he would kill her." It seemed abundantly clear that Robin sought a final parting, but within a month or two, Robin had a change of heart. By December, he asked Rinah's master, Ichabod Watson, for "permission to visit" her. Watson understood that "they had parted" and, apparently aware of their turbulent history, "thought they had best remain so." But Robin was insistent in stating that "he did not wish to give her up." That night, Watson summoned the pair to inquire into the matter, and Rinah expressed her preference to remain apart because Robin had been so abusive toward her. Robin begged Rinah "if she would not give him a chance" and extracted an agreement from Watson whereby Robin would get "two or three days" over the Christmas holiday in which to persuade his ex-wife to "reconcile." When that failed, Watson ordered Robin off with instructions to "not come inside of his lot any more." The despondent Robin later murdered his former wife.[97]

Perhaps pushing Robin over the edge was the fact that Rinah had moved on, striking up a new relationship with a slave named Isaac. A bondwoman's taking up with someone else was at times the final straw capable of driving a former slave husband to commit murder. Well aware of Isaac, Robin grew insanely jealous and possessive, informing one bondwoman "that Rinah never should enjoy another man in the world as long as he lived." He expressed the same sentiment to another: "by God if he couldn't enjoy her no body else should." Fellow slaves attempted to cheer Robin by noting that "there were other women in the world besides Rinah." "[S]o there was," Robin conceded, "and better too." That acknowledgment notwithstanding, he could not tamp down his obsession. Robin came to see himself as the victim of the drama he lived, carping to one elderly slave woman that "they had taken his wife away." Self-pity only hardened his murderous resolve. "Some people think old Robin's a fool," he said of himself, but "he didn't intend to stand it": "I intend to put her to an end." Having telegraphed his crime to several bondpeople, Robin then carried out his deadly threat. After he murdered Rinah, he confessed to another slave that "he struck her three times" with an axe. He had tried one last time to reunite, but Rinah again rejected him, and Robin "got so dam mad with her he could not pacify her any way" shy of killing her.[98]

Court records show that bondmen were at least as likely to vent their rage not on the former wife who was moving on but on the enslaved man who took up with her. Caswell County, North Carolina, cross-plantation slave couple Samuel and Mima "had cohabited as man and wife for about ten years successively, and had . . . five children," but at Samuel's instigation, the pair split. After their separation, Mima remarried, and Samuel allegedly murdered the bondman who replaced him as her husband. Allen, enslaved in Georgia, was another bondman to die at the hands of a wife's ex-lover. At the time of his death in 1846, Allen and the bondwoman Eliza were a couple, but only a year or so before, Eliza "had been living as man & wife" with Tom. "Tom has been in the habit of coming to see me for the last 6 years," Eliza explained. But in 1844, Tom "took up with a girl at Mrs Gibsons." Demanding an exclusive, monogamous relationship with her husband, Eliza separated from Tom and gave him a choice: "she was willing to take up with him again," but only on the condition that he "quit Mrs Gibson's girl." Tom refused to be served the ultimatum, so Eliza began a relationship with Allen. Unwilling to accept Eliza's new union, Tom told Allen, "I give you Hell," fatally stabbed his rival twice in the chest "with a common pocket knife," and "stamped him" as he attempted to flee. Tom's story was not unique. In Anderson District, South Carolina, the bondman Warren repeatedly threatened to kill an enslaved adversary named Dan. Although Warren and his wife had been "apart 12 months," he charged Dan with "being after" her and believed them altogether "too thick." Separated for a year, Warren still could not stomach the thought of his one-time spouse with another man.[99]

Some attempts to control and dominate a former spouse and punish her new partner backfired tragically for ex-husbands, and they, though the aggressors, were killed. The enslaved couple Hannah and Tom of Washington County, Virginia, "had a falling out, on account . . . of her intimacy with Green," a bondman recently arrived from Tennessee. Hannah believed herself effectively divorced. Tom had complained that "she and Green were too thick together," "had not been to see her for four weeks," and explicitly "told her he never intended to come back to see her again." The message could hardly have been clearer, but ultimately Tom was not prepared to dissolve their relationship permanently. "I am the most miserable man that ever lived," he moaned to another bondman. Unlucky in love, he explained, "This is [the] second wife I have had, and I never had any confidence in either of them." Tom was not one to wallow in self-pity, however. "I have stabbed one damned negro on account of my first wife," he confessed, "and I'll cut Greens damned heart out of him" for his liaison with Hannah. Tom intimated to other slaves that he would give Green "an unmerciful thrashing." Quite the opposite actually happened. Despite Tom's size advantage over his rival, he got the worst of his encounter with Green, who cut him mortally in the throat and chest. In a similar case, the bondman Gustavus appeared before the Lynchburg city Hustings Court in January 1845 for stabbing Barney several times from behind, with a dagger, in retribution for his liaison with a former spouse. "I was married to Gustavus 6 or 7 years ago," explained the bondwoman Patsy. "Last July, a year ago, Gustavus came to me with a Deacon of the Church, and said that 'I was no more his wife,' and we parted." Gustavus later reconsidered his casting off of Patsy. As Patsy herself related, "he has been several times to see me, but I would not make up with him." Gustavus watched with simmering resentment as Patsy launched a budding romance with the enslaved man Barney. He therefore hatched a plot to lie in ambush for his ex-wife's new love and attack him by surprise. On one occasion when Barney went to visit Patsy, Gustavus "sprung from under the steps of the porch, and halloed at him 'You wont get in so easy tonight.'" He then thrust a knife repeatedly into Barney's lower back and left shoulder, inflicting wounds that eventually killed him.[100]

The broken relationships inside the quarters that incited such violence also held ramifications for southern slave law. Could enslaved husbands and wives, for instance, testify against the other in court? Whites embroiled in litigation could not be lawfully compelled to give evidence against a spouse. Did the same standard apply to slaves? "[T]he . . . question," acknowledged one high court in the South, ". . . is one of great interest." The Supreme Court of North Carolina established the precedent through which almost all southern states ruled the testimony of an enslaved spouse against his or her partner admissible evidence in the eyes of the law. Caswell County bondman Samuel had left his wife Mima but allegedly murdered the man who replaced him as her husband. During Samuel's trial, Mima was called to testify against her former spouse of ten years and father of her five children. Samuel's counsel objected, arguing that "cohabitation between slaves, constitutes, in this state, a marriage, or rather such a marriage as produces incompetency to give evidence." Mutual consent of the parties involved, it was suggested, rather than formal recognition by the law, made the marital union. In its verdict from 1836, the North Carolina Supreme Court disagreed: "The marriage of slaves in this State, consisting of cohabitation merely, by the permission of their owners, does not constitute the relation of husband and wife, so as to attach to them the privileges and disabilities, incident to that relation by the common law." In assessing the competency of enslaved husbands and wives to testify against the other, Judge Thomas Ruffin explained that "only a marriage de jure, will exclude one of the parties from giving evidence for or against the other"; "a marriage de facto will not." In short, "the only test of competency is this: are they in fact and in law husband and wife?" Legally, Mima was never Samuel's wife, regardless of their decade as a couple. Eliminating all doubt as to Mima's ability to give evidence against Samuel, the Court also noted that her testimony "would undoubtedly be admissible after they had separated, and she had become the wife of another slave." Enslaved spouses could testify against the other under all circumstances, "even in a capital case."[101]

Nearly all other slaveholding states followed the precedent set in North Carolina. The Supreme Court of Alabama referenced the *State v. Samuel* decision in a similar case one decade later. In 1845, the Dallas County Circuit Court convicted the bondman Smith "for the murder of one Edmund, also a slave." During that trial, the state, in attempting to establish Smith's jealousy toward Edmund, called Smith's "own wife ... as a witness against him." Smith's counsel argued, "All the reasons which exclude the wife from being a witness for and against her husband, apply as well to slaves as free persons, and there is nothing in the condition of slavery which calls for the application of other than the general rules." Prosecutors challenged this assertion. "The laws of the State recognize no such relation as husband and wife between slaves," they explained. "It is true, morality and decency require, and religion commands, that the moral relation shall exist, and be faithfully observed, but no rights or disabilities ensue from the relation, when slaves are the subject of it." The lower court permitted Smith's wife to testify, and the Supreme Court of Alabama saw nothing improper about that decision. "Slaves," ruled the high court, "though living together as husband and wife, may be witnesses for or against each other, in a criminal case." Conceding the "moral obligation" of "the relation of husband and wife," Alabama law nevertheless failed to acknowledge slave marriages and thus the prohibition against spousal testimony. Likewise, "the legal relation of husband & wife [did] not exist between slaves in Virginia." As a result, when the bondman Tom's counsel objected to Abby as a witness because she was married to the accused, a Louisa County Court of Oyer and Terminer promptly overruled the defense and judged her competent to testify. In Texas, too, "Slaves could not marry ... so as to constitute them husband and wife, and protect them from being witnesses against each other."[102]

Of the slaveholding states, only Georgia ruled the testimony of enslaved spouses inadmissible, just as it was for white couples. In the case of William, found guilty in Thomas County of the wartime murder of another slave, the Supreme Court of Georgia reversed the judgment against him because the lower court had allowed the testimony of his enslaved wife Ann. "On the trial of slaves or free persons of color in this State," proclaimed the high court in 1864, "the husband or wife is not admissible as a witness for or against each other." Legally, Georgia recognized the marital relations of slave and free black couples, "or what passes with them" as such. William's conviction was therefore overturned and a new trial ordered.[103]

Although Georgia was unique in exempting the testimony of enslaved spouses against one another, the standard of proof required for conviction was quite low. Guilt did not require reasonable doubt; circumstantial evidence alone sufficed. The Baldwin County bondman John allegedly committed murder in 1862 because "his wife's affections had been stolen from him by another"—a slave named Jackson. Despite a lack of eyewitness testimony, jurors on the Baldwin County Superior Court found John guilty. On appeal, the state Supreme Court affirmed the verdict. Although the high court expressed "pity" for the cuckolded slave, Judge Joseph Henry Lumpkin observed that John had a plausible "motive for committing the crime. He was actuated by jealousy, of a most malignant and terrible character ... This passion had taken entire possession of his bosom, and shook the throne of reason to its very centre." "[M]addened" by loss of sexual proprietorship over his wife, "revenge prompted the deed," and "every blow was guided by the most intense malice." Neighboring Alabama maintained an equally minimal threshold for conviction. In Dallas County, the enslaved couple Baalam and Ellen "quarreled and separated" a full year prior to Ellen's murder. Even though they "continued on good terms with each other," the circuit court convicted Baalam for the crime on the basis of an unproven "old grudge." On appeal, the hypothesis of the ex-husband's presumptive guilt passed muster with the Supreme Court of Alabama. The court conceded that "there was no direct proof implicating the accused in the commission of the crime," but some circumstantial evidence suggested as much. No one was able to show that Baalam and Ellen had ever fully reconciled, and witnesses had seen them together the day of the murder. Moreover, Baalam was barefooted, and at the murder site were tracks of someone not wearing shoes. "This evidence was exceedingly remote and entitled to but little weight from the jury in coming to a conclusion as to the guilt or innocence of the prisoner," acknowledged the Supreme Court, "but we cannot say that the [circuit] court erred in admitting it": "[T]hough weak and inconclusive," circumstantial evidence "is nevertheless admissible." Baalam's conviction and death sentence stood.[104]

Attorneys for some slaves accused of murder argued that adultery as a precipitating motive for homicide ought to mitigate the charge against them to manslaughter. In Craven County, North Carolina, John tracked down his straying wife Flora at her mother's house and informed her that, at the first opportunity, "he intended to kill Ben Shipman," another slave, for fooling around with her. At the instigation of their mother, Flora and her sister went to warn Ben, who lived only "about ten steps distant." Ben was not home, so the sisters "commenced sewing" by firelight as they waited inside his cabin. When Ben soon appeared, they alerted him to John's threat. Ben closed and locked the door and laid down to rest in an adjacent room. Before long, John rapped at the door, and when Flora refused to open it as he commanded, John broke in and bludgeoned Ben Shipman to death with a piece of iron. At trial, John's counsel contended that a longstanding "adulterous intercourse" between Flora and Ben "would extenuate the offence to manslaughter." Cuckolding had caused John to suffer "mental alienation to such an extent as to render him incapable of committing a crime." That night, according to witnesses, John "seemed to be crazy and not in his right mind." In truth, it was reported, strange was normal for John. As he went about a typical day painting houses, he was "in the habit of talking to himself, and frequently swearing as if he were angry." The evening of the murder, however, "he seemed to be much enraged, and said he would have his wife out of Ben's house." John's lawyers proposed that their client "was labouring under monomania"—a form of insanity—"on the subject of the adultery of his wife." The Craven County Superior Court rejected this line of argumentation, and the North Carolina Supreme

Court upheld the decision. "[T]o extenuate the offence," explained the court, "the husband must find the deceased in the very act of adultery with his wife."[105]

Southern courts took note of whether intraracial slave homicides resulted from passion or premeditation. The Supreme Court of North Carolina entertained the theoretical possibility that catching a spouse *in flagrante delicto* might reduce a charge from murder to manslaughter. "It is the sudden fury excited by finding a man in the very act of shame with his wife, which mitigates the offence of the husband," explained the Court. But the wronged husband must kill "his wrongdoer at the instant" to have meaningful implications at law: "The law extends its indulgence to a transport of passion justly excited, and acting before reason has time to subdue it, but not to a settled purpose of vengeance, no matter how great the injury, or gross the insult." For slaves as well as whites, men could escape a murder charge for the homicide of a wife's paramour, but they were required to act immediately upon making the shocking discovery. Revenge taken at any later time smacked of premeditation and rendered the murderer fully culpable for his crime. Had the Virginia bondman Moses actually carried out his plan to murder Elic because "Elic kept his wife," there could have been no reduction of charge because Moses had purchased a dirk from McGhee's Reuben, another slave, with the avowed intention of killing his rival. That Adam failed to kill Fanny upon catching her in the act of adultery or "immediately after the separation" convinced a Jones County, Georgia, inferior court that his deadly act was thoroughly contemplated and deliberate. He was convicted, sentenced to hang "until he be dead," and accordingly led to the place of public execution to meet his scheduled fate. An Alabama slave named Sam, jealous after having found his wife and the bondman Edmund "together," reportedly threatened to kill the interloper four times, the last of which was just two weeks prior to Edmund's death. At a "negro house" the night Edmund was killed, Sam explained to another slave that "he must return home," for he anticipated finding "Edmund and his wife together." Edmund was later "found dead at the root of a tree."[106]

If threats indicated premeditation, so did attempts to establish an alibi. In Georgia, testimony at the trial of the bondman John showed that he had labored proactively to disguise his murderous plans for Jackson, the slave who had "stolen" his wife's affections. John's deception began by supplying misinformation to a marshal that a runaway slave wielding both an axe and a hatchet was lurking in the neighborhood and "that he was afraid he would kill some one if he was not caught." After the murder, John dismissed the blood splatters on his clothes by claiming to have just "killed a pig," portions of which he said he delivered to his mother-in-law Dinah and to another enslaved woman named Lucretia. The pair of bondwomen eviscerated John's alibi, however, when they each testified that he "did not bring me a pig, or any part of one, any time about the homicide." John spun some plausible tales to shield himself from suspicion in Jackson's death, but his extensive efforts ironically reinforced the impression that the crime was premeditated.[107]

For slaves convicted of murdering other bondpeople, written appeals by whites to state governors marked the last, best hope for a reduction of sentence or, on rare occasion, a full pardon. In the 1850s, one North Carolinian requested that Governor Thomas Bragg show mercy to a male slave who killed the bondman who had cuckolded him. The correspondent argued that "the defects in the moral and mental training" of slaves abrogated his responsibility for the crime. More frequently, memorials presented by whites acknowledged at least a modicum of sympathy with the plights of convicted slaves. Petitioners on their behalf often drew comparisons to hypothetical trial outcomes had the assailant and victim been white. In their 1842 plea to Virginia's governor, lawyers for the enslaved Emanuel asserted, "We are confident that the prisoner would have been acquitted had the affray occurred between white men. Such was the sentiment of the bystanders." Less than a decade before, Harry's counsel expressed to the governor their confidence "that had the parties been white men, the prisoner, upon the same evidence, would have been convicted of no higher offence than manslaughter." The implicit recognition of a two-tiered legal system in Virginia, in which cases were adjudicated differently on the basis of the defendant's race or color, is unmistakable.[108]

Petitioners—all of whom were white men—exhibited the greatest empathy for cuckolded slave men who murdered their competition for a bondwoman's affection. Attorney William Daniel Jr. wrote Virginia's governor to introduce a petition with more than one hundred signatures in support of his client Gustavus, a bondman sentenced to death in Lynchburg for the murder of the slave Barney. Petitioners noted that Gustavus was driven to commit the crime "by a well founded jealousy against the deceased for criminal intimacy and adulterous intercourse with his lawful wife." As a lawyer, Daniel understood, first, that a slave could not have a "lawful wife" and, second, that the homicidal slave's motivation "cannot be ground of legal justification." But he added that, when combined with the court's recommendation for gubernatorial mercy and Gustavus's "unusually good character," the bondman's request for reprieve merited serious consideration. In 1849, thirteen petitioners from Louisa County strongly suspected that the bondman Tom had killed John when he discovered his wife "in an act of Adultery" with him—"circumstances so provoking" as not to constitute murder "but only manslaughter of the lowest degree." They and two Louisa County magistrates who did not officiate at Tom's trial recommended a complete pardon. Even William J. Robertson, the attorney who prosecuted the case against Tom, appealed to the governor for "a mitigation of punishment." In 1818, forty-five white men, including the prosecuting attorney, six other lawyers, three sheriffs, three magistrates, and the clerk and deputy clerk of Caroline County, Virginia, signed a petition for the outright pardon of the enslaved man John. "John[']s character stands as fair as any black man's in this Commonwealth," they declared, but "he was prompted to commit the unfortunate act"—the murder of a slave named Sam—"by the strongest passion that can possibly aggitate the human mind": "jealousy." Sam had been "caught in bed with the said John[']s wife" and "constantly visit[ed]" her, "keeping alive the aforementioned angry passion." In the world of southern honor these white male petitioners inhabited, defense of family and loved ones was paramount. Gender conventions demanded it. Tom and John had fulfilled their masculine responsibilities appropriately. Although they were held in bondage, the homicides they committed seemed to a number of white men perfectly justified.[109]

Violence played a crucial role in the creation and defense of enslaved families. Slave marriages were legally illusory, and masters regularly defiled them through the sexual and economic decisions they made. But enslaved unions' vulnerabilities did not dampen bondpeople's interests in forging and maintaining them. When bondmen—and occasionally even bondwomen—smited an enslaved rival, protected their families through violence, or physically punished other slaves for infringing upon existing relationships, they policed the slave community internally and enforced a moral and ethical code forged in the crucible of the quarters. Violence provided one method for upholding cultural expectations regarding love, courtship, and marriage. Yet the functional, constructive power of violence stands as only part of the story.

Violence assumed a fundamentally different character when an enslaved spouse, inequitably fond of, respectful, or devoted to his or her partner, physically abused the other or when one member of an enslaved couple refused to allow an ailing, unsatisfying relationship to die. During these moments, the destructive potential of violent behaviors became evident. Slave marriage was always a tenuous institution. White contemporaries understood that "many cases arise in which separations among married slaves, occur from voluntary abandonment of duty by the parties themselves, or from circumstances beyond their control." As their observation suggested, impediments to slaves' marital harmony sometimes emanated from within. A fraction of enslaved husbands committed violent acts upon family members to exercise physical domination in the slave cabin, enforce their vision of domesticity, or grasp at some semblance of patriarchal control over their wives and children otherwise denied them under the system of slavery. But the more formidable sets of challenges to slave unions were external. Sales and compulsory removals devastated slave families as well as the broader neighborhoods to which bondpeople belonged. Whatever the cause of separation, voluntary or involuntary, violence might be the result as enslaved men struggled to maintain failing marriages, pursued reunions unsuccessfully with former spouses, or wrought vengeance upon an ex-wife or her new love interest. Altogether, violence proved a prominent feature in the destruction of many enslaved unions.[110]

Chapter 7

HONOR, VIOLENCE, AND ENSLAVED MASCULINITY

ON A SATURDAY NIGHT in 1840, Cupe, enslaved in Russell County, Virginia, chatted up "a woman of Mr. Alexanders by the name of Patsy, and asked her if she would go with him." According to one enslaved informant, "some three or four years ago Cupe claimed this woman ... as his wife," but apparently their relationship had soured. In the intervening time, Cupe had taken a different woman as his partner, but now, perhaps acting upon residual feelings of love and affection, Cupe attempted to rekindle his dormant relationship with Patsy. When Patsy declined, Cupe "abused her." Cupe repeated his inquiry, and Patsy relaxed her defenses. But when she refused to go with him at the very moment he insisted, the bondman suddenly turned menacing. He "talked of knocking her out of the home or into the fire." As tensions mounted, another slave within earshot, named Richard, injected himself into the conversation. Richard, who did harbor some unspecified grievance against Cupe, instructed his fellow slave that "he should not abuse the woman." His valiant stand on Patsy's behalf enraged Cupe. Cursing, he asked Richard, "do you take it up?" "Yes," replied the bondman as he shed his coat in preparation for a scuffle. They quarreled and "abused one another and gave each other the lie." Their clash resulted in Richard suffering a fatal stab wound to the thigh.[1]

Although there is no evidence to suggest any "intimacy ... between Richard and Patsy," it was not unheard of for an enslaved man to kill a rival for a sweetheart's love. Recall that the Louisa County, Virginia, bondwoman Abby acquiesced to her parents' wish that she not marry John. Instead, she married Tom, but while Tom passed muster with Abby's parents, the young bondwoman's heart apparently remained with her forbidden love. Threatened by John's lingering presence, Tom fractured his challenger's skull with a stick of wood, killing him. Richard, however, appears to have interceded largely out of a sense of chivalry and may well have thought his deed admirable. Patsy may have neither wanted nor needed Richard's aid, but the bondman took it upon himself to defend the enslaved woman from her former lover's threats. Protecting and defending women was just one component of a masculine honor code prevalent in the Old South. Men asserted their manhood when they guarded wives and preserved reputations of self and family. Southern whites would not have assumed Richard, as a slave, capable of honor, but that fact was altogether irrelevant in his dispute with Cupe. Though enslaved, bondmen such as Richard laid claim to a system of honor widely understood in the slave quarters, one that often coincided, invisibly to their owners, with white notions of honor. As with southern white male honor, however, enslaved male honor went hand in hand with violent behavior.[2]

Scholars have long noted that a culture of honor flourished among southern white men, but John C. Willis and Bertram Wyatt-Brown excepted, southern historians have been much slower than their counterparts studying Latin America to recognize honor among slaves.[3] Sociologist Orlando Patterson famously defined the slave as a "person without honor." Yet in denying honor to slaves, most scholars have unwittingly adopted masters' perspective.[4] Slaveholders upheld honor as their special preserve, a possession bestowed upon them by others but one that was nevertheless uniquely theirs. Honor—a gauge of one's standing or respect in the community—was not distributed equally. In the Old South, elite white men conferred honor most generously upon their own. Occasionally masters grudgingly conceded limited honor to respectable, non-slaveholding whites, but they excluded slaves (as well as poor whites) altogether from the honor code. In failing to acknowledge the honor of slaves, southern whites recognized only the vertical dimension of honor, in which inferiors granted respect to those who outranked them in the social hierarchy. As such, white men expected deference from women, children, and blacks, all of whom were their subordinates. In contrast to whites, slaves more keenly understood honor's horizontal component, in which respect was distributed among equals. Individuals achieved horizontal honor by earning it from their peer group. Whites' refusal to grant honor unto slaves was irrelevant because, for bondpeople, the pertinent audience of reference was black, however degraded they were in wider southern society. Meritorious behavior and demonstrations of desirable traits brought respect, and no single class or race could stake a monopoly on it. In this context, Wyatt-Brown observes, "Male honor was richly prized" among slaves, albeit "confined to the slave quarters." The degradation slaves suffered in white society served only to enhance the sense of honor among themselves. Their heightened sensitivity demanded constant, conscientious accounting of their status relative to one another and a quick response to any challenge to honor. As North Carolina jurist Thomas Ruffin perceptively noted in 1849, slaves "sometimes kill each other in heat of blood" because they were "sensible to the dishonor in their own caste."[5]

Slaves' honor was fundamentally a gendered concept intimately related to white and black definitions of manhood. (I discuss enslaved female honor and femininity in the next chapter.) Southern whites virtually never recognized honor among slaves. To the contrary, they routinely dishonored slaves in their daily lives. Commodified slave bodies were hired out without regard to slaves' own preferences, mortgaged as collateral for loans, insured like other valuable goods, and regularly bought and sold in a thriving domestic slave trade. Purveyors of human flesh stripped bondpeople publicly for intrusive inspection at slave auctions, and masters and overseers inflicted whippings in full view of spouses, children, and friends. The disfiguring scars of the lash permanently imprinted on bondpeople's backs indelible markers of their subordination. But absent an acute understanding of honor—and its inverse, shame—they would not have felt the profound humiliation of a whipping so evident in their narratives and autobiographies.[6]

Slaves' systematic degradation in southern society undergirded white male claims to manhood. Historian Lorri Glover has described manhood as a journey— "the culmination of a process"—that "included but transcended honor." Southern white men defined manhood, in part, in contradistinction to slaves. Manhood encompassed a set of admirable traits—independence, assertiveness, and self-confidence, among them—antithetical to slavery. Indeed, masters conscientiously strove to avoid cultivating such potentially dangerous characteristics in their bondmen. Slaves thus functioned as a convenient cultural foil. Slaveholders' domination over their chattel—slaves' dishonor—contributed to the construction of southern white men's senses of honor and mastery. The exercise of southern white manhood required the differentiation of white men from slaves. The result was a paradox: in fashioning an identity as self-assured, independent men, slaveholders were highly dependent upon their slaves.[7]

If the institution of slavery buttressed southern white manhood, bondage directly challenged enslaved manhood. White male mastery and identity were predicated upon the denial of black manhood and the exercise of dominion over slaves. In a seminal essay from 1959, Stanley M. Elkins stoked controversy when he argued that bondage "emasculated" slaves. Writing as though all slaves were men, Elkins described a process of infantilization through which slaves were transformed into docile, childlike, dependent, and submissive Sambos. The Sambo personality type was the product of masters' creation, Elkins argued; for them, the ideal slave man was a perpetual "boy," easily controlled and utterly harmless. After decades of unrelenting attacks by John W. Blassingame, Eugene D. Genovese, Herbert G. Gutman, and countless others, Elkins's interpretation lost credibility, and modern scholars of masculinity do not couch discussion in his terms.[8]

Nevertheless, much about the institution of slavery was inimical to the development of traditionally masculine roles and responsibilities. Enslavement was particularly disorienting for first-generation bondmen forcibly plucked from Africa in the colonial era. Captivity itself marked a devastating assault on African manhood for individuals who prided themselves as warriors. Because they had been dislodged from their familiar cultural matrix, African men's past military feats and accomplishments were rendered suddenly meaningless. Labor regimes in the Americas also marked a cultural assault upon African notions of masculinity. Whereas in much of West Africa, agricultural work was gendered female, eighteenth-century southern masters dispatched the overwhelming majority of male slaves into rice and tobacco fields to perform "women's work." Agricultural work in Africa was also sometimes relegated to those defeated in battle and enslaved. The Fulani warrior Abd-al-Rahman Ibrahima, reduced to slavery in what became Mississippi, was appalled by the prospect of field work. He shunned agricultural labor as appropriate only for enemies conquered in combat. For all generations of enslaved men, masters exercised the final authority over enslaved families. Without legal sanction to slave marriages, slaveholders retained the power to break up the enslaved family unit and sell off its members at any time. Enslaved husbands could not protect their wives or daughters from the physical or sexual abuse of the owner without risking great bodily harm. When masters whipped enslaved men in front of their families, they undercut male slaves' pretensions to authority as husbands and fathers. Moreover, despite the efforts of enslaved men to provide basic necessities and material comforts for their families via the slave economy, they typically did not supply the bulk of the household's essential needs. All of these factors deprived male slaves of the control and authority customarily accorded men in their day-to-day lives.[9]

Inevitably, the crisis of enslaved masculinity informed abolitionists' rhetorical flourishes. "The Slave is not treated as a Man, is not looked upon as a man," bemoaned New England minister Joshua Young in one of his antislavery sermons. To enslave someone, "you unmake him, *unman* him; . . . you *crush out of him the very consciousness that he is a man.*" Under slavery, preached the Reverend William H. Marsh of Connecticut, "the manhood with which God endowed him, is shrunk into a mere piece of living property." Even Lewis Clarke, himself an escaped fugitive, memorably lamented, "A SLAVE CAN'T BE A MAN!" Militant black abolitionists in particular invoked the language of black manhood in their appeals. In his 1843 "Address to the Slaves," newspaper editor and minister Henry Highland Garnet of New York scolded enslaved men and spurred them to action: "you tamely submit while your lords tear your wives from your embraces and defile them before your eyes. In the name of God, we ask you, are you men?" The refrain was a familiar one. Abolitionist David Walker, a North Carolina–born free black, beseeched his "coloured brethren" in 1829 "to prove to the Americans and the world, that we are MEN, and not *brutes*." "[W]hen shall we arise from this death-like apathy?" he inquired, "And be men!!"[10]

Despite the pronouncements of Clarke and others, enslaved men successfully overcame the obstacles they faced to construct masculine identities. "The typical slave," wrote John Blassingame in rebuttal to the Elkins thesis, "preserved his manhood in the quarters." Away from white surveillance, "the slave . . . could be a man." Burgeoning scholarship continues to explore the ways in which enslaved men actively created their own paradigms of masculinity. The affirmation and performance of manhood assumed many possible forms. Often it involved risk-taking behaviors, such as theft from the master or evading the patrol, both of which exhibited courage and daring. Male slaves across the South acted as men when they took the initiative in courtship, making illicit visits to a sweetheart in defiance of masters and patrollers, exerting themselves physically through dance, bestowing small gifts (possibly pilfered from the master) upon the object of their desires, or protecting and defending the women they loved. Taking advantage of opportunities afforded by the internal economy, enslaved men who hunted, fished, and cultivated foodstuffs to augment their families' diet or to supply other commodities that made the slaves' lives or cabins more comfortable staked a claim to manhood as well. Henry "Box" Brown, for example, encountered one slave who had sold "a few hickory nuts" at market for "36 cents," which he promptly turned over to his wife "to furnish her with some little articles of comfort." Less altruistically, some enslaved men used recreational activities such as homosocial drinking and gambling to demonstrate manhood. Boxing and wrestling matches, foot races, jumping contests, and other competitive sporting events channeled enslaved men's energies for more than mere leisurely amusement. Such public performances showcased their physical prowess and marked affirmative displays of masculinity to audiences of enslaved peers, including the women whom they hoped to impress. Enslaved men also expressed their manhood bodily "through clothing, speech, dance, song, eating, lovemaking, and fighting [whites]." Edward E. Baptist detected several different models of enslaved manhood in his work on the cotton frontier of the antebellum South. As he explained, some enslaved men acted heroically by running away, fighting masters or overseers, or otherwise defying white authority. Others served as caretakers for new families cobbled together from the shards of broken ones. Having been torn from families and communities in older slaveholding states, they cultivated new relationships that invested them with masculine responsibilities. Still others acted independently, as atomized individuals, rejecting altogether emotional ties to other slaves. All represented attempts to forge a masculine identity amid the chaos of forced migration.[11]

Darlene Clark Hine and Earnestine Jenkins observe that enslaved men exercised a masculinity of resistance. Although they caution against "becoming ensnared in the trap of equating manhood with violence," violent, aggressive behaviors were crucial to the construction of masculinity and the functioning of the honor code for southern men, whether white or black.[12] Nothing predetermined the centrality of violence to the lives of antebellum southern men. As cultural constructs, definitions of masculinity varied from one society to the next. Middle-class northern whites and Englishmen in the Victorian era, for example, lauded control over one's passions and restraint from violence. Through a process Freud described as the "sublimation of instinct," civilization demanded the suppression of humans' innate aggressive impulses. In civilized societies, Freud explained, people's "instinct of destruction" was not expressed outwardly, for a well-developed sense of guilt neutralized aggression by channeling it inward. To behave violently, therefore, was not "manly"; doing so signaled a surrender to passion, the immature act of a child rather than the responsible conduct of a civilized adult. But such beliefs were subjective, and antebellum southern men, white and black, subscribed to a different understanding of manhood. When they engaged in violent behaviors to defend their status and reputation over real or imagined slights, they engaged in behavior that they considered masculine. For them, violence marked the appropriate response when challenged.[13]

Just as southern white gentlemen engaged in duels and lower-class white men fought rough-and-tumble brawls and eye-gouging matches, slaves, too, employed violence as one possible outlet for the expression of manhood.[14] Bondmen sometimes declared limits to the punishments administered by whites to which they would willingly submit and defied white authority figures through individual acts of confrontation. Frederick Douglass's epic fight with the slave breaker Covey offers the most famous example. After their purported two-hour altercation, Douglass recorded, "My long-crushed spirit rose, cowardice departed, bold defiance took its place." Douglass found redemption through violence. "This battle with Mr. Covey," he reflected, "... revived within me a sense of my own manhood." The Mississippi bondman Alfred probably felt the same way when he avenged his wife's rape by killing their white overseer. On a larger scale, slave rebels such as Nat Turner or those aboard the slaving vessels *Amistad* and *Creole* "came to be associated with manhood and masculinity" because their physically violent actions marked "an unequivocal challenge to white male authority." The final generation of black men enslaved in the American South confronted a unique opportunity to claim manhood by serving in the official capacity of U.S. soldiers during the latter half of the Civil War. Some 110,000 former bondmen donned Union blue, willing to prove their mettle in combat. The significance of this watershed moment for black masculinity was not lost on the soldiers. "I's a man now," said one. Even a white soldier acknowledged of his black comrades-in-arms, "Put a United States uniform on his back and the *chattel* is a *man*."[15]

Throughout the history of American slavery, however, bondmen were less likely to assault whites in manly acts of resistance than to inflict injury upon their counterparts in bondage. Slaves often thought of violent conduct toward other bondmen in positive terms. As we have seen in previous chapters, enslaved men sometimes fought at work and at play, to enforce claims to property and uphold business dealings, to establish or maintain supremacy over the household, to defend the women they claimed and take vengeance upon male slave interlopers, and to punish slaves who violated social expectation. Culturally, enslaved men expected violence in certain situations. Among bondmen, the refusal to fight invited ridicule. As Lewis Clarke recorded, "them as won't fight, is called Poke-easy."[16] An analysis of the words that enslaved men uttered during confrontations, the circumstances that prompted their violent encounters, and the fighting techniques they utilized reveals that the ethic of honor so prevalent in southern white society was ingrained in masculine slave culture as well. For some enslaved men, violence in the quarters afforded one means to construct a masculine identity within the context of a white society that routinely denied their manhood. However detrimental or disruptive conflicts were to the harmony and solidarity of the slave community, physical aggression was often crucial to the definition of enslaved masculinity.

The provenance of enslaved honor in the American South is impossible to pinpoint with precision. Recent scholarship has revealed the centrality of honor codes across many African cultures. Across the African continent, honor assumed many different forms.[17] Yet violence was inextricably interwoven into a number of African honor codes. Men who were insulted or challenged avenged themselves physically. T. J. Desch Obi has studied martial arts traditions originating in Africa. Although some African honor systems, such as that of the Kunene, emphasized self-control and restraint, many others demanded violent responses to aspersions against honor. To protect and defend honor, African men developed and perfected distinctive fighting styles, such as leg wrapping, foot fighting, and head butting. Angolans settled affairs of honor through stick fighting. Those who excelled in the performance of these martial arts gained acclaim. By no coincidence, the powerful leader Okonkwo, the protagonist in Nigerian novelist Chinua Achebe's *Things Fall Apart* (1958), was a local wrestling champion in his fictional Igbo village. The real-life African men displaced from their homes and forcibly conveyed via the Middle Passage carried their specialized combat traditions with them to the Americas. Enslaved Africans kicked, butted heads, battled with sticks, wrestled, boxed, ran, and jumped in contests of physical prowess that displayed their masculinity and conferred honor upon the victors. So did their male descendants.[18]

The rich African heritage of honor and violence transmitted to the American South meant that enslaved honor need not have been learned from or purely imitative of southern white culture. From the late seventeenth century to the end of the colonial era, slaves imported directly from Africa or by way of the Caribbean disembarked from slave ships in major American ports for sale. The stream of fresh arrivals kept African culture alive, particularly in the majority black Carolina lowcountry. Eventually, the imperial conflict between Great Britain and its aggrieved American colonists interfered with these continuous cultural infusions from Africa. The transatlantic slave trade came under direct assault with the approach of the American Revolution. Colonial governments banned the African trade as part of a broader economic boycott against Britain, and with independence declared in 1776, most of the newly created state governments prohibited the importation of slaves from abroad. In 1798, Georgia became the last of the original thirteen states to ban the traffic in human cargoes, although South Carolina subsequently revived its participation in the international slave trade in 1803. The U.S. government formally terminated the country's lawful participation in the transatlantic traffic at the earliest constitutionally authorized date, in 1808. Yet the closure of the African trade did nothing to diminish the significance of honor and violence in the lives of southern slaves.[19]

Even as death claimed the lives of native-born African slaves and cultural injections direct from Africa diminished, notions of honor remained strong among enslaved African Americans. With only a small number of exceptions, attempting to disaggregate which honorific forms characteristic of slaves were derived from Africa from those with European roots is a virtually impossible task. Processes of cultural transmission, adaptation, and fusion are complicated and notoriously difficult to trace. In the slaveholding South, blacks and whites regularly and mutually borrowed across cultural boundaries. Although generations of African tradition may have informed the behavior of enslaved men in the Old South, most nineteenth-century African American slaves had been born and reared in the land of their bondage. In addition, whites outnumbered them demographically in most localities across the South and in all states except Mississippi and South Carolina. No doubt the environment in which they lived greatly conditioned the way honor manifested itself in the quarters. As John C. Willis rhetorically asked, "Could any people living so intimately with . . . honor-obsessed white Southerners have remained ignorant of the features and workings of their code?" By the end of the antebellum era, the influence of purely African cultural forms and inheritances had waned significantly, which is not to argue that slaves' honor merely mimicked that of whites. Slaves could maintain their own sense of honor without simply replicating white codes. Willis himself discerned a "distinct slave honor" borne out of the oppression of bondage and therefore necessarily different from that of white honor. Specifically, he highlighted group loyalty, pride in appearance, and the exacting of vengeance when dishonored as key components of an enslaved honor rooted in a culture that was itself the product of slaves' inferior status and degraded existence.[20]

Without disputing Willis's contention that slaves possessed a system of honor uniquely forged in the crucible of bondage, this chapter points out that the honor codes of whites and slaves in the Old South mirrored one another in many ways. One important point of intersection was the primacy attached to acts of violence. Honor sometimes achieved expression through nonviolent means; nevertheless, it also explained much of the violent conflict not only among southern white men, as scholars have long noted, but among the enslaved as well. As Edward L. Ayers observed in the context of the late nineteenth century, "Accounts of Southern black violence" were arrestingly similar to episodes of "honor-related violence among whites." His insight applies equally well to the violent encounters among slaves in the antebellum decades. Lower-court records from Virginia, South Carolina, and other southern states chronicle the honor-bound behaviors of enslaved men that culminated in the violent defense of slaves' honor. In the Old South, violence marked one common, overlapping feature in the honor cultures of southern white and enslaved black men.[21]

Trial testimony recorded in southern courtrooms offers clues to enslaved men's senses of honor and masculinity. Contrary to southern physician Samuel A. Cartwright's contention that "the sentiment of honor or duty . . . has no place in their language," black men's conversations as recalled in court transcripts reveal acute concern about manhood and honor. A language of honor infused both their speech and behavior. During one dispute among slaves in Adams County, Mississippi, in 1834, "Anthony asked Henry if he was a man." Henry's reply in the affirmative was not enough to dissuade Anthony from clubbing him with "a certain billet of wood." At one point during a scuffle in Albemarle County, Virginia, the bondman William instructed Washington to "behave like a man." Often, behaving like a man meant not backing down from a challenge. Recalled one former Alabama slave, "It used to be that one man would walk up to another and say, 'You ain't no good.' And the other one would say, 'All right, le's see.' And they would rassle" to determine the better man.[22]

Wrestling matches or other physical contests helped establish plantation hierarchies, but not all such challenges to rank were similarly good-natured. One Virginia bondman unexpectedly "knocked" Primus into the fire burning inside a Pittsylvania County kitchen in 1819. Primus regained his balance, regrouped, and cursed his adversary: "God Damn him let him come again, he was ready for him." They then engaged in a mortal fray. Shortly before the bondman Bill stabbed Caesar in Muscogee County, Georgia, in 1854, he "dared" his foe "to make a riffle towards him, and [said] he would cut his heart out of him." In Civil War–era Richmond, words passed between slaves Jim and Andrew in Judith Roane's boardinghouse. The pair had been at odds for at least a month, and when Andrew hit Jim on the side of the head, Jim warned, "You had better let me alone." "Damn you," Andrew replied, "I dare you into the yard." The two proceeded to the boardinghouse porch, where Jim stabbed him with a bowie knife. Andrew perhaps spent some of the last remaining minutes of his life regretting having goaded Jim into a fight.[23]

Unlike Andrew's challenge, a dare issued in front of a Baton Rouge barber shop lacked any hostile intent but proved no less tragic. In 1857, as an anonymous "black boy" passed by, the bondman Alex eagerly showed him "an old gun in his hand." The possession of guns was outlawed to slaves, and Alex was perhaps fascinated with the deadly weapon he wielded. The gun itself had "for a long time" sat in the barber shop, seemingly a prop to keep customers entertained. It "had been often snapped before, and no one thought it loaded." Thus, when "some words" passed "in jest" between the two slaves, and the enslaved passerby "dared Alex to shoot," he did. To the shock of witnesses, the gun discharged. Alex, reportedly "a peaceable, harmless and well disposed boy," was distraught in the aftermath of the accidental shooting.[24]

Possessing their own keenly developed sense of honor, enslaved men valued status and reputation. With honor at a premium, they vocalized their readiness to perpetrate violence. Words held tremendous potency in the oral culture of the Old South. Compared to the written or printed word, speech was more immediate and forceful. For enslaved men, it marked the proper medium for asserting masculinity, whether through threats, boasts, or insults. (And most slaves were illiterate anyway.) Identifying no particular target of his hostility, a Wake County, North Carolina, bondman declared that "he intended Bursting two or three Negroes he[a]ds open before he died." Even this vague threat enhanced his identity as a man. Other enslaved men addressed more specific targets. Isham, enslaved in Prince Edward County, Virginia, and carrying a stick, announced to a circle of acquaintances the same day in which he later murdered Bob that "he would give Bob that stick to his hearts content." After the bondman Harry recklessly brandished a switchblade knife at a "negro dance" in Kanawha County, Sam, clutching a piece of coal, publicly threatened the assembled partygoers, regardless of race: "[T]he first man, that he saw (white or black) with a knife, he would knock down with the coal." However emboldened Sam perhaps was by drink, his declaration not only provided a warning to potential adversaries but also announced to enslaved audiences and anyone within earshot that he would not submit meekly to challenge, threat, or insult by another slave and, in this case, even a white person. Boldly raising the prospect of violence demonstrated enslaved men's sense of masculinity.[25]

Threats preceded violence between slaves from mere moments to weeks, months, and even years before a confrontation occurred. In Anderson District, South Carolina, the affronted slave "Charles said that he would knock Moses head off" before they in fact "attempted to kill Each other contrary to the lawes of this state." Also in Anderson District, Jake informed Baylis that "he could whip him" and "put his hand on him as he pleased" before he shoved "his fist in Baylis' face" and "[p]ut his hands on his shoulders." Baylis gave Jake a sharp kick in retribution for the violation of his physical space. Elsewhere in the South Carolina upcountry, Spartanburg District slave Jason confronted the bondman Larken to confirm the rumor that Larken claimed he could "whip" Jason. Not backing down, Larken replied, "Goddamn you if you will follow me to the end of the lane I can do it."[26]

The opportunity for violent redress was longer in coming for Rutherford County, Tennessee, slave Sam. He believed that the bondman Nelson had either poisoned his whiskey or conjured him by "put[ting] something down so that . . . Sam . . . walked over it." Either way, Sam "had been in bad health through the winter" and held Nelson accountable for the debilities he suffered. He announced that "the first time he caught him in his neighborhood, or from home, he would whip Nelson, or Nelson should whip him." More than a year later, they clashed, and Nelson emerged the victor. Sam missed his opportunity to avenge the wrong he had long endured. Not so for Julius, enslaved in Rockbridge County, Virginia. His revenge was nonetheless a dish served cold. On a February Saturday in 1817 devoted primarily to chopping wood, he hacked his adversary Ned in the neck with an axe to avenge "an old grudge of better than two years."[27]

Maintaining control over or defending a spouse and the integrity of the enslaved family fueled intense, impassioned threats against fellow slaves. Not merely rhetorical devices, such pronouncements sometimes portended conflict and even death. In Virginia, the bondman Tom "had had a falling out" with his wife Hannah but had grown jealous and angry when she developed an "intimacy with Green," another slave. Many slaves "understood" that "Tom intended to beat" or whip Green. Substantially larger than his adversary, Tom was described as "a stout man" and an "overmatch" for the smaller Green. Perhaps his size advantage inspired Tom to declare that "if he ever caught Green out of town he would break every limb he had" or "give him an unmerciful thrashing." "I'll cut Greens damned heart out of him," Tom vowed. When one slave relayed these messages to Green, the diminutive bondman appeared nonplussed, confident in his own abilities. Green replied nonchalantly that "if Tom attacked him," he would "make sure work of him." Three or four weeks later, on a snowy Sunday evening, Tom spied Green entering Hannah's cabin. Minutes later, Tom approached, "broke open the door," and announced to Green, "dam you I'm here too." After an exchange of "loud talk" that filtered into an adjoining room, interrupting the sleep of another bondman, the two scuffled, and Green used a knife to dispatch his much larger opponent. Tom proved unable to deliver upon his threats.[28]

Enslaved men voiced their willingness to defend the sanctity of not only the family but also the physical space of the slave cabin itself. Although often deserted during the day, slave quarters bustled with activity in the evenings. The conclusion of the day's labor for the master meant the beginning of domestic chores about the slave houses. Enslaved women returning from the fields immediately set to work preparing food, cleaning, and doing laundry. Abuzz with motion, slave cabins failed to fulfill the domestic ideal of the home as a sanctuary of peace and serenity. On one Pittsylvania County, Virginia, plantation, the enslaved cook Sally occupied a room adjoining a kitchen with Henry, presumably her spouse. Sally was responsible for baking bread for all of her master's slaves and distributing it to them when they arrived at her dwelling. As one slave explained, "All the hands were in the habit of going . . . in the early part of the night to get their bread" from Sally. Sally's home, bakery, and shop were thus one and the same, and the conflation of private and public space provoked conflict. One night in December 1863, the bondman Kit did not attempt to retrieve his bread until midnight, after Sally had gone to sleep. The tardy slave then engaged in a heated exchange with Henry, who protested Kit's arrival at such a late hour as a violation of neighborly common sense. The testimony of an enslaved witness allows us to reconstruct their conversation:

Kit: "I must have some bread."
Henry: "I don't know where you are going to get it from. I don't have any here." (Either the evening's loaves had already been distributed, or Henry simply did not wish to be disturbed.)
Kit: "By God, I am going to bake some then."
Henry: "Where are you going to bake it?"
Kit: "I am going to bake it in here."
Henry: "Why can't you go to your own house & bake bread as well as you can in here? It is a pretty unreasonable time of night to come to anybody's house to bake bread. I am going to bed."
Kit: "I am going to bake the bread in here. My baking it won't hurt you. I have got as much liberty to bake bread in here as you."
Henry: "You have no more liberty than I have. If you put any bread in the fire here I'll tear it all to pieces."
Kit: "I'll show you whether I've got any liberty in here. If you tear this bread to pieces I'll tear you all to pieces."
Henry: "I have said mighty near as much to you as I intend to say. The thing is mighty near decided between you and me anyway. If there is any bread put in this fire tonight there will be death in this house. You'll cut my

throat or I'll cut yours, one or the other."
Kit: "There won't be any throat cut here tonight."
Henry, grabbing a shovel: "Do not talk too big."

Henry then smashed the shovel against Kit's head and stabbed his bread-seeking adversary. In so doing, Henry claimed authority over the physical space he and Sally occupied and reasserted some semblance of privacy over their dwelling. As one witness testified, "Kit did not stay in the room and had no right in there."[29]

Henry's caution to Kit—"Do not talk too big"—was well placed. Male slaves' ritual boasts and challenges reverberated throughout the quarters. The highest court in Mississippi commented dismissively that "idle braggadocia ... may at any time be overheard in the conversation of negroes." Among slaves, however, language was no trivial matter. Although not as elaborate or fanciful in their inflated words as the bragging of the "half horse, half alligator" Mike Fink and other semi-legendary or wholly fictional characters in the southwestern humor genre, slaves nevertheless employed the exaggeration and masculine boasting reminiscent of the Old Southwest's tall tales. Mississippi bondman "Horace cursed & roared a good deal" and boldly announced that "he wouldn't be whipped" before fatally stabbing his enslaved nemesis Stuart on the streets of Natchez. Enslaved men's inflated pronouncements were not merely the product of the southern frontier, however. Back east, in Lynchburg, Virginia, a "very muscular" slave named Barney informed the bondman Gustavus and an enslaved ally of Gustavus, "If you want any thing out of me, come on and get it. I can whip you and John both." In Norfolk, the enslaved Bill Williams stumbled upon "a Quarrel" between two black boys and proclaimed that "he could whip four such boys." Similar boasts could be heard not only in urban locales such as Natchez, Lynchburg, and Norfolk but in the countryside as well. The day before two rural Chesterfield County, Virginia, bondmen came to blows, Fleming warned John at breakfast that he could "put him in Hell in three minutes."[30]

The boasting of male slaves often featured direct references to enslaved manhood, toughness, and readiness to take on challengers physically. "[L]et them be white or black," bellowed the bondman Edmond at a Fauquier County, Virginia, dance. "I am a man as well as they." Central to bondmen's hostile speech was the denial of fear. Anderson District, South Carolina, bondman "Len spoke very independent" in declaring "that he was not afraid of negroes." Dismissing possible adversaries as weak, insignificant, and no cause for concern was common. Quarreling with Bob in Lunenburg County, Virginia, Nelson proclaimed "that he did not fear him or any other man." A Nansemond County slave elevated himself above his rival when he told his opponent, "God dam you, I dont care for no man." Male claims to superiority over other bondmen rankled fellow slaves. After a day's labor at a Kentucky brick kiln, Daniel and George refreshed themselves with liquor in sufficient quantities to loosen Daniel's tongue. He declared that "he was the best man that was ever on that walk," prompting a fatal confrontation with his enslaved co-worker and erstwhile drinking buddy. In upcountry South Carolina, a dispute erupted at a corn shucking in which "Aron boasted of his manhood" and crowed that "he was the best man there"; another slave similarly declared himself "the best man of the Turff." Such proclamations invited one's comeuppance, though. When the bondman Lewis averred that Jackson Wilson's "Ben nor no other man should curse him," Ben countered him by daring to say that "he would curse him or any other man." Lewis shoved Ben, who retaliated by stabbing him with a knife.[31]

The possession of deadly weapons emboldened slave men in their speech. On the way back from a Christmas ball, the slave Ed engaged in loud talk, bragging that he "could whip any man in the crowd except freinds." He "jumped up[,] slap[p]ed his hands together[,] and said ... I dont fear no man." For good reason: Ed staked his claim to masculinity when he "drew a pistol" and warned his fellow slave revelers to "stand back Gentlemen." In the American South, many slaves regularly carried knives as necessary accouterments for the completion of their labors, but firearms were lawfully prohibited and another class of weapon altogether. When one voice in the crowd, perhaps incredulous at the scene before him, questioned whether Ed really did have a gun, the armed slave snapped "that he did not tell no damned nigger what he had." Wielding a firearm enhanced Ed's self-esteem and, as he believed, commanded the respect of all his fellow slaves, whom he degraded beneath himself in dismissing them as "damned nigger[s]." Nero displayed similar bravado when he declared "that he was man a nuff" to draw his knife and stab Griffin Brazeale's slave Sam multiple times, even though knives did not merit the same respect in the quarters as did firearms.[32]

Complementing these kinds of braggadocio, verbal assaults frequently served as a prelude to physically violent encounters among slaves. Insults offer an instructive pathway into the culture in which the offending words were uttered. Individual cultures betray certain patterns of insults reflective of those cultures' values. Insults function by way of a shared cultural language. They make sense because they strike inversely at that which society deems proper, respectable, and desirable, thereby revealing, in the negative, the social values of a given culture. Although whites insulted their foes as well, analyzing insults is particularly useful in the study of subaltern peoples, such as slaves, who leave relatively little written documentation of their own creation. Insults often provoke violence, which, when sufficiently serious in its consequences, can generate a paper trail of official records. Although these records are filtered through a white prism, reading such evidence of insults backward exposes social tensions and the origins of disputes, laying bare the mutual cultural understandings of the parties involved.[33]

By their nature, insults show disrespect, attack honor, and damage reputation. Offensive speech impugned one's social rank and status, elevating the slanderer and degrading the slandered. In the oral societies of Africa, insults carried great weight. Many peoples, including the Kuba of the Congo, esteemed the oratorical arts and verbally jousted "with a refinement that made European visitors feel boorish." African honor codes demanded that insult be redressed. In centralized states such as the Asante kingdom, the appropriate response to insult, slander, or defamation was often litigation. For stateless peoples, offensive verbal exchanges more commonly prompted violence. Africans taken captive and transported to the American South as slaves persisted in their obsession with words. Enslaved Africans and their descendants in the Old South showed remarkable sensitivity to seemingly harmless slights uttered by fellow slaves. Insults hurled by the master, overseer, or other whites were often disregarded. However personally hurtful whites' words may have been, collectively slaves already occupied a debased position in southern society and so were not fundamentally reduced by the offensive words. Most slights coming from the mouths of whites went ignored altogether, although occasionally a slave struck out violently at a verbally abusive master or overseer or took revenge opportunistically through "Snopesian crimes" such as theft or arson. By contrast, when slaves spit verbal venom upon one another, it stung. Just as southern white men bristled at the insults of other white men, slaves could not dismiss the insults of their peers. Slaves inhabited the same social plane, and if one's equal voiced the insult, it mattered: one slave was attempting to establish superiority or dominance over another and deny the second slave's expectation of treatment as an equal. Their relationship was no longer reciprocal but imbalanced. With social identity challenged through insult, the target of the offensive language might resort to violence to reestablish the social equilibrium, restore honor, and enact manhood. The Virginia bondman Nelson generally "bears a good character, is humble and obedient," explained master Reuben Vaughn, "but [is] passionate when he considers himself insulted." Another of Vaughn's slaves concurred. When affronted, the normally "peaceably disposed" Nelson could "strike in a minute," "like a rattle snake": "he was a very devil."[34]

Southern court records reveal a limited range of insults slaves hurled at one another. Students of African American culture have described creative verbal sparring and dueling among blacks—playing the dozens—as a ritual contest. The very structure of these oral performances instilled discipline and emotional control in the participants, precluding the eruption of violence. With only rare exception (one Virginia slave said that another "was so Lazy that the Bugs Knatts and flies followed him"), the known insults slaves employed lacked the oral agility and theatrical wordplay of the dozens. To the contrary, their blunt, forceful, and offensive words provoked violence. Some trial papers and other sources document only that a slave engaged in unspecified name-calling, uttered "a gross insult," or used "sasey language," but at times the records are more explicit, providing a verbatim transcript as recalled by the witnesses. Bondpeople adopted "bitch" when referring to an enslaved woman and "son of a bitch" to describe an enslaved man, verbally locating their adversary on the subhuman level of dogs. In Anderson District, South Carolina, the slave Ed called George a "damned son of a bitch" for "bed[ding] up with my wife every night," and bondman "Jeff said Emory was a reel footed sun of a bitch." Bondmen sometimes called male slaves "rascals" or "rogues" as well. When Lunenburg County, Virginia, slave Bob asserted that "Nelson was a damd Rascal and every body that [k]new him knew it," Nelson beat his detractor to death with a hoe. In Amherst County, the bondman John Red administered a mortal blow to his enemy Alfred and repeatedly gloated, "I have killed the damned rascal." During an altercation between slaves in Brunswick County, "Stephen and Cary . . . called each other Rogue several times and made use of other provoking language." The terms "rascal" and "rogue" both denoted someone judged dishonest, unprincipled, or mischievous, suggesting slaves' reverence for honesty, fairness, and trustworthiness in the quarters. By identifying the scoundrels among them, slaves demarcated clear boundaries that excluded certain slaves from the social group for violating cultural expectations of approved behavior.[35]

Inebriation only magnified slaves' sensitivity to slights. Many insults passed among slaves gathered at corn shuckings and other events that simultaneously incorporated work and leisure. Amid the "corn Husking" festivities in the vicinity of Lewisburg, Virginia, the enslaved Sam partook generously enough of "spirituous liquors" to demonstrate "a good humour & a lively mood," declaring "at Table after we are done [with] Supper [that] we will be all Great Men." The joviality of the occasion quickly soured, however. Sam and another slave began "running the rig on each other" and "appeared very Warm in Conversation." When the other slave "got up from [the] Table and Gathered up the Crum[b]s of the Table in a Pile," Sam observed, "if that was in Frankfort it would be a show," adding that "there was not as clever People in Frankfort as there was here." Sam's unflattering remarks toward the people of Frankford, Virginia, some ten miles north of Lewisburg, revealed a sense of provincial pride and contempt for those outside his neighborhood. But working socials often brought together slaves from widely scattered holdings, and Sam's careless speech sparked an apparent local rivalry. Offended by Sam's words, the other slave, perhaps from or with family in Frankford, stabbed him.[36]

Enslaved men often responded with violence when those people most dear to them were insulted. The ethic of southern honor demanded prompt retaliation for insults directed against loved ones. Bondmen were typically unable to exercise the privilege of standing up for those they cared about when whites heaped verbal abuse upon them. The prudent slave dared not use words to antagonize whites and risk punishment.[37] In contrast, male slaves had the opportunity to behave as honorable men when they quickly defended wives, family, and friends from any slights or aspersions cast by fellow slaves. In so doing, their performance of honor coincided with that of southern white men, who also reacted violently to insults directed against loved ones. At a "Dancing party" held on Daniel Vasser's Pittsylvania County, Virginia, plantation the day after Christmas 1819, "some of the Company" offended the bondwoman Dilsey by saying that "she danced as if she had a pound of Lead to her feet." Aware of the significance Dilsey and many other enslaved women attached to bodily movement, control, and performance, her husband Primus "got angry" and manfully declared that he "would stand at his Wifes Back." North Carolina bondman Nelson told fellow slave Gabriel that "he would kill any man if he talked about his wife," then administered him a mortal whack on the side of the head with "a piece of Fence-rail." Spartanburg District, South Carolina, bondman Bassett likewise struck fellow slave Joseph with "a large stick" for "abusing his wife."[38]

Spouses were not the only recipients of enslaved male chivalry. When Pendleton District slave Leu "Cursed Dianna" "& Calld her a Damnd Bitch," Dianna's sibling Jack immediately cried out, "Dont you abuse my sister," and assaulted Leu. Aron Motes, a slave in Laurens District, complained that other bondpeople at a corn shucking "were trying to run over Perry," a fellow Motes family slave, "and he would not allow it." When the loyal Aron determined that "they should not impose on Perry or he would bust their heads," he rallied in support of his own. As with southern whites, slaves might invoke the concept of honor to justify violence or the threat of it.[39]

Entrenched in the honor of the quarters, slaves also bristled when other bondmen gave them the lie. "Giving the lie"—calling someone a liar, questioning his word, and hence divorcing him from the culture of honor—provoked countless battles in honor-bound southern white society but is unexplored among the enslaved. Masters assumed that slaves chronically lied; bondpeople told falsehoods, feigned illness and broke or "lost" tools to avoid work, and stole with impunity. Such behaviors demonstrated to whites that slaves' word could not be trusted and rationalized the exclusion of slave testimony against white defendants in southern courtrooms. "Whites," Kenneth Greenberg writes, "assumed that slaves lied all the time—and that their lies were intimately connected to their position as slaves." Many slaves "are in the habit of telling stories," explained several white men before a Tennessee court, "and are not entitled to full credit." If the law questioned the veracity of bondpeople's statements, so did southern churches, which expelled enslaved members infinitely more often than white congregants for the "telling of lies," a charge positively correlated with accusations of theft. Slaves did lie, not because they were devoid of honor but because lying was a necessary part of their performance—of the mask they wore—in the presence of whites.[40]

But whereas slaves routinely lied to whites as a means of navigating bondage from day to day, they expected honesty and truthfulness among themselves and abhorred deceit or a lack of transparency. Even as young children, slaves enforced a code of integrity in the quarters. An Orange County, North Carolina, youngster pushed his sister into a fire because she "called me a lie." The plantation mistress whipped him to atone for the burns his sibling suffered. As a boy enslaved in Mississippi, Jake Dawkins recalled that, when "some of de other kids would say I was tellin' a story I'd jump on dem and start a fight." But Dawkins devised a clever strategy to reduce the severity of his punishment for roughhousing. When the mistress called him to account for his misbehavior, he explained that "I fit cause somebody called me a lie and I ain't never tell a lie cause she don't low dat." With a slight flush of pride, the mistress "sorter smile" and "don't whip me so hard."[41]

As boys matured into men, the physical dangers of giving the lie escalated, and adult slaves knew it. When the Wake County, North Carolina, bondman Gabriel reported that Nelson "had cursed the whole plantation at Col. Mangum's at the log rolling," Nelson denied it, saying "it was a lie," and accused Gabriel of trying to instigate a "fuss." Fusses often resulted when enslaved men gave the lie to one another. Three bondmen from antebellum Anderson District, South Carolina, took umbrage when fellow slaves accused them of deceit. "[T]he dam lie passed" between bondmen George and Jim, a trio of slaves "heard Bas give Joe the Dam lie," and the bondman Dandy "threw a stone and hit Jim" because Jim "give the God dam lye."[42]

The obsession with lies in upcountry South Carolina was not unique. Across the South, slaves violently objected to charges of dishonesty. In Monroe County, Virginia, the bondman "Will charged Moses with telling a lie on him." Moses denied it, and in the ensuing "scuffle," "Will threw ... Moses in the fire." Recovering his footing, Moses "swore by the Lord Jesus Christ he would Kill Will that night if he laid his Hands upon him in anger." Moses immediately followed through on his threat and was convicted in January 1811 of fatally stabbing his adversary. Farther south, in Chatham County, Georgia, a fugitive slave named Prince killed the bondman July in 1827 because "July told a lie upon him." A drunken Prince was in a boat in Hog Marsh one winter Sunday after midnight when he heard July singing as he paddled a canoe nearby. Prince, July, and three other slaves lived together in the same remote camp, but Prince thought July a "damned rascal." He turned to his companions and identified him as "one damned negro I want to kill." Over his compatriots' objections, Prince hailed July, and when the unsuspecting slave maneuvered his craft side by side with Prince's, Prince "col[l]ared him from [the] Boat," brandished a sword, and hacked away at his enemy, nearly severing a hand and striking several blows to the side of the head. July's alleged lies earned him a mortal wound that "penetrated the Brain." On the cotton frontier, too, giving the lie was cause for offense. Marion County, Mississippi, slaves Harry and Claiborne Faulk "had a quarrel with Green ... in which the 'damn lie' and other offensive epithets of like character" were passed. Only the intervention of a white man "prevent[ed] a more serious difficulty." If slaves possessed no sense of honor, as southern whites claimed, it would not have mattered whether another bondman had "given the lie." That enslaved men across the South responded promptly and violently suggests a compelling need to defend the honor they knew they possessed.[43]

Court records typically do not document the specific circumstances that triggered enslaved men to "give the lie." In those rare cases that afford some clues, many of the slaves' disputes appear remarkably petty. In Henrico County, Virginia, bondmen Martin and Bartlett—"strangers" to one another—"got to quarrelling about their knowledge of the situation of different places about town." However trifling their impromptu competition, Martin discounted Bartlett's claims and labeled him "a damned liar." Such a serious affront issued by a man Bartlett barely knew (the two "had met for the first time only a few minutes previous to the quarrel") demanded a violent response. Sometimes allegations of lying stemmed from slaves' workday activities. In 1798, shortly before Charles Loadnum killed his brother Jacob in a disagreement over the oxen they managed, their master Joseph David "heard Jacob calling Charles a damn liar." Even though southern whites denied honor to enslaved men, surely David recognized the potency of the slur and understood what would have ensued had whites used the same language.[44]

Black men sometimes "gave the lie" about matters of property or money. A disagreement over meat in Warwick County, Virginia, between the slave Caesar Old and the free black George Owens in 1860 resulted in mutual charges of dishonesty: "Caesar disputed George's word," and "George called Caesar a liar." In Pittsylvania County, slaves Shadrack and George had a similar confrontation over pilfered meat. Shadrack complained that "that son of a bitch [George] . . . was mad with him . . . because I said he stole meat out of the cellar." They exchanged heated words:

George: "[D]o you know I am mad with you."
Shadrack: "[B]ecause I said you stole the meat and you did steal it."
George: "If I stole it you helped me."
Shadrack: "You are a damned liar."
George: "[Y]ou are a damned liar."
Shadrack: "[D]on[']t you give me the damned lie."
George: "[I]f you give me the damned lie I will give it you again."

Both clutched weapons as they reciprocated their allegations, but Shadrack's language turned more menacing when he threatened to "knock [George's] damn brains out." "God Damn you I mean to kill you," Shadrack fumed. "God Damn you, and the head man, plantation, and all on it."[45]

On a Sunday evening in Petersburg, Virginia, an aged and inebriated bondman named John approached two fellow slaves, Knight and William, inquiring, "Gents[,] have any of you money to get drinks?" The pair replied in the negative. John seemed unconvinced. "It was not worth while to tell a damned lie about money," he said as he departed, surely disappointed. After John left, his words continued to simmer inside William. Having "worked himself up in a passion" over John's remarks, William took off in pursuit of the elder slave, complaining to a few slaves he encountered that John "called me a damned lie about my own money." Overtaking the senior slave, William said, "look here old man[:] you called me a damned lie," adding, "what is my money to you"? He then struck John on the head. A second blow sent John reeling. He staggered, collapsed to the ground, and expired within a few minutes. William was sentenced to die, and Governor William Smith found "no Ground for Interference in this case." Whereas whites might be excused before the law for exacting violent retribution on those who called them liars, southern governors were disinclined to show slave convicts leniency under similar circumstances. William's expeditious execution for murder confirmed that white society did not permit enslaved men the same exercise of the prerogatives of honor afforded white men.[46]

When bondmen fought over lies, enslaved women were often somehow involved. Giving the lie was gendered masculine; to give the lie *to* a bondwoman was almost unheard of. Nevertheless, enslaved men responded, sometimes with violence, when female slaves purveyed falsehoods. Ralph, a Botetourt County slave, beat Fan, "a trifling old negroe" woman, in the head with a stick in 1814 because "she was very quarrelsome & told lies on him." Male conversations *about* female slaves sometimes invited charges of lying. In Mecklenburg County, the bondmen Bob and Lee "were talking about the Gals" in 1846 when Lee said, "Bob you are sort of a liar." Precisely what Bob had stated to spur Lee's disbelief is subject to speculation. Perhaps he claimed an unlikely conquest or exaggerated his sexual prowess. Regardless, Bob, insulted, immediately picked up a stick and struck Lee a fatal blow to the head. In Chesterfield County, Essex suspected that the bondman Archer had "been too intimate with his wife." Confronting him, Essex asked, "Archer can you swear you never had to do with my wife?" Archer replied, "yes I can swear I never had to do with your wife." Then "you are a liar," Essex retorted. But Archer shot back, "you are the father of it." At that point, Essex "struck Archer with a stick" and fatally stabbed him.[47]

Most often, enslaved men defended the bondwomen they loved or cared for from the lies told about them. The Essex County, Virginia, bondman John, the property of William L. Waring, asked Peter, enslaved on a nearby estate, whether he "had not been telling lies upon his wife, by saying that his wife was to leave Capt. Waring's at the end of the year and that she would leave something behind that would last three of them as long as they lived." Was Peter suggesting that John's wife—Celia—was to be hired out or sold, and that she would give birth sometime prior to her departure? Was Peter further implying that Celia had slept with either her master, overseer, or a bondman other than her husband? The details remain sketchy, but Peter was adamant that he heard the news straight from Celia. "[S]he did say so," he insisted, "and if she had it not she would sell one of her dresses to get it." Enraged at Peter's alleged rumormongering, John attempted to strike and kick the other bondman, who in turn stabbed John in the belly. John soon "expired in the arms of his wife." Distraught, Celia "ordered [Peter] off, and struck him" herself.[48]

Slaves dwelled in circumscribed social spaces in which face-to-face encounters punctuated their daily lives. Studies have shown that codes of honor tend to thrive in such locations and societies where personal relationships more than anonymous bureaucratic structures shape the contours of human existence. The overwhelmingly rural South thus afforded fertile ground for the cultivation of honor. Most slaves operated within a narrow radius of home. Enslaved boatmen, various slaves possessing valuable, specialized skills, and those slaves dispatched by the master on distant errands—all almost always men—defied the "geography of containment," but they marked the exceptions to the rule that masters significantly restricted slaves' movement. Under such circumstances, slaves knew the other bondpeople in their neighborhood by both name and reputation. Any lying, telling of tales, or rumormongering that damaged one's position relative to fellow bondpeople must be addressed. Consequently, in Elbert County, Georgia, Ben went to Peter's house one Sunday night in 1837 and demanded an explanation of Peter for "those tales that had been told," tales that a female slave named Eddy confirmed Peter had indeed related. According to a witness to their conversation, "Ben told Peter he did not want to have any difficulty with him," but he did ask him "twice to confess to the lie that was told." "What . . . made you tell such a tale?" inquired Ben. Quickly growing hostile, Peter replied, "Damn it, what tale is it?" "You know what it is," Ben retorted. Peter, however, replied that "he would be damned if he would not die on the cause before he would be scandalized so." He even claimed a willingness to "loose part of his life before he would own that he told it." His patience soon depleted by Ben's persistent nagging, Peter delivered the first in a series of blows exchanged between the two slaves.[49]

The derogatory "fighting words" anchored in the idiom of honor sparked conflicts involving fists, sticks, rocks, knives, farm implements, and fence rails. Especially in the eighteenth and early nineteenth centuries, men enslaved on southern soil sometimes utilized traditional African fighting techniques such as head butting. At a Rockbridge County, Virginia, husking in 1814, for example, bondman Ned "butted" Julius, "which vexed him." (Two years later, Julius nearly severed Ned's head with an axe.) Still later, in 1830, King George County slave Hubard "butted Tom on the head and Tom fell down." If enslaved men sometimes drew upon African tradition in battles among themselves, they also utilized the rough-and-tumble fighting techniques common to lower-class southern white brawlers. Rough-and-tumble fighting flourished in the southern backwoods and upcountry regions not yet fully incorporated into the market economy. There, values of the market had yet to penetrate and overwhelm the rural values of a semi-subsistence agricultural society. In such close-knit localities, the ethic of honor bound neighbors together. Southern gentlemen scoffed at lower-class claims to honor, but the rough-and-tumbles characteristic of poor whites showed that, despite their socioeconomic inferiority, they were no less men. They willingly sacrificed their bodies, exposing themselves to ear bitings and eye gougings, in defense of honor, reputation, and community standing.[50]

In rough-and-tumble contests analogous to those among white participants, enslaved men vied for rank and honor among themselves. As former slave John Finnely of Alabama made clear, occasionally masters orchestrated no-holds-barred wrestling matches between bondmen. Finnely's owner frequently pitted a favorite slave renowned as a "powerful good fighter" against various enslaved challengers, allowing the combatants "to do anything with dey hands and head and teeth." They were at liberty to "hit and kick and bite and butt anywhere and any place for to best de udder," Finnely explained. "Nothin' barred 'cept de knife and de club." Yet Finnely's master carefully monitored these bouts and brought them to an abrupt halt when necessary. No prudent slaveholder wished to risk serious injuries detrimental to the value of enslaved property. For that reason, masters abhorred slaves' rough-and-tumbles outside slaveholder supervision. Contests among enslaved men that employed the fighting styles of lower-class whites brought real dangers of permanent scarring, maiming, and mutilation. In early nineteenth-century Petersburg, Virginia, Dick reportedly did "Bite of the Ear" of the slave Jacob with the intention of disfiguring him. The Petersburg Hustings Court also punished the bondman Tom "for biting off the ear and lip of another slave." In upcountry South Carolina, the Pendleton District slave "Jack bit off p[ar]t of one of Lue⁵ Ears," Pickens District bondman Jesse was charged with "Biting Wiley['s] Right year off," and, when the slave Ned attacked Steve in Anderson District, he "bit of[f] a peace of his year." The Anderson District bondman Elijah "gouged ... and scr[at]ched" Dick, another slave, in 1845. Slave narratives reinforce impressions gleaned from court records concerning the unrestrained character of some slaves' violent behaviors. When an "old negro driver" attempted to beat slave autobiographer William Grimes with a stick, Grimes "let him have it in old Virginia style, (which generally consists in gouging, biting and butting)." Gouging was a fighting technique unknown among the indigenous inhabitants of Africa and therefore not part of the repertoire of southern slaves' inherited combat traditions, yet Elijah and Grimes apparently learned of it through the observation of poor white scrappers. According to Wilma King, a leading scholar of slave childhood, enslaved parents did not promote rough-and-tumble fighting, yet they could not wholly shield their offspring from witnessing the wrestling matches arranged by masters or the ghastly, bloody contests between white competitors. As with lower-class whites, then, for some enslaved men, the ritual violence of ear biting, eye gouging, and scratching represented a form of manly assertion in a society that denied their claims to honor. Male slaves who participated in rough-and-tumbles verified their manhood to themselves as well as to enslaved spectators.[51]

Whatever precise form their violence took, the prelude to enslaved men's honorific battles was often a symbolic and practical shedding of clothes. The ritual of "stripping to fight" was customary for black fighters as well as white.[52] It sometimes meant only the removal of a coat or outer garment; at other times, foes jettisoned their shirts as well to battle bare-chested. Half-clad combatants showcased their physiques, highlighting not only the sinews of their musculature but also the enduring scars from previous encounters. Battle-worn bare skin that betrayed a contestant as a veteran of such frays played a role in the mental gamesmanship of violent clashes, serving as a means of intimidating an opponent. More practically, bodies emancipated of fabric enjoyed freedom of movement. Fights were physically demanding, and having full range of motion, flexibility, and mobility was an asset during a bout. Absent restrictive clothing, moreover, fighters could not use a shirt, for example, to hold opponents in place, fling them to the ground, or choke them. And for enslaved men especially, stripping their clothing to fight spared their limited wardrobes from rips, tears, and bloodstains. Their clothes would remain unsullied. They would not need to have them mended or cleaned, and they would not be accountable for explaining to the master the damage to their raiment. Thus, in Rockbridge County, Virginia, Ned met Julius's challenge to fight on one condition: that "he would let him shed his clothes." Likewise, the Russell County bondman Richard "jumped up and took off his coat" in preparation for battle with Cupe, and Abram of Pittsylvania County "strip[p]ed himself" before engaging in his fray with Primus.[53]

Enslaved men, then, protected the women they claimed, settled scores with enemy bondmen, issued threats, boasted of their manhood, brooked no insults, and entered into rough-and-tumbles designed to inflict permanent scars on the loser. The parallels with southern white masculine culture were unmistakable. Specifically, the honor of enslaved men shared many of the trappings of southern white honor as demonstrated in patterns of lower-class white behavior, not that male slaves necessarily mimicked the actions of neighborhood whites. African codes of honor intersected with those of the American South in many respects. Jealously guarding women and avenging insult, for instance, were familiar to peoples on the African continent as well as to southern white men. Independent of white cultural influences, generations of tradition informed the honorific behavior of enslaved men carried from Africa to the colonial South. African influences continued to be felt through the late eighteenth and early nineteenth centuries. But with the passage of time, the cultural ties to Africa weakened. By the antebellum decades, most slaves had been born and reared in the South. The environment in which slaves lived greatly conditioned the way honor and masculinity manifested in the quarters. In southern society, blacks and whites participated in a thriving social and cultural commerce, borrowing from one another freely and frequently. It was no coincidence that in Virginia, the South Carolina upcountry, and elsewhere, many of the hallmarks of enslaved masculinity neatly coincided with those of poor white men, for they shared a common culture of honor and violence. Through their routine contacts—drinking, gambling, socializing, trading—slaves and poor whites engaged in a process of cultural exchange. As these transactions accumulated over time, male slaves absorbed lower-class white definitions and expressions of honor. After Jesse accused fellow bondman Wiley of stealing his tobacco, white onlooker James P. Jenkins of Pickens District, South Carolina, informed Wiley that if he "wo[u]ld tak[e] the like of that he was no man attall." Jenkins took it as his prerogative to interject into their dispute, providing guidance on how a man would properly respond. A brawl commenced between the two slaves only after a white man reminded one of the bondmen of the rules of honor as he understood them. But was his prompt necessary? Jesse and Wiley may have been preparing to rumble anyway, or they may have preferred to delay their confrontation until no whites were present. If so, Jenkins's remark only reinforced sentiments already welling up inside the bondmen and gave them permission to unleash their violent emotions in his presence without delay or fear of reprisal. Or maybe Jenkins was simply picking a fight between two bondmen for his own amusement.[54]

Enslaved men understood that their sense of honor had its limitations within the constraints of southern white society. Highly structured, ritualistic duels as practiced by elite southern white men, for example, were almost exclusive to their race and class. Poor white men preferred the riotous rough-and-tumble, as did male slaves. Although dueling was not common to all African cultures, various forms of it, often involving stick fighting or head butting, were practiced in Africa. Henry Bibb, an escaped slave from Kentucky, recalled contests reminiscent of these African duels adapted to the setting of the antebellum South and the condition of bondage. On the Sabbath, Bibb explained, enslaved men engaged in "wrestling, fighting, . . . and butting each other like sheep" for the amusement of slaveholders. Masters encouraged bondmen to spar, supplied the combatants whiskey, and wagered on the outcomes of the matches. Bibb described one technique for provoking a fight that involved masters "laying chips on one slave's head, and daring another to tip it off with his hand; and if he tipped it off, it be called an insult, and cause a fight." Slaves were "not allowed to fight a duel," however, "nor to use weapons [of] any kind," Bibb clarified. Nevertheless, as with duels, "Before fighting, the parties choose their seconds to stand by them while fighting; a ring or a circle is formed to fight in, and no one is allowed to enter the ring while they are fighting, but their seconds, and they white gentlemen." During the bouts, Bibb continued, "blows are made by kicking, knocking, and butting with their heads; they grab each other by their ears, and jam their heads together like sheep." Under the master's close supervision, the violence was not allowed to exceed a critical threshold. "If they are likely to hurt each other very bad," Bibb noted, "their masters would rap them with their walking canes, and make them stop." Thus, the sort of contest Bibb witnessed during his enslavement blended select cultural forms of elite southern white men's duels with fighting techniques indigenous to Africa.[55]

Rarely, reports surfaced of slaves participating in the duels typical of southern white gentlemen. Like elite white men, male slaves across the South sought "satisfaction" for affronts to their honor. When Delaware slaves Anderson and Emory quarreled at a camp meeting in 1857, Anderson assured Emory "that if he would follow him off the camp ground he would give him satisfaction." The product or reward of an honorific encounter, "satisfaction" might be granted through any number of violent means. But in 1830s Mississippi, two enslaved men mirrored elite white behavior all too closely by dueling with pistols. Throughout the South, accounts of duels appeared in newspaper columns, set communities abuzz with conversation, and became the stuff of legend. Most slaves heard—and a few even read—tales of lost honor regained through the duel, and some had the opportunity to witness one firsthand. As a result, even without reading a published guidebook to dueling, they were familiar with the elaborate ritual inherent in the gentlemanly practice. In a few scattered cases, they put their knowledge to work. An enslaved Mississippi newspaper courier "Alfred, a colored man, had an unfortunate misunderstanding with another servant which terminated in an *'affair of honor'* between the parties. They met with pistols, at five paces, loaded with three balls, and both fired at nearly the same instant. Alfred received a severe wound in the right arm, after which, both parties expressed their entire satisfaction, and the affair terminated." Alfred sustained injury but survived. As was often the case with duels, no one died, but a death was not requisite for the duel to fulfill its cultural function. Alfred and his opponent each enacted their manhood through the performance of the duel. In each other's eyes, they manfully confronted the specter of death for the sake of upholding the honor they knew they had. They had indeed achieved "satisfaction."[56]

Another pair of bondmen met with less success in their attempt to emulate a duel. Certainly legal restrictions against slaves' purchase or possession of firearms limited bondmen's ability to replicate gentlemanly duels in every detail, but that did not stop them from re-creating honorific encounters with only minor modifications. In Kershaw District, South Carolina, Paul and Solomon had a dispute over a "negro girl" in 1817 in which they exchanged words and resolved "to have a Civil fight." Paul "agreed to fight with Solomon," testimony revealed, "because the latter was always picking at him," and now Paul would respond like a man. As in a duel, the combatants each had "seconds." Solomon had three seconds, Paul seven. Like any responsible seconds, they "advised them to not fight" and "endeavoured to make peace." Solomon's seconds included bondmen Kildare and Frank, who had a vested interest in their man's safety. They wished "no injury should be done Solomon" after the fight, for all three shared the same master, and Kildare feared that their owner "should blame him if any thing happened." One of Paul's seconds, an enslaved friend named Eben, was equally interested in guaranteeing "a fair fight." As insurance, Eben concealed "two bricks in his [own] pockets," ready to be wielded as weapons on Paul's behalf, if necessary. Unsuccessful in negotiations, the seconds could not avert the impending duel. In the absence of pistols, however, what resulted was a strange hybrid, a brawl initially shrouded in decorum. Paul knocked Solomon down, but Solomon soon gained the advantage. As one of the seconds parted the "duelists," a second from the opposing side misinterpreted the action, believing he was joining the fray. Rushing to the defense of his man, a violent free-for-all ensued. Curiously, John Martin and at least one other white were present throughout the episode. Martin played a murky role during the bondmen's duel, acting almost in the capacity of judge. Amid the chaos of the brawl, Eben threatened to hit Kildare, but first "he asked permission of the white people who were there," who disallowed it. Martin and at least one other white person apparently refereed the entire confrontation, perhaps part of the slaves' effort to add legitimacy to their ritual. Their resort to the dueling grounds likely resolved none of the slaves' differences, however, as they all appeared in court, charged with a "riot."[57]

Enslaved men understood that they could not flaunt their honor too overtly without possibly inviting various forms of retribution, not only at the hands of whites but by fellow slaves as well. In Anderson District, South Carolina, for instance, the bondman Lewis had jettisoned his hat and umbrella while frantically escaping the patrol, earning himself notice in the quarters. Slave Aaron boldly remarked "that he would have fought a duel before any body should have taken his hat from him that way" and that he was willing to "loose every drop of blood in him before he would give up his hat and umbrella" as Lewis had. "Six or Eight negroes" who heard Aaron's statement "all busted out in a Laugh." Aaron's braggadocio had instantly transformed him into the subject of sportive mockery. What was so funny? Interpreting humor over time proves difficult because modern observers of the past must reconstruct the cultural matrix in which the humorous comment or situation occurred. At the most basic level, the slaves who overheard the conversation may have considered it ridiculous to risk one's life over a hat and umbrella. The value of the property was not worth the potential harm to the body. More substantially, the comment may have evoked laughter because Aaron was asserting a foolish willingness to stand up to the patrol, or exhibiting an inflated sense of honor that vastly exceeded reason, elevating himself socially to the level of the white patrollers. Perhaps the mention of "a duel" elicited the laughter. Duels were clearly the preserve of elite white gentlemen; lower-class southern whites did not even participate in them, so the thought of a slave, so inferior a member of southern society, drawing a pistol in a duel might have struck the "Six or Eight negroes" as humorous. Duels were also always fought among participants who considered themselves social equals. That Aaron's hypothetical duel would have pitted him on the grounds against a white rival may have exacerbated the humor of the mental picture the amused slaves were drawing. Whatever the reason, Aaron got the joke, for he, too, "Joined in the laugh."[58]

To varying degrees, for those enslaved and white men who attended worship services in the pre–Civil War South, performing manhood was fraught with complications unknown among the unchurched. From its inception in the late eighteenth-century South, evangelical religion presented distinct challenges to southern white manhood and the region's culture of honor. Early churches undermined many of the hierarchies that traditionally governed society. They interfered directly in family life, subverting fathers' and husbands' patriarchal authority over the household. They permitted women to speak publicly, undercutting the gendered privileges customarily accorded men. Racially, churches openly appealed to slaves as the spiritual equals of whites. And power invested in youthful clergy upended conventional hierarchies of age and experience. The public conversions expected of all members exposed male emotional vulnerability and risked men's sense of mastery over themselves and others. Evangelical men were not to fight when an opponent challenged them, a proscription anathema to the ethic of southern honor. Moreover, strictures against the secular pastimes central to masculine culture—the drinking and gambling, music making and dancing—were enforced. The persistent ban on worldly leisure pursuits notwithstanding, southern evangelical churches undertook a spate of accommodations designed to bridge the chasm between the values of evangelical religion and honorable manhood and make their brand of religiosity more palatable to respectable southern white men.[59]

As the eighteenth century transitioned into the nineteenth, southern evangelical churches grew increasingly accepting of the violence committed by white male churchgoers. Unless accompanied by drunkenness or other sins, acts of violence did not automatically prompt the expulsion of white men. Gregory A. Wills calculates that male defendants charged with perpetrating violence were excommunicated 41 percent of the time. In my sample of nine Baptist churches in Southside Virginia, congregations forgave white male members for violent acts against other white men almost two-thirds of the time. Virginia's pattern of lenience toward white male violence was not unique. In the South Carolina upcountry, accusations of fighting outnumbered all other charges against white men, drinking notwithstanding. Church disciplinary committees virtually always forgave white men's first infraction for fighting; expulsions were usually reserved for recidivists. Altogether, in fourteen upcountry South Carolina churches, white male churchgoers successfully "gave satisfaction" for their violent affrays with other whites in four out of every five cases. The twenty-three Baptist churches in Middle Georgia examined for this study were not as forgiving but still pardoned white men more than half the time when they attacked other whites.[60] Exoneration required a simple, albeit humbling and genuine, act of public contrition. More often than not, an apology accompanied by a promise to behave better served as a satisfactory acknowledgment of the sin of fighting.[61]

White men's exclusion from southern Baptist churches for fighting grew increasingly rare after the first decade of the nineteenth century. Evangelical churches' emerging acceptance of violence as an expression of white male masculinity is evident through their handling of those congregants who issued a challenge to duel. Accusations of churchgoers' dueling flew freely prior to about 1800. After that point, no other accusation of dueling was levied in the forty-six total Baptist churches examined in Virginia, South Carolina, and Georgia for almost five decades.[62] Biblical injunctions against fighting never wavered; what changed over time was evangelicals' waning resolve to enforce them vis-à-vis white male churchgoers. Pleas of self-defense or shows of regret for the circumstances that sparked violence, rather than for the violent actions themselves, were oftentimes sufficient to earn white men absolution for fighting.[63] Others shielded themselves from reproach by claiming their masculine obligation to defend women, wives, or family—a rationale with which church leaders surely empathized.[64] To retain fellowship, white male churchgoers merely needed to demonstrate that their violent conduct toward other white men was "justifiable."[65] Upon explaining the extenuating circumstances that mitigated their culpability for the infraction, they were often excused.

As Robert Elder has recently shown, for white men, the dictates of evangelical religion and southern honor were not necessarily antagonistic. A man of honor could worship comfortably in an antebellum evangelical church without sacrificing his masculine identity. Churches deemed white male violence socially and theologically acceptable under circumstances tacitly understood by the congregation. Because white men, themselves the products of the southern culture of honor, held the leadership positions within the region's evangelical churches, the willingness to absolve white male members who fought comes as little surprise. In reality, southern evangelical churches established a remarkably high threshold for the expulsion of churchgoing white men who committed violent acts.[66] When their victims were black, odds of exclusion were even lower. Only as attempted murder shaded into outright homicide did southern white evangelical men exceed churches' limits of permissible violent masculine expression. Otherwise, by the antebellum decades, southern churches established standards for exclusion that granted white male church members ample leeway to enact their manhood through violence.[67]

If antebellum southern evangelical churches shied away from infringing on white masculine prerogatives, they did not grant the same wide latitude to enslaved congregants. Gregory A. Wills's investigation of Baptist disciplinary records revealed that "[f]or violent offenses . . . , black defendants suffered exclusion one and a half times more often" than whites. Church disciplinary committees did not automatically condemn all violent expressions of enslaved masculinity, but they did hold them in check. As one might expect, churches adopted a harsher stance against enslaved male violence when the victim was white rather than black. My sample churches from Virginia and South Carolina excluded all slave members charged with fighting masters, overseers, or other unidentified whites. In Georgia, however, there were exceptions. One enslaved man in Jones County's Salem Baptist Church and another in Hancock County's Island Creek Baptist Church gave satisfactory acknowledgments, respectively, for "fitting the overseer" and "for Striking . . . his Master" as the owner "cor[r]ect[ed] him for Disobeying."[68]

Expulsion proved much rarer when the victim was black. When enslaved churchgoers in Georgia assaulted fellow slaves, they were excluded approximately 57 percent of the time; in South Carolina, the figure stood at closer to 40 percent. On the whole, when black churchgoers assaulted other blacks, they were expelled somewhat more frequently than when whites attacked whites. As with accused whites, the preemptive confessions of slave aggressors sometimes elicited a congregation's forgiveness. At Brushy Creek Baptist Church in 1821, "John a Black man came forward and acknowledged that he was wrong for getting angry and stricking a Blackman . . . two or three times without any provocation." The church deemed his acknowledgment "satisfactory." In 1842, Brother Israel, a black deacon at Fishing Creek Baptist Church, "made acknowledgement for having been engaged in a fight with one of his fellow servants, & professed sorrow & repentance for his conduct." Although the church quickly accepted his apology, the enslaved Sister Rose reflected for another month before she, too, "professed satisfaction." In the late 1850s, Fishing Creek Baptist also forgave the contrite, enslaved Brother North twice for fighting. After a third charge for the same offense in a little more than one year, however, the congregation expelled him.[69]

Typically, southern evangelical churches did not show such patience or toleration toward violent enactments of enslaved manhood. They imposed strict limitations upon the performance of black masculinity. Sometimes threats alone were sufficient to merit expulsion. In Hancock County, Georgia, Powelton Baptist Church investigated the bondman Simon for "threatening to kill one of his fellow servants." Despite the accumulated evidence against him, Simon denied the charge, "which the brethren think was wrong." Nearby, Bethel Baptist Church expelled the bondman Frank for having "made some threats of taking the lives of his fellow servants." Churches also refused to forgive slaves accused of the attempted murder of another, valuable bondman. Broad Run Baptist Church in Fauquier County, Virginia, excluded the enslaved member Moses on that charge. Congregations generally expelled slaves even for violent acts that lacked deadly intent. In 1835, Big Creek Baptist Church in Anderson District, South Carolina, was distressed to learn that "Mr. Owenses ben had acted disorderly in striking his fellowservant." Only three years earlier, the same church had dismissed "Brother Ceasor . . . fornocking down his fellow servent with an Ax." Evangelical Christianity, in short, showed greater hostility toward enslaved men's violent expressions of honor than toward those of free white men.[70]

At times, church membership seemingly enhanced enslaved masculinity. Evangelical churches granted black men nominal claims to spiritual equality with whites, authorized them to participate in "colored conferences" that oversaw black congregants, and permitted some the opportunity to become spiritual leaders within the church and the surrounding neighborhood. The apex of black religious involvement, confined exclusively to men, was the ability to preach or otherwise sing, pray, or speak publicly. In the first decades of the nineteenth century, many southern evangelical churches granted enslaved men permission to exhort or preach to black audiences, pending the master's consent. Churches that entrusted the spiritual needs of black congregants to enslaved male leaders allowed those individuals an alternative path to masculinity that did not involve violence. In West Africa, John Iliffe explains, the introduction of formal religion to unchurched people was capable of challenging ingrained codes of honor. The infusion of Islam into the African continent was particularly transformative. Islam rejected honor's "egotistical pursuit of rank and personal reputation," tempered the influence of the heroic ethic, and instead granted new emphasis to a competing ethic of respectability. Similarly, in the American South, the evangelical religions first introduced to slaves in the late eighteenth and early nineteenth centuries seemed in many ways incompatible with the region's honor culture familiar to both blacks and whites. As Kathleen M. Brown observes, "Christian piety... created a dilemma for black manhood. It celebrated the combination of deference, dutifulness, and humility that was supposed to mark the character of the ideal slave, but left little room for slave manhood... [P]iety smacked of subordination and submission rather than masculine assertion." Yet the roles that enslaved male exhorters and preachers played in southern evangelical churches afforded them respect, admiration, and prestige as men of God, at least among black churchgoers. Religion provided them another means of constructing enslaved manhood. The southern racial hierarchy never dissolved, however, and white congregants' racial anxieties never relaxed. Powelton Baptist Church of Hancock County, Georgia, and many other congregations thought it only prudent for whites to observe and supervise "the publick exercises of our Black Brethren."[71]

White evangelicals reasserted their authority over enslaved preachers and exhorters whenever and however they saw fit, undercutting black male claims to manhood. At its mildest form, white oversight meant only a reprimand for behavior whites perceived as misguided. If Powelton Baptist's white observers found black services "not conducted according to the Spirit of the Gospel,... they shall give them such advice[,] admonition[,] or reproof as may appear necessary and proper." Enslaved male religious figures who overstepped their authority merited quick censure. In 1823, Flint Hill Baptist Church in York District, South Carolina, granted "Brother Antoney a black man" "liberty to ex[h]ort his fellow servents in a publick manner." More than four years later, accusations of Antoney's improper conduct convinced the church to circumscribe his ministry geographically. Henceforth, he was permitted "to exercise his gift publickly [only] within the bounds of the road leading from Charlotte to rockets Ferry on the Catawba & as far as Dr. Polks plantation near Charlotte and from thence to the South line and Catawba River." When, in 1809, Padgett's Creek Baptist Church allowed "Negroe Tom" to "Exercise his Gift of Singing, prayer, & Exhortation," the congregation also delineated precise boundaries inside of which he was permitted to perform the work of the Lord. Other enslaved men had their authority to exercise their spiritual gifts revoked altogether. Philips Mill Baptist Church of Wilkes County, Georgia, "admonish[ed]" the bondman Daniel to cease "speaking in publick after he has been silenced by the church." Also in Wilkes County, the congregation of Sardis Baptist heard rumors that "brother Dick has been attempting to preach contrary to the order of the Church to the injury of her feelings." Sardis dispatched three white brethren "to admonish him to silence once more."[72]

White vigilance over enslaved men's preaching heightened dramatically in the aftermath of the August 1831 insurrection led by Nat Turner. An enslaved prophet or preacher, Turner, in company with some seventy followers, massacred approximately sixty whites in their Southampton County, Virginia, neighborhood before the uprising was quelled. Although rapidly mobilized whites guaranteed that the rebellion remained localized, its ramifications were profound. Virtually overnight, the revolt prompted the Virginia House of Delegates to ponder the gradual abolition of slavery in the Commonwealth. Unable to reach a consensus on that monumental step, Virginia lawmakers instead passed legislation restricting a range of slaves' activities, including unsupervised black religious gatherings. Slave preaching was also forbidden. As Lower Banister Church of Pittsylvania County understood, in the wake of Nat Turner, "no collerd member shal[l] preach under the penalty of the laws." Feeling the reverberations from the Turner revolt, other southern states quickly followed suit, imposing stricter slave codes. Individual churches responded to the Turner uprising accordingly. Within two months of the rebellion, the Lincoln County, Georgia, congregation at Goshen Baptist pondered the "regulation of the coloured members of this church" and elected to ban "all assembling of the coloured people of this neighbourhood separate & apart from their masters Mistresses or other heads of authority," even if for purportedly religious purposes. Slaves needed permission to attend any religious service and would be expelled if found loitering during or after church "in crowds with others of their colour." In addition, the congregation determined that "all Further attempts of preaching or exhorting by the coloured people of this church be expressly Forbidden & that in [the] future no coloured person a member of this church shall be permitted to take upon himself the task of the ministry by preaching exhortation or in any other mode of public address whatever." Exceptions were possible, however, if a potential enslaved preacher was "First regularly examined & found adequate to the work." He would then be "accordingly licensed." In York District, South Carolina, Flint Hill Baptist Church conformed to state law in July 1832 when it resolved to "put a stop to the black members preaching out of the Church." Nearby, in Greenville District, Dr. William Butler's bondman Hampton "app[l]ied for permission to Exercise a publick gift" in early 1840, but Brushy Creek Baptist Church "decided that they would withhold from Coloured Members the liberty of preaching." Eight years later, Hampton repeated his request. Again, the church determined "Not to suffer him to preach" because "the Laws of the Land for bid Large Gro[u]ps of Negros convineing to Gather with out some white person to se[e] to the[i]r Good behaviour."[73]

After the Turner revolt, enslaved men found it more difficult to harness the power of evangelical religion to construct a masculine identity based, not on violence, but on leadership within the church. Churches required a prospective black preacher to audition before the congregation so that it might "Judge of his gifts." Pending the successful demonstration of his oratorical skills and knowledge of scripture, churches decided whether to authorize his preaching and under what conditions. Horeb Baptist Church in Hancock County, Georgia, crafted a policy whereby enslaved men "passed through a long probation, and furnished evidence of being able to teach," before being allowed to preach. Only the white members of the church "adjudged" their readiness. In the immediate wake of the Turner revolt, many enslaved men who "exercised" their gifts were denied the privilege to preach, but some defied the restrictions against them. In Georgia, Wilkes County's Fishing Creek Baptist Church alone charged three enslaved men in the 1830s with "having exercised in publick without leave from the church." The congregation retained each offender in fellowship but admonished the violators.[74]

With the passage of time, congregations grew somewhat more lax in enforcing the letter of the law. As the memory of Nat Turner and the panic he incited receded, many began granting conditional permission to preach. The master's consent was required for slave preaching, and it was routine for "responsible white persons" to be present during meetings. Some enslaved male religious figures were allowed to preach only in the quarters. After hearing the slaves Edmond and James "Exercise in Prayer" in 1844, Wilkes County's Beaverdam Baptist Church "granted them the Priviliege of Exersising at home among there families and Fellowservants." In South Carolina, Brushy Creek Baptist extended to Brother Isham in 1856 "Liberty to pray and Exhort with his own collor." Other bondmen, such as "Hudson a black member" of upcountry South Carolina's Pleasant Grove Baptist Church, were required to preach within the confines of the church. Brushy Creek Baptist authorized "Brother Charles a colloured member" to preach "in the bounds of the Church" but further stipulated that he could only do so "in the daytime."[75] By the 1850s, though, a number of enslaved men were once again permitted wide latitude to spread the word outside the walls of the church, almost as if the Turner revolt had never happened. In 1853, Georgia's Goshen Baptist granted an enslaved member named Charles the opportunity "to exercise his gift in publick."[76]

Whatever personal satisfaction enslaved preachers derived from their elevated positions as leaders within a church, they could not press their advantage too hard at the risk of losing their religious privileges. In 1844, Horeb Baptist Church cautioned enslaved preachers that "the first act of imprudence shall subject a slave so exercising to an open reprimand by the Moderator of the Church...

[B]y a second offense he shall forfeit his privilege" to speak. "Bro[ther] Billy Lennard... a colored man" understood the tenuous position enslaved church leaders occupied. He began preaching at Washington First Baptist Church in Wilkes County, Georgia, in 1836. Church records document that in June 1837, while still "on probation," he "exercised his Gift of preaching and exhortation" from the tenth chapter of Hosea, the latter portion of verse 12: "for it is time to seek the lord, until he comes and showers righteousness on you." Although Billy Lennard's words were never recorded, presumably the selected passage, on the Lord raining righteousness upon the wicked, held peculiar resonance for bondpeople. Nevertheless, the white congregants of Washington First Baptist appeared oblivious to the delicious irony of a slave expounding on such a verse before an audience that included slaveholding whites. Indeed, it is easy to imagine a clever enslaved preacher taking immense delight in using one set of words to communicate dual meanings simultaneously to the respective races gathered in the pews. Active in his faith for decades, Brother Lennard remained in the good graces of white leadership. In 1854, he transferred to Wilkes County's Fishing Creek Baptist and became a deacon there.[77]

The previous decade, Fishing Creek's black deacon had become mired in controversy over his excessively enthusiastic, hyper-vigilant surveillance of the slave quarters. Brother Israel frequently aired grievances between slaves before the church, publicly levying charges against fellow bondpeople. In April 1843, for example, he exposed "a difficulty" between the enslaved women Ailsey and Harriet. In 1845, he also charged the bondwoman Olive "for stealing calico." All three of the accused were excluded from church membership. Israel was perhaps attempting to impose a form of patriarchal authority over the women he charged. He may also have been involved in a dispute with a Brother Gabriel as well. In June 1845, the colored conference cited Israel "for exercising too much authority as deacon" over his fellow black members. Apparently Israel's spiritual zealotry had strained his relationship not only with black congregants but with white churchgoers as well. The aggressively vigilant slave was removed as deacon and possibly either censured by or expelled from the church. By November 1845, he must have made amends, for "he was restored to full fellowship," no doubt humbled. As his case demonstrated, the church carefully guarded against individual bondmen from becoming too religiously powerful.[78]

Just as southern evangelical churches required acts of public mortification from purportedly wayward congregants, slaves accused of wrongdoing on southern plantations or in courts of law often faced the humiliation of shaming punishments. Under bondage, black bodies were physically vulnerable to the whims of white tempers and daily subject to possible brutality and dishonor. Many native-born Africans displaced by the Diaspora to the American South and other New World slave societies were already familiar with the use of ridicule and disgrace for disciplinary purposes. On the African continent, different peoples employed various techniques to dishonor those who violated social convention. Belonging to a society that valued martial honor, an Asante man who proved cowardly in battle might be forced to dress as a woman and compelled to allow another man to seduce his wife. The Igbo shamed thieves by tying them up in public and exposing them to taunting and mockery. Africans held in bondage by other Africans also suffered degradation consistent with their enslaved status. The Beti people made slaves visually conspicuous in humiliating ways: they "cut one ear from an adult male slave, scored his body, and made him go naked." Funj masters branded their slaves with the same marks that were seared into animal flesh. Those Africans enslaved in the colonial South were also subject to a host of mortifying—and unequivocally gruesome—punishments. Philip J. Schwarz located ample evidence of slaves in eighteenth-century Virginia forced to stand at the pillory, where some had their ears cropped, or nailed to the wooden framework and then cut or pulled off. Other slaves had their toes amputated for their alleged misdeeds.[79]

Another mutilation punishment employed in the colonial and early nineteenth-century South was castration, the literal and figurative emasculation of a convicted slave criminal. Castration was legal in North Carolina from 1758 to 1764, and in Virginia it was a lawful punishment for a range of criminal offenses until 1769, after which it was restricted to enslaved men found guilty of the rape or attempted rape of white women. Of the thirty-six bondmen convicted of those two crimes between 1740 and 1785, one was castrated for rape and three others for attempted rape. (Most were instead hanged.) The Virginia slave code instituted in 1792 made hanging the legal punishment for rape, permitting castration only in cases of attempted rape. But by 1823, the law also made attempted rape punishable by death, terminating the lawful castration of enslaved men in Virginia. Later, a Missouri law of 1845 authorized the castration of enslaved or free black rapists, and one black man indeed suffered that sentence in 1853. But as Daniel J. Flanigan observes, after decades of being permitted only as punishment for the sexual violation of white women, "castration . . . fell into nearly universal disuse by 1860."[80]

Even as southern whites largely abandoned ear cropping, castration, and other inhumane punishments more typical of the eighteenth century, shaming punishments persevered in the antebellum decades. During a two-year sojourn in the United States, Swedish traveler Fredrika Bremer encountered a slave prisoner in Richmond. The "negro, whose feet ... were fettered by heavy irons," she reported, had refused to work the coal pits as ordered. The master planned to sell him but in the meantime had the slave "put ... in irons, just to mortify him." The slaveholder's efforts were successful. "The poor fellow was ... annoyed and ashamed," Bremer explained.[81]

For slaves, whipping, too, qualified as a shaming punishment. Along with iron shackles, cuffs, and chains, the whip marked one of the most potent symbols of slavery in the American South. Slavery as an institution could only persist through the use of violence or the threat of it, and whipping was slaveholders' preferred, day-to-day method for enforcing discipline. For slaves, whipping was insulting. It was most dishonorable to be lashed in the presence of family and friends. For that very reason, slaves took great satisfaction in the physical, mental, and spiritual liberation derived from resisting a beating at the hands of the master, overseer, or patroller. Just as Frederick Douglass's victory over the slave-breaker Covey rekindled within him his own flagging sense of manhood, the Virginia bondman Tom, who shot and killed a white man named Henry C. Williams in the 1850s, explained that "Williams had whipped him once, but should not do so again." The bondman Samuel of Concordia Parish, Louisiana, boldly informed his white overseer, "I am not going to be whipped by anybody, either black or white." After his master whipped him for the first time, one affronted bondman, proud of never before having been whipped, "struck off the upper half of his right hand" with an axe. "You have mortified me," he informed his owner, holding up a bloody stump for inspection, "so I have made myself useless."[82]

Slaves sought vengeance upon other bondpeople for whom they blamed their whippings. In 1829, Pittsylvania County slave George gave an unfavorable report about fellow bondman Shadrack to their master, Allen Womack. They had been fighting when Womack approached and inquired about them. George volunteered that "Shadrack had been fighting him, and had hit him with a Rock," prompting Womack to administer lashes to Shadrack. Soon thereafter, Shadrack waylaid George with a shovel, fracturing his skull. Shadrack vowed that "he would be damned if he would not kill any negro that would make his master take his shirt off."[83]

Although southern masters did not brand their slaves with the same daily regularity as they employed the whip, branding was nevertheless included in slaveholders' repertoire of domination. In the colonial era, captive Africans were sometimes branded before ever being herded onto slave ships for the transatlantic crossing. Branding represented an assault upon manhood as the mark reduced an individual to the property of another. Some masters scattered across the South branded slaves as they did cattle to signify ownership and to aid in the recovery of runaways. The most taciturn captured fugitive could easily be identified by brand if apprehended within the orbit of the knowledge of a master's mark or if a runaway advertisement alerted strangers to be on the lookout for a specific letter or symbol. Branding also served as a form of punishment. Masters occasionally burned the flesh of their slaves, usually with a letter or combination of letters as shorthand for the offense they committed. Slaveholders' brutal artistry met with varying degrees of success. A North Carolina master in 1838 used "a hot iron" to try to burn a letter onto the left side of the bondwoman Betty's face, but botched the job. To discipline the enslaved man Jack for visiting his wife on a nearby plantation without permission, a Georgia slaveholder "had Jack stripped and tied up to a rough red oak tree, his hands being made fast round the tree, so that he embraced it." The master "then took a branding-iron ... which he heated red hot at the kitchen fire, and applied [it] to the fleshy part of Jack's loins." Jack shrieked in pain and, to escape the branding iron, scraped his way in a circle around the tree he involuntarily hugged. The master feared the slave's movement "would cause him to make what is called a miss-letter, so he followed Jack round the tree till the iron was quite buried in the flesh." Jack screamed throughout the horrifying ordeal, "smoke from his burning flesh rising high and white." When the torture of the branding finally ceased, Jack was untied. Inching frantically around the tree as he had, the bark had scoured "all the flesh from his chest," which bled profusely.[84]

If masters sometimes branded slaves, branding was also a lawful punishment, dating from the colonial era. Whites—most frequently indentured servants—and slaves alike might suffer branding, although as time went on, the practice targeted black convicts more often than white criminals. In 1737, authorities in York County, Virginia, branded a slave's thumb with the letter T, signifying the crime of theft. Although more common in the colonial period, branding was not unheard of as a legal penalty during the early republic and antebellum decades. Many southern states utilized branding, at least for a time, for a range of offenses. In Virginia, the future slave conspirator Gabriel was branded in the late eighteenth century for attacking a white man and biting off part of his ear. Several slaves in the 1802 plot in northeastern North Carolina were also branded. An enslaved arsonist in antebellum Georgia was branded on one cheek with an H and on the other with a B to denote house burning. Some states employed the branding of bondpeople as an alternative to capital punishment. Prior to 1847, for example, slaves in the Commonwealth of Kentucky could claim the benefit of clergy. In keeping with this feature of the law, Kentucky courts were empowered to order literate slaves—those capable of reading the Bible—whipped and branded rather than hanged. In much of the Old South, slaves convicted of injuring or killing other bondpeople were among the more likely candidates for branding. Branding clearly identified enslaved troublemakers in the community without forcing masters to sacrifice the lives of valuable bondpeople or compelling the state to reimburse slaveholders for slaves either executed or transported. In 1828, the Hustings Court of Petersburg, Virginia, ordered the bondman Tom burned on the hand and whipped twenty-five lashes for injuring a fellow slave.[85]

Slaves convicted of the manslaughter, rather than murder, of other slaves often earned a letter M on either the hand or face. After the Delaware slave Charles Loadnum was convicted of manslaughter in the death of his brother Jacob in 1798, Charles was ordered to "be burnt in the brawn of the left thumb with the letter M." In 1825, a thirteen-year-old bondperson in Washington, D.C., named John Clark was found guilty of manslaughter in the death of a fellow slave two years his senior. Besides receiving ten stripes, Clark was ordered "to be burnt in the hand." The Alabama Supreme Court held in 1827 that any slave guilty of the manslaughter of a fellow slave or free black could be punished with as many as one hundred lashes and branded in the hand. South Carolina forbade branding in 1833, but the practice persisted after that date in other southern states. In Mississippi, "Little Jorden a negro slave" of Adams County fatally stabbed "Big Jorden" with a knife in 1854. Upon his conviction for manslaughter the next year, Little Jorden was "Sentenced to be branded in the hand [with an] M." The Mississippi law code of 1857 affirmed the continued use of branding as punishment for slaves convicted of noncapital crimes.[86]

No southern state seemed to employ branding as frequently as Georgia. Several times Georgia's governors requested that the state legislature outlaw the practice, but lawmakers refused to budge. Decade after decade, Georgia slaves were branded upon their convictions for crimes, including the deaths of fellow bondpeople. In Chatham County, "Adam a man of color and slave" killed "Bob a slave the property of Thomas Mitchell Esquire" in June 1819. The Chatham County Inferior Court sentenced Adam to receive "three times thirty nine lashes on his bare back on three different days at the market": Thursday, Saturday, and the Tuesday of the following week. Following the third and final day of whipping, Adam was ordered "branded on the fleshy part of the Thumb of the right hand with the letter M and then discharged." Decades later, in 1853, a Greene County court found the bondman Simon guilty of voluntary manslaughter in the death of another slave. Simon was punished with thirty-nine total lashes and a brand of M on the right cheek.[87]

The surviving inferior court records of the five Middle Georgia counties of Baldwin, Hancock, Jones, Lincoln, and Putnam identify 8 slave men accused of murdering fellow bondmen between 1815 and 1849. Of the 8, 2 were acquitted, 6 found guilty. Two of those condemned were found guilty of murder as charged, with the other 4 convicted of the reduced charge of manslaughter. Only 1 of the 6 bondmen found guilty—Adam of Jones County—was executed by hanging. The other 5 escaped the gallows to suffer a combination of lashes—ranging from 100 to 500, with 117 (39 lashes on 3 separate days) being the most common—and branding. Former slave Carrie Mason of Baldwin County, Georgia, remembered, "Effen a man or a 'oman kilt another one den dey wuz branded wid er hot i'on. Er big S wuz put on dey face somewhars. S stood fer 'slave,' an' evvybody knowed dey wuz er mudderer." Her recollections were partly accurate. A slave convicted in Georgia of killing another bondman was branded on the face, but with the letter M for murder or manslaughter. (Slaves branded with an S were guilty of theft, or stealing.)[88]

Although increasingly rare by the late antebellum era, branding as a punishment was emblematic of the Old South's honor culture. To whites, permanent scarring lowered slaves' property value but served the useful function of offering a visible, conspicuous caution to otherwise unwitting potential buyers. The appearance of lash marks and brands stymied the kinds of deception endemic to southern slave markets. The effect on purchasers must have been ambiguous, however. Slaves marked as troublemakers were risky investments, but they were also less expensive than similar bondmen without telltale symbols of a rebellious spirit. For white authorities who inflicted the scars, shaming punishments were designed to deter crime rather than reform the convict. Branded slaves enjoyed no hope of ever erasing the mark to make a fresh start. As Ben Simpson, himself branded by his Norcross, Georgia, master, explained, "they was no way to get that off. It was put on there with [a] hot iron."[89]

Certainly the excruciating pain and the permanence of branding were intended to discourage misbehavior as defined by masters and the southern legal culture. But did shaming punishments such as branding also imply white recognition of enslaved honor? Many southern whites denied that slaves suffered shame through the punishments inflicted upon them. Justice Richmond M. Pearson of the North Carolina Supreme Court opined that bondpeople were so "accustomed... to constant humiliation" that " a blow inflicted upon a slave is not attended with any feeling of degradation, by reason of his lowly condition." The Supreme Court of Texas concurred, sharing the widely held belief among whites that whipping "to a slave was no disgrace."[90] A portion of all southern whites, including the master who put his slave in irons "just to mortify him," did understand that slaves could be humiliated and dishonored, yet shaming a slave was a fundamentally redundant act in that slaves were already degraded members of southern society. Lacerated or burned flesh only reinforced preexisting white perceptions of slave inferiority.

Southern whites probably never considered that the true shame associated with slaves' punishments of humiliation derived from the possible meaning of the scar within the slave community. Whereas countless slaves had indelible marks from the lash upon their backs, comparatively few slaves had letters denoting crimes burned into their skin. Among bondpeople, could the relative rarity of branding marks have stigmatized those slaves forced to bear them? Slave narratives and autobiographies are silent on the matter. It is likely that slaves branded for crimes against whites suffered no disgrace in the quarters. By contrast, brands incurred for the manslaughter of a fellow bondman may have generated shame, depending on the circumstances of the case and the reputation and place of the deceased in the slave community. On the one hand, if slaves on a plantation suffered the loss of a popular, respected bondman, they may have ostracized the branded slave for his crime. If, on the other hand, the murder victim was a deviant bondman unloved in the quarters, the brand itself may have been worn as a badge of honor by the wearer, who had accomplished the welcome disposal of an enslaved outcast.

The profound humiliation of whippings and other shaming punishments represented just one of many challenges to their masculinity that enslaved men confronted. On a daily basis, southern whites dishonored slaves and implicitly dismissed notions of black honor. But enslaved men rejected white claims that they lacked honor and took measures to assert their manhood and maintain the honor they knew they possessed. When male slaves behaved in ways informed by and consistent with their honor code, they behaved as men. Bondage fully defined neither their identity nor their lives. Enslaved men had many different models of masculinity available to them, some violent and some not. Bondmen who employed violence to redress grievances and thereby prevent any loss of honor demonstrated but one version of manliness evident in early nineteenth-century America. Scholars of the American South have overlooked honor as a source of conflict among slaves, but a masculine code of honor influenced male slaves no less than southern white men. In the Old South, enslaved men and poor white men, in particular, shared a common culture of honor and violence that overlapped in many respects.

Although southern whites mocked slave pretensions to honor, enslaved men's degradation in white society only enhanced their sense of honor among enslaved peers. Dishonor stung, striking at slaves' identity as men. One loss of honor prompted a touching turn of events on the plantation of Spartanburg District, South Carolina, farmer David Golightly Harris. "York and Old Will had a fight," Harris's wife recorded, and the elder slave's defeat at the hands of the younger York humbled him. No longer comfortable remaining on the plantation where York cost him honor among his fellow slaves (and perhaps still menaced him), Old Will asked his mistress for permission to locate a new master. As Emily Liles Harris explained of her aged bondman, "York has given him a whipping and he wishes to leave the place." The elderly slave's request suggests the pride that bondpeople maintained in the face of bondage.[91]

Other slaves responded to dishonor in different—and oftentimes more violent—ways. In Nansemond County, Virginia, the bondman Sam was depressed that "somebody," presumably a slave, "said I was nothing." Though Sam was enslaved, through the force of horizontal honor, the belittling remark nonetheless hurt. A fellow slave named Simon quickly denied that he was the "somebody" in question. Sam acknowledged as much but grew suddenly angry anyway. In a likely case of misplaced aggression, he lashed out at Simon both verbally and physically. "God dam you," Sam replied, "I'll let you know who did [say I was nothing]." He then attacked Simon with a pine stick and a knife, killing him. Elsewhere, Brunswick County, Virginia, bondman Stephen refused to admit defeat in a fight he had had with an enslaved man named Cary. When the enslaved observer Adam said to Stephen, "I reckon he has whipped you," Stephen refuted the charge: "[N]o he has not." He then resumed his battle with Cary and murdered his opponent.[92]

Constantly vigilant of their honor within the slave community, enslaved men often displayed weapons as a demonstration of masculinity. They routinely carried knives in their day-to-day lives as tools necessary for their labors, but such implements could also serve more sinister, deadly purposes. In the early nineteenth century, Monroe County, Virginia, bondman Moses kept his knife at the ready, as he explained, "for the purpose of stab[b]ing any Negro larger than himself who should interrupt him." Smaller, weaker, or younger slave men, especially, may have found confidence in wielding a deadly weapon. The night that Henrico County slave Martin killed the bondman Lewis in 1837, Martin had informed a third slave "that he had his instruments in his pocket to fix any man." In New Orleans, one bondman concerned about a fellow slave's growing arsenal observed that "you have to[o] many weapons about you for any good." "[N]ever mind," came the curt reply, "they are my weapons." The security of a weapon at hand emboldened enslaved men and enhanced their masculinity. The bondman Cornelius may have gotten a perverse thrill when he entered his master's kitchen in 1861 and casually pointed an unloaded gun at Nancy, another slave. Although the bondwoman scolded him for his irresponsibility, Cornelius probably reveled in the sense of power the firearm bestowed. When one slave affirmed at a trial in Anderson District, South Carolina, that the gun the bondman George clutched in his hand the night of a violent affray was authentic "& not merely a representation made of wood," he suggested that some slaves actually carried fake, wooden pistols (and other homemade weaponry) as an exhibition of manhood. In a botched quasi-duel held in Kershaw District, South Carolina, Eben, an enslaved man acting as a second, brandished a makeshift sword described as "some three edged thing . . . with a cob stuck on the end of it for a handle." When a white man ordered Eben to relinquish the weapon, the bondman "replied he could not give it up any how and live." He then tossed it down and fled the dueling grounds.[93]

Confronting daily challenges to their masculinity, enslaved men negotiated and renegotiated claims to manhood throughout their adult lives. Violence afforded them one avenue to display manhood in the quarters and to avenge any loss of honor. Although it risks reinforcing modern stereotypes of black deviance or criminality, examining slave life through the lens of violence is useful in prying into the culture of enslaved men. Bondmen had at their disposal many models of masculinity, but in the context of antebellum southern society, it would have been surprising had violence not become enmeshed in their definitions of manhood and honor.[94]

Chapter 8

HONOR, VIOLENCE, AND ENSLAVED FEMININITY

DURING THE CIVIL WAR, on a plantation in northeastern Louisiana, the bondwomen "Jane ... and Aunt Lucy had a terrible row." Jane, a "very surly" and "powerful" slave woman "nearly six feet tall," possessed "a fearful temper" and "fire in her eyes"; even whites were "afraid" and "stood in wholesome dread of her." But because she was such "a splendid cook," her white mistress grudgingly tolerated her baneful presence. On the night of the altercation, "Jane cut a great gash in Lucy's face with a blow from a chair and hurt her severely." The "scene of terror" rattled the plantation: "The quarreling and screaming, the blood streaming down Lucy's face, Jane's fiery looks and speeches" were all too much for her owner's family to bear. "We felt her a constant menace," one member confessed to her journal. Accordingly, when Jane fled after the incident, the white family was "thankful to get rid her": "we are all glad she has gone."[1]

The details of this incident mark it as unusual in a number of ways. Jane's imposing physique and intimidating demeanor set her apart from the masses of female slaves. The sheer brutality of her assault was also atypical for a bondwoman. That an enslaved woman committed such a violent, bloody attack at all made it comparatively remarkable. Enslaved men perpetrated acts of physical violence upon their peers in bondage far more frequently than did enslaved women. As we saw in the last chapter, for some male slaves, violence played a significant role in constructing masculinity within the quarters. But as Victoria E. Bynum, Laura F. Edwards, and a small number of other historians have shown, the Old South's "unruly women," whether black or white, occasionally carried out violent acts of their own. Incidents involving violence committed by enslaved women, though relatively rare, are nonetheless instructive, helping to recover the meanings of black femininity and enslaved female honor in the American South as well as the peculiar stresses that bondage placed on female slaves.[2]

This chapter examines bondwomen as both perpetrators and victims of intraracial slave violence. Although bondwomen committed fewer physically violent acts than bondmen, their violent altercations with enslaved women and men and their assaults upon slave infants and children provide an unusual avenue through which to explore the construction of enslaved femininity. Bondwomen's violent acts carried out upon other female slaves, bondmen, and infants and children all offer clues into enslaved women's conceptions of honor. Physical clashes with other bondwomen often began as verbal disagreements. Their disputes over lies, insults, and other offensive words mirrored bondmen's obsession with honor and reputation within the slave community. Female slaves also staked a claim to a form of sexual honor familiar to antebellum southern white women, despite the many obstacles the institution of slavery erected in fulfilling that vision. Whereas enslaved women endured countless rapes and sexual assaults committed by white men, they claimed the right to deny consent to predatory bondmen. When those who sought to violate them were similarly enslaved, bondwomen were better able to seize control of their sexuality and violently defend themselves. The most frequent targets of enslaved female violence, however, were children. Whereas much of this violence was standard parental discipline or displaced aggression, surviving records better document the more exceptional cases of infanticide and child murder perpetrated by bondwomen. These episodes further suggest slave women's concern with sexual honor, character, and standing in the quarters. Altogether, what emerges from the records is a portrait of enslaved femininity fundamentally at variance with contemporary whites' characterizations of unrestrained black female sexuality. No wonder that, in ex-slave recollections, violent slave women "were often described with affection or even pride." Gazing through the lens of violence helps sharpen a developing picture of enslaved female honor.[3]

Scholarly discussions of southern honor have long been confined to whites. Honor appears in the literature as an overwhelmingly if not exclusively white male prerogative, with white women marginalized when not overlooked altogether. Whereas among white men honor was inequitably distributed by class, with elite white men staking a greater claim to honor than white men of lower social standing, white women have often been portrayed either as not possessing honor unto themselves or as mere repositories of a collective, familial honor. To the extent that female honor existed, it was something for southern white men to guard, often through violence but occasionally through religious institutions or legal channels. The social anthropologist Julian Pitt-Rivers explains succinctly the difference between male and female honor: "Male honor is something to be won, increased, and defended against a rival; female honor is something to be conserved and protected." On the whole, female honor appears fundamentally passive in the scholarship.[4]

Yet in the culture of southern honor, white women were paradoxically both powerless and powerful. However peripheral they have been to scholarly discussions of honor, they were nonetheless crucial to the functioning of the code. White women both judged male performances of honor and possessed the ability to shame spouses and disgrace families and kin. Female power expressed itself most forcefully in the sexual arena. Honorable women maintained their chastity and preserved their virtue. The young woman who gave birth out of wedlock "ruined" herself by her shame, the adulterous woman who cuckolded her husband dishonored him, and the promiscuous woman besmirched the family name. Social convention held that fathers, husbands, and brothers act as guardians of female virtue; hence, white women's sexual misconduct demonstrated that the men in the family ineffectually exercised patriarchal authority over their households and exposed them to public opprobrium. The potential ramifications of female behavior thus reached far beyond the individual: white women of the Old South might either validate or undercut male pretensions to honor. The ethic of honor inextricably bound the sexes together.[5]

Not all white women whose own sense of honor was impugned sat idly by and waited for men to defend them. Some of them may not have had a male figure in their lives to protect them at all. Unattached, single, and therefore socially dangerous women often received unwanted community scrutiny of their behavior and struggled to uphold claims to respectability as they labored outside the home. Whether as substitutes for or auxiliaries to patriarchal protection, some "unruly women" took the initiative in seeking redress, resorting even to violence. Southern evangelical churches afforded a more respectable avenue through which white women sometimes asserted their own sense of honor. They might charge fellow sisters with sexual improprieties or for spreading malicious falsehoods about the accuser's sexual misconduct. The sacred space of the church even empowered women to levy accusations against male congregants who gave them the lie or "circulat[ed] . . . scandalous report[s]" of a sexual nature. As reluctant as churches often were to censure men when women brought charges against them, some southern white women found in evangelical churches a convenient resource to draw upon to enforce claims to female honor.[6]

In the Old South, enslaved women occupied a cultural space entirely outside the boundaries of respectable womanhood. A widespread stereotype of black women as promiscuous Jezebels gripped the southern white imagination. White southerners detected and frequently criticized the rampant moral depravity they perceived among bondwomen pathologically addicted to sex, and no women of such reputedly loose morals could lay successful claim to honor. That it was often masters, overseers, and other white men who made enslaved women prematurely knowledgeable of sexual matters made no difference; the irony garnered the polite silence of the southern white masses. At the same time, the slave quarters did foster a sense of sexual morality distinct from that of white society. The moral code of the quarters, for instance, more readily countenanced premarital sex, but not unconditionally. The bondman Harry McMillan reported to an interrogator from the American Freedmen's Inquiry Commission in 1863 that enslaved women did sometimes give birth prior to marriage, but as he further clarified, it would be a mistake to conclude that the quarters were therefore sites of sexual license and moral bankruptcy. According to McMillan, enslaved women "are thought low of among their companions unless they get a husband before the child is born[,] and if they cannot the shame grows until they do get a husband." McMillan's remarks about the shame bondwomen felt suggest the presence of an enslaved female code of honor entirely unrecognized by nineteenth-century white society. As the inverse of honor, shame cannot be felt without it. Both functioned in tandem inside the quarters.[7]

John Iliffe's work on honor in African societies shows the various ways in which native Africans defined honor. Women in Africa, Iliffe observes, generally valued fertility and domestic acumen, including the skills to raise and care for children and to support the household economically. Compared to that in the American South, female honor in Africa was less contingent upon sexual conduct. Although in eastern and southern Africa women's honor was grounded in virginity at the time of marriage, many West African peoples—the Yoruba probably excepted—placed little premium on premarital virginity. According to Iliffe, "Men, especially in West Africa, did not necessarily expect their brides to be virgins." The "Asante thought it foolish to marry without first living experimentally with the intended partner." Moreover, in Africa "there was little sense that the woman's behaviour shamed her own family," as was true among southern whites. The apparent licentiousness antebellum whites perceived in the slave quarters, then, may be traced in part to the lingering cultural effects of African conceptions of honor—notions that conflicted with those of their enslavers.[8]

By the nineteenth century, however, most southern slaves had not been born in Africa, and doubtless African definitions of honor did not survive decades of slavery completely intact, unaffected by the new environment. An exploration of violence committed by female slaves in Virginia and other states offers clues into their gendered identity as enslaved women. This chapter draws upon slave narratives and autobiographies as well as "white" sources such as court records, which often recorded verbatim testimony of enslaved eyewitnesses to violent crimes, and petitions explaining why bondwomen convicted of violent offenses upon other slaves were deserving of gubernatorial clemency. Through these sources, motivations lurking behind homicides and other violent acts committed by female slaves come more clearly into focus. The resulting glimpse into enslaved women's values and their perceptions of themselves and their place as women within the quarters hints at the continuing significance of honor in their lives in defiance of the degradation of slavery.

Ex-slave respondents to Works Progress Administration interviewers affirmed the presence of cantankerous and physically aggressive bondwomen in the quarters. Mary Dodson of Fayette County, Texas, recalled that her sister Maria "was a devil fo' fightin'." She frequently "would git mad and try to pass a lick at somebody." Former slaves occasionally attributed their own fiery temperaments to their mothers. "I was mean like my mammy," admitted Susan Snow, born into slavery in Wilcox County, Alabama. "Always a-fightin' an' scratchin' wid white an' black." Anderson Furr of Hall County, Georgia, likewise confessed that "I'se lak my Ma. I'se a fighter. Ma would jump on anybody what looked at her twice."[9]

To an even greater extent than among enslaved men, bondwomen's violent outbursts were punished on the plantation where the offense occurred. "Fighting, particularly amongst women, . . . is to be always rigorously punished," one southern master instructed his overseer. This customarily meant whipping. One former slave recalled that "de women uster git whuppins fer fightin'." Eliza Evans, enslaved in Dallas County, Alabama, remembered a fight between her mother and another bondwoman. In consequence of the fray, she said, "My mother got ten licks and de other woman got twenty-five." Defiantly, a small number of female ex-slaves reveled in the punishments they endured. Susan Snow practically boasted when she admitted that, on account of her meanness, "I got more whuppin's dan any other Nigger on de place."[10]

Churchgoing bondwomen sometimes also faced religious censure for their nonlethal assaults upon other slaves. Sardis Baptist Church in Wilkes County, Georgia, excluded Letty and Elsey, both of whom were found "Guilty of [the] sin of Quarreling and using Bad Language," but retained in fellowship "a black woman . . . named Beck for quarrelling with and threat[e]ning to stick a knife in one of her fellow servants." Rabun Creek Baptist Church in Laurens District, South Carolina, displayed similar generosity of spirit in restoring fellowship to

"Mrs. Boyce's Lorrissa" after she acknowledged "a fight or Difference with a black Woman of Mr Choices" in which she had followed and struck her enslaved female adversary. Churches deemed bondwomen's disputes within the quarters as sufficiently insignificant to warrant automatic expulsion.[11]

Bondwomen in Virginia and other states rarely engaged in violent acts serious enough to gain the attention of the judicial system. Between 1796 and 1864, Virginia's records of condemned blacks executed or transported, governors' papers, and county court order books document thirty-nine female slaves convicted of the murders of at least forty-one other bondpeople. These figures are minimums but still miniscule for a female slave population that exceeded 200,000 in the antebellum decades. Enslaved women accounted for 31 percent of all intraracial slave homicides unearthed in the records after 1796, a figure vastly higher than among whites, where women were rarely convicted of murder in a society rife with violence. On average, enslaved women in Virginia are known to have killed one fellow bondperson every twenty months. Their enslaved victims included equal numbers of women and men—a paltry seven apiece, or one male and one female victim, on average, per decade—and twenty-seven infants or children born into bondage, the equivalent of one murder every two and a half years. Aided by the fact that bondwomen were found guilty of killing their own offspring in almost two-thirds of the cases in which they were charged with the death of another bondperson, and by the fact that they enjoyed little freedom of movement off the home plantation, convicted slave female murderers belonged to the same master as their victims 85 percent of the time.

When their intended victims were male, enslaved women were most likely to use deadly toxins to achieve their goal. As tough as they were, with muscles hardened through manual labor, female slaves generally avoided physical conflicts with even stronger enslaved men. Poisoning, a technique long employed to eliminate despised masters or other whites, could achieve all the anticipated benefits of an enemy's death without direct confrontation. Furthermore, enslaved women's important role in food preparation made poisoning a sensible option for them. In Prince Edward County, Virginia, the bondwomen Rinah and Fanny, mother and daughter, were charged in 1832 "with feloniously preparing, exhibiting and administering medicine to Oxford a negro man slave," killing him. Rinah served Oxford a toxic "broth" containing "two or three doses of Hemlock." The slave Louisa, of Fauquier County, slipped arsenic to George "with intent... to injure and Kill." Many of the poisons employed could be readily obtained from natural sources. Rinah's daughter Fanny, for instance, had dug up "red hemlock" or gathered the "highland hemlock" her mother mixed into her lethal soup. Another bondwoman administered a fatal concoction of "Buckeye and James town weed," reputed to be as effective, within twenty-four hours, "as the snap of a gun."[12]

Whereas bondwomen tended to poison male slaves, they drew upon a broad range of weapons in disposing of their enslaved female victims. Some of their murders proved quite grisly. In dispatching Aunt Sally in 1852, Mahala, of Giles County, Virginia, followed through on her threat to "cut her up with an axe." Other women stabbed their female adversaries with knives. Two whipped out knives concealed "under their Aprons" to hack away at their common enemy. Eschewing sharp instruments, other bondwomen used blunt objects to bludgeon their female foes. The enslaved Clara confessed to a Spotsylvania County magistrate that she killed the bondwoman Grace "with a stone, by striking her above the ear, & laying her head on another stone & beating her until she was dead." These were exceptionally bloody and brutal methods enslaved women sometimes used to murder other female slaves. Viney, enslaved in Bedford County, Virginia, chose the less confrontational technique of poisoning more commonly reserved for attempts to kill masters or enslaved men. She purchased an ounce of arsenic from a white storekeeper under the pretense that she wanted "to catch a weazel" that was "killing fowls in the Coop." Instead, Viney used the poison to murder "a negro girl slave named Jane," to whom she delivered fatal, arsenic-laden *"puffs or crackers"* for her to eat as well as a spiked "bowl of tea."[13]

Of all the enslaved women convicted in Virginia courts of murdering fellow slaves between 1796 and 1864, two-thirds were sentenced to hang. (See table 8.1.) Death was the standard sentence for murder, but in actuality, only eight enslaved women, or 21 percent of those found guilty, were executed for the homicide of another slave, the last in 1853. Bondwomen were no more or less likely to die at the end of the hangman's noose based on the sex of their adult victims, but they would almost assuredly escape execution in cases of infanticide and child murder. Though tragic, the deaths of unproductive slave infants and children were not as immediately detrimental to masters' economic interests as the loss of adult slave men and women. Virginia governors frequently commuted death sentences, often on the basis of the youth or character of the black female convict. Mahala, the fourteen-year-old convicted murderer of the elderly Aunt Sally, was not among them. Despite appeals to the governor based on her "tender years," she was not spared execution. A counterpetition from 120 Giles County citizens objected to any reprieve, stating that, "whilst . . . Mahala is not over fifteen years of

Table 8.1. Sentences and Punishments of Convicted Female Murderers in Virginia, 1796–1864

	Enslaved Victims						
	Infants/Children		Men		Women		
Punishment	Sentence	Actual	Sentence	Actual	Sentence	Actual	Total
Execution	15 (65%)	2 (9%)	5 (63%)	3 (38%)	6 (75%)	3 (38%)	8 (21%)
Sale & transportation	8 (35%)	19 (83%)	2 (25%)	2 (25%)	2 (25%)	4 (50%)	25 (64%)
Public works	0 (0%)	2 (9%)	0 (0%)	1 (13%)	0 (0%)	1 (13%)	4 (10%)
Whipping & mutilation	0 (0%)	0 (0%)	1 (13%)	1 (13%)	0 (0%)	0 (0%)	1 (3%)
Pardoned	0 (0%)	0 (0%)	0 (0%)	1 (13%)	0 (0%)	0 (0%)	1 (3%)
	23	23	8	8	8	8	39

Source: Appendix.

age ... she is remarkably developed both phisically and mentally ... [and] shrewd, sensible, cunning and artfull remarkably so for one of her age." Any pardon, insisted the signers, "would be ... productive of Great mischief and danger in every community in this Commonwealth where slaves are found." Mahala earned distinction as one of only three female slaves to die for killing another adult bondwoman.[14]

The foremost alternative to hanging for convicted female slave murderers in Virginia was sale and transportation out of the United States. Petitioners on behalf of Halifax County's Lizzy, convicted in the homicide of a fellow bondwoman, pleaded for the governor's mercy because "[s]he is a young woman ... who if guilty at all was named to participate in the murder wholly by the influence of her mother" Sally, also convicted of the same crime. Whereas Sally hanged as scheduled, Lizzy was reprieved for sale and transportation. Removal marked the ultimate fate of twenty-five bondwomen (64 percent) held responsible for the death of a slave and of 83 percent of those convicted of killing enslaved infants and children. Another four female slave convicts were spared hanging and were instead condemned to hard labor on the public works, a legal option beginning in 1858. One was pardoned altogether; far less fortunate, one, in 1799, received thirty-nine lashes and had her ears cut off. Still, probably because authorities perceived women as less dangerous than men, female slaves generally fared better in the distribution of punishments. Male slaves found guilty of murdering another bondperson confronted nearly equal chances of hanging or sale.[15]

The Old Dominion compensated masters the market value of slave convicts regardless of whether they were executed, sold and transported, or sent to the public works. Justices appraised enslaved women found guilty of murder from a low of $50 for an exceptionally notorious bondwoman in 1832 to a high, in 1864, of $3,000 in increasingly worthless, depreciated Confederate currency, with an average valuation of between $500 and $600. Virginia recouped at least a portion of its expenditures to masters when it sold slave convicts confined in the state penitentiary in Richmond. There, slaves found guilty of murder awaited sale to passing traders, assuming the price was right. In 1856, trader John T. Lewis offered the state $500 for the purchase of Opha Jane, a Powhatan County slave found guilty of infanticide, but his offer proved too low for the state to accept.[16]

One of the few scholars to address the disputes that erupted between bondwomen in the plantation South, Deborah Gray White argues that "sisterhood could coexist with discord" and suggests it would have been unrealistic not to expect some infighting among female slaves. Slave women enjoyed even fewer opportunities than enslaved men to travel with permission off the home estate or to earn a break from their routine, day-to-day responsibilities as wives, mothers, and workers. As a result, they encountered a relatively narrow set of fellow bondpeople repeatedly as they went about their labors. "Conflict occurred *because* women were in close daily contact with each other," Gray White observes. Bondwomen's "constant jockeying for 'occupational' and social status created an atmosphere rife with smouldering jealousies and antipathies." Harriet Ware, a Boston missionary in wartime South Carolina, recognized as much. Writing of lowcountry black women in August 1863, she observed that "[j]ealousy is the foundation of a great deal of trouble among them." She furthermore noted, with a tone of Yankee moral condescension, that "there is often too much foundation for it."[17]

Accounts of the violence that erupted between enslaved women, though small in number, often smacked of a sense of honor that closely resembled that of enslaved men. Take, for example, female slaves' physical disputes over speech, lies, and insults. As was true of enslaved men, bondwomen often fell out over the words that passed between them. Georgia planter Charles Colcock Jones opined that, as far as he could tell, "[t]he women quarrel more than the men, and fight oftener." After observing a fight among lowcountry blacks, Harriet Ware conceded that "I don't know what the trouble was," but she strongly suspected it was "the tongues of the women." We might dismiss these critical pronouncements were it not for the recollections of former slaves that validated white impressions. Former Alabama bondwoman Eliza Evans recalled one fight that erupted after "[a] woman cussed my mother and it made her mad."[18]

No less than their fathers, husbands, and brothers, bondwomen betrayed a prickliness about lies. According to the report of an overseer on the Allston family rice plantation in lowcountry South Carolina, "a goodeal of Quarling and disputeing & teling [of] lies" took place on the estate, "[m]ostly mongst the Women." Female slaves often took umbrage when another bondperson, male or female, questioned the truth of their word. Former slave Hector Godbold's mother got in an argument with a slave named John because, as she explained, "John call me a liar en I never take it." Bondwomen also accused one another of lying, a charge capable of producing violence. In Greensville County, Virginia, Frankey informed Clary that she "should not call her a liar" immediately before Clary stabbed her. A pair of Halifax County bondwomen killed a third enslaved woman because she charged them with fatally poisoning her spouse. Amey, the property of William Link, suffered a great personal loss when her husband of four or five years died. She accused Dr. James Singleton's enslaved cook Sally "of poisoning him . . . by putting something in his brandy." The allegation "made Salley mad." A livid Sally told one slave "that if she was to see Amey dead & laid out & the dogs eating her she would not drive them off of her." So when Amey unexpectedly turned up dead, suspicion naturally fell to Sally. Court records reveal that Amey was spinning cotton one night in November 1853 when a knock at the door interrupted her labors. When she answered, standing in her doorway were Singleton's Sally and Sally's daughter, the house servant Lizzy. Both assaulted Amey with knives, "[s]awing on her neck" and "cutting away on her." Amey succumbed to her wounds two weeks later. Despite defense efforts to cast doubt as to the true perpetrators of the crime, the Court of Oyer and Terminer convicted the enslaved mother and daughter of Amey's murder.[19]

Bondwomen's resentment of lies extended to all manner of gossip circulated about them. In 1844, the bondwoman Maria, a twenty-six-year-old domestic servant in Pendleton County, Virginia, approached a free black woman named Ruth and entered into a hostile exchange. "I understand you have been talking about me," Maria alleged. Ruth, described by Maria's master as "an abandoned free Negro girl," had previously threatened to kill her enslaved female adversary. Now it was Maria who shook her cane menacingly above Ruth's head and "told her she would beat her if she did not mind." Ruth denied "carrying a knife" for Maria, but Maria was not similarly free of a vengeful spirit. "[Y]es I do carry a knife for you," she admitted, "with which I will see your heart[']s blood or the heart[']s blood of any of your protectors." Maria stood ready to bring a violent end to Ruth's rumormongering.[20]

Enslaved women also demonstrated bondmen's acute concern with insults. One former Georgia slave related the story of "de Nigger 'omans" Rita and Retta, who, in retaliation for a perceived affront, gave "pizen [poisoned] . . . collards" to "Aunt Vira and her baby to eat." At a frolic, Vira "had been laughin' at a man 'cause his coattail was a-flappin' so funny whilst he was dancin'," but her merriment was misinterpreted. The "two Jezebels" Rita and Retta "thought she was makin' fun of dem," and their misunderstanding prompted them to seek vengeance for the supposed mockery.[21]

The circumstances swirling around bondwomen's violent encounters suggest a blurring of the boundaries between "masculine" and "feminine" in slave society. Compared to whites, gendered expectations of proper conduct among slaves were relatively less sharply differentiated. Like bondmen, most bondwomen in their workaday lives toiled in the fields, even though no respectable white woman did so. Similarly, away from work, female slaves could take certain liberties that would have been entirely unbecoming white women. Bondwomen might act upon aggressive impulses with proportionally less fear of censure or scandal for violating social protocol. Depending upon the particulars, their conduct might even meet with assent in the quarters. Informed by a similar sense of honor, enslaved women as well as men understood that violence could mark the appropriate response to honor slighted.

Bondwomen could be reasonably confident that, if they did not respond personally to an assault upon their honor, a bondman who loved them would. Enslaved men willingly—even eagerly—defended enslaved female honor from the aspersions cast upon bondwomen's character through offensive speech. The festive revelry at a post-Christmas "Dancing Party" held on one Pittsylvania County, Virginia, plantation in 1819 quickly soured when "some of the Company" remarked that the female slave Dilsey "danced as if she had a pound of Lead to her feet." Such a slight cut to the heart of Dilsey's identity as a woman. Stephanie M. H. Camp writes of the immense pleasure female slaves took in their bodily performances at dances. Bondwomen's ability to control and skillfully manipulate their bodies through space was a source of pride and self-expression that helped define a female gendered identity entirely divorced from their working life for the master. It represented the enactment of the honor that they knew they possessed. The criticism of Dilsey's dancing technique thus must have stung her deeply, and the holiday gathering intended to draw slaves together for recreation and enjoyment undermined the very sense of community it otherwise might have fostered.[22] When Dilsey's husband Primus heard the insult heaped upon his wife—that she "danced as if she had a pound of Lead to her feet"—he instantly took offense and declared that "he would stand at his Wifes Back." Perhaps no greater evidence for the existence of female honor in the slave quarters can be found than the willingness of enslaved men to protect it. Bondwomen fortunate enough to escape the familial devastation of the domestic slave trade took confidence in the knowledge that the significant men in their lives, whether husbands, brothers, or other kin, were prepared to fulfill their masculine responsibility to guard the women they loved from slights or assaults upon their character. The Pendleton County, Virginia, bondwoman Maria informed her enemy, the free black woman Ruth, that she "carried a pistol and if she could not shoot[,] her brother could."[23]

Male slaves were indeed prepared to protect bondwomen's sexual honor. Whereas enslaved men had but little choice to endure white men's sexual assaults upon female slaves, they need not tolerate similar violations committed by other male slaves. If they could not prevent them, they could at least seek vengeance upon the transgressor. One night as she slept, testified the Chesterfield County, Virginia, bondwoman Isabel, a slave named Archer placed "a handkerchief over her mouth," pinned her arms, and "nearly done what he wanted to do" before she awoke and prevented penetration. Isabel "was very much offended" by the assault but successfully "repulsed him." Although Archer pleaded for her "not to tell her husband" Essex, she did. At the same time, Isabel, anticipating her spouse's violent response, admonished Essex "to command his passion." Essex did not take the news of his wife's attempted rape lightly. Ignoring his wife's caution, the aggrieved husband killed his loved one's assailant, stabbing Archer multiple times "with a shoe knife." Through violent payback, Essex reclaimed his wife's honor as well as his own, making amends for his dereliction of duty in preventing the attack by a fellow slave. Even though the court that heard his case found Essex guilty and sentenced him to die, the justices understood his motivation because it would have been no different in southern white society. They therefore recommended him to the governor "as a proper object of mercy." Essex earned a reprieve to sale and transportation.[24]

As the conflict between Essex and Archer shows, just as some male slaves stood as guardians of enslaved female honor, others attempted to violate it. The masses of bondwomen across the American South were perpetually vulnerable to rape and sexual assault. Typically, their attackers were white men. Countless masters, overseers, poor whites, and others extracted sex from women in the slave quarters without fear of legal reprisal for violating black female bodies. Legally, enslaved women were, in Victoria Bynum's memorable term, "unrapeable." Southern law refused to define violent sexual attacks on female slaves as criminal. As a rule, southern whites denied that black women could be raped at all because they were presumed to be promiscuous Jezebels who craved sex and were utterly incapable of withholding consent, the necessary precondition for the crime. With such widespread attitudes entrenched in the minds of whites, many enslaved women suffered through the horrors of forced or coerced sex either occasionally or chronically.[25]

Uncritically accepting the pronouncements of nineteenth-century white men leads to the conclusion that enslaved women lacked any sense of sexual honor. Whereas southern whites detected pervasive moral depravity among bondwomen, antislavery writers deflected blame from the victim of sexual assault and placed it instead upon the general immorality fomented by the system of bondage. Yet even well-intentioned abolitionist allies accepted the racial assumption that bondwomen indiscriminately consented to sex. To the contrary, perhaps inspired by the moral instruction of the slave family or the more formal efforts of southern churches, some bondwomen refused to submit meekly to the unwanted sexual advances of white men. As Harriet Jacobs's autobiography and a number of other female slave narratives show, enslaved women struggled valiantly to elude rape and sexual exploitation by masters, overseers, and others. Jacobs wrote explicitly about her efforts to maintain her virtue, which, ironically, led to her sleeping with a white man of her own choosing to spite her master. Jacobs apologized to her readers for her course of action and noted her pious grandmother's acute disappointment in the choice she had made. Though on the whole more vulnerable to sexual depredation than white women, female slaves still evinced concern for sexual honor.[26]

Compared to the assaults of white men, female slaves could more readily resist—and resist with violence—the unwanted overtures of male slaves. Whereas historians have for decades explored white men's sexual exploitation of bondwomen, there remains practically no scholarship that investigates incidents of rape or sexual assault in which both victim and perpetrator were held in bondage. Historian Wilma King commented years ago that a study of slave-slave rape was still needed. Intraracial slave rapes certainly occurred, and, as with the anguish inflicted on slave families when white men frequented the quarters for salacious purposes, they devastated the female victim as well as her husband, if she was married, or enslaved suitor who might have been courting her at the time. An enslaved rapist or other sexually abusive bondman also incurred the wrath of the quarters if and when his actions were exposed. Momentously disruptive to the slave community, slave-slave rapes are notoriously difficult to document since, a few odd exceptions notwithstanding, raping a bondwoman was not a crime.[27]

On the basis of admittedly scarce evidence from randomly scattered southern court records, it appears that, most often, when female slaves attacked male slaves, bondwomen were not the aggressors. Certainly in the courtroom they justified their assaults as self-defense, a common tactic for anyone accused of violent crime. The Pendleton County, Virginia, bondwoman Maria denied any intention to murder the enslaved man Washington, or Wash, that December day in 1843 in which she thrust a butcher knife into his chest. The incident began with a dispute "in Dr. Newmans Kitchen" between Maria and the free black woman Ruth. Wash entered the room during their quarrel and instructed the pair to "quit your fuss." As Maria strode across the kitchen to leave, Wash blocked her, but she pushed her way out. Wash warned her, "you had better take care or you may land in hell to night." Later that night, however, it was Wash who ended up dead and Maria charged with murder. Court records do not reveal the precise relationship between Wash and Maria, but according to the slave Cyrus, Wash "seemed to be in a great rage with her because She had quarreled with the free Negro Ruth," possibly Wash's wife or love interest. A witness to the fray, Cyrus came forward only after Maria was tried, convicted, and sentenced to death for her crime. Because he had been off the plantation without permission the night he spied the murder, Cyrus feared being punished if he divulged what he had seen. But with Maria's life hanging in the balance, Cyrus's conscience overwhelmed him. He broke his silence, revealing that Washington had followed Maria, overtaken her, and assaulted her, saying *"damn you I will kill you this night, and bury your soul in the regions of hell."* Maria stabbed him to save her own life. The new evidence Cyrus supplied prompted Virginia's governor to issue Maria a rare full pardon.[28]

In the preponderance of cases in which female slaves violently attacked enslaved men, they were defending their honor from sexually predatory bondmen. The most fortunate bondwomen need not commit violence to spare themselves. They escaped violation through a simple scream of alarm. In September 1774, a nocturnal visitor crept into a Virginia nursery where Sukey, "a plump, sleek, likely Negro Girl about sixteen," was sleeping. Sukey awoke to discover a man in her bed. Veiled in darkness, the mysterious guest "lying by her Side" *"tickled* her, & said *whish, whish."* Sukey leapt out of bed with a cry to alert the other "young Ladies" slumbering in the nursery, but the unknown intruder fled, vanishing unseen into the night. Although some slaves attributed the incident to a ghost, chances are the entity in the bed was less spectral than physical. As one observer conjectured, it was probably "one of the warm-blooded, well fed young Negroes, trying for the company of buxom *Sukey.*"[29]

When screams like Sukey's did not frighten off an enslaved attacker, female slaves might prevent their sexual victimization through a resort to violence. Summoning their strength, they physically seized possession and exclusive control of their own bodies. Malinda of Southampton County, Virginia, offers one example of a bondwoman defending her sexual honor from the advances of a fellow slave. In 1840, the bondman Allen, owned by the same master as Malinda, made her uncomfortable through his repeated, uninvited touching. According to the testimony of an eyewitness, Allen approached Malinda and "laid his arm on her shoulder" but was met with rebuke. Malinda "told him to get away" and threatened to "stick the knife in him" if he refused. Allen persisted in his harassment, and in the tussle that followed, Malinda nicked Allen's jacket and inflicted a minor cut upon his arm. Later the same day, when the relentless Allen pressed his body against hers, sandwiching her between him and a post, Malinda fatally stabbed him in the chest. The Court of Oyer and Terminer sentenced her to death for her crime but also "recommend[ed] to the Executive to commute the punishment . . . to Transportation," which the governor did. Malinda's master would have been compensated equally by the state whether she were hanged or deported, so considerations of her owner's property rights would not have entered into the decision to recommend mercy. The court could not allow Malinda to go entirely unpunished for her extreme action against a valuable slave, but something about the particular circumstances of her case compelled the justices to urge gubernatorial leniency. They may well have understood Malinda within her rights to protect herself from Allen's unwanted attention. Self-defense would hardly have carried any weight with the justices were her victim a white man; that case would not even have gone to trial. That her attacker was a fellow slave made all the difference. The court thus balanced the conflicting demands of justice in law with justice for Malinda by recommending a severe punishment short of execution.[30]

Whereas Malinda confidently and competently wielded her knife to preserve her virtue, other bondwomen were less successful in their resistance. Some who claimed the right to deny consent to sex with a bondman paid for it with their lives. Jim, of Bedford County, Virginia, used a razor to slit the throat of the bondwoman Esther in July 1838. The pair had a history. Two years before, Esther had "refused to marry him." Her rejection had not deterred Jim from wanting to have his way with her, however. An enslaved housemate of Jim's had at least twice discovered the bondman attempt to enter the bed where Esther slept, although he was not sure whether Jim "hated or loved" her. In March, "there was a little roughing between them," but nothing to compare to the attack in July. When Jim's master William Woodford discovered Esther's lifeless body, "her outside dress was pulled over her head and her under clothes were about her knees," obvious indicators of a rape attempt. Another white witness observed that Esther's "clothes were rip[ped] as high as her hips." Only when Woodford lowered the bondwoman's dress to its proper position on her body did he see that her throat had been slashed. For the viciousness of the assault, a Bedford County Court of Oyer and Terminer sentenced Jim to death and *"unanimously* overruled" a motion from Jim's counsel to recommend the convict "to the mercy of the Executive." Jim hanged in October.[31]

An even more complicated relationship involving Appomattox County, Virginia, slaves Nelson and Catharine, or Kitty, also resulted in a bondwoman's death. Catharine angered Nelson by withholding sex from him. Nelson struck her in the head and neck with a seven-pound axe, he explained, after "he tried to get in the bed with Catharine" and "she forbid it." "Nelson had been in the habit of sleeping with Kitty," reported the slaves who lived in the same house. On the night of her death, however, she refused him. Nelson was undeterred: "He told her that he had laid with her [before] and would do it again." But if Nelson had previously slept with Catharine, Catharine had also previously denied consent. According to one female slave, "some times she would not let him sleep with her," and "Nelson would ... get mad." On this night, too, "Kitty ... told him to go away" and threatened to tell their master so that Nelson might be punished. Nelson replied that if Catharine "did not consent for him to lay with her, that he would kill her at the risk of his life." The bondman thus simultaneously acknowledged Catharine's right to refuse him but then, through a threat of violence, attempted to deprive her of that choice. What made this refusal different from previous denials was that Catharine had recently "persuaded" Nelson "to leave his wife," "who lived about a quarter of a mile off" on another estate. Although married to a bondwoman nearby, Nelson had not been a faithful husband. In fact, Nelson's master strongly suspected that Nelson had fathered the youngest of Catharine's four children. Kitty had never been heard "complaining of Nelson's going to see the other woman," but she may have bottled her emotions. Nelson had once left his wife "but had gone back to her," quite possibly over Catharine's objections, and perhaps she had finally given him an ultimatum. Now that "Nelson had quit his wife" for good, he was driven to commit murder when Catharine "refused to receive him as her husband." Now committed to Catharine exclusively, Nelson anticipated unrestricted conjugal access that the bondwoman proved unwilling to grant. As Nelson himself explained, "he . . . determined that if she did him no good that she should not do any body else any."[32]

Slavery bred conditions conducive to the sexual abuse of bondwomen perpetrated by male slaves. Hidden deep inside the slave quarters, most rapes or attempted rapes of enslaved women by enslaved men never garnered whites' attention. If violated bondwomen reported such incidents at all, it was more likely to a family member than to the master, and some of those slaveholders who were informed of sexual improprieties among their bondpeople elected not to pursue the allegation. The master, indeed, stood to profit from male slaves' exploitation of the owner's bondwomen should the assault result in pregnancy. The South Carolina lowcountry bondman Prince Robinson, for example, "took advantage" of Phoebe Brown and "got her in the family way," to the betterment of the master's finances. On some plantations, then, the lack of certain punishment for sexual assaults presented no deterrent to enslaved wrongdoers' exploitive behaviors. Masters' at times callous pairing of enslaved men and women without regard for their own preferences also established the context for rape. As a sixteen-year-old slave girl in Bell County, Texas, Rose Williams fought off the "bully" Rufus, the enslaved man her master chose to father her children. When Rufus attempted to share her bed, Williams "give him a shove" onto the floor and beat him over the head with a "poker."[33]

Although most of the sexually abusive encounters bondwomen endured at the hands of male slaves remain shrouded in mystery, the most common culprits appear to have been slave drivers. Like masters or overseers, drivers held positions of authority that emboldened them to take license with enslaved women. They also possessed the physicality to overpower them. In the late 1830s, for example, the driver Morris on one Georgia plantation raped the female slave Sophy. "[H]e have strength to make me," Sophy lamented. The South Carolina lowcountry bondwoman Lydia Brown birthed three children prior to her marriage, all the products of rapes committed by the slave driver. In Mississippi, Anna Baker's mother refused to submit. When "de Nigger overseers . . . kep' a-tryin' to mess 'roun' wid her," Baker recalled, "she wouldn' have nothin' to do wid 'em." On one occasion, a driver "asked her to go over to de woods wid him," and she fled the plantation.[34]

Although Michael Stephen Hindus has argued that "whites . . . could not conceptualize the rape of a slave by a fellow slave," shards of evidence suggest otherwise. One slave runaway advertisement from Maryland, for example, explained that the fugitive had raped a female slave prior to absconding. Enslaved women who mustered the courage to complain directly to the master or mistress of rape by a slave might enjoy the satisfaction of seeing an attacker punished. Slaveholders did sometimes whip enslaved men in retribution for their sexual assaults upon female slaves. Legally, however, throughout almost all of the South and for almost the full duration of slavery, statutes did not classify the rape of one slave by another as a crime. Eugene D. Genovese observes that "when a black man sexually attacked a black woman . . . no way existed to bring him to trial or to convict him if so brought." Yet there were the odd exceptions.[35]

Most known cases of enslaved men charged with the rape of black women come from the Commonwealth of Virginia. The circumstances through which these isolated cases appeared before Virginia courts are murky, especially since, by strict accordance with statute, no rape of a bondwoman should ever have been prosecuted in the Old Dominion. As Glenn M. McNair has explained with respect to Georgia, "when slave women were raped it was not viewed as a crime against the woman but as a trespass against the property interests of her owner." Hence, documented allegations of the rape of enslaved women by enslaved men in Virginia almost always involved parties belonging to different masters. Were the two slaves property of the same owner, a master made aware of the attack would have either whipped or otherwise punished the slave rapist without recourse to law or perhaps ignored the drama altogether. In those few cases that went to court, the enslaved female victim or possibly a friend or ally in the quarters must have reported the assault to her owner, who then instigated the suit against the enslaved perpetrator.[36]

But why did slave owners bother pursuing court action? A fraction may have acted out of ignorance to the law, oblivious to the fact that the rape of a slave woman was not a criminal act. They filed suit because that was the appropriate step to take when someone was raped. Some masters may have been genuinely sympathetic to the enslaved woman and justifiably outraged by the violation of her person. That they took the case to court at all may suggest some recognition of black female sexual rights, vis-à-vis bondmen at any rate, and that not all masters automatically dismissed female slaves as lusty, libidinous Jezebels. Simultaneously, however, the enslaved woman was also the master's property, and perhaps he had his own designs on her and resented the imposition on him the rape symbolized. Maybe he had plans to pair her with another slave of his choosing. Conventional antebellum southern medical wisdom maintained that women could not become pregnant without taking pleasure in the carnal act, which would not have been the case with forced sex. This belief, conveniently, validated white preconceptions of female slaves as Jezebels and may have palliated the minds of masters whose own sexual dalliances in the quarters produced enslaved, mixed-race children, since their victims must have enjoyed the encounter. More to the point, it meant that, even though masters would become the lawful owners of any "increase" born of slave women as the result of sex forced upon them by enslaved men, slaveholders may not necessarily have understood the possible financial benefits that might accrue to them in consequence of intra-slave rapes. They therefore did not necessarily grasp the economic irrationality of taking a neighbor's offending bondman to court. Finally, rape allegations may have served a master no other purpose than to afford the pretense to seek redress from a rival planter against whom he maintained some longstanding, simmering grievance. Possibly the infraction of rape gave some slaveholders the opportunity to settle old scores. For a number of reasons, then, cases of rape involving residents of the slave quarters might course their way through formal legal channels, in spite of the letter of the law.

When they did, the path to conviction was long and anything but certain. In some cases, the charge was dropped. Loudoun County, Virginia, bondman "William, a slave the property of Hamilton Rogers" was charged in April 1858 with a sexual assault upon Annette, a nineteen-year-old slave belonging to Matilda R. Adams. William allegedly "did violently and against her will, by force, feloniously ravish and carnally Know" the female slave, but the following month, the Commonwealth attorney opted not to prosecute, and William was released. Court records do not share the attorney's rationale for discharging William. We may speculate that there was not enough evidence, that the crime did not merit the time or energy of the court, or that the attorney believed it was not worth pursuing the case if its outcome could be potentially detrimental to masters' economic interests in enslaved property. In neighboring North Carolina, a grand jury in Chowan County found a true bill against the slave George for allegedly raping "a negroe Girl named Juno" in 1824. The evidentiary trail runs suddenly cold, so it is not clear precisely what happened to George. His case, too, may never have gone to trial.[37]

A few cases did make it to trial, but convictions were almost impossible to secure. The "Negro Man Slave" Kitt of Westmoreland County, Virginia, was charged with "Committing a Rape on the Body of Fan a Negro woman Slave" in 1783, but the case concluded abruptly in July when no one appeared in court to testify against the accused. On October 1, 1824, jurors in Chowan County, North Carolina, presented a "negro man Slave named Tom" for raping a "negro woman slave named Annis" "against the will of her the said Annis." Testimony from the case does not survive, but the jury, which by North Carolina law consisted exclusively of slaveholders, was not convinced of Tom's guilt. Jurors concluded either that the evidence against Tom was not strong enough or that his offense was so trifling as not to merit punishment.[38]

In only a few known Virginia cases, decades apart, did Courts of Oyer and Terminer find enslaved men guilty of raping enslaved women. The first, in Westmoreland County in 1778, involved Robert Carter's bondman Kitt, charged with "having forcibly and against her will had Carnal Knowledge of the Body of Sarah a Negro Woman Slave the property of the said Carter." Convicted, Kitt was ordered to the gallows. Second, in September 1796, a Loudoun County Court of Oyer and Terminer sentenced a slave named Luke to hang for the rape of "one Luce a negroe Girl Slave." At the same time, the justices recommended Luke "to his Excellency the Governor and Council as a proper object of Mercy." Such language encouraged the governor to commute the sentence from execution to sale and transportation out of the United States, a practice that was in use by the time of Luke's trial in the late eighteenth century despite not yet being codified into Virginia law. A private petition containing three signatures also reached the desk of Governor Robert Brooke asking for clemency for Luke. Petitioners explained that he had already received thirty-nine lashes for his offense, which they deemed more than adequate punishment considering the trifling magnitude of the crime. Moreover, they continued, "the Girl had lived in the Family w[ith] Luke & ... there might have been some consent at the beginning of the business which was denied afterwards." On this almost singular occasion, three white men recognized an enslaved woman's right to grant or withhold consent for sex, at least from a black man. In the tale spun by petitioners, Luce was not a sexually insatiable Jezebel but rather a purported tease, having withdrawn the consent formerly conferred. Although Luke's ultimate fate remains unknown, at least one Virginia slave man was convicted of raping an enslaved woman and subsequently deported. In December 1850, Spotsylvania County slave John was found guilty of the rape of the bondwoman Eliza and sentenced to sale and transportation outside the United States. Justices authorized John's master $550 in compensation for the loss of his bondman.[39]

Convictions of enslaved men in Virginia for rapes of free black or mulatto women proved almost as rare as those committed against female slaves, but the penalties tended to be more severe. A small number of convicted slave rapists, such as Charles of Halifax County, were sentenced to "sale and transportation for the rape on a free colored Girl." Other slaves found guilty of raping free women of color were sentenced to death, a fate almost unheard of for raping a female slave. In New Kent County, "Tom a negro man slave ... was tried ... on suspicion of Having committed a rape upon the Body of Dolly Boasman a free mulatto woman." The Court of Oyer and Terminer condemned Tom in January 1810 "to be Hang[ed] by the neck untill He be Dead" but also recommended him to the executive "as a fit object for transportation." Governor and future president John Tyler reprieved Tom for sale and transportation, sparing him from the gallows. No such mercy awaited the Surry County slave Peter, "charged with feloniously committing a rape on the body of Dolly Walden a free mulatto woman" in 1797. The court found him guilty and ordered him hanged, a sentence that was carried out per the justices' instructions. In Tennessee, the state Supreme Court observed in 1841 that rape "committed on a *black woman,* would not be punished with death" because the "enormity" of the offense was contingent upon the race of the victim. The full force of the law in the Volunteer State, the Court suggested, would only be brought to bear when the violated woman was white. In Virginia, by contrast, rapes of free women of color sometimes earned their perpetrators the death sentence. We cannot say with absolute confidence, however, that the rape of an adult female slave resulted in the execution of any Virginia bondman.[40]

Southern courts took somewhat more seriously very rare allegations of male slaves' rapes of underage slave girls. Individual states defined the lawful age of consent differently, usually ten or twelve but as young as a very tender seven in Delaware. Virginia court documents specified that alleged rape victims were "over the age of twelve years" or, conversely, as in the case of the Mecklenburg County slave girl Harriett, "under the age of twelve," in which case she was incapable of granting consent. Harriett's precise age is not stated in the records, which refer to her as "a coloured infant." This "coloured infant" offered graphic testimony on her own behalf during the November 1856 trial of the slave Coleman for raping her, so true infancy had long since passed. The circumstances surrounding the case were extraordinary. On Monday, October 13, 1856, a white boy identified as the roughly fifteen-year-old Ben Green chanced upon Harriett near the plantation of Alexander Jones in Mecklenburg County, Virginia. Perhaps wanting to exercise his white racial prerogative over a female slave and practice sowing his wild, teenage oats, Green "asked her if she would not go around the stack with him." Harriett refused and fled, but Green overtook and captured her. Up to this point, Harriett's account mimicked the horrors suffered by countless female slaves across the antebellum South, relentlessly pursued by masters and other white men for sexual gratification. But Harriett's drama then deviated sharply from the customary rape narrative. Once Green caught Harriett, he called to the young slave Coleman and invited him "to get in and do his part." Green then restrained the slave girl Harriett as Coleman raped her. Coleman "had my clothes up and ... his pantaloons down," Harriett recounted. Green "held my feet" while Coleman "held my arms and put all his weight on me and hurt me." Coleman "hurt me," Harriett elaborated, "when he first got on" and "when he was in me": "he hurt me by pushing and trying to get it in me so deep." Harriett's personal hell then took another unconventional turn. After Coleman "had done his part," he and "the white boy" exchanged places, and Coleman pinned her down as Green had his way with her. Harriett thus found herself the victim of an interracial gang rape. Two or three days after the rape, her master, by sheer coincidence a physician, "examined the girl and found that the mark of virginity had been destroyed."[41]

At Coleman's trial, Harriett relived the horrific experience of the assault. As would be expected of any "respectable" woman, Harriett struggled throughout the ordeal and attempted to escape, but to no avail. Her wrenching testimony before the court struck a chord with the justices. Despite Coleman's plea of not guilty, the court ruled that the bondman did indeed "carnally know and abuse" Harriett. It found him guilty and ordered him "transported beyond the limits of the United States." The five justices valued Coleman at $900, the sum his owner, Martha L. Nelson, would receive in compensation for her loss.[42]

Despite Virginia's built-in legal safeguards to reimburse masters for slaves either sold and transported or executed, there were whites who petitioned Virginia's governor on Coleman's behalf. Sixty-seven individuals signed a memorial begging for Coleman's full pardon. They noted that the slave "has heretofore behaved with exemplary obedience and deportment." One signer noted, "I have hired the said boy Coleman and he has always been a dutiful servant." Coleman was known, in short, as "an excellent boy." Given his history as a model slave, petitioners expressed their suspicion "that whatever part he took in the offence" was done under "the pressure of a white person under whose control he then was." Put another way, the white male signers of the petition excused Coleman of any culpability in the assault because he was merely following the orders of a white teenager who, quite conveniently, never could (and did not) suffer any consequences for his role in the incident. The petitioners also noted that Coleman was "wholly ignorant" of Virginia law and implied that an immature conscience rendered him unable to distinguish right from wrong. Many whites regarded blacks as hypersexual beings who recklessly pursued their animalistic passions, and the coded language of the petition perhaps disguised such lurking assumptions held by its signers. Complicating matters further, Coleman's owner was a white woman, and although petitioners did not couch their appeal in these terms, they may have thought of themselves as performing their masculine duty in protecting her interests. In the end, Governor Henry A. Wise was unpersuaded. He rejected the petition, and Coleman was presumably sold and transported as sentenced.[43]

One Virginia bondman who had raped an enslaved girl of six *is* known to have hanged, in August 1859. A bondman named Ned, of Spotsylvania County, worked as a groundskeeper. Approximately fifty years old, Ned was a pedophiliac and employed strategies common to the type: he enticed his victims with promises of treats and threatened to kill them if they told anyone what he had done. Although an enslaved girl named Betty Gordon was named in the charge against Ned, likely as a courtesy to a community outraged by his sexual assaults on underage victims, raping her was not a crime. Ned almost assuredly went to the gallows because his victims also included a nine-year-old white girl, whose rape, by law, demanded a punishment commensurate with the heinousness of the crime. Betty Gordon's rape was incidental to the charge.[44]

Of all the slaveholding states, only Mississippi took steps to criminalize slave-slave rape before the Civil War. A Madison County jury convicted the bondman George of a sexual assault upon a slave girl less than ten years old and sentenced him to death, but upon appeal in 1859, the state Supreme Court reversed the judgment against him. More than any other case, the trial of George exposed the gaping legal holes that left female slaves of any age vulnerable to rape. As one of the lawyers explained, "The crime of rape does not exist in this State between African slaves ... The regulations of law, as to the white race, on the subject of sexual intercourse, do not and cannot, for obvious reasons, apply to slaves; their intercourse is promiscuous, and the violation of a female slave by a male slave would be a mere assault and battery." Legally, "a slave can only commit a rape upon a white woman" or, as of 1858 in Mississippi, "Indian women" as well. The law, in short, had "no application to the sexual intercourse of African slaves." In handing down the verdict of the Mississippi Supreme Court, Justice William Harris agreed that neither common law nor the statutory law of that state "specifically include[d] rape by a slave on a female slave": "From a careful examination of our legislation on this subject, we are satisfied that there is no act which embraces either the attempted or actual commission of a rape by a slave on a female slave." Among whites, it was "a penitentiary offence" to gain "unlawful carnal knowledge of a child under the age of ten years," but "the carnal knowledge of a slave girl under 10 years of age by a slave is not a capital offense under our laws." A slave who committed rape, even upon the body of a young girl, Harris explained, "could be ... punished only at the suit of the master." As such, George was discharged.[45]

Setting aside issues of race and color, public outrage mounted. Pressured by their constituents' objections to the release of an enslaved pedophiliac rapist, the very next year, in 1860, Mississippi state legislators made "the actual or attempted commission of a rape by a negro or mulatto on a female negro or mulatto, under twelve years of age," a crime "punishable with death or whipping." As applied to black Mississippians, the law thus made the criminalization of rape a function of age rather than simply sex. Limited in its scope, it did not apply equally to all black women. Put bluntly, black men in Mississippi could legally rape black women, but not black girls. Despite the statute, female slaves and free blacks in Mississippi would remain vulnerable to intraracial rape throughout the greater portion of their lives.[46]

Adult women of color did gain, belatedly, some legal protection from rape in Georgia. In 1861, the state legislature redefined rape as "the carnal knowledge of a woman, *whether slave or free,* forcibly and against her will," but with the outbreak of Civil War and the demise of slavery as an institution four years later, no enslaved or free black man was charged, prosecuted, or convicted of raping a black woman by war's end. Antebellum southern white society proved slow to acknowledge black women's need for legal protection from the sexual depredations of black men. Most states passed no legislation whatsoever for their benefit.

The two states that did pass protective statutes either imposed narrow restrictions on the basis of age or were so tardy in crafting legislation that the law had no practical effect prior to abolition.[47]

The only possible source of institutional protection afforded female slaves' sexual honor came from southern evangelical churches. Enslaved women or the men concerned about their welfare on very rare occasion reported churchgoing slave sexual offenders to their local congregations. Disciplinary committees then dispensed with their cases. In July 1821, Fishing Creek Baptist Church in Wilkes County, Georgia, expelled the slave Isham for "attempting to defile a fellow servants wife." At Clarke's Station Baptist Church, the "Coloured Conference" charged the bondman "Emry for attempting to be intimate with Judah also a servant of J.H. Willis." After a thorough investigation, the church excluded Emry in March 1851, only to restore him eight months later upon "acknowledgements of his misconduct." Incidents of church intervention were so infrequent, however, that they made little difference for the masses of bondwomen. Across the South, punishment of an enslaved man's rape or attempt rape of a female slave was generally left to the discretion of the master, if it involved whites at all.[48]

Female slaves directed most of the violence they committed not at adult bondmen or bondwomen but at infants and children. From birth, enslaved children were raised within a framework of violence. Slaves daily confronted the potential wrath of white and black authority figures. Tender young eyes witnessed the master's, overseer's, or driver's lashing of parents, older siblings, extended kin, and other familiar folk in the quarters. Their ears heard the crack of the whip and the howls of pain. Odds were high that one day those infants and toddlers, too, would suffer the lash. Yet most slave children were more likely to be physically abused by a parent than by a master. Parental violence was common in the nineteenth century, more so among the poor and uneducated, irrespective of race, than among middle-class contemporaries. Under slavery, either parent might exercise harsh discipline, but mothers' primary role in raising children assured that they inflicted much of the violence enslaved children suffered.

The institution of slavery did nothing to stay parents' hand. Raising children, a challenging task under the best of circumstances, was made more difficult by the added strains bondage imposed upon slave parents. As Deborah Gray White, Wilma King, and others have noted, many enslaved mothers and fathers rationalized their seemingly cruel or abusive behaviors as an essential part of responsible parenting as slaves. Beating one's children instilled the discipline necessary for their offspring to survive in a world of slavery, imparting valuable lessons that would prevent future and even more severe whippings at the hands of the master. Parentally administered beatings gave enslaved children a fleeting taste of the type of pain the master had the power to inflict. King has also suggested that, since enslaved parents were sometimes whipped in the presence of their children, their own harsh correction of their children reestablished respect for parental authority.[49] Efforts to employ that strategy may have backfired, however, as undeveloped childhood minds may have failed to differentiate the abusive treatment meted out by parents from that administered by slaveholders. Enslaved children's mental fusion of distinct authority figures into one would have had ramifications for slave youngsters' impressions of their parents.

Even with the passage of decades, those held in slavery as children tended not to appreciate parents' violent correction. In WPA and other narratives, a number of former slaves characterized their parents as inordinately cruel. They of course may have disparaged them for the edification of their interviewers, who typically were whites receptive to hearing stories that confirmed their perceptions of blacks' poor parenting skills. Slaves' statements nevertheless merit consideration. Susan Snow, born into slavery in Wilcox County, Alabama, claimed a "wild and mean" mother who "was so mean to me I couldn't believe she was my mammy." Snow's mother may have believed strict, even harsh, parenting essential for instilling in her daughter the discipline necessary to navigate a life in bondage. But if that was the case, Snow evinced no indication of gratitude for the lessons imparted through her mother's technique. Considering that Snow's mother and other enslaved parents grew up in a world of whippings, beating their children likely seemed normative. Corporal punishment, perhaps administered to excess, also provided a means through which enslaved parents might displace their own aggression onto their children, an essentially defenseless population without the ability to effectively resist. No wonder, then, that decades removed from bondage, slave respondents recollecting their childhoods often remained resentful of abusive upbringings.[50]

Masters took note of the harsh parenting practiced in the quarters. Ironically, the very same owners who viewed whipping as a necessary form of correction for their bondpeople constructed an alternate narrative to explain the violence that took place on the plantation, one that recast paternalistic whites as the guardians and protectors of their enslaved people from the dangers posed by other slaves. "Unless the Negroes are carefully watched and made accountable for power lodged in their hands, it will be abused," declared the Reverend Charles Colcock Jones of Liberty County, Georgia. Just as enslaved husbands beat their wives, or slave drivers the charges under their command, "Parents will beat their children." Master Robert Collins of Macon reserved particular censure for female slaves. Enslaved mothers, he declared, will abuse their children so severely "that it becomes a prominent duty of owners and overseers, to keep peace, and prevent quarreling and disputes among them." Should conflict erupt, he continued, "summary punishment should follow." As slaveholders thus explained it, masters were needed to save slaves from themselves. "[W]e cannot help flogging them sometimes, when they ... fight," maintained one overseer on a Louisiana sugar plantation. "They would stab one another, if we did not interfere with the whip." Slaveholders believed themselves obligated to intervene in slaves' conflicts of all stripes to stave off violent outbreaks or to punish those that had already erupted.[51]

In their telling, whites frequently interceded on behalf of enslaved children to spare them the excessive abuse suffered at the hands of their parents. A South Carolina master "one time" whipped the mother of former slave Jake McLeod, as he remembered, "cause she whip me." The owner assuredly believed his intervention necessary, either to spare the youngster physical harm or to impart the paternalistic message that the master behaved in the impressionable slave boy's best interests. Former slaves occasionally professed that the white master or mistress of a plantation treated them better than their own enslaved parents did. "Ole Missus wuz kinder ter me den ma wuz," related Emily Dixon of Mississippi. "She ust [to] make her quit whipping me fer ma beat me to[o] hard." The apparent concern shown by Dixon's mistress and other slaveholders may have been less humanitarian than crassly economic. They may have interfered for no other reason than to preserve slaves' monetary value, or perhaps to wrest parental authority away from the enslaved mother and reaffirm where true power was deposited. But from the perspective of enslaved children such as Dixon, white persons had rescued them from their mothers' perceived maltreatment.[52]

Paradoxically, the same masters who deplored slaves' parental violence at times implemented plantation policies conducive to violence among enslaved children. On larger holdings, as the adult slaves toiled in the fields and older children delivered pails of water or performed other age-appropriate tasks, enslaved toddlers and other youngsters gathered in plantation nurseries tended by enslaved women no longer suitable for field labor. Enslaved "nurses"—essentially daycare workers—faced the unenviable task, recalled George Austin of

Cass County, Texas, of keeping "weuns out of fights[,] and dat was a man size job." Roughhousing commonly broke out in the nursery. Then as now, childhood play routinely turned mildly aggressive, from verbal bullying, teasing, and mocking, to more physical wrestling matches and outright fights. Although enslaved children's spats derived from a lack of restraint commensurate with their age rather than from any explicit desire to maim or kill, the challenge to corral misbehaving youngsters was nonetheless real for the bondwomen running plantation nurseries. The "nursery am wo'k aplenty fo' de womens dat runs it," conceded one ex-slave and product of a nursery, "'cause dey am s'posed to keep de kids outer fights." Every time the nurses' backs were turned, it seemed, a new row commenced.[53]

Teshan Young of Harrison County, Texas, and other enslaved nurses found mealtime the most challenging. No masters wished to see their slaves of any age inadvertently injured, but as Young knew from firsthand experience, "chilluns... gits to fightin' b'fo' you know it. 'Specially w'en dey eats." Many enslaved children on plantations across the Deep South ate unceremoniously from troughs, although the practice appears to have been more common in the more westerly slaveholding states. The children under Young's supervision were among those who ate from a "long bowl." Communal feeding tempted slave children to mischief. At the feeding trough, Mississippi-born Aron Carter could not resist the opportunity to "smear some tatters right smack in somebodys face." Whereas good-spirited humor shaded Carter's recollection of shenanigans at the trough, other slaves remembered it as a site of fierce competition where youngsters jockeyed for sustenance. A few shoves or solidly thrown elbows might make the difference between hunger and a belly not entirely empty. For ravenous young slaves at the trough, jostling for "co'n bread an' sweet milk or clabber," scrumptious morsels of cake, or pot liquor was well worth the effort. Armed with tin cups, wooden spoons, other utensils, or nothing more than their hands, children plunged into the free-for-all, all vying for one more mouthful of food at the expense of their enslaved playmates. That was when "de a'guments an' de fights" began.[54]

Close monitoring was required to preempt potential injury through fisticuffs at the trough. As the enslaved children under her watch fed on "mush, milk, bread, lasses, veg'tables an' sich," nurse Teshan Young patrolled the length of the trough with a "long switch... to make dem debils behabe" and avert any scuffles. Nearby in Harrison County, Texas, the master of Amy Else monitored mealtime personally. "He stood right there by us with a walking cane," Else reported. "If we got to fighting over the vitels, he whacked us over the head with his cane." Former slave Tom Hawkins understood how competition for the tasty scraps in the trough could prompt fights among his master's bondpeople, but thanks to strict patrolling, the slaves "all knowed better'n" to start trouble. Close supervision and fear of the repercussions minimized but never completely eliminated childhood sparring at dinner time.[55]

As nurse Teshan Young's experiences patrolling the trough suggest, enslaved children were sometimes disciplined at the hands of slaves other than their parents. Beyond mothers and fathers, the extended family of the slave quarters sometimes corrected errant offspring. When Dora Franks of Choctaw County, Mississippi, asked the elderly cook Aunt Caroline "for a piece o' white bread like de white folks eat," the aged bondwoman took it upon herself to contribute to the informal education of the youngster by smacking her in the face. Based on her years of experience in bondage and an adult's awareness of the harsh realities of slavery, Aunt Caroline felt obligated to teach the child a lesson about wanting things not suitable to her station. In response, she herself was punished for bloodying the girl's nose.[56]

Enslaved parents did not always appreciate the intervention of fellow slaves in the discipline of their children; to the contrary, some were defensive and outright hostile. Masters commonly appropriated the role of disciplinarian from enslaved mothers and fathers, but parents in the quarters need not tolerate that sort of meddling from fellow slaves. Enslaved mothers, in particular, were loathe to surrender the right to correct their offspring to another slave. That duty was incumbent upon them. William Flannagan, formerly enslaved in Attala County, Mississippi, recalled "his mother and another woman ... fighting over their children" until the owner intervened. As a young slave in Mississippi's Jefferson County, J. T. Tims bit his master's daughter. The white girl summoned William, another slave, "to come and beat me," Tims remembered, but "Ma had been peeping out from the kitchen watchin' the whole thing. When William come up to beat me, she come out with a big carving knife and told him, 'That's my child and if you hit him, I'll kill you.'" Had the white girl called her father, Tims's mother would have had little choice but to remain in the kitchen. She could not have contradicted a slave owner as boldly as she did William and the order from the master's young daughter.[57]

In conflicts with other bondpeople, enslaved mothers willingly defended with violence their right to discipline their children. Two bondwomen living on the same plantation in McLennan County, Texas, quarreled in 1863 over the punishment of an enslaved youngster. Mary asked Maria to whip Maria's daughter for lying and threatened to inflict the punishment herself if Maria refused. "I will not," Maria replied, "and if you do it there will be ... a big fuss." Half an hour later, Mary "found the child in the cook-house" and "smacked" her "on the bottom with her hand." At that moment, Maria rushed in and cried out, "You whip my child, God drast your eyes! I will kill you! I will cut your heart-strings out." She then made a bloody assault upon Mary with a butcher knife. Mary lingered in agony in bed for more than a month before dying of her injuries.[58]

Enslaved mothers stripped of parental control over their offspring might bring the weight of their church to bear on their behalf if the transgressor was also a churchgoer. Although it is not entirely clear how the case came to Island Creek Baptist Church's attention, odds are good that the bondwoman Sister Ginny initiated an investigation of the enslaved Brother Nat by complaining to the congregation that he disciplined her daughter without Ginny's consent. Nor can we be certain whether Nat was a slave driver exercising too much authority over Ginny's child or if this was a private affair between a stepfather, mother, and daughter that had become public. In any event, the congregation of Island Creek "had no fellowship for such Conduct." It declared Brother Nat "no Longer a member of this Church" in part due to his "unbrotherly conduct towards Sister Ginny in forcing her to stay in the House while he was Giving her Daughter the Lash."[59]

If the discipline of enslaved children rarely became a matter of church concern, neither was the issue often aired in southern courtrooms. The preponderance of all violence enslaved adults inflicted upon slave youngsters qualified as routine physical discipline, and the severity of the injuries incurred did not warrant any sort of court action. Tamer, an enslaved nurse in Kershaw District, South Carolina, proved an exception. She was arrested in 1844 for allegedly burning to death "the little girl Ann," another slave belonging to her master. In her capacity as nurse, Tamer was responsible for childcare and childrearing. Among her charges was the bondwoman Betsy's daughter Ann, who was still learning to master control of her bowels. According to slave witnesses, Tamer beat Ann "with a Leather Strap," tied "her hands and feet with cotton and Leather Strings," and developed "the habit of holding" Ann "to the fire as ... punishment" whenever the youngster dirtied the bed. One day the torture went too far, and Ann sustained injuries serious enough to result in her death. Tamer reportedly threatened another slave girl with identical treatment "if she said any thing about it," but her deed was exposed. A Court of Magistrates and Freeholders sentenced her to one month in jail and one hundred lashes. Several slaves testified that Tamer burned the youngster with Betsy's permission. The mother denied the allegation, insisting that she "would rather whip her" herself.[60] Betsy's account is probably more credible, for enslaved parents preferred to reserve for themselves the right to discipline their children inasmuch as that was possible in a slave society.

Though frequently the victims of their mothers' or fathers' aggression, enslaved children occasionally lashed out violently against their parents as well. When they did, depending upon the severity of the attack, masters, churches, or the law might become involved. Laurens District, South Carolina, slaveholder Thomas Hood owned an enslaved man named Frank, charged by Poplar Springs Baptist Church in 1853 "For whipping Vine his Mother." Another slave of Hood's, Moriah, was also accused at the same time of the identical "Crime of Whipin His mother." The brief entry in the church minutes offers no indication of the cause or causes lurking behind the allegations. Nor does it state if these were separate incidents or if Frank and Moriah were brothers who together beat the mother they shared. Both slaves acknowledged that they "done Rong," and the church, accepting their apologies as sincere, forgave them.[61]

Other attacks upon older slaves suggest a generational divide within the slave community. Elderly slaves viewed their world differently than younger ones, perhaps having reconciled themselves to bondage over the course of a lifetime in ways that headstrong adolescents had not. In January 1852, an incident involving two Giles County, Virginia, slaves revealed the resentment younger slaves sometimes felt toward their elders. Fourteen-year-old slave girl Mahala attacked the aged Aunt Sally with an axe because she considered her "the meanest negro in the world." According to fellow bondwomen, Mahala "hated aunt Sally as she did the devil" because "the old negro woman" was "in the habit of telling news on her," informing the master of "every thing she did." After the crime, Mahala attempted to deflect suspicion away from her by tearfully informing a white man of the terrible news of Sally's demise, but her own carelessness was her undoing. Mahala owned an incriminating "bloody apron," which she explained away by telling some that "[s]he had killed a chicken that morning" and others that she had been "chopping meat." In addition to the inconsistency of her stories, several slaves testified in court that they recalled hearing Mahala a month or two before the murder vow to kill Sally. Numerous witnesses, including one white woman, had all heard Mahala say that she could kill "aunt Sally ... as freely as ever she eat a mouthful of bread. That she could cut her up with an axe." Mahala thus telegraphed her crime. A spirited youth, Mahala supplied plenty of unspecified "news" for Sally to report to the master. Whatever her particular transgressions, they annoyed the elder bondwoman, whose life experience may have suggested that the best way to cope with bondage was to cooperate with the master, inform on errant bondpeople, and reap the potential rewards for loyalty.[62]

Most corporal punishment enslaved children endured qualified as standard childhood discipline. Because it was generally so utterly unremarkable, it generated few records despite its commonality. In contrast, cases of infanticide were rare but generated ample documentation. Female slaves were far more often convicted in courts of law for murdering not enslaved adults but rather infants and children. Virginia courts found bondwomen guilty of murdering almost twice as many slave infants and children as adult male and female slave victims combined, not that infanticide and child murder were either common or normal in the slaveholding South. The best proof is demographic. The total slave population of the United States grew from 1.1 million in 1810 to almost 4 million by 1860. Since the United States ceased its legal participation in the transatlantic slave trade on January 1, 1808, almost all of the increase in the number of slaves after that date was due to natural reproduction, along with some tens of thousands of slaves smuggled into country illegally thereafter. The rarity of infanticide and child murder assured that news of such tragedies elicited shock among white neighbors and other contemporaries. Despite bondwomen's degraded status, whites still recognized infanticide as "contrary to the laws of nature" regardless of race or color. "That a Mother should be the murderer of her own offspring ... at the moment of its birth," wrote one Tidewater Virginia master, "seems ... improbable," a "monstrous and unnatural ... deed."[63]

By its very nature, the frequency of infanticide is impossible to quantify. Masters typically handled infanticide cases privately on the plantation, determining for themselves the appropriate number of lashes for punishment. Slaveholders would have had little motivation for prosecuting in court a female slave who murdered her own children. They stood to lose not only the murdered newborn or child but a valuable, verifiably fecund bondwoman as well. Still, it happened. Some masters may not have wanted to keep a female slave capable of murder and might have preferred the compensation granted by the state. Moreover, in some cases the pregnancy or the circumstances surrounding the infanticide were so public and notorious that the murder could hardly have been concealed or confined to the plantation. As a result, while anecdotal evidence of infanticides appears sporadically in plantation records, slave narratives, abolitionist propaganda, and newspaper reports, the most thorough and systematic accounts available for analysis come from court records and the petitions the cases inspired.[64]

When cases of slave infanticide and child murder went before southern courts of law, there were no predetermined outcomes. Many times the legal system refused to punish enslaved women accused of such crimes. In Davidson County, North Carolina, the bondwoman Mary stood accused of killing her infant son in 1849. According to the indictment against her, after Mary delivered the child, she beat it "in and upon the head, temples, throat, windpipe, stomach, back, and sides," leaving "mortal bruises." Despite the gruesome and horrific description of the crime, the twelve-man jury found Mary not guilty. North Carolina law mandated that all jurors hold slaves, and the average juror in Mary's case owned about seventeen.[65]

Masters' economic interests undoubtedly contributed to many of the acquittals of female slaves charged with infanticide or child murder. Slaveholders served on juries or, in states such as Virginia or South Carolina without jury trials for slave crimes, as magistrates or freeholders. From these positions of authority, masters protected the interests of fellow slaveholders. Bondwomen who reportedly murdered their children already deprived their masters of future labor. If southern courts convicted female slaves and sentenced them to the maximum penalty of death, they robbed masters of yet another slave as well as her future offspring. Such thinking may have compelled the acquittals of Fauquier County, Virginia, slave Sall; bondwomen Jenny and Nancy, respectively from Richmond and Petersburg; and the enslaved Matilda of Chambers County, Alabama, all charged with infanticide or child murder. At the opposite end of the spectrum, the "Negro Woman Slave" Sall of Brunswick County, Virginia, was sentenced to hang after she confessed to "Feloniously Murdering her own Child." Between these extremes, a range of other punishments for infanticide was also possible. The Reverend Charles Colcock Jones of Georgia took his enslaved woman Lucy to court, charging her with the murder of her newborn baby. Lucy received a scant eight days in jail along with an assuredly painful ninety lashes. Polly, "a negro Girl" of Fairfield District, South Carolina, was to remain lodged in jail until all two hundred stripes of her sentence were administered in increments of seventy-five, seventy-five, and fifty. Union District bondwoman Clarissa, "tried in 1838 ... for killing her child Rachel," was slated "to be removed from the State & sold," a punishment tantamount to death for slaves permanently separated from their families.[66]

Virginia court records document few infanticides. From 1799 to 1860, at least

23 enslaved women and 1 enslaved man were convicted of no fewer than 28 cases of infanticide or child murder. Three female slaves were found guilty of killing more than 1 child. The bondwoman Jenny from Powhatan County murdered her 2 sons and a daughter, making her responsible for the deaths of more Virginia slaves than any other known bondperson. Neonaticides, defined as murders of newborns less than a day old, made up 17 (61 percent) of the 28 total deaths. The remaining 11 deaths (39 percent) qualified as filicides, or murders of any child older than 1 day. The 28 known infanticide and child murder cases in the 61 years from 1799 to 1860—a rate of 1 approximately every 2 years—represent, by modern standards, a remarkably low tally in a state with a slave population that grew from less than 350,000 in 1800 to almost half a million by 1860. Certainly an untold number of black infanticides are unaccounted for in the statistics, but even the small quantity of known infanticides and other murders of slave youngsters in Virginia outnumber the cases in which bondwomen murdered white children. Overall, it was more common for white women in Virginia than for female slaves to be prosecuted for infanticide.[67]

Infanticide cases pose distinct interpretive challenges for historians. Distinguishing genuine infanticides and child murders from other causes of death proves a virtually impossible task. Some enslaved women knew and attempted to exploit the fact that infanticide might be disguised as a stillbirth; conversely, stillbirth might also be mistaken for infanticide. When Fanny, "the milker" and occasional cook for Albemarle County, Virginia, master Alexander Terrell, was charged with infanticide, Terrell observed that Fanny had given birth to a stillborn infant in the past. Perhaps she had, or maybe this was the second child she had murdered.[68]

Some alleged infanticides may actually have been very late-term abortions. Enslaved women frequently consulted—often secretly, without their masters' knowledge—elderly female slaves, African American midwives, or other respected slaves with expertise regarding medicinal roots and herbs capable of treating a range of gynecological conditions and maladies. Expectant slave mothers occasionally terminated a pregnancy through the use of natural abortifacients. Sometimes one or more parents forced their hand. In June 1853, Warrior Creek Baptist Church in Laurens District, South Carolina, excluded "Limas a Black Brother" for "giving his daughter Medison [medicine]"—a tea—"to make her misscarry." Church records do not state whether it was the father's or daughter's idea to instigate the attempt to destroy the unborn child.[69]

If some apparent infanticides were abortions, others may have been tragic miscarriages. Enslaved women nurtured new life under less-than-optimal conditions, performing their normal work routines up to the time of delivery. When the Orange County, North Carolina, bondwoman Charity gave birth to a baby girl in May 1830, she concealed the live infant "under a large log lying ... in a secret and unfrequented spot." Charity explained that "she did not expect to have the child for five or six weeks." Although somewhat premature, the infant might well have lived, were it not for the blow Charity purportedly inflicted upon its head. Charity stated, however, that "if any injury had been done the child it was from the way it came into the world." One Surry County, Virginia, master was prepared to believe that his bondwoman Lizza had not murdered her newborn but, rather, that the injuries to the infant's face were "occasioned by the fall of the Child at its birth," since "no Person was present" to assist Lizza during delivery. Lizza may have consciously chosen to give birth alone and in secret so that she might more easily destroy the child, but her master was willing to give her the benefit of the doubt. Newborns were subject to a host of potential, life-threatening dangers during delivery that may have projected the appearance of infanticide.[70]

In the twenty-seven cases of infanticide and child murder for which enslaved women in Virginia were convicted, the deceased newborns and youngsters purportedly died from beatings, choking or suffocation, drowning, knife wounds, or exposure to the elements, among other causes. A coroner's inquest determined that Lizza had beaten her infant "against the Fence." Patrick County bondwoman Milly purportedly destroyed her infant child "by mashing the head and body" with "a certain large stone weighing fifty five pounds." In Missouri, the enslaved woman Jane of Callaway County failed in her attempt to poison her "infant child, Angeline." Days later, Jane "choked, suffocated and smothered" Angeline with "bed clothes" to complete the infant's demise.[71]

Infants' and children's corpses were found hidden in any number of locations: under a pile of leaves "at the root of a Poplar tree," "in a heap of Brush," "in the creek," "in a gully," "in one corner of the garden," "in [a] Plough furrow," in a deep ditch "covered ... over with some turf," "under a barrel in the yard," "in a hole in the stable yard (from which a post had been recently taken) [and] covered over with manure."[72] Matching the lifeless bodies to uncooperative mothers could be no simple task. Whereas a few, such as the enslaved woman Milly in Patrick County, "acknowledged freely and voluntarily" that a tiny corpse was that of "her child" and "that it was alive" when born, far more often, female slaves suspected of infanticide denied their pregnancies. Forced to work as normal throughout virtually the entirety of gestation, enslaved women often delivered babies with low birth weights. Physically, many would have lacked the abdominal rotundity characteristic of a robust, healthy pregnancy and could therefore realistically think they could cast doubt upon their condition. Time and again in court records, masters and others noted that an enslaved woman "seemed to be pregnant" or that they had "reason to suppose" a baby had been born. Female slaves capitalized on this uncertainty. In Prince Edward County, Virginia, Martha, who delivered an "infant boy child" on April 4, 1827, "denied she had any child." The Albemarle County bondwoman Fanny "emphatically denied" having committed infanticide, "stating that she had not been pregnant for the last three years." She added bluntly "that she was sick with her regular 'monthly courses.'"[73]

Denials of pregnancy sometimes withered in the face of evidence to the contrary. In Richmond, the enslaved woman Charlotte acknowledged that she delivered a baby only after the infant's body was found. She had given birth outdoors, "cut the umbilical cord with a pair of scissors," and thrown the afterbirth "in the yard" of a neighboring white man. Albemarle County's Fanny disavowed her pregnancy even when another female slave on her master's plantation "heard a child cry once" and "heard a snuffling in [the] next room." Not until presented "the placenta or afterbirth" did she relent. Fanny's fellow bondwoman also observed that Fanny "was *smaller* than usual," another useful piece of evidence for those inquiring into infanticide cases. Suspicious of a bondwoman's recent delivery, testified a white woman in Amherst County, "I put my hand around [the] waist" of Mary "& found that she was reduced."[74]

If unable to sustain the fiction that they had never been pregnant, some enslaved women insisted that their children were stillborn. Trapped in her lie that she had not been pregnant, Fanny of Albemarle County at last admitted she gave birth to a child "but stated that it was born dead, and that she had thrown it to the hogs and had seen them eat it." The full-term baby girl may have been stillborn, but the dead infant was discovered "concealed in the bed." Likewise, after her original denials of pregnancy were proven false, Prince Edward County's Martha reportedly placed her child in the garden because she "thought it was dead."[75]

In cases of doubt over pregnancies or stillbirths, masters often summoned a local doctor to complete an invasive gynecological exam over the spoken or silent objections of the enslaved woman. Even after a physician in Albemarle County "made an examination and found conclusive evidences of a recent delivery," Fanny persisted in her denials. In contrast, testified Dr. John E. Mount in Loudoun County, Virginia, the bondwoman Marietta "admitted it" after "I examined her." Marietta then claimed that the baby—by then "a good deal torn by dogs"—"was a still born child." Richmond slave Lucy admitted her pregnancy after Dr. James Beale's intimate investigations "found that she had been recently delivered of a child." Exposed both literally and figuratively, Lucy, like Marietta and many other female slaves accused of killing a newborn, then made the plausible assertion that the infant in question had been "born dead." In fact, Lucy insisted (until her baby's corpse was discovered) "that she had a miscarriage," in which "she had been delivered [only] of a mass of bones, as long as her hand." Doctors discounted slave mothers' claims of stillbirth in all known antebellum Virginia cases, most frequently determining instead that strangulation terminated the life of a living child. In Lucy's case, by contrast, Dr. Beale's postmortem examination revealed that the newborn died from "a blow on the side of its face."[76]

In at least four infanticide cases from the 1850s alone, Virginia physicians employed a forensic technique known as the hydrostatic test to determine if dead infants had been stillborn or murdered. Variously called the flotation test or the lung test, the hydrostatic test had been in use since the seventeenth century to detect infant murder. During an autopsy, doctors extracted the lungs, placed them in water, and observed their buoyancy. The test proceeded under the premise that lungs floated if respiration had occurred, as the air inhaled into the lungs made the organs lighter than water. Thus, for antebellum Virginia physicians, buoyant lungs were indicative of infanticide: the child had been born alive and breathed. Lungs that sank suggested stillbirth. Dr. Beale declared unequivocally in 1855 that the bondwoman Lucy's "child was born alive . . . : the lungs were filled with air, and floated in water when taken out."[77]

Although modern medicine confirms that the hydrostatic test for infanticide is neither definitive nor foolproof, nineteenth-century southern whites readily accepted any evidence of enslaved women as bad mothers. Cases of infanticide and child murder confirmed widespread assumptions about enslaved mothers' negligence and innate incompetence. According to one Georgia doctor, "many planters suppose . . . an unnatural tendency in the mother to destroy her offspring." One commentator in Virginia blamed the death of an enslaved infant on "the unnatural neglect of his infamous mother" and believed a second baby "murdered right out by his mother's neglect and barbarous cruelty." To believe the rhetoric, antebellum black women habitually killed their offspring, ignored enslaved children's basic needs, and treated them without the love and care expected of good, responsible mothers.[78]

In antebellum-era discourse, enslaved women's carelessness and incompetence as mothers was best exhibited through their purportedly pronounced tendency to smother their children. An overseer on the plantation of future president James Knox Polk recorded in late 1833 that "Elizabeth's child died last night." The bondwoman, he believed, "smothered it somehow." Reportedly, female slaves frequently rolled over onto their offspring as they co-slept, resulting in the suffocations of countless infants and children. A fraction of these overlaying deaths no doubt could be attributed to maternal exhaustion. New mothers, already residually tired from the physical ordeals of pregnancy and childbirth and now with added parental responsibilities, often returned to their customary work routines within a short month or so. Little surprise, then, that one former Mississippi field slave admitted that she fell asleep "nussin'" her infant son "and rolled over on him and smothered him to death." Between 1790 and 1860, more than 60,000 slave infants were allegedly smothered. In 1850 alone, slaves accounted for 82 percent of the more than 900 suffocation deaths in the United States. Of all enslaved infants who died that year, 9.3 percent had supposedly suffocated, compared to 1.2 percent of white infants. Michael P. Johnson's study of infanticide in the slave South concludes, however, that enslaved women neither intentionally nor accidentally smothered their children, as white contemporaries so often assumed. His study shows, rather, that slave infants suffered from an unusually high incidence of sudden infant death syndrome (SIDS). Gross disregard for proper prenatal care, female slaves' grueling work regimens late into their pregnancies, and nutritional deficiencies in their diet combined to make SIDS more prevalent among slave than white infants. Those same factors could have contributed to the delivery of stillborn babies.[79]

But occasionally, as Kelli M. Black has observed, "'smothering' was simply 'smothering.'" For enslaved mothers seeking to destroy an infant or child, suffocation was clean, bloodless, and relatively nonviolent. Deaths by smothering appeared natural and might be attributed to other causes, thereby deflecting suspicion away from the mother. If punished at all, the crime of smothering was addressed on the plantation. All of those enslaved women charged in Virginia courts of law with choking or suffocating their children had allegedly been more aggressive in completing their acts of murder. In Culpeper County, the whites who examined the corpse of Suckey's child in 1857 "found that a string of linsey cloth was wrapped twice tightly around the neck and tied fast." They concluded that "the pressure of the string was sufficient to have produced suffocation." Prince Edward County slave Martha similarly attempted to strangle her infant son, but "the string was not strong [and] it broke." She instead smashed his skull. When discovered, the boy was barely alive and making "a noise something like a puppy" as "blood discharged from the eye, mouth and nose." Hanover County, Virginia, slave woman Caroline allegedly "choak[ed], suffocate[d], and strangle[d]" her newborn daughter with her bare hands and cloths before leaving her out to freeze in "the night air." Violent, sensational strangulations that created a neighborhood stir invited court actions, but comparatively benign smotherings did not.[80]

Infanticide ended a child's life and changed that of the mother forever. It was a desperate action indicative of profound emotional strain and turmoil. As historian Kirsten Fischer has observed, those enslaved women who ultimately disposed of their children felt "the burden of an undesired pregnancy" and refused "to accept fertility as fate." But their odds of successfully committing infanticide without facing potentially dire consequences were slim. Any woman whose belly swelled noticeably, making it impossible to conceal her pregnancy, was automatically disadvantaged. The slave quarters—and early nineteenth-century American society generally—lacked privacy. Keeping a pregnancy secret was difficult when one or perhaps two families shared a small, crowded slave cabin. Moreover, infanticide was no easy crime to commit. Enslaved women needed to select a secluded location, deliver the baby, cut the umbilical cord, kill the infant quickly and quietly, dispose of the body, clean or destroy any bloodied, incriminating sheets or clothing, and then look, work, and act as normal, as if nothing had happened. Assuming no enslaved woman could accomplish all of these steps undetected, infanticide, finally, demanded a conspiracy of silence among the residents of the quarters. Polly, held in slavery in Fairfield District, South Carolina, confronted this host of challenges when she committed infanticide in 1860. One of her own daughters could not help but notice that, one morning, "her mother was not as large as she formaly was." The inquisitive girl "went in the field," "hunted in a gul[l]y," and located a dead infant, "covered up." When she presented the corpse to her mother, the bondwoman acknowledged her deed.[81]

What provoked enslaved women to kill their children? They must have had a compelling rationale for committing such a serious, irreversible crime. "It is impossible . . . to discern all of the complex motives behind such acts," historian Steven Deyle correctly observes. The records available to scholars, declares Kelli M. Black, "are practically useless for ascertaining an infanticidal mother's real motivation." It is in fact easy to disbelieve the statement of the Powhatan County, Virginia, bondwoman Jenny who, when asked why she drowned her three children, replied, "it was because she could not make the oldest boy obey her and mind the other children." Nevertheless, courtroom testimony from Virginia offers some indication of motivation, and even more telling are the various petitions for clemency filed with the governors of the Commonwealth. Enslaved female convicts frequently garnered petitions on their behalf from masters and other white male citizens of the neighborhood who were acquainted with them. The vast majority of all memorials submitted in favor of enslaved women sought mercy for bondwomen found guilty of infanticide and pleaded not for a complete pardon but rather, out of respect for the judicial system, for a reduction in sentence from execution to sale and transportation. Such petitions provide some of the most intriguing content regarding slave infanticide and child murder cases and their possible motives.[82]

The "real motivation" may in fact often have been what would be diagnosed today as postpartum depression. Despite some contemporary physicians' or midwives' recognition of a psychological condition labeled "puerperal insanity" or "puerperal mania" that manifested in some recently delivered women, most nineteenth-century southerners would have been unaware of these discussions and not made that medical assessment. Nevertheless, hormonal changes associated with a recent birth probably did factor into some portion of the infanticides and child murders committed by bondwomen. Struggling to explain their actions, more than one infanticidal slave mother concluded that "the Devil made her" kill her child. In the nineteenth century, such language served as code for biological or chemical processes not yet understood by science, much less the public. Witnesses familiar with the enslaved mother Vicy of Madison County, Missouri, recognized that "she was not at herself" when she reportedly smothered her six-month-old son Stephen in 1845, or "else she would not have done the act." As it was, "there was such a weight upon her she was obliged to kill it." Although it was standard practice for antebellum court records to state that bondwomen charged with infanticide were "Moved and Seduced by the Instigation of the Devil," the words used in indictments also betrayed nineteenth-century struggles to come to terms with physical, mental, and emotional states they lacked the knowledge to comprehend or articulate fully.[83]

Infants or children were sometimes casualties of murder-suicides initiated by depressed, despondent mothers. In 1796, an enslaved woman in Savannah hurled her five- and ten-year-old sons into a well before leaping in behind them. Unwilling to tolerate slavery any longer, the mother resolved to commit suicide, but she refused to abandon her children to the torments of bondage in her absence. In another, nearly identical case from Georgia, the twenty-six-year-old domestic servant Becky dumped her three children into a well in 1860 and then jumped in herself. The following day, Becky's master fished her out alive, but all the children had perished. According to Becky's own confession, she was simply "tired of life" and decided to end her suffering. She committed the three murders because she "didn't want to leave any children behind her." Becky's motivation may have been multilayered, however. Becky admitted that she hoped to damage her owner's family financially by destroying her children. In a separate, conflicting confession, she claimed the only reason she had jumped into the well at all was to make sure that her offspring drowned.[84]

In the most widely publicized infanticide case of the antebellum era, an enslaved woman preferred that her children die rather than live under slavery. Margaret Garner, a runaway slave trapped by slave catchers with her fugitive family in a Cincinnati, Ohio, cabin, declared in 1856 "that she would kill herself and her children before she would return to bondage." Frantic and desperate, she slashed her three-year-old daughter's throat with a butcher knife to prevent her recapture and return to slavery. Using either the same knife or a coal shovel, she attempted to take the lives of her other three children as well but was restrained before accomplishing her object. After her apprehension and return to Kentucky, Garner was sold to Mississippi. En route to the Deep South, the boat she was aboard collided with another vessel on the Ohio River. Either the force of the impact threw Garner and an infant daughter into the water, or Garner took advantage of the chaotic moment to throw the girl in before making her own suicidal plunge. A black cook aboard one of the boats rescued Garner, but her baby girl drowned. Garner was ecstatic. She demonstrated "frantic joy" that death had liberated a second of her children. The institution of slavery could turn protective maternal instincts on their heads as a few mothers concluded that dying represented the best protection from bondage.[85]

Several historians have depicted infanticide as a form of resistance to the system of slavery. For years, scholars defined "resistance" narrowly, referring to slave runaways and rebels, the overwhelming majority of whom were male. They also recognized breaking or "losing" tools, working slowly when the master's back was turned, and theft as forms of "day-to-day" resistance. More recently, historians have examined the theme of slave resistance through a consciously gendered lens. Stephanie M. H. Camp, Jennifer L. Morgan, and others indicate the ways peculiar to their sex in which enslaved women challenged the terms and conditions of bondage. In such studies, female reproduction emerges as contested terrain, a form of gendered resistance rooted in the enslaved female body. In addition to bondwomen regulating their own fertility or inducing abortion, infanticide may be understood within this same conceptual framework. Infanticide as a form of "gynecological resistance," one scholar suggests, represented a covert exercise of bodily autonomy. Through infanticide, enslaved women seized control of their bodies and rejected the expectation of virtually all masters that female slaves reproduce and thereby augment the wealth of their owners. When they killed their children they wreaked vengeance upon their masters by depriving them of the next generation of bound labor. In this way, infanticide marked an egregious infringement on the master's property rights.[86]

Various efforts to spite the master did make casualties of enslaved infants and children. In retribution for a punishment she deemed too harsh for striking another bondwoman with a hoe, Betty seized and "threw her little son, Simon, in the well." The murder earned her compulsory conveyance from Alabama to the dreaded state of Louisiana. A Civil War–era Georgia bondwoman named Becky defied her master's authority by feigning pregnancy to avoid work. Skeptical, her owner scheduled her a gynecological appointment and threatened to whip her if it was proven she had deceived him. To the master's surprise, the midwife summoned to examine Becky announced that the slave woman had already given birth. Through no coincidence, however, a nine-month-old baby disappeared from a neighboring plantation at the same time. Either Becky or an accomplice had kidnapped the child and, to perpetuate her ruse that it was hers, extracted its teeth and cut off the tip of its navel to give it the appearance of a newborn. The missing infant was located in Becky's cabin, but the amateur surgeries it suffered were enough to kill it. Becky was convicted of manslaughter and sentenced to two hundred stripes.[87]

Under bondage, infanticide may be construed as a product of love and maternal affection warped by the institution of slavery. A minute fraction of all enslaved mothers preferred that their children die than live in chains. The Madison County, Missouri, bondwoman Vicy reportedly pondered killing her infant son for "about three weeks" before committing the deed. She later confessed "that she had smothered her baby on purpose" because now "it was free." The distorted form of liberation achieved through death spared children the horrors of slavery and a lifetime of abuse. In his travels, Frederick Law Olmsted heard about the case of an enslaved woman in Alabama who confessed to murdering her child because her mistress—also the wife of the child's father—"treated it so cruelly." The mother therefore "killed it to save it from further suffering." In Georgia, an enslaved woman named Rene killed her two girls, Amanda and Fanny, in 1858. Rene explained that their master, Ephraim Gross, abused them, and "she would rather that they were dead." After failing in her attempt to drown the children, Rene cut their throats with an axe and dumped the bodies in a Dade County spring.[88]

Infanticidal slave mothers do not appear to have disproportionately targeted children of one sex or the other. Many enslaved girls and women experienced the sexual abuse and exploitation of masters, overseers, and other white men. Possibly acquainted with the hazards peculiar to their sex, enslaved mothers might have employed infanticide more frequently against daughters than sons as a possible means of sparing them a future of sexual violence with which many bondwomen were all too familiar. In the documented cases from antebellum Virginia, however, daughters proved no more likely to be victims of infanticide than sons; indeed, in the eighteen cases for which the sex of the victim is known, there were an equal number of male and female victims. Infanticides and child murders terminated the lives and denied masters the future labor of at least nine girls and at least nine boys born in bondage, with the sex of ten victims unknown. (See table 8.2.) Infanticide marked less a gender-specific assault upon slaveholders' claims of mastery over enslaved sexuality than a broad rejection of the institution of slavery altogether.

In particular, stories abound of infanticides and child murders designed to prevent the division of enslaved families through sale. These violent actions implicitly and dramatically condemned the domestic slave trade. Infanticides, too, severed enslaved parents from their children, but separation took place on slaves' own terms. Wherever there were surplus slaves, most commonly in the Upper South and, by the 1820s, in the older slaveholding states of the South Atlantic seaboard, enslaved mothers might employ this strategy to prevent their children from being carried away to the cotton frontier or, worse still by reputation, the sugar plantations of Louisiana. The formerly enslaved Lewis Clarke of Kentucky recorded in his autobiography that one distraught "slave mother . . . took her child into the cellar and killed it . . . to prevent being separated from her child" by the commerce in slaves. An enslaved mother in Tennessee, dreading her impending sale from family, fell into a "frenzy and drowned her two Children." One respondent to a WPA interviewer related the story of a bondwoman whose master had made a habit of selling her children once they reached the age of one or two: "he'd sell them and it would break her heart. She never got to keep them." Forced to surrender three children already, the woman determined not to let her owner sell her fourth baby. Instead, when the infant was about two months old,

Table 8.2. Virginia Infanticide and Child Murder Victims by Sex, 1799–1860

Victim's Sex	Infant*	Child	Total
Male	4	5	9
Female	5	4	9
Unknown	8	2	10
	17	11	28**

* Infant here is defined as a newborn only. In one case, a six-week-old is counted as a child.
** Only one of the total of twenty-eight, a child of unknown sex, was killed by an enslaved man.

she "give it something out of a bottle" that fatally poisoned it. "'Course didn't nobody tell on her" because the other slaves understood her rationale. The system of slavery had driven her to desperation and the decision to kill a baby whom she loved.[89]

Such stories became potent weapons in abolitionists' arsenal. Propaganda pieces condemned slavery not only for breaking apart enslaved families through sale but also for imposing stresses on families that resulted in the tragic deaths of innocent children. It is impossible to gauge with any precision how common infanticide or child murder was, for any reason, but scholars agree that such forms of violence did not pose a serious threat to the institution of slavery. Eugene D. Genovese observes that infanticide constituted neither "a major problem" nor "an ordinary form of 'resistance' for the slaves." Although infanticide can be understood within the resistance paradigm, virtually all enslaved mothers loved their children too much to sacrifice them for the sake of making a political statement.[90]

Records from antebellum Virginia suggest that shame, grounded in enslaved women's own sense of gendered identity, provided another possible motivation for infanticide and child murder. In early America, infanticide was almost exclusively a female crime, with far more documented cases among whites than blacks. Courts typically prosecuted for infanticide unmarried white women accused of murdering their newborns. Recent research suggests that, among white women of the poor and laboring class, poverty motivated a substantial portion of all infanticides. Short on time and money, working-class white women unable to afford or care for a baby destroyed it at birth. But as Georgia's Reverend Charles

Colcock Jones argued, for female slaves, the institution of slavery removed the economic inducement to infanticide prevalent among poor white women. "[T]he crime of *Infanticide*," he wrote, is "restrained in good measure" within the slave community in part because bondwomen could count on their owners' financial support for their offspring. Moreover, he added, the punishments meted out for infanticide and child murder offered a sufficient deterrent to the crime.[91]

Jones also posited that infanticide was so rare among slaves because the innate "moral degradation of the people ... takes away the disgrace of bastardy." American society often presumed that white women committed infanticide in a desperate attempt to hide the shame of an illegitimate birth, and some certainly did. Respectable society demanded the careful guardianship of white female chastity. In contrast, southern whites commonly accepted a contradictory image for enslaved women, the Jezebel stereotype of unrestrained passion and promiscuity. The white popular imagination alleged that female slaves lacked virtue and therefore could not suffer the shame and dishonor associated with certain pregnancies that might prompt a white woman to murder her offspring. But in one exception to the general rule, petitioners on behalf of the Prince Edward County, Virginia, bondwoman Martha asserted "that the injuries done [her infant] were inflicted ... to conceal the shame of b[e]aring a child" out of wedlock.[92]

Martha's white petitioners made a curious argument since slaves could not lawfully marry. In chastising a perceived lack of sexual ethics among slave women, Jones and other whites frequently overlooked the structural fact that southern legal codes' refusal to recognize slave marriages made bastards of *all* enslaved newborns. The clerk of the Orange County, North Carolina, court that heard the case of the bondwoman Charity, "a single woman" charged in 1830 with killing "her female infant child by means of neglect & unlawful violence," had a better grasp of the legal reality. He recorded explicitly that the "said female child was by the laws of this State a bastard." That bastardy was the legal norm for births among bondwomen might have reduced bondwomen's feelings of dishonor associated with bearing children out of wedlock.[93]

But in defiance of legal statute, slave marriages proved so deeply entrenched and widely recognized by custom throughout the South that some female slaves indeed expressed the shame attached to childbirth in the absence of a husband. A Culpeper County, Virginia, court believed that the slave Suckey murdered her baby girl "not from any feelings of malice but from a sense of shame & pride of character." Suckey's master testified during his slave's trial that "she had been married a good many years ago to a slave belonging to a neighbor ... and by him had two children." Unfortunately for Suckey, "her husband had been carried off to the South several years ago," a victim of the internal slave trade. Ever since her domestic arrangements had been irreversibly altered, her master continued, she "had maintained a good character in all respects," a remark that implied Suckey's fidelity to an absent spouse. Therefore, when her owner "suspected from her appearance and other symptoms that she was pregnant," he sent for a physician from Alexandria, who concurred that Suckey "was *probably* pregnant." Suckey, however, "protested with great earnestness that she was not." We cannot know the precise source or sources of her objections. They perhaps stemmed from fears that her master would someday separate her from her child. If among the minority of all slaves exposed to Christian religious teachings, she may have suffered from a heightened sense of guilt over the extramarital sex responsible for her pregnancy. Or she may have fretted over a loss of honor among her fellow slaves after moving on from her prior marital commitment.[94]

In scattered infanticide cases, Virginia bondwomen clearly indicated that white paternity was a source of shame. Many slaveholders across the South exercised sexual mastery in the quarters, extorting sexual favors from enslaved women or blatantly forcing themselves upon them against their will. Scholars have noted that bondwomen felt "the dishonor of rape" by masters or other white men, and inevitably some of these encounters resulted in pregnancy. It makes abundant sense that some enslaved women might have wished to abort or kill the by-products of sexual coercion and rape. Under such conditions, infanticidal violence became a means to terminate an unwanted pregnancy that was itself the result of violence. Although we usually cannot know the specific context in which conception took place, Brooke County, Virginia, slave Letty, convicted of infanticide, said "that if the child had been one of her own color she would not have done as she had done." If Letty intended only to damage the economic interests of her master in an act of resistance, the infant's particular hue was irrelevant. Her remark raises the prospect that a mixed-race child proved an embarrassment for some black mothers in the quarters, a living reminder of sexual coercion and exploitation and an affront to enslaved husbands. Under this scenario, killing the newborn destroyed the evidence of an unwanted encounter while it simultaneously—if the father was the owner—spited the master by denying him her offspring. It may have been no accident that the runaway bondwoman Margaret Garner, the infamous child murderer, slit the throat of her daughter just as her master burst into the room where her family was sheltered. According to reports, "The murdered child was almost white, and was a little girl of rare beauty." Gazing upon the horrific scene, Garner's distraught master—and probable father of the child—took up the small corpse, clutched it close, and refused to surrender it to white authorities.[95]

Masters who found sexual pleasure in the quarters augmented their property holdings when their dalliances produced children, but not all white fathers welcomed the arrival of enslaved progeny. Petitioners for Letty stated that the unidentified father of her "illegitimate child" was a married "free white man" who "may have moved her to the commission of the crime," perhaps to conceal his sexual indiscretions from his wife, family, or larger community. In a similar case, "the Common report" about Lucy, an "unhappy Black girl" in Lewis County, Virginia, was "that her Child was by a Whight Man," and according to the slave, "her life was threaten[e]d if she . . . should ever let her case be known." The abandonment and subsequent death of her child reportedly "was actuated by fear, occasioned by threats of the consequences, in case she should have another Molatto child[,] She having had one some time before." White fathers may have forced Letty and Lucy to kill their infants or played another, even more direct and insidious role in their deaths.[96]

Regardless of a child's paternity, bondwomen's sense of shame over infanticide charges pulsates through many of the court records and governors' petitions documenting their turmoil. Enslaved women charged with infanticide frequently expressed intense anxiety over their characters and reputations. Fanny, of Albemarle County, denied strangling her full-term baby girl, explained her owner, because "[t]he prisoner is a woman of great pride, and thinks a great deal of her virtue." After finally admitting that she had given birth, Fanny begged either the master or the doctor who examined her "to conceal the fact and not expose her" because she dreaded others learning of either her pregnancy or her crime. When the Henrico County bondwoman Kesiah gave birth in 1834, she covered the infant's mouth with her hand to muffle the cries that might draw attention to her, she "being very much ashamed at her having had a child." Both of these accounts suggest a form of sexual virtue present among bondwomen that would have been all too familiar to their female counterparts in respectable, nineteenth-century white society.[97]

White petitioners to the governor on Kesiah's behalf suggested that the slave's age—"not more than seventeen years old"—may also have been a source of shame. Studies have shown that the typical bondwoman did not bear her first child until she reached her very late teens or early twenties, so Kesiah did deliver her baby somewhat earlier than was typical.[98] Penitentiary and court records from Vir-

Table 8.3. Ages of Female Slaves in Virginia Convicted of Murder

Year	County	Name	Age
Infanticides and child murders			
1818	Buckingham	Polly	18
1819	Surry	Liza/Lizza	17/18
1822	Brooke	Letty/Letitia	28
1824	Louisa	Milly/Mildred	30
1827	Prince Edward	Martha	18
1833	Fairfax	Ally/Alley	19
1834	Henrico	Kesiah	17/18
1855	Richmond (city)	Lucy	16/18
1860	Amherst	Mary	18
Other murders			
1833	Greensville	Clary/Clara	30
1837	Bedford	Viney/Lavinia	25
1840	Southampton	Malinda	20
1843	Pendleton	Maria McCoy	26
1852	Giles	Mahala	14/15

ginia supply the specific ages of fourteen enslaved women found guilty of murder. Of the five convicted of killing adults, the average age was twenty-three. Of the nine convicted of infanticide or child murder, the average fell closer to twenty, but seven were teenagers. For such young bondwomen, barely removed from childhood themselves, bearing a child may have brought with it a certain stigma within the quarters.[99] (See table 8.3.)

Signers of memorials to the governor on convicted bondwomen's behalf often noted the respectability of the white petitioners themselves or the upwelling of popular sentiment in the local white community in favor of leniency, but they cited most frequently the youthful age and heretofore "excellent character" of the convicted.[100] In one petition to Virginia's governor, the five magistrates who presided over the trial as well as a physician shifted blame for an infanticide from a teenaged slave to her mother. The signers described "Maria the Mother of Lucy," the convict, as "more guilty than Lucy. Lucy was under her control, almost constantly under her eye, slept in the same room with her, and could not have committed the act without her knowledge." Suspicion was strong that Maria had helped keep Lucy's pregnancy secret, cut the umbilical cord during delivery, and concealed the infant's death. "[W]e ... do not think," the memorialists concluded, "that the thought of murdering the child originated with [Lucy]." The magistrates stated that they would have preferred to commute Lucy's punishment "from death to ... transportation, if we had believed that we had the legal power to do so." They therefore appealed to the governor for mercy.[101]

The Virginia courts that adjudicated the trials of enslaved women convicted of infanticide or child murder regularly urged gubernatorial clemency. After finding the bondwoman Ally guilty of infanticide in 1833, "three of the Justices ... recommend[ed] the said Ally to the Executive as a fit subject to be transported." One favored a complete pardon. Another court "earnestly recommend[ed] to the Executive to commute the punishment of ... slave Lucy," just sentenced to death for infanticide in 1852, "to sale and transportation, because of her youth and the excellent character which she has borne up to the time of this crime."[102]

If petitions in convicted bondwomen's favor may be read as something more than merely a projection of white values onto female slaves, young or unmarried slave mothers, much like white women who proved careless with their virtue, at times did feel stigmatized, either in the quarters or in the broader community, when they violated social convention. At least some female slaves who gave birth either out of wedlock, to a mixed-race child, or at a young age believed that the delivery impugned the good character they possessed and strove to maintain. The inevitable question is whether the "shame" Virginia whites found so apparent within bondwomen such as Suckey, Fanny, or Kesiah was imagined, genuine, or a clever performance calculated to extract sympathy in a time of personal desperation by exploiting commonly held white assumptions. We cannot know with absolute certainty. Although it is possible that white observers detected and magnified issues of sexual honor in slave infanticide cases because they were culturally predisposed to see them, bondwomen themselves voiced expressions of concern over their reputations and shame. If their stated anxieties were somehow not legitimate, at the very least female slaves betrayed a remarkably acute understanding of gendered notions of sexual honor and nineteenth-century conventions of proper female sexual comportment.

Isolated cases of slave suicide reinforce the pattern of enslaved female honor evident in so many episodes of infanticide. Ex-slave H. C. Bruce's autobiography confirms the significance that many female slaves attached to childbirth within the confines of marriage. Bruce related the story of a "very good-looking" slave girl in Missouri who drowned herself in 1858 to avoid the "dishonor and loss of character" associated with giving birth outside the bonds of matrimony. As a few southern whites realized, this was distinctly not the moral code of the Jezebel. The white Elizabeth Lyle Saxon reminisced decades after the Civil War that her hired slave Nellie and Nellie's sister Clara each "felt the disgrace" of Nellie becoming a mother "so keenly they attempted suicide."[103]

Aided in their decision-making process by petitions that emphasized female slaves' worthy character, Virginia's governors frequently granted clemency to those enslaved women convicted of infanticide. Of the twenty-three Virginia bondwomen found guilty of that crime between 1799 and 1860, fifteen were condemned to "suffer death for Child murder" and eight to sale and transportation out of the United States. Almost assuredly, however, bondwomen escaped execution, with only two of the twenty-three (9 percent) meeting their fate at the gallows. Enslaved women garnered far more petitions to the governor on their behalf than did the typical male slave found guilty of murder. Governors always needed to weigh the social, economic, and political costs and benefits of executing a convicted slave, but they generally looked more favorably upon appeals to spare bondwomen rather than bondmen. Male slaves with violent proclivities posed the greater physical threat to slaveholding society. The pattern of gubernatorial clemency also suggested some possible gender-based squeamishness about executing female slaves, whose procreative power replicated the institution of slavery. Governors' intervention was most forthcoming, reductions of sentences most generously dispensed, in cases of infanticide or child murder. Though tragic, the deaths of unproductive slave infants and children affected slaveholder profits in the distant future and were not as immediately detrimental to masters' economic interests as the loss of adult slave men and women.

Nevertheless, no enslaved woman found guilty of infanticide or child murder received a full pardon. Three members of the Hustings Court in Richmond sought executive clemency for the bondwoman Charlotte in 1854, offering assurances "that such exercise of the pardoning power will not be attended by bad consequences," but the governor disagreed and rejected the appeal. To excuse infanticides and child murders altogether set too dangerous an example in a slaveholding society. Instead, Virginia governors reprieved two female slaves convicted of infanticide (9 percent) to hard labor on the public works, but nineteen of the twenty-three (83 percent) were sold and transported out of the United States. In the case of Prince Edward County bondwoman Martha, Governor William B. Giles initially "determined not to interfere" "and leave the law to take its course" but then changed his mind. Martha was sold and transported. Upon "careful examination" of the 1857 trial record of Powhatan County slave Opha Jane, wrote Governor Henry A. Wise, "I ordered the sentence of death to be commuted to sale and transportation, for reason of uncertainty in the evidence, and because the prisoner was recommended by the court to the mercy of the executive." The same day, Wise commuted the sentence of Culpeper County slave Suckey to sale and transportation as well. Wise's interventions should not suggest that Virginia's governors automatically reduced the sentences of female slave convicts recommended to mercy. Despite the reputed "excellent good Character" of Patrick County bondwoman Milly prior to her smashing her infant with a "large stone," Governor John Tyler twice "refuse[d] to interfere" with her sentence. In 1826, Milly became the last bondwoman in Virginia to hang for committing infanticide.[104]

A look at courtroom testimony, gubernatorial petitions, and slave narratives concerning bondwomen's violent behaviors hints at the priorities of enslaved femininity. Although less numerous than episodes involving enslaved men exclusively, incidents of enslaved female violence offer unexpected insights into bondwomen's lives. Female slaves' assaults upon other bondwomen, the rapes inflicted upon them by slave men, parental violence, and cases of infanticide and child murder all combine to expose the values of enslaved women and to tell us something about bondwomen's gendered identities in slavery. Against other female slaves they employed violence to preserve relationships and families and to maintain their good word and reputation inside the slave community. In these ways, enslaved female honor coincided with that of enslaved men. Yet bondwomen's honor also intersected with that of white women. Although vulnerable to white male sexual assaults, female slaves, like their white sisters, did make efforts to seize control over their sexual lives and protect their sexual honor. When the violators of enslaved female bodies were white men, options for resisting were limited. But when male slaves attempted to have their way with a bondwoman, she could more readily seize control of her sexuality, deny consent, and violently defend herself from assault. Whenever possible, bondwomen not only asserted control over their own bodies but also the lives of those they brought into the world. For female slaves, childbirth fostered a range of possible emotions, from joy to shame and bittersweet feelings in between. Through violent discipline, enslaved women laid claim to their rights as parents but also vented their own aggression against the one group of slaves more vulnerable than them. Defenseless infants and children sometimes became victims in bondwomen's violent efforts to govern their own reproductive powers, to deny masters a future generation of enslaved labor, or to uphold enslaved women's own notions of female honor based on a set of sexual ethics uniquely forged in the crucible of slavery. Violence played an essential role in bondwomen's process of defining enslaved femininity.

EPILOGUE
"Black-on-Black Violence" in Historical Perspective

BORN INTO BONDAGE in Bedford County, Tennessee, in 1851, George W. Arnold recalled decades later a violent altercation he had with an enslaved cook named Johny Sims. Sims had overimbibed a quantity of "Holland rum" prior to a much anticipated candy pull. But he had not yet had his fill. Armed with a full "quart bottle," he planned to continue his merriment at the event. Arnold and the others in his company debated whether their inebriated compatriot should join them in attendance. "Don't you see he is drunk?" asked one. The prospect of one drunken slave spoiling the festivities was far too great a risk for the other bondmen to tolerate. Arnold, who described Sims as "my friend, my more than brother," casually slung an arm "about his shoulders and tried to tell him he had better sleep a while before we started." Unexpectedly, Sims, his inhibitions liberated by intoxication, "drew out his knife" from his pocket "and with one thrust, cut a deep gash" in Arnold's neck. In the "terrible fight" that ensued, Arnold was "knocked over" and hit his head. His defensive instincts then kicked in. He grabbed the nearest weapon at hand—an axe—and struck his attacker and erstwhile friend. As Arnold explained it, "The thud of the ax brought me to my senses as our blood mingled." Mental clarity returned suddenly to Sims as well. "Oh, George," he cried, "what an awful thing we have done? We have never said a cross word to each other and now, look at us both." Injured and bleeding, a dispirited Sims ambled off into the night and "was never seen again." Neither the attempt to follow the trail of blood, inquiries made throughout the neighborhood, nor a telltale circling of buzzards overhead provided any clue to Sims's whereabouts. Though he was presumed dead, his body was never found.[1]

Such violent episodes nourished nineteenth-century blacks' widespread belief in the supernatural. Remorseful, wracked by anguish, and denied the benefit of closure, Arnold could not help but replay the nightmarish series of events in his head. "For two years," Arnold recounted, Sims "haunted my pillow and went beside me night and day. His blood was on my hands." Sims's spectral presence stalked Arnold "beyond endurance." To escape the dogged phantom shadowing him, Arnold secured work on a river because folk wisdom maintained "that the ghost of a person you had wronged would not cross water to haunt you." In another case, former Floyd County, Georgia, bondwoman Callie Elder remembered that, on the plantation where she resided, "One of de cabins was allus ha'nted atter some of de slaves got kilt in it whilst dey was fightin'. Nobody never could live in dat cabin no more atter dat widout ha'nts gittin' atter 'em." The restless spirits dwelling within constantly moved chairs and made knocking sounds on the walls to the torment of any living occupants.[2]

Much like in these two tales related by respondents to Works Progress Administration interviewers, the metaphorical ghost of violence continues to haunt contemporary discussions of the black community. The politically loaded notion of "black-on-black violence" gained sudden currency in the 1980s. During the Reagan era, argued geographer David Wilson, conservatives and liberals alike were complicit in the popularization and politicization of the term. Conservative commentators criticized raging, uncontrolled black youth for the growing plague of inner-city violence and condemned broken, dysfunctional black families as agents in transmitting destructive values to black children. Proclaiming the death of racism, they argued that it was time for black Americans to step up, take personal responsibility for their own fates, and stop blaming a racist society for their problems. Conservatives thus portrayed "black-on-black violence" as the by-product of defective values and a pathological culture, and only black people themselves could remedy the situation by resolving, through force of will, to change course.[3]

Liberals, Wilson continued, aided and abetted in the social construction of "black-on-black violence." Although they claimed to challenge the conservative portrait of black America, liberals allowed conservatives to set the terms of the debate. The liberal discourse, too, spoke of decaying inner cities, troubled black youth, and "cultural dysfunction" rather than the institutional and structural forces contributing to "black-on-black violence" that conservatives ignored or denied, such as economic inequalities and racism. Both sides of the political debate accepted a belief in an "underclass culture" distinguished by high levels of interpersonal violence, and "[a]t the core of this violence," Wilson observed, "... was blackness rather than poverty, economics, or class." Liberals stressed the need to draw upon blacks' collective energies to launch a cultural revival, reverse black fortunes, and reinvigorate the black community. They further argued that government intervention, through the creation of various social programs, was needed to respond to the social crisis. But liberals' political position to the left of their conservative opponents, Wilson contends, was nevertheless fundamentally "imaginary." Regardless of ideology or party affiliation, politicians from the left and the right alike employed racially coded language that vilified an entire segment of the population by associating it with violence and criminality. In labeling African Americans as socially deviant, they collaborated to spin a racialized narrative that diverted attention from systemic economic problems by blaming black lifestyles, values, and culture. Liberals thus inadvertently "helped reproduce a cultural racism that conservatives flagrantly and boldly offered."[4]

The broader social conversation Wilson analyzes emerged well before the 1980s. Certainly the discussion was well under way in the 1960s, driven by such factors as the publication of the Moynihan Report and the increasingly fractious, sometimes violent, course of the civil rights movement after 1965. Although elected officials, members of the press, and social commentators sprinkled across the political spectrum disagreed on the causes of "black-on-black violence" and prescribed different remedies for it, they all identified the phenomenon as alarmingly real, and a depressing array of statistics bore them out. Escalating numbers of news reports cited an "epidemic" of homicides as the leading cause of death among black men aged fifteen to twenty-four. One in three black deaths in that age bracket was attributable to murder, disproportionately at the hands of other blacks. Throughout the era of reliable recordkeeping, black homicide rates have been four to ten times higher than those for whites. In 1992, wrote political scientist James W. Clarke, "the homicide rate for black males between the ages of twelve and twenty-four was 114.9 per 100,000, nearly ten times the rate for white males of the same ages and fourteen times the national average." By 2000, statistics showed that African Americans committed almost 82 percent of all the violent crimes against fellow black people. A U.S. Justice Department report observed that, in 2005, almost half of all homicide victims across the country were black, even though African Americans comprised just 13 percent of the total population. Young black men made up but 3 percent of the population yet accounted for more than 40 percent of all murders and roughly half of all violent crime nationwide. Fully 93 percent of black murder victims were killed by other members of the same race. By 1994, black activist Jesse Jackson decried "black-on-black violence" as the "No. 1 civil rights issue."[5]

This book does not pretend to hold the solutions to modern debates over "black-on-black violence" in the United States, but it does seek to inform the dialogue by placing the subject in the broadest historical context possible: the slaveholding South. Most studies of "black-on-black violence" have examined the urban North of the 1960s and later, although there were some investigations made earlier in the twentieth century. Already by the 1930s, black scholars W. E. B. Du Bois and E. Franklin Frazier detected a scourge of violence between and among black Americans. At the start of the twentieth century, homicide rates among blacks in both New York and Philadelphia exceeded those of whites by a factor of between 2 and 3. Nationally, by the 1920s, intraracial homicides were 7 times higher among blacks than whites. In Philadelphia alone, the black homicide rate outpaced that of whites 12-fold. In 1925, the black murder rate in Chicago was 103 per 100,000 people (versus 11 for whites); in Cincinnati, 190; in East St. Louis, 229; and in more southerly Miami, 276. "Between 1918 and 1927," observed James W. Clarke, "the national mean annual homicide rate for blacks was 37 deaths per 100,000 persons, compared to a white rate of 5," and the disparity only grew with time. By the 1930s, the figure for blacks had grown to 75 deaths per 100,000 while the rate remained less than 10 for whites. Even the initially high murder rates present among Irish and Italian immigrants declined within a generation to levels below those of blacks. Irrespective of race, homicide rates were consistently 2 to 5 times higher in urban areas than in the countryside, but even the rate for rural blacks exceeded that of urban whites.[6]

"Black-on-black" conflicts have earned only tangential mention in studies of post–Civil War, Reconstruction-era violence. During those tumultuous years, evidence reveals no sudden epidemic of intraracial homicide among blacks. To the contrary, blacks' primary assailants were whites, confused and disoriented by the profound social and political changes attending the close of the war and the emancipation of slaves. According to one tabulation for the state of Texas, blacks killed 48 other blacks between 1865 and 1868, just 11 percent of the African Americans murdered in Texas during those years and 5 percent of the 939 total homicides in the Lone Star State over that span of time. Specific numbers differed in a more comprehensive set of data from the Texas Freedmen's Bureau, but the overall pattern was clear: Reconstruction-era black Texans committed few murders upon one another (and even fewer upon whites) and were victimized by whites far more often than by fellow blacks for a range of criminal offenses. (See table E.1.) The story was similar in rural Louisiana. Gilles Vandal examined almost 4,000 homicide cases from 1865 to 1884, only 551 of which (13.8 percent) qualified as "black-on-black." African Americans accounted for 72 percent of all homicide victims in Louisiana but represented only 25 percent of the murderers. As in Texas, white assailants killed vastly more blacks than did black

Table E.1. Racial Distribution of Selected Violent Crimes in Texas, 1865–1868

Violent Act	White-on-Black	Black-on-Black	Black-on-White	White-on-White	Total
Murder	499 (62%)	48 (6%)	15 (2%)	241 (30%)	803
(Aggravated) Assault & battery	487 (78%)	90 (14%)	9 (1%)	38 (6%)	624
Assault w/ intent to kill	61 (48%)	17 (13%)	2 (2%)	47 (37%)	127
Shooting	81 (76%)	3 (3%)	5 (5%)	17 (16%)	106
Assault	50 (70%)	5 (7%)	3 (4%)	13 (18%)	71
Shooting at	28 (72%)	5 (13%)	1 (3%)	5 (13%)	39
Stabbing	14 (93%)	0 (0%)	0 (0%)	1 (7%)	15
Totals	1,220 (68%)	168 (9%)	35 (2%)	362 (20%)	1,785

Source: Barry A. Crouch, "A Spirit of Lawlessness: White Violence; Texas Blacks, 1865–1868," *Journal of Social History* 18 (Winter 1984): 220.

murderers. Indeed, intraracial homicide rates among Louisiana blacks proved lower than those among whites throughout the years of Vandal's study.[7]

Emancipation, in short, did not liberate slaves to kill one another. Southern whites nevertheless detected a penchant among postbellum blacks to commit violent acts upon their own. According to one observer, "The murderer and murdered are regularly of the same race and the same social class." The southern press, too, perceived a rash of postwar intraracial homicides. One newspaper remarked that blacks "kill those of their own color to an extent that shocks all who remember how few homicides or grave crimes were committed by this race when they were in a state of slavery. Freedom with them means license." The press thus purveyed an image of southern blacks run amok once liberated from bondage. Released from their chains, ex-slaves fought over the pettiest and most trivial of causes, more than ever before with guns. Black men, one Greensboro, North Carolina, newspaper complained in 1890, always seemed to possess "some kind of firearm," and they stood ready to "use the pistol on the slightest provocation." The upending of the familiar social order no doubt sensitized bitter, resentful whites to any signs of blacks' aggression that validated formerly holding them in bondage, but statistics also illustrate the ways in which the perception of rampant "black-on-black violence" was cultivated. After the war, blacks charged other blacks in 56 percent of the assault cases that appeared before Freedmen's Bureau courts in Kentucky, South Carolina, and Virginia. And although Reconstruction-era blacks were responsible for few violent crimes, in Texas, fellow blacks were the victims in 89 percent of all the assaults and 76 percent of all the homicides alleged to have been committed by blacks between 1865 and 1868. Similarly, in Reconstruction Louisiana, 77 percent of blacks' murder victims belonged to the same race as their attackers, and that figure rose somewhat after Reconstruction, to 83 percent for the 1877 to 1884 timeframe. These figures show, primarily, that southern blacks were overwhelmingly smart enough not to attack whites in the racially charged climate of the postwar South, knowing the possible consequences, legal or extralegal, that might befall them. It was true that blacks generally assaulted other blacks rather than whites, but the number of cases was still comparatively small.[8]

How do scholars explain the transition from the low rates of intraracial black homicide during the Reconstruction years to the much higher rates evident by the start of the twentieth century? Motives for postwar nineteenth-century violence probably did not vary from the 1870s to 1900, just as they differed little from those lurking behind violent confrontations in the antebellum decades. Gilles Vandal's research dismissed economic disputes as a bone of contention in the postwar years, a dubious assertion given the significance of conflicts over money and goods during slavery and, as Dylan Penningroth's research has shown, among former slaves navigating the social and economic transformations of a post-emancipation world. That exception notwithstanding, all of the major causes Vandal discerned for violence in the latter nineteenth century mirrored those evident under bondage. Many of the exact same reasons that compelled slaves to commit violent acts held for former bondpeople as well. Late nineteenth-century blacks, Vandal explained, fought at the gaming table, particularly when inebriated and armed. "Familial and marital quarrels were the second major category of criminality among blacks," he continued. "Quarrels over women and disputes of passion" spurred many black freemen to violence, but another substantial portion of the intraracial violence within the context of the family occurred as freedmen and freedwomen negotiated new understandings of household relations. That black men claimed increased authority over wives and that black women lost the master's possible protection produced conditions conducive to domestic abuse. But for late nineteenth-century blacks, Vandal concluded, violence was most significant in that it marked "an extra-legal means of defending their honor and gaining respect within their own communities." They "killed each other over personal grudges, in self-defense, and as a result of minor disputes." Though nominally free, black men nevertheless struggled to lay claim to manhood. Generally impoverished and still socially degraded, they fought so hard among themselves, ironically, because the stakes were so low. Inflicting violence upon a wife or girlfriend or upon one's peers marked one avenue for the extraction of some small shred of honor and respect from others within their reference group. The increasingly widespread practice among late nineteenth-century black men of carrying of pistols enhanced their self-esteem and provided them a potent weapon with which they might defend themselves. The same was true decades later, well into the twentieth century. As one man who grew up in Harlem after World War II explained, "nothing was more strongly impressed upon me than the fact that you had to fight and that you should fight" when circumstances warranted. "[T]hey used to say on the streets," he continued, "'Don't mess with a man's money, his woman, or his manhood.'"[9]

Sociologist Marvin E. Wolfgang, in collaboration with Franco Ferracuti, developed the subculture of violence theory to make sense of differential levels of criminality among various segments within a larger population. In some contexts, Wolfgang explained in 1958, "there may be a sub-culture of violence which does not define personal assaults as wrong or antisocial," where "physical aggression is . . . socially approved and expected." Whereas members of the dominant culture would dismiss most "insult[s] or argument[s] . . . as trivial and petty," in "a sub-cultural tradition" those same actions would be understood as "signals for physical attack."[10] Members of the subculture lived under constant expectation of violent assault, armed themselves in preparation for that eventuality, and readily wielded those weapons as required. "Quick resort to physical combat as a measure of daring, courage, or defense of status appears to be a cultural expression," Wolfgang and Ferracuti concluded, "especially for lower socioeconomic class males of both races." When a subculture tolerated and even encouraged violence as normative, and members of that subculture mutually agreed upon the cultural meaning and significance of their encounter, deadly "physical assaults, altercations, and violent domestic quarrels . . . are likely to be common." For Wolfgang and Ferracuti, then, violence was not simply an expression of social or economic frustration; culture was the central variable. Did the culture condone violence or not? The answer depended upon "[t]he value system" of the group and its "ideas and attitudes toward the use of violence."[11]

Scholars interested in "black-on-black violence" in the late nineteenth century, including historian Edward L. Ayers and political scientist James W. Clarke,

EPILOGUE

have applied Wolfgang and Ferracuti's subculture of violence theory to the post–Civil War surge in intraracial black violence. Under slavery, the argument runs, masters, overseers, and the southern legal system took acute interest in disputes among bondpeople because slaves counted as valuable white property. As such, whites actively intervened in the conflicts that erupted in the quarters. With slaves' liberation from bondage, however, whites no longer considered African Americans useful members of society worthy of whites' time or trouble. Although black crimes against whites were punished promptly and severely, white police officers and the southern criminal justice system in general paid little heed to former slaves' internal quarrels and altercations. As one southern white policeman pithily explained, "If a nigger kills a white man, that's murder. If a white man kills a nigger, that's justifiable homicide. If a nigger kills another nigger, that's one less nigger." The emerging reality of southern law enforcement bred among blacks distrust in white institutional authority. Absent recourse to law, African Americans took the policing of intrablack crime into their own hands, physically, and "black-on-black violence" soared. Substituting for more conventional paths to justice, blacks were granted unusual license to settle their own affairs without fear of reprisal, establishing a custom of extralegal black self-regulation that has lasted for generations. The greater prevalence of intraracial violence could furthermore be attributed to postbellum constructions of masculinity. Ayers and Clarke each argued that black male obsessions with honor exploded after emancipation. Denied paths to economic prosperity and success, such as land ownership and educational opportunities, African American men increasingly relied on intraracial violence to define black manhood in the decades after the Civil War.[12]

In tracing "black-on-black violence" to the first generation of emancipated slaves, Clarke viewed the phenomenon as historical product, a mental "scar" of bondage and "the damaging effects of countless generations of cruelty and injustice" done unto blacks by whites. Whites' repeated victimization of blacks through violence, Clarke argued, generated among blacks a subculture of violence that valued aggressive behavior as a means of achieving status and respect. The argument falls short on at least two major points, however. The first error is chronological. Clarke (and Ayers) mistakenly date the rise of "black-on-black violence" from the immediate post–Civil War years rather than from the close of Reconstruction. As we have seen, statistics now show that intraracial black violence—homicides, specifically—erupted with increasing frequency not with the conclusion of the war but in the last quarter of the nineteenth century. If the racial injustices suffered under bondage were responsible for the creation of a violent subculture among blacks, former slaves must have repressed their reputed cultural inclination toward violence for some years after the war ended because any violent subculture that was present remained latent during Reconstruction. Taking advantage of the resources available to them, African Americans instead resolved many of their differences by consulting Freedmen's Bureau agents to mediate their disputes and by taking their first tentative steps into southern courtrooms as plaintiffs. Only with the termination of the Freedmen's Bureau and the rise of Democratic, Redeemer governments not only unsympathetic and unresponsive but openly hostile to blacks did "black-on-black violence" increase.[13]

Second, Clarke's interpretation accepts "black-on-black violence" as culturally deviant. According to Wolfgang and Ferracuti, however, "a subculture of violence could exist" only "so long as nonviolence is the governing principle within the social and political life of the group." The values of the dominant culture, in short, define the subculture. By this standard, a black subculture of violence in the late nineteenth-century United States could only have existed if the urban North was the frame of reference. In northern cities such as Philadelphia, for example, "white homicide rates declined while black homicide rates increased" and "continued to climb in the twentieth century." This divergence in black and white patterns of intraracial homicide by the start of the twentieth century is necessary for the notion of a subculture of violence to retain any meaning. In contrast to their counterparts in the North, southern blacks could not have lived within a subculture of violence because contemporary southern white society was itself incredibly violent. Historian Stephen A. West has described how non-elite southern white men in the post–Civil War era gave up the rough-and-tumble fights characteristic of the antebellum decades but instead began carrying guns as symbols of manhood. When they resolved disputes through the use of pistols rather than wrestling matches, the number of deaths rose sharply. As a result, West observed, "by 1890 the rate of homicide prosecutions against white men was more than twice what it had been during the 1850s." The late nineteenth-century increase in homicides involving southern whites thus paralleled and coincided with the rise involving the region's black population. The subculture of violence theory similarly crumbles in the context of the slaveholding South. The pre–Civil War South was a remarkably violent place, and by any quantifiable measure, whites committed at least as many if not more homicidal acts per capita than did slaves. Because violence was very much a distinguishing feature of the dominant white southern culture, and because antebellum blacks cannot be proven demonstrably more (or even as) violent, slaves cannot be said to have dwelled within a subculture of violence.[14]

Some social commentators continue to embrace cultural explanations for the modern dilemma of "black-on-black violence" in America's inner cities. They identify such factors as parental negligence, broken homes, absent fathers, and widespread access to guns as conspiring to break down the discipline of black youth and to create a culture whose value system condones violence among the alienated and disaffected, particularly in a misguided quest for black manhood. Anthropologist Elijah Anderson, for one, analyzed the unwritten set of rules governing the "code of the street" that, in bleak, impoverished urban neighborhoods, comprised an oppositional culture valorizing values antithetical to those of mainstream, middle-class whites. Not all scholars are equally swayed by cultural explanations, however. If historical experience has cultivated among African Americans values inimical to those of the dominant society, they ask, why are some individuals born into an oppositional culture (or subculture) that accepts violence nonviolent? Why are some inner cities more violent than others? Why would black crime rates differ, as they do, from one urban area to the next?[15]

Critics of cultural theories of violence deny that there is anything defective or pathological about black culture that predisposes African Americans to crime. It is neither blacks themselves nor black families, they argue, who require repair. They instead explain "black-on-black violence" by noting the systemic, structural inequalities that breed aggression. Poverty and economic deprivation, high rates of unemployment, and a lack of education and job skills necessary to succeed economically are frequently cited as culprits lurking behind high rates of black crime against whites as well as other blacks. Other observers point to white racial discrimination as the cause, most often evident in the treatment of blacks by police officers and the criminal justice system. When African Americans commit crimes against fellow blacks, they are more likely to escape the full brunt of the law than if their victims were white. Those scholars who focus on these structural concerns contend that remedying the forces conducive to "black-on-black violence" will stem the tide of intrablack conflict.[16]

There remains no scholarly consensus on the precise causes of "black-on-black violence," but regardless of its true origins, wrote one student of the subject, "it is imperative that more historical ... knowledge be applied to the problem."[17] The purpose of this book is not to assess and critique any of the reputed causes of "black-on-black violence" but to place the concept in broad historical perspective. That said, it is impossible, given the available evidence, to draw an unbroken line linking the intraracial violence among blacks during bondage and that of modern times, as though "black-on-black violence" as the term is used today describes a continuous, centuries-old phenomenon. To be sure, one might advance the psychological argument that, beginning in the colonial era and through the present day, frustrated black Americans coped with the pressures of racial oppression by redirecting their rage and aggression inwardly and cathartically upon the black community, rather than outwardly, upon socially dominant whites whose victimization would expose black assailants to the harshest punishments before the law.[18]

Yet the magnitude of intraracial black violence was not constant throughout the centuries in which enslaved Africans and their descendants lived on American soil. Although high among the first generation of bondpeople imported from Africa, it soon receded but rose somewhat after the American Revolution. Although surviving records permit few firm conclusions, the incidence of intraracial slave homicide likely remained fairly stable during the antebellum era, rising only the last decade before the Civil War. With emancipation, violent encounters between freedpeople continued as they navigated the transition from slavery to ostensible freedom, but there was no pronounced jump in homicidal conflicts internal to the black community until after Reconstruction, when murderous black violence turned increasingly intraracial.[19]

In historicizing the social construction of "black-on-black violence," this book tackles the arresting juxtaposition between the media's widely reported epidemic of modern-day intraracial homicide and historians' long-held assumptions of a peculiarly harmonious slave community. The examination of slaves' violent encounters reveals no consistent pattern of elevated rates of violence among black Americans over time and discounts any suggestion that contemporary "black-on-black violence" may be explained as the residual aftereffect of slavery. But it does tell us a great deal about the experience of bondage itself. For decades, scholars' emphasis on slaves' "community" successfully showed that slaves were not simply objects of white treatment and celebrated their ability to combat the dehumanization of bondage. By overlooking slaves' arguments, conflicts, and foibles, however, much of the literature improperly canonized the enslaved population. Paradoxically, the "slave community" paradigm constructed to restore slaves as agents worked to dehumanize bondpeople by depriving them of the full range of human emotion. Rage, resentment, and passion sometimes did overwhelm restraint and culminate in violence. Any failure to recognize that fact clouds our understanding of slavery and slaves' values. Although discussions

EPILOGUE

of "black-on-black violence" are often fraught with controversy, tainted by participants' economic or political agendas and subject to misuse and abuse, investigating the various fault lines and fissures that tore through the slave community neither necessarily denigrates bondpeople nor implies any intrinsic weakness of character. What it does offer is a more realistic appraisal of slave life. The entire slaveholding South constituted a culture of violence, and slaves were part of it, but not to such an extent that we should automatically construe their battles as indicative of deviance or pathology. The violent acts slaves committed upon other bondpeople undermine scholars' notion of a unified "community," but they also contributed to the creation of the very communities that sustained slaves. When slaves fought over what they valued, they revealed the senses of fairness, justice, honor, and pride that they relied upon to persevere against and resist the terms and conditions of bondage. Slaves' violent conflicts exposed the energy and fervor percolating inside the quarters even as they produced pain, suffering, and sometimes death. Violence was very much part of slaves' lives, but all that meant was that they were southern.

APPENDIX
Intraracial Slave Homicides in Virginia, 1777–1864

Date of Trial:			Convicted						
Year	Month	County	Murderer	Convict's Master	Victim	Victim's Master	Sentence	Outcome	Valuation
n.d.	n.d.	Lunenburg	Dollen	James Reynolds	Mercer	Cornelius Crenshaw	hanging	execution	£30
1777	Jan.	Cumberland	John	William Anderson	Buckner	William Anderson	hanging	execution	£95
1777	Apr.	Cumberland	Jeffrey	George Welton	Colby	Steger	hanging	execution	£100
1782	Aug.	Powhatan	Sam	Benjamin Harris	Gill	William Fence	hanging	execution	£60
1786	Dec.	Rockbridge	York	Andrew Reid	Tom	Andrew Reid	hanging	execution	£80
1792	Jan.	Halifax	Gumbo Billey	Walter Coles	Nim	Walter Coles	hanging	execution	£74
1792	Nov.	Cumberland	Will	John Thornton	"negroe girl"	John Childres	hanging	execution	£85; $283.33
1793	Mar.	Louisa	George	Matthew Farrar	Ann	Matthew Farrar	hanging	execution	£65
1794	Jan.	Orange	Charles	Alexander Shepherd	Reuben	William Bell	hanging	execution	£80; $266.66
1794	July	Spotsylvania	Harry	Jeremiah Morton	James	Jeremiah Morton	hanging	execution	£60
1794			Ned	Margaret Chew Carter	James	Jeremiah Morton	hanging	execution	£80; $266.66
1795	Sept.	Middlesex	Peter	George Dillard	Alice	Robert Boyd	hanging	execution	£65
1796	Feb.	Mecklenburg	Stepney	John Hutcheson	Tom	Miles Hall	hanging	execution	£70
1796	July	Shenandoah	Fortune	Wm. Aylett Boothe	Sukey	Wm. Aylett Boothe	hanging	execution	£80; $266.66
1796	Oct.	Halifax	Moll	Thomas Stanfield	Joe	Thomas Stanfield	hanging	execution	£60; $200
1796	Nov.	Rockingham	Daniel	Gabriel Jones	Joseph	Gabriel Jones	hanging	execution	$300
1798	Feb.	Greensville	Abram	William Maclin	Holland	William Maclin	hanging	execution	$783.34
1799	Mar.	Pittsylvania	Hannah	George Robertson	Brandon	George Robertson	39 lashes, ears cut off		n.a.
1799	May	King & Queen	Amey	John Gresham	Isbell (ch)	John Gresham	hanging	execution	£70; $233.33
			Amey	John Gresham	Harrison (ch)	John Gresham			
1800	Oct.	Dinwiddie	Peter	William P. Claiborne	Matt	William P. Claiborne	hanging	execution	£90; $300
1801	Feb.	Henrico	Stephen	Lucy Redford	Aaron	Miles Selden	hanging	execution	£100; $333.33

Year	Month	County	Slave	Owner	Victim	Method	Outcome	Value
1802	Jan.	Mecklenburg	Hall	David Walker	William	Samuel Holmes	hanging	execution	£108
1802	Apr.	Norfolk?	Jonas	George Martin	Betty	Mary Ann Miller	hanging	execution	$400
1803	May	Nottoway	Tom	Dicey Bagley	Titus	Grandison Bagley	hanging	sale & trans.	£130; $433.33
1811	Jan.	Monroe	Moses	Samuel Ewing	Will	Oliver Ewing	hanging	execution	$275
1813	June	Chesterfield	Essex	James F. Foesie	Archer	Henry Cox	hanging	sale & trans.	$475
1813	June	Prince Edward	Isham	Jonah Parkinson	Bob	Jacob Waddell	hanging	execution	$500
1814	July	Botetourt	Ralph	Barcley Kyle	Fan	William Kyle	hanging	execution	$500
1814	Sept.	New Kent	Jim	Francis Tyree	Claiborne	John Carter	hanging	sale & trans.	$400
1815	Sept.	Powhatan	Jenny	Peter Stratton	Anderson (ch)	Peter Stratton	hanging	sale & trans.	$400
			Jenny	Peter Stratton	Julius (ch)	Peter Stratton			
			Jenny	Peter Stratton	Violett (ch)	Peter Stratton			
1816	May	Rockbridge	Matt	Henry Salling	Mike	Henry Salling	hanging	execution	$420
1816	June	Northampton	Matthew	Marriott Willis	Ben	Stokely Wilson	hanging	pardon	$550
1816	Sept.	Spotsylvania	Clara	Thomas Shelton	Grace	Thomas Shelton	hanging	execution	$400
1817	Jan.	Southampton	Hubbard	Fanny Blow	West	James Barnett	hanging	sale & trans.	$780
1817	Feb.	Rockbridge	Julius	Andrew Reid	Ned	Matthew Houston	hanging	sale & trans.	$400
1817	July	Harrison	David	John G. Jackson	Isaac	Thomas Millar	hanging	sale & trans.	$650
1818	Aug.	Caroline	John	John Thornton	Sam	Charles Young	hanging	execution	$800
1818	Nov.	Buckingham	Polly	William Toney	infant (unk)	William Toney	hanging	sale & trans.	$600
1819	Nov.	Lewis	Lucy	Thomas Batton	infant (m)	Thomas Batton	hanging	sale & trans.	$500
1819	Nov.	Surry	Lizza	William Spratley	infant (unk)	William Spratley	hanging	sale & trans.	$400
1820	Jan.	Amherst	Robin	Charles Taliaferro	Isaac	Charles Taliaferro	hanging	execution	$600
1820	Jan.	Pittsylvania	Primus	Ayres Hodnett	Abraham	Pleasant Waller	hanging	sale & trans.	$700
1820	Feb.	James City	Abram	John Crowdas	Nat	Archer Hawkins	hanging	execution	$360
1820	May	Cumberland	Jim	Edward T. Coleman	Daniel	Josiah Chambers	hanging	sale & trans.	$650

Date of Trial: Year	Month	County	Convicted Murderer	Convict's Master	Victim	Victim's Master	Sentence	Outcome	Valuation
1821	Mar.	Orange	John Miller	William Shepherd	King	William Lindsay	hanging	execution	$430
1822	July	Brooke	Letty	Robert Hartford	infant (unk)	Robert Hartford	hanging	sale & trans.	$300
1822	Aug.	Bedford	Plato	William Milner	Edy	William Milner	hanging	execution	$500
1823	May	Lunenburg	Scott	Peter Jones	Bob	Joel Blankwell	hanging	execution	$450
1823	Nov.	Accomack	Daniel	Tully Lillistone	Levi	John W. Barstow	hanging	sale & trans.	$350
1824	Mar.	Chesterfield	Henry	James B. Scott	John	James B. Scott	hanging	sale & trans.	$500
1824	July	Louisa	Milly	Garland Walton Jr.	child (f)	Garland Walton Jr.	hanging	sale & trans.	$250
1824	Nov.	Brunswick	Stephen	Lewis Kelly	Cary	Martha Raney	hanging	execution	$375
1824	Nov.	Greenbrier	Sam	Charles MClung	Sam	John Neal	hanging	sale & trans.	$300
1824	Dec.	Nansemond	Sam	John H. Wilkinson	Simon	Harrison King	hanging	execution	$350
1825	Aug.	Hanover	Moses	Miles Macon	Armistead	n.a.	hanging	execution	$450
1826	Mar.	King & Queen	Bartlett	Thomas Lumpkin	Jack	Ralph Bland	hanging	sale & trans.	$350
1826	June	Patrick	Milly	Gabriel Hanly	infant (unk)	Gabriel Hanly	hanging	execution	$400
1826	Oct.	Essex	Peter	Thomas Hart	John	William L. Waring	hanging	sale & trans.	$200
1827	May	Lunenburg	Nelson	Reuben Vaughn	Bob	Upton Edmondson	hanging	sale & trans.	$540
1827	May	Prince Edward	Martha	Richard McDearmon	infant (m)	Richard McDearmon	hanging	sale & trans.	$300
1828	Mar.	Madison	Sawney	George Smith	James Huston	James Madison	hanging	sale & trans.	$375
1828			Tom	George Smith	James Huston	James Madison	hanging	sale & trans.	$350
1828			Jere	Milly Smith	James Huston	James Madison	hanging	sale & trans.	$375
1829	Apr.	Pittsylvania	Shadrack	Allen Womack	George	Allen Womack	hanging	execution	$400
1830	Jan.	Henry	Reubin	Rhoda Hunt	Frederick	Jane S. Colland	hanging	execution	$350
1830	May	King George	Hubard	Nathaniel H. Hooe	Tom	Nathaniel H. Hooe	hanging	sale & trans.	$400

Year	Month	County	Slave	Owner	Method	Outcome	Value
1831	Sept.	Spotsylvania	Jarret	Thomas Coleman	Reuben L. Coleman	hanging	execution	$25
			Jarret	Thomas Coleman	Reuben L. Coleman			
1832	June	Northampton	Solomon	Littleton W. Tazewell	Littleton W. Tazewell	hanging	sale & trans.	$400
1832	Aug.	Prince Edward	Rinah	Henry Dawson Jr.	Henry Dawson Jr.	hanging	execution	$50
			Fanny	Henry Dawson Jr.	Henry Dawson Jr.	hanging	execution	$200
1833	Feb.	Fairfax	Ally	George Millan	George Millan	hanging	sale & trans.	$300
1833	Oct.	Buckingham	Israel	William D. Jones	Jacob Woodson	hanging	sale & trans.	$550
1833	Dec.	Greensville	Clary	Geo. M. Williamson	Geo. M. Williamson	hanging	sale & trans.	$325
1834	Feb.	Kanawha	Harry	Ann Pollard	Levi Welch	hanging	sale & trans.	$400
1834	May	Henrico	Kesiah	Henry L. Carter	Henry L. Carter	hanging	sale & trans.	$440
1837	Feb.	Henrico	Martin	John Talley	John Enders	hanging	sale & trans.	$2,000
1837	Sept.	Appomattox	Reuben	Willie Ann Jones	Willie Ann Jones	hanging	execution	$400
1837	Dec.	Bedford	Viney	William Terry	William Terry	hanging	sale & trans.	$580
1838	July	Bedford	Jim	William Woodford	Henry Latham	hanging	execution	$750
1839	May	Buckingham	Tom	Thomas G. Noel	Elizabeth Mosby	hanging	sale & trans.	$700
1840	Feb.	Southampton	Malinda	Thomas Newsom	Thomas Newsom	hanging	sale & trans.	$450
1840	June	Nottoway	Ransom	Asa Oliver	Asa Oliver	hanging	execution	$630
1840	Aug.	Nottoway	Lewis	Miles A. Giles	William Hardaway	hanging	execution	$575
1840	Nov.	Nelson	Joe Wills	Robert T. Hubard	Robert T. Hubard	hanging	sale & trans.	$700
1840	Dec.	Russell	Cupe	Aaron Hendricks	Aaron Hendricks	hanging	sale & trans.	$400
1842	Nov.	Richmond city	Emanuel	Samuel Clark	n.a.	hanging	sale & trans.	$480
1842	Dec.	Chesterfield	Fleming	Henry T. Drewry	Henry T. Drewry	hanging	execution	$390
1843	Dec.	Pendleton	Maria McCoy	William McCoy	John McClure	hanging	pardon	n.a.
1844	Jan.	Pittsylvania	Robin	Charles F. Adams	Ichabod T. Watson	hanging	execution	$340
1845	Jan.	Lynchburg c.	Gustavus	David R. Edley	Cabell	hanging	sale & trans.	$743.20

Rose — Rose's child — Ben — (Northampton 1832)
Oxford — child (unk) — Joe (1833)
Franky — Dennis (1833)
infant (f) — Lewis (1834)
Tom — Jane (1837)
Esther — Davy (1838)
Allen — Tom (1840)
Ben — Little Joe (1840)
Richard — Isaac (1840)
John — Washington (1843)
Barney (1845)

Date of Trial:			Convicted						
Year	Month	County	Murderer	Convict's Master	Victim	Victim's Master	Sentence	Outcome	Valuation
1845	Nov.	Albemarle	Washington	George Rives	William	Daniel Scott	hanging	sale & trans.	$485
1846	Oct.	Mecklenburg	Bob	Dorothy Turberville	Lee	Paschall Bracey	hanging	sale & trans.	$515
1848	Mar.	Henrico	King	Richard Gooch	Moses	John B. Young	hanging	execution	$600
1848	Mar.	Petersburg c.	Billy	Lilly Hunnicutt	John	Joel Sturdivant Jr.	hanging	execution	$540
1848	Sept.	Kanawha	John	John D. Lewis	Yamma	John D. Lewis	hanging	execution	$600
1849	June	Louisa	Tom	John Bibb	John	Nathaniel W. Harris	hanging	sale & trans.	$550
1850	Sept.	Prince Edward	Ned	James H. C. Leach	Stephen	James H. C. Leach	sale & trans.	sale & trans.	$450
1851	Jan.	Mecklenburg	Hainey	Francis W. Boyd	Tucker (ch), Amy (ch)	n.a.	sale & trans.	sale & trans.	$590
			Dick	Francis W. Boyd	Tucker (ch), Amy (ch)	n.a.	hanging	execution	$870
			Nelson	Amanda Dedman	Tucker (ch), Amy (ch)	n.a.	sale & trans.	sale & trans.	$700
			Daniel	Francis W. Boyd	Tucker (ch), Amy (ch)	n.a.	sale & trans.	sale & trans.	$770
1851	Apr.	Hanover	Caroline	Hugh McDowell	infant (f)	Hugh McDowell	sale & trans.	sale & trans.	$500
1851	Aug.	Petersburg c.	Jesse	Napoleon Archer	George	Robert Justice	sale & trans.	sale & trans.	$600
1851	Aug.	Rappahannock	Martin	Frances Burgess	Martha	Frances Burgess	sale & trans.	sale & trans.	$850
1852	Feb.	Washington	Green	Thomas Wilson	Tom	William Y. C. White	sale & trans.	sale & trans.	$500
1852	Mar.	Giles	Mahala	William B. Mason	Sally	William B. Mason	hanging	execution	$800
1852	Aug.	Albemarle	Fanny	Alexander Terrell	infant (f)	Alexander Terrell	sale & trans.	sale & trans.	$650
1852	Sept.	Charlotte	Albert	Bouldin family	Mike	Abram H. Roberts	sale & trans.	sale & trans.	$580

Year	Month	County	Slave	Owner	Victim	Victim's Owner	Sentence	Disposition	Value
1852	Sept.	Richmond city	Lucy	Judith Fore	infant (m)	Judith Fore	hanging	sale & trans.	$650
1853	Nov.	Rockbridge	Jim Gooch	Creed Taylor	Sam	William, John Pogue	hanging	execution	$350
1853	Dec.	Halifax	Sally	James Singleton Sr.	Amey	William Link	hanging	execution	$450
1853	Dec.	Halifax	Lizzy	James Singleton Sr.	Amey	William Link	hanging	sale & trans.	$850
1854	Mar.	Spotsylvania	Beverley	William T. J. Richards	Jacob	Sanford Chancellor	sale & trans.	sale & trans.	$1,350
1854	Sept.	Richmond city	Charlotte	Hay Holmes	infant (m)	Hay Holmes	sale & trans.	sale & trans.	$700
1854	Oct.	Chesterfield	Sprig	A. F. D. Gifford	William	Macon Trabue	sale & trans.	sale & trans.	$800
1854	Nov.	Richmond city	Edward	Elizabeth Slaughter	John	William W. Wingo	sale & trans.	sale & trans.	$840
1855	Mar.	Prince Edward	Frank	Thomas J. Owen	Violet	n.a.	hanging	execution	$600
1855	Apr.	Chesterfield	Johnson	Chastain H. Findley	Edmund	George W. Scully	sale & trans.	sale & trans.	$600
1855	Apr.	Richmond city	Lucy	Samuel Ellis	infant (unk)	Samuel Ellis	hanging	sale & trans.	$700
1855	June	Fauquier	Louisa	Mrs. W. A. Brown	George	William A. Bowen	sale & trans.	sale & trans.	$700
1856	Feb.	Charlotte	Julius	Mary Bouldin	Richard/Dick	Henry Carrington	hanging	execution	$650
1856	May	Powhatan	Opha Jane	n.a.	infant (unk)	n.a.	hanging	sale & trans.	n.a.
1856	Nov.	Amherst	Allen	Augustus Leftwich	Pleasant	n.a.	sale & trans.	sale & trans.	$800
1856	Nov.	Hardy	Mary J. Willis	B. F. Warden	infant (unk)	B. F. Warden	sale & trans.	sale & trans.	n.a.
1857	June	Culpeper	Suckey	Charles Wm. Ashby	infant (f)	Charles Wm. Ashby	hanging	sale & trans.	$1,000
1857	June	Fauquier	Richard	Alexander Campbell	Edmond	S. D. Armstrong	sale & trans.	sale & trans.	$1,000
1857	Nov.	Caroline	James	n.a.	"a slave"	n.a.	sale & trans.	sale & trans.	n.a.
1858	Jan.	Middlesex	Levi	Mary E. Bohannan	Mortimer	Thomas Parren	sale & trans.	sale & trans.	$900
1858	May	Gloucester	Augustine Read	Nancy Johnson	Frank	n.a.	sale & trans.	sale & trans.	$900
1858	Aug.	Rappahannock	Ellen	James Thornhill	child (m)	James Thornhill	sale & trans.	sale & trans.	$875
1858	Oct.	Fluvanna	James	Beverly Fox	George	Oliver	sale & trans.	public works	$1,100
1858	Nov.	Loudoun	Marietta	John Francis	infant (f)	John Francis	sale & trans.	public works	$800
1859	May	Amherst	John Red	D. Lee Powell	Alfred	Philip H. Geo. Ambler	sale & trans.	public works	$700

| Date of Trial: | | County | Convicted Murderer | Convict's Master | Victim | Victim's Master | Sentence | Outcome | Valuation |
Year	Month								
1859	Nov.	Richmond city	Scott	Jackson B. Wood	Priscilla	Richard Alvey	hanging	public works	$400
1860	June	Madison	Philip	Mariah Kemper	Alfred	William Tutz	sale & trans.	public works	$1,200
1860	Sept.	Amherst	Mary	R. H. Cox	infant (unk)	R. H. Cox	sale & trans.	public works	$1,200
1860	Oct.	Prince George	Betsey	John P. Wilcox	Patty	John P. Wilcox	sale & trans.	public works	$200
1861	Jan.	Appomattox	Britton	Thomas Womack	John Robert	Samuel D. Sears	sale & trans.	public works	$800
1861	Jan.	Fauquier	Adam	John Martin	Walker	Gustavus S. Ficklin	sale & trans.	public works	$500
1861	Feb.	Stafford	Jeff Brooker	John Hare	John Brooker	John Hare	sale & trans.	public works	$850
1861	May	Pulaski	Margaret	David C. Kent	Jacob	Francis Bell	sale & trans.	public works	$620
1861	Nov.	Appomattox	Nelson	Joel W. Coleman	Catharine	Joel W. Coleman	hanging	execution	$676
1862	May	Richmond city	James	Johan Tuning	Andrew	n.a.	sale & trans.	public works	$800
1863	Dec.	Pittsylvania	Henry	Azariah G. Walters	Kit	Azariah G. Walters	sale & trans.	public works	$3,000
1864	Oct.	Charlotte	Harriett	G. J. W. Roberts	Matilda	Joseph H. Roberts	sale & trans.	sale & trans.	$3,000

Source: Auditor of Public Accounts, Condemned Blacks Executed or Transported, Records—Condemned Slaves, Court Orders, and Valuations, 1781–1865, Misc. Reels 2449–2555, LVA; Executive Papers, LVA.

NOTES

ABBREVIATIONS

ACCCHNF   Adams County Courthouse Collection, Historic Natchez Foundation, Natchez, Miss.
- GA   Georgia Archives, Morrow
- LVA   Library of Virginia, Richmond
- MDAH   Mississippi Department of Archives and History, Jackson
- NCDAH   North Carolina Department of Archives and History, Raleigh
- NOPL   New Orleans Public Library, New Orleans
- SBHLA   Southern Baptist Historical Library and Archives, Nashville, Tenn.
- SCDAH   South Carolina Department of Archives and History, Columbia
- SCL   South Caroliniana Library, University of South Carolina, Columbia
- SHC   Southern Historical Collection, Wilson Library, University of North Carolina at Chapel Hill
- SWBTS   Southwestern Baptist Theological Seminary, Fort Worth, Tex.

INTRODUCTION

1. *Lewis, a slave v. State* (1847), Supreme Court of Mississippi, 17 Miss. 115, 1847 Miss. LEXIS 95, 9 S. & M. 115.

2. Various studies have identified such factors as frontier conditions, an ethic of honor, and a transplanted Celtic cultural tradition as explanations for violence committed by southern whites. On antebellum southern violence, see W. J. Cash, *The Mind of the South* (1941; reprint, New York: Vintage, 1991); John Hope Franklin, *The Militant South, 1800–1861* (Cambridge: Harvard University Press, 1956); Dickson D. Bruce Jr., *Violence and Culture in the Antebellum South* (Austin: University of Texas Press, 1979); Bertram Wyatt-Brown, *Southern Honor: Ethics and Behavior in the Old South* (New York: Oxford University Press, 1982); Edward L. Ayers, *Vengeance and Justice: Crime and Punishment in the 19th-Century American South* (New York: Oxford University Press, 1984); Elliott J. Gorn, "'Gouge and Bite, Pull Hair and Scratch': The Social Significance of Fighting in the Southern Backcountry," *American Historical Review* 90 (February 1985): 18–43; Grady McWhiney, *Cracker Culture: Celtic Ways in the Old South* (Tuscaloosa: University of Alabama Press, 1988); Kenneth S. Greenberg, "The Nose, the Lie, and the Duel in the Antebellum South," *American Historical Review* 95 (February 1990): 57–74; Victoria E. Bynum, *Unruly Women: The Politics of Social and Sexual Control in the Old South* (Chapel Hill: University of North Carolina Press, 1992); Laura F. Edwards, "Law, Domestic Violence, and the Limits of Patriarchal Authority in the Antebellum South," *Journal of Southern History* 65 (November 1999): 733–770; Edward E. Baptist, "'My Mind Is to Drown You and Leave You Behind': 'Omie Wise,' Intimate Violence, and Masculinity," in *Over the Threshold: Intimate Violence in Early America*, ed. Christine Daniels and Michael V. Kennedy (New York: Routledge, 1999), 94–110; and Loren Schweninger, "Slavery

and Southern Violence: County Court Petitions and the South's Peculiar Institution," *Journal of Negro History* 85 (Winter-Spring 2000): 33-35.

3. Nell Irvin Painter, *Southern History across the Color Line* (Chapel Hill: University of North Carolina Press, 2002), 6; Ayers, *Vengeance and Justice*, 132-133; Peter Kolchin, *American Slavery, 1619-1877* (New York: Hill and Wang, 1993), 160. See, for example, David W. Blight, ed., *Narrative of the Life of Frederick Douglass, an American Slave, Written by Himself* (New York: Bedford Books of St. Martin's Press, 1993); and Melton A. McLaurin, *Celia, a Slave* (Athens: University of Georgia Press, 1991; reprint, New York: Perennial, 2002). Among revisionist scholars of the 1970s, Eugene D. Genovese, *Roll, Jordan, Roll: The World the Slaves Made* (1974; reprint, New York; Vintage, 1976), 622-637, was unique in his somewhat more extensive recognition of violence among slaves. Genovese explored intraracial slave violence in a sixteen-page section titled "Brothers, Sisters, and No-'Counts."

4. Stanley M. Elkins, *Slavery: A Problem in American Institutional and Intellectual Life*, 3rd ed. (Chicago: University of Chicago Press, 1976); John W. Blassingame, *The Slave Community: Plantation Life in the Antebellum South*, rev. ed. (New York: Oxford University Press, 1979), 190, 226, 238, 293, 305, 312, 313, 320, 321 (same quotation 238 and 320). For more on Sambo, see also Bertram Wyatt-Brown, "The Mask of Obedience: Male Slave Psychology in the Old South," *American Historical Review* 93 (December 1988): 1239, 1240, 1242, 1245, 1249.

5. In addition to Blassingame's *Slave Community*, some of the most significant works include Genovese, *Roll, Jordan, Roll*; Herbert G. Gutman, *The Black Family in Slavery and Freedom, 1750-1925* (New York: Pantheon Books, 1976); Leslie Howard Owens, *This Species of Property: Slave Life and Culture in the Old South* (New York: Oxford University Press, 1976); Lawrence W. Levine, *Black Culture and Black Consciousness: Afro-American Folk Thought from Slavery to Freedom* (New York: Oxford University Press, 1977); Albert J. Raboteau, *Slave Religion: The "Invisible Institution" in the Antebellum South* (New York: Oxford University Press, 1978); and Sterling Stuckey, *Slave Culture: Nationalist Theory and the Foundations of Black America* (New York: Oxford University Press, 1987). On *The Slave Community*'s reception by historians, see Mary Frances Berry, "*The Slave Community*: A Review of Reviews," in *Revisiting Blassingame's The Slave Community: The Scholars Respond*, ed. Al-Tony Gilmore (Westport, Conn.: Greenwood Press, 1978), 3, 14-15.

6. Peter Kolchin, "Reevaluating the Antebellum Slave Community: A Comparative Perspective," *Journal of American History* 70 (December 1983): 581. See also Kolchin, *American Slavery*, 148-155; Clarence E. Walker, *Deromanticizing Black History: Critical Essays and Reappraisals* (Knoxville: University of Tennessee Press, 1991), xi-xviii; and Philip D. Morgan, *Slave Counterpoint: Black Culture in the Eighteenth-Century Chesapeake and Lowcountry* (Chapel Hill: University of North Carolina Press, 1998), xxiv, 442-443.

7. Morgan, *Slave Counterpoint*, 442; Jean Butenhoff Lee, "The Problem of Slave Community in the Eighteenth-Century Chesapeake," *William & Mary Quarterly* 3rd ser., 43 (July 1986): 334, 338, 340, 343, 348, 350, 361; Kolchin, "Reevaluating the Antebellum Slave Community," 584, 588; Genovese, *Roll, Jordan, Roll*, 628. Painter, *Southern History across the Color Line*, 30, estimates that perhaps half of all slaves were not part of a "slave community" because they did not live on plantations with twenty or more slaves.

8. Henry Bibb, *Narrative of the Life and Adventures of Henry Bibb, an American Slave, Written*

NOTES TO PAGES 4-6

by Himself (New York: The Author, 1849), 33; Kenneth M. Stampp, *The Peculiar Institution: Slavery in the Ante-Bellum South* (New York: Alfred A. Knopf, 1956), 333, 334, 337, 338, 339; Christopher Morris, "The Articulation of Two Worlds: The Master-Slave Relationship Reconsidered," *Journal of American History* 85 (December 1998): 1002; D. R. Hundley, *Social Relations in Our Southern States* (New York: Henry B. Price, 1860; reprint, New York: Arno Press, 1973), 332.

9. C. W. Harper, "House Servants and Field Hands: Fragmentation in the Antebellum Slave Community," *North Carolina Historical Review* 55 (January 1978): 42–59 (quotation 47); idem, "Black Aristocrats: Domestic Servants on the Antebellum Plantation," *Phylon* 46 (June 1985): 123–135; Michael P. Johnson, "Work, Culture, and the Slave Community: Slave Occupations in the Cotton Belt in 1860," *Labor History* 27 (Summer 1986): 325–355; George P. Rawick, ed., *The American Slave: A Composite Autobiography*, vol. 3, pt. 4 (Westport, Conn.: Greenwood Publishing Company, 1972), 148. Blassingame noted that many field slaves viewed house servants with mistrust. See Blassingame, *Slave Community*, 316. Genovese, however, denied that house servants were the spies or betrayers of field hands and instead demonstrated a general solidarity with them. See Genovese, *Roll, Jordan, Roll*, 623. For a succinct discussion of occupational stratification among slaves and social divisions generally, see Kolchin, *American Slavery*, 107–111. Kolchin stresses a lack of differentiation except on the largest of slaveholdings. On status in the quarters, see also Philip J. Schwarz, *Twice Condemned: Slaves and the Criminal Laws of Virginia, 1705–1865* (Baton Rouge: Louisiana State University Press, 1988), 250–252.

10. William L. Van Deburg, *The Slave Drivers: Black Agricultural Labor Supervisors in the Antebellum South* (Westport, Conn.: Greenwood Press, 1979); Kolchin, "Reevaluating the Antebellum Slave Community," 596.

11. Stampp, *Peculiar Institution*, 339; Harper, "House Servants and Field Hands," 47; Brenda E. Stevenson, "Distress and Discord in Virginia Slave Families, 1830–1860," in *In Joy and in Sorrow: Women, Family, and Marriage in the Victorian South, 1830–1900*, ed. Carol Bleser (New York: Oxford University Press, 1991), 112, 114, 115; idem, "Gender Convention, Ideals, and Identity among Antebellum Virginia Slave Women," in *More Than Chattel: Black Women and Slavery in the Americas*, ed. David Barry Gaspar and Darlene Clark Hine (Bloomington: Indiana University Press, 1996), 173–174; idem, *Life in Black and White: Family and Community in the Slave South* (New York: Oxford University Press, 1996), 255; Rawick, *American Slave*, vol. 3, pt. 4, 148. Eugene D. Genovese downplayed hostility based on differences of skin color. See Genovese, *Roll, Jordan, Roll*, 429.

12. Michael P. Johnson, "Runaway Slaves and the Slave Communities in South Carolina, 1799 to 1830," *William & Mary Quarterly* 3rd ser., 38 (July 1981): 419 (quotation), 429, 433.

13. Kolchin, "Reevaluating the Antebellum Slave Community," 596, 597 (quotation), 600; Anthony E. Kaye, "Neighbourhoods and Solidarity in the Natchez District of Mississippi: Rethinking the Antebellum Slave Community," *Slavery & Abolition* 23 (April 2002): 12, 14–16. C. W. Harper observed that house servants, more closely allied with their white owners, proved more likely than field slaves to expose the discovery of a runaway. See Harper, "House Servants and Field Hands," 54.

14. Wyatt-Brown, "Mask of Obedience," 1247.

15. Kolchin, *American Slavery*, 148–149; Paul Lachance, "Use and Misuse of the Slave Community Paradigm," *Canadian Review of American Studies* 17 (Winter 1986): 449–458 (quotation

456); Wyatt-Brown, "Mask of Obedience," 1251; Kolchin, *American Slavery*, 155. The pervasiveness of the slave community paradigm was evident in the titles of many important works on slavery, including George P. Rawick, *From Sundown to Sunup: The Making of the Black Community* (Westport, Conn.: Greenwood Publishing Company, 1972); Thomas L. Webber, *Deep Like the Rivers: Education in the Slave Quarter Community, 1831–1865* (New York: Norton, 1978); Charles Joyner, *Down by the Riverside: A South Carolina Slave Community* (Urbana: University of Illinois Press, 1984); and Lorena Seebach Walsh, *From Calabar to Carter's Grove: The History of a Virginia Slave Community* (Charlottesville: University Press of Virginia, 1997).

16. Stevenson, "Distress and Discord"; idem, "Gender Convention"; idem, *Life in Black and White*; Christopher Morris, "Within the Slave Cabin: Violence in Mississippi Slave Families," in *Over the Threshold: Intimate Violence in Early America*, ed. Christine Daniels and Michael V. Kennedy (New York: Routledge, 1999), 268–285; Dylan C. Penningroth, *The Claims of Kinfolk: African American Property and Community in the Nineteenth-Century South* (Chapel Hill: University of North Carolina Press, 2003), 8; Kaye, "Neighbourhoods and Solidarity," 2, 3, 5, 6, 18 (first quotation), 8 (second quotation), 12, 14–16. Kaye notes that former slaves preferred the term "neighborhood" and did not speak in terms of "community" in the Southern Claims Commission records until the 1890s. With the linguistic shift, they then used "community" and "neighborhood" interchangeably. For historians, however, "community" subsequently lost the sense of place so important to the slaves. Kaye, "Neighbourhoods and Solidarity," 17–18. Based on his study of Piedmont Virginia, John T. Schlotterbeck concurs that "[t]he neighborhood, not the plantation, became the unit of the slave community." See John T. Schlotterbeck, "The Internal Economy of Slavery in Rural Piedmont Virginia," in *The Slaves' Economy: Independent Production by Slaves in the Americas*, ed. Ira Berlin and Philip D. Morgan (London: Frank Cass, 1991), 172. Dylan Penningroth also implicitly agrees with Kaye's idea of neighborhood when he writes that "slaves themselves carefully set boundaries regarding who 'their people' were." See Penningroth, *Claims of Kinfolk*, 88.

17. Ned Blackhawk, *Violence over the Land: Indians and Empires in the Early American West* (Cambridge: Harvard University Press, 2006), 5–6; Laurence Shore, "The Poverty of Tragedy in Historical Writing on Southern Slavery," *South Atlantic Quarterly* 85 (Spring 1986): 148, 160, 164 (quotation). See also Orlando Patterson, "Whatever Happened to the Horrors of Slavery?" presentation at the Rice Center for Cultural Studies, Moral Sensibilities in Cultural and Historical Context Session No. 11, January 19, 1989.

18. Walter Johnson, "On Agency," *Journal of Social History* 37 (Fall 2003): 114, 115 (first, fourth, and fifth quotations), 116, 121 (sixth quotation); Kolchin, *American Slavery*, 155 (second and third quotations).

19. Johnson, "On Agency," 121.

20. Philip J. Schwarz, "The Transportation of Slaves from Virginia, 1801–1865," *Slavery & Abolition* 7 (December 1986): 216; Executive Papers, John Letcher, Misc. Reel 4709, Box 3, Folder 8, Frame 520, LVA.

21. On the history and workings of the South Carolina Courts of Magistrates and Freeholders, see Terry W. Lipscomb and Theresa Jacobs, "The Magistrates and Freeholders Court," *South Carolina Historical Magazine* 77 (January 1976): 62–65; William Henderson, "The Slave Court System in Spartanburg County," *Proceedings of the South Carolina Historical Association* (1976):

31–37; Robert Olwell, *Masters, Slaves, & Subjects: The Culture of Power in the South Carolina Low Country, 1740–1790* (Ithaca: Cornell University Press, 1998), 73–77, 90; and W. J. Megginson, *African American Life in South Carolina's Upper Piedmont, 1780–1900* (Columbia: University of South Carolina Press, 2006), ch. 5. For statistical data on the South Carolina upcountry, see Joseph C. G. Kennedy, *Agriculture of the United States in 1860; Compiled from the Original Returns of the Eighth Census, Under the Direction of the Secretary of the Interior*, vol. 2 Agriculture (Washington: Government Printing Office, 1864), 214, 129; *Compendium of the Enumeration of the Inhabitants and Statistics of the United States* (Washington: T. Allen, 1841), 191–192; J. D. B. DeBow, *The Seventh Census of the United States: 1850* (Washington: R. Armstrong, 1853), 346–347; and Jeff Forret, "Conflict and the 'Slave Community': Violence among Slaves in Upcountry South Carolina," *Journal of Southern History* 74 (August 2008): 555–558.

22. Historical Census Browser, University of Virginia, Geospatial and Statistical Data Center (2004): http://fisher.lib.virginia.edu/collections/stats/histcensus/index.html. On Adams County, Mississippi, in other academic works, see James Oakes, *The Ruling Race: A History of American Slaveholders* (1982; reprint, New York: W. W. Norton & Company, 1998), ch. 3; Winthrop D. Jordan, *Tumult and Silence at Second Creek: An Inquiry into a Civil War Slave Conspiracy* (Baton Rouge: Louisiana State University Press, 1993), 46; and Michael Wayne, *Death of an Overseer: Reopening a Murder Investigation from the Plantation South* (New York: Oxford University Press, 2001).

23. Randolph Roth, *American Homicide* (Cambridge: Belknap Press of Harvard University Press, 2009), 101.

24. Scott R. Reisinger, "Let Justice Be Done to Slavery: The White Virginia Baptist Clergy and the Slaves, 1840–1865," *Virginia Baptist Register* 33 (1994): 1666; James David Essig, "A Very Wintry Season: Virginia Baptists and Slavery, 1785–1797," *Virginia Magazine of History and Biography* 87 (April 1980): 170; Christine Leigh Heyrman, *Southern Cross: The Beginnings of the Bible Belt* (Chapel Hill: University of North Carolina Press, 1998).

25. Gregory A. Wills, *Democratic Religion: Freedom, Authority, and Church Discipline in the Baptist South, 1785–1900* (New York: Oxford University Press, 1997), 31.

26. Hundley, *Social Relations*, 332; Roth, *American Homicide*, 136; Genovese, *Roll, Jordan, Roll*, 631; Schwarz, *Twice Condemned*, 231; Glenn M. McNair, "Justice Bound: Aframericans, Crime, and Criminal Justice in Georgia, 1751–1865" (Ph.D. diss., Emory University, 2001), 120; Thomas D. Morris, *Southern Slavery and the Law, 1619–1860* (Chapel Hill: University of North Carolina Press, 1996), 300; Gilles Vandal, "Black Violence in Post–Civil War Louisiana," *Journal of Interdisciplinary History* 25 (Summer 1994): 63.

27. See, for example, Deborah Gray White, *Ar'n't I a Woman? Female Slaves in the Plantation South*, rev. ed. (New York: Norton, 1999); Stephanie M. H. Camp, *Closer to Freedom: Enslaved Women and Everyday Resistance in the Plantation South* (Chapel Hill: University of North Carolina Press, 2004); and Jennifer L. Morgan, *Laboring Women: Reproduction and Gender in New World Slavery* (Philadelphia: University of Pennsylvania Press, 2004).

28. Dea H. Boster, *African American Slavery and Disability: Bodies, Property, and Power in the Antebellum South, 1800–1860* (New York: Routledge, 2013), 115–117; Fredrika Bremer, *The Homes of the New World; Impressions of America*, trans. Mary Howitt, vol. 2 (1853; reprint, New York: Negro Universities Press, 1968), 533; Max L. Grivno, *Gleanings of Freedom: Free and Slave Labor along the Mason-Dixon Line, 1790–1860* (Urbana: University of Illinois Press, 2011), 75–

76; Damian Alan Pargas, *The Quarters and the Fields: Slave Families in the Non-Cotton South* (Gainesville: University Press of Florida, 2010), 178; Steven Deyle, *Carry Me Back: The Domestic Slave Trade in American Life* (New York: Oxford University Press, 2005), 254, 256; Walter Johnson, *Soul by Soul: Life inside the Antebellum Slave Market* (Cambridge: Harvard University Press, 1999), 11, 33; Jonathan D. Martin, *Divided Mastery: Slave Hiring in the American South* (Cambridge: Harvard University Press, 2004), 51–52, 55; Harriet Martineau, *Society in America*, vol. 2 (London: Saunders and Otley, 1837; reprint, New York: AMS Press, 1966), 321; Stampp, *Peculiar Institution*, 128.

29. John Iliffe, *Honour in African History* (Cambridge: Cambridge University Press, 2005), 74, 76, 77, 87, 131; Blassingame, *Slave Community*, 7; Michael A. Gomez, *Exchanging Our Country Marks: The Transformation of African Identities in the Colonial and Antebellum South* (Chapel Hill: University of North Carolina Press, 1998), 164; Genovese, *Roll, Jordan, Roll*, 639; Terri L. Snyder, "Suicide, Slavery, and Memory in North America," *Journal of American History* 97 (June 2010): 40; Werner Sollors, ed., *The Interesting Narrative of the Life of Olaudah Equiano, or Gustavus Vassa, the African, Written by Himself* (New York: Norton, 2001), 39, 41; quoted in Blassingame, *Slave Community*, 9.

30. Gomez, *Exchanging Our Country Marks*, 120, 117; Stephanie E. Smallwood, *Saltwater Slavery: A Middle Passage from Africa to American Diaspora* (Cambridge: Harvard University Press, 2007), 145, 186; Genovese, *Roll, Jordan, Roll*, 639; J. William Harris, *The Hanging of Thomas Jeremiah: A Free Black Man's Encounter with Liberty* (New Haven: Yale University Press, 2009), 26–27; Gomez, *Exchanging Our Country Marks*, 116, 117, 119, 120, 131; Snyder, "Suicide," 39.

31. Genovese, *Roll, Jordan, Roll*, 639; Theodore Dwight Weld, *American Slavery As It Is: Testimony of a Thousand Witnesses* (New York: American Anti-Slavery Society, 1839), 102; quoted in Genovese, *Roll, Jordan, Roll*, 639; Gomez, *Exchanging Our Country Marks*, 120; Genovese, *Roll, Jordan, Roll*, 639, 640 (quotation).

32. Edward E. Baptist, *Creating an Old South: Middle Florida's Plantation Frontier Before the Civil War* (Chapel Hill: University of North Carolina Press, 2002), 78; Snyder, "Suicide," 42, 46; Schwarz, *Twice Condemned*, 80; Stampp, *Peculiar Institution*, 128, 129; James L. Smith, *Autobiography of James L. Smith, Including, Also, Reminiscences of Slave Life, Recollections of the War, Education of Freedmen, Causes of the Exodus, Etc.* (Norwich, Conn.: Press of the Bulletin Company, 1881), 19; Ralph Betts Flanders, *Plantation Slavery in Georgia* (Chapel Hill: University of North Carolina Press, 1933; reprint, Cos Cob, Conn.: John E. Edwards, 1967), 270; John Houston Bills Diary #2245, Box 1, Folder 10, Folder 11, June 30, 1854, SHC; Douglas R. Egerton, *Gabriel's Rebellion: The Virginia Slave Conspiracies of 1800 and 1802* (Chapel Hill: University of North Carolina Press, 1993), 113.

33. W. Wells Brown, *Three Years in Europe; or Places I Have Seen and People I Have Met* (Edinburgh: Oliver and Boyd, 1852), xv; Harris, *Hanging of Thomas Jeremiah*, 49; Johnson, *Soul by Soul*, 195, 207.

34. Rawick, *American Slave*, vol. 15, pt. 2, 333; Grivno, *Gleanings of Freedom*, 76; David L. Lightner, *Slavery and the Commerce Power: How the Struggle Against the Interstate Slave Trade Led to the Civil War* (New Haven: Yale University Press, 2006), 107; Deyle, *Carry Me Back*, 179; Charles Ball, *Fifty Years in Chains; or, The Life of An American Slave* (New York: H. Dayton, 1859), 35.

35. Quoted in Johnson, *Soul by Soul*, 34; Goshen Baptist Church (Lincoln County, Ga.), Rec-

ords and Minutes, 1802–1869, June 1816, GA; Rehoboth Baptist Church (Wilkes County, Ga.), Minutes, 1806–1933, July 1845, Drawer 45, Reel 15, GA.

36. Genovese, *Roll, Jordan, Roll,* 639; David Silkenat, *Moments of Despair: Suicide, Divorce, and Debt in Civil War Era North Carolina* (Chapel Hill: University of North Carolina Press, 2011), 14–21; Jessica Millward, "'As Cool as I Now Am': Identity, Abortion and Infanticide in the Slave South" (M.A. thesis, UCLA, 1997), 23; Daniel P. Black, "The Black Male Concept of Manhood as Portrayed in Selected Slave and Free Narratives (1794–1863)" (Ph.D. diss., Temple University, 1993), 82–85; Snyder, "Suicide," 42, 43, 57.

37. Roth, *American Homicide,* 101; Powhatan County, Order Book 12, 1814–1816, Reel 27, LVA; Deyle, *Carry Me Back,* 256.

38. Roth, *American Homicide,* 101; Genovese, *Roll, Jordan, Roll,* 633; Schwarz, *Twice Condemned,* 79 (quotation).

39. Dylan C. Penningroth, "My People, My People: The Dynamics of Community in Southern Slavery," in *New Studies in the History of American Slavery,* ed. Edward E. Baptist and Stephanie M. H. Camp (Athens: University of Georgia Press, 2006), 168–169, 175n11.

1. ORIGINS, PREVALENCE, AND PATTERNS

1. Baldwin County, Georgia, Inferior Court Minutes, Trial of Slaves, 1812–1828.

2. Randolph Roth, *American Homicide* (Cambridge: Belknap Press of Harvard University Press, 2009), 100; Alexander Falconbridge, *An Account of the Slave Trade on the Coast of Africa* (London: J. Phillips, 1788), 14 (quotation), 18.

3. Quoted in Michael A. Gomez, *Exchanging Our Country Marks: The Transformation of African Identities in the Colonial and Antebellum South* (Chapel Hill: University of North Carolina Press, 1998), 116 (first quotation); Falconbridge, *Account of the Slave Trade,* 22 (second and third quotations), 20 (fourth and fifth quotations); Marcus Rediker, *The Slave Ship: A Human History* (New York: Viking, 2007), 271 (sixth quotation).

4. Werner Sollors, ed., *The Interesting Narrative of the Life of Olaudah Equiano, or Gustavus Vassa, the African, Written by Himself* (New York: Norton, 2001), 39 (first and second quotations); David Eltis, *The Rise of African Slavery in the Americas* (Cambridge: Cambridge University Press, 2000), 230 (third quotation), 229 (eighth quotation), 232, 233 (ninth quotation); Anthony S. Parent Jr., *Foul Means: The Formation of a Slave Society in Virginia, 1660–1740* (Chapel Hill: University of North Carolina Press, 2003), 138; Rediker, *Slave Ship,* 272 (fourth and fifth quotations); Stephanie E. Smallwood, *Saltwater Slavery: A Middle Passage from Africa to American Diaspora* (Cambridge: Harvard University Press, 2007), 180 (sixth and seventh quotations).

5. Rediker, *Slave Ship,* 271; Roth, *American Homicide,* 99–100; Ira Berlin, *Many Thousands Gone: The First Two Centuries of Slavery in North America* (Cambridge: Belknap Press of Harvard University Press, 1998), 104 (first quotation); Philip D. Morgan, *Slave Counterpoint: Black Culture in the Eighteenth-Century Chesapeake and Lowcountry* (Chapel Hill: University of North Carolina Press, 1998), 458; T. J. Desch Obi, *Fighting for Honor: The History of African Martial Art Traditions in the Atlantic World* (Columbia: University of South Carolina Press, 2008), 77 (second quotation).

6. Eltis, *Rise of African Slavery,* 230; Peter H. Wood, *Black Majority: Negroes in Colonial South Carolina from 1670 through the Stono Rebellion* (1974; reprint, New York: Norton, 1975), 252; Jen-

nifer L. Morgan, *Laboring Women: Reproduction and Gender in New World Slavery* (Philadelphia: University of Pennsylvania Press, 2004), 134; Berlin, *Many Thousands Gone*, 104.

7. Berlin, *Many Thousands Gone*, 129, 142; Morgan, *Slave Counterpoint*, 459, 614; Philip J. Schwarz, *Twice Condemned: Slaves and the Criminal Laws of Virginia, 1705–1865* (Baton Rouge: Louisiana State University Press, 1988), 90–91n44, 154, 108; Cumberland County, Order Book, 1752–1758, Reel 23, LVA; Cumberland County, Order Book, 1762–1764, Reel 24, LVA.

8. Roth, *American Homicide*, 124; Cotton Mather, *Tremenda. The Dreadful Sound with Which the Wicked Are to Be Thunderstruck. In a Sermon Delivered Unto a Great Assembly, in Which Was Present, a Miserable African, Just Going to Be Executed for a Most Inhumane and Uncommon Murder. At Boston, May 25th, 1721. To Which is Added, a Conference Between a Minister and the Prisoner, on the Day Before His Execution* (Boston: B. Green, 1721), 34; Executive Papers, James Patton Preston, February 1817, Box 1, Folder 6, LVA.

9. Steven Deyle, *Carry Me Back: The Domestic Slave Trade in American Life* (New York: Oxford University Press, 2005), 13; Eugene D. Genovese, *Roll, Jordan, Roll: The World the Slaves Made* (1974; reprint, New York; Vintage, 1976), 625.

10. Deyle, *Carry Me Back*, 251; quoted in Walter Johnson, *Soul by Soul: Life inside the Antebellum Slave Market* (Cambridge: Harvard University Press, 1999), 68.

11. David L. Lightner, *Slavery and the Commerce Power: How the Struggle Against the Interstate Slave Trade Led to the Civil War* (New Haven: Yale University Press, 2006), 63–64; Deyle, *Carry Me Back*, 254–255.

12. Genovese, *Roll, Jordan, Roll*, 624–625; Executive Papers, Joseph Johnson, February–April 1852, Box 411, Folder March 1852, LVA; George P. Rawick, ed., *The American Slave: A Composite Autobiography*, vol. 12, pt. 2 (Westport, Conn.: Greenwood Publishing Company, 1972), 138.

13. Quoted in Johnson, *Soul by Soul*, 196; Christopher Morris, *Becoming Southern: The Evolution of a Way of Life, Warren County and Vicksburg, Mississippi, 1770–1860* (New York: Oxford University Press, 1995), 81, 82.

14. Quoted in Genovese, *Roll, Jordan, Roll*, 620; Francis Terry Leak Diary #1095 [typescript vol. 3], SHC; Schwarz, *Twice Condemned*, 150; Spartanburg District, Court of Magistrates and Freeholders, Trial Papers, Reel C2920, Case #11, SCDAH; Anderson District, Court of Magistrates and Freeholders, Reel C2917, Case #189, SCDAH.

15. Russell County, Law Order Book 11, 1838–1846, Reel 17, LVA.

16. Executive Papers, Wilson Cary Nicholas, April 1816–October 1816, Misc. Reel 239, LVA; Kershaw District, Court of Magistrates and Freeholders, Trial Papers, 1800–1861, Box 1, Folder 7, SCDAH; Executive Papers, William B. Giles, May 1827, Box 1, Folder 6, LVA; Pendleton District, Court of Magistrates and Freeholders, Reel C2916, Case #24, SCDAH; Executive Papers, John Letcher, Misc. Reel 4715, Box 5, Folder 7, Frames 343–348, LVA; *William (a slave) v. the State* (1855), Supreme Court of Georgia, 18 Ga. 356, 1855 Ga. LEXIS 202.

17. Rediker, *Slave Ship*, 273; Executive Papers, William Smith, January–April 1848, Box 390, Folder March 1848, LVA.

18. *U.S. v. Clark* (1825), 25 Fed. Cas. 441 (2 Cranch C.C. 620), in *Judicial Cases Concerning American Slavery and the Negro*, vol. 4, ed. Helen Tunnicliff Catterall (Washington, D.C.: Carnegie Institution of Washington, 1936); 176; *William (a slave) v. the State* (1855), Supreme Court of Georgia, 18 Ga. 356, 1855 Ga. LEXIS 202.

19. Roth, *American Homicide*, 101; Halifax County, Minutes 14, 1847–1850, June 1847, LVA; Francois-Xavier Martin, *Martin's Reports of Cases Argued and Determined in the Supreme Court of the State of Louisiana*, vol. 4 (New Orleans: J. B. Steel, 1853), 176.

20. *Laura, a slave v. the State of Mississippi* (1852), Box 5830, Case 6763, MDAH; *Sam, a slave v. the State of Mississippi* (1857), Box 5842, Case 7910, MDAH.

21. Genovese, *Roll, Jordan, Roll*, 622; *Re Chaperon's Slave* (1745), 14 La. Hist. Q. 97, in *Judicial Cases Concerning American Slavery and the Negro*, vol. 3, ed. Helen Tunnicliff Catterall (Washington, D.C.: Carnegie Institution of Washington, 1932), 419; *Re Negro Pedro* (1774), 10 La. Hist Q. 455, in *Judicial Cases*, vol. 3, 431; Morgan, *Slave Counterpoint*, 463, 468; Morris, *Becoming Southern*, 81; John Ernest, ed., *Narrative of the Life of Henry Box Brown, Written by Himself* (Chapel Hill: University of North Carolina Press, 2008), 58; Genovese, *Roll, Jordan, Roll*, 629.

22. Morgan, *Slave Counterpoint*, 468; Norman R. Yetman, ed., *Life under the "Peculiar Institution": Selections from the Slave Narrative Collection* (New York: Holt, Rinehart and Winston Inc., 1970), 142; Race and Slavery Petitions Project, #11383403, Ser. I, Reel 11, 0106; Race and Slavery Petitions Project, #11382410, Ser. I, Reel 10, 0244.

23. Morgan, *Slave Counterpoint*, 470; Schwarz, *Twice Condemned*, 89; Douglas R. Egerton, *Gabriel's Rebellion: The Virginia Slave Conspiracies of 1800 and 1802* (Chapel Hill: University of North Carolina Press, 1993), 149, 173–175; Glenn M. McNair, "Justice Bound: Aframericans, Crime, and Criminal Justice in Georgia, 1751–1865" (Ph.D. diss., Emory University, 2001), 20.

24. Quoted in Schwarz, *Twice Condemned*, 247; John C. Willis, "Behind 'Their Black Masks': Slave Honor in Antebellum Virginia" (M.A. thesis, University of Virginia, 1987), 23 (quotation), 24. See, alternatively, idem, "From the Dictates of Pride to the Paths of Righteousness: Slave Honor and Christianity in Antebellum Virginia," in *The Edge of the South: Life in Nineteenth-Century Virginia*, ed. Edward L. Ayers and John C. Willis (Charlottesville: University Press of Virginia, 1991), 41; Pittsylvania County, Court Records 27, 1827–1829, Reel 55, LVA; Genovese, *Roll, Jordan, Roll*, 635.

25. Edward L. Ayers, *Vengeance and Justice: Crime and Punishment in the 19th-Century American South* (New York: Oxford University Press, 1984), 133; Kenneth M. Stampp, *The Peculiar Institution: Slavery in the Ante-Bellum South* (New York: Alfred A. Knopf, 1956), 335; Genovese, *Roll, Jordan, Roll*, 635; Emily West, *Chains of Love: Slave Couples in Antebellum South Carolina* (Urbana: University of Illinois Press, 2004), 44; Ayers, *Vengeance and Justice*, 133; McNair, "Justice Bound," 52, 48–49, 372.

26. Rawick, *American Slave*, vol. 12, pt. 2, 108; George P. Rawick, ed., *The American Slave: A Composite Autobiography, Supplement, Series 1*, vol. 3, pt. 1 (Westport, Conn: Greenwood Press, 1977), 64 (hereinafter cited as SS1); quoted in Thomas D. Morris, *Southern Slavery and the Law, 1619–1860* (Chapel Hill: University of North Carolina Press, 1996), 299; Charles C. Jones, *The Religious Instruction of the Negroes. In the United States* (Savannah: Thomas Purse, 1842), 136; Charles Lyell, *Second Visit to North America*, vol. 1, 3rd ed. (London: John Murray, 1855), 358. See also Genovese, *Roll, Jordan, Roll*, 635.

27. Roth, *American Homicide*, 101 (first and second quotations), 127, 226 (third and fourth quotations), 227. In antebellum Florida, blacks committed 51 of at least 401 homicides that occurred from 1821 to 1861. The 51 included victims of all races. James M. Denham and Randolph Roth placed "[t]he homicide rate for black adults" at some "10 to 14 per 100,000 persons per year,

a bit higher than the 8 per 100,000" in the 4 Virginia counties of Amelia, Lancaster, Rockbridge, and Surry examined for their sample. The Florida estimate was consistent with their findings for Horry and Edgefield Districts in South Carolina and the Georgia counties of Franklin, Jasper, and Wilkes. See James M. Denham and Randolph Roth, "Why Was Antebellum Florida Murderous? A Quantitative Analysis of Homicide in Florida, 1821–1861," *Florida Historical Quarterly* 86 (Fall 2007): 218, 224.

28. Eric H. Monkkonen, *Murder in New York City* (Berkeley: University of California Press, 2001), 149, 138 (quotations); Roger Lane, *Murder in America: A History* (Columbus: Ohio State University Press, 1997), 116–117; Historical Census Browser, University of Virginia, Geospatial and Statistical Data Center (2004): http://fisher.lib.virginia.edu/collections/stats/histcensus/index.html.

29. McNair, "Justice Bound," 360.

30. *State v. Caesar, a slave* (1849), 9 Ired. 391, 31 N.C. 391 (N.C.), 1849 WL 1307 (N.C.); Edward E. Baptist, *Creating an Old South: Middle Florida's Plantation Frontier Before the Civil War* (Chapel Hill: University of North Carolina Press, 2002), 233 (first and second quotations), 204 (third quotation).

31. Robert M. Saunders, "Crime and Punishment in Early National America: Richmond, Virginia, 1784–1820," *Virginia Magazine of History and Biography* 86 (January 1978): 44; Mecklenburg County, Virginia, Order Book 6, 1853–1858 (County Court), Reel 120, LVA. See also Michael Stephen Hindus, *Prison and Plantation: Crime, Justice, and Authority in Massachusetts and South Carolina, 1767–1878* (Chapel Hill: University of North Carolina Press, 1980), 140–142, 144.

32. The sample nine Baptist churches in Southside Virginia include, in Charlotte County, Antioch, Keysville, Mossingford, Mt. Tirzah, and Shiloh; Mount Vernon, in Halifax County; Buffalo, in Mecklenburg County; and Cascade Primitive and Lower Banister, both in Pittsylvania County, all LVA. The fifteen Baptist churches in the South Carolina upcountry are, in Greenville District, Abner Creek, Brushy Creek, Clear Springs, and Milford; in Kershaw District, Beaverdam Primitive; in Laurens District, Bethabara, Chestnut Ridge, Huntsville, Poplar Springs, Rabun Creek, and Warrior Creek; in Union District, Padgett's Creek, Union, and Upper Fairforest; and Flint Hill in York District, all SCL. The twelve sample Middle Georgia Baptist churches are, in Lincoln County, Goshen, Greenwood, Hephzibah, New Hope, and Salem; and in Wilkes County, Beaverdam, Clarke's Station, Fishing Creek, Philips Mill, Rehoboth, Sardis, and Washington First, all GA.

33. Brushy Creek Baptist Church (Greenville District, S.C.), Minutes, 1794–1927, SCL; Genovese, *Roll, Jordan, Roll,* 636.

34. Morris, *Southern Slavery and the Law,* 299; Schwarz, *Twice Condemned,* 238–240, 105; Robert Olwell, *Masters, Slaves, & Subjects: The Culture of Power in the South Carolina Low Country, 1740–1790* (Ithaca: Cornell University Press, 1998), 79. Olwell's finding runs counter to Philip D. Morgan's observation that, in the colonial era, slaves murdered as many blacks as whites. See Morgan, *Slave Counterpoint,* 473. The contrast between the rural U.S. South and urban Latin America is striking. As Herbert S. Klein notes, "Two-thirds of the victims of crimes in the city of Rio de Janeiro between 1810 and 1821 were slaves assaulted by their fellow slaves." See Herbert S. Klein, *African Slavery in Latin America and the Caribbean* (New York: Oxford University Press, 1986), 214.

35. Philip J. Schwarz, *Slave Laws in Virginia* (Athens: University of Georgia Press, 2010), 33; idem, *Twice Condemned,* 247, 152.

36. Jeff Forret, *Race Relations at the Margins: Slaves and Poor Whites in the Antebellum Southern Countryside* (Baton Rouge: Louisiana State University Press, 2006); Roth, *American Homicide,* 99 (quotation), 101; Index, Court of General Sessions Records, Laurens District, SCDAH; Index, Court of General Sessions Records, Spartanburg District, SCDAH; ACCCHNF; Albemarle County Commonwealth Causes, LVA; Mecklenburg County, Virginia, Order Book 6, 1853–1858 (County Court), Reel 120, LVA; Roth, *American Homicide,* 226. Much more research needs to be completed at the county court level to provide a more precise picture of comparative rates of violence between whites and blacks.

37. Schwarz, *Twice Condemned,* 63, 90, 153, 64 (quotation); Morgan, *Slave Counterpoint,* 472–473.

38. Albemarle County Commonwealth Causes, LVA.

39. Ulrich B. Phillips, "Slave Crime in Virginia," *American Historical Review* 20 (January 1915): 337; Daniel J. Flanigan, *The Criminal Law of Slavery and Freedom 1800–1868* (New York: Garland Publishing, Inc., 1987), 49, 404; Schwarz, *Twice Condemned,* 232.

40. Schwarz, *Twice Condemned,* 90; Anthony E. Kaye, *Joining Places: Slave Neighborhoods in the Old South* (Chapel Hill: University of North Carolina Press, 2007), 120, 124; Laurens District, Court of Magistrates and Freeholders, Trial Papers, 1808–1865, Box 1, Folder 67, SCDAH. From 1785 to 1864, Philip J. Schwarz uncovered 31 cases of slaves killed by another slave owned by the same master, 67 cases of slaves killed by a slave belonging to a different master, and 23 cases of infanticide, for a total of 121. See Schwarz, *Twice Condemned,* 232. Over that same period, 34 slaves were convicted of murdering a slave owned by the same master, 69 slaves were convicted of murdering a slave owned by a different master, and 19 were convicted of infanticide. See Schwarz, *Twice Condemned,* 233. According to Schwarz, by the late eighteenth century and into the nineteenth, the number of cross-plantation slave homicides declined somewhat. Of slave-slave murders between 1785 and 1834, he writes, "the killing of slaves from other plantations was not [as] predominant as it was in the early and mid-eighteenth century." Schwarz, *Twice Condemned,* 247.

41. The same was true postwar. See Gilles Vandal, "'Bloody Caddo': White Violence against Blacks in a Louisiana Parish, 1865–1876," *Journal of Social History* 25 (Winter 1991): 374–375; and idem, "Black Violence in Post–Civil War Louisiana," *Journal of Interdisciplinary History* 25 (Summer 1994): 63.

42. Auditor of Public Accounts, Condemned Blacks Executed or Transported, Records—Condemned Slaves, Court Orders, and Valuations, 1794–1809, Misc. Reel 2550, Frame 326, LVA. See also Auditor of Public Accounts, Condemned Blacks Executed or Transported, Records—Condemned Slaves, Court Orders, and Valuations, 1846–1857, Misc. Reel 2554, Frame 880, LVA; Auditor of Public Accounts, Condemned Blacks Executed or Transported, Records—Condemned Slaves, Court Orders, and Valuations, 1781–1793, Misc. Reel 2549, Frame 721, LVA.

43. McNair, "Justice Bound," 115, 117; Schwarz, *Twice Condemned,* 154, 247; Executive Papers, John Floyd, January–February 1851, Box 403, Folder February 11–20, 1851, LVA; Executive Papers, Henry Lee, Oversized Box 9, Folder 59, Frame 478, Misc. Reel 5054, LVA; Madison County, Order Book 7, Reel 25, LVA; Prince Edward County, County Court Orders No. 23 1832–1837, Reel 30, LVA; Auditor of Public Accounts, Condemned Blacks Executed or Transported, Records—Condemned Slaves, Court Orders, and Valuations, 1823–1832, Misc. Reel 2552, Frame

1188, LVA; Executive Papers, Joseph Johnson, March–May 1854, Box 424, Folder March 1854, LVA; *Frank et al. (slaves) v. State* (1855), Supreme Court of Alabama, 27 Ala. 37, 1855 Ala. LEXIS 7.

44. Schwarz, *Twice Condemned*, 153–154; Auditor of Public Accounts, Condemned Blacks Executed or Transported, Records—Condemned Slaves, Court Orders, and Valuations, 1794–1809, Misc. Reel 2550, Frame 305, LVA; Powhatan County, Order Book 12, 1814–1816, Reel 27, LVA; Auditor of Public Accounts, Condemned Blacks Executed or Transported, Records—Condemned Slaves, Court Orders, and Valuations, 1823–1832, Misc. Reel 2552, Frame 1166, LVA.

45. Schwarz, *Twice Condemned*, 90. In Adams County, Mississippi, court records, no enslaved woman committed an act of violence against another slave. All but one victim of enslaved male violence were men.

46. Roth, *American Homicide*, 124; Schwarz, *Twice Condemned*, 153.

47. Morgan, *Slave Counterpoint*, 166–167.

48. Jones, *Religious Instruction of the Negroes*, 136; Henry Bibb, *Narrative of the Life and Adventures of Henry Bibb, an American Slave, Written by Himself* (New York: The Author, 1849), 23; Anne Newport Royall, *Letters from Alabama, 1817–1822*, ed. Lucille Griffith (Tuscaloosa: University of Alabama Press, 1969), 248–249; Spartanburg District, Court of Magistrates and Freeholders, Reel C2920, Case #131, SCDAH; *The Star, and North-Carolina State Gazette* (Raleigh), September 30, 1825. Joe was found guilty and sentenced to twenty-three lashes. Sunday was the common day for violent intraracial conflicts after slavery as well. See Vandal, "Black Violence," 62.

49. Jones, *Religious Instruction of the Negroes*, 136; Ayers, *Vengeance and Justice*, 101; Genovese, *Roll, Jordan, Roll*, 635; Judith Kelleher Schafer, "Slaves and Crime: New Orleans, 1846–1862," in *Local Matters: Race, Crime, and Justice in the Nineteenth-Century South*, ed. Christopher Waldrep and Donald G. Nieman (Athens: University of Georgia Press, 2001), 54; First District Court of New Orleans, NOPL; *State v. Henry, slave of Mr. Jennings* (1853), First District Court of New Orleans, 9144, NOPL.

50. On the spatial distribution of intraracial violence in postwar Louisiana, see Vandal, "Black Violence," 57–58. There, one-third of black intraracial murders in the entire state were confined to the Red River Delta region.

51. McNair, "Justice Bound," 118; ACCCHNF; author's database of cases from South Carolina and Virginia; Auditor of Public Accounts, Condemned Blacks Executed or Transported, Records—Condemned Slaves, Court Orders, and Valuations, 1794–1809, Misc. Reel 2550, Frames 937, LVA; *State v. Prince*, 1827, Chatham County, Georgia, Inferior Court Trial Docket, 1813–1827, Drawer 90, Reel 33. Stephen A. West, "From Yeoman to Redneck in Upstate South Carolina, 1850–1915" (Ph.D. diss., Columbia University, 1998), 139, observed that, among whites in the South Carolina upcountry, minor assaults were frequent but rarely involved knives. Slaves, however, frequently used them. Studies have shown that, in the twentieth century, blacks were five times more likely than whites to commit murder with a knife or other sharp object. See Marvin E. Wolfgang, *Patterns in Criminal Homicide* (1958; reprint, Montclair, N.J.: Patterson Smith, 1975), 86.

52. *State v. Sanite, slave of Alexis Faurie* (1855), First District Court of New Orleans, 9934, NOPL (first three quotations); Executive Papers, James Patton Preston, January 1817, Box 1, Folders 3, 6, LVA (fourth and fifth quotations); Schwarz, *Twice Condemned*, 96, 108 (seventh quotation), 109, 203 (sixth quotation); Cumberland County, Order Book, 1762–1764, Reel 24, LVA (eighth quotation). Schwarz further explains that only 23 of the 117 total convictions for poison-

ing or administering poison (20 percent) between 1750 and 1784 were for harming or attempting to harm fellow bondpeople. Of the sixteen not slated to hang, eleven were granted benefit of clergy and five escaped with a misdemeanor conviction. See Schwarz, *Twice Condemned*, 203, 96.

53. Schwarz, *Twice Condemned*, 96, 203n5. Caroline County, Order Book, 1759–1763, Reel 16, LVA. In 1765, a Cumberland County court ordered Peter, charged with preparing and delivering poison "to Bella a negro woman slave," to die for his crime. Middlesex County bondman Lewis stood accused in 1772 of having "wilfully and feloniously prepare[d] and exhibit[ed] certain poisonous Medicines unto" Burgess, John, and "divers[e] other Slaves" of his master, Gavin Corbin. Although Burgess and John both died, Lewis was found not guilty in the death of the former "but Guilty of the other Murder and Felonies in the Indictment." The court scheduled him to hang in late May. The same fate awaited Lunenburg County slave Dollen, executed for preparing and delivering poison to the bondman Mercer. See Cumberland County, Order Book, 1764–1767, Reel 24, LVA; Middlesex County, Order Book 1769–1772, Reel 39, LVA; Auditor of Public Accounts, Condemned Blacks Executed or Transported, Records—Condemned Slaves, Court Orders, and Valuations, 1781–1793, Misc. Reel 2549, Frames 425–426, LVA. According to Schwarz, at least one bondperson convicted of poisoning was pardoned.

54. Orange County, Order Book 5, 1747–1754, Reel 32, LVA; Powhatan County, Order Book 1, 1777–1784, Reel 22, LVA; Powhatan County, Order Book 2, 1784–1786, Reel 22, LVA; Schwarz, *Twice Condemned*, 100–101, 107, 109.

55. Caroline County, Order Book, 1741–1746 (Parts 1 & 2), Reel 14, LVA; Cumberland County, Order Book, 1772–1774, Reel 25, LVA. In another case, Cumberland County's "Tim a negro man slave" supposedly administered "sundry poisonous medicines" to the bondwoman Sue in 1765. The court found Tim not guilty as charged but ordered him to "receive thirty nine lashes on his bare back well laid on" "at the common whipping post" because he was still "guilty of threatening the life of the said Sue." Cumberland County, Order Book, 1764–1767, Reel 24, LVA.

56. D. R. Hundley, *Social Relations in Our Southern States* (New York: Henry B. Price, 1860; reprint, New York: Arno Press, 1973), 332; Schwarz, *Twice Condemned*, 296; *Mississippi Territory v. Peter a slave* (1812), Case 6793, Group 1810, Box 27, File 42, ACCCHNF. In Lincoln County, Georgia, Elick allegedly used a "large quantity of the Root of Hemlock" to "secretly mix & mingle into the food or infuse in water" so that "Bob should eat & swallow down into his boddy the said root of Hemlock." The concoction produced "sickness & distemper of Boddy" as well as the ultimate "death of negro Bob." But Elick was not held legally responsible. Likewise six Spartanburg District, South Carolina, slaves were found not guilty of an alleged poisoning that "cause[d] the death of a certain Negro woman Ann" in the fall of 1843. A vigilant and suspicious young white woman had "found something in a handkerchief" that she assumed was poison but that one of the accused dismissed as harmless "potatoe starch." A medical doctor who twice visited a failing Ann testified "that he had no suspicions at the time" of possible poisoning and that he was not convinced her symptoms, including a "tongue [that] swelled verry quickly," were consistent with poisoning. All the enslaved defendants were discharged. Lincoln County, Georgia, Inferior Court, Docket of Slaves indicted for capital crimes, 1814–1838; Spartanburg District, Court of Magistrates and Freeholders, Reel C2920, Case #66, SCDAH.

57. Auditor of Public Accounts, Condemned Blacks Executed or Transported, Records—Condemned Slaves, Court Orders, and Valuations, 1794–1809, Misc. Reel 2550, Frames 305–306, LVA;

Mississippi Territory v. Negro man Milo (1814), Case 6794, Group 1810, Box 27, File 1, ACCCHNF. In one case from Adams County, Mississippi, an available piece of discarded lumber sufficed. After the bondman Johnson "got into a quarrel" and struck his fellow slave Ellis with a "Press Iron (usually called an arrow)," Ellis retaliated by fatally whacking his foe on the head with a worthless wooden plank about three feet in length. The wounds inflicted by "a certain brickbat of no value" led to the bondman John's death on Christmas day 1854. *State v. Ellis, a slave* (1840), Case 10566, Group 1840, Box 7, File 24, ACCCHNF; *State v. Henry, a slave, and West, a slave* (1855), Case 10300, Group 1850, Box 26, File, 67, ACCCHNF.

58. *State v. Anthony, a slave* (1834), Case 22977, Group 1830, Box 66, File 50, ACCCHNF; Executive Papers, William B. Giles, May 1827, Box 1, Folder 6, LVA; Executive Papers, James Pleasants, November 1824, Box 5, Folder 12, LVA; *Jordan, a slave v. the State of Mississippi* (1856), Box 5842, Case 7834, MDAH; *State v. Little Jordan, a slave* (1855), Case 10301, Group 1850, Box 26, File 68, ACCCHNF; *State v. Horace, a slave* (1860), Case 10416, Group 1860, Box 1, File 76, ACCCHNF; *State v. George, a slave* (1840), Case 10575, Group 1840, Box 7, File, 34, ACCCHNF; Harrison County, Minute Book, 1816–1818, Reel 7, LVA. In 2012 dollars, all of these murder weapons ranged in value from between $1.36 and $26.62.

59. Middlesex County, Orders 1794–1797, Reel 43, LVA; Executive Papers, Henry Lee, Oversized Box 9, Folder 59, Frame 478, Misc. Reel 5054, LVA; Auditor of Public Accounts, Condemned Blacks Executed or Transported, Records—Condemned Slaves, Court Orders, and Valuations, 1781–1793, Misc. Reel 2549, Frame 669, LVA; *State v. Horace, a slave* (1860), Case 10416, Group 1860, Box 1, File 76, ACCCHNF. Also in Natchez, Isaac, for reasons never stated in the trial papers, struck Lewis two or three times in the face. Lewis called Isaac "crazy," and after the latter grabbed "an axe helve and a dirk," Lewis "picked up a billet of wood to defend himself" and delivered a fatal blow to Isaac. *State v. Lewis, a slave* (1834), Case 22984, Group 1830, Box 66, File 53, ACCCHNF.

60. Nicolas W. Proctor, *Bathed in Blood: Hunting and Mastery in the Old South* (Charlottesville: University Press of Virginia, 2002), 162; Morgan, *Slave Counterpoint*, 386, 389–391; McNair "Justice Bound," 119. Exceptions continued to exist in the antebellum decades, however. Proctor located rare examples of slaves who owned a gun or received one as a gift. See Proctor, *Bathed in Blood*, 163.

61. Executive Papers, John Floyd, April–June 1849, Box 394, Folder June 1849, LVA; Anderson District, Court of Magistrates and Freeholders, Reel C2918, Case #278, SCDAH; *State v. Negro Bill Jefferson, a slave* (1842), Court of General Sessions of Delaware, 3 Del. 571, 1842 Del. LEXIS 58, 3 Harr. 571; Jones County, Georgia, Inferior Court Minutes, 1818–1846.

62. Executive Papers, Henry A. Wise, Misc. Reel 4208, Frames 148–149, LVA. Bertie County, North Carolina's, "Dempsy a negro man slave the property of John Rowan" stood charged in 1804 "with shooting a negro man slave named March the property of Mrs. Ann B. Pollock." In 1812, the bondman Carter of Chatham County, Georgia, visited master Edward Harden's Mulberry Grove plantation and "feloniously wilfully and of his malice aforethought, shot and murdered a negro man slave named John, the property of . . . Edward Harden." One slave owner in the Province of West Florida complained to the Escambia County court in 1821 that a bondman named Tom "maliciously and without provocation shot" her slave Harry and "wounded Him mortally." Bertie County, Criminal Papers, 1803–1819, Folder Criminal 1803–1805, NCDAH; *State v. Carter* (1813),

Chatham County, Georgia, Inferior Court Trial Docket, 1813–1827, Drawer 90, Reel 33, GA; Race and Slavery Petitions Project, #20582102, Ser. II, Reel 5, 0710.

63. Proctor, *Bathed in Blood*, 147, 163; Executive Papers, John Letcher, Misc. Reel 4724, Box 8, Folder 4, Frames 201–206, LVA; *State v. Cornelius (slave)* (1861), First District Court of New Orleans, 15361, NOPL; *State v. Moses, a slave* (1830), Supreme Court of North Carolina, 13 N.C. 452, 1830 N.C. LEXIS 82; *Jim, a slave, v. the State* (1843), Supreme Court of Tennessee, 23 Tenn. 289, 1843 Tenn. LEXIS 85, 4 Hum. 289; *Jim, a slave, v. the State* (1844), Supreme Court of Tennessee, 24 Tenn. 145, 1844 Tenn. LEXIS 46, 5 Hum. 145; McNair, "Justice Bound," 119.

64. Schwarz, *Twice Condemned*, 155, 231.

2. SLAVES, MASTERS, CHURCH, AND THE CIVIL LAW OF SLAVERY

1. Governor's Papers, Gov. Edward B. Dudley, G.P. 90, Folder Correspondence, Petitions, etc. Oct. 1, 1839–Oct. 28, 1839, NCDAH.

2. James O. Breeden, ed., *Advice among Masters: The Ideal in Slave Management in the Old South* (Westport, Conn.: Greenwood Press, 1980), 58–59, 60, 55; Bocock quoted in Eugene D. Genovese, *Roll, Jordan, Roll: The World the Slaves Made* (1974; reprint, New York; Vintage, 1976), 634; George P. Rawick, ed., *The American Slave: A Composite Autobiography*, vol. 12, pt. 1 (Westport, Conn.: Greenwood Publishing Company, 1972), 84.

3. Philip J. Schwarz, *Slave Laws in Virginia* (Athens: University of Georgia Press, 2010), 87; Christopher Morris, "Within the Slave Cabin: Violence in Mississippi Slave Families," in *Over the Threshold: Intimate Violence in Early America*, ed. Christine Daniels and Michael V. Kennedy (New York: Routledge, 1999), 275; Rawick, *American Slave*, vol. 2, pt. 2, 129–130; idem, ed., *The American Slave: A Composite Autobiography, Supplement, Series 1*, vol. 9, pt. 4 (Westport, Conn.: Greenwood Press, 1977), 1743, 1657; idem, *American Slave*, vol. 2, pt. 2, 31.

4. Wilmington *Recorder*, reprinted in *The Star, and North-Carolina State Gazette* (Raleigh), August 14, 1828; Beaufort (S.C.) *Banner*, reprinted in *The North Carolinian* (Fayetteville), October 27, 1855.

5. Breeden, *Advice among Masters*, 58; Charles C. Jones, *The Religious Instruction of the Negroes. In the United States* (Savannah: Thomas Purse, 1842), 136; Lorri Glover, *Southern Sons: Becoming Men in the New Nation* (Baltimore: Johns Hopkins University Press, 2007), 176.

6. John Hammond Moore, ed., *A Plantation Mistress on the Eve of the Civil War: The Diary of Keziah Goodwyn Hopkins Brevard, 1860–1861* (Columbia: University of South Carolina Press, 1993), 100.

7. Rawick, *American Slave*, vol. 12, pt. 2, 75; idem, ed., *The American Slave: A Composite Autobiography, Supplement, Series 2*, vol. 10, pt. 9 (Westport, Conn.: Greenwood Press, 1979), 3981 (hereinafter cited as SS2); idem, *American Slave*, vol. 13, pt. 3, 54; Steven Hahn, *A Nation under Our Feet: Black Political Struggles in the Rural South, from Slavery to the Great Migration* (Cambridge: Belknap Press of Harvard University Press, 2003), 37; Executive Papers, John M. Gregory, November 1842, Box 2, Folder 7, LVA; T. J. Desch Obi, *Fighting for Honor: The History of African Martial Art Traditions in the Atlantic World* (Columbia: University of South Carolina Press, 2008), 100; James Mellon, ed., *Bullwhip Days: The Slaves Remember* (New York: Weidenfeld &

Nicolson, 1988), 138; Harry Smith, *Fifty Years of Slavery in the United States of America* (Grand Rapids: West Michigan Printing Co., 1891), 135, 136.

8. Essex County, Order Book 45, 1823–1826, Reel 94, LVA; Executive Papers, John Letcher, Misc. Reel 4767, Box 22, Folder 4, Frames 46–48, LVA. Following a Nelson County, Virginia, corn shucking in 1840, "there was some dispute . . . between Brents Harry and boy," and a slave known as Little Joe labored "to make peace" between them. In Richmond, the slave William "urged Isaac," then stewing in his own hatred for tobacco factory co-worker Emanuel, "to give over his threats and behave himself." Nelson County, County Court Minute Book, Vol. 8, 1835–1840, Reel 27, LVA; Executive Papers, John M. Gregory, November 1842, Box 2, Folder 4, LVA.

9. Pittsylvania County, Court Records 27, 1827–1829, Reel 55, LVA. During the altercation, Shadrack had arrived for breakfast shortly before George. Shadrack threatened to kill George if he went into the house to eat. As George attempted to enter, another bondman named Stephen "pushed him back & told him he wanted no fuss there," but his efforts were insufficient. At that point, Aunt Philis stepped in.

10. Executive Papers, John Letcher, Misc. Reel 4783, Box 28, Folder 8, Frames 608–612, LVA; Executive Papers, Thomas Walker Gilmer, August 1840, Box 2, Folder 1, LVA; Executive Papers, William B. Giles, May 1827, Box 1, Folder 6, LVA. When her son Richard got into a fistfight with the bondman Cupe in her Russell County slave cabin, the enslaved mother Phillis "told Richard to let him alone." Richard's brother and fellow slave Brittain Tully stepped in and "pulled Richard off him." Russell County, Law Order Book 11, 1838–1846, Reel 17, LVA.

11. Executive Papers, John Floyd, February 1834, Box 12, Folder 4, LVA; *State v. Prince* (1827), Chatham County, Georgia, Inferior Court Trial Docket, 1813–1827, Drawer 90, Reel 33, GA. See also the incidents involving Stephen, Cary, and Jim, in Executive Papers, James Pleasants, November 1824, Box 5, Folder 12, LVA; Billy, John, and Knight, in Executive Papers, William Smith, January–April 1848, Box 390, Folder March 1848, LVA; Hilliard and three other slaves, in Madison County, Order Book 7, Reel 25, LVA; Jim, Andrew, and Jefferson, in Executive Papers, John Letcher, Misc. Reel 4767, Box 22, Folder 4, Frames 46–48, LVA; Kit, Henry, and Nathan, in Executive Papers, John Letcher, Misc. Reel 4783, Box 28, Folder 8, Frames 608–612, LVA; Shadrack, George, and Stephen, in Pittsylvania County, Court Records 27, 1827–1829, Reel 55, LVA.

12. Executive Papers, David Campbell, May 1839, Box 6, Folder 2, LVA.

13. *State v. Cornelius (slave)* (1861), First District Court of New Orleans, 15361, NOPL; Executive Papers, William Smith, August–October 1848, Box 392, Folder October 1848, LVA; Madison County, Order Book 7, Reel 25, LVA.

14. Genovese, *Roll, Jordan, Roll,* 635; Executive Papers, David Campbell, May 1839, Box 6, Folder 2, LVA; Executive Papers, Henry A. Wise, Misc. Reel 4195, Box 2, Folder 5, Frames 3–11, April 1856, LVA; Rawick, SS1, vol. 7, pt. 2, 772; Jones, *Religious Instruction of the Negroes,* 130; Pittsylvania County, Court Records 21, 1819–1820, Reel 54, Frames 28–33, LVA.

15. Jones, *Religious Instruction of the Negroes,* 130, 131; Madison County, Order Book 7, Reel 25, LVA.

16. Executive Papers, William Smith, Misc. Reel 5022, Box 4, Folder 4, Frames 59–69, LVA; Executive Papers, William Smith, August–October 1848, Box 392, Folder October 1848, LVA; Essex County, Order Book 45, 1823–1826, Reel 94, LVA; Executive Papers, William B. Giles, May 1827, Box 1, Folder 6, LVA.

NOTES TO PAGES 79-84

17. Executive Papers, John Letcher, Misc. Reel 4715, Box 5, Folder 7, Frames 343–348, LVA; Auditor of Public Accounts, Condemned Blacks Executed or Transported, Records—Condemned Slaves, Court Orders, and Valuations, 1823–1832, Misc. Reel 2552, Frames 1158–1159, LVA; Executive Papers, James Pleasants, November 1824, Box 5, Folder 12, LVA.

18. Pittsylvania County, Court Records 27, 1827–1829, Reel 55, LVA; Executive Papers, Wyndham Robertson, Box 3, Folder 3, LVA; *Green, a slave v. the State of Mississippi* (1849), Box 5817, Case 2915, MDAH; Executive Papers, James Pleasants, November 1824, Box 5, Folder 12, LVA; Rawick, *American Slave*, vol. 3, pt. 3, 283; idem, SS1, vol. 8, pt. 3, 1232; Race and Slavery Petitions Project, #11383402, Ser. I, Reel 11, 0092.

19. Randolph Roth, *American Homicide* (Cambridge: Belknap Press of Harvard University Press, 2009), 227; Madison County, Order Book 7, Reel 25, LVA; Executive Papers, James Patton Preston, February 1817, Box 1, Folder 6, LVA; King George County, Order Book 12 1827–1833, Reel 32, LVA; Pittsylvania County, Court Records 27, 1827–1829, Reel 55, LVA; Executive Papers, Wyndham Robertson, Box 3, Folder 3, LVA; Governor's Papers, Gov. Edward B. Dudley, G.P. 90, Folder Correspondence, Petitions, etc. Oct. 1, 1839–Oct. 28, 1839, NCDAH; Russell County, Law Order Book 11, 1838–1846, Reel 17, LVA.

20. *State v. Charles Loadnum* (1798), Court of Oyer and Terminer of Delaware, Kent, 2 Del. Cas. 240, 1798 Del. LEXIS 42; Pittsylvania County, Court Records 21, 1819–1820, Reel 54, Frames 28–33, LVA; Executive Papers, James Barbour, July 1814, Box 13, Folder 1, LVA.

21. Essex County, Order Book 45, 1823–1826, Reel 94, LVA; Executive Papers, John Floyd, February 1834, Box 12, Folder 4, LVA; Executive Papers, William B. Giles, May 1827, Box 1, Folder 6, LVA; Auditor of Public Accounts, Condemned Blacks Executed or Transported, Records—Condemned Slaves, Court Orders, and Valuations, 1823–1832, Misc. Reel 2552, Frames 1158–1159, LVA; Executive Papers, Thomas Walker Gilmer, August 1840, Box 2, Folder 1, LVA; Race and Slavery Petitions Project, #11083102, Ser. I, Reel 3, 0433; Jones County, Georgia, Inferior Court Minutes, 1818–1846. Duckworth was awarded $210.25 for his time and trouble. In a similar case, John Broughton petitioned the general assembly of Tennessee in 1835 for the reimbursement of expenses incurred in pursuing and seizing "a free man of colour named Henry Ransom," who had killed "an old man the slave of Phillip Shute," and returning him for trial in Nashville. See Race and Slavery Petitions Project, #11483528, Ser. I, Reel 13, 0536.

22. Kenneth M. Stampp, *The Peculiar Institution: Slavery in the Ante-Bellum South* (New York: Alfred A. Knopf, 1956), 224; Drew Gilpin Faust, ed., *The Ideology of Slavery: Proslavery Thought in the Antebellum South, 1830–1860* (Baton Rouge: Louisiana State University Press, 1981), 190; Breeden, *Advice among Masters*, 57; Glenn M. McNair, "Justice Bound: Aframericans, Crime, and Criminal Justice in Georgia, 1751–1865" (Ph.D. diss., Emory University, 2001), 153; Michael Stephen Hindus, *Prison and Plantation: Crime, Justice, and Authority in Massachusetts and South Carolina, 1767–1878* (Chapel Hill: University of North Carolina Press, 1980), 139; Rawick, *American Slave*, vol. 7 Mississippi, 23; *Maria (a freedwoman) v. State*, Supreme Court of Texas, December 1866, 28 Tex. 698, 1866 WL 4062.

23. Genovese, *Roll, Jordan, Roll*, 634; Breeden, *Advice among Masters*, 51; Executive Papers, James Pleasants, November 1824, Box 5, Folder 12, LVA.

24. Quoted in Ulrich Bonnell Phillips, *American Negro Slavery: A Survey of the Supply, Employment and Control of Negro Labor as Determined by the Plantation Régime* (New York: Peter

Smith, 1952), 270; Rawick, *American Slave*, vol. 3, pt. 3, 157; idem, *American Slave*, vol. 4, pt. 2, 195; idem, *American Slave*, vol. 3, pt. 3, 182; idem, SS2, vol. 2, pt. 1, 408; idem, SS1, vol. 7, pt. 2, 772; Pittsylvania County, Court Records 27, 1827–1829, Reel 55, LVA; Rawick, *American Slave*, vol. 4, pt. 1, 191; idem, SS1, vol. 6, 130; Margaret Abruzzo, *Polemical Pain: Slavery, Cruelty, and the Rise of Humanitarianism* (Baltimore: Johns Hopkins University Press, 2011), 210. In Baton Rouge, Louisiana, "A town ordinance ordered the immediate flogging on the spot of any slave caught in a fight." See William L. Richter, "Slavery in Baton Rouge, 1820–1860," *Louisiana History* 10 (Spring 1969): 139. See also Ralph Betts Flanders, *Plantation Slavery in Georgia* (Chapel Hill: University of North Carolina Press, 1933; reprint, Cos Cob, Conn.: John E. Edwards, 1967), 255–256; Rawick, *American Slave*, vol. 7 Oklahoma, 94; idem, *American Slave*, vol. 13, pt. 3, 151; idem, SS2, vol. 2, pt. 1, 408; idem, SS1, vol. 7, pt. 2, 772; Pittsylvania County, Court Records 27, 1827–1829, Reel 55, LVA.

25. Rawick, SS2, vol. 2, pt. 1, 146; idem, *American Slave*, vol. 4, pt. 2, 195; quoted in Phillips, *American Negro Slavery*, 270; Rawick, *American Slave*, vol. 7 Oklahoma, 94; idem, *American Slave*, vol. 12, pt. 2, 57; idem, SS1, vol. 7, pt. 2, 441, 732.

26. Rawick, *American Slave*, vol. 12, pt. 1, 14; idem, *American Slave*, vol. 13, pt. 4, 129; idem, *American Slave*, vol. 7 Oklahoma, 346; idem, SS1, vol. 5, 160.

27. Rawick, SS2, vol. 4, pt. 3, 1033; idem, SS2, vol. 6, pt. 5, 2271; idem, SS1, vol. 9, pt. 4, 1663–1664, 1666; idem, SS1, vol. 8, pt. 3, 1186; idem, *American Slave*, vol. 12, pt. 1, 348, 310.

28. Rawick, *American Slave*, vol. 7 Oklahoma, 160; idem, *American Slave*, vol. 2, pt. 2, 9–10; Edwin Morris Betts, ed., *Thomas Jefferson's Farm Book with Commentary and Relevant Extracts from Other Writings* (Princeton: Princeton University Press, 1953), 19. On Jefferson and Cary, see also Mary Beth Norton, Herbert G. Gutman, and Ira Berlin, "The Afro-American Family in the Age of Revolution," in *Slavery and Freedom in the Age of the American Revolution*, ed. Ira Berlin and Ronald Hoffman (Charlottesville: University Press of Virginia, 1983), 184; and Steven Deyle, *Carry Me Back: The Domestic Slave Trade in American Life* (New York: Oxford University Press, 2005), 231.

29. Schwarz, *Slave Laws in Virginia*, 52; Patience Essah, "Slavery and Freedom in the First State: The History of Blacks in Delaware from the Colonial Period to 1865" (Ph.D. diss., UCLA, 1985), 104; Race and Slavery Petitions Project, #20379102, Ser. II, Part B, 0174; Race and Slavery Petitions Project, #20379507, Ser. II, Part B, 0287.

30. Brushy Creek Baptist Church (Greenville District, S.C.), Minutes, 1794–1927, April 1832, May 1832, SCL; Mt. Tirzah Baptist Church (Charlotte County, Va.), Minute Book, 1834–1915, January 1838, LVA; Mossingford Baptist Church (Charlotte County, Va.), Minute Book, 1823–1869, July 1859, LVA.

31. Flint Hill Baptist Church (York District, S.C.), Church Records, 1792–1899, December 1856, January 1857, SCL; Powelton Baptist Church (Hancock County, Ga.), Minutes, 1786–1916, February 1849, Drawer 32, Reel 76, GA.

32. Philips Mill Baptist Church (Wilkes County, Ga.), Minutes, 1785–1948, September 1791, Drawer 45, Reel 13, GA; Powelton Baptist Church (Hancock County, Ga.), Minutes, 1786–1916, December 1808, Drawer 32, Reel 76, GA; Lower Duncan's Creek Baptist Church (Laurens District, S.C.), Minutes, 1841–1884, July 1864, October 1864, SCL; Mt. Tirzah Baptist Church (Charlotte County, Va.), Minute Book, 1834–1915, June 1860, LVA; Washington First Baptist Church (Wilkes County, Ga.), Records, 1827–1903, March 1861, Drawer 45, Reel 14, GA.

33. Mt. Tirzah Baptist Church (Charlotte County, Va.), Minute Book, 1834–1915, October 1850, LVA; Lower Banister Church (Pittsylvania County, Va.), 1798–1845, December 1834, September 1835, March 1843, LVA; Sardis Baptist Church (Wilkes County, Ga.), Minutes, 1805–1951, October 1856, September 1856, Drawer 45, Reel 24, GA; Rabun Creek Baptist Church (Laurens District, S.C.), Church Book, 1828–1913, August 1843, LVA.

34. Roanoke District Association (Baptist), Minute Book, 1789–1831, 1789, Article 2, p. 2, LVA; Shiloh Baptist Church (Charlotte County, Va.), Minute Book, 1825–1873, Covenant, LVA; Poplar Springs Baptist Church (Laurens District, S.C.), Minutes, 1794–1937, p. 1, SCL; Di Ann Vick, *Minutes, 1858–1890, First Baptist Church, Hemphill, Texas* (Hemphill, Tex.: The Church, 1982), 7; Flint Hill Baptist Church (York District, S.C.), Church Records, 1792–1899, p. 52, SCL; Roanoke District Association (Baptist), Minute Book, 1789–1831, October 1797, LVA. The First Baptist Church of Hemphill listed in Article 4 of its covenant the scriptural justifications for the public airing of members' sins: Romans 16:17–18; Galatians 5:19–21; and 1 Corinthians 5:11.

35. Poplar Springs Baptist Church (Laurens District, S.C.), Minutes, 1794–1937, October 1853, SCL; Philips Mill Baptist Church (Wilkes County, Ga.), Minutes, 1785–1948, 1790, Drawer 45, Reel 13, GA; Sardis Baptist Church (Wilkes County, Ga.), Minutes, 1805–1951, April 1808, Drawer 45, Reel 24, GA; Horeb Baptist Church (Hancock County, Ga.), Minutes, 1792–1916, January 1850, March 1850, Drawer 32, Reel 77, GA; First Baptist Church (Houston, Tex.), Minutes, 1841–1881, May 1850, SWBTS.

36. Rehoboth Baptist Church (Wilkes County, Ga.), Minutes, 1806–1933, March 1830, Drawer 45, Reel 15, GA; Powelton Baptist Church (Hancock County, Ga.), Minutes, 1786–1916, November 1803, Drawer 32, Reel 76, GA; Goshen Baptist Church (Lincoln County, Ga.), Records and Minutes 1802–1869, June 1826, GA; Sardis Baptist Church (Wilkes County, Ga.), Minutes, 1805–1951, June 1860, Drawer 45, Reel 24, GA; Washington First Baptist Church (Wilkes County, Ga.), Records, 1827–1903, May 1831, September 1848, Drawer 45, Reel 14, GA. See also Philips Mill Baptist Church (Wilkes County, Ga.), Minutes, 1785–1948, September 1791, Drawer 45, Reel 13, GA.

37. Fishing Creek Baptist Church (Wilkes County, Ga.), Minutes, 1821–1873, August 1822–January 1831, Drawer 171, Reel 28, GA; Beaverdam Baptist Church (Wilkes County, Ga.), Minutes, 1836–1855, August 1844, Drawer 9, Reel 22, GA; First Baptist Church (Houston, Tex.), Minutes, 1841–1881, November 1850, SWBTS; Sardis Baptist Church (Wilkes County, Ga.), Minutes, 1805–1951, June 1860, Drawer 45, Reel 24, GA.

38. Sardis Baptist Church (Wilkes County, Ga.), Minutes, 1805–1951, December 1808, Drawer 45, Reel 24, GA; Washington First Baptist Church (Wilkes County, Ga.), Records, 1827–1903, July 1838, Drawer 45, Reel 14, GA; Lower Banister Church (Pittsylvania County, Va.), 1798–1845, November 1826, October 1826, July 1811, LVA. See also Philips Mill Baptist Church (Wilkes County, Ga.), Minutes, 1785–1948, February 1829, Drawer 45, Reel 13, GA; Shiloh Church (San Augustine County, Tex.), Church Records, 1850–1977, January 1851, MF5330, Reel 1, SBHLA.

39. Mt. Tirzah Baptist Church (Charlotte County, Va.), Minute Book, 1834–1915, November 1835, December 1835, LVA; Padgett's Creek Baptist Church (Union District, S.C.), Church Book, vol. 2, 1837–1874, August 1844, SCL; Ash Camp (Keysville) Baptist Church (Charlotte County, Va.), Minute Book, 1813–1872, November 1849, LVA; Poplar Springs Baptist Church (Laurens District, S.C.), Minutes, 1794–1937, June 1853, SCL.

40. First Baptist Church (Houston, Tex.), Minutes, 1841–1881, February 1852, SWBTS;

Bethabara Baptist Church (Laurens District, S.C.), Records, 1801–1881, July 1857, SCL; Mt. Tirzah Baptist Church (Charlotte County, Va.), Minute Book, 1834–1915, April 1853, LVA; Mossingford Baptist Church (Charlotte County, Va.), Minute Book, 1823–1869, May 1853, July 1861, LVA.

41. Flint Hill Baptist Church (York District, S.C.), Church Records, 1792–1899, May 1814, SCL; Sardis Baptist Church (Wilkes County, Ga.), Minutes, 1805–1951, June 1846, Drawer 45, Reel 24, SCL; Clarke's Station Baptist Church (Wilkes County, Ga.), Minutes, 1835–1896, June 1845, September 1850; Washington First Baptist Church (Wilkes County, Ga.), Records, 1827–1903, May 1840, Drawer 45, Reel 14, GA; Mossingford Baptist Church (Charlotte County, Va.), Minute Book, 1823–1869, September 1853, June 1859, November 1860, LVA.

42. Fishing Creek Baptist Church (Wilkes County, Ga.), Minutes, 1821–1873, October 1832, August 1835, Drawer 171, Reel 28, GA; Island Creek Baptist Church (Hancock County, Ga.), Minutes, 1806–1873, May 1861, July 1863, Drawer 31, Reel 80, GA. On outcomes of black votes, see, for example, Washington First Baptist Church (Wilkes County, Ga.), Records, 1827–1903, October 1840, Drawer 45, Reel 14, GA; Shiloh Church (San Augustine County, Tex.), Church Records, 1850–1977, December 1855, MF5330, Reel 1, SBHLA.

43. Washington First Baptist Church (Wilkes County, Ga.), Minutes, 1858–1923, 1924–1936, April 1862, May 1862, Drawer 45, Reel 23, GA.

44. Daniel L. Fountain, *Slavery, Civil War, and Salvation: African American Slaves and Christianity, 1830–1870* (Baton Rouge: Louisiana State University Press, 2010), 32.

45. Beaverdam Baptist Church (Wilkes County, Ga.), Minutes, 1836–1855, August 1844, Drawer 9, Reel 22, GA; Rabun Creek Baptist Church (Laurens District, S.C.), Church Book, 1828–1913, May 1835, SCL.

46. Warrior Creek Baptist Church (Laurens District, S.C.), Records, 1843–1896, January 1848, SCL; Rawick, SS1, vol. 6, pt. 1, 104. Due to a lack of data, the South Carolina figures cannot be adjusted for the relative sizes of the white and black populations in the sample churches.

47. Chestnut Ridge Baptist Church (Laurens District, S.C.), Minutes, 1816–1934, June 1847, SCL.

48. On southern disinterest in prosecuting violence within the slave community, see Thomas D. Morris, *Southern Slavery and the Law, 1619–1860* (Chapel Hill: University of North Carolina Press, 1996), 299–300; and Daniel J. Flanigan, *The Criminal Law of Slavery and Freedom 1800–1868* (New York: Garland Publishing, Inc., 1987), 50.

49. Thomas D. Morris, "'As If the Injury Was Effected by the Natural Elements of Air, or Fire': Slave Wrongs and the Liability of Masters," *Law & Society Review* 16, no. 4 (1982): 570, 573 (first quotation), 574 (fourth and fifth quotations), 580, 584, 589; idem, *Southern Slavery and the Law*, 354, 362, 365; *Wright v. Weatherly* (1835), 15 Tenn. 367, 1835 WL 860 (Tenn. Err. & App.), 7 Yer. 367 (second and third quotations).

50. Morris, "As If the Injury Was Effected by the Natural Elements," 570, 575, 585 (first and second quotations), 584; idem, *Southern Slavery and the Law*, 362, 354; *Gaillardet v. Demaries* (1841), 18 La. 490, 1841 WL 1433 La. 1841 (third quotation).

51. *Steel v. Cazeaux* (1820), Supreme Court of the State of Louisiana, Eastern District, 8 Mart. (o.s.) 318, 1820 La. LEXIS 79; Morris, "As If the Injury Was Effected by the Natural Elements," 580; *Maille v. Blas* (1860), Supreme Court of Louisiana, New Orleans, 15 La. Ann. 100, 1860 La. LEXIS 537; *State v. Jack (slave)* (1858), First District Court of New Orleans, 13653, NOPL; Morris, "As If the Injury Was Effected by the Natural Elements," 583.

52. William Goodell, *The American Slave Code in Theory and Practice: Its Distinctive Features Shown by Its Statutes, Judicial Decisions, and Illustrative Facts* (1853; reprint, New York: Negro Universities Press, 1968), 203, 205–206; *Jourdan v. Patton* (1818), 5 Mart. (o.s.) 615, 1818 WL 1606 (La.).

53. *Sterling v. Luckett* (1828), 7 Mar. N.S. 198, in *Judicial Cases Concerning American Slavery and the Negro*, vol. 3, ed. Helen Tunnicliff Catterall (Washington, D.C.: Carnegie Institution of Washington, 1932), 485; *Steel v. Cazeaux* (1820), Supreme Court of the State of Louisiana, Eastern District, 8 Mart. (o.s.) 318, 1820 La. LEXIS 79.

54. *Steel v. Cazeaux* (1820), Supreme Court of the State of Louisiana, Eastern District, 8 Mart. (o.s.) 318, 1820 La. LEXIS 79.

55. Morris, "As If the Injury Was Effected by the Natural Elements," 585; idem, *Southern Slavery and the Law*, 362–363; *Steel v. Cazeaux* (1820), Supreme Court of the State of Louisiana, Eastern District, 8 Mart. (o.s.) 318, 1820 La. LEXIS 79.

56. *Steel v. Cazeaux* (1820), Supreme Court of the State of Louisiana, Eastern District, 8 Mart. (o.s.) 318, 1820 La. LEXIS 79; *Arnoult v. Deschapelles* (1849), 4 La. Ann. 41, 1849 WL 5446, La. 1849. In *Hynson v. Meuillon* (1847), the Supreme Court of Louisiana maintained that a master retained the right to abandon a slave under Article 181 of the Civil Code even as the bondperson was imprisoned for a term of years, rather than life, in the penitentiary. Slaves' "temporary confinement by the State," the Court ruled, "does not affect the rights of property of the master. In the eye of the law, he continues to possess, though he may not enjoy." See *Hynson v. Meuillon* (1847), 2 La. Ann. 798, 1847 WL 3615, La. 1847.

57. Morris, "As If the Injury Was Effected by the Natural Elements," 575, 577, 578, 583; *Ewing v. Thompson* (1850), Supreme Court of Missouri, 13 Mo. 132, 1850 Mo. LEXIS 34.

58. *Wright v. Weatherly* (1835), 15 Tenn. 367, 1835 WL 860 (Tenn. Err. & App.), 7 Yer. 367; *Ewing v. Thompson* (1850), Supreme Court of Missouri, 13 Mo. 132, 1850 Mo. LEXIS 34; *Maille v. Blas* (1860), Supreme Court of Louisiana, New Orleans, 15 La. Ann. 100, 1860 La. LEXIS 537.

59. *Wright v. Weatherly* (1835), 15 Tenn. 367, 1835 WL 860 (Tenn. Err. & App.), 7 Yer. 367. See also Morris, "As If the Injury Was Effected by the Natural Elements," 587; idem, *Southern Slavery and the Law*, 357, 364.

60. Morris, "As If the Injury Was Effected by the Natural Elements," 587–588, 589, 592, 595; idem, *Southern Slavery and the Law*, 365; *Ewing v. Thompson* (1850), Supreme Court of Missouri, 13 Mo. 132, 1850 Mo. LEXIS 34 [italics mine]; *Ewing v. Thompson* (1850), 13 Mo. 132, 1850 WL 4160.

61. *Leggett v. Simmons* (1846), 7 Smedes & M. 348, 15 Miss. 348, 1846 WL 2992, Miss. Err. App. 1846.

62. Race and Slavery Petitions Project, #20883737, Ser. II, Part F, Reel 10, 0279.

63. Race and Slavery Petitions Project, #20883737, Ser. II, Part F, Reel 10, 0279; Race and Slavery Petitions Project, #20884749, Ser. II, Part F, Reel 13, 0411. The Louisiana Supreme Court later ordered a new trial against Hebert.

64. Virginia, General Assembly, Legislative Petitions, King & Queen County, 1776–1859, Reel 101, Box 132, Folder 45, LVA; Race and Slavery Petitions Project, #11284806, Ser. I, Reel 7, 0312; Race and Slavery Petitions Project, #11382407, Ser. I, Reel 10, 0231.

65. Race and Slavery Petitions Project, #11682003, Ser. I, Reel 18, 0239.

3. INTRARACIAL SLAVE HOMICIDE AND THE CRIMINAL LAW OF SLAVERY

66. Race and Slavery Petitions Project, #11381717, Ser. I, Reel 9, 0409; Race and Slavery Petitions Project, #11380004, Ser. I, Reel 8, 0545.

1. Executive Papers, Joseph Johnson, June–September 1852, Box 2, Folder 8, LVA; Charlotte County, Order Book 23, 1820–1823, Reel 32, LVA; Executive Papers, Joseph Johnson, August–October 1852, Box 413, Folder September 1852, LVA; Charlotte County, Order Book 34, 1852–1857, Reel 36, LVA. Some enslaved women in Virginia committed infanticide or child murder in twos or threes. One enslaved man killed a bondwoman and her child.

2. Executive Papers, Joseph Johnson, August–October 1852, Box 413, Folder September 1852, LVA; Thomas D. Morris, "'As If the Injury Was Effected by the Natural Elements of Air, or Fire': Slave Wrongs and the Liability of Masters," *Law & Society Review* 16, no. 4 (1982): 580; idem, *Southern Slavery and the Law, 1619–1860* (Chapel Hill: University of North Carolina Press, 1996), 300; Philip J. Schwarz, *Twice Condemned: Slaves and the Criminal Laws of Virginia, 1705–1865* (Baton Rouge: Louisiana State University Press, 1988), 89, 289n14, 154; Michael Stephen Hindus, *Prison and Plantation: Crime, Justice, and Authority in Massachusetts and South Carolina, 1767–1878* (Chapel Hill: University of North Carolina Press, 1980), 159.

3. Schwarz, *Twice Condemned*, 89, 289.

4. Christopher Morris, "Within the Slave Cabin: Violence in Mississippi Slave Families," in *Over the Threshold: Intimate Violence in Early America*, ed. Christine Daniels and Michael V. Kennedy (New York: Routledge, 1999), 271; Hindus, *Prison and Plantation*, 139; quoted in Glenn M. McNair, "Justice Bound: Aframericans, Crime, and Criminal Justice in Georgia, 1751–1865" (Ph.D. diss., Emory University, 2001), 40.

5. Hindus, *Prison and Plantation*, 160; Daniel J. Flanigan, *The Criminal Law of Slavery and Freedom 1800–1868* (New York: Garland Publishing, Inc., 1987), 50; George P. Rawick, ed., *The American Slave: A Composite Autobiography*, vol. 12, pt. 1 (Westport, Conn.: Greenwood Publishing Company, 1972), 310; idem, ed., *The American Slave: A Composite Autobiography, Supplement, Series 1*, vol. 3, pt. 1 (Westport, Conn: Greenwood Press, 1977), 64; Morris, *Southern Slavery and the Law*, 301; Nathan Neal to Father and Mother, 2 September 1857, Folder 13: Aaron Neal and Elizabeth Fox Neal, Neal Family Papers, SHC.

6. Jones County, Georgia, Inferior Court Minutes, 1818–1846.

7. Spartanburg District, Court of Magistrates and Freeholders, Reel C2920, Cases #128, #131.

8. John Berkley Grimball Diary, 5–6 May 1840 [typescript vol. 2, pp. 54–55], Box 4, Folder 19, SHC.

9. Philip J. Schwarz, *Slave Laws in Virginia* (Athens: University of Georgia Press, 2010), 71–72, 201n12; Thad W. Tate, *The Negro in Eighteenth-Century Williamsburg* (Williamsburg, Va.: The Colonial Williamsburg Foundation, 1965), 93; William Waller Hening, *The Statutes at Large; Being a Collection of All the Laws of Virginia from the First Session of the Legislature, in the Year 1619*, vol. 8 (Richmond: J. & G. Cochran, 1821), 138.

On the history and workings of the South Carolina Courts of Magistrates and Freeholders, see Terry W. Lipscomb and Theresa Jacobs, "The Magistrates and Freeholders Court," *South Carolina Historical Magazine* 77 (January 1976): 62–65; William Henderson, "The Slave Court

NOTES TO PAGES 114-116

System in Spartanburg County," *Proceedings of the South Carolina Historical Association* (1976): 31-37; Hindus, *Prison and Plantation,* 131, 154-155; Robert Olwell, *Masters, Slaves, & Subjects: The Culture of Power in the South Carolina Low Country, 1740-1790* (Ithaca: Cornell University Press, 1998), 73-77, 90; and W. J. Megginson, *African American Life in South Carolina's Upper Piedmont, 1780-1900* (Columbia: University of South Carolina Press, 2006), ch. 5.

On Louisiana, see Judith Kelleher Schafer, "Slaves and Crime: New Orleans, 1846-1862," in *Local Matters: Race, Crime, and Justice in the Nineteenth-Century South,* ed. Christopher Waldrep and Donald G. Nieman (Athens: University of Georgia Press, 2001), 56-57, 59; *State v. Isaac* (1848), Supreme Court of Louisiana, New Orleans, 3 La. Ann. 359, 1848 La. LEXIS 186; *State v. Hannah (a slave)* (1855), 10 La. An. 131, in *Judicial Cases Concerning American Slavery and the Negro,* vol. 3, ed. Helen Tunnicliff Catterall (Washington, D.C.: Carnegie Institution of Washington, 1932), 634.

10. McNair, "Justice Bound," 164. On North Carolina, see Marvin L. Michael Kay and Lorin Lee Cary, "'The Planters Suffer Little or Nothing': North Carolina Compensations for Executed Slaves, 1748-1772," *Science and Society* 40 (Fall 1976): 291; John Spencer Bassett, *Slavery in the State of North Carolina* (Baltimore: Johns Hopkins Press, 1899), 11-12. On Georgia, see McNair, "Justice Bound," 15, 28-29, 157, 372, 22-23, 160, 162; idem, "Slave Women, Capital Crime, and Criminal Justice in Georgia," *Georgia Historical Quarterly* 93 (Summer 2009): 149; Ralph Betts Flanders, *Plantation Slavery in Georgia* (Chapel Hill: University of North Carolina Press, 1933; reprint, Cos Cob, Conn.: John E. Edwards, 1967), 233-235. See also E. Merton Coulter, "Four Slave Trials in Elbert County, Georgia," *Georgia Historical Quarterly* 41 (Fall 1957): 237-246; John C. Edwards, "Slave Justice in Four Middle Georgia Counties," *Georgia Historical Quarterly* 57 (Summer 1973): 265-273; Royce Gordon Shingleton, "The Trial and Punishment of Slaves in Baldwin County, Georgia, 1812-1826," *Southern Humanities Review* 8 (Winter 1974): 67-73. On Alabama, see James Benson Sellers, *Slavery in Alabama* (Tuscaloosa: University of Alabama Press, 1950), 215.

11. Bassett, *Slavery in the State of North Carolina,* 11; Caleb Perry Patterson, *The Negro in Tennessee, 1790-1865* (1922; reprint, New York: Negro Universities Press, 1968), 29; McNair, "Justice Bound," 164, 373, 180, 150, 179, 165; Sellers, *Slavery in Alabama,* 212. On jury trials in other states, see, for example, Orville W. Taylor, *Negro Slavery in Arkansas* (Durham: Duke University Press, 1958), 235; and Ivan E. McDougle, *Slavery in Kentucky, 1792-1865* (1918; reprint, Westport, Conn.: Negro Universities Press, 1970), 35-36.

12. *Seaborn and Jim v. State* (1852), Supreme Court of Alabama, 20 Ala. 15, 1852 Ala. LEXIS 294; *Crockett (a slave) v. State* (1862), Supreme Court of Alabama, 38 Ala. 387, 1862 Ala. LEXIS 35; *State v. Dick* (1849), Supreme Court of Louisiana, New Orleans, 4 La. Ann. 182, 1849 La. LEXIS 117; *State v. Jerry* (1849), Supreme Court of Louisiana, New Orleans, 4 La. Ann. 190, 1849 La. LEXIS 125; *William (a slave) v. the State* (1855), Supreme Court of Georgia, 18 Ga. 356, 1855 Ga. LEXIS 202.

13. Taylor, *Negro Slavery in Arkansas,* 234; *Crockett (a slave) v. State* (1862), Supreme Court of Alabama, 38 Ala. 387, 1862 Ala. LEXIS 35; Sellers, *Slavery in Alabama,* 221, 223; *State v. Anderson* (1858), Houst. Cr. Cas. 38, Delaware, in *Judicial Cases Concerning American Slavery and the Negro,* vol. 4, ed. Helen Tunnicliff Catterall (Washington, D.C.: Carnegie Institution of Washington, 1936), 237; Schwarz, *Slave Laws in Virginia,* 71; Executive Papers, John Floyd, February 1834,

NOTES TO PAGES 116-120

Box 12, Folder 4, LVA; Auditor of Public Accounts, Condemned Blacks Executed or Transported, Records—Condemned Slaves, Court Orders, and Valuations, 1846-1857, Misc. Reel 2554, Frame 374, LVA.

14. *William (a slave) v. the State* (1855), Supreme Court of Georgia, 18 Ga. 356, 1855 Ga. LEXIS 202; Schafer, "Slaves and Crime," 74-75; *State v. Jack (slave)* (1858), First District Court of New Orleans, 13653, NOPL; *State v. slave Jack* (1859), Supreme Court of Louisiana, New Orleans, 14 La. Ann. 385, 1859 La. LEXIS 229.

15. Morris, *Southern Slavery and the Law*, 300; *State v. Horace, a slave* (1860), Case 10416, Group 1860, Box 1, File 76, ACCCHNF; Executive Papers, William B. Giles, May 1827, Box 1, Folders 6-7, LVA; Executive Papers, Henry A. Wise, Misc. Reel 4217, Box 20, Folder 6, Frames 317-323, LVA. On manslaughter in various southern states, see, for example, Sellers, *Slavery in Alabama*, 260; Shingleton, "Trial and Punishment of Slaves," 73n6; McDougle, *Slavery in Kentucky*, 38.

16. *State v. Horace, a slave* (1860), Case 10416, Group 1860, Box 1, File 76, ACCCHNF; Governor's Papers, Gov. Edward B. Dudley, G.P. 90, Folder October 1839, NCDAH; Executive Papers, Henry A. Wise, Misc. Reel 4217, Box 20, Folder 6, Frames 317-323, LVA.

17. *The North Carolinian* (Fayetteville), January 30, 1847; *The North Carolinian* (Fayetteville), May 8, 1847; *Souther v. Commonwealth* (1851), Supreme Court of Virginia, 48 Va. 673, 1851 Va. LEXIS 28, 7 Gratt. 673; George P. Rawick, ed., *The American Slave: A Composite Autobiography, Supplement, Series 2*, vol. 3, pt. 2 (Westport, Conn.: Greenwood Press, 1979), 649. See also Edward E. Baptist, "The Absent Subject: African American Masculinity and Forced Migration to the Antebellum Plantation Frontier," in *Southern Manhood: Perspectives on Masculinity in the Old South*, ed. Craig Thompson Friend and Lorri Glover (Athens: University of Georgia Press, 2004), 152.

18. Schwarz, *Twice Condemned*, 235; Elizabeth City County, Order Book, 1731-1747, Reel 17, LVA; Spartanburg District, Court of Magistrates & Freeholders, Reel C2922, Cases #270, #271, SCDAH. In 1762, a Caroline County court found "Sam a negro man slave," charged, along with another slave, with administering deadly "medicine" to a bondwoman, "not guilty of the several facts in the Indictment" but sentenced him to "Thirty Nine Lashes on his bare back at the whipping post" for being "Guilty of a misdemeanor." Pompey and James, a pair of Spotsylvania County slaves arrested "on Suspicion of murdering Nero," were also ruled innocent of the murder but guilty of a lesser charge. They met the same fate as Sam. See Caroline County, Order Book, 1759-1763, Reel 16, LVA; Spotsylvania County, Minutes, 1755-1765, Reel 45, LVA.

19. *Commonwealth vs. Billy a Negro Slave* (1818), Albemarle Court Records, County Court Commonwealth Causes, 1818-1819, Box 11, LVA; Baldwin County, Georgia, Inferior Court Minutes, Trial of Slaves, 1812-1828; *State v. Cornelius (slave)* (1861), First District Court of New Orleans, 15361, NOPL.

20. *State v. Henry, slave of Mr. Jennings* (1853), First District Court of New Orleans, 9144, NOPL; Chatham County, Georgia, Inferior Court Trial Docket, 1813-1827, Drawer 90, Reel 33, GA; *State v. Titus* (1820), Lincoln County, Georgia, Inferior Court, Docket of Slaves indicted for capital crimes, 1814-1838; *Commonwealth vs. Harry a Negro Man Slave* (1826), Albemarle County Court Records Commonwealth Causes, 1826, Box 15, LVA; *Commonwealth vs. Armstead a Negro Man Slave* (1841), Albemarle County Court Records Commonwealth Causes, 1841, Box 28, LVA; *Commonwealth vs. Bartlett a Negro Man Slave* (1826), Albemarle County Court Records Commonwealth Causes, 1826, Box 15, LVA; Richmond City, Hustings Court Minutes 15,

1842–1844, Reel 90, LVA; Halifax County, Pleas (Court Orders), No. 18 1796–1798, Reel 61, LVA; *Commonwealth vs. Isaac a Negro Man Slave* (1824), Albemarle County Commonwealth Causes, 1824–1825, Box 14, LVA; Madison County, Order Book 7, Reel 25, LVA. See also *Commonwealth vs. Carter a Negro Man Slave* (1826), Albemarle County Court Records Commonwealth Causes, 1826, Box 15, LVA; Giles (1855), Mecklenburg County, Order Book 6, 1853–1858 (County Court), Reel 120, LVA; Doctor (1861), Halifax County, Minutes 19, 1859–1862, Reel 74, LVA; Davy (1864), Mecklenburg County, Order Book 7, 1859–1865 (County Court), Reel 120, LVA.

21. McNair, "Justice Bound," 112, 102, 216, 354, 357; James Campbell, "'The victim of prejudice and hasty consideration': The Slave Trial System in Richmond, Virginia, 1830–61," *Slavery & Abolition* 26 (April 2005): 75, 76; *Ready v. the Commonwealth* (1839), Court of Appeals of Kentucky, 39 Ky. 38, 1839 Ky. LEXIS 72, 9 Dana 38. McNair observes that, irrespective of the victim's race, Georgia blacks tried for murder were convicted 86 percent of the time between 1812 and 1849. See McNair, "Justice Bound," 201.

22. McNair, "Justice Bound," 348; *Maria (a freedwoman) v. State* (1866), Supreme Court of Texas, 28 Tex. 698, 1866 WL 4062; James M. Denham and Randolph Roth, "Why Was Antebellum Florida Murderous? A Quantitative Analysis of Homicide in Florida, 1821–1861," *Florida Historical Quarterly* 86 (Fall 2007): 218; Mecklenburg County, Order Book 7, 1859–1865 (County Court), Reel 120, Frame 149, LVA; Halifax County, Minutes 19, 1859–1862, Reel 74, LVA; Albemarle County, Minute Book, 1842–1844, Reel 58, LVA; *Commonwealth vs. Reuben a Slave* (1843), Albemarle County Court Records Commonwealth Causes, 1843, Box 30, LVA; Lancaster County, Orders No. 7, 1721–1729, Reel 27, LVA; York County, Order Book 5, 1784–1787, Reel 33, LVA; *Commonwealth vs. Isaac a Negro Man Slave* (1835), Albemarle County Court Records Commonwealth Causes, 1835, Box 22, LVA; Albemarle County, Minute Book, 1834–1836, June 1835, Reel 57, LVA; *Commonwealth vs. Archer a Negro Man Slave* (1824), Albemarle County Commonwealth Causes, 1824–1825, Box 14, LVA; Albemarle County, Order Book 1824, Reel 54, LVA. In addition to administering thirty-nine stripes, the sheriff of King and Queen County in 1797 "burned in the left hand" and "in open Court" the bondman Willoughby for striking Bob on the side of the head with "a Footadz." See Virginia, General Assembly, Legislative Petitions, King & Queen County, 1776–1859, Reel 101, Box 132, Folder 45, LVA.

23. Robert M. Saunders, "Crime and Punishment in Early National America: Richmond, Virginia, 1784–1820," *Virginia Magazine of History and Biography* 86 (January 1978): 42, 43; Hening, *Statutes at Large*, vol. 8, 139; Bassett, *Slavery in the State of North Carolina*, 12; J. Winston Coleman, *Slavery Times in Kentucky* (Chapel Hill: University of North Carolina Press, 1940), 263; Hindus, *Prison and Plantation*, 155n64; Schwarz, *Twice Condemned*, 289, 291; Henrico County, Minute Book 1847–1848, Reel 83, LVA.

24. *State v. Charles Loadnum* (1798), Court of Oyer and Terminer of Delaware, Kent, 2 Del. Cas. 240, 1798 Del. LEXIS 42; *State v. Little Jordan, a slave* (1855), Case 10301, Group 1850, Box 26, File 68, ACCCHNF. On individual slaveholding states' use of branding, see, for example, Sellers, *Slavery in Alabama*, 244; Taylor, *Negro Slavery in Arkansas*, 15; Edwards, "Slave Justice in Four Middle Georgia Counties," 272; Shingleton, "Trial and Punishment of Slaves in Baldwin County, Georgia," 69, 70; McDougle, *Slavery in Kentucky*, 37; Coleman, *Slavery Times in Kentucky*, 263.

25. *State v. Peter* (1827), Supreme Court of Alabama, Tuscaloosa, 1 Stew. 38, 1827 Ala. LEXIS 24; Flanigan, *Criminal Law of Slavery*, 25; McNair, "Justice Bound," 335–336, 342–343, 337; Flan-

ders, *Plantation Slavery in Georgia,* 255, 257–259. McNair notes that, in Georgia, "certain kinds of whips" were used to reduce the dangers of traumatic physical injury. See McNair, "Justice Bound," 342.

The six sample Georgia cases in which slaves were charged with murder but convicted of manslaughter and sentenced to be whipped and branded are those of Tom (1815), Baldwin County, Georgia, Inferior Court Minutes, Trial of Slaves, 1812–1828; Adam (1819), Chatham County, Georgia, Inferior Court Trial Docket, 1813–1827, Drawer 90, Reel 33, GA; Peter (1821), Baldwin County, Georgia, Inferior Court Minutes, Trial of Slaves, 1812–1828; Dick (1831), Putnam County, Georgia, Inferior Court Records, 1813–1843, Record of the Proceeds of the Court for Trial of Slaves; Thomas (1846), Jones County, Georgia, Inferior Court Minutes, 1818–1846; and Warren (1949), Hancock County, Georgia, Inferior Court Minutes, County Purposes & Lunacy, 1843–1850.

26. Morris, *Southern Slavery and the Law,* 302; Kershaw District, Court of Magistrates and Freeholders, Trial Papers, 1800–1861, Box 2, Folder 82, SCDAH; Laurens District, Court of Magistrates and Freeholders, Trial Papers, 1808–1865, Box 1, Folder 67, SCDAH; Spartanburg District, Court of Magistrates and Freeholders, Reel C2922, Case #296, SCDAH; Race and Slavery Petitions Project, #21384617, Ser. II, Part D, 0853; Fairfield District, Court of Magistrates and Freeholders, Trial Papers, 1839–1865, Cases 1–54, Folder 44, SCDAH.

27. Thomas D. Morris, "Slaves and the Rules of Evidence in Criminal Trials," in *Slavery and the Law,* ed. Paul Finkelman (Madison, Wis.: Madison House, 1997), 221; Pittsylvania County, Court Records 9 1798–1801, Reel 49, LVA; Schwarz, *Twice Condemned,* 82, 155n42; Amelia County, Order Book 1A (Minutes), 1746–1751, LVA; Ulrich B. Phillips, "Slave Crime in Virginia," *American Historical Review* 20 (January 1915): 338; idem, *American Negro Slavery: A Survey of the Supply, Employment and Control of Negro Labor as Determined by the Plantation Régime* (New York: Peter Smith, 1952), 459.

28. Helen Tunnicliff Catterall, ed., *Judicial Cases Concerning American Slavery and the Negro,* vol. 3 (Washington, D.C.: Carnegie Institution of Washington, 1932), 439.

29. Flanigan, *Criminal Law of Slavery,* 13; *State v. Dabney Green, slave of Capt. Thomas J. Casey* (1853), First District Court of New Orleans, 8608, NOPL; *State v. James, slave of Widow Bouny* (1846), First District Court of New Orleans, 181, NOPL; *State v. Henry Payton, slave of John Eaton* (1846), First District Court of New Orleans, 186, NOPL; Kenneth M. Stampp, *The Peculiar Institution: Slavery in the Ante-Bellum South* (New York: Alfred A. Knopf, 1956), 227; *Louisiana Advertiser,* reprinted in *North Carolina Watchman* (Salisbury) June 25, 1836; Taylor, *Negro Slavery in Arkansas,* 235–236. See also *State v. Frederick (slave)* (1858), First District Court of New Orleans, 13652, NOPL.

30. James W. Clarke, *The Lineaments of Wrath: Race, Violent Crime, and American Culture* (New Brunswick, N.J.: Transaction Publishers, 1998), 23; Stampp, *Peculiar Institution,* 227; Schwarz, *Twice Condemned,* 231; McNair, "Justice Bound," 352, 358, 367; Glenn M. McNair, "The Trials of Slaves in Baldwin County, Georgia, 1812–1838" (M.A. thesis, Georgia College and State University, 1996), 27, 66, 72, 75, 107; Sellers, *Slavery in Alabama,* 250–251.

31. McNair, "Justice Bound," 9, 352, 354, 360; Flanders, *Plantation Slavery in Georgia,* 257; *State v. Carter* (1813), Chatham County, Georgia, Inferior Court Trial Docket, 1813–1827, Drawer 90, Reel 33, GA; Jones County, Georgia, Inferior Court Minutes, 1818–1846; Coulter, "Four Slave

Trials," 238; Shingleton, "Trial and Punishment of Slaves in Baldwin County, Georgia," 68; Rawick, *American Slave*, vol. 12, pt. 1, 208.

32. Philip J. Schwarz, "The Transportation of Slaves from Virginia, 1801–1865," *Slavery & Abolition* 7 (December 1986): 219; Hindus, *Prison and Plantation*, 156; McNair, "Justice Bound," 52, 50; Schwarz, *Twice Condemned*, 25, 289, 291, 247n24. These findings disagree with those of Schwarz, who argues that "more and more men and women were executed . . . for killing other slaves" after 1848. See Schwarz, *Twice Condemned*, 289.

33. McNair, "Justice Bound," 256; Auditor of Public Accounts, Condemned Blacks Executed or Transported, Records—Condemned Slaves, Court Orders, and Valuations, 1823–1832, Misc. Reel 2552, Frame 1166, LVA; Auditor of Public Accounts, Condemned Blacks Executed or Transported, Records—Condemned Slaves, Court Orders, and Valuations, 1846–1857, Misc. Reel 2554, Frame 111, LVA; Auditor of Public Accounts, Condemned Blacks Executed or Transported, Records—Condemned Slaves, Court Orders, and Valuations, 1810–1822, Misc. Reel 2551, Frame 48, LVA; Auditor of Public Accounts, Condemned Blacks Executed or Transported, Records—Condemned Slaves, Court Orders, and Valuations, 1810–1822, Misc. Reel 2551, Frames 375–376, LVA.

34. Quoted in Morris, "Slaves and the Rules of Evidence," 211; Thomas D. Condy, *A Digest of the Laws of the United States & the State of South-Carolina, Now of Force, Relating to the Militia; with an Appendix, Containing the Patrol Laws; the Laws for the Government of Slaves and Free Persons of Colour; the Decisions of the Constitutional Court and Court of Appeals of South-Carolina Thereon; and an Abstract from the Rules and Regulations of the United States' Army, &c.* (Charleston: A. E. Miller, 1830), 153; Jenny Bourne Wahl, *The Bondsman's Burden: An Economic Analysis of the Common Law of Southern Slavery* (Cambridge: Cambridge University Press, 1998), 171; McNair, "Justice Bound," 332; Morris, *Southern Slavery and the Law*, 253; Hindus, *Prison and Plantation*, 156, 159; Kay and Cary, "The Planters Suffer Little or Nothing," 290.

35. Morris, *Southern Slavery and the Law*, 254, 255; Kay and Cary, "The Planters Suffer Little or Nothing," 293; Bassett, *Slavery in the State of North Carolina*, 14; McDougle, *Slavery in Kentucky*, 37; Lawrence M. Friedman, *A History of American Law*, 2nd ed. (New York: Touchstone, 1985), 228n74; Morris, *Southern Slavery and the Law*, 255, 253.

36. Quoted in Kay and Cary, "The Planters Suffer Little or Nothing," 290; Morris, *Southern Slavery and the Law*, 254, 255; Sellers, *Slavery in Alabama*, 220–221, 251; J. T. Currie, "From Slavery to Freedom in Mississippi's Legal System," *Journal of Negro History* 65 (Spring 1980): 114–115; *Maria (a freedwoman) v. State* (1866), Supreme Court of Texas, 28 Tex. 698, 1866 WL 4062; Bassett, *Slavery in the State of North Carolina*, 14; Joe Gray Taylor, *Negro Slavery in Louisiana* (Baton Rouge: Louisiana Historical Association, 1963), 207; Schafer, "Slaves and Crime," 59; *Acts Passed by the Second Legislature of the State of Louisiana, at Its First Session, Held and Begun in the Town of Baton Rouge, on the 16th January, 1854* (New Orleans: Emile La Sere, 1854), 149; Morris, *Southern Slavery and the Law*, 254, 255; John Belton O'Neall, *The Negro Law of South Carolina* (Columbia: John G. Bowman, 1848), 45; Hindus, *Prison and Plantation*, 156; Wahl, *Bondsman's Burden*, 259n157; Campbell, "Victim of Prejudice," 77; Schwarz, "Transportation," 230.

37. Morris, *Southern Slavery and the Law*, 254; Kay and Cary, "The Planters Suffer Little or Nothing," 292, 299, 302; Bassett, *Slavery in the State of North Carolina*, 14; Sellers, *Slavery in Alabama*, 244; Hindus, *Prison and Plantation*, 156.

38. Hindus, *Prison and Plantation*, 156; Morris, *Southern Slavery and the Law*, 255; Schafer,

"Slaves and Crime," 59; Bassett, *Slavery in the State of North Carolina*, 14; Sellers, *Slavery in Alabama*, 220–221; McDougle, *Slavery in Kentucky*, 37. On exclusions in colonial South Carolina, see Morris, *Southern Slavery and the Law*, 254.

39. Flanders, *Plantation Slavery in Georgia*, 235; Shingleton, "Trial and Punishment of Slaves in Baldwin County, Georgia," 73n5; McNair, "The Trials of Slaves in Baldwin County, Georgia," 67; idem, "Justice Bound," 28, 332, 334, 342.

40. Morris, *Southern Slavery and the Law*, 253–254; Schwarz, "Transportation," 220; Joseph Tate, *Digest of the Laws of Virginia, which are of a Permanent Character and General Operation; Illustrated by Judicial Decisions: to which is Added, an Index of the Names of the Cases in the Virginia Reporters*, 2nd ed. (Richmond: Smith and Palmer, 1841), 274; Auditor of Public Accounts, Condemned Blacks Executed or Transported, Records—Condemned Slaves, Court Orders, and Valuations, 1833–1845, Misc. Reel 2553, Frame 682, LVA.

41. Kay and Cary, "The Planters Suffer Little or Nothing," 294; Auditor of Public Accounts, Condemned Blacks Executed or Transported, Records—Condemned Slaves, Court Orders, and Valuations, 1833–1845, Misc. Reel 2553, Frame 452, LVA; Auditor of Public Accounts, Condemned Blacks Executed or Transported, Records—Condemned Slaves, Court Orders, and Valuations, 1823–1832, Misc. Reel 2552, Frame 1188, LVA; Auditor of Public Accounts, Condemned Blacks Executed or Transported, Records—Condemned Slaves, Court Orders, and Valuations, 1823–1832, Misc. Reel 2552, Frame 1166, LVA.

42. Auditor of Public Accounts, Condemned Blacks Executed or Transported, Records—Condemned Slaves, Court Orders, and Valuations, 1781–1793, Misc. Reel 2549, Frame 207, LVA; Auditor of Public Accounts, Condemned Blacks Executed or Transported, Records—Condemned Slaves, Court Orders, and Valuations, 1794–1809, Misc. Reel 2550, Frames 935–936, LVA; Auditor of Public Accounts, Condemned Blacks Executed or Transported, Records—Condemned Slaves, Court Orders, and Valuations, 1823–1832, Misc. Reel 2552, Frame 593, LVA; Executive Papers, Joseph Johnson, March–May 1854, Box 424, Folder March 1854, LVA; Auditor of Public Accounts, Condemned Blacks Executed or Transported, Records—Condemned Slaves, Court Orders, and Valuations, 1810–1822, Misc. Reel 2551, Frame 510, LVA.

43. Auditor of Public Accounts, Condemned Blacks Executed or Transported, Records—Condemned Slaves, Court Orders, and Valuations, 1858–1865, Misc. Reel 2555, Frame 572, 424, 539, 821, LVA.

44. Schwarz, "Transportation," 215, 216, 217–218, 220; Auditor of Public Accounts, Condemned Blacks Executed or Transported, Records—Condemned Slaves, Court Orders, and Valuations, 1794–1809, Misc. Reel 2550, LVA; Executive Papers, James Pleasants, December 1824, Box 6, Folder 1, LVA. One study of slave crime in Richmond, Virginia, found that, between 1830 and 1860, only five of the forty-five slaves slated for execution were actually put to death. Virginia governors prevented the executions of more than 80 percent of the slaves condemned to die in antebellum Richmond. See Campbell, "Victim of Prejudice," 74, 78.

45. Auditor of Public Accounts, Condemned Blacks Executed or Transported, Records—Condemned Slaves, Court Orders, and Valuations, 1846–1857, Misc. Reel 2554, Frame 374, LVA; Richmond City, Hustings Court Minutes 28, 1862–1863, Reel 96, LVA; Schwarz, *Slave Laws in Virginia*, 84; idem, "Transportation," 219; Executive Papers, James Pleasants, August 1825, Box 7, Folder 11, LVA.

NOTES TO PAGES 137–146

46. McNair, "Justice Bound," 370–371; Stampp, *Peculiar Institution*, 227; John Berkley Grimball Diary, 9 May 1840 [typescript vol. 2, pp. 55–56], Box 4, Folder 19, SHC; Race and Slavery Petitions Project, #21385347, Ser. II, Part D, 0183; Race and Slavery Petitions Project, #21384617, Ser. II, Part D, 0853. In 1857, Fairfield District bondmen Sampson and Manuel fell into a quarrel while fishing, and Manuel ended up dead. Convicted, Sampson was sentenced to 5 months' imprisonment and 150 lashes, followed by transportation out of South Carolina. Fairfield District, Court of Magistrates and Freeholders, Trial Papers, 1839–1865, Cases 1–54, Folder 34, SCDAH.

47. Schwarz, "Transportation," 216, 223–224, 225, 215–216; Executive Papers, James Barbour, June 1813, Box 7, Folder 6, LVA; Campbell, "Victim of Prejudice," 82.

48. Executive Papers, Thomas Mann Randolph, January 1820, Box 1, Folder 6, LVA.

49. Violence among southern white men was most common in the identical age range. See Stephen Alan West, "From Yeoman to Redneck in Upstate South Carolina, 1850–1915" (Ph.D. diss., Columbia University, 1998), 136–137.

50. Richmond City, Hustings Court Minutes 21, 1853–1855, Reel 93, LVA.

51. Executive Papers, Henry A. Wise, May 1856, Box 3, Folder 2, LVA.

52. Morris, *Southern Slavery and the Law*, 254; Schwarz, "Transportation," 215, 216, 219, 220, 223; Executive Papers, Thomas Mann Randolph, August 1822, Box 7, Folder 3, LVA; Auditor of Public Accounts, Condemned Blacks Executed or Transported, Records—Condemned Slaves, Court Orders, and Valuations, 1858–1865, Misc. Reel 2555, Frames 1021, 1026, LVA.

53. Auditor of Public Accounts, Condemned Blacks Executed or Transported, Records—Condemned Slaves, Court Orders, and Valuations, 1858–1865, Misc. Reel 2555, Frames 1011 (Viney); 1017, 1019, 1021 (James); 1009, 1011 (Martin), LVA; Schwarz, "Transportation," 226; quoted in Campbell, "Victim of Prejudice," 83.

54. Walter Johnson, *Soul by Soul: Life inside the Antebellum Slave Market* (Cambridge: Harvard University Press, 1999).

55. Campbell, "Victim of Prejudice," 79, 87n33; Schwarz, "Transportation," 220, 224; McNair, "Justice Bound," 370–371.

56. Schwarz, "Transportation," 228, 229; Auditor of Public Accounts, Condemned Blacks Executed or Transported, Records—Condemned Slaves, Court Orders, and Valuations, 1858–1865, Misc. Reel 2555, Frame 425, LVA; Auditor of Public Accounts, Condemned Blacks Executed or Transported, Records—Condemned Slaves, Court Orders, and Valuations, 1858–1865, Misc. Reel 2555, Frame 595, LVA; Executive Papers, John Letcher, Misc. Reel 4709, Box 3, Folder 5, Frames 28–31, LVA; Campbell, "Victim of Prejudice," 85.

57. *Acts Passed at the First Session of the Sixteenth Legislature of the State of Louisiana, Began and Held in the City of New Orleans, on the 2d Day of January, 1843* (New Orleans: Alexander C. Bullitt, 1843), 70. See also *Official Journal of the Proceedings of the House of Representatives of the State of Louisiana. Second Session—Sixteenth Legislature January 1, 1844* (New Orleans: n.p., 1844), 31; *Acts Passed at the Second Session of the Sixteenth Legislature of the State of Louisiana, Begun and Held in the City of New Orleans, on the 1st Day of January, 1844* (New Orleans: Alexander C. Bullitt, 1844), 27, 41. On the incarceration of slaves in Louisiana, see Jeff Forret, "Before Angola: Enslaved Prisoners in the Louisiana State Penitentiary," *Louisiana History* 54 (Spring 2013): 133–171.

58. *Official Journal of the Proceedings of the House of Representatives of the State of Louisiana.*

NOTES TO PAGES 146–148

Second Session—Sixteenth Legislature January 1, 1844, 3; *Baton Rouge Gazette,* April 30, 1842; Susan Wurtzburg and Thurston H. G. Hahn III, *Hard Labor: History and Archaeology at the Old Louisiana State Penitentiary, Baton Rouge, Louisiana* (Fort Worth: General Services Administration, 1991), 5, state that antebellum black prisoners labored on the levees because it was an unhealthy and dangerous task white men eschewed and one that planters refused to let their valuable bondmen perform.

59. *Report on the Penitentiary, by a Joint Committee of the Senate and House of Representatives. J. Bernard, Chairman,* n.p.; *Baton Rouge Gazette,* April 30, 1842; *Acts Passed at the First Session of the Seventeenth Legislature of the State of Louisiana, Began and Held in the City of New Orleans, on the 6th Day of January 1845* (New Orleans: Magne & Weisse, 1845), 28; *Report of the Joint Committee on the Penitentiary* (New Orleans: Emile La Sere, 1854), 4; *Minority Report of the Committee on the Penitentiary* (Baton Rouge: Winfree & Bryan, 1852), 15.

60. Gilles Vandal, "Regulating Louisiana's Rural Areas: The Function of Parish Jails, 1840–1885," *Louisiana History* 42 (Winter 2001): 59–92; *State v. Sanite, slave of Alexis Faurie* (1855), First District Court of New Orleans, 9934, NOPL; Betty Wood, "Prisons, Workhouses, and the Control of Slave Labour in Low Country Georgia, 1763–1815," *Slavery & Abolition* 8 (December 1987): 247–271; McNair, "Justice Bound," 161, 273; Coulter, "Four Slave Trials," 238; Hindus, *Prison and Plantation,* 145; Tate, *Negro in Eighteenth-Century Williamsburg,* 96; Anderson District, Court of Magistrates and Freeholders, Reel C2918, Case #278, SCDAH; Kershaw District, Court of Magistrates and Freeholders, Trial Papers, 1800–1861, Box 2, Folders 114, 105, SCDAH; Laurens District, Court of Magistrates and Freeholders, Trial Papers, 1808–1865, Box 1, Folder 67, SCDAH; Spartanburg District, Court of Magistrates and Freeholders, Reel C2922, Case #296; Clarendon District, Court of Magistrates and Freeholders, Trial Papers, 1863–1865, Folder 4, SCDAH; Race and Slavery Petitions Project, #11385006, Ser. I, Reel 11, 0503; Race and Slavery Petitions Project, #11677805, Ser. I, Reel 16, 0033.

61. Rawick, SS1, vol. 6, pt. 1, 317; T. Lynn Smith and Homer L. Hitt, "The Composition of the Population of Louisiana State Penitentiary, 1859, 1860, and 1861," *Southwestern Social Science Quarterly* 20 (March 1940): 365; Wood, "Prisons, Workhouses, and the Control of Slave Labour," 248; Jim Rice, "'This Province, So Meanly and Thinly Inhabited': Punishing Maryland's Criminals, 1681–1850," *Journal of the Early Republic* 19 (Spring 1999): 19; Flanigan, *Criminal Law of Slavery,* 21; *Acts Passed by the Second Legislature of the State of Louisiana, at Its First Session, Held and Begun in the Town of Baton Rouge, on the 16th January, 1854* (New Orleans: Emile La Sere, 1854), 149; Edward L. Ayers, *Vengeance and Justice: Crime and Punishment in the 19th-Century American South* (New York: Oxford University Press, 1984), 61.

62. Flanigan, *Criminal Law of Slavery,* 21; Ayers, *Vengeance and Justice,* 295n56. In the North, gradual or immediate emancipation laws passed in the wake of the Revolution undermined or eliminated altogether the institution of slavery. The North's slave population was therefore in decline before northern penitentiaries were built. Among northern states, only Pennsylvania, which abolished slavery gradually by law in 1780 and founded its penitentiary a mere decade later, stood a reasonable chance of incarcerating slaves in any numbers. In fact, dozens of runaways from the Upper South and the neighboring states of New York and New Jersey counted among the inmates of Pennsylvania's Walnut Street Prison in the 1790s. See Gary B. Nash, *Forging Freedom: The Formation of Philadelphia's Black Community, 1720–1840* (Cambridge: Har-

vard University Press, 1988), 138. For a demographic study of Walnut Street Prison, see Leslie Patrick-Stamp, "Numbers That Are Not New: African Americans in the Country's First Prison, 1790–1835," *Pennsylvania Magazine of History and Biography* 119 (January–April 1995): 95–128. Although Patrick-Stamp's article focuses on the issue of race, it neglects the phenomenon of slave prisoners, making no distinction between slave and free black convicts.

63. J. Thorsten Sellin, *Slavery and the Penal System* (New York: Elsevier, 1976), 144; Rice, "This Province, So Meanly and Thinly Inhabited," 35. Marvin E. Gettleman notes that, while Maryland's law of 1818 eliminated slaves from the penitentiary, free blacks still entered, numbering one-third of new inmates in 1834 and more than half in 1839. See Marvin E. Gettleman, "The Maryland Penitentiary in the Age of Tocqueville, 1828–1842," *Maryland Historical Magazine* 56 (September 1961): 276–277. Flanigan discusses a subsequent effort to imprison slaves in Maryland later in the antebellum period. See Flanigan, *Criminal Law of Slavery*, 22–23.

64. Josiah Gould, *Digest of the Statutes of Arkansas: Embracing All Laws of a General and Permanent Character in Force at the Close of the Session of the General Assembly of 1856: Together with Notes of the Decisions of the Supreme Court upon the Statutes, and an Appendix Containing Forms for Justices of the Peace* (Little Rock: Johnson & Yerkes, 1858), 385; Flanigan, *Criminal Law of Slavery*, 23.

65. Ayers, *Vengeance and Justice*, 61; Auditor of Public Accounts, Condemned Blacks Executed or Transported, Records—Condemned Slaves, Court Orders, and Valuations, 1846–1857, Misc. Reel 2554, Frames 374, 397, 405, 518, 862, LVA. Virginia slaves slated for execution remained confined in the local city or county jail.

66. *State v. Fleming, slave of Casimire Lacoste* (1848), First District Court of New Orleans, 1945, NOPL; *State v. Cuffy, property of the New Orleans and Carrollton Railroad* (1848), First District Court of New Orleans, 3016, NOPL; *State v. Tom Evans (slave)* (1855), First District Court of New Orleans, 10487, NOPL; *State v. Jack (slave)* (1858), First District Court of New Orleans, 13653, NOPL; *State v. Hannah (a slave)* (1855), 10 La. An. 131, in Catterall, *Judicial Cases*, vol. 3, 634.

67. Taylor, *Negro Slavery in Louisiana*, 207; *Report of the Board of Directors, of the Louisiana Penitentiary to the Governor of Louisiana*, 2; *Daily Gazette & Comet* (Baton Rouge), January 22, 1857; *Report on the Penitentiary, by a Joint Committee of the Senate and House of Representatives. J. Bernard, Chairman*, n.p. (quotation). See also *Message of Robert C. Wickliffe, Governor of the State of Louisiana, Together with an Appendix, Containing the Report of the Penitentiary Agents for the Year 1856* (Baton Rouge: Office of the Daily Advocate, 1857), 21.

68. Coulter, "Four Slave Trials," 240; Hindus, *Prison and Plantation*, 158; Schwarz, *Slave Laws in Virginia*, 72; McNair, "Justice Bound," 167; A. E. Kier Nash, "The Texas Supreme Court and Trial Rights of Blacks, 1845–1860," *Journal of American History* 58 (December 1971): 629; *Calvin, a slave v. State* (1860), Supreme Court of Texas, 1860 Tex. LEXIS 118; *John (a slave) v. State* (1852), Supreme Court of Mississippi, 24 Miss. 569, 1852 Miss. LEXIS 103; *Allen, a slave v. the State* (1851), Supreme Court of Georgia, 9 Ga. 492, 1851 Ga. LEXIS 43; *John (a slave) v. the State* (1858), Supreme Court of Tennessee, 38 Tenn. 49, 1858 Tenn. LEXIS 116, 1 Head 49.

69. *Jack, a slave v. State* (1861), Supreme Court of Texas, 26 Tex. 1, 1861 Tex. LEXIS 1; Hancock County, Georgia, Inferior Court Minutes, County Purposes & Lunacy, 1843–1850; *Henry, a slave, v. the State* (1863), Supreme Court of Georgia, 33 Ga. 441, 1863 Ga. LEXIS 6; *Jim, a slave, v. the State* (1843), Supreme Court of Tennessee, 23 Tenn. 289, 1843 Tenn. LEXIS 85, 4 Hum. 289.

Other lawyers in slave-slave homicide cases filed appeals concerning the court's instructions to the jury. See, for example, *Nelson v. the State* (1852), Supreme Court of Tennessee, 32 Tenn. 237, 1852 Tenn. LEXIS 58, 2 Swan 237.

70. Morris, "Slaves and the Rules of Evidence," 221, 220, 223; Thomas R. R. Cobb, *An Inquiry into the Law of Negro Slavery in the United States of America. To Which is Prefixed, an Historical Sketch of Slavery*, vol. 1 (Savannah: W. Thorne Williams, 1858), 271–272. Cobb's remarks echoed those of Chief Justice Leonard Henderson of North Carolina, who observed in *State v. Charity* (1830) that the slave's "confessions are made, not from a love of truth, not from a sense of duty, not to speak a falsehood, but to please his master; and it is in vain, that his master tells him to speak the truth ... The slave will ... mould his answer accordingly. We therefore more often get the wishes of the master, or the slave's belief of his wishes, than the truth." See *State v. Charity, a slave* (1830), Supreme Court of North Carolina, 13 N.C. 543, 1830 N.C. LEXIS 108.

71. Orange County, Minutes, Superior Court, 1821–1833, NCDAH; *State v. Charity* (1830), 13 N.C. 543, Reel 41, Case 1802, pp. 352–357; *State v. Charity, a slave* (1830), Supreme Court of North Carolina, 13 N.C. 543, 1830 N.C. LEXIS 108.

72. *Simon (a slave) v. State* (1858), Supreme Court of Mississippi, 37 Miss. 288, 1858 Miss. LEXIS 75; *Simon, a slave v. State* (1859), Supreme Court of Mississippi, 36 Miss. 636, 1859 Miss. LEXIS 77.

73. Executive Papers, James Barbour, July 1814, Box 13, Folder 1, LVA.

74. *Seaborn and Jim v. State* (1852), Supreme Court of Alabama, 20 Ala. 15, 1852 Ala. LEXIS 294.

75. *William (a slave) v. State* (1865), Supreme Court of Alabama, 39 Ala. 532, 1865 Ala. LEXIS 5; *State v. Isaac* (1848), Supreme Court of Louisiana, New Orleans, 3 La. Ann. 359, 1848 La. LEXIS 186.

76. *Jordan, a slave v. State* (1856), Supreme Court of Mississippi, 32 Miss. 382, 1856 Miss. LEXIS 222.

77. Cumberland County, Order Book, 1774–1778, Reel 26, LVA; Virginia, General Assembly, Legislative Petitions, Cumberland County, 1776–1837, May 10, 1777, Reel 44, Box 61, Folder 5, Frames 35–37, LVA. See also Race and Slavery Petitions Project, #11677701, Ser. I, Reel 16, 0008.

78. Race and Slavery Petitions Project, #11380403, Ser. I, Reel 9, 0032; David J. McCord, *The Statutes at Large of South Carolina; Edited, Under Authority of the Legislature*, vol. 6 (Columbia: A. S. Johnston, 1839), 188; Race and Slavery Petitions Project, #11384202, Ser. I, Reel 11, 0332. Robert Stinson of Lancaster District owned a slave named Bob, hanged in October 1830 for having murdered Stinson's bondwoman Sabry. Stinson wrote the South Carolina House of Representatives to guarantee that he would be allowed "the usual compensation." Lawmakers granted his request. See Race and Slavery Petitions Project, #11383001, Ser. I, Reel 10, 0607.

79. Race and Slavery Petitions Project, #11380004, Ser. I, Reel 8, 0545; Executive Papers, Henry A. Wise, Misc. Reel 4201, Frame 512, LVA.

80. Auditor of Public Accounts, Condemned Blacks Executed or Transported Records—Condemned Slaves, Court Orders, and Valuations, 1810–1822, Misc. Reel 2551, Frames, 610–614, LVA.

81. *Re Negro Tom*, 32 Md. Arch. 333, February 1770, in *Judicial Cases Concerning American Slavery and the Negro*, vol. 4, ed. Helen Tunnicliff Catterall (Washington, D.C.: Carnegie Institution of Washington, 1936), 48.

82. Campbell, "Victim of Prejudice," 79; Executive Papers, Wilson Cary Nicholas, April 1816–

October 1816, Misc. Reel 239, LVA; Executive Papers, James McDowell, February 1844, Box 3, Folder 4, LVA. On gubernatorial pardons in Georgia, see McNair, "Justice Bound," 234, 266.

83. Taylor, *Negro Slavery in Louisiana*, 207; State Auditor's Account Book 1, March 20, 1847, to December 30, 1848, P1978-189, 320, Louisiana State Archives, Baton Rouge; State Auditor's Account Book 4, January 1, 1857, to December 30, 1859, P1978-189, 167, Louisiana State Archives, Baton Rouge; *Report of the Board of Directors of the Louisiana Penitentiary* (New Orleans: Emile La Sere, 1854), 4; *Acts Passed by the Fifth Legislature of the State of Louisiana, at Its First Session, Held and Begun in the City of Baton Rouge, on the 16th of January, 1860* (Baton Rouge: J. M. Taylor, 1860), 148.

84. Morris, *Southern Slavery and the Law*, 301; Race and Slavery Petitions Project, #21384617, Ser. II, Part D, 0853; Race and Slavery Petitions Project, #11383402, Ser. I, Reel 11, 0092.

85. Chesterfield County, Order Book 24, 1822–1824, Reel 49, LVA; Executive Papers, John M. Gregory, November 1842, Box 2, Folder 4, LVA; Essex County, Order Book 45, 1823–1826, Reel 94, LVA.

86. Executive Papers, James Barbour, October 1814, Box 14, Folder 4, LVA; Executive Papers, John Floyd, February 1834, Box 12, Folder 4, LVA.

87. Executive Papers, John Floyd, February 1834, Box 12, Folder 4, LVA; Executive Papers, William B. Giles, March 1828, Box 4, Folder 3, LVA.

88. Madison County, Order Book 7, Reel 25, LVA; Executive Papers, John Floyd, April–June 1849, Box 394, Folder June 1849, LVA; Executive Papers, Henry A. Wise, Misc. Reel 4202, Box 8, Folder 4, Frames 690–698, LVA.

89. Executive Papers, John M. Gregory, November 1842, Box 2, Folder 4, LVA.

90. Governor's Papers, Gov. Edward B. Dudley, G.P. 90, Folder Correspondence, Petitions, etc. Oct. 1, 1839–Oct. 28, 1839, NCDAH; GLB 32 Gov. Letter Book, Edward B. Dudley 1837–1840, p. 331, NCDAH.

91. Henrico County, Order Book 2, 1784–1787, Reel 69, LVA; Schwarz, *Twice Condemned*, 24; *State v. William Dillahunt, negro* (1840), Court of General Sessions of Delaware, 3 Del. 551, 1840 Del. LEXIS 43, 3 Harr. 551.

92. Auditor of Public Accounts, Condemned Blacks Executed or Transported, Records—Condemned Slaves, Court Orders, and Valuations, 1810–1822, Misc. Reel 2551, Frames 510, 508, LVA; Powhatan County, Order Book 12, 1814–1816, Reel 27, LVA; Schwarz, *Twice Condemned*, 253; Executive Papers, James Pleasants, August 1824, Box 5, Folder 5, LVA.

93. Executive Papers, John Floyd, February 1834, Box 12, Folder 4, LVA; Executive Papers, James Pleasants, December 1824, Box 6, Folder 1, LVA; Executive Papers, Henry Lee, Box 3, Folder 15, Misc. Reel 5050, Frame 920, LVA; Auditor of Public Accounts, Condemned Blacks Executed or Transported, Records—Condemned Slaves, Court Orders, and Valuations, 1781–1793, Misc. Reel 2549, Frame 733, LVA.

94. Executive Papers, Henry Lee, Box 3, Folder 15, Misc. Reel 5050, Frame 920, LVA; Governor's Papers, Gov. Edward B. Dudley, G.P. 90, Folder Correspondence, Petitions, etc. Oct. 1, 1839–Oct. 28, 1839, NCDAH; GLB 32 Gov. Letter Book, Edward B. Dudley 1837–1840, p. 331, NCDAH; Executive Papers, William B. Giles, March 1828, Box 4, Folder 3, LVA; Executive Papers, Wyndham Robertson, Box 3, Folder 3, LVA; Executive Papers, John M. Gregory, November 1842, Box 2,

NOTES TO PAGES 166–169

Folder 4, LVA. See also the case of Bourbon County, Kentucky, bondman Daniel in Morris, *Southern Slavery and the Law,* 301.

4. VIOLENCE AT WORK AND PLAY

1. Executive Papers, John Letcher, Misc. Reel 4721, Box 7, Folder 5, Frames 406–412, LVA.

2. Executive Papers, John Letcher, Misc. Reel 4721, Box 7, Folder 5, Frames 406–412, LVA. Britton was eventually found guilty of second-degree murder and sentenced to sale and transportation out of the United States. Virginia's governor commuted his sentenced to labor on the public works for life. See Auditor of Public Accounts, Condemned Blacks Executed or Transported, Records—Condemned Slaves, Court Orders, and Valuations, 1858–1865, Misc. Reel 2555, Frame 552, LVA.

3. Executive Papers, John Letcher, Misc. Reel 4721, Box 7, Folder 5, Frames 406–412, LVA; Ira Berlin and Philip D. Morgan, eds., *Cultivation and Culture: Labor and the Shaping of Slave Life in the Americas* (Charlottesville: University Press of Virginia, 1993). Recent scholarship has paid greater attention to the centrality of work in slaves' lives.

4. Sergio Lussana, "To See Who Was Best on the Plantation: Enslaved Fighting Contests and Masculinity in the Antebellum Plantation South," *Journal of Southern History* 76 (November 2010): 905, 916–917; Executive Papers, John Letcher, Misc. Reel 4721, Box 7, Folder 5, Frames 406–412, LVA. On slaves' leisure-time activities, see David K. Wiggins, "Good Times On the Old Plantation: Popular Recreations of the Black Slave in Ante Bellum South, 1810–1860," *Journal of Sport History* 4 (Fall 1977): 260–284; idem, "The Play of Slave Children in the Plantation Communities of the Old South, 1820–1860," *Journal of Sport History* 7 (Summer 1980): 21–39; and James Walvin, "Slaves, Free Time and the Question of Leisure," *Slavery & Abolition* 16 (April 1995): 1–13.

5. George P. Rawick, ed., *The American Slave: A Composite Autobiography, Supplement, Series 2,* vol. 3, pt. 2 (Westport, Conn.: Greenwood Press, 1979), 505; idem, ed., *The American Slave: A Composite Autobiography, Supplement, Series 1,* vol. 9, pt. 4 (Westport, Conn.: Greenwood Press, 1977), 1451.

6. Eugene D. Genovese, *Roll, Jordan, Roll: The World the Slaves Made* (1974; reprint, New York; Vintage, 1976), 339, 338, 341, 342; Michael P. Johnson, "Work, Culture, and the Slave Community: Slave Occupations in the Cotton Belt in 1860," *Labor History* 27 (Summer 1986): 345–347; George P. Rawick, ed., *The American Slave: A Composite Autobiography,* vol. 2, pt. 1 (Westport, Conn.: Greenwood Publishing Company, 1972), 225; idem, *American Slave,* vol. 3, pt. 4, 2; Emily West, *Chains of Love: Slave Couples in Antebellum South Carolina* (Urbana: University of Illinois Press, 2004), 106. See also C. W. Harper, "House Servants and Field Hands: Fragmentation in the Antebellum Slave Community," *North Carolina Historical Review* 55 (January 1978): 42–59; idem, "Black Aristocrats: Domestic Servants on the Antebellum Plantation," *Phylon* 46 (June 1985): 123–135. Harper proposes that masters selected house servants on the basis of innate qualities such as intelligence or skin color and that house servants in turn benefited intellectually through increased contact with whites.

7. Genovese, *Roll, Jordan, Roll,* 620; Philip D. Morgan, *Slave Counterpoint: Black Culture in the Eighteenth-Century Chesapeake and Lowcountry* (Chapel Hill: University of North Carolina Press, 1998), 467.

8. Charles C. Jones, *The Religious Instruction of the Negroes. In the United States* (Savannah:

Thomas Purse, 1842), 136; John Hammond Moore, ed., *A Plantation Mistress on the Eve of the Civil War: The Diary of Keziah Goodwyn Hopkins Brevard, 1860–1861* (Columbia: University of South Carolina Press, 1993), 88.

9. Elizabeth Ware Pearson, ed., *Letters from Port Royal, 1862–1868* (New York: Arno Press and the New York Times, 1969), 113; J. Mason Brewer, *American Negro Folklore* (Chicago: Quadrangle Books, 1968), 233; Race and Slavery Petitions Project, #21284804, Ser. II, Part D, 0015; Harrison County, Minute Book, 1816–1818, Reel 7, LVA. On David and Isaac, see also Philip J. Schwarz, *Twice Condemned: Slaves and the Criminal Laws of Virginia, 1705–1865* (Baton Rouge: Louisiana State University Press, 1988), 250.

10. *William (a slave) v. the State* (1855), Supreme Court of Georgia, 18 Ga. 356, 1855 Ga. LEXIS 202; *State v. Elbert* (1863), Records of the Superior Court of Newton County, Drawer 11, Reel 3, GA, in Glenn M. McNair, "Justice Bound: Aframericans, Crime, and Criminal Justice in Georgia, 1751–1865" (Ph.D. diss., Emory University, 2001), 121–122; Executive Papers, Wyndham Robertson, Box 3, Folder 3, LVA; Executive Papers, John M. Gregory, November 1842, Box 2, Folder 4, LVA; *State v. Horace, a slave* (1860), Case 10416, Group 1860, Box 1, File 76, ACCCHNF.

11. Executive Papers, Henry A. Wise, Misc. Reel 4206, Box 11, Folder 4, Frames 413–421, LVA; *Wilmington Journal,* reprinted in *The North Carolinian,* September 3, 1853. Horrified by what he had done and likely fearful of the punishment that awaited him, Hamilton "committed suicide by jumping into the river from a wharf near the Distillery, . . . drowning himself." Hamilton did not live long enough to learn that the slave he had knifed recovered; his victim even attended his funeral.

12. *State v. Nelson* (1853), Records of the Superior Court of Habersham County, Drawer 80, Box 64, GDAH, in McNair, "Justice Bound," 123. Asked about Young's whereabouts, his nemesis suggested that the deceased could be found "in hell." He also warned a different foe that he might "end up like" the deceased Young, for he would "knock his brains out with a hand spike." Later still, he suggested that Young was "at the upper end of the plantation in a gold pit," precisely where his corpse was located. The assembled evidence was enough to convince the jury of his guilt.

13. Race and Slavery Petitions Project, #11382902, Ser. I, Reel 10, 0510; Race and Slavery Petitions Project, #11382904, Ser. I, Reel 10, 0518. Inabinet petitioned the South Carolina legislature for compensation to recoup the loss of "a slave worth six hundred Dollars" while in service to the state but was refused.

14. *State v. Cuffy* (1848), 3016, First District Court of New Orleans, NOPL.

15. *John (a slave) v. State* (1852), Supreme Court of Mississippi, 24 Miss. 569, 1852 Miss. LEXIS 103. See also Helen Tunnicliff Catterall, ed., *Judicial Cases Concerning American Slavery and the Negro,* vol. 3 (Washington, D.C.: Carnegie Institution of Washington, 1932), 329.

16. *The Crescent,* reprinted in *Daily Gazette and Comet* (Baton Rouge), October 5, 1858; Manuscript Census Returns, Eighth Census of the United States, 1860, Orleans Parish, Louisiana, Schedule 1, Free Population, National Archives Microfilm Series M-653, Roll 418, p. 715.

17. *State v. Negro Will* (1834), 1 Dev. & Bat. 121, 18 N.C. 121.

18. Spartanburg District, Court of Magistrates and Freeholders, Trial Papers, Reel C2922, Case #270, SCDAH; *State v. Charles Loadnum* (1798), Court of Oyer and Terminer of Delaware, Kent, 2 Del. Cas. 240, 1798 Del. LEXIS 42; Randolph Roth, *American Homicide* (Cambridge: Belknap Press of Harvard University Press, 2009), 227.

19. Executive Papers, Henry A. Wise, Misc. Reel 4211, Box 15, Folder 5, Frames 220–225, LVA.

20. *State v. Johnson* (1852), Records of the Superior Court of Bibb County, Drawer 183, Reel 12, GA, in McNair, "Justice Bound," 128.

21. Genovese, *Roll, Jordan, Roll*, 393; Kenneth M. Stampp, *The Peculiar Institution: Slavery in the Ante-Bellum South* (New York: Alfred A. Knopf, 1956), 336, 337; *Simon, a slave v. the State of Mississippi* (1859), Box 5849, Case 8900, MDAH.

22. Executive Papers, Thomas Mann Randolph, June 1820, Box 2, Folder 3, LVA.

23. Jonathan D. Martin, *Divided Mastery: Slave Hiring in the American South* (Cambridge: Harvard University Press, 2004); David E. Paterson, "Slavery, Slaves, and Cash in a Georgia Village, 1825–1865," *Journal of Southern History* 75 (November 2009): 922.

24. Dylan C. Penningroth, *The Claims of Kinfolk: African American Property and Community in the Nineteenth-Century South* (Chapel Hill: University of North Carolina Press, 2003), 80–81; Executive Papers, Henry A. Wise, Misc. Reel 4208, Frames 329–331, LVA; Executive Papers, Henry A. Wise, Misc. Reel 4214, Box 18, Folder 3, Frames 487–492, LVA.

25. McNair, "Justice Bound," 249; Executive Papers, John Floyd, January–February 1851, Box 403, Folder February 11–20, 1851, LVA.

26. Frances Anne Kemble, *Journal of a Residence on a Georgian Plantation in 1838–1839*, ed. John A. Scott (New York: Alfred A. Knopf, 1961), 281, 305; Moore, *Plantation Mistress*, 88; Stampp, *Peculiar Institution*, 335; Abbeville *Banner*, reprinted in *The Raleigh Star, and North Carolina Gazette*, March 4, 1846; Bertram Wyatt-Brown, *Southern Honor: Ethics and Behavior in the Old South* (New York: Oxford University Press, 1982), 290–291.

27. Abbeville *Banner*, reprinted in *The Raleigh Star, and North Carolina Gazette*, March 4, 1846; Paul D. Escott et al., *Major Problems in the History of the American South*, vol. 1, 2nd ed. (New York: Houghton Mifflin, 1999), 216.

28. James Mellon, ed., *Bullwhip Days: The Slaves Remember* (New York: Weidenfeld & Nicolson, 1988), 138; Rawick, *American Slave*, vol. 2, pt. 2, 49, 237, 310.

29. Rawick, *American Slave*, vol. 2, pt. 2, 212; idem, *American Slave*, vol. 11 Missouri, 27; idem, *American Slave*, vol. 3, pt. 3, 49; Norman R. Yetman, ed., *Life under the "Peculiar Institution": Selections from the Slave Narrative Collection* (New York: Holt, Rinehart and Winston Inc., 1970), 55; Rawick, *American Slave*, vol. 2, pt. 2, 310–311.

30. Rawick, SS2, vol. 10, pt. 9, 4346–4347; Joe Gray Taylor, *Negro Slavery in Louisiana* (Baton Rouge: Louisiana Historical Association, 1963), 202; William Grimes, *Life of William Grimes, the Runaway Slave, Brought Down to the Present Time. Written by Himself* (New Haven, Conn.: The Author, 1855), 44. In Richmond, Virginia, Edward was dismayed to see his housemate John "whipping" a slave named Henry. The following day, Edward asked Henry "what he let John whip him for," declaring that if it had been him, "he would have knocked John in the head." Indeed, Edward resolved to do just that, "as he had something against him." Edward went to the house he shared with John, challenged him to a fight outdoors, and struck a mortal blow to his head with an axe. Executive Papers, Joseph Johnson, October–December 1854, Box 423, Folder November 1854, LVA.

31. Yetman, *Life under the "Peculiar Institution,"* 55; Randy J. Sparks, *On Jordan's Stormy Banks: Evangelicalism in Mississippi, 1773–1876* (Athens: University of Georgia Press, 1994), 168; *Re Negro Pedro* (1774), 10 La. Hist Q. 455, in Catterall, *Judicial Cases*, vol. 3, 431; Genovese, *Roll, Jordan, Roll*, 372; *Ned and Taylor (slaves) v. State* (1857), Supreme Court of Mississippi, 33 Miss. 364, 1857 Miss. LEXIS 48.

32. Executive Papers, John Letcher, Misc. Reel 4724, Box 8, Folder 4, Frames 201–206, LVA.

33. Stampp, *Peculiar Institution,* 332; Charles L. Perdue Jr., Thomas E. Barden, and Robert K. Phillips, eds., *Weevils in the Wheat: Interviews with Virginia Ex-Slaves* (Charlottesville: University Press of Virginia, 1976), 280; Yetman, *Life under the "Peculiar Institution,"* 13; Executive Papers, Wyndham Robertson, Box 3, Folder 3, LVA; Stephanie M. H. Camp, *Closer to Freedom: Enslaved Women and Everyday Resistance in the Plantation South* (Chapel Hill: University of North Carolina Press, 2004), 86–87; Sue Eakin, *Solomon Northup's* Twelve Years a Slave *and Plantation Life in the Antebellum South* (Lafayette: Center for Louisiana Studies, University of Louisiana at Lafayette, 2007), 255–256.

34. Rawick, *American Slave,* vol. 5, pt. 3, 4; idem, *American Slave,* vol. 10, pt. 6, 337.

35. *Ben (a slave) v. State* (1861), Supreme Court of Alabama, 37 Ala. 103, 1861 Ala. LEXIS 35; Genovese, *Roll, Jordan, Roll,* 623; Pittsylvania County, Court Records 40, 1848–1850, Reel 59, LVA.

36. *Prince, a slave v. State of Mississippi* (1856), Box 5837, Case 7376, MDAH.

37. *Jim, a slave, v. the State* (1844), Supreme Court of Tennessee, 24 Tenn. 145, 1844 Tenn. LEXIS 46, 5 Hum. 145. See also *Jim, a slave v. the State* (1843), Supreme Court of Tennessee, 23 Tenn. 289, 1843 Tenn. LEXIS 85, 4 Hum. 289; Stampp, *Peculiar Institution,* 332; and Helen Tunnicliff Catterall, ed., *Judicial Cases Concerning American Slavery and the Negro,* vol. 2 (Washington, D.C.: Carnegie Institution of Washington, 1929), 522–523; Yetman, *Life under the "Peculiar Institution,"* 13.

38. *Jordan, a slave v. the State of Mississippi* (1856), Box 5842, Case 7834, MDAH; *Jordan, a slave v. State* (1856), Supreme Court of Mississippi, 32 Miss. 382, 1856 Miss. LEXIS 222.

39. Race and Slavery Petitions Project, #11381405, Ser. I, Reel 9, 0232; Race and Slavery Petitions Project, #11381507, Ser. I, Reel 9, 0290.

40. Rawick, *American Slave,* vol. 7, pt. 2, 12; Race and Slavery Petitions Project, #11383803, Ser. I, Reel 11, 0231.

41. Race and Slavery Petitions Project, #11383803, Ser. I, Reel 11, 0231.

42. Norfolk *Herald,* reprinted in *The Raleigh Star, and North Carolina Gazette,* June 12, 1844; McNair, "Justice Bound," 147; Box 2E776, Folder 3: Civil and Criminal Court Cases, Warren County, Mississippi, 1849–1863 and undated, Natchez Trace Slaves and Slavery Collection, Center for American History, University of Texas, Austin. See also William L. Richter, "Slavery in Baton Rouge, 1820–1860," *Louisiana History* 10 (Spring 1969): 133.

43. McNair, "Justice Bound," 61; *State v. Winningham* (1857), 10 Richardson 257, in Catterall, *Judicial Cases,* vol. 2, 452–453.

44. Rawick, *American Slave,* vol. 13, pt. 4, 73; idem, *American Slave,* vol. 13, pt. 3, 238; idem, SS1, vol. 10, pt. 5, 2149, 2315, 2301; idem, *American Slave,* vol. 7 Oklahoma, 142; T. J. Desch Obi, *Fighting for Honor: The History of African Martial Art Traditions in the Atlantic World* (Columbia: University of South Carolina Press, 2008), 92–97; Rawick, SS1, vol. 7, pt. 2, 622.

45. Executive Papers, James Pleasants, August 1825, Box 7, Folder 12, LVA; Rawick, *American Slave,* vol. 4, pt. 1, 240–241.

46. Rawick, SS1, vol. 10, pt. 5, 2361; idem, *American Slave,* vol. 4, pt. 2, 37; idem, SS2, vol. 5, pt. 4, 1886; idem, SS1, vol. 7, pt. 2, 748; Desch Obi, *Fighting for Honor,* 98–100. On arranged fights, see Lussana, "To See Who Was Best on the Plantation."

47. Roger D. Abrahams, *Singing the Master: The Emergence of African American Culture in*

the Plantation South (New York: Penguin, 1993), 78, 249–250, 255; Daina Ramey Berry, *"Swing the Sickle for the Harvest Is Ripe": Gender and Slavery in Antebellum Georgia* (Urbana: University of Illinois Press, 2007), 3, 10, 60, 61; Rawick, *American Slave*, vol. 14, pt. 1, 265.

48. Lussana, "To See Who Was Best on the Plantation," 908–909, 920; Rawick, *American Slave*, vol. 12, pt. 1, 71; idem, SS2, vol. 5, pt. 4, 1886; idem, *American Slave*, vol. 12, pt. 1, 312; idem, *American Slave*, vol. 13, pt. 3, 334.

49. Executive Papers, James Pleasants, December 1824, Box 6, Folders 1, 4, LVA; Nelson County, County Court Minute Book, Vol. 8, 1835–1840, Reel 27, LVA.

50. Jeff Forret, *Race Relations at the Margins: Slaves and Poor Whites in the Antebellum Southern Countryside* (Baton Rouge: Louisiana State University Press, 2006); Stephen A. West, "From Yeoman to Redneck in Upstate South Carolina, 1850–1915" (Ph.D. diss., Columbia University, 1998), 188–189, 199; Executive Papers, Thomas Mann Randolph, August 1822, Box 7, Folder 3, LVA; *Isaac Franklin v. William Grissam* (1825), Case 24224, Group 1820, Box 44, File 1, ACCCHNF.

51. Genovese, *Roll, Jordan, Roll*, 627; Spartanburg District, Court of Magistrates and Freeholders, Reel C2920, Case #105, SCDAH; Rawick, *American Slave*, vol. 12, pt. 1, 350; idem, *American Slave*, vol. 12, pt. 2, 143.

52. James O. Breeden, ed., *Advice among Masters: The Ideal in Slave Management in the Old South* (Westport, Conn.: Greenwood Press, 1980), 263–264.

53. Rawick, *American Slave*, vol. 13, pt. 3, 283.

54. Executive Papers, James Monroe, January 1811, Box 1, Folder 1, LVA. In another incident, ten slaves in Rutherford County, Tennessee, gathered "in the woods" to drink whiskey purchased from a white man named Forbes. Altogether the bondmen had bought "a quart of liquor," which Forbes poured into Simon's "tickler" and Harkless's bottle. Sam had also "got from Forbes a glass as near full as he could carry it." After drinking, eight of the slaves departed, leaving only Sam and Nelson. "Sam and Nelson were friendly when I left them in the cedars," reported one of the slaves, but when Daniel McClary, master of Harkless, next saw Sam, the slave's "bowels" were spilling out of a four-inch cut in his belly, "and a spelling book" the slaves had somehow acquired "had been placed in the wound to keep them in." Sam's prognosis was grim. Had he lived, he might have counted among the many former bondmen who admitted in slave narratives that they were drunk when they got in fights with other blacks. See *Nelson v. the State* (1852), Supreme Court of Tennessee, 32 Tenn. 237, 1852 Tenn. LEXIS 58, 2 Swan 237. Several episodes of "black-on-black violence" in the WPA narratives appear to document conflicts that took place after slavery. See, for example, Rawick, SS1, vol. 8, pt. 3, 1145; idem, SS1, vol. 9, pt. 4, 1460, 1586, 1587.

55. Rawick, *American Slave*, vol. 4, pt. 1, 246–247; idem, *American Slave*, vol. 12, pt. 2, 120; idem, SS2, vol. 8, pt. 7, 3052; idem, SS1, vol. 10, pt. 5, 2361–2362; idem, SS1, vol. 9, pt. 4, 1657.

56. Anderson District, Court of Magistrates and Freeholders, Trial Papers, Reel C2919, Case #292, SCDAH.

57. Executive Papers, Henry A. Wise, Misc. Reel 4202, Box 8, Folder 4, LVA; Manuscript Census Returns, Eighth Census of the United States, 1860, Alexandria County, Virginia, Schedule 1, Free Population, National Archives Microfilm Series M-653, Roll 1331, p. 691.

58. Executive Papers, Henry A. Wise, Misc. Reel 4202, Box 8, Folder 4, Frames 670–683, LVA.

59. Executive Papers, Henry A. Wise, Misc. Reel 4202, Box 8, Folder 4, Frames 672–674, 688–689, 697–698, LVA.

60. Executive Papers, Henry A. Wise, Misc. Reel 4202, Box 8, Folder 4, Frames 677–681, LVA. Richard was found guilty of second-degree murder and sentenced to sale and transportation. See Fauquier County, Minute Book 1856–1857, Reel 61, LVA.

61. Rawick, SS1, vol. 9, pt. 4, 1432–1433; *Aaron, a slave v. the State of Mississippi* (1859), Box 5835, Case 7111, MDAH; *Leggett v. Simmons* (1846), 7 Smedes & M. 348, 15 Miss. 348, 1846 WL 2992, Miss. Err. App. 1846; Rawick, *American Slave,* vol. 6 Indiana, 107; Spartanburg District, Court of Magistrates and Freeholders, Trial Papers, Reel C2921, Case #135, SCDAH.

62. Executive Papers, John Floyd, February 1834, Box 12, Folder 4, LVA.

63. Spartanburg District, Court of Magistrates and Freeholders, Trial Papers, Reel C2921, Case #191, SCDAH; Anderson District, Court of Magistrates and Freeholders, Trial Papers, Reel C2919, Case #327, SCDAH; Rockbridge County, Minute Book, 1852–1854, Reel 43, LVA.

64. Rockbridge County, Minute Book, 1852–1854, Reel 43, LVA.

65. D. R. Hundley, *Social Relations in Our Southern States* (New York: Henry B. Price, 1860; reprint, New York: Arno Press, 1973), 332; Executive Papers, Henry A. Wise, Misc. Reel 4214, Box 18, Folder 3, Frames 487–492, LVA; Auditor of Public Accounts, Condemned Blacks Executed or Transported, Records—Condemned Slaves, Court Orders, and Valuations, 1858–1865, Misc. Reel 2555, Frame 398, LVA. Although sentenced to sale and transportation outside the United States, Red had his punishment reduced by Virginia's governor to labor on the public works for life.

66. Beaverdam Baptist Church (Wilkes County, Ga.), Minutes, 1836–1855, April 1850, Drawer 9, Reel 22, GA; Powelton Baptist Church (Hancock County, Ga.), Minutes, 1786–1916, August 1815, Drawer 32, Reel 76, GA; Cascade Primitive Baptist Church (Pittsylvania County, Va.), Minute Book, 1809–1913, October 1810, Misc. Reel 390, LVA; First Baptist Church (Houston, Tex.), Minutes, 1841–1881, July 1852, SWBTS; Mt. Tirzah Baptist Church (Charlotte County, Va.), Minute Book, 1834–1915, April 1842, LVA. One church in Union District, South Carolina, ferreted out all of its members who attended a cakewalk but reached the consensus that "no harm was intended." See Padgett's Creek Baptist Church (Union District, S.C.), Church Book, vol. 2, 1837–1874, December 1864, February 1865, SCL.

67. Lower Banister Church (Pittsylvania County, Va.), 1798–1845, November 1830, July 1831, LVA; New Hope Baptist Church (Lincoln County, Ga.), Minutes, 1831–1866, June 1846, Drawer 19, Reel 1, GA; Island Creek Baptist Church (Hancock County, Ga.), Minutes, 1806–1873, December 1816, April 1817, Drawer 31, Reel 80, GA; First Baptist Church (Huntsville, Tex.), Record and Minutes, 1844–1890, January 1864, November 1856, Newton Gresham Library, Sam Houston State University, Huntsville, Tex. On racing horses and horse racing, see Bethabara Baptist Church (Laurens District, S.C.), Records, 1801–1881, February 1816, December 1835, SCL; and Brushy Creek Baptist Church (Greenville District, S.C.), Minutes, 1794–1927, October 1839, SCL; Bethabara Baptist Church (Laurens District, S.C.), Records, 1801–1881, September 1857, SCL.

68. Flint Hill Baptist Church (York District, S.C.), Church Records, 1792–1899, September 1861, SCL; Greenwood Baptist Church (Lincoln County, Ga.), Minutes, 1798–1880, August 1837, Drawer 90, Reel 23. On whites disciplined for violating musical taboos, see, for example, County Line Primitive Baptist Church (Jones County, Ga.), Minutes, 1809–1830, September 1818, Drawer 218, Reel 15, GA; Crooked Creek Primitive Baptist Church (Putnam County, Ga.), Minutes, 1807–1846, June 1810 [typescript], GA; Powelton Baptist Church (Hancock County, Ga.), Minutes, 1786–1916, September 1834, Drawer 32, Reel 76, GA; Union Baptist Church (Union

District, S.C.), Records, 1804–1843, 1807, SCL; Lower Banister Church (Pittsylvania County, Va.), 1798–1845, November 1830, LVA; Poplar Springs Baptist Church (Laurens District, S.C.), Minutes, 1794–1937, September 1846, SCL.

69. See, for example, Warrior Creek Baptist Church (Laurens District, S.C.), Records, 1843–1896, November 1847, SCL; Rehoboth Baptist Church (Wilkes County, Ga.), Minutes, 1806–1933, December 1854, January 1855, Drawer 45, Reel 15, GA; Mount Vernon Church (Halifax County, Va.), Minute Book, 1837–1868, December 1857, LVA.

70. On condemnations of dancing, see Mt. Tirzah Baptist Church (Charlotte County, Va.), Minute Book, 1834–1915, February 1849, LVA; Washington First Baptist Church (Wilkes County, Ga.), Minutes, 1858–1923, 1924–1936, January 1864, Drawer 45, Reel 23, GA; Island Creek Baptist Church (Hancock County, Ga.), Minutes, 1806–1873, January 1829, Drawer 31, Reel 80, GA; Middle Ground Baptist Church (Screven County, Ga.), Minutes, 1850–1888, August 1856, Drawer 22, Reel 77, GA; Horeb Baptist Church (Hancock County, Ga.), Minutes, 1792–1916, October 1839, Drawer 32, Reel 77, LVA.

71. Mt. Tirzah Baptist Church (Charlotte County, Va.), Minute Book, 1834–1915, March 1859, LVA; Ash Camp (Keysville) Baptist Church (Charlotte County, Va.), Minute Book, 1813–1872, July 1856, August 1856, June 1857, January 1858, March 1858, LVA. In addition to dancing or holding dances, another way for whites to earn church scrutiny was for Baptist parents to send their children "to a dancing School for instruction." Several churches established rules against the practice. See Powelton Baptist Church (Hancock County, Ga.), Minutes, 1786–1916, August 1799, Drawer 32, Reel 76, GA; Bethabara Baptist Church (Laurens District, S.C.), Records, 1801–1881, July 1842, SCL; Rabun Creek Baptist Church (Laurens District, S.C.), Church Book, 1828–1913, March 1847, SCL; First Baptist Church (Houston, Tex.), Minutes, 1841–1881, May 1852, SWBTS.

72. Darien Baptist Church (Hancock County, Ga.), Minutes, 1794–1816, November 1813, Drawer 148, Reel 53, GA; Powelton Baptist Church (Hancock County, Ga.), Minutes, 1786–1916, July 1841, September 1841, Drawer 32, Reel 76, GA; Rehoboth Baptist Church (Wilkes County, Ga.), Minutes, 1806–1933, April 1855, Drawer 45, Reel 15, GA.

5. VIOLENCE AND THE SLAVE ECONOMY

1. *Henry, a slave v. the State* (1863), Supreme Court of Georgia, 33 Ga. 441, 1863 Ga. LEXIS 6. See also Helen Tunnicliff Catterall, ed., *Judicial Cases Concerning American Slavery and the Negro*, vol. 3 (Washington, D.C.: Carnegie Institution of Washington, 1932), 86; Eugene D. Genovese, *Roll, Jordan, Roll: The World the Slaves Made* (1974; reprint, New York; Vintage, 1976), 607; and Glenn M. McNair, "Justice Bound: Aframericans, Crime, and Criminal Justice in Georgia, 1751–1865" (Ph.D. diss., Emory University, 2001), 61–62.

2. *Henry, a slave v. the State* (1863), Supreme Court of Georgia, 33 Ga. 441, 1863 Ga. LEXIS 6. The Supreme Court of Georgia reversed the guilty verdict handed down by the Dougherty County court. Not only did the higher court see no malicious intent in Henry's actions; it also maintained that a slave could not legally control a blacksmith or any other shop.

3. Dylan C. Penningroth, *The Claims of Kinfolk: African American Property and Community in the Nineteenth-Century South* (Chapel Hill: University of North Carolina Press, 2003), ch. 2.

4. On the internal economy of the lowcountry, see Philip D. Morgan, "Work and Culture: The

Task System and the World of Lowcountry Blacks, 1700 to 1880," *William & Mary Quarterly* 3rd ser., 39 (October 1982): 563–599; idem, "The Ownership of Property by Slaves in the Mid-Nineteenth-Century Low Country," *Journal of Southern History* 49 (August 1983): 399–420; Betty Wood, "'White Society' and the 'Informal' Slave Economies of Lowcountry Georgia, c. 1763–1830," *Slavery & Abolition* 11 (December 1990): 313–331; idem, *Women's Work, Men's Work: The Informal Slave Economies of Lowcountry Georgia* (Athens: University of Georgia Press, 1995); and Robert Olwell, *Masters, Slaves, & Subjects: The Culture of Power in the South Carolina Low Country, 1740–1790* (Ithaca: Cornell University Press, 1998), ch. 4. On the internal economy outside the lowcountry, see Lawrence T. McDonnell, "Money Knows No Master: Market Relations and the American Slave Community," in *Developing Dixie: Modernization in a Traditional Society*, ed. Winfred B. Moore Jr., Joseph F. Tripp, and Lyon G. Tyler Jr. (Westport, Conn.: Greenwood Press, 1988), 31–44; John Campbell, "As 'A Kind of Freeman'? Slaves' Market-Related Activities in the South Carolina Upcountry, 1800–1860," in *The Slaves' Economy: Independent Production by Slaves in the Americas*, ed. Ira Berlin and Philip D. Morgan (London: Frank Cass, 1991), 131–169; John T. Schlotterbeck, "The Internal Economy of Slavery in Rural Piedmont Virginia," in *The Slaves' Economy: Independent Production by Slaves in the Americas*, ed. Ira Berlin and Philip D. Morgan (London: Frank Cass, 1991), 170–181; Loren Schweninger, "The Underside of Slavery: The Internal Economy, Self-Hire, and Quasi-Freedom in Virginia, 1780–1865," *Slavery & Abolition* 12 (September 1991): 1–22; idem, "Slave Independence and Enterprise in South Carolina, 1780–1865," *South Carolina Historical Magazine* 93 (April 1992): 101–125; Joseph P. Reidy, "Obligation and Right: Patterns of Labor, Subsistence, and Exchange in the Cotton Belt of Georgia, 1790–1860," in *Cultivation and Culture: Labor and the Shaping of Slave Life in the Americas*, ed. Ira Berlin and Philip D. Morgan (Charlottesville: University Press of Virginia, 1993), 138–154; Larry E. Hudson Jr., "'All That Cash': Work and Status in the Slave Quarters," in *Working toward Freedom: Slave Society and Domestic Economy in the American South*, ed. Larry E. Hudson Jr. (Rochester: University of Rochester Press, 1994), 77–94; idem, *To Have and to Hold: Slave Work and Family Life in Antebellum South Carolina* (Athens: University of Georgia Press, 1997), ch. 1; Penningroth, *Claims of Kinfolk*, ch. 2; Jeff Forret, "Slaves, Poor Whites, and the Underground Economy of the Rural Carolinas," *Journal of Southern History* 70 (November 2004): 783–824; Kathleen Mary Hilliard, "Spending in Black and White: Race, Slavery, and Consumer Values in the Antebellum South" (Ph.D. diss., University of South Carolina, 2006); and David E. Paterson, "Slavery, Slaves, and Cash in a Georgia Village, 1825–1865," *Journal of Southern History* 75 (November 2009): 879–930.

5. Penningroth, *Claims of Kinfolk*, 80, 82; Hudson, "All That Cash," 77, 83; Robert William Fogel and Stanley L. Engerman, *Time on the Cross: The Economics of American Negro Slavery* (1974; reprint, New York: W. W. Norton & Company, 1995), 127, 151; Hilliard, "Spending in Black and White," 102–104; McDonnell, "Money Knows No Master," 37–38; Ira Berlin, *Many Thousands Gone: The First Two Centuries of Slavery in North America* (Cambridge: Belknap Press of Harvard University Press, 1998), 138; Dylan C. Penningroth, "My People, My People: The Dynamics of Community in Southern Slavery," in *New Studies in the History of American Slavery*, ed. Edward E. Baptist and Stephanie M. H. Camp (Athens: University of Georgia Press, 2006), 166–176; Charles C. Jones, *The Religious Instruction of the Negroes. In the United States* (Savannah: Thomas Purse, 1842), 136.

6. Penningroth, *Claims of Kinfolk*, 80, 91, 94–95, 99. Penningroth discusses violence briefly, but only in the context of the postwar, Reconstruction South. See Penningroth, *Claims of Kinfolk*, 122–123. He does offer one example of violence among slaves in Penningroth, "My People, My People," 172.

7. Alexander Falconbridge, *An Account of the Slave Trade on the Coast of Africa* (London: J. Phillips, 1788), 23; *Ben (a slave) v. State* (1861), Supreme Court of Alabama, 37 Ala. 103, 1861 Ala. LEXIS 35; Penningroth, *Claims of Kinfolk*, 89–90. See also Catterall, *Judicial Cases*, vol. 3, 245.

8. Deborah Gray White, *Ar'n't I a Woman? Female Slaves in the Plantation South*, rev. ed. (New York: Norton, 1999), 143, 134; Stephanie M. H. Camp, *Closer to Freedom: Enslaved Women and Everyday Resistance in the Plantation South* (Chapel Hill: University of North Carolina Press, 2004), 78; Shane White and Graham White, *Stylin': African American Expressive Culture from Its Beginnings to the Zoot Suit* (Ithaca: Cornell University Press, 1998), ch. 1; Robert G. McPherson, "Georgia Slave Trials, 1837–1849," *American Journal of Legal History* 4 (October 1960): 375–376; Norman R. Yetman, ed., *Life under the "Peculiar Institution": Selections from the Slave Narrative Collection* (New York: Holt, Rinehart and Winston, Inc., 1970), 13; George P. Rawick, ed., *The American Slave: A Composite Autobiography, Supplement, Series 1*, vol. 7, pt. 2 (Westport, Conn.: Greenwood Press, 1977), 623; Elizabeth Ware Pearson, ed., *Letters from Port Royal, 1862–1868* (Boston: W. B. Clarke Company, 1906; reprint, New York: Arno Press and the New York Times, 1969), 113, 211.

9. George P. Rawick, ed., *The American Slave: A Composite Autobiography*, vol. 7 Mississippi (Westport, Conn.: Greenwood Publishing Company, 1972), 163; C. Vann Woodward, ed., *Mary Chesnut's Civil War* (New Haven: Yale University Press, 1981), 829; Executive Papers, William Smith, Misc. Reel 5022, Box 4, Folder 4, Frames 59–69, LVA.

10. Executive Papers, William Smith, Misc. Reel 5022, Box 4, Folder 4, Frames 59–69, LVA.

11. Executive Papers, James Pleasants, 1824 Pardons, Box 6, Folder 4, LVA; Executive Papers, John M. Gregory, November 1842, Box 2, Folder 7, LVA; Executive Papers, Henry A. Wise, Misc. Reel 4208, Frames 329–331, LVA; Executive Papers, Wilson Cary Nicholas, April 1816–October 1816, Misc. Reel 239, LVA.

12. Executive Papers, Wilson Cary Nicholas, April 1816–October 1816, Misc. Reel 239, LVA; Executive Papers, John Letcher, Misc. Reel 4722, Box 7, Folder 8, Frames 308–316, 321–323, LVA; Race and Slavery Petitions Project, #20582102, Ser. II, Reel 5, 0710.

13. Executive Papers, James Monroe, January 1811, Box 1, Folder 1, LVA; *Simon, a slave v. the State of Mississippi* (1859), Box 5849, Case 8900, MDAH.

14. *State v. Jones* (1857), Houst. Cr. Cas. 21, in *Judicial Cases Concerning American Slavery and the Negro*, vol. 4, ed. Helen Tunnicliff Catterall (Washington, D.C.: Carnegie Institution of Washington, 1936), 237; *Nelson v. the State* (1852), Supreme Court of Tennessee, 32 Tenn. 237, 1852 Tenn. LEXIS 58, 2 Swan 237.

15. Hudson, "All That Cash," 77; Walter Johnson, "Clerks All! Or, Slaves with Cash," *Journal of the Early Republic* 26 (Winter 2006): 641–651; Michael Wayne, *Death of an Overseer: Reopening a Murder Investigation from the Plantation South* (New York: Oxford University Press, 2001), 94; Executive Papers, John Tyler, March 1826, Box 1, Folder 7, LVA; Hilliard, "Spending in Black and White," 73; Pearson, *Letters from Port Royal*, 112.

16. Hudson, "All That Cash," 77, 83, 84; Johnson, "Clerks All!" 649–650.

17. Hudson, "All That Cash," 86; Executive Papers, Henry A. Wise, Misc. Reel 4202, Box 8, Folder 4, LVA.

18. Hilliard, "Spending in Black and White," 85–88; Executive Papers, John Letcher, Misc. Reel 4724, Box 8, Folder 4, Frames 201–206, LVA; Auditor of Public Accounts, Condemned Blacks Executed or Transported Records—Condemned Slaves, Court Orders, and Valuations, 1810–1822, Misc. Reel 2551, Frame 998, LVA; Auditor of Public Accounts, Condemned Blacks Executed or Transported, Records—Condemned Slaves, Court Orders, and Valuations, 1833–1845, Misc. Reel 2553, Frame 814, LVA; *State v. Daniel G. Smith* (1854), Case 21846, Group 1850, Box 16, File 21, ACCCHNF; Executive Papers, Henry A. Wise, Misc. Reel 4202, Box 8, Folder 4, LVA.

19. Executive Papers, William Smith, August–October 1848, Box 392, Folder October 1848, LVA.

20. Jones, *Religious Instruction of the Negroes*, 135; Alex Lichtenstein, "'That Disposition To Theft, With Which They Have Been Branded': Moral Economy, Slave Management, and the Law," *Journal of Social History* 21 (Spring 1988), 415; John Ernest, ed., *Narrative of the Life of Henry Box Brown, Written by Himself* (Chapel Hill: University of North Carolina Press, 2008), 52; Genovese, *Roll, Jordan, Roll*, 606; Jeff Forret, *Race Relations at the Margins: Slaves and Poor Whites in the Antebellum Southern Countryside* (Baton Rouge: Louisiana State University Press, 2006), ch. 2. Compared to thefts from the master, thefts among slaves have received very little scholarly attention, although they are mentioned in Genovese, *Roll, Jordan, Roll*, 606–607, 631; and Penningroth, "My People, My People," 171–172. Less understood still are thefts from slaves by whites. In 1853, for example, a white man in Mississippi robbed a slave of a $15 gold watch and some money. See *State v. Daniel G. Smith* (1854), Case 21846, Group 1850, Box 16, File 21, ACCCHNF. On theft within the quarters in the colonial era, see Philip D. Morgan, *Slave Counterpoint: Black Culture in the Eighteenth-Century Chesapeake and Lowcountry* (Chapel Hill: University of North Carolina Press, 1998), 469–470.

21. Auditor of Public Accounts, Condemned Blacks Executed or Transported Records—Condemned Slaves, Court Orders, and Valuations, 1810–1822, Misc. Reel 2551, Frame 922, LVA; Historical Census Browser, University of Virginia, Geospatial and Statistical Data Center (2004): http://fisher.lib.virginia.edu/collections/stats/histcensus/index.html [accessed March 17, 2012]; Auditor of Public Accounts, Condemned Blacks Executed or Transported, Records—Condemned Slaves, Court Orders, and Valuations, 1781–1793, Misc. Reel 2549, Frame 439, LVA.

22. Penningroth, *Claims of Kinfolk*, 97; Charles B. Dew, "Disciplining Slave Ironworkers in the Antebellum South: Coercion, Conciliation, and Accommodation," *American Historical Review* 79 (April 1974): 411, 412.

23. Wayne, *Death of an Overseer*, 12–13; Auditor of Public Accounts, Condemned Blacks Executed or Transported Records—Condemned Slaves, Court Orders, and Valuations, 1810–1822, Misc. Reel 2551, Frame 998, LVA; Executive Papers, James Patton Preston, February–May 1818, Box 4, Folder 1, LVA.

24. Pickens District, Court of Magistrates and Freeholders, Trial Papers, 1829–1862, Folder 11, SCDAH; Campbell, "A Kind of Freeman?" 147–148, 153. On slaves' ability to save money, including for such long-term purposes as purchasing freedom, see Hilliard, "Spending in Black and White," 90–93 and ch. 6.

25. McDonnell, "Money Knows No Master," 37; Genovese, *Roll, Jordan, Roll*, 607; William Thomson, *A Tradesman's Travels in the United States and Canada, in the Years 1840, 41, & 42*

(Edinburgh: Oliver & Boyd, 1842), 189; Jones, *Religious Instruction of the Negroes*, 135; William Howard Russell, *My Diary North and South*, ed. Fletcher Pratt (New York: Harper & Brothers, 1954), 77, 78; Charles Lyell, *A Second Visit to the United States of North America*, vol. 1 (New York: Harper & Brothers, 1849), 264; Charles Sackett Sydnor, *Slavery in Mississippi* (New York: D. Appleton-Century Company, 1933), 41; Frederick Law Olmsted, *A Journey in the Seaboard Slave States, with Remarks on Their Economy* (New York: Dix & Edwards, 1856), 111–112; Executive Papers, William Smith, Misc. Reel 5022, Box 4, Folder 4, Frames 59–69, LVA.

26. Executive Papers, William Smith, Misc. Reel 5022, Box 4, Folder 4, Frames 59–69, LVA; Executive Papers, Henry A. Wise, Misc. Reel 4202, Box 8, Folder 4, Frame 690, LVA; *Henry, a slave v. the State* (1863), Supreme Court of Georgia, 33 Ga. 441, 1863 Ga. LEXIS 6.

27. Morgan, *Slave Counterpoint*, 469; Sally E. Hadden, *Slave Patrols: Law and Violence in Virginia and the Carolinas* (Cambridge: Harvard University Press, 2001); Camp, *Closer to Freedom*, ch. 1; Ernest, *Narrative of the Life of Henry Box Brown*, 55.

28. Anthony E. Kaye, *Joining Places: Slave Neighborhoods in the Old South* (Chapel Hill: University of North Carolina Press, 2007).

29. L.A. Chamerovzow, ed., *Slave Life in Georgia: A Narrative of the Life, Sufferings, and Escape of John Brown, a Fugitive Slave, Now in England* (London: n.p., 1855), 83; *Narratives of the Sufferings of Lewis and Milton Clarke, Sons of a Soldier of the Revolution, during a Captivity of More Than Twenty Years among the Slaveholders of Kentucky, One of the So Called Christian States of North America. Dictated by Themselves* (Boston: Bela Marsh, 1846), 119–120.

30. J. S. Buckingham, *The Slave States of America*, vol. 2 (1842; reprint, New York: Negro Universities Press, 1968), 87: Hilliard, "Spending in Black and White," 161, 166.

31. *Laura, a slave v. the State of Mississippi* (1852), Box 5830, Case 6763, MDAH; Penningroth, *Claims of Kinfolk*, 99.

32. Anderson District, Court of Magistrates and Freeholders, Trial Papers, Reel C2775, Case #400, SCDAH; Spartanburg District, Court of Magistrates and Freeholders, Trial Papers, Reel C2922, Case #296, SCDAH. George was found guilty of manslaughter, jailed for two months, and given three hundred total lashes distributed in weekly increments of fifty. See also McDonnell, "Money Knows No Master," 37, 38.

33. Sue Eakin, *Solomon Northup's Twelve Years a Slave and Plantation Life in the Antebellum South* (Lafayette: Center for Louisiana Studies, University of Louisiana at Lafayette, 2007), 241–242.

34. Genovese, *Roll, Jordan, Roll*, 607; *Henry, a slave v. the State* (1863), Supreme Court of Georgia, 33 Ga. 441, 1863 Ga. LEXIS 6.

35. Auditor of Public Accounts, Condemned Blacks Executed or Transported, Records—Condemned Slaves, Court Orders, and Valuations, 1794–1809, Misc. Reel 2550, Frame 252, LVA; Auditor of Public Accounts, Condemned Blacks Executed or Transported, Records—Condemned Slaves, Court Orders, and Valuations, 1833–1845, Misc. Reel 2553, Frames 166, 814, LVA.

36. *Re Clement and Jacobo* (1777), 12 La. Hist. Q. 682, in Catterall, *Judicial Cases*, vol. 3, 437–438; *John (a slave) v. State* (1852), Supreme Court of Mississippi, 24 Miss. 569, 1852 Miss. LEXIS 103; Lunenburg County, Order Book 24, 1821–1823, Reel 34, LVA.

37. Quoted in Hilliard, "Spending in Black and White," 140–141; *Henry, a slave v. the State* (1863), Supreme Court of Georgia, 33 Ga. 441, 1863 Ga. LEXIS 6; Auditor of Public Accounts,

Condemned Blacks Executed or Transported Records—Condemned Slaves, Court Orders, and Valuations, 1810–1822, Misc. Reel 2551, Frame 919, LVA; Genovese, *Roll, Jordan, Roll*, 607; James O. Breeden, ed., *Advice among Masters: The Ideal in Slave Management in the Old South* (Westport, Conn.: Greenwood Press, 1980), 51.

38. Amherst County, Order Book 1815–1820, Reel 30, LVA; *Simon, a slave v. the State of Mississippi* (1859), Box 5849, Case 8900, MDAH.

39. Executive Papers, James Patton Preston, February–May 1818, Box 4, Folder 1, LVA.

40. Executive Papers, James Patton Preston, February–May 1818, Box 4, Folder 1, LVA; Hilliard, "Spending in Black and White," 178.

41. Penningroth, *Claims of Kinfolk*, 100–101; Bethabara Baptist Church (Laurens District, S.C.), Records, 1801–1881, September 1837, p. 48, SCL; Beaverdam Baptist Church (Wilkes County, Ga.), Minutes, 1836–1855, August 1849, Drawer 9, Reel 22, GA; Bethel Baptist Church (Hancock County, Ga.), Minutes, 1828–1887, December 1839, Drawer 77, Reel 26, GA; Fishing Creek Baptist Church (Wilkes County, Ga.), Minutes, 1821–1873, September 1855, Drawer 171, Reel 28, GA.

42. Philips Mill Baptist Church (Wilkes County, Ga.), Minutes, 1785–1948, June 1822, September 1822, Drawer 45, Reel 13, GA; Beaverdam Baptist Church (Wilkes County, Ga.), Minutes, 1836–1855, May 1850, Drawer 9, Reel 22, GA; Horeb Baptist Church (Hancock County, Ga.), Minutes, 1792–1916, July 1838, Drawer 32, Reel 77, GA.

43. Jacob Stroyer, *Sketches of My Life in the South. Part I* (Salem, Mass.: Salem Press, 1879), 47–50. See also Herbert G. Gutman, *The Black Family in Slavery and Freedom, 1750–1925* (New York: Pantheon Books, 1976), 279–282.

44. *Henry, a slave v. the State* (1863), Supreme Court of Georgia, 33 Ga. 441, 1863 Ga. LEXIS 6; Stroyer, *Sketches of My Life*, 50; *State v. Neil* (1853), Records of the Superior Court of Muscogee County, Drawer 80, Reel 64, GA, in McNair, "Justice Bound," 120–121.

45. Buckingham, *Slave States of America*, vol. 2, 87–88; Executive Papers, John M. Gregory, November 1842, Box 2, Folder 4, LVA.

46. Anderson District, Court of Magistrates and Freeholders, Trial Papers, Reel C2917, Case #154, SCDAH; Anderson District, Court of Magistrates and Freeholders, Trial Papers, Reel C2918, Case #289, SCDAH. On Florilla, see also McDonnell, "Money Knows No Master," 37.

47. Anderson District, Court of Magistrates and Freeholders, Trial Papers, Reel C2918, Case #268, SCDAH.

48. Pickens District, Court of Magistrates and Freeholders, Trial Papers, 1829–1862, Folder 11, SCDAH; *State v. Neil* (1853), Records of the Superior Court of Muscogee County, Drawer 80, Reel 64, GA, in McNair, "Justice Bound," 121. In Pickens District, both slaves ultimately received more than three dozen lashes for "Fighting on the sabeth and gaming."

49. *State v. Elbert* (1863), Records of the Superior Court of Newton County, Drawer 11, Reel 3, GA, in McNair, "Justice Bound," 121–122; Executive Papers, Henry A. Wise, Misc. Reel 4195, Box 2, Folder 5, Frames 3–11, April 1856, LVA.

50. Breeden, *Advice among Masters*, 58; Hilliard, "Spending in Black and White," 123; David Silkenat, *Moments of Despair: Suicide, Divorce, and Debt in Civil War Era North Carolina* (Chapel Hill: University of North Carolina Press, 2011), 151; E. Merton Coulter, "Four Slave Trials in Elbert County, Georgia," *Georgia Historical Quarterly* 41 (Fall 1957): 243; Penningroth, *Claims of Kinfolk*, 84.

51. Auditor of Public Accounts, Condemned Blacks Executed or Transported, Records—Condemned Slaves, Court Orders, and Valuations, 1810–1822, Misc. Reel 2551, Frame 843, LVA; Philip J. Schwarz, *Twice Condemned: Slaves and the Criminal Laws of Virginia, 1705–1865* (Baton Rouge: Louisiana State University Press, 1988), 226; McNair, "Justice Bound," 65; Coulter, "Four Slave Trials," 243; Penningroth, *Claims of Kinfolk*, 122. In a pair of unusual cases from Adams County, Mississippi, whites owed money to slaves. With the aid of her master, "Elizabeth a Negro woman servant" brought suit in 1800 to recover $62 from Maria Williams for "money lent." The jury found in the slave's favor. Seventeen years later, John White beat an enslaved woman named Amy because she asked him "for mon[e]y he owed" in the presence of other white people. The jury fined White $40 for assault and battery. See, respectively, *Elizabeth a Negro Woman v. Maria Williams* (1800), Case 2662, Group 1800, Box 23, File 65, ACCCHNF; and *State v. John White* (1818), Case 7877, Group 1810, Box 39, File 27, ACCCHNF.

52. Quoted in Hilliard, "Spending in Black and White," 89; Executive Papers, John Floyd, February 1834, Box 12, Folder 4, LVA; Executive Papers, Thomas Mann Randolph, February 1820, Box 1, Folder 6, LVA; *The State of Mississippi v. York, a slave* (1861), Box 11675, Case 1, MDAH.

53. Executive Papers, James McDowell, November 1845, Box 7, Folder 5, LVA.

54. Anderson District, Court of Magistrates and Freeholders, Trial Papers, Reel C2917, Case #185, SCDAH; *State v. James, slave of Widow Bouny* (1846), 181, First District Court of New Orleans, NOPL. The case with Amos and Andrew is also mentioned in McDonnell, "Money Knows No Master," 37. On *State v. James*, see also Judith Kelleher Schafer, "Slaves and Crime: New Orleans, 1846–1862," in *Local Matters: Race, Crime, and Justice in the Nineteenth-Century South*, ed. Christopher Waldrep and Donald G. Nieman (Athens: University of Georgia Press, 2001), 73.

55. Auditor of Public Accounts, Condemned Blacks Executed or Transported Records—Condemned Slaves, Court Orders, and Valuations, 1810–1822, Misc. Reel 2551, Frame 616, LVA; Executive Papers, William B. Giles, January 1830, Box 8, Folder 3, LVA; *State v. James, slave of Widow Bouny* (1846), 181, First District Court of New Orleans, NOPL; Accomack County, Order Book 1822–1824, Reel 96, LVA; *Slavery in the United States: A Narrative of the Life and Adventures of Charles Ball* (New York: John S. Taylor, 1837), 191; Campbell, "A Kind of Freeman?" 147–148, 153; *The State of Mississippi v. York, a slave* (1861), Box 11675, Case 1, MDAH. In the antebellum era, knives often sold for between ten and fifty cents. On affrays for seemingly petty sums, see also Randolph Roth, *American Homicide* (Cambridge: Belknap Press of Harvard University Press, 2009), 227.

56. Executive Papers, William B. Giles, January 1830, Box 8, Folder 3, LVA.

57. Executive Papers, James McDowell, November 1845, Box 7, Folder 5, LVA.

58. Anderson District, Court of Magistrates and Freeholders, Trial Papers, Reel C2917, Case #160, SCDAH.

59. Accomack County, Order Book 1822–1824, Reel 96, LVA.

60. Auditor of Public Accounts, Condemned Blacks Executed or Transported Records—Condemned Slaves, Court Orders, and Valuations, 1810–1822, Misc. Reel 2551, Frames 615–617, LVA. On Hubbard and West, see also Penningroth, *Claims of Kinfolk*, 99.

61. Anderson District, Court of Magistrates and Freeholders, Trial Papers, Reel C2919, Case #368, SCDAH; Auditor of Public Accounts, Condemned Blacks Executed or Transported Records—Condemned Slaves, Court Orders, and Valuations, 1810–1822, Misc. Reel 2551, Frame 617, LVA.

62. Powelton Baptist Church (Hancock County, Ga.), Minutes, 1786–1916, July 1805, November 1805, Drawer 32, Reel 76, GA.

63. Powelton Baptist Church (Hancock County, Ga.), Minutes, 1786–1916, October 1854, Drawer 32, Reel 76, GA. Sometime prior to May 1860, Abner was restored to the flock at Powelton Baptist, but that month, he was again excluded "for imposing a two dollar bill of no worth in a public collection and receiving in change $1.75." This time, Abner claimed that Herbert's Paul was the guilty party, a charge borne out by the findings of the church investigating committee. Nonetheless, the church opted not to readmit Abner into fellowship. Slaves were still pawning off too many illegitimate Macon bank notes. See Powelton Baptist Church (Hancock County, Ga.), Minutes, 1786–1916, May 1860, June 1860, Drawer 32, Reel 76, GA.

64. Bethel Baptist Church (Hancock County, Ga.), Minutes, 1828–1887, March 1829, p. 10, Drawer 77, Reel 26, GA; Padgett's Creek Baptist Church (Union District, S.C.), Church Book, vol. 2, 1837–1874, August 1860, May 1861, pp. 135, 138, SCL.

65. Essex County, Order Book 45, 1823–1826, Reel 94, LVA.

66. Spartanburg District, Court of Magistrates and Freeholders, Trial Papers, Reel C2920, Case #117, SCDAH; Pendleton District, Court of Magistrates and Freeholders, Trial Papers, Reel C2916, Case #35, SCDAH.

67. Executive Papers, John Letcher, Misc. Reel 4767, Box 22, Folder 4, Frames 46–48, LVA; Auditor of Public Accounts, Condemned Blacks Executed or Transported, Records—Condemned Slaves, Court Orders, and Valuations, 1823–1832, Misc. Reel 2552, Frames 1158–1159, LVA.

68. Executive Papers, Henry A. Wise, Misc. Reel 4217, Box 20, Folder 6, Frames 317–323, LVA.

69. Race and Slavery Petitions Project, #11383402, Ser. I, Reel 11, 0092; King George County, Order Book 12 1827–1833, Reel 32, LVA.

70. Executive Papers, John Letcher, Misc. Reel 4715, Box 5, Folder 7, Frames 343–348, LVA; Executive Papers, William B. Giles, May 1827, Box 1, Folder 6, LVA.

71. Hudson, "All That Cash," 90; Hilliard, "Spending in Black and White," 29–30.

6. VIOLENCE IN THE CREATION, MAINTENANCE, AND DESTRUCTION OF SLAVE UNIONS

1. George P. Rawick, ed., *The American Slave: A Composite Autobiography*, vol. 10, pt. 6 (Westport, Conn.: Greenwood Publishing Company, 1972), 191.

2. According to Eugene D. Genovese's reckoning, the majority of intraracial violence in the quarters was related to the family, the product of passions suddenly roused rather than simmering, long-term grudges. Eugene D. Genovese, *Roll, Jordan, Roll: The World the Slaves Made* (1974; reprint, New York; Vintage, 1976), 636.

3. Calvin Schermerhorn, *Money over Mastery, Family over Freedom: Slavery in the Antebellum Upper South* (Baltimore: Johns Hopkins University Press, 2011), 132; T. J. Desch Obi, *Fighting for Honor: The History of African Martial Art Traditions in the Atlantic World* (Columbia: University of South Carolina Press, 2008), 116.

4. Michael Wayne, *Death of an Overseer: Reopening a Murder Investigation from the Plantation South* (New York: Oxford University Press, 2001), 94; Deborah Gray White, *Ar'n't I a Woman? Female Slaves in the Plantation South*, rev. ed. (New York: Norton, 1999), 151.

5. Herbert G. Gutman, *The Black Family in Slavery and Freedom, 1750–1925* (New York: Pantheon Books, 1976), 309–320. Many other prominent scholars of Gutman's era embraced his interpretation. See, for example, John W. Blassingame, *The Slave Community: Plantation Life in the Antebellum South*, rev. ed. (New York: Oxford University Press, 1979), 171–172, 191; Genovese, *Roll, Jordan, Roll*, 451–452, 491; and Robert William Fogel and Stanley L. Engerman, *Time on the Cross: The Economics of American Negro Slavery* (1974; reprint, New York: W. W. Norton & Company, 1995), 141.

6. Nell Irvin Painter, *Southern History across the Color Line* (Chapel Hill: University of North Carolina Press, 2002), 21.

7. Brenda E. Stevenson, "Distress and Discord in Virginia Slave Families, 1830–1860," in *In Joy and in Sorrow: Women, Family, and Marriage in the Victorian South, 1830–1900*, ed. Carol Bleser (New York: Oxford University Press, 1991), 103–124; Ann Patton Malone, *Sweet Chariot: Slave Family and Household Structure in Nineteenth-Century Louisiana* (Chapel Hill: University of North Carolina Press, 1992), ch. 8; idem, "Gender Convention, Ideals, and Identity among Antebellum Virginia Slave Women," in *More Than Chattel: Black Women and Slavery in the Americas*, ed. David Barry Gaspar and Darlene Clark Hine (Bloomington: Indiana University Press, 1996), 173–174; idem, *Life in Black and White: Family and Community in the Slave South* (New York: Oxford University Press, 1996); Christopher Morris, "Within the Slave Cabin: Violence in Mississippi Slave Families," in *Over the Threshold: Intimate Violence in Early America*, ed. Christine Daniels and Michael V. Kennedy (New York: Routledge, 1999), 268–285; Emily West, "Surviving Separation: Cross-Plantation Marriages and the Slave Trade in Antebellum South Carolina," *Journal of Family History* 24 (April 1999): 212–231; Wayne, *Death of an Overseer;* Stephanie M. H. Camp, "The Pleasures of Resistance: Enslaved Women and Body Politics in the Plantation South, 1830–1861," *Journal of Southern History* 68 (August 2002): 557–558; Wilma A. Dunaway, *The African-American Family in Slavery and Emancipation* (New York: Cambridge University Press, 2003), esp. 268–274; Stephanie M. H. Camp, *Closer to Freedom: Enslaved Women and Everyday Resistance in the Plantation South* (Chapel Hill: University of North Carolina Press, 2004), 76; Emily West, "Tensions, Tempers, and Temptations: Marital Discord among Slaves in Antebellum South Carolina," *American Nineteenth Century History* 5 (Summer 2004): 1–18; idem, *Chains of Love: Slave Couples in Antebellum South Carolina* (Urbana: University of Illinois Press, 2004), ch. 2; Anthony E. Kaye, *Joining Places: Slave Neighborhoods in the Old South* (Chapel Hill: University of North Carolina Press, 2007), 80; and Jeff Forret, "Conflict and the 'Slave Community': Violence among Slaves in Upcountry South Carolina," *Journal of Southern History* 74 (August 2008): 551–588.

8. Quoted in Drew Gilpin Faust, ed. *The Ideology of Slavery: Proslavery Thought in the Antebellum South, 1830–1860* (Baton Rouge: Louisiana State University Press, 1981), 292.

9. Rebecca Griffin, "Courtship Contests and the Meaning of Conflict in the Folklore of Slaves," *Journal of Southern History* 71 (November 2005): 786n51, 770, 771, 780, 785, 799, 800, 801; Rebecca J. Fraser, *Courtship and Love among the Enslaved in North Carolina* (Jackson: University Press of Mississippi, 2007), 7; White, *Ar'n't I a Woman?* 144; Philip J. Schwarz, *Twice Condemned: Slaves and the Criminal Laws of Virginia, 1705–1865* (Baton Rouge: Louisiana State University Press, 1988), 62, 153; Damian Alan Pargas, *The Quarters and the Fields: Slave Families in the Non-Cotton South* (Gainesville: University Press of Florida, 2010), 140, 162; West, "Surviving Separa-

tion," 223; Emily West, "The Debate on the Strength of Slave Families: South Carolina and the Importance of Cross-Plantation Marriages," *Journal of American Studies* 33 (August 1999): 227; idem, "Masters and Marriages, Profits and Paternalism: Slave Owners' Perspectives on Cross-Plantation Unions in Antebellum South Carolina," *Slavery & Abolition* 21 (April 2000): 58, 66.

10. Fogel and Engerman, *Time on the Cross*, 142; West, *Chains of Love*, 27, 37, 58; Rawick, *American Slave*, vol. 3, pt. 3, 78–79; idem, *American Slave*, vol. 2, pt. 1, 43–44; idem, ed., *The American Slave: A Composite Autobiography, Supplement, Series 1*, vol. 3, pt. 1 (Westport, Conn.: Greenwood Press, 1977), 64; idem, ed., *The American Slave: A Composite Autobiography, Supplement, Series 2*, vol. 1 (Westport, Conn.: Greenwood Press, 1979), 401–402.

11. White, *Ar'n't I a Woman?* 136, 137, 151, 133–134; Executive Papers, Wilson Cary Nicholas, April 1816–October 1816, Misc. Reel 239, LVA; Spotsylvania County, Minute Book, 1815–1819, Reel 51, LVA. Other female slaves delegated violent deeds to enslaved men whom they aided or even manipulated. Details surrounding the wartime murder of Troup County, Georgia, slave Isaac in 1863 are sketchy, but a bondwoman was undoubtedly complicit in his demise at the hands of the bondman Willis. Willis had a longstanding grievance against Isaac. More than a year before the killing, Willis had been overheard saying that "he would be the death of Isaac ... if it took him five years." For reasons known only to her, one bondwoman shared Willis's interest in killing Isaac, and the pair conspired to kill him. The bondwoman asked that Isaac catch some fish for her. Isaac consented, and Willis tagged along. As the unsuspecting Isaac cast his line from the bank of a creek, Willis struck him two fatal blows on the head with an axe. He then returned to his female accomplice, who promptly inquired whether he had done as "promised." Willis may have willingly murdered Isaac without any urging from the bondwoman, but it is likely that female persuasion and encouragement steeled him to commit the deed. Their plot succeeded in achieving the mutual goal of Isaac's destruction. *State v. Willis* (1863), Records of the Superior Court of Troup County, Drawer 155, Box 22, GA, quoted in Glenn M. McNair, "Justice Bound: Aframericans, Crime, and Criminal Justice in Georgia, 1751–1865" (Ph.D. diss., Emory University, 2001), 122. Although Willis made the ultimate sacrifice, hanging for his crime, the bondwoman and possible mastermind of their plan was neither charged nor punished.

12. Charles C. Jones, *The Religious Instruction of the Negroes. In the United States* (Savannah: Thomas Purse, 1842), 136; Camp, *Closer to Freedom*, 61; Sue Eakin, *Solomon Northup's Twelve Years a Slave and Plantation Life in the Antebellum South* (Lafayette: Center for Louisiana Studies, University of Louisiana at Lafayette, 2007), 218; Rawick, *American Slave*, vol. 7 Oklahoma, 58; Kaye, *Joining Places*, 6.

13. Executive Papers, John Floyd, April–June 1849, Box 394, Folder June 1849, LVA; Fraser, *Courtship and Love*, 46.

14. Justin Labinjoh, "The Sexual Life of the Oppressed: An Examination of the Family Life of Ante-Bellum Slaves," *Phylon* 35, no. 4 (1974): 386; Haywood County, Records of Slaves and Free Persons of Color, n.d., 1823–1868, Folder 1851–1859, NCDAH.

15. Camp, *Closer to Freedom*, 77; Executive Papers, James McDowell, February 1844, Box 3, Folder 4, LVA.

16. Executive Papers, James Monroe, Box 3, Folder 8, Frames 14–15, Misc. Reel 5337, LVA. In a different case, it is not clear whether the enslaved John Miller of Orange County, Virginia, was a former husband, ex-boyfriend, spurned lover, or rejected suitor, but in 1821 he was angry

when he fought with the bondwoman Sally in a slave kitchen. Miller "complained of the ... woman's conduct," apparently dissatisfied with her marriage to an enslaved man named King. Miller stormed off but vowed to "be done with them all after to night." He later returned to find Sally in the laundry room with King. "[W]hat are you doing here you grand villain[?]" Miller inquired of the husband. "I have business here," King replied. Miller shot back, "you have her you grand rascal," but he determined to change that. He left the laundry, retrieved an axe from the adjoining kitchen, promptly returned, and smashed the blade into King's forehead. King "staggered and fell" as Miller "repeated the blows three or four times." Turning to Sally, Miller observed, "you are married but you shall soon be unmarried for I will"—and in fact just did—"Kill him on sight." Miller eliminated King, but his own subsequent execution for the crime kept Sally from him. Orange County, Order Book (Minutes) 1820–1825, Reel 35, LVA.

17. Executive Papers, Henry A. Wise, Misc. Reel 5205, Box 10, Folder 4, Frame 471, LVA.

18. Lewis W. Paine, *Six Years in a Georgia Prison: Narrative of Lewis W. Paine* (Boston: Bela Marsh, 1852), 152; Frederick Douglass, *My Bondage and My Freedom* (New York: Miller, Orton & Mulligan, 1855), 86; quoted in West, *Chains of Love*, 67; Executive Papers, John Floyd, April–June 1849, Box 394, Folder June 1849, LVA; *State v. John Harding* (1866), Box 5, File 71, ACCCHNF.

19. Genovese, *Roll, Jordan, Roll*, 467; quoted in Guion Griffis Johnson, *Ante-bellum North Carolina: A Social History* (Chapel Hill: University of North Carolina Press, 1937), 538; Philip D. Morgan, *Slave Counterpoint: Black Culture in the Eighteenth-Century Chesapeake and Lowcountry* (Chapel Hill: University of North Carolina Press, 1998), 553–554; Eakin, *Solomon Northup's Twelve Years a Slave*, 221; Rawick, SS1, vol. 9, pt. 4, 1524.

20. Quoted in Leslie A. Schwalm, *A Hard Fight for We: Women's Transition from Slavery to Freedom in South Carolina* (Urbana: University of Illinois Press, 1997), 53; Frances Anne Kemble, *Journal of a Residence on a Georgian Plantation in 1838–1839*, ed. John A. Scott (New York: Alfred A. Knopf, 1961), 247–248; Schwalm, *A Hard Fight for We*, 54; Pittsylvania County, Court Records 21, 1819–1820, Reel 54, Frames 28–33, LVA; Executive Papers, Henry A. Wise, Misc. Reel 4206, Box 11, Folder 4, Frames 413–421, LVA.

21. Stevenson, *Life in Black and White*, 241 (first and fourth quotations); Blassingame, *Slave Community*, 164; Leslie Howard Owens, "Blacks in *The Slave Community*," in *Revisiting Blassingame's* The Slave Community: *The Scholars Respond*, ed. Al-Tony Gilmore (Westport, Conn.: Greenwood Press, 1978), 65 (second and third quotations).

22. Stevenson, *Life in Black and White*, 244; Elizabeth Fox-Genovese, *Within the Plantation Household: Black and White Women of the Old South* (Chapel Hill: University of North Carolina Press, 1988), 327; Genovese, *Roll, Jordan, Roll*, 632; Anderson District, Court of Magistrates and Freeholders, Trial Papers, Reel C2917, Case #185, SCDAH; Laurens District, Court of Magistrates and Freeholders, Trial Papers, 1808–1865, Box 1, Folder 67, SCDAH; Fairfield District, Court of Magistrates and Freeholders, Trial Papers, 1839–1865, Folder 34, SCDAH.

23. Fraser, *Courtship and Love*, 7; West, "Surviving Separation," 222–223; idem, "Debate on the Strength of Slave Families," 221–222, 227; idem, "Masters and Marriages," 56–58, 66; John Ernest, ed., *Narrative of the Life of Henry Box Brown, Written by Himself* (Chapel Hill: University of North Carolina Press, 2008), 55–56; Executive Papers, John Letcher, Misc. Reel 4760, Box 19, Folder 3, Frames 14–21, LVA.

24. Blassingame, *Slave Community*, 164; West, "Debate on the Strength of Slave Families,"

223, 236; idem, "Masters and Marriages," 64; Anthony E. Kaye, "Neighbourhoods and Solidarity in the Natchez District of Mississippi: Rethinking the Antebellum Slave Community," *Slavery & Abolition* 23 (April 2002): 7; White, *Ar'n't I a Woman?* 76; Genovese, *Roll, Jordan, Roll,* 472–475.

25. West, "Surviving Separation," 223; idem, "Masters and Marriages," 57.

26. West, "Debate on the Strength of Slave Families," 239; Rebecca Griffin, "'Goin' Back Over There to See That Girl': Competing Social Spaces in the Lives of the Enslaved in Antebellum North Carolina," *Slavery & Abolition* 25 (April 2004): 94–113. On the concept of "rival geography" applied to southern slaves, see Stephanie M. H. Camp, "'I Could Not Stay There': Enslaved Women, Truancy and the Geography of Everyday Forms of Resistance in the Antebellum Plantation South," *Slavery & Abolition* 23 (December 2002): 1–20; and idem, *Closer to Freedom*.

27. West, "Surviving Separation," 223; idem, "Debate on the Strength of Slave Families," 236; idem, "Masters and Marriages," 64, 65; Executive Papers, Henry A. Wise, Misc. Reel 4214, Box 18, Folder 1, Frame 342, LVA.

28. West, "Debate on the Strength of Slave Families," 223 (first quotation), 222, 238 (second quotation); idem, "Masters and Marriages," 56 (third quotation); idem, "Surviving Separation," 212, 213, 217, 220, 222, 224, 225, 228.

29. Peter Kolchin, "Reevaluating the Antebellum Slave Community: A Comparative Perspective," *Journal of American History* 70 (December 1983): 584.

30. Genovese, *Roll, Jordan, Roll,* 474; Spartanburg District, Court of Magistrates and Freeholders, Trial Papers, Reel C2920, Case #58, SCDAH.

31. West, "Tension," 5; Anderson District, Court of Magistrates and Freeholders, Trial Papers, Reel C2918, Case #278, SCDAH; Anderson District, Court of Magistrates and Freeholders, Trial Papers, Reel C2918, Case #264, SCDAH; Rawick, *American Slave,* vol. 2, pt. 2, 129; Spartanburg District, Court of Magistrates and Freeholders, Trial Papers, Reel C2920, Case #58, SCDAH; Clarendon District, Court of Magistrates and Freeholders, Trial Papers, 1863–1865, Folder 4, SCDAH. Henry was found guilty and sentenced to two weeks in prison and 150 lashes. For a case of two slaves fighting over an enslaved woman in Virginia, see Joshua D. Rothman, *Notorious in the Neighborhood: Sex and Families across the Color Line in Virginia, 1787–1861* (Chapel Hill: University of North Carolina Press, 2003), 147–148.

32. Records of Eastern State Hospital, Register of Patients, 1852–1853, vol. 028, pp. 275, 313, LVA.

33. D. R. Hundley, *Social Relations in Our Southern States* (New York: Henry B. Price, 1860; reprint, New York: Arno Press, 1973), 332; *State v. Anthony, a slave* (1834), Case 22977, Group 1830, Box 66, File 50, ACCCHNF; quoted in Morris, "Within the Slave Cabin," 272; Laura F. Edwards, *Gendered Strife and Confusion: The Political Culture of Reconstruction* (Urbana: University of Illinois Press, 1997), 178–179. Peter spent nine and one-half months as a patient at the institution; Stafford died after a little more than two.

34. *William, a slave v. the State* (1864), Supreme Court of Georgia, 33 Ga. 85, 1864 Ga. LEXIS 57.

35. Gutman, *Black Family in Slavery and Freedom,* 67; Executive Papers, John Floyd, January–February 1851, Box 403, Folder February 11–20, 1851, LVA; Executive Papers, James Barbour, June 1813, Box 7, Folder 6, LVA.

36. Executive Papers, Thomas Walker Gilmer, June 1840, Box 1, Folder 7, LVA; Executive Papers, Thomas Walker Gilmer, June 1840, Box 1, Folder 7, LVA; Pittsylvania County, Court Records 21, 1819–1820, Reel 54, Frames 28–33, LVA.

37. David Gavin Diary, July 9, 1856 [typescript p. 44], SHC; *Laura, a slave v. the State of Mississippi* (1852), Box 5830, Case 6763, MDAH; Harriet Martineau, *Society in America*, vol. 2 (London: Saunders and Otley, 1837), 333–334; Executive Papers, John Floyd, December 1833, Box 11, Folder 8, LVA.

38. Executive Papers, William Smith, Misc. Reel 5022, Box 4, Folder 4, Frames 59–69, LVA; David Gavin Diary, July 9, 1856 [typescript p. 44], SHC.

39. Genovese, *Roll, Jordan, Roll*, 467; Jeff Forret, "Slaves, Sex and Sin: Adultery, Forced Separation and Baptist Church Discipline in Middle Georgia," *Slavery & Abolition* 33 (September 2012): 343.

40. Stevenson, *Life in Black and White*, 255 (first and second quotations); idem, "Distress and Discord," 122–123; *George (a slave) v. State* (1859), Supreme Court of Mississippi, 37 Miss. 316, 1859 Miss. LEXIS 20; Gutman, *Black Family in Slavery and Freedom*, 67; David Silkenat, *Moments of Despair: Suicide, Divorce, and Debt in Civil War Era North Carolina* (Chapel Hill: University of North Carolina Press, 2011), 89; Pittsylvania County, Court Records 21, 1819–1820, Reel 54, Frames 28–33, LVA.

41. *Simon, a slave v. the State of Mississippi* (1859), Box 5849, Case 8900, MDAH; Executive Papers, Wyndham Robertson, Box 3, Folder 3, LVA.

42. Jones, *Religious Instruction of the Negroes*, 133, 131; *George (a slave) v. State* (1859), Supreme Court of Mississippi, 37 Miss. 316, 1859 Miss. LEXIS 20; quoted in Drew Gilpin Faust, *James Henry Hammond and the Old South: A Design for Mastery* (Baton Rouge: Louisiana State University Press, 1982), 85. On church disciplinary action concerning adultery cases, see Forret, "Slaves, Sex and Sin."

43. For a letter written by a slave to her mistress to complain of an adulterous son-in-law and beg for intervention, see Stephanie McCurry, *Masters of Small Worlds: Yeoman Households, Gender Relations, and the Political Culture of the Antebellum South Carolina Low Country* (New York: Oxford University Press, 1995), 199–200.

44. West, "Tensions," 7, 11; Philadelphia Baptist Church (Pauline, S.C.), Minutes, 1803–1919, April–May 1839, SCDAH; Fox-Genovese, *Within the Plantation Household*, 327.

45. Executive Papers, James McDowell, February 1844, Box 3, Folder 4, LVA; Pittsylvania County, Court Records 40, 1848–1850, Reel 59, LVA.

46. *State v. George, slave of James Hopkins, Jr.* (1856), First District Court of New Orleans, 12584, NOPL. George's crime earned him a life sentence in the Louisiana State Penitentiary.

47. James Campbell, "'The victim of prejudice and hasty consideration': The Slave Trial System in Richmond, Virginia, 1830–61," *Slavery & Abolition* 26 (April 2005): 76; *Smith (a slave) v. State* (1846), Supreme Court of Alabama, 9 Ala. 990, 1846 Ala. LEXIS 209; Anderson District, Court of Magistrates and Freeholders, Trial Papers, Reel C2919, Case #292, SCDAH.

48. Anderson District, Court of Magistrates and Freeholders, Trial Papers, Reel C2918, Case #278, SCDAH.

49. Genovese, *Roll, Jordan, Roll*, 474; *John, a slave v. State* (1862), Supreme Court of Georgia, 33 Ga. 257, 1862 Ga. LEXIS 23.

50. Pendleton District, Court of Magistrates and Freeholders, Trial Papers, Reel C2916, Case #9, SCDAH; Anderson District, Court of Magistrates and Freeholders, Trial Papers, Reel C2775, Case #398, SCDAH. John Iliffe discussed the "sexual jealousy" prevalent among various Afri-

can peoples. Asante men considered adultery a form of property dispute over the commodified woman. If an elite man was cuckolded, penalties might include slow death for the male interloper. More commonly, financial compensation to the cuckold was the appropriate response. See John Iliffe, *Honour in African History* (New York: Cambridge University Press, 2005), 79, 85, 96.

51. Executive Papers, John Floyd, April–June 1849, Box 394, Folder June 1849, LVA.

52. King George County, Order Book 12 1827–1833, Reel 32, LVA.

53. Johnson, *Ante-bellum North Carolina*, 539; *Arnoult v. Deschapelles* (1849), 4 La. An. 41, in *Judicial Cases Concerning American Slavery and the Negro*, vol. 3, ed. Helen Tunnicliff Catterall (Washington, D.C.: Carnegie Institution of Washington, 1932), 594; James Patton Preston, Executive Papers, August 1818, Box 5, Folder 9, LVA.

54. *State v. Frank (a slave)* (1858), Supreme Court of North Carolina, 50 N.C. 384, 1858 N.C. LEXIS 60, 5 Jones Law 384.

55. Executive Papers, John Floyd, October 1833, Box 11, Folder 1, LVA.

56. Executive Papers, John Floyd, October 1833, Box 11, Folder 1, LVA.

57. Executive Papers, John Letcher, Misc. Reel 4715, Box 5, Folder 7, Frames 343–348, LVA.

58. West, "Tensions," 6, 67; idem, *Chains of Love: Slave Couples in Antebellum South Carolina* (Urbana: University of Illinois Press, 2004), 60–61; Edwards, *Gendered Strife and Confusion*, 178; Schwalm, *A Hard Fight for We*, 234, 260–263, 265; Morris, "Within the Slave Cabin," 271; Fox-Genovese, *Within the Plantation Household*, 296; Stevenson, "Distress and Discord," 117–118, 122.

59. Quoted in Faust, *Ideology of Slavery*, 292; Race and Slavery Petitions Project, #11383402, Ser. I, Reel 11, 0092.

60. Louis B. Wright and Marion Tinling, eds., *The Secret Diary of William Byrd of Westover 1709–1712* (Richmond, Va.: Dietz Press, 1941), 192; Jack P. Greene, ed., *The Diary of Colonel Landon Carter of Sabine Hall, 1752–1778*, vol. 1 (Charlottesville: University Press of Virginia, 1965), 383; Camp, *Closer to Freedom*, 41. See also Randolph Roth, *American Homicide* (Cambridge: Belknap Press of Harvard University Press, 2009), 124. Other cases of male assaults of female slaves in the colonial period are only suggestive of spousal violence. The lack of detail in the trial records precludes absolute certainty, but it is highly likely that a Henrico County, Virginia, "negro woman named Nell" was killed in 1721 by her own husband. Both she and her assailant Peter, found guilty of delivering the fatal "blow on the Crown of her head," belonged to the same master. Goochland County slaveholder Joseph Anthony owned both "Davy a Negro Slave" and Nanny, the "negro woman" he was charged with murdering in 1741. Convicted of Nanny's death and sentenced to die, Davy was also shown to have "so badly used" another of Anthony's bondwomen that she absconded from her master's plantation and hoped "to Complain ... of the abuse she had receiv'd from the said Davy." Meanwhile, she hid out "in the Woods" and "among the Mountains" but in so doing grew so "weak and Sickly" for lack of provision "that she dyed soon after she was found." See Henrico County, Minute Book, 1719–1724, Reel 66, LVA; Goochland County, Order Book 5, 1741–1744, Reel 22, LVA.

61. George P. Rawick, ed., *The American Slave: A Composite Autobiography, Supplement, Series 1*, vol. 7, pt. 2 (Westport, Conn.: Greenwood Press, 1977), 624; idem, SS1, vol. 6, pt. 1, 325; idem, ed., *The American Slave: A Composite Autobiography*, vol. 9, pt. 4 (Westport, Conn.: Greenwood Publishing Company, 1972), 13; Rawick, SS1, vol. 7, pt. 2, 444.

62. Genovese, *Roll, Jordan, Roll*, 490–491, 494; Blassingame, *Slave Community*, 164–165, 172;

Fox-Genovese, *Within the Plantation Household*, 296–297, 326, 374; Stevenson, *Life in Black and White*, 161, 240; idem, "Distress and Discord," 108, 111–113, 120–121; Morris, "Within the Slave Cabin," 271, 273; West, "Tensions," 4; Stevenson, "Gender Convention, Ideals, and Identity," 180; Melton A. McLaurin, *Celia, a Slave: A True Story* (New York: Perennial, 2002), 139–140; Joshua D. Rothman, *Notorious in the Neighborhood: Sex and Families across the Color Line in Virginia, 1787–1861* (Chapel Hill: University of North Carolina Press, 2003), 139; Wayne, *Death of an Overseer*, 105.

63. Morris, "Within the Slave Cabin," 273; Blassingame, *Slave Community*, 311, 322; Bertram Wyatt-Brown, "The Mask of Obedience: Male Slave Psychology in the Old South," *American Historical Review* 93 (December 1988): 1246; Stevenson, "Distress and Discord," 115.

64. Morris, "Within the Slave Cabin," 272; Rawick, SS1, vol. 10, pt. 5, 2232.

65. Robert Collins, *Essay on the Treatment and Management of Slaves. Written for the Seventh Annual Fair of the Southern Central Agricultural Society*, 2nd ed. (Boston: Eastburn's Press, 1853), 11; James W. Clarke, "Black-on-Black Violence," *Society* 33, no. 5 (July–August 1996): 48; Morris, "Within the Slave Cabin," 272, 273; West, *Chains of Love*, 67; Kaye, *Joining Places*, 70; Labinjoh, "Sexual Life of the Oppressed," 393.

66. *State v. John Williams* (1866), Box 5, File 69, ACCCHNF; *State v. John Harding* (1866), Box 5, File 71, ACCCHNF; Schwalm, *A Hard Fight for We*, 262–263.

67. Executive Papers, Joseph Johnson, March–May 1855, Box 426, Folder March 1855, LVA; Edwin Adams Davis, ed., *Plantation Life in the Florida Parishes of Louisiana, 1836–1846 as Reflected in the Diary of Bennet H. Barrow* (New York: Columbia University Press, 1943), 139.

68. Charles Ball, *Fifty Years in Chains; or, The Life of an American Slave* (New York: H. Dayton, 1859), 197; Steven Hahn, *A Nation under Our Feet: Black Political Struggles in the Rural South, from Slavery to the Great Migration* (Cambridge: Belknap Press of Harvard University Press, 2003), 40; Fox-Genovese, *Within the Plantation Household*, 327; B. A. Botkin, ed., *Lay My Burden Down: A Folk History of Slavery* (Chicago: University of Chicago Press, 1973), 125. Edwards, *Gendered Strife and Confusion*, 21, observes that household negotiations of power between formerly enslaved men and women continued after emancipation.

69. Edwards, *Gendered Strife and Confusion*, 112; Spartanburg District, Court of Magistrates and Freeholders, Trial Papers, Reel C2920, Case #106, SCDAH; Genovese, *Roll, Jordan, Roll*, 483; Morris, "Within the Slave Cabin," 274; West, *Chains of Love*, 65. There is no conclusive evidence that Asa and Peggy were a couple; however, the case does smack of a domestic squabble.

70. Hahn, *Nation under Our Feet*, 40; Camp, *Closer to Freedom*, 38; West, *Chains of Love*, 65–66 (quotation 66); *State v. John, a slave* (1848), Supreme Court of North Carolina, 30 N.C. 330, 1848 N.C. LEXIS 81, 8 Ired. Law 330; Christopher Morris, *Becoming Southern: The Evolution of a Way of Life, Warren County and Vicksburg, Mississippi, 1770–1860* (New York: Oxford University Press, 1995), 63, 77. On gender roles and marital expectations in the postbellum black family, see Edwards, *Gendered Strife and Confusion*, 178. She observes that domestic abuse not related to infidelity often hinged on male and female responsibilities and the delegation of power within the household.

71. Auditor of Public Accounts, Condemned Blacks Executed or Transported Records—Condemned Slaves, Court Orders, and Valuations, 1810–1822, Misc. Reel 2551, LVA, Frames 863, 865; Island Creek Baptist Church (Hancock County, Ga.), Minutes, 1806–1873, May 1834, Drawer 31, Reel 80, GA; Mt. Tirzah Baptist Church (Charlotte County, Va.), Minute Book, 1834–1915, July

1860, August 1860, November 1860, March 1861, LVA. In the post–Civil War era, freedwomen also complained about freedmen who failed to provide. See Schwalm, *A Hard Fight for We*, 263–264, 265.

72. Race and Slavery Petitions Project, #11383402, Ser. I, Reel 11, 0092; George P. Rawick, ed., *The American Slave: A Composite Autobiography, Supplement, Series 2*, vol. 5, pt. 4 (Westport, Conn.: Greenwood Press, 1979), 1446.

73. Morris, "Within the Slave Cabin," 270, 273; James O. Breeden, ed., *Advice among Masters: The Ideal in Slave Management in the Old South* (Westport, Conn.: Greenwood Press, 1980), 51, 55, 308, 55.

74. West, *Chains of Love*, 65; Breeden, *Advice among Masters*, 51.

75. Pendleton District, Court of Magistrates and Freeholders, Trial Papers, Reel C2916, Case #9, SCDAH; Laurens District, Court of Magistrates and Freeholders, Trial Papers, 1808–1865, Box 1, Folder 9, SCDAH.

76. Stephen Alan West, "From Yeoman to Redneck in Upstate South Carolina, 1850–1915" (Ph.D. diss., Columbia University, 1998), 111–112; *State v. Hussey* (1852), Busb. 123, 1852 WL 1248; Stephanie Cole, "Keeping the Peace: Domestic Assault and Private Prosecution in Antebellum Baltimore," in *Over the Threshold: Intimate Violence in Early America*, ed. Christine Daniels and Michael V. Kennedy (New York: Routledge, 1999), 148–149, 162.

77. John Hammond Moore, ed., *A Plantation Mistress on the Eve of the Civil War: The Diary of Keziah Goodwyn Hopkins Brevard, 1860–1861* (Columbia: University of South Carolina Press, 1993), 102; Rawick, *American Slave*, vol. 6 Alabama, 216.

78. Ball, *Fifty Years in Chains*, 197; Executive Papers, James McDowell, February 1844, Box 3, Folder 4, LVA.

79. Botkin, *Lay My Burden Down*, 125.

80. Morris, "Within the Slave Cabin," 270; Breeden, *Advice among Masters*, 308, 55.

81. Genovese, *Roll, Jordan, Roll*, 462, 464; Stevenson, "Distress and Discord," 117–118, 122; Daina Ramey Berry, *"Swing the Sickle for the Harvest Is Ripe": Gender and Slavery in Antebellum Georgia* (Urbana: University of Illinois Press, 2007), 10, 84; Rawick, *American Slave*, vol. 5, pt. 4, 177; Jones, *Religious Instruction of the Negroes*, 134.

82. Powelton Baptist Church (Hancock County, Ga.), Minutes, 1786–1916, Drawer 32, Reel 76, April 1842, GA.

83. Philips Mill Baptist Church (Wilkes County, Ga.), Minutes, 1785–1948, April 1808, Drawer 45, Reel 13, GA; Rehoboth Baptist Church (Wilkes County, Ga.), Minutes, 1806–1933, June 1841, Drawer 45, Reel 15, GA; Philips Mill Baptist Church (Wilkes County, Ga.), Minutes, 1785–1948, December 1846, Drawer 45, Reel 13, GA.

84. Rawick, SS1, vol. 3, pt. 1, 94. In 1804, the congregation of Goshen Baptist Church in Lincoln County, Georgia, simultaneously excommunicated the bondman Mark "for living in Adultery with his daughter" and Chloe "for living in Adultery with her Father." Some three decades later, Bethabara Baptist Church in Laurens District, South Carolina, "declared a non fellowship with ... and excluded" the "black brother Ned" for "living in an incestious marriage." Some of the few churchgoing bondmen ever charged with incest did not actually have sexual relations with women biologically related to them. Various hiring and rental agreements, sales, and deaths all affected the composition of enslaved families and households, forcing slaves to improvise in the

reconstitution of their domestic arrangements. Bondmen sometimes took up with women understood as family but who were not genetically so. Rose, "a member of Couler" at Sardis Baptist Church, complained in 1824 that "Reuben her Husband . . . had without any provocation left her and taken up with her own daughter." The girl was identified as Rose's daughter—not Reuben's—and was probably, more accurately, his stepdaughter. Nevertheless, the congregation declared that Reuben was "no longer to be considered as one of us." In Laurens District, the enslaved "Brother Frank" charged himself in January 1840 with "lying on a bed with a girl he *claims* as his daughter." Frank may have been the girl's stepfather or merely fictive kin acting as a substitute for her deceased, sold, or otherwise absent biological dad. In any case, Frank, wracked by guilt for violating the parameters of their relationship, threw himself upon the mercy of the church. The congregation at Rabun Creek initially forgave him his transgression but upon reconsideration the following month excluded him. By April, however, he was back in the fold. See Goshen Baptist Church (Lincoln County, Ga.), Records and Minutes, 1802–1869, December 1804, GA; Bethabara Baptist Church (Laurens District, S.C.), Records, 1801–1881, July 1837, SCL; Sardis Baptist Church (Wilkes County, Ga.), Minutes, 1805–1951, April 1824, May 1824, Drawer 45, Reel 24, GA; Rabun Creek Baptist Church (Laurens District, S.C.), Church Book, 1828–1913, January 1840, February 1840, April 1840, SCL [italics mine].

85. Island Creek Baptist Church (Hancock County, Ga.), Minutes, 1806–1873, September 1828, Drawer 31, Reel 80, GA.

86. Robert G. Gardner, "Virginia Baptists and Slavery, 1759–1790, Part I," *Virginia Baptist Register* 24 (1985): 1214; John Leland and L. F. Greene, *The Writings of the Late Elder John Leland: Including Some Events in His Life* (New York: G. W. Wood, 1845), 95; Padraig Riley, "Slavery and the Problem of Democracy in Jeffersonian America," in *Contesting Slavery: The Politics of Bondage and Freedom in the New American Nation*, ed. John Craig Hammond and Matthew Mason (Charlottesville: University of Virginia Press, 2011), 230.

87. Glenda Riley, *Divorce: An American Tradition* (Lincoln: University of Nebraska Press, 1997), 35–36; Executive Papers, John Letcher, Misc. Reel 4715, Box 5, Folder 7, Frames 343–348, LVA. See also Eakin, *Solomon Northup's Twelve Years a Slave*, 186.

88. Quoted in Schwalm, *A Hard Fight for We*, 53; quoted in Ulrich Bonnell Phillips, *American Negro Slavery: A Survey of the Supply, Employment and Control of Negro Labor as Determined by the Plantation Régime* (1918; reprint, New York: Peter Smith, 1952), 269; Eakin, *Solomon Northup's Twelve Years a Slave*, 221; Martha von Briesen, ed., *The Letters of Elijah Fletcher* (Charlottesville: University Press of Virginia, 1965), 23; Fishing Creek Baptist Church (Wilkes County, Ga.), Minutes, 1821–1873, May 1835, Drawer 171, Reel 28, GA; Philips Mill Baptist Church (Wilkes County, Ga.), Minutes, 1785–1948, December 1819, Drawer 45, Reel 13, GA; Horeb Baptist Church (Hancock County, Ga.), Minutes, 1792–1916, July 1841, Drawer 32, Reel 77, GA; Sardis Baptist Church (Wilkes County, Ga.), Minutes, 1805–1951, September 1851, Drawer 45, Reel 24, GA. See also Wayne, *Death of an Overseer*, 94.

89. Rawick, SS1, vol. 7, pt. 2, 606; Executive Papers, John Floyd, April–June 1849, Box 394, Folder June 1849, LVA; quoted in Gutman, *Black Family in Slavery and Freedom*, 67, 67–68; quoted in White, *Ar'n't I a Woman?* 156–157; Rawick, SS1, vol. 9, pt. 4, 1892.

90. Michael Tadman, *Speculators and Slaves: Masters, Traders, and Slaves in the Old South* (Madison: University of Wisconsin Press, 1989), 171; Leland and Greene, *Writings of the Late*

Elder John Leland, 95; Island Creek Baptist Church (Hancock County, Ga.), Minutes, 1806–1873, February 1862, April 1862, Drawer 31, Reel 80, GA.

91. Executive Papers, Joseph Johnson, February–April 1852, Box 411, Folder March 1852, LVA; *William, a slave v. the State* (1864), Supreme Court of Georgia, 33 Ga. 85, 1864 Ga. LEXIS 57.

92. Ernest, *Narrative of the Life of Henry Box Brown,* 74; Executive Papers, Henry A. Wise, Misc. Reel 4195, Box 2, Folder 5, Frames 3–11, April 1856, LVA.

93. Executive Papers, John Floyd, October 1833, Box 11, Folder 1, LVA; *John, a slave v. State* (1862), Supreme Court of Georgia, 33 Ga. 257, 1862 Ga. LEXIS 23; Executive Papers, James McDowell, February 1844, Box 3, Folder 4, LVA.

94. Executive Papers, Thomas Mann Randolph, August 1822, Box 7, Folder 3, LVA.

95. *State v. Samuel, a slave* (1836), Supreme Court of North Carolina, 19 N.C. 177, 1836 N.C. LEXIS 60, 2 Dev. & Bat. Law 177; Executive Papers, Joseph Johnson, February–April 1852, Box 411, Folder March 1852, LVA; Executive Papers, James McDowell, February 1844, Box 3, Folder 4, LVA; Executive Papers, Henry A. Wise, Misc. Reel 4217, Box 20, Folder 6, Frames 317–323, LVA.

96. Executive Papers, John Tyler, August 1810, Box 5, Folder 5, LVA; J. Mason Brewer, *American Negro Folklore* (Chicago: Quadrangle Books, 1968), 229.

97. Jones County, Georgia, Inferior Court Minutes, 1818–1846; Executive Papers, James McDowell, February 1844, Box 3, Folder 4, LVA.

98. Executive Papers, James McDowell, February 1844, Box 3, Folder 4, LVA.

99. *State v. Samuel, a slave* (1836), Supreme Court of North Carolina, 19 N.C. 177, 1836 N.C. LEXIS 60, 2 Dev. & Bat. Law 177; Jones County, Georgia, Inferior Court Minutes, 1818–1846; Anderson District, Court of Magistrates and Freeholders, Trial Papers, Reel C2775, Case #394, SCDAH.

100. Executive Papers, Joseph Johnson, February–April 1852, Box 411, Folder March 1852, LVA; Executive Papers, James McDowell, February 1845, Box 5, Folder 9, LVA.

101. *State v. Samuel, a slave* (1836), Supreme Court of North Carolina, 19 N.C. 177, 1836 N.C. LEXIS 60, 2 Dev. & Bat. Law 177.

102. *Smith (a slave) v. State* (1846), Supreme Court of Alabama, 9 Ala. 990, 1846 Ala. LEXIS 209; Executive Papers, John Floyd, April–June 1849, Box 394, Folder June 1849, LVA; *Timmins v. Lacy* (1867), 30 Tex. 115, 1867 WL 4571 Tex. 1867.

103. *William, a slave v. the State* (1864), Supreme Court of Georgia, 33 Ga. 85, 1864 Ga. LEXIS 57. See also McNair, "Justice Bound," 231.

104. *John, a slave v. State* (1862), Supreme Court of Georgia, 33 Ga. 257, 1862 Ga. LEXIS 23. See also McNair, "Justice Bound," 247–248. *Baalam, a slave v. State* (1850), Supreme Court of Alabama, 17 Ala. 451, 1850 Ala. LEXIS 70.

105. *State v. John, a slave* (1848), Supreme Court of North Carolina, 30 N.C. 330, 1848 N.C. LEXIS 81, 8 Ired. Law 330.

106. *State v. John, a slave* (1848), Supreme Court of North Carolina, 30 N.C. 330, 1848 N.C. LEXIS 81, 8 Ired. Law 330; Executive Papers, James Pleasants, August 1825, Box 7, Folder 12, LVA; Jones County, Georgia, Inferior Court Minutes, 1818–1846; *Smith, a slave, v. State* (1846), Supreme Court of Alabama, 9 Ala. 990, 1846 Ala. LEXIS 209.

107. *John, a slave v. State* (1862), Supreme Court of Georgia, 33 Ga. 257, 1862 Ga. LEXIS 23.

108. Quoted in Victoria E. Bynum, *Unruly Women: The Politics of Social and Sexual Control in*

the Old South (Chapel Hill: University of North Carolina Press, 1992), 84; Rothman, *Notorious in the Neighborhood,* 161; Executive Papers, John M. Gregory, November 1842, Box 2, Folder 4, LVA; Executive Papers, John Floyd, February 1834, Box 12, Folder 4, LVA.

109. Executive Papers, James McDowell, February 1845, Box 5, Folder 9, LVA; Executive Papers, John Floyd, April–June 1849, Box 394, Folder June 1849, LVA; Executive Papers, James Patton Preston, August 1818, Box 5, Folder 9, LVA. On the case of Sam and John, see also Rothman, *Notorious in the Neighborhood,* 147–148.

110. *Report of the Special Committee Appointed by the Protestant Episcopal Convention, at Its Session in 1858, to Report on the Duty of Clergymen in Relation to the Marriage of Slaves* (Charleston: Walker, Evans, 1859), in *Defending Slavery: Proslavery Thought in the Old South: A Brief History with Documents,* ed. Paul Finkelman (Boston and New York: Bedford/St. Martin's, 2003), 120; Camp, *Closer to Freedom,* 77.

7. HONOR, VIOLENCE, AND ENSLAVED MASCULINITY

1. Russell County, Law Order Book 11, 1838–1846, Reel 17, LVA.

2. Russell County, Law Order Book 11, 1838–1846, Reel 17, LVA; Executive Papers, John Floyd, April–June 1849, Box 394, Folder June 1849, LVA; T. J. Desch Obi, *Fighting for Honor: The History of African Martial Art Traditions in the Atlantic World* (Columbia: University of South Carolina Press, 2008), 117.

3. On honor in the Old South, see Bertram Wyatt-Brown, *Southern Honor: Ethics and Behavior in the Old South* (New York: Oxford University Press, 1982); Edward L. Ayers, *Vengeance and Justice: Crime and Punishment in the 19th-Century American South* (New York: Oxford University Press, 1984); Kenneth S. Greenberg, *Honor & Slavery: Lies, Duels, Noses, Masks, Dressing as a Woman, Gifts, Strangers, Humanitarianism, Death, Slave Rebellions, the Proslavery Argument, Baseball, Hunting, and Gambling in the Old South* (Princeton: Princeton University Press, 1996); and Bertram Wyatt-Brown, *The Shaping of Southern Culture: Honor, Grace, and War, 1760s–1880s* (Chapel Hill: University of North Carolina Press, 2001). On honor among slaves, see John C. Willis, "Behind 'Their Black Masks': Slave Honor in Antebellum Virginia" (M.A. thesis, University of Virginia, 1987); idem, "From the Dictates of Pride to the Paths of Righteousness: Slave Honor and Christianity in Antebellum Virginia," in *The Edge of the South: Life in Nineteenth-Century Virginia,* ed. Edward L. Ayers and John C. Willis (Charlottesville: University Press of Virginia, 1991); Bertram Wyatt-Brown, "The Mask of Obedience: Male Slave Psychology in the Old South," *American Historical Review* 93 (December 1988): 1228–1252; Jeff Forret, "Slave-Poor White Violence in the Antebellum Carolinas," *North Carolina Historical Review* 81 (April 2004): 144–146; Desch Obi, *Fighting for Honor,* 111–121; and the following works on Latin America: Sandra Lauderdale Graham, "Honor among Slaves," in *The Faces of Honor: Sex, Shame, and Violence in Colonial Latin America,* ed. Lyman L. Johnson and Sonya Lipsett-Rivera (Albuquerque: University of New Mexico Press, 1998), 201–228; Richard Boyer, "Honor among Plebeians," in *Faces of Honor,* 161–164; and Lyman L. Johnson, "Dangerous Words, Provocative Gestures, and Violent Acts," in *Faces of Honor,* 130, 141.

4. Orlando Patterson, *Slavery and Social Death: A Comparative Study* (Cambridge: Harvard University Press, 1982), 12. See, for example, Ayers, *Vengeance and Justice,* 13, 26; Stephen A.

West, "From Yeoman to Redneck in Upstate South Carolina, 1850–1915" (Ph.D. diss., Columbia University, 1998), 161.

5. Wyatt-Brown, "Mask of Obedience," 1249 (both quotations); idem, *Shaping of Southern Culture*, 3, 303; Willis, "Behind 'Their Black Masks,'" 4, 16, 17; Glenn M. McNair, "Justice Bound: Aframericans, Crime, and Criminal Justice in Georgia, 1751–1865" (Ph.D. diss., Emory University, 2001), 126; J. G. Peristiany and Julian Pitt-Rivers, "Introduction," in *Honor and Grace in Anthropology*, ed. J. G. Peristiany and Julian Pitt-Rivers (New York: Cambridge University Press, 1992), 4; *State v. Caesar, a slave* (1849), 9 Ired. 391, 31 N.C. 391 (N.C.), 1849 WL 1307 (N.C.). On vertical and horizontal honor, see John Iliffe, *Honour in African History* (Cambridge: Cambridge University Press, 2005), 4, 119–120, 123; and Desch Obi, *Fighting for Honor*, 213, 239n98. Under certain circumstances, white men may have acknowledged that enslaved men had honor with respect to one another, but not relative to any white man. See Joshua D. Rothman, *Notorious in the Neighborhood: Sex and Families across the Color Line in Virginia, 1787–1861* (Chapel Hill: University of North Carolina Press, 2003), 161.

6. Willis, "Behind 'Their Black Masks,'" 19; Desch Obi, *Fighting for Honor*, 111; Ariela J. Gross, *Double Character: Slavery and Mastery in the Antebellum Southern Courtroom* (Princeton: Princeton University Press, 2000), 51–52. On shame, see Eugene D. Genovese, *Roll, Jordan, Roll: The World the Slaves Made* (1974; reprint, New York; Vintage, 1976), 120–123; and Willis, "Behind 'Their Black Masks,'" 14.

7. Lorri Glover, *Southern Sons: Becoming Men in the New Nation* (Baltimore: Johns Hopkins University Press, 2007), 3 (first quotation), 2 (second quotation), 26–27, 169; Craig Thompson Friend and Lorri Glover, "Rethinking Southern Masculinity: An Introduction," in *Southern Manhood: Perspectives on Masculinity in the Old South*, ed. Craig Thompson Friend and Lorri Glover (Athens: University of Georgia Press, 2004), x–xi; Drew Gilpin Faust, *James Henry Hammond and the Old South: A Design for Mastery* (Baton Rouge: Louisiana State University Press, 1982); Stephanie McCurry, *Masters of Small Worlds: Yeoman Households, Gender Relations, and the Political Culture of the Antebellum South Carolina Low Country* (New York: Oxford University Press, 1995); McNair, "Justice Bound," 124.

8. Stanley M. Elkins, *Slavery: A Problem in American Institutional and Intellectual Life*, 3rd ed. (Chicago: University of Chicago Press, 1976); John W. Blassingame, *The Slave Community: Plantation Life in the Antebellum South*, rev. ed. (New York: Oxford University Press, 1979), 164–165, 172; Genovese, *Roll, Jordan, Roll*, 149, 490–494; Herbert G. Gutman, *The Black Family in Slavery and Freedom, 1750–1925* (New York: Pantheon Books, 1976).

9. Desch Obi, *Fighting for Honor*, 191; Daniel P. Black, "The Black Male Concept of Manhood as Portrayed in Selected Slave and Free Narratives (1794–1863)" (Ph.D. diss., Temple University, 1993), 4, 70–72, 121, 128; Jennifer L. Morgan, *Laboring Women: Reproduction and Gender in New World Slavery* (Philadelphia: University of Pennsylvania Press, 2004), 145–146; Wyatt-Brown, "Mask of Obedience," 1229; Genovese, *Roll, Jordan, Roll*, 490–491, 494; Blassingame, *Slave Community*, 164–165, 172; Elizabeth Fox-Genovese, *Within the Plantation Household: Black and White Women of the Old South* (Chapel Hill: University of North Carolina Press, 1988), 296–297, 326, 374; Brenda E. Stevenson, *Life in Black and White: Family and Community in the Slave South* (New York: Oxford University Press, 1996), 161, 240; idem, "Distress and Discord in Virginia Slave Families, 1830–1860," in *In Joy and in Sorrow: Women, Family, and Marriage in the Victo-*

rian South, 1830–1890, ed. Carol Bleser (New York: Oxford University Press, 1991), 108, 111–113, 120–121; Christopher Morris, "Within the Slave Cabin: Violence in Mississippi Slave Families," in *Over the Threshold: Intimate Violence in Early America,* ed. Christine Daniels and Michael V. Kennedy (New York: Routledge, 1999), 271, 273; Emily West, "Tensions, Tempers, and Temptations: Marital Discord among Slaves in Antebellum South Carolina," *American Nineteenth Century History* 5 (Summer 2004): 4; Brenda E. Stevenson, "Gender Convention, Ideals, and Identity among Antebellum Virginia Slave Women," in *More Than Chattel: Black Women and Slavery in the Americas,* ed. David Barry Gaspar and Darlene Clark Hine (Bloomington: Indiana University Press, 1996), 180; Melton A. McLaurin, *Celia, a Slave: A True Story* (New York: Perennial, 2002), 139–140; Rothman, *Notorious in the Neighborhood,* 139.

10. Joshua Young, *God Greater Than Man: A Sermon Preached June 11th, After the Rendition of Anthony Burns* (Burlington: Samuel B. Nichols, 1854), 19, 17–18; Rev. William H. Marsh, *God's Law Supreme: A Sermon, Aiming to Point Out the Duty of a Christian People in Relation to the Fugitive Slave Law: Delivered at Village Corners, Woodstock, Conn., on the Day of the Annual Thanksgiving, Nov. 28, 1850; and Subsequently Repeated, by Request, in Southbridge, Mass.* (Worcester, Mass.: Henry J. Howland, n.d.), 17; Lewis Clarke, "Leaves from a Slave's Journal of Life," *The Anti-Slavery Standard,* October 20, 1842; Henry Highland Garnet, "An Address to the Slaves of the United States," 1843, http://www.blackpast.org/; David Walker, *Walker's Appeal, in Four Articles; Together with a Preamble, to the Coloured Citizens of the World, But in Particular, and Very Expressly, to Those of the United States of America, Written in Boston, State of Massachusetts, September 28, 1829,* 3rd ed. (Boston: David Walker, 1830), 35, 70.

11. Blassingame, *Slave Community,* 322, 311; Rebecca J. Fraser, *Courtship and Love among the Enslaved in North Carolina* (Jackson: University Press of Mississippi, 2007), esp. 73–74, 79, 78; idem, "Negotiating Their Manhood: Masculinity amongst the Enslaved in the Upper South, 1830–1861," in *Black and White Masculinity in the American South, 1800–2000,* ed. Lydia Plath and Sergio Lussana (Newcastle upon Tyne, U.K.: Cambridge Scholars Publishing, 2009), 76–94; David E. Paterson, "Slavery, Slaves, and Cash in a Georgia Village, 1825–1865," *Journal of Southern History* 75 (November 2009): 919; John Ernest, ed., *Narrative of the Life of Henry Box Brown, Written by Himself* (Chapel Hill: University of North Carolina Press, 2008), 58; Sergio Lussana, "To See Who Was Best on the Plantation: Enslaved Fighting Contests and Masculinity in the Antebellum Plantation South," *Journal of Southern History* 76 (November 2010): 901–922; Brown, "Strength of the Lion," 173; Edward E. Baptist, "The Absent Subject: African American Masculinity and Forced Migration to the Antebellum Plantation Frontier," in *Southern Manhood: Perspectives on Masculinity in the Old South,* ed. Craig Thompson Friend and Lorri Glover (Athens: University of Georgia Press, 2004), 136–173. See also Darlene Clark Hine and Earnestine Jenkins, eds., *A Question of Manhood: A Reader in U.S. Black Men's History and Masculinity,* vol. 1 (Bloomington: Indiana University Press, 1999). Michael J. Goleman, "'To Become Men: Resistance, Revolt, and Masculinity in Antebellum Rural Slave Communities" (M.A. thesis, Mississippi State University, 2006), 24, argues that those with the speed and savvy to abscond from plantation labor and evade detection, or with the intelligence to trick or outwit masters, overseers, and patrollers laid claim to a form of manhood through resistance.

12. Hine and Jenkins, *A Question of Manhood,* 1, 30. As James Oliver Horton and Lois E. Horton stated, "Aggression, and sometimes sanctioned violence, was a common thread in American

ideals of manhood." See James Oliver Horton and Lois E. Horton, "Violence, Protest, and Identity: Black Manhood in Antebellum America," in *A Question of Manhood: A Reader in U.S. Black Men's History and Masculinity*, vol. 1, ed. Darlene Clark Hine and Earnestine Jenkins (Bloomington: Indiana University Press, 1999), 382.

13. Sigmund Freud, *Civilization and Its Discontents*, trans. James Strachey (New York: Norton, 1962), 44 (first quotation), 62, 67 (second quotation), 70–71.

14. On antebellum southern violence, see W. J. Cash, *The Mind of the South* (1941; reprint, New York: Vintage, 1991); John Hope Franklin, *The Militant South, 1800–1861* (Cambridge: Belknap Press of Harvard University Press, 1956); Dickson D. Bruce Jr., *Violence and Culture in the Antebellum South* (Austin: University of Texas Press, 1979); Wyatt-Brown, *Southern Honor;* Ayers, *Vengeance and Justice;* Elliott J. Gorn, "'Gouge and Bite, Pull Hair and Scratch': The Social Significance of Fighting in the Southern Backcountry," *American Historical Review* 90 (February 1985): 18–43; Grady McWhiney, *Cracker Culture: Celtic Ways in the Old South* (Tuscaloosa: University of Alabama Press, 1988); Kenneth S. Greenberg, "The Nose, the Lie, and the Duel in the Antebellum South," *American Historical Review* 95 (February 1990): 57–74; Victoria E. Bynum, *Unruly Women: The Politics of Social and Sexual Control in the Old South* (Chapel Hill: University of North Carolina Press, 1992); Laura F. Edwards, "Law, Domestic Violence, and the Limits of Patriarchal Authority in the Antebellum South," *Journal of Southern History* 65 (November 1999): 733–770; Edward E. Baptist, "'My Mind Is to Drown You and Leave You Behind': 'Omie Wise,' Intimate Violence, and Masculinity," in *Over the Threshold: Intimate Violence in Early America*, ed. Christine Daniels and Michael V. Kennedy (New York: Routledge, 1999), 94–110; and Loren Schweninger, "Slavery and Southern Violence: County Court Petitions and the South's Peculiar Institution," *Journal of Negro History* 85 (Winter–Spring 2000): 33–35.

15. Peter Kolchin, *Unfree Labor: American Slavery and Russian Serfdom* (Cambridge: Belknap Press of Harvard University Press, 1987), 265; Philip J. Schwarz, *Twice Condemned: Slaves and the Criminal Laws of Virginia, 1705–1865* (Baton Rouge: Louisiana State University Press, 1988), 239; David W. Blight, ed., *Narrative of the Life of Frederick Douglass, an American Slave, Written by Himself* (Boston: Bedford Books of St. Martin's Press, 1993), 79; *Alfred (a slave) v. State* (1859), Supreme Court of Mississippi, 37 Miss. 296, 1859 Miss. LEXIS 19; Hine and Jenkins, *A Question of Manhood*, 37; Maggie Montesinos Sale, *The Slumbering Volcano: American Slave Ship Revolts and the Production of Rebellious Masculinity* (Durham: Duke University Press, 1997), 54, 108, 124; Jim Cullen, "'I's a Man Now': Gender and African American Men," in *Divided Houses: Gender and the Civil War*, ed. Catherine Clinton and Nina Silber (New York: Oxford University Press, 1992), 77, 85, 91. See also Heather Andrea Williams, "'Commenced to Think Like a Man': Literacy and Manhood in African American Civil War Regiments," in *Southern Manhood: Perspectives on Masculinity in the Old South*, ed. Craig Thompson Friend and Lorri Glover (Athens: University of Georgia Press, 2004), 196–219. Abolitionist writers agonized over the subject of black aggression. Although its goal was the eradication of slavery, abolitionist literature could not portray slaves engaged in violent acts without potentially alienating white readers threatened by assertive black men or reinforcing white stereotypes of black savagery and animalistic proclivities. Even Frederick Douglass acted defensively, employing violence only as a last resort to counter his chronic abuse. This served as one strategy to confront the challenge of establishing the manhood of enslaved protagonists; however, black violence never meshed comfortably with

the need to cultivate a sympathetic response among white audiences. See Cynthia Griffin Wolff, "'Masculinity' in *Uncle Tom's Cabin,*" *American Quarterly* 47 (December 1995): 595–618; Richard Yarborough, "Race, Violence, and Manhood: The Masculine Ideal in Frederick Douglass's 'The Heroic Slave,'" in *Haunted Bodies: Gender and Southern Texts,* ed. Anne Goodwyn Jones and Susan V. Donaldson (Charlottesville: University Press of Virginia, 1997), 159–184; and Sarah N. Roth, "'How a Slave was Made a Man': Negotiating Black Violence and Masculinity in Antebellum Slave Narratives," *Slavery & Abolition* 28 (August 2007): 255–275. Post-emancipation, Frederick Douglass embraced violence as an expression of black manhood. See Celeste-Marie Bernier, "'Emblems of Barbarism': Black Masculinity and Representations of Toussaint L'Ouverture in Frederick Douglass's Unpublished Manuscripts," *American Nineteenth Century History* 4 (Fall 2003): 97, 98, 105, 110–111.

16. Lewis Clarke, "Leaves from a Slave's Journal of Life."

17. Patterson, *Slavery and Social Death,* 82–83; Iliffe, *Honour in African History,* 1, 120, 69–70, 67, 71, 82, 100; Kathleen M. Brown, "'Strength of the Lion . . . Arms Like Polished Iron': Embodying Black Masculinity in an Age of Slavery and Propertied Manhood," in *New Men: Manliness in Early America,* ed. Thomas A. Foster (New York: New York University Press, 2011), 175–176; McNair, "Justice Bound," 125.

18. Iliffe, *Honour in African History,* 88, 100; Desch Obi, *Fighting for Honor,* 113, 33, 34, 78, 87, 111, 88, 142; Lussana, "To See Who Was Best on the Plantation," 901–922. Special thanks to David Owusu-Ansah for the reference to Chinua Achebe's novel *Things Fall Apart.* The works of Iliffe and Desch Obi call into question Glenn M. McNair's statement that "Little in the West African experience prepared slaves for the levels of personal violence they would encounter in America." See McNair, "Justice Bound," 76.

19. Desch Obi, *Fighting for Honor,* 111; Jeff Forret, *Slavery in the United States* (New York: Facts on File, 2012), ch. 3.

20. Emily West, *Chains of Love: Slave Couples in Antebellum South Carolina* (Urbana: University of Illinois Press, 2004), 21: Willis, "Behind 'Their Black Masks,'" 4 (first quotation), 8–9, 6 (second quotation), 15, 21, 9; Desch Obi, *Fighting for Honor,* 111–112.

21. McNair, "Justice Bound," 124; Ayers, *Vengeance and Justice,* 234.

22. S. A. Cartwright, "Slavery in the Light of Ethnology," in *Cotton is King, and Pro-Slavery Arguments Comprising the Writings of Hammond, Harper, Christy, Stringfellow, Hodge, Bledsoe, and Cartwright, on This Important Subject,* ed. E. N. Elliott (1860; reprint, New York: Negro Universities Press, 1969), 717–718; *State v. Anthony, a slave* (1834), Case 22977, Group 1830, Box 66, File 50, ACCCHNF; Executive Papers, James McDowell, November 1845, Box 7, Folder 5, LVA; George P. Rawick, ed., *The American Slave: A Composite Autobiography,* vol. 9, pt. 4 (Westport, Conn.: Greenwood Publishing Company, 1972), 12.

23. Pittsylvania County, Court Records 21, 1819–1820, Reel 54, Frames 28–33, LVA; *William (a slave) v. the State* (1855), Supreme Court of Georgia, 18 Ga. 356, 1855 Ga. LEXIS 202; Executive Papers, John Letcher, Misc. Reel 4767, Box 22, Folder 4, Frames 46–48, LVA.

24. *Daily Gazette & Comet* (Baton Rouge), March 28, 1857.

25. McNair, "Justice Bound," 126–127; Governor's Papers, Gov. Edward B. Dudley, G.P. 90, Folder Correspondence, Petitions, Etc. Oct. 1, 1839–Oct. 28, 1839; Prince Edward County, County Court Orders, No. 17 1811–1813, Reel 27, LVA; Executive Papers, John Floyd, February 1834, Box

12, Folder 4, LVA. At a 1795 wedding, an irate, axe-wielding mulatto named Bob threatened "with great passion" to "split down any fellows that were saucy." See *Respublica v. Mulatto Bob* (1795), Supreme Court of Pennsylvania, 4 U.S. 145, 1 L. Ed. 776, 1795 U.S. LEXIS 332, 4 Dall. 145.

26. Anderson District, Court of Magistrates and Freeholders, Trial Papers, Reel C2919, Case #371, SCDAH; Anderson District, Court of Magistrates and Freeholders, Trial Papers, Reel C2917, Case #160, SCDAH; Spartanburg District, Court of Magistrates and Freeholders, Trial Papers, Reel C2920, Case #117, SCDAH.

27. *Nelson v. the State* (1852), Supreme Court of Tennessee, 32 Tenn. 237, 1852 Tenn. LEXIS 58, 2 Swan 237; Executive Papers, James Patton Preston, February 1817, Box 1, Folder 6, LVA. Hostile, threatening exchanges between bondmen were common. Big Joe, of Nelson County, Virginia, cautioned Little Joe "to hold your tongue or he would take his life." But even after his larger namesake twice threw him out of the slave kitchen, Little Joe defiantly claimed that "if he put his hands on him again that night he would stab him with a knife." See Nelson County, County Court Minute Book, Vol. 8, 1835–1840, Reel 27, LVA.

28. Executive Papers, Joseph Johnson, February–April 1852, Box 411, Folder March 1852, LVA.

29. Wendy Gamber, "Tarnished Labor: The Home, the Market, and the Boardinghouse in Antebellum America," *Journal of the Early Republic* 22 (Summer 2002): 177–204; Executive Papers, John Letcher, Misc. Reel 4783, Box 28, Folder 8, Frames 608–612, LVA. At one point during their exchange, Kit, "a much stronger man," wrested the shovel from Henry and struck him four times with it, one blow "almost knock[ing] his right eye out."

30. *Jordan, a slave v. State* (1856), Supreme Court of Mississippi, 32 Miss. 382, 1856 Miss. LEXIS 222; Gorn, "Gouge and Bite," 28–31; Edward E. Baptist, "Accidental Ethnography in an Antebellum Southern Newspaper: Snell's Homecoming Festival," *Journal of American History* 84 (March 1998): 1355–1383; *State v. Horace, a slave* (1860), Case 10416, Group 1860, Box 1, File 76, ACCCHNF; Executive Papers, James McDowell, February 1845, Box 5, Folder 9, LVA; Norfolk City, Order Book 16, 1807–1808, LVA; Executive Papers, John M. Gregory, November 1842, Box 2, Folder 7, LVA.

31. Executive Papers, Henry A. Wise, Misc. Reel 4202, Box 8, Folder 4, Frame 677, LVA; Anderson District, Court of Magistrates and Freeholders, Reel C2918, Case #278, SCDAH; Executive Papers, William B. Giles, May 1827, Box 1, Folder 6, LVA; Executive Papers, James Pleasants, December 1824, Box 6, Folder 1, LVA; quoted in Thomas D. Morris, *Southern Slavery and the Law, 1619–1860* (Chapel Hill: University of North Carolina Press, 1996), 301; Laurens District, Court of Magistrates and Freeholders, Trial Papers, 1808–1865, Box 1, Folder 67, SCDAH; Pendleton District, Court of Magistrates and Freeholders, Trial Papers, Reel C2916, Case #20, SCDAH; Anderson District, Court of Magistrates and Freeholders, Reel C2917, Case #195, SCDAH.

32. Anderson District, Court of Magistrates and Freeholders, Trial Papers, Reel C2919, Case #292, SCDAH; Anderson District, Court of Magistrates and Freeholders, Trial Papers, Reel C2917, Case #189, SCDAH. Desch Obi, *Fighting for Honor,* 192, observed a relationship between carrying a knife and masculinity among some African tribes.

33. On insults providing clues to culture in the Americas, see Peter N. Moogk, "'Thieving Buggers' and 'Stupid Sluts': Insults and Popular Culture in New France," *William & Mary Quarterly* 3rd ser., 36 (October 1979): 524–547; Mary Beth Norton, "Gender and Defamation in Seven-

teenth-Century Maryland," *William & Mary Quarterly* 3rd ser., 44 (January 1987): 3–39; Cheryl English Martin, "Popular Speech and Social Order in Northern Mexico, 1650–1830," *Comparative Studies in Society and History* 32 (April 1990): 305–324; Kirsten Fischer, "'False, Feigned, and Scandalous Words': Sexual Slander and Racial Ideology among Whites in Colonial North Carolina," in *The Devil's Lane: Sex and Race in the Early South,* ed. Catherine Clinton and Michele Gillespie (New York: Oxford University Press, 1997), 139–153; Richard Boyer, "Respect and Identity: Horizontal and Vertical Reference Points in Speech Acts," *Americas* 54 (April 1998): 491–509; and Sonya Lipsett-Rivera, "*De Obra Y Palabra:* Patterns of Insults in Mexico, 1750–1856," *Americas* 54 (April 1998): 511–539.

34. Iliffe, *Honour in African History,* 97 (quotation), 107, 88, 155, 143; Genovese, *Roll, Jordan, Roll,* 630; Schwarz, *Twice Condemned,* 250; Ayers, *Vengeance and Justice,* 133; Desch Obi, *Fighting for Honor,* 111, 113–115; Executive Papers, William B. Giles, May 1827, Box 1, Folder 6, LVA.

35. Lawrence W. Levine, *Black Culture and Black Consciousness: Afro-American Folk Thought from Slavery to Freedom* (New York: Oxford University Press, 1977), 347–348, 358; Executive Papers, James Pleasants, 1824 Pardons, Box 6, Folder 4, LVA; Roger D. Abrahams, *Singing the Master: The Emergence of African American Culture in the Plantation South* (New York: Penguin, 1992), 267; Governor's Papers, Gov. Edward B. Dudley, G.P. 90, Folder October 1839, NCDAH; Kershaw District, Court of Magistrates and Freeholders, Trial Papers, 1800–1861, Box 1, Folder 33, SCDAH; Anderson District, Court of Magistrates and Freeholders, Trial Papers, Reel C2919, Case #292, SCDAH; Anderson District, Court of Magistrates and Freeholders, Trial Papers, Reel C2918, Case #264, SCDAH; Executive Papers, William B. Giles, May 1827, Box 1, Folder 7, LVA; Executive Papers, Henry A. Wise, Misc. Reel 4214, Box 18, Folder 3, Frames 487–492, LVA; Executive Papers, James Pleasants, November 1824, Box 5, Folder 12, LVA. In Georgia, Pressley murdered fellow slave Boston "because Boston called him a d——d white-eyed son of a b——h." See *Pressley (a slave) v. State* (1855), 19 Ga. 192, in *Judicial Cases Concerning American Slavery and the Negro,* vol. 3, ed. Helen Tunnicliff Catterall (Washington, D.C.: Carnegie Institution of Washington, 1932), 46. In South Carolina, the bondman Henry called John "a dam raskel," and Jake complained that "Baylis had cursed him like a dammd rascal." See Clarendon District, Court of Magistrates and Freeholders, Trial Papers, 1863–1865, Folder 4, SCDAH; Anderson District, Court of Magistrates and Freeholders, Trial Papers, Reel C2917, Case #160, SCDAH.

36. Ayers, *Vengeance and Justice,* 234; Executive Papers, James Pleasants, December 1824, Box 6, Folder 1, LVA; Executive Papers, James Pleasants, 1824 Pardons, Box 6, Folder 4, LVA.

37. Wyatt-Brown, *Southern Honor,* 53. In one unusual case, an enslaved man in North Carolina talked to a white woman "till she cried." Their chickens had fought, and the slave "came to my house and cursed and abused me and threttend to spill my dam[n]ed Brains out," the woman explained. But tongue-lashing a white was foolhardy for any bondperson interested in self-preservation. The irate and "sassy" bondman was fortunate that the woman's husband merely ordered him off after he returned home. As the woman herself said, "if she had been a man she would of tore Him all to Mash." See Governor's Papers, Gov. Edward B. Dudley, G.P. 90, Folder Correspondence, Petitions, Etc. Oct. 1, 1839–Oct. 28, 1839.

38. Pittsylvania County, Court Records 21, 1819–1820, Reel 54, Frames 28–33, LVA; Stephanie M. H. Camp, *Closer to Freedom: Enslaved Women and Everyday Resistance in the Plantation South* (Chapel Hill: University of North Carolina Press, 2004); Governor's Papers, Gov. Edward

B. Dudley, G.P. 90, Folder Correspondence, Petitions, Etc. Oct. 1, 1839–Oct. 28, 1839; Spartanburg District, Court of Magistrates and Freeholders, Trial Papers, Reel C2920, Case #128, SCDAH.

39. Pendleton District, Court of Magistrates and Freeholders, Trial Papers, Reel C2916, Case #20, SCDAH; Laurens District, Court of Magistrates and Freeholders, Trial Papers, 1808–1865, Box 1, Folder 67, SCDAH.

40. Greenberg, *Honor & Slavery,* 8, 12, 40, 11 (quotation), 32; *Jim, a slave v. the State* (1844), Supreme Court of Tennessee, 24 Tenn. 145, 1844 Tenn. LEXIS 46, 5 Hum. 145. See, for example, Shiloh Baptist Church (Charlotte County, Va.), Minute Book, 1825–1873, June 1847, LVA.

41. Rawick, *American Slave,* vol. 15, pt. 2, 418–419; idem, ed., *The American Slave: A Composite Autobiography, Supplement, Series 1,* vol. 7, pt. 2 (Westport, Conn.: Greenwood Press, 1977), 596.

42. Governor's Papers, Gov. Edward B. Dudley, G.P. 90, Folder Correspondence, Petitions, Etc. Oct. 1, 1839–Oct. 28, 1839; Anderson District, Court of Magistrates and Freeholders, Trial Papers, Reel C2919, Case #292, SCDAH; Anderson District, Court of Magistrates and Freeholders, Trial Papers, Reel C2917, Case #185, SCDAH; Anderson District, Court of Magistrates and Freeholders, Trial Papers, Reel C2775, Case #384, SCDAH.

43. Executive Papers, James Monroe, January 1811, Box 1, Folder 1, LVA; *State v. Prince* (1827), Chatham County, Georgia, Inferior Court Trial Docket, 1813–1827, Drawer 90, Reel 33, GA; *Green, a slave v. the State of Mississippi* (1849), Box 5817, Case 2915, MDAH. In Copiah County, Mississippi, slave Simon confessed in 1857 to killing Norvall "because the deceased had told lies on him." See *Simon (a slave) v. State* (1858), Supreme Court of Mississippi, 37 Miss. 288, 1858 Miss. LEXIS 75; Helen Tunnicliff Catterall, ed., *Judicial Cases Concerning American Slavery and the Negro,* vol. 3 (Washington, D.C.: Carnegie Institution of Washington, 1932), 356.

44. Executive Papers, Wyndham Robertson, Box 3, Folder 3, LVA; *State v. Charles Loadnum* (1798), Court of Oyer and Terminer of Delaware, Kent, 2 Del. Cas. 240, 1798 Del. LEXIS 42.

45. Executive Papers, John Letcher, Misc. Reel 4722, Box 7, Folder 8, Frames 308–316, 321–323, LVA; Pittsylvania County, Court Records 27, 1827–1829, Reel 55, LVA.

46. Executive Papers, William Smith, January–April 1848, Box 390, Folder March 1848, LVA.

47. Executive Papers, James Barbour, July 1814, Box 13, Folder 1, LVA; Mecklenburg County, Order Book 4, 1844–1848 (County Court), Reel 119, LVA; Executive Papers, James Barbour, June 1813, Box 7, Folder 6, LVA.

48. Essex County, Order Book 45, 1823–1826, Reel 94, LVA. In Meriwether County, Georgia, a bondman named Nathan and his sister objected to the slave Stephen's bothersome presence. Defending his sibling, Nathan chastised Stephen for having "imposed" upon them. Stephen called Nathan a "damned liar" for levying the charge. In the argument that followed, Stephen inquired whether Nathan thought he was "afraid to give you the damn lie here tonight." "See that you don't do it," Nathan advised. Defiantly, Stephen told Nathan, "You are a damn liar." Nathan immediately struck Stephen on the side of the head with an axe. Stephen lingered several agonizing weeks before dying. *State v. Nathan* (1850), Records of the Superior Court of Meriwether County, Drawer 12, Box 59, GA, quoted in McNair, "Justice Bound," 127.

49. Camp, *Closer to Freedom;* Anthony E. Kaye, *Joining Places: Slave Neighborhoods in the Old South* (Chapel Hill: University of North Carolina Press, 2007); Robert G. McPherson, "Georgia Slave Trials, 1837–1849," *American Journal of Legal History* 4 (July 1960): 262–263. See also *State v. Peter* (1837), Records of the Inferior Court of Elbert County, Drawer 2, Box 76, GA, in E.

Merton Coulter, "Four Slave Trials in Elbert County, Georgia," *Georgia Historical Quarterly* 41 (Fall 1957): 241–242; and McNair, "Justice Bound," 126.

50. William B. Taylor, *Drinking, Homicide, and Rebellion in Colonial Mexican Villages* (Stanford: Stanford University Press, 1979), 159; Executive Papers, James Patton Preston, February 1817, Box 1, Folder 6, LVA; King George County, Order Book 12 1827–1833, Reel 32, LVA; Gorn, "Gouge and Bite," 34, 21, 33, 41.

51. Rawick, *American Slave*, vol. 4, pt. 2, 37; Desch Obi, *Fighting for Honor*, 81, 80; quoted in Thomas D. Morris, *Southern Slavery and the Law, 1619–1860* (Chapel Hill: University of North Carolina Press, 1996), 302; Pendleton District, Court of Magistrates and Freeholders, Trial Papers, Reel C2916, Case #20, SCDAH; Pickens District, Court of Magistrates and Freeholders, Trial Papers, 1829–1862, Folder 11, SCDAH; Anderson District, Court of Magistrates and Freeholders, Trial Papers, Reel C2918, Case #261, SCDAH; Anderson District, Court of Magistrates and Freeholders, Reel C2917, Case #167, SCDAH; William Grimes, *Life of William Grimes, the Runaway Slave, Brought Down to the Present Time. Written by Himself* (New Haven, Conn.: The Author, 1855), 44; Desch Obi, *Fighting for Honor*, 79, 87; Wilma King, *Stolen Childhood: Slave Youth in Nineteenth-Century America* (Bloomington: Indiana University Press, 1995), 47.

On rare occasions, enslaved men utilized the rough-and-tumble fighting techniques of lower-class whites against white adversaries. In Virginia, the future slave conspirator Gabriel was branded for attacking a white man and biting off part of his ear. Enraged after receiving an undeserved lick, an Alabama slave seized the whip and gun of his overseer and bit off a chunk of his ear. In Issaquena County, Mississippi, the enslaved Sam struck his sleeping master in the face with an axe and "cut off his nose" in 1857. Court records attributed the gruesome injury to poor aim, although Sam may very well have understood the symbolic importance southern white men attached to their noses. Sam immediately delivered a second blow, however, that killed his owner. See Douglas R. Egerton, *Gabriel's Rebellion: The Virginia Slave Conspiracies of 1800 and 1802* (Chapel Hill: University of North Carolina Press, 1993), 32; Peter Kolchin, *American Slavery 1619–1877* (New York: Hill and Wang, 1993), 160; *Sam, a slave v. the State of Mississippi* (1857), Box 5842, Case 7910, MDAH. On the importance of noses, see Greenberg, *Honor & Slavery*, ch. 1.

52. In the 1830s, the white Henry W. Coleman of Pittsylvania County, Virginia, "pulled off his coat to fight." In a separate incident, James J. Hardwick similarly "threw off his cloak to fight" in Hancock County, Georgia. Lower Banister Church (Pittsylvania County, Va.), Minute Book, 1798–1845, February 1830, LVA; Powelton Baptist Church (Hancock County, Ga.), Minutes, 1786–1916, September 1834, Drawer 32, Reel 76, GA. For other examples of white men stripping to fight, see Philips Mill Baptist Church (Wilkes County, Ga.), Minutes, 1785–1948, May 1794, Drawer 45, Reel 13, GA; Lower Banister Church (Pittsylvania County, Va.), Minute Book, 1798–1845, October 1804, LVA; County Line Primitive Baptist Church (Jones County, Ga.), Minutes, 1809–1830, May 1820, Drawer 218, Reel 15, GA; and Cascade Primitive Baptist Church (Pittsylvania County, Va.), Minute Book, 1809–1913, November, 1824, Misc. Reel 390, LVA.

53. Executive Papers, James Patton Preston, February 1817, Box 1, Folder 6, LVA; Russell County, Law Order Book 11, 1838–1846, Reel 17, LVA. Pittsylvania County, Court Records 21, 1819–1820, Reel 54, Frames 28–33, LVA. In Essex County, the slaves Peter, John, and Tom all shed their coats in advance of their fight. Essex County, Order Book 45, 1823–1826, Reel 94, LVA.

54. Iliffe, *Honour in African History;* Jeff Forret, *Race Relations at the Margins: Slaves and Poor*

Whites in the Antebellum Southern Countryside (Baton Rouge: Louisiana State University Press, 2006); Pickens District, Court of Magistrates and Freeholders, Trial Papers, 1829–1862, Folder 11, SCDAH. Lawrence T. McDonnell underestimates the cultural interplay between black and white when he writes that slaves "emulated manly white behavior, boasting, carrying weapons, . . . parading a desperate, overblown, paper-thin honor." See McDonnell, "Money Knows No Master," 38.

55. Desch Obi, *Fighting for Honor*; Iliffe, *Honour in African History*, 26, 88; *Narrative of the Life and Adventures of Henry Bibb, an American Slave, Written by Himself with an Introduction by Lucius C. Matlack* (New York: published by the author, 1849), 23. On the nature of honor and dueling among whites, see Steven M. Stowe, *Intimacy and Power in the Old South: Ritual in the Lives of the Planters* (Baltimore: Johns Hopkins University Press, 1987), ch. 1.

56. *State v. Anderson* (1858), Houst. Cr. Cas. 38, in *Judicial Cases Concerning American Slavery and the Negro*, vol. 4, ed. Helen Tunnicliff Catterall (Washington, D.C.: Carnegie Institution of Washington, 1936), 237; *The Liberator* (Boston), March 14, 1835. As they were crossing a river in Prince Edward County, Virginia, in 1813, Isham "asked Bob . . . three or four times if he was satisfied. Bob made no answer." Isham scoffed, "if you are I am not." Prince Edward County, County Court Orders, No. 17 1811–1813, Reel 27, LVA.

57. Kershaw District, Court of Magistrates and Freeholders, Trial Papers, 1800–1861, Box 1, Folder 24, SCDAH.

58. Desch Obi, *Fighting for Honor*, 265n204; Anderson District, Court of Magistrates and Freeholders, Trial Papers, Reel C2917, Case #185, SCDAH; Gorn, "Gouge and Bite," 41.

59. Christine Leigh Heyrman, *Southern Cross: The Beginnings of the Bible Belt* (Chapel Hill: University of North Carolina Press, 1998); Janet Moore Lindman, "Acting the Manly Christian: White Evangelical Masculinity in Revolutionary Virginia," *William & Mary Quarterly* 3rd ser., 57 (April 2000): 393–416; Glover, *Southern Sons*, 21; Gregory A. Wills, *Democratic Religion: Freedom, Authority, and Church Discipline in the Baptist South, 1785–1900* (New York: Oxford University Press, 1997), 37.

60. Robert Elder, "Southern Saints and Sacred Honor: Evangelicalism, Honor, Community, and the Self in South Carolina and Georgia, 1784–1860" (Ph.D. diss., Emory University, 2011), 141; Wills, *Democratic Religion*, 56; West, "From Yeoman to Redneck," 168.

61. Churches did occasionally expel white men for fighting, but in those relatively rare cases of exclusion, fighting was often linked to a plethora of related sins, such as drinking and gambling. At other times, churches were forced to exclude white male members because, rather than exhibiting proper penitence, the accused remained defiant. Lower Banister Church (Pittsylvania County, Va.), Minute Book, 1798–1845, January 1803, May 1804, LVA; Padgett's Creek Baptist Church (Union District, S.C.), Church Book, vol. 1, 1784–1837, October 1804, October 1788, SCL.

62. Philips Mill Baptist Church (Wilkes County, Ga.), Minutes, 1785–1948, June 1791, February 1795, Drawer 45, Reel 13, GA; Darien Baptist Church (Hancock County, Ga.), Minutes, 1794–1816, January 1800, Drawer 148, Reel 53, GA; Ash Camp (Keysville) Baptist Church (Charlotte County, Va.), Minute Book, 1813–1872, July 1848, LVA.

63. Elder, "Southern Saints and Sacred Honor," 148–149; Rabun Creek Baptist Church (Laurens District, S.C.), Church Book, 1828–1913, August 1853, July 1858, SCL; Mount Zion Baptist Church (Hancock County, Ga.), Minutes, 1833–1849, December 1842, Drawer 240, Reel 37, GA; Bethel Baptist Church (Hancock County, Ga.), Minutes, 1828–1887, October 1841, Drawer 77, Reel

26, GA. See also Warrior Creek Baptist Church (Laurens District, S.C.), Records, 1843–1896, June 1846, February 1856, SCL; and Buffalo Baptist Church (Mecklenburg County, Va.), Record Book, 1852–1880, February 1856, Misc. Reel 291, LVA; Shiloh Baptist Church (Charlotte County, Va.), Minute Book, 1825–1873, June 1842, July 1842, June 1856, July 1856, LVA; Poplar Springs Baptist Church (Laurens District, S.C.), Minutes, 1794–1937, January 1858, SCL; Island Creek Baptist Church (Hancock County, Ga.), Minutes, 1806–1873, July 1831, Drawer 31, Reel 80, GA.

64. Elder, "Southern Saints and Sacred Honor," 148; Abner Creek Baptist Church of Christ (Greenville District, S.C.), Church Book, 1834–1870, December 1860, SCL; Fishing Creek Baptist Church (Wilkes County, Ga.), Minutes, 1821–1873, July 1833, Drawer 171, Reel 28, GA; Beaverdam Primitive Baptist Church (Kershaw District, S.C.), Minutes, 1844–1882, October 1851, SCL.

65. Cascade Primitive Baptist Church (Pittsylvania County, Va.), Minute Book, 1809–1913, April 1834, Misc. Reel 390, LVA (quotation); Horeb Baptist Church (Hancock County, Ga.), Minutes, 1792–1916, July 1834, Drawer 32, Reel 77, GA; Powelton Baptist Church (Hancock County, Ga.), Minutes, 1786–1916, May 1849, Drawer 32, Reel 76, GA; Greenwood Baptist Church (Lincoln County, Ga.), Minutes, 1798–1880, October 1856, Drawer 90, Reel 23, GA.

66. Elder, "Southern Saints and Sacred Honor," ch. 3; Flint Hill Baptist Church (York District, S.C.), Church Records, 1792–1899, July 1845, SCL; Brushy Creek Baptist Church (Greenville District, S.C.), Minutes, 1794–1927, March 1825, SCL; Buffalo Baptist Church (Mecklenburg County, Va.), Record Book, 1852–1880, June 1853, Misc. Reel 291, LVA; Poplar Springs Baptist Church (Laurens District, S.C.), Minutes, 1794–1937, December 1850, SCL.

67. Rehoboth Baptist Church (Wilkes County, Ga.), Minutes, 1806–1933, July 1840, October 1841, Drawer 45, Reel 15, GA; Ash Camp (Keysville) Baptist Church (Charlotte County, Va.), Minute Book, 1813–1872, March 1817, LVA; Shiloh Baptist Church (Charlotte County, Va.), Minute Book, 1825–1873, August 1842, September 1842, LVA; Crooked Creek Primitive Baptist Church (Putnam County, Ga.), Minutes, 1807–1846, April 1823, GA; Middle Ground Baptist Church (Screven County, Ga.), Minutes, 1850–1888, January 1852, Drawer 22, Reel 77, GA.

68. Wills, *Democratic Religion*, 66; Salem Baptist Church (Jones County, Ga.), Minutes, 1839–1870, May 1862, Drawer 227, Reel 29, GA; Island Creek Baptist Church (Hancock County, Ga.), Minutes, 1806–1873, March 1827, Drawer 31, Reel 80, GA.

69. Brushy Creek Baptist Church (Greenville District, S.C.), Minutes, 1794–1927, November 1821, SCL; Fishing Creek Baptist Church (Wilkes County, Ga.), Minutes, 1821–1873, March 1842, April 1842, January 1858, October 1858, February 1859, Drawer 171, Reel 28, GA.

70. Powelton Baptist Church (Hancock County, Ga.), Minutes, 1786–1916, June 1792, Drawer 32, Reel 76, GA; Bethel Baptist Church (Hancock County, Ga.), Minutes, 1828–1887, February 1848, April 1848, Drawer 77, Reel 26, GA; Willis, "Behind 'Their Black Masks,'" 63; Big Creek Baptist Church (Williamston, S.C.), Minutes, 1801–1836, September 1835, May 1832, Microfilm Reel R5, SCL.

71. Iliffe, *Honour in African History*, 1, 31 (quotation), 53; Brown, "Strength of the Lion," 183; Powelton Baptist Church (Hancock County, Ga.), Minutes, 1786–1916, February 1809, Drawer 32, Reel 76, GA.

72. Powelton Baptist Church (Hancock County, Ga.), Minutes, 1786–1916, February 1809, Drawer 32, Reel 76, GA; Flint Hill Baptist Church (York District, S.C.), Church Records, 1792–1899, December 1823, June 1828, SCL; Padgett's Creek Baptist Church (Union District, S.C.),

Church Book, vol. 1, 1784–1837, September 1809, SCL; Philips Mill Baptist Church (Wilkes County, Ga.), Minutes, 1785–1948, January 1829, Drawer 45, Reel 13, GA; Sardis Baptist Church (Wilkes County, Ga.), Minutes, 1805–1951, August 1820, Drawer 45, Reel 24, GA.

73. Lower Banister Church (Pittsylvania County, Va.), Minute Book, 1798–1845, April 1845, LVA; Goshen Baptist Church (Lincoln County, Ga.), Minutes, 1802–1869, October 1831, August 1853, GA; Flint Hill Baptist Church (York District, S.C.), Church Records, 1792–1899, July 1832, SCL; Brushy Creek Baptist Church (Greenville District, S.C.), Minutes, 1794–1927, February 1840, June 1840, September 1848, SCL.

74. Brushy Creek Baptist Church (Greenville District, S.C.), Minutes, 1794–1927, February 1840, SCL; Horeb Baptist Church (Hancock County, Ga.), Minutes, 1792–1916, August 1844, Drawer 32, Reel 77, GA; Fishing Creek Baptist Church (Wilkes County, Ga.), Minutes, 1821–1873, November 1831, September 1835, August 1839, Drawer 171, Reel 28, GA.

75. Washington First Baptist Church (Wilkes County, Ga.), Records, 1827–1903, October 1840, Drawer 45, Reel 14, GA; Beaverdam Baptist Church (Wilkes County, Ga.), Minutes, 1836–1855, October 1844, Drawer 9, Reel 22, GA; Brushy Creek Baptist Church (Greenville District, S.C.), Minutes, 1794–1927, October 1856, SCL; Pleasant Grove Baptist Church (Greenville District, S.C.), Records, 1833–1922, March 1843, SCL; Brushy Creek Baptist Church (Greenville District, S.C.), Minutes, 1794–1927, March 1838, SCL.

76. Goshen Baptist Church (Lincoln County, Ga.), Minutes, 1802–1869, August 1853, GA. The bondman Sam enjoyed almost as much freedom to preach as did Charles. See Rabun Creek Baptist Church (Laurens District, S.C.), Church Book, 1828–1913, June 1854, SCL.

77. Horeb Baptist Church (Hancock County, Ga.), Minutes, 1792–1916, August 1844, Drawer 32, Reel 77, GA; Washington First Baptist Church (Wilkes County, Ga.), Records, 1827–1903, March 1836, June 1837, Drawer 45, Reel 14, GA; Fishing Creek Baptist Church (Wilkes County, Ga.), Minutes, 1821–1873, January 1854, June 1854, Drawer 171, Reel 28, GA.

78. Fishing Creek Baptist Church (Wilkes County, Ga.), Minutes, 1821–1873, April 1843, July 1843, March 1845, June 1845, November 1845, Drawer 171, Reel 28, GA.

79. Iliffe, *Honour in African History,* 123, 86, 116, 122 (quotation); Schwarz, *Twice Condemned,* 61, 114, 78, 80. On slaves and shame, see Genovese, *Roll, Jordan, Roll,* 120–123.

80. Morris, *Southern Slavery and the Law,* 305; Schwarz, *Twice Condemned,* 22, 157, 150, 206, 208, 292; Daniel J. Flanigan, *The Criminal Law of Slavery and Freedom 1800–1868* (New York: Garland Publishing, Inc., 1987), 16. On the bodily scars of African American men and women in literature, see Jennifer Putzi, *Identifying Marks: Race, Gender, and the Marked Body in Nineteenth-Century America* (Athens: University of Georgia Press, 2006), chs. 4–5.

81. Fredrika Bremer, *The Homes of the New World; Impressions of America,* trans. Mary Howitt, vol. 2 (1853; reprint, New York: Negro Universities Press, 1968), 534.

82. Justin Labinjoh, "The Sexual Life of the Oppressed: An Examination of the Family Life of Ante-Bellum Slaves," *Phylon* 35, no. 4 (1974): 394; Desch Obi, *Fighting for Honor,* 115, 118–119, 121; Executive Papers, Henry A. Wise, Misc. Reel 4198, Box 5, Folder 5, Frame 735, LVA; Joe Gray Taylor, *Negro Slavery in Louisiana* (Baton Rouge: Louisiana Historical Association, 1963), 203; Harriet Martineau, *Society in America,* vol. 2 (London: Saunders and Otley, 1837; reprint, New York: AMS Press, 1966), 321.

83. Pittsylvania County, Court Records 27, 1827–1829, Reel 55, LVA.

84. Black, "Black Male Concept of Manhood," 88–89; Kenneth M. Stampp, *The Peculiar Institution: Slavery in the Ante-Bellum South* (New York: Alfred A. Knopf, 1956), 188; L. A. Chamerovzow, ed., *Slave Life in Georgia: A Narrative of the Life, Sufferings, and Escape of John Brown, a Fugitive Slave, Now in England* (London: n.p., 1855), 62–63.

85. Schwarz, *Twice Condemned*, 79; Egerton, *Gabriel's Rebellion*, 32, 145; Coulter, "Four Slave Trials," 246; Flanigan, *Criminal Law of Slavery*, 15–16; Stampp, *Peculiar Institution*, 188; Morris, *Southern Slavery and the Law*, 302.

86. *State v. Charles Loadnum* (1798), Court of Oyer and Terminer of Delaware, Kent, 2 Del. Cas. 240, 1798 Del. LEXIS 42; *U.S. v. Clark* (1825), 25 Fed. Cas. 441 (2 Cranch C.C. 620), in Catterall, *Judicial Cases*, vol. 4, 176; Flanigan, *Criminal Law of Slavery*, 25, 14; *State v. Peter* (1827), Supreme Court of Alabama, Tuscaloosa, 1 Stew. 38, 1827 Ala. LEXIS 24; Catterall, *Judicial Cases*, vol. 3, 134; Michael Stephen Hindus, *Prison and Plantation: Crime, Justice, and Authority in Massachusetts and South Carolina, 1767–1878* (Chapel Hill: University of North Carolina Press, 1980), 102; *State v. Little Jordan, a slave* (1855), Case 10301, Group 1850, Box 26, File 68, ACCCHNF; Flanigan, *Criminal Law of Slavery*, 15.

87. Flanigan, *Criminal Law of Slavery*, 15; *State v. Adam* (1819), Chatham County (Ga.), Inferior Court Trial Docket, 1813–1827, Drawer 90, Reel 33, GA; McNair, "Justice Bound," 343.

88. Rawick, SS1, vol. 4, pt. 2, 423. Of the five slaves from our sample sentenced to whipping and branding, Jones County bondman Tom, found guilty of killing Allen, escaped with the lightest but nevertheless severe sentence. In addition to having "the letter M" seared "on the right cheek," he suffered 100 lashes—30 on both Monday and Tuesday, 40 on Wednesday. Baldwin County bondmen Tom and Peter, convicted of manslaughter in 1815 and 1821, respectively, each received 39 lashes for 3 consecutive days, for a total of 117 lashes apiece. Tom had a "Letter M" burnt onto "each cheek," Peter "upon the right cheek" only. Putnam County bondman Dick, held responsible for the death of "Toney the property of Sarah Roper," had an M imprinted on his cheek but had his 117 stripes spaced out, enduring 39 on Saturday, Monday, and Wednesday. Hancock County slave Warren fared worst of all. He was "sentenced to receive on his bare back Five hundred lashes"—in 50-stripe increments "to be executed with regard to Humanity" over the course of a month—"and to be branded with the Letter M on his left Cheek." Jones County (Ga.), Inferior Court Minutes, 1818–1846; Baldwin County (Ga.), Inferior Court Minutes, Trial of Slaves, 1812–1828; Putnam County (Ga.), Inferior Court Records, 1813–1843; Hancock County (Ga.), Inferior Court Minutes, County Purposes & Lunacy.

89. Flanigan, *Criminal Law of Slavery*, 14; McNair, "Justice Bound," 343; Walter Johnson, *Soul by Soul: Life inside the Antebellum Slave Market* (Cambridge: Harvard University Press, 1999); Hindus, *Prison and Plantation*, 102, 100; George P. Rawick, ed., *The American Slave: A Composite Autobiography, Supplement, Series 2*, vol. 9, pt. 8 (Westport, Conn.: Greenwood Press, 1979), 3552.

90. *State v. Caesar, a slave* (1849), 9 Ired. 391, 31 N.C. 391 (N.C.), 1849 WL 1307 (N.C.); *Maria (a freedwoman) v. State* (1866), Supreme Court of Texas, 28 Tex. 698, 1866 WL 4062. Dea H. Boster, *African American Slavery and Disability: Bodies, Property, and Power in the Antebellum South, 1800–1860* (New York: Routledge, 2013), 48–49, briefly mentions the dishonor associated with branding.

91. Philip N. Racine, ed., *Piedmont Farmer: The Journals of David Golightly Harris, 1855–1870* (Knoxville: University of Tennessee Press, 1990), 354, 356.

92. Executive Papers, James Pleasants, December 1824, Box 6, Folder 1, LVA; Executive Papers, James Pleasants, November 1824, Box 5, Folder 12, LVA.

93. Executive Papers, James Monroe, January 1811, Box 1, Folder 1, LVA; Executive Papers, Wyndham Robertson, Box 3, Folder 3, LVA; *State v. Cornelius (slave)* (1861), First District Court of New Orleans, 15361, NOPL; Anderson District, Court of Magistrates and Freeholders, Trial Papers, Reel C2918, Case #278, SCDAH; Kershaw District, Court of Magistrates and Freeholders, Trial Papers, 1800–1861, Box 1, Folder 24, SCDAH.

94. David Wilson, *Inventing Black-on-Black Violence: Discourse, Space, and Representation* (Syracuse: Syracuse University Press, 2005).

8. HONOR, VIOLENCE, AND ENSLAVED FEMININITY

1. John Q. Anderson, ed., *Brokenburn: The Journal of Kate Stone 1861–1868* (Baton Rouge: Louisiana State University Press, 1972), 170–172. See also Stephanie M. H. Camp, *Closer to Freedom: Enslaved Women and Everyday Resistance in the Plantation South* (Chapel Hill: University of North Carolina Press, 2004), 77.

2. Victoria E. Bynum, *Unruly Women: The Politics of Social and Sexual Control in the Old South* (Chapel Hill: University of North Carolina Press, 1992); Laura F. Edwards, "Law, Domestic Violence, and the Limits of Patriarchal Authority in the Antebellum South," *Journal of Southern History* 65 (November 1999): 733–770.

3. Christopher Morris, "Within the Slave Cabin: Violence in Mississippi Slave Families," in *Over the Threshold: Intimate Violence in Early America*, ed. Christine Daniels and Michael V. Kennedy (New York: Routledge, 1999), 272 (quotation). For a brief overview of the place of sexuality in the slave quarters, see Steven E. Brown, "Sexuality and the Slave Community," *Phylon* (First Quarter [Spring] 1981): 1–10. Rebecca J. Fraser, *Courtship and Love among the Enslaved in North Carolina* (Jackson: University Press of Mississippi, 2007), 47, hints that there was sexual honor among enslaved women.

4. Glenn M. McNair, "Justice Bound: Aframericans, Crime, and Criminal Justice in Georgia, 1751–1865" (Ph.D. diss., Emory University, 2001), 230, observes that "women were not thought to possess honor." Bertram Wyatt-Brown, *Southern Honor: Ethics and Behavior in the Old South* (New York: Oxford University Press, 1982), 39; idem, *The Shaping of Southern Culture: Honor, Grace, and War, 1760s–1880s* (Chapel Hill: University of North Carolina Press, 2001), 75; Julian Pitt-Rivers, "Postscript: The Place of Grace in Anthropology," in *Honor and Grace in Anthropology*, ed. J. G. Peristiany and Julian Pitt-Rivers (New York: Cambridge University Press, 1992), 226.

5. Wyatt-Brown, *Southern Honor*, 52, 40, 54, 233, 294, 253; idem, *Shaping of Southern Culture*, 75. On the significance of female sexual restraint in the Mediterranean context, see J. G. Peristiany, ed., *Honour and Shame: The Values of Mediterranean Society* (Chicago: University of Chicago Press, 1966), 45, 146, 182.

6. Bynum, *Unruly Women;* Powelton Baptist Church (Hancock County, Ga.), Minutes, 1786–1916, February 1845, Drawer 32, Reel 76, GA; Rabun Creek Baptist Church (Laurens District, S.C.), Church Book, 1828–1913, May 1838, SCL; New Hope Baptist Church (Lincoln County, Ga.), Minutes, 1831–1866, September 1843, Drawer 19, Reel 1, GA.

7. Jessica Millward, "'As Cool as I Now Am': Identity, Abortion and Infanticide in the Slave

South" (M.A. thesis, UCLA, 1997), 9; Deborah Gray White, *Ar'n't I a Woman? Female Slaves in the Plantation South*, rev. ed. (New York: Norton, 1999), 29–46. McMillan quoted in Herbert G. Gutman, *The Black Family in Slavery and Freedom, 1750–1925* (New York: Pantheon Books, 1976), 70.

  8. John Iliffe, *Honour in African History* (New York: Cambridge University Press, 2005), 116, 262, 80, 115 (first and third quotations), 263 (second quotation).

  9. George P. Rawick, ed., *The American Slave: A Composite Autobiography, Supplement, Series 2*, vol. 4, pt. 3 (Westport, Conn.: Greenwood Press, 1979), 1211; idem, ed., *The American Slave: A Composite Autobiography*, vol. 7 Mississippi (Westport, Conn.: Greenwood Publishing Company, 1972), 138; idem, *American Slave*, vol. 12, pt. 1, 348.

  10. John Spencer Bassett, *The Southern Plantation Overseer as Revealed in His Letters* (Northampton, Mass.: Smith College, 1925), 32; Rawick, *American Slave*, vol. 12, pt. 2, 57; idem, *American Slave*, vol. 7 Oklahoma, 94; idem, SS2, vol. 4, pt. 3, 1211; idem, *American Slave*, vol. 7 Mississippi, 138.

  11. Sardis Baptist Church (Wilkes County, Ga.), Minutes, 1805–1951, June 1840, February 1813, April 1813, Drawer 45, Reel 24, GA; Rabun Creek Baptist Church (Laurens District, S.C.), Church Book, 1828–1913, May 1835, SCL.

  12. Auditor of Public Accounts, Condemned Blacks Executed or Transported, Records—Condemned Slaves, Court Orders, and Valuations, 1823–1832, Misc. Reel 2552, Frames 1188, 1190, LVA; Prince Edward County, County Court Orders, No. 23, 1832–1837, Reel 30, LVA; Auditor of Public Accounts, Condemned Blacks Executed or Transported, Records—Condemned Slaves, Court Orders, and Valuations, 1846–1857, Misc. Reel 2554, Frame 911, LVA; Executive Papers, John Floyd, January–February 1851, Box 403, Folder February 11–20, 1851, LVA.

  13. Executive Papers, Joseph Johnson, February–April 1852, Box 411, Folder April 1852, LVA; Executive Papers, John Floyd, December 1833, Box 11, Folder 8, LVA; Executive Papers, Joseph Johnson, March–May 1854, Box 424, Folder March 1854, LVA; Executive Papers, William Smith, Misc. Reel 5022, Box 4, Folder 4, Frames 59–69, LVA; Executive Papers, Wilson Cary Nicholas, April 1816–October 1816, Misc. Reel 239, LVA; Spotsylvania County, Minute Book, 1815–1819, Reel 51, LVA; Executive Papers, David Campbell, December 1837, Box 2, Folder 7, LVA.

  14. Executive Papers, Joseph Johnson, February–April 1852, Box 411, Folder April 1852, LVA.

  15. Executive Papers, Joseph Johnson, March–May 1854, Box 424, Folder March 1854, LVA. One petition to the governor on behalf of Mahala offered a principled critique of the death penalty itself. The findings for convicted female slave murderers in Virginia do not support Deborah Gray White's contention that "the penalties for venting anger on other women were not as severe as those for striking out at men, either black or white." See White, *Ar'n't I a Woman?* 137.

  16. Executive Papers, Henry A. Wise, May 1856, Box 3, Folder 2, LVA.

  17. White, *Ar'n't I a Woman?* 137 (first two quotations), 133 (third quotation); Elizabeth Ware Pearson, ed., *Letters from Port Royal, 1862–1868* (Boston: W. B. Clarke Company, 1906; reprint, New York: Arno Press and the New York Times, 1969), 211.

  18. Charles C. Jones, *The Religious Instruction of the Negroes. In the United States* (Savannah: Thomas Purse, 1842), 136; Pearson, *Letters from Port Royal*, 211; Rawick, *American Slave*, vol. 7 Oklahoma, 94.

  19. J. H. Easterby, ed., *The South Carolina Rice Plantation as Revealed in the Papers of Robert F. W. Allston* (Chicago: University of Chicago Press, 1945), 291; Rawick, *American Slave*, vol. 2, pt.

2, 144; Executive Papers, John Floyd, December 1833, Box 11, Folder 8, LVA; Executive Papers, Joseph Johnson, March–May 1854, Box 424, Folder March 1854, LVA.

20. Executive Papers, James McDowell, February 1844, Box 3, Folder 4, LVA.

21. Rawick, *American Slave,* vol. 13, pt. 4, 104. See also Camp, *Closer to Freedom,* 78.

22. Pittsylvania County, Court Records 21, 1819–1820, Reel 54, Frames 28–33, LVA; Camp, *Closer to Freedom,* 7, ch. 3; T. J. Desch Obi, *Fighting for Honor: The History of African Martial Art Traditions in the Atlantic World* (Columbia: University of South Carolina Press, 2008), 130.

23. Pittsylvania County, Court Records 21, 1819–1820, Reel 54, Frames 28–33, LVA; Executive Papers, James McDowell, February 1844, Box 3, Folder 4, LVA.

24. Executive Papers, James Barbour, June 1813, Box 7, Folder 6, LVA.

25. Bynum, *Unruly Women,* 118; White, *Ar'n't I a Woman?* 78; Catherine Clinton, "'Southern Dishonor': Flesh, Blood, Race, and Bondage," in *In Joy and in Sorrow: Women, Family, and Marriage in the Victorian South, 1830–1900,* ed. Carol Bleser (New York: Oxford University Press, 1991), 66. Even some northern enemies of slavery, such as Joseph J. Blunt, reflected southern white sentiments when they declared that "[t]he female slave is prevented by no fear of scorn or loss of reputation, from gratifying the desires of her master." Marcus [Joseph J. Blunt], *An Examination of the Expediency and Constitutionality of Prohibiting Slavery in the State of Missouri* (New York: C. Wiley, 1819), 9.

26. Harriet A. Jacobs, *Incidents in the Life of a Slave Girl Written by Herself,* ed. Jean Fagan Yellin (Cambridge: Harvard University Press, 2000). See also Melton A. McLaurin, *Celia, a Slave: A True Story* (New York: Perennial, 2002). According to abolitionist Joseph J. Blunt, "it is not surprising that she [the slave woman] is easily persuaded to overstep the bounds of modesty, and to consent to acts at which decency recoils." She had been "[b]rought up in entire ignorance of the obligations of morality and religion, knowing no law but her master's will." Marcus, *Examination of the Expediency,* 9.

27. Camp, *Closer to Freedom,* 65. Sexual assaults no doubt triggered some cases in which bondwomen attacked bondmen, but often the circumstances leading to the assaults were neglected in the sources. A Charleston, South Carolina, newspaper reported that an anonymous "Negro Woman" stabbed a "very valuable Negro Man" in 1817 but failed to state her motivation. Likewise, in 1829, Island Creek Baptist Church in Hancock County, Georgia, charged both Brother Flournoy's bondman Sesar and Brother Hubert's bondwoman Liza with "fighting with Sticks and knife on Last Sabbath" without delving into the circumstances of their affray. *Charleston Courier,* reprinted in *Raleigh Minerva,* August 29, 1817; Island Creek Baptist Church (Hancock County, Ga.), Minutes, 1806–1873, October 1829, Drawer 31, Reel 80, GA.

28. Executive Papers, James McDowell, February 1844, Box 3, Folder 4, LVA. Maria's master William McCoy interceded on her behalf, hoping to get her death sentence commuted to sale and transportation. On January 2, 1844, he offered to pay her "full value" to the state "and give the most ample security to have her carried beyond the limits of the United States, never to return." McCoy hoped Maria could be sent "to Liberia or to some other place of refuge, where she might devote the remainder of her days, under proper care and protection." The governor's full pardon must have taken McCoy by surprise.

29. Hunter Dickinson Farish, ed., *Journal and Letters of Philip Vickers Fithian 1773–1774: A Plantation Tutor of the Old Dominion* (Charlottesville, Va.: Dominion Books, 1957), 184–185. In

1840, a free black man in Kershaw District, South Carolina, named William Pettifoot was accused of the attempted rape of a bondwoman named Dinah. See Kershaw District, Court of Magistrates and Freeholders, Trial Papers, 1800–1861, Box 2, Folders 83, 91, SCDAH.

30. Executive Papers, David Campbell, November 1839, Box 7, Folder 8, LVA. See also Joshua D. Rothman, *Notorious in the Neighborhood: Sex and Families across the Color Line in Virginia, 1787–1861* (Chapel Hill: University of North Carolina Press, 2003), 159–160.

31. Executive Papers, David Campbell, July 1838, Box 4, Folder 1, LVA; Auditor of Public Accounts, Condemned Blacks Executed or Transported, Records—Condemned Slaves, Court Orders, and Valuations, 1833–1845, Misc. Reel 2553, Frame 515, LVA.

32. Executive Papers, John Letcher, Misc. Reel 4760, Box 19, Folder 3, Frames 14–21, LVA.

33. Quoted in Leslie A. Schwalm, *A Hard Fight for We: Women's Transition from Slavery to Freedom in South Carolina* (Urbana: University of Illinois Press, 1997), 52; Rawick, *American Slave*, vol. 5, pt. 4, 176–177.

34. White, *Ar'n't I a Woman?* 152; Wilma King, *Stolen Childhood: Slave Youth in Nineteenth-Century America* (Bloomington: Indiana University Press, 1997), 108; Emily West, *Chains of Love: Slave Couples in Antebellum South Carolina* (Urbana: University of Illinois Press, 2004), 68; Anthony E. Kaye, *Joining Places: Slave Neighborhoods in the Old South* (Chapel Hill: University of North Carolina Press, 2007), 59, 60, 66, 79, 142, 143; Frances Anne Kemble, *Journal of a Residence on a Georgian Plantation in 1838–1839*, ed. John A. Scott (New York: Alfred A. Knopf, 1961), 270; Schwalm, *A Hard Fight for We*, 52; Rawick, *American Slave*, vol. 7, pt. 2 Mississippi, 13.

35. Michael Stephen Hindus, *Prison and Plantation: Crime, Justice, and Authority in Massachusetts and South Carolina, 1767–1878* (Chapel Hill: University of North Carolina Press, 1980), 144; West, *Chains of Love*, 68; Eugene D. Genovese, *Roll, Jordan, Roll: The World the Slaves Made* (1974; reprint, New York; Vintage, 1976), 33.

36. McNair, "Justice Bound," 82.

37. Loudoun County, Minute Book, 1856–1858, Reel 89, LVA; Thomas D. Morris, *Southern Slavery and the Law, 1619–1860* (Chapel Hill: University of North Carolina Press, 1996), 306; Chowan County, Slave Records, Criminal Actions Concerning Slaves 1767–1829, Folder 1824, NCDAH. On the Loudoun County, Virginia, case, see also Philip J. Schwarz, *Twice Condemned: Slaves and the Criminal Laws of Virginia, 1705–1865* (Baton Rouge: Louisiana State University Press, 1988), 293.

38. Westmoreland County, Orders, 1776–1786, Reel 61, LVA; Chowan County, Slave Records, Criminal Actions Concerning Slaves 1767–1829, Folder 1824, NCDAH; Chowan County, Minute Docket, Superior Court, 1809–1828, NCDAH. In Norfolk County, Virginia, the slave Toby was charged in 1783 "with house breaking rob[b]ery hog stealing and committing a rape on [a] negro girl." The county Court of Oyer and Terminer ordered "that he be burned in the hand and receive 39 Lashes on his bare back," but it is not certain for which infraction or combination of crimes. The court judged him not guilty of the burglary and guilty only of an unspecified "felony." The rape allegation likely had nothing to do with his sentence. Norfolk County, Minute Book, 1782–1783, Reel 62a, LVA.

39. Morris, *Southern Slavery and the Law*, 306; Executive Papers, Robert Brooke, Box 4, Folder November 17, Misc. Reel 5214, Frames 427, 429–430, LVA; Schwarz, *Twice Condemned*, 293; Spotsylvania County, Order Book, 1849–1858, Reel 55, LVA. The case of Luke challenges

Philip J. Schwarz's assertion that "No eighteenth-century Virginia court whose records have survived ever convicted a slave of raping another slave." See Schwarz, *Twice Condemned*, 156.

40. Auditor of Public Accounts, Condemned Blacks Executed or Transported, Records—Condemned Slaves, Court Orders, and Valuations, 1846–1857, Misc. Reel 2554, Frame 1116, LVA; Auditor of Public Accounts, Condemned Blacks Executed or Transported, Records—Condemned Slaves, Court Orders, and Valuations, 1810–1822, Misc. Reel 2551, Frame 32, LVA; Auditor of Public Accounts, Condemned Blacks Executed or Transported, Records—Condemned Slaves, Court Orders, and Valuations, 1781–1793, Misc. Reel 2549, Frame 174, LVA; McNair, "Justice Bound," 82; *Grandison (a slave) v. State*, 2 Humphreys 451 (December 1841), in *Judicial Cases Concerning American Slavery and the Negro*, vol. 2, ed. Helen Tunnicliff Catterall (Washington, D.C.: Carnegie Institution of Washington, 1929), 513. The Mecklenburg County, Virginia, slave Lewis also hanged for raping a free black woman.

41. Wilma King, "'Mad' Enough to Kill: Enslaved Women, Murder, and Southern Courts," *Journal of African American History* 92 (Winter 2007): 40; Loudoun County, Minute Book, 1856–1858, Reel 89, LVA; Spotsylvania County, Order Book, 1849–1858, Reel 55, LVA; Mecklenburg County, Virginia, Order Book 6, 1853–1858 (County Court), Reel 120, Frame 353, LVA; Executive Papers, Henry A. Wise, Misc. Reel 4198, Box 5, Folder 4, Frames 482–483, LVA. See also Auditor of Public Accounts, Condemned Blacks Executed or Transported, Records—Condemned Slaves, Court Orders, and Valuations, 1823–1832, Misc. Reel 2552, Frame 1056, LVA. The age of consent varied over time within the same state. By a Virginia law of 1792, it was ten. As of 1822 in Mississippi, it was twelve.

42. Mecklenburg County, Virginia, Order Book 6, 1853–1858 (County Court), Reel 120, Frame 353, LVA; Executive Papers, Henry A. Wise, Misc. Reel 4198, Box 5, Folder 4, Frames 482–483, LVA. See also Auditor of Public Accounts, Condemned Blacks Executed or Transported, Records—Condemned Slaves, Court Orders, and Valuations, 1823–1832, Misc. Reel 2552, Frame 1056, LVA.

43. Executive Papers, Henry A. Wise, Misc. Reel 4198, Box 5, Folder 4, Frames 666, 718, LVA.

44. King, "'Mad' Enough to Kill," 40–41.

45. *George (a slave) v. State*, Supreme Court of Mississippi, October 1859, 37 Miss. 316, 1859 Miss. LEXIS 20. See also Helen Tunnicliff Catterall, ed., *Judicial Cases Concerning American Slavery and the Negro*, vol. 3 (Washington, D.C.: Carnegie Institution of Washington, 1932), 363; Clinton, "Southern Dishonor," 66; White, *Ar'n't I a Woman?* 152–153.

46. *George (a slave) v. State*, Supreme Court of Mississippi, October 1859, 37 Miss. 316, 1859 Miss. LEXIS 20; White, *Ar'n't I a Woman?* 152–153; Peter W. Bardaglio, *Reconstructing the Household: Families, Sex, and the Law in the Nineteenth-Century South* (Chapel Hill: University of North Carolina Press, 1995), 68–69.

47. McNair, "Justice Bound," 82.

48. Fishing Creek Baptist Church (Wilkes County, Ga.), Minutes, 1821–1873, July 1821, Drawer 171, Reel 28, GA; Clarke's Station Baptist Church (Wilkes County, Ga.), Minutes, 1835–1896, September 1850, March 1851, November 1851.

49. White, *Ar'n't I a Woman?* 9; King, *Stolen Childhood*, 97; Thaviola Glymph, *Out of the House of Bondage: The Transformation of the Plantation Household* (New York: Cambridge University Press, 2008), 56; Morris, "Within the Slave Cabin," 271.

50. Norman R. Yetman, ed., *Life under the "Peculiar Institution": Selections from the Slave Narrative Collection* (New York: Holt, Rinehart and Winston Inc., 1970), 290.

51. Charles C. Jones, *The Religious Instruction of the Negroes. In the United States* (Savannah: Thomas Purse, 1842), 137; Robert Collins, *Essay on the Treatment and Management of Slaves. Written for the Seventh Annual Fair of the Southern Central Agricultural Society*, 2nd ed. (Boston: Eastburn's Press, 1853), 11; Margaret Abruzzo, *Polemical Pain: Slavery, Cruelty, and the Rise of Humanitarianism* (Baltimore: Johns Hopkins University Press, 2011), 235; Francis Pulszky and Theresa Pulszky, *White, Red, Black: Sketches of American Society in the United States During the Visit of Their Guests*, vol. 2 (New York: Redfield, 1853), 107.

52. George P. Rawick, ed., *The American Slave: A Composite Autobiography*, vol. 3, pt. 3 (Westport, Conn.: Greenwood Publishing Company, 1972), 158; idem, ed., *The American Slave: A Composite Autobiography, Supplement, Series 1*, vol. 7, pt. 2 (Westport, Conn.: Greenwood Press, 1977), 621.

53. George P. Rawick, ed., *The American Slave: A Composite Autobiography, Supplement, Series 2*, vol. 2, pt. 1 (Westport, Conn.: Greenwood Press, 1979), 104; idem, SS2, vol. 7, pt. 6, 2875. See also idem, SS2, vol. 5, pt. 4, 1733; and idem, SS2, vol. 8, pt. 7, 3033.

54. Rawick, SS2, vol. 10, pt. 9, 4319; idem, SS1, vol. 7, pt. 2, 356; idem, SS2, vol. 2, pt. 1, 104; idem, SS2, vol. 8, pt. 7, 3034; idem, *American Slave*, vol. 2, pt. 2, 267; idem, SS2, vol. 7, pt. 6, 2875. See also idem, ed., *The American Slave: A Composite Autobiography, Supplement, Series 1*, vol. 7, pt. 2 (Westport, Conn.: Greenwood Press, 1977), 749.

55. Rawick, SS2, vol. 10, pt. 9, 4319; idem, SS2, vol. 4, pt. 3, 1301; idem, *American Slave*, vol. 12, pt. 2, 128.

56. Yetman, *Life under the "Peculiar Institution,"* 127.

57. Rawick, SS1, vol. 7, pt. 2, 732; idem, *American Slave*, vol. 10, pt. 6, 337.

58. *Maria (a freedwoman) v. State*, Supreme Court of Texas, December 1866, 28 Tex. 698, 1866 WL 4062.

59. Island Creek Baptist Church (Hancock County, Ga.), Minutes, 1806–1873, May 1829, Drawer 31, Reel 80, GA.

60. Kershaw District, Court of Magistrates and Freeholders, Trial Papers, 1800–1861, Box 2, Folder 105, SCDAH.

61. Poplar Springs Baptist Church (Laurens District, S.C.), Minutes, 1794–1937, November 1841, July 1853, August 1853, October 1853, SCL.

62. Executive Papers, Joseph Johnson, February–April 1852, Box 411, Folder April 1852, LVA.

63. Genovese, *Roll, Jordan, Roll*, 496; White, *Ar'n't I a Woman?* 88; Historical Census Browser, University of Virginia, Geospatial and Statistical Data Center (2004): http://fisher.lib.virginia.edu/collections/stats/histcensus/index.html [accessed January 17, 2012]; Executive Papers, James Pleasants, August 1824, Box 5, Folder 5, LVA; Executive Papers, James Patton Preston, December 1819, Box 9, Folder 4, LVA.

64. Steven Deyle, *Carry Me Back: The Domestic Slave Trade in American Life* (New York: Oxford University Press, 2005), 232; Kelli M. Black, "Creating Infanticide: A Comparative Study of Early Modern British Servant and Antebellum American Slave Women" (M.A. thesis, San Diego State University, 2003), 15, 24–25, 20.

65. Davidson County, Records of Slaves and Free Persons of Color, n.d., 1826–1896, Folder

1840, 1843, 1844, NCDAH; Davidson County, County Court Minutes, 1824–1860, n.p.; Seventh Census of the United States, 1850, Slave Schedule: Davidson County, North Carolina.

66. McNair, "Justice Bound," 131–132; Morris, *Southern Slavery and the Law*, 301; Edward L. Ayers, *Vengeance and Justice: Crime and Punishment in the 19th-Century American South* (New York: Oxford University Press, 1984), 134; Brunswick County, Order Book 12, 1772–1774, Reel 33, LVA; Fairfield District, Court of Magistrates and Freeholders, Trial Papers, 1839–1865, Cases 1–54, Folder 44, SCDAH; Race and Slavery Petitions Project, #21385347, Ser. II, Part D, 0183; Deyle, *Carry Me Back*, 232–233.

67. Powhatan County, Order Book 12, 1814–1816, Reel 27, LVA; McNair, "Justice Bound," 128; Daniel J. Flanigan, *The Criminal Law of Slavery and Freedom 1800–1868* (New York: Garland Publishing, Inc., 1987), 51; Black, "Creating Infanticide," 19–20. Census data come from Historical Census Browser, University of Virginia, Geospatial and Statistical Data Center (2004): http://fisher.lib.virginia.edu/collections/stats/histcensus/index.html. The remaining figures are based on the data assembled in the appendix.

According to official Federal Bureau of Investigation statistics, the rate of infanticides in 2005 stood at 2.2 per year per 100,000 whites and 6.6 per year per 100,000 blacks. If these rates had been true for Virginia slaves, approximately 30 slaves would have been infanticide victims in 1860 alone. Black, "Creating Infanticide," 20, suggests "that infanticide occurred more often than suggested by recent scholarship." Unlike in the antebellum era, in the modern United States men commit a majority of all infanticides. For infanticide data compiled from FBI Supplementary Homicide Reports, 1976–2005, see James Alan Fox and Marianne W. Zawitz, "Homicide Trends in the United States," http://www.bjs.gov/index.cfm?ty=pbdetail&iid=966.

For a case study of infanticide in the Spanish context, see Jane Landers, "'In Consideration of Her Enormous Crime': Rape and Infanticide in Spanish St. Augustine," in *The Devil's Lane: Sex and Race in the Early South*, ed. Catherine Clinton and Michele Gillespie (New York: Oxford University Press, 1997), 205–217.

68. Schwarz, *Twice Condemned*, 252; Executive Papers, Joseph Johnson, August–October 1852, Box 413, Folder October 1–12, 1852, LVA.

69. Sharla M. Fett, *Working Cures: Healing, Health, and Power on Southern Slave Plantations* (Chapel Hill: University of North Carolina Press, 2002); Warrior Creek Baptist Church (Laurens District, S.C.), Records, 1843–1896, May–June 1853, SCL. On the use of birth control in the slave quarters, see Liese M. Perrin, "Resisting Reproduction: Reconsidering Slave Contraception in the Old South," *Journal of American Studies* 35 (August 2001): 255–274.

70. Black, "Creating Infanticide," 40; Orange County, Slave Records, n.d., 1783–1865, Folder 1825–1831, NCDAH; Executive Papers, James Patton Preston, December 1819, Box 9, Folder 4, LVA.

71. Executive Papers, James Patton Preston, December 1819, Box 9, Folder 4, LVA; Executive Papers, John Tyler, June 1826, Box 2, Folder 1, LVA; *Jane (a slave) v. State*, Supreme Court of Missouri, Bowling Green District, April 1831, 3 Mo. 61, 1831 Mo. LEXIS 22. On Jane, see also Catterall, *Judicial Cases*, vol. 5, 139.

72. Executive Papers, James Patton Preston, November 1819, Box 9, Folder 3, LVA; Executive Papers, James Patton Preston, December 1819, Box 9, Folder 4, LVA; Louisa County, Minute Book, 1822–1826, Reel 36, LVA; Executive Papers, John Tyler, June 1826, Box 2, Folder 1, LVA; Prince Edward County, County Court Orders, No. 21 1824–1828, Reel 29, LVA; Executive Papers,

John Floyd, February 1833, Box 9, Folder 4, LVA; Henrico County, Minute Book 1833–1835, Reel 81, LVA; Executive Papers, Joseph Johnson, March–May 1855, Box 426, Folder April 1855, LVA; Executive Papers, Henry A. Wise, Misc. Reel 4202, Box 8, Folder 3, Frames 527–532, LVA.

73. Executive Papers, John Tyler, June 1826, Box 2, Folder 1, LVA; Executive Papers, Joseph Johnson, August–September 1854, Box 422, Folder September 1854, LVA; Prince Edward County, County Court Orders, No. 21 1824–1828, Reel 29, LVA; Executive Papers, Joseph Johnson, August–October 1852, Box 413, Folder October 1–12, 1852, LVA. See also the case of Richmond slave Lucy, in Executive Papers, Joseph Johnson, March–May 1855, Box 426, Folder April 1855, LVA.

74. Executive Papers, Joseph Johnson, August–September 1854, Box 422, Folder September 1854, LVA; Executive Papers, Joseph Johnson, August–October 1852, Box 413, Folder October 1–12, 1852, LVA; Executive Papers, John Letcher, Misc. Reel 4714, Box 5, Folder 4, Frames 187–191, LVA.

75. Black, "Creating Infanticide," 46; Executive Papers, Joseph Johnson, August–October 1852, Box 413, Folder October 1–12, 1852, LVA; Prince Edward County, County Court Orders, No. 21 1824–1828, Reel 29, LVA. See also Executive Papers, James Patton Preston, November 1818, Box 6, Folder 4, LVA; and Executive Papers, Joseph Johnson, August–September 1854, Box 422, Folder September 1854, LVA.

76. Executive Papers, Joseph Johnson, August–October 1852, Box 413, Folder October 1–12, 1852, LVA; Executive Papers, Henry A. Wise, Misc. Reel 4211, Box 15, Folder 5, Frames 382–387, LVA; Executive Papers, Joseph Johnson, March–May 1855, Box 426, Folder April 1855, LVA. Fett, *Working Cures,* discusses the invasive white doctors who practiced in the antebellum South, much to the displeasure of female slaves who preferred enslaved healers and midwives.

77. Executive Papers, Joseph Johnson, March–May 1855, Box 426, Folder April 1855, LVA. In the infanticide cases of Marietta, of Loudoun County; Charlotte, of Richmond; and Suckey, of Culpeper County, physicians all employed the hydrostatic test to conclude that the dead infants had been murdered rather than stillborn. See Executive Papers, Henry A. Wise, Misc. Reel 4211, Box 15, Folder 5, Frames 382–387, LVA; Executive Papers, Joseph Johnson, August–September 1854, Box 422, Folder September 1854, LVA; Executive Papers, Henry A. Wise, Misc. Reel 4202, Box 8, Folder 3, Frames 527–532, LVA.

78. Quoted in Kenneth M. Stampp, *The Peculiar Institution: Slavery in the Ante-Bellum South* (New York: Alfred A. Knopf, 1956), 306, 346; White, *Ar'n't I a Woman?* 89.

79. Bassett, *Southern Plantation Overseer,* 59; White, *Ar'n't I a Woman?,* 89, 88; Marie Jenkins Schwartz, *Born in Bondage: Growing Up Enslaved in the Antebellum South* (Cambridge: Harvard University Press, 2000), 55–58; King, *Stolen Childhood,* 11; Rawick, SS1, vol. 6, pt. 1, 3–4; Robert William Fogel and Stanley L. Engerman, *Time on the Cross: The Economics of American Negro Slavery* (1974; reprint, New York: W. W. Norton & Company, 1995), 125; Michael P. Johnson, "Smothered Slave Infants: Were Slave Mothers at Fault?" *Journal of Southern History* 47 (November 1981): 493–520, esp. 495, 494. On SIDS, see also Todd L. Savitt, *Medicine and Slavery: The Diseases and Health Care of Blacks in Antebellum Virginia* (1978; reprint, Urbana: University of Illinois Press, 2002), 122–127. The scholarship of both White and King is sympathetic to the SIDS thesis. Even with changes in the work routines of black women after the Civil War, suffocations among black infants continued. See King, *Stolen Childhood,* 11. For an analysis of the role of slave infanticide in antislavery fiction, see Sarah N. Roth, "'The Blade Was in My Own Breast': Slave Infanticide in 1850s Fiction," *American Nineteenth Century History* 8 (June 2007): 169–185.

80. Black, "Creating Infanticide," 10; Executive Papers, Henry A. Wise, Misc. Reel 4202, Box 8, Folder 3, Frames 527–532, LVA; Prince Edward County, County Court Orders, No. 21 1824–1828, Reel 29, LVA; Executive Papers, John Floyd, March–May 1851, Box 404, Folder April 1851, LVA.

81. Black, "Creating Infanticide," 85, 59; Kirsten Fischer, *Suspect Relations: Sex, Race, and Resistance in Colonial North Carolina* (Ithaca: Cornell University Press, 2002), 105–106; Millward, "As Cool as I Now Am," 36; Fairfield District, Court of Magistrates and Freeholders, Trial Papers, 1839–1865, Cases 1–54, Folder 44, SCDAH.

82. Deyle, *Carry Me Back*, 232; Black, "Creating Infanticide," 45; Powhatan County, Order Book 12, 1814–1816, Reel 27, LVA.

83. King, "'Mad' Enough to Kill," 43; Robeson County, Records Concerning Slaves and Free Persons of Color, 1814–1839, Folder 1834, NCDAH; Race and Slavery Petitions Project, #21184501, Ser. II, Part E, Reel 7, 0374. Postpartum depression probably also contributed to a Bibb County, Georgia, bondwoman's decision to commit suicide in 1829 at the age of thirty. Pounds, as she was called, had recently given birth to a healthy baby. See Ralph Betts Flanders, *Plantation Slavery in Georgia* (Chapel Hill: University of North Carolina Press, 1933; reprint, Cos Cob, Conn.: John E. Edwards, 1967), 269.

84. McNair, "Justice Bound," 129, 130–131.

85. Gerda Lerner, ed., *Black Women in White America: A Documentary History* (New York: Pantheon, 1972), 61; Julius Yanuck, "The Garner Fugitive Slave Case," *Mississippi Valley Historical Review* 40 (June 1953): 47–66. On Margaret Garner, see also Black, "Creating Infanticide," 22, 50–51; Millward, "As Cool as I Now Am," 2–3; and Steven Weisenburger, *Modern Medea: A Family Story of Slavery and Child-Murder from the Old South* (New York: Hill and Wang, 1999), 222–225. The Garner case became the basis for the Toni Morrison novel *Beloved*. In Granville County, North Carolina, the bondwoman Hannah only partially succeeded in committing a murder-suicide. In 1835, she killed her son Solomon by stabbing him in the throat with a corn knife, but the self-inflicted wound in her own neck failed to achieve its goal, and she instead went to trial for Solomon's murder. Granville County, Criminal Actions Concerning Slaves and Free Persons of Color, 1820–1837, Folder State vs. Hannah (a slave of Colo John G. Hart) 1836.

86. Camp, *Closer to Freedom*; Jennifer L. Morgan, *Laboring Women: Reproduction and Gender in New World Slavery* (Philadelphia: University of Pennsylvania Press, 2004), ch. 6; Caroline Elizabeth Neely, "'Dat's One Chile of Mine You Ain't Never Gonna Sell': Gynecological Resistance Within the Plantation Community" (M.A. thesis, Virginia Polytechnic Institute and State University, 2000), 55–62; Black, "Creating Infanticide," 43; Millward, "As Cool as I Now Am," vi, 7, 39. Quantitative historians Robert William Fogel and Stanley L. Engerman disputed the notion of infanticide as a form of resistance. If conditions under slavery were "so unbearable," they argued, the suicide rate among slaves should have been dramatically higher than it was. As it stood, "Less than one slave in every ten thousand committed suicide in 1850," a rate only one-third as high as that among whites. See Fogel and Engerman, *Time on the Cross*, 124.

87. J. Mason Brewer, *American Negro Folklore* (Chicago: Quadrangle Books, 1968), 233; Flanders, *Plantation Slavery in Georgia*, 264–265.

88. Millward, "As Cool as I Now Am," 9, 41; Race and Slavery Petitions Project, #21184501, Ser. II, Part E, Reel 7, 0374; Frederick Law Olmsted, *Journey in the Seaboard Slave States, with*

Remarks on Their Economy (New York: Dix & Edwards, 1856), 602; White, *Ar'n't I a Woman?* 88; McNair, "Justice Bound," 129–130.

89. Black, "Creating Infanticide," 49; Lewis Clarke, *Narrative of the Sufferings of Lewis Clarke, During a Captivity of More Than Twenty-Five Years, Among the Algerines of Kentucky, One of the So-Called Christian States of North America. Dictated by Himself* (Boston: David H. Ela, 1845), 76; Race and Slavery Petitions Project, #11481901, Tennessee, 1819, http://library.uncg.edu/slavery/index.aspx; Rawick, *American Slave*, vol. 7 Oklahoma, 302; White, *Ar'n't I a Woman?* 88. When a Fairfax County, Virginia, slave owner asked his bondwoman Ally why she murdered her infant child, she replied, "She was afraid he would whip her or sell her." In one of the very few known cases of an enslaved man committing infanticide or child murder, an Alabama slave slated for sale away from his children grew so despondent that he lashed out at his owner and knifed his two children to death. As reported in the newspaper, "It is supposed he was urged to the horrid deed by the idea of parting with them." Executive Papers, John Floyd, February 1833, Box 9, Folder 4, LVA; Deyle, *Carry Me Back*, 254.

90. White, *Ar'n't I a Woman?* 87; Genovese, *Roll, Jordan, Roll*, 497.

91. Katie M. Hemphill, "'Driven to the Commission of This Crime': Women and Infanticide in Baltimore, 1835–1860," *Journal of the Early Republic* 32 (Fall 2012): 438; Jones, *Religious Instruction of the Negroes*, 135.

92. Jones, *Religious Instruction of the Negroes*, 135; Hemphill, "Driven to the Commission of This Crime," 437; Merril D. Smith, "'Unnatural Mothers': Infanticide, Motherhood, and Class in the Mid-Atlantic, 1730–1830," in *Over the Threshold*, 177, 173; White, *Ar'n't I a Woman?* 29–46; Executive Papers, William B. Giles, May 1827, Box 1, Folder 7, LVA.

93. Jones, *Religious Instruction of the Negroes*, 135; Orange County, Slave Records, n.d., 1783–1865, Folder 1825–1831, NCDAH.

94. Culpeper County, Minute Book 23, 1853–1858, Reel 47, LVA; Executive Papers, Henry A. Wise, Misc. Reel 4202, Box 8, Folder 3, Frames 527–532, LVA.

95. Desch Obi, *Fighting for Honor*, 115 (quotation); Deyle, *Carry Me Back*, 232; Black, "Creating Infanticide," 44, 56; Millward, "As Cool as I Now Am," 28; Executive Papers, Thomas Mann Randolph, August 1822, Box 7, Folder 3, LVA; Lerner, *Black Women*, 61; Weisenburger, *Modern Medea*, 47–48, 76. Historian Leslie A. Schwalm has documented that, after the Civil War, freedwomen expressed shame for the mixed-race children resulting from masters' rapes. See Schwalm, *A Hard Fight for We*, 248.

96. Executive Papers, Thomas Mann Randolph, August 1822, Box 7, Folder 3, LVA; Executive Papers, James Patton Preston, November 1819, Box 9, Folder 3, LVA.

97. Executive Papers, Joseph Johnson, August–October 1852, Box 413, Folder October 1–12, 1852, LVA; Henrico County, Minute Book 1833–1835, Reel 81, LVA.

98. Henrico County, Minute Book 1833–1835, Reel 81, LVA; Schwartz, *Born in Bondage*, 189; James Trussel and Richard Steckel, "The Age of Slaves at Menarche and Their First Birth," *Journal of Interdisciplinary History* 8 (Winter 1978): 477–505.

99. Penitentiary records, Auditor of Public Accounts, Condemned Blacks Executed or Transported, Records—Condemned Slaves, Court Orders, and Valuations, 1858–1865, Misc. Reel 2555, Frames 997–998, LVA; Executive Papers, James McDowell, February 1844, Box 3, Folder 4, LVA; Executive Papers, Joseph Johnson, February–April 1852, Box 411, Folder April 1852, LVA; Ex-

ecutive Papers, Joseph Johnson, March–May 1855, Box 426, Folder April 1855, LVA; Executive Papers, John Letcher, Misc. Reel 4714, Box 5, Folder 4, Frames 187–191, LVA.

100. On the respectability of petitioners or the force of popular sentiment in the community, see, for example, Executive Papers, James Patton Preston, November 1819, Box 9, Folder 3, LVA; Executive Papers, Thomas Mann Randolph, August 1822, Box 7, Folder 3, LVA; and Executive Papers, Joseph Johnson, March–May 1854, Box 424, Folder March 1854, LVA. On youth and good character, see, for example, Executive Papers, James Patton Preston, December 1819, Box 9, Folder 4, LVA; Auditor of Public Accounts, Condemned Blacks Executed or Transported, Records—Condemned Slaves, Court Orders, and Valuations, 1846–1857, Misc. Reel 2554, LVA; and Executive Papers, Joseph Johnson, August–September 1854, Box 422, Folder September 1854, LVA.

101. Executive Papers, Joseph Johnson, March–May 1855, Box 426, Folder April 1855, LVA.

102. Executive Papers, John Floyd, February 1833, Box 9, Folder 4, LVA; Auditor of Public Accounts, Condemned Blacks Executed or Transported, Records—Condemned Slaves, Court Orders, and Valuations, 1846–1857, Misc. Reel 2554, Frame 516, LVA. In 1818, a Buckingham County court recommended the bondwoman Polly "to the mercy of the Executive on account of her youth, and former good character." Auditor of Public Accounts, Condemned Blacks Executed or Transported Records—Condemned Slaves, Court Orders, and Valuations, 1810–1822, Misc. Reel 2551, Frame 731, LVA. See also Executive Papers, Joseph Johnson, March–May 1855, Box 426, Folder April 1855, LVA.

103. H. C. Bruce, *Twenty-Nine Years a Slave, Twenty-Nine Years a Free Man: Recollections of H. C. Bruce* (York, Pa.: Anstadt & Sons, 1895), 75; Elizabeth Lyle Saxon, *A Southern Woman's War Time Reminiscences* (Memphis: Pilcher Printing Co., 1905), 30–31.

104. Executive Papers, Joseph Johnson, August–September 1854, Box 422, Folder September 1854, LVA; Auditor of Public Accounts, Condemned Blacks Executed or Transported, Records—Condemned Slaves, Court Orders, and Valuations, 1823–1832, Misc. Reel 2552, Frame 741, LVA; Executive Papers, Henry A. Wise, Misc. Reel 4205, Box 10, Folder 3, Frame 232, LVA; Executive Papers, Henry A. Wise, Misc. Reel 4205, Box 10, Folder 3, Frame 235, LVA; Executive Papers, John Tyler, June 1826, Box 2, Folder 1, LVA. Unlike black women, white women found guilty of infanticide commonly received full gubernatorial pardons. For sample cases in North Carolina, see those of Sally Barneycastle of Mecklenburg County in 1832 and Catharine Bastian of Cabarrus County in 1833, respectively, in Governor's Papers, Gov. Montfort Stokes, vol. 64, p. 118, NCDAH; and Governor's Papers, Gov. David L. Swain, vol. 66, p. 47, NCDAH.

EPILOGUE

1. George P. Rawick, ed., *The American Slave: A Composite Autobiography*, vol. 6 Indiana (Westport, Conn.: Greenwood Publishing Company, 1972), 3–4.

2. Rawick, *American Slave*, vol. 6 Indiana, 4; idem, *American Slave*, vol. 12, pt. 1, 313.

3. David Wilson, *Inventing Black-on-Black Violence: Discourse, Space, and Representation* (Syracuse: Syracuse University Press, 2005), x, 6, 5, 51, 58, 70–72, 77–78.

4. Wilson, *Inventing Black-on-Black Violence*, 79–80, 104 (first quotation), xi (second quotation), 4 (third and fourth quotations), 99, 103–104, 127 (fifth quotation), 126 (sixth quotation). Following Wilson's example, I place quotation marks around the term "black-on-black violence"

"to connote its socially constructed nature." See David Wilson, "Colouring the City: 'Black-on-Black Violence' and Liberal Discourse," *Journal of Economic & Social Geography* 92, no. 3 (2001): 275n1. On the overuse of the phrase "black-on-black" perpetuating negative stereotypes, see Robert L. Bing, "Politicizing Black-on-Black Crime: A Critique of Terminological Preference," in *Black on Black Crime: Facing Facts—Challenging Fictions,* ed. P. Ray Kedia (Bristol, Ind.: Wyndham Hall Press, 1994), 245.

5. Jack E. White, "When Brother Kills Brother," *Time,* September 16, 1985, 32; James W. Clarke, *The Lineaments of Wrath: Race, Violent Crime, and American Culture* (New Brunswick, N.J.: Transaction Publishers, 1998), 1; James W. Clarke, "Black-on-Black Violence," *Society* 33 (July–August 1996): 46; Renford Reese, *American Paradox: Young Black Men* (Durham, N.C.: Carolina Academic Press, 2004), 167; "At hate crimes rally, some will decry black-on-black violence," *USA Today,* November 16, 2007; Elizabeth Gleick, "Stand and Deliver: The Reverend Jesse Jackson targets schools in his new crusade to combat the violence that blacks are doing to themselves," *People,* April 11, 1994, 100. Jackson convened a three-day conference in Washington, D.C., in January 1994 to discuss "black-on-black violence."

6. Clarke, "Black-on-Black Violence," 46–47.

7. Barry A. Crouch, "A Spirit of Lawlessness: White Violence; Texas Blacks, 1865–1868," *Journal of Social History* 18 (Winter 1984): 219; Gilles Vandal, "Black Violence in Post–Civil War Louisiana," *Journal of Interdisciplinary History* 25 (Summer 1994): 53. An older, smaller data set appears in Gilles Vandal, "'Bloody Caddo': White Violence against Blacks in a Louisiana Parish, 1865–1876," *Journal of Social History* 25 (Winter 1991): 374–388.

8. Edward L. Ayers, *Vengeance and Justice: Crime and Punishment in the 19th-Century American South* (New York: Oxford University Press, 1984), 231 (first quotation), 233 (third and fourth quotations); Vandal, "Black Violence," 47, 48 (second quotation), 49, 54; Dylan C. Penningroth, *Claims of Kinfolk: African American Property and Community in the Nineteenth-Century South* (Chapel Hill: University of North Carolina Press, 2003), 122; Crouch, "Spirit of Lawlessness," 220.

9. Vandal, "Black Violence," 59, 61–62, 60 (first quotation), 60–61 (second quotation), 59 (third quotation), 62 (fourth quotation); Penningroth, *Claims of Kinfolk,* 123; Laura F. Edwards, "Sexual Violence, Gender, Reconstruction, and the Extension of Patriarchy in Granville County, North Carolina," *North Carolina Historical Review* 68 (July 1991): 237–260; Christopher Morris, "Within the Slave Cabin: Violence in Mississippi Slave Families," in *Over the Threshold: Intimate Violence in Early America,* ed. Christine Daniels and Michael V. Kennedy (New York: Routledge, 1999), 280; Ayers, *Vengeance and Justice,* 234–235; Claude Brown, *Manchild in the Promised Land* (New York: Macmillan, 1965), 253 (fifth quotation), 255 (sixth and seventh quotations).

10. Marvin E. Wolfgang, *Patterns in Criminal Homicide* (1958; reprint, Montclair, N.J.: Patterson Smith, 1975), 329.

11. Marvin E. Wolfgang and Franco Ferracuti, *The Subculture of Violence: Towards an Integrated Theory in Criminology* (New York: Tavistock, 1967), 153 (first three quotations), 152 (fourth quotation), 154 (fifth quotation).

12. Clarke, "Black-on-Black Violence," 47–48; Ayers, *Vengeance and Justice,* 231 (quotation), 234–235; Clarke, *Lineaments of Wrath,* 4. See also Eugene D. Genovese, *Roll, Jordan, Roll: The World the Slaves Made* (1974; reprint, New York; Vintage, 1976), 632; and Roger Lane, *Murder in America: A History* (Columbus: Ohio State University Press, 1997), 351.

13. Clarke, *Lineaments of Wrath*, 4, 31 (first quotation), 293 (second quotation).

14. Wolfgang and Ferracuti, *Subculture of Violence*, 271; Eric H. Monkkonen, *Murder in New York City* (Berkeley: University of California Press, 2001), 134; Clarke, "Black-on-Black Violence," 47; Stephen A. West, "From Yeoman to Redneck in Upstate South Carolina, 1850–1915" (Ph.D. diss., Columbia University, 1998), 24–25 (quotation), 25n23.

15. Robert J. Sampson and Lydia Bean, "Cultural Mechanisms and Killing Fields: A Revised Theory of Community-Level Racial Inequality," in *The Many Colors of Crime: Inequalities of Race, Ethnicity, and Crime in America*, ed. Ruth D. Peterson, Lauren J. Krivo, and John Hagan (New York: New York University Press, 2006), 23; C. Eric Lincoln, *Coming through the Fire: Surviving Race and Place in America* (Durham: Duke University Press, 1996), 126; Elijah Anderson, *Code of the Street: Decency, Violence, and the Moral Life of the Inner City* (New York: Norton, 1999), 32–33; Roger D. Turner, "Black on Black Violence: Moving Towards Realistic Explanations and Solutions," in *Black on Black Crime: Facing Facts—Challenging Fictions*, ed. P. Ray Kedia (Bristol, Ind.: Wyndham Hall Press, 1994), 4; Robert J. Sampson and William Julius Wilson, "Toward a Theory of Race, Crime, and Urban Inequality," in *Crime and Inequality*, ed. John Hagan and Ruth D. Peterson (Stanford: Stanford University Press, 1995), 41.

16. Aldore Collier, "What's Behind the Black-on-Black Violence at Movie Theaters," *Ebony* 46 (October 1991): 98, 100, 102; Jack E. White, "Endangered Species," *Time*, March 1, 1999, 40; Clarke, *Lineaments of Wrath*, 3; Claire Potter, review of *The Lineaments of Wrath: Race, Violent Crime, and American Culture*, by James W. Clarke, *Journal of American History* 86 (June 1999): 325; Paul Stretesky, review of *The Lineaments of Wrath: Race, Violent Crime, and American Culture*, by James W. Clarke, *American Political Science Review* 93 (December 1999): 971; Turner, "Black on Black Violence," 4, 11; Amos N. Wilson, *Black-on-Black Violence: The Psychodynamics of Black Self-Annihilation in Service of White Domination* (New York: Afrikan World Infosystems, 1990), xii–xiv; Lincoln, *Coming through the Fire*, 127, 153.

Some scholars have attempted to unite the cultural and structural explanations for violence. Drawing upon social disorganization theory, for example, Robert J. Sampson and William Julius Wilson examine the interplay between structural forces and local, community contexts that can give rise to cultures valuing violence. See Sampson and Wilson, "Toward a Theory of Race, Crime, and Urban Inequality," 37–54; and Sampson and Bean, "Cultural Mechanisms and Killing Fields," 8–36.

17. Turner, "Black on Black Violence," 19. See also Lincoln, *Coming through the Fire*, 151, who argued that "to accept the grotesquely inflated ratio of racial violence implied in our official reckoning is to ignore the evidence of history, which after all may be the only reliable index we have."

18. John Dollard, *Caste and Class in a Southern Town*, 3rd ed. (Garden City, N.Y.: Doubleday, 1957), 269–272. Dollard's interpretation has been invoked in Sheldon Hackney, "Southern Violence," *American Historical Review* 74 (February 1969): 921–922; Edward E. Baptist, *Creating an Old South: Middle Florida's Plantation Frontier Before the Civil War* (Chapel Hill: University of North Carolina Press, 2002), 203; Glenn M. McNair, "Justice Bound: Aframericans, Crime, and Criminal Justice in Georgia, 1751–1865" (Ph.D. diss., Emory University, 2001), 119.

19. Vandal, "Black Violence," 45, 63.

BIBLIOGRAPHY

PRIMARY SOURCES
Manuscripts and Archival Collections
Library of Virginia, Richmond

Auditor of Public Accounts, Condemned Blacks Executed or Transported, Records—
 Condemned Slaves, Court Orders, and Valuations
Church Records, Baptist
 Antioch, Ash Camp (Keysville), Buffalo, Cascade Primitive, Lower Banister, Mossingford, Mt. Tirzah, Mount Vernon, Shiloh
Court Records
 Accomack County, Order Books
 Albemarle County, Court Records, Commonwealth Causes
 Albemarle County, Minute Books
 Albemarle County, Order Books
 Amelia County, Order Book 1A (Minutes)
 Amherst County, Order Books
 Brunswick County, Order Books
 Caroline County, Order Books
 Charlotte County, Order Books
 Chesterfield County, Order Books
 Culpeper County, Minute Books
 Cumberland County, Order Books
 Elizabeth City County, Order Books
 Essex County, Order Books
 Fauquier County, Minute Books
 Halifax County, Minutes
 Halifax County, Pleas (Court Orders)
 Harrison County, Minute Books
 Henrico County, Minute Books
 Henrico County, Order Books
 King George County, Order Books
 Lancaster County, Orders
 Loudoun County, Minute Books
 Louisa County, Minute Books
 Lunenburg County, Order Books
 Madison County, Order Books

BIBLIOGRAPHY

    Mecklenburg County, Order Books
    Middlesex County, Order Books
    Middlesex County, Orders
    Nelson County, County Court Minute Books
    Norfolk City, Order Books
    Norfolk County, Minute Books
    Orange County, Order Book (Minutes)
    Pittsylvania County, Court Records
    Powhatan County, Order Books
    Prince Edward County, County Court Orders
    Richmond City, Hustings Court Minutes
    Rockbridge County, Minute Books
    Russell County, Law Order Books
    Spotsylvania County, Minute Books
    Spotsylvania County, Minutes
    Spotsylvania County, Order Books
    Westmoreland County, Orders
    York County, Order Books
Executive Papers
    Henry Lee, Robert Brooke, James Monroe, John Tyler, James Barbour, Wilson Cary Nicholas, James Patton Preston, Thomas Mann Randolph, James Pleasants, William B. Giles, John Floyd, Littleton W. Tazewell, Wyndham Robertson, David Campbell, Thomas Walker Gilmer, John M. Gregory, James McDowell, William Smith, John Buchanan Floyd, Joseph Johnson, Henry A. Wise, John Letcher
Legislative Petitions, Virginia General Assembly
Records of Eastern State Hospital, Register of Patients
Roanoke District Association (Baptist), Minute Book

North Carolina Department of Archives and History, Raleigh

Bertie County, Criminal Papers
Chowan County, Minute Docket, Superior Court
Chowan County, Slave Records, Criminal Actions Concerning Slaves
Davidson County, County Court Minutes
Davidson County, Records of Slaves and Free Persons of Color
Governor's Letter Book, Edward B. Dudley
Governor's Papers
    Edward B. Dudley, Montfort Stokes, David L. Swain
Granville County, Criminal Actions Concerning Slaves and Free Persons of Color
Haywood County, Records of Slaves and Free Persons of Color

BIBLIOGRAPHY

Orange County, Minutes, Superior Court
Orange County, Slave Records
Robeson County, Records Concerning Slaves and Free Persons of Color

Southern Historical Collection, Wilson Library, University of North Carolina at Chapel Hill

John Houston Bills Diary
David Gavin Diary
John Berkley Grimball Diary
Francis Terry Leak Diary
Neal Family Papers

South Carolina Department of Archives and History, Columbia

Courts of Magistrates and Freeholders, Trial Papers
    Anderson, Clarendon, Fairfield, Kershaw, Laurens, Pendleton, Pickens, Spartanburg Districts
Index, Court of General Sessions Records
    Laurens, Spartanburg Districts
Philadelphia Baptist Church, Minutes

South Caroliniana Library, University of South Carolina, Columbia

Church Records, Baptist
    Abner Creek, Beaverdam Primitive, Bethabara, Brushy Creek, Chestnut Ridge, Clear Springs, Flint Hill, Huntsville, Milford, Padgett's Creek, Poplar Springs, Rabun Creek, Union, Upper Fairforest, Warrior Creek

Georgia Archives, Morrow

Baldwin County, Inferior Court Minutes, Trial of Slaves
Chatham County, Inferior Court Trial Docket
Church Records, Baptist
    Beaverdam, Bethel, Clarke's Station, County Line Primitive, Crooked Creek Primitive, Darien, Fishing Creek, Goshen, Greenwood, Hephzibah, Horeb, Island Creek, Middle Ground, Mount Zion, Mountain Springs Primitive, New Hope, Philips Mill, Powelton, Rehoboth, Salem (Jones), Salem (Lincoln), Sardis, Washington First
Hancock County, Inferior Court Minutes, County Purposes & Lunacy
Jones County, Inferior Court Minutes

BIBLIOGRAPHY

Lincoln County, Inferior Court, Docket of Slaves Indicted for Capital Crimes
Minutes of the Georgia Baptist Association, 1803–1866
Putnam County, Inferior Court Records, Record of the Proceeds of the Court for Trial of Slaves

Mississippi Department of Archives and History, Jackson

Green, a slave v. the State of Mississippi (1849)
Laura, a slave v. the State of Mississippi (1852)
Jordan, a slave v. the State of Mississippi (1856)
Prince, a slave v. State of Mississippi (1856)
Sam, a slave v. the State of Mississippi (1857)
Aaron, a slave v. the State of Mississippi (1859)
Simon, a slave v. the State of Mississippi (1859)
The State of Mississippi v. York, a slave (1861)

Adams County Courthouse Collection, Historic Natchez Foundation, Natchez, Miss.

Elizabeth a Negro Woman v. Maria Williams (1800)
Mississippi Territory v. Peter a slave (1812)
Mississippi Territory v. Negro man Milo (1814)
State v. John White (1818)
George Howell v. William Cooper (1824)
Isaac Franklin v. William Grissam (1825)
John A. Miller v. Frederick Stanton (1831)
Theodore D. Elliott v. John Robson (1832)
State v. Anthony, a slave (1834)
State v. Lewis, a slave (1834)
State v. Ellis, a slave (1840)
State v. George, a slave (1840)
State v. Daniel G. Smith (1854)
State v. Henry, a slave, and West, a slave (1855)
State v. Little Jordan, a slave (1855)
State v. Horace, a slave (1860)
State v. John Harding (1866)

New Orleans Public Library

First District Court of New Orleans Records

BIBLIOGRAPHY

Louisiana State Archives, Baton Rouge

State Auditor's Account Books

Southern Baptist Historical Library and Archives, Nashville, Tenn.

Bethel Baptist Church, Church Records
First Baptist Church (Honey Grove, Tex.), Church Records
First Baptist Church (Port Lavaca, Tex.), Minutes
Lonesome Dove Baptist Church, Church Records
Mud Creek Primitive Baptist Church, Church Records
Salem Baptist Church, Church Records
Shiloh Church, Church Records

Center for American History, University of Texas, Austin

Natchez Trace Slaves and Slavery Collection

Carroll Library, Baylor University, Waco, Tex.

Black Jack Springs Baptist Church, Church Membership Records and Minutes
Liberty Baptist Church, Church Membership Records and Minutes

Herzstein Library, San Jacinto Museum of History, LaPorte, Tex.

Mount Pleasant Regular United Baptist Church of Christ, Records
Pilgrim Predestinarian Regular Baptist Church, Church Book, Walston Family Papers

Newton Gresham Library, Sam Houston State University, Huntsville, Tex.

First Baptist Church (Huntsville), Record and Minutes

Rosenberg Library, Galveston, Tex.

First Baptist Church (Galveston), Minutes

Southwestern Baptist Theological Seminary, Fort Worth, Tex.

Concord Baptist Church, Minutes
First Baptist Church (Houston), Minutes

BIBLIOGRAPHY

Published Church Records

Conference Minutes of the Salem Baptist Church, Larissa, Cherokee County, Texas, 1849–1899. 1989.

First Book of Church Minutes, 1838–1872: Old North Baptist Church, Nacogdoches, Texas. Nacogdoches, Tex.: Old North Baptist Church, 1987.

Hill, J. Edd. *Goshen Baptist Church, Lincoln County, Georgia, Records, 1802–1869 and Later.* Danielsville, Ga.: Heritage Papers, 1989.

Vick, Di Ann. *Minutes, 1858–1890, First Baptist Church, Hemphill, Texas.* Hemphill, Tex.: The Church, 1982.

State Supreme Court Cases

Catterall, Helen Tunnicliff, ed. *Judicial Cases Concerning American Slavery and the Negro.* 5 vols. Washington, D.C.: Carnegie Institution of Washington, 1926–1937.

Alabama

State v. Peter (1827)
Smith (a slave) v. State (1846)
Baalam, a slave v. State (1850)
Seaborn and Jim v. State (1852)
Frank, et al. (slaves) v. State (1855)
Ben (a slave) v. State (1861)
Crockett (a slave) v. State (1862)
William (a slave) v. State (1865)

Delaware

State v. Charles Loadnum (1798)
State v. William Dillahunt, negro (1840)
State v. Negro Bill Jefferson, a slave (1842)

Georgia

Allen, a slave v. the State (1851)
William (a slave) v. the State (1855)
John, a slave v. State (1862)
Henry, a slave, v. the State (1863)
William, a slave v. the State (1864)

BIBLIOGRAPHY

Kentucky

Ready v. the Commonwealth (1839)

Louisiana

Jourdan v. Patton (1818)
Steel v. Cazeaux (1820)
Gaillardet v. Demaries (1841)
Hynson v. Meuillon (1847)
State v. Isaac (1848)
Arnoult v. Deschapelles (1849)
State v. Dick (1849)
State v. Jerry (1849)
State v. slave Jack (1859)
Maille v. Blas (1860)

Mississippi

Leggett v. Simmons (1846)
Lewis, a slave v. State (1847)
John (a slave) v. State (1852)
Jordan, a slave v. State (1856)
Ned and Taylor (slaves) v. State (1857)
Simon (a slave) v. State (1858)
George (a slave) v. State (1859)
Simon, a slave v. State (1859)

Missouri

Jane (a slave) v. State (1831)
Ewing v. Thompson (1850)

North Carolina

State v. Charity, a slave (1830)
State v. Moses, a slave (1830)
State v. Samuel, a slave (1836)
State v. John, a slave (1848)
State v. Caesar, a slave (1849)
State v. Frank (a slave) (1858)

BIBLIOGRAPHY

Pennsylvania

Respublica v. Mulatto Bob (1795)

Tennessee

Wright v. Weatherly (1835)
Jim, a slave, v. the State (1843)
Jim, a slave, v. the State (1844)
Nelson v. the State (1852)
John (a slave) v. the State (1858)

Texas

Calvin, a slave v. State (1860)
Jack, a slave v. State (1861)
Maria (a freedwoman) v. State (1866)
Timmins v. Lacy (1867)

Virginia

Souther v. Commonwealth (1851)

Laws, Legal Reports, Legislative Journals, and Petitions

Acts Passed by the Fifth Legislature of the State of Louisiana, at Its First Session, Held and Begun in the City of Baton Rouge, on the 16th of January, 1860. Baton Rouge: J. M. Taylor, 1860.

Acts Passed at the First Session of the Seventeenth Legislature of the State of Louisiana, Began and Held in the City of New Orleans, on the 6th Day of January 1845. New Orleans: Magne & Weisse, 1845.

Acts Passed at the First Session of the Sixteenth Legislature of the State of Louisiana, Began and Held in the City of New Orleans, on the 2d Day of January, 1843. New Orleans: Alexander C. Bullitt, 1843.

Acts Passed by the Second Legislature of the State of Louisiana, at Its First Session, Held and Begun in the Town of Baton Rouge, on the 16th January, 1854. New Orleans: Emile La Sere, 1854.

Acts Passed at the Second Session of the Sixteenth Legislature of the State of Louisiana, Begun and Held in the City of New Orleans, on the 1st Day of January, 1844. New Orleans: Alexander C. Bullitt, 1844.

BIBLIOGRAPHY

Annual Report of the Board of Directors of the Louisiana Penitentiary, to the Governor of the State of Louisiana. January, 1856. New Orleans: John Claiborne, 1856.

Condy, Thomas D. *A Digest of the Laws of the United States & the State of South-Carolina, Now of Force, Relating to the Militia; with an Appendix, Containing the Patrol Laws; the Laws for the Government of Slaves and Free Persons of Colour; the Decisions of the Constitutional Court and Court of Appeals of South-Carolina Thereon; and an Abstract from the Rules and Regulations of the United States' Army, &c.* Charleston: A. E. Miller, 1830.

Goodell, William. *The American Slave Code in Theory and Practice: Its Distinctive Features Shown by Its Statutes, Judicial Decisions, and Illustrative Facts.* 1853. Reprint. New York: Negro Universities Press, 1968.

Gould, Josiah. *Digest of the Statutes of Arkansas: Embracing All Laws of a General and Permanent Character in Force at the Close of the Session of the General Assembly of 1856: Together with Notes of the Decisions of the Supreme Court upon the Statutes, and an Appendix Containing Forms for Justices of the Peace.* Little Rock: Johnson & Yerkes, 1858.

Hening, William Waller. *The Statutes at Large; Being a Collection of All the Laws of Virginia from the First Session of the Legislature, in the Year 1619.* Vol. 8. Richmond: J. & G. Cochran, 1821.

Martin, Francois-Xavier. *Martin's Reports of Cases Argued and Determined in the Supreme Court of the State of Louisiana.* Vol. 4. New Orleans: J. B. Steel, 1853.

McCord, David J. *The Statutes at Large of South Carolina; Edited, Under Authority of the Legislature.* Vol. 6. Columbia: A. S. Johnston, 1839.

Message of Robert C. Wickliffe, Governor of the State of Louisiana, Together with an Appendix, Containing the Report of the Penitentiary Agents for the Year 1856. Baton Rouge: Office of the Daily Advocate, 1857.

Minority Report of the Committee on the Penitentiary. Baton Rouge: Winfree & Bryan, 1852.

Official Journal of the Proceedings of the House of Representatives of the State of Louisiana. Second Session—Sixteenth Legislature January 1, 1844. New Orleans: n.p., 1844.

O'Neall, John Belton. *The Negro Law of South Carolina.* Columbia: John G. Bowman, 1848.

Race and Slavery Petitions Project. Digital Library on American Slavery. University of North Carolina at Greensboro. https://library.uncg.edu/slavery/.

Report of the Board of Directors of the Louisiana Penitentiary. New Orleans: Emile La Sere, 1854.

Report of the Joint Committee on the Penitentiary. New Orleans: Emile La Sere, 1854.

Report on the Penitentiary, by a Joint Committee of the Senate and House of Representatives. J. Bernard, Chairman. No publication information.

Tate, Joseph. *Digest of the Laws of Virginia, which are of a Permanent Character and General Operation; Illustrated by Judicial Decisions: to which is Added, an Index of the Names of the Cases in the Virginia Reporters.* 2nd ed. Richmond: Smith and Palmer, 1841.

Slave Narratives

Ball, Charles. *Fifty Years in Chains; or, The Life of An American Slave.* New York: H. Dayton, 1859.

Bibb, Henry. *Narrative of the Life and Adventures of Henry Bibb, an American Slave, Written by Himself.* New York: The Author, 1849.

Blight, David W., ed. *Narrative of the Life of Frederick Douglass, an American Slave, Written by Himself.* New York: Bedford Books of St. Martin's Press, 1993.

Brown, W. Wells. *Three Years in Europe; or Places I Have Seen and People I Have Met.* Edinburgh: Oliver and Boyd, 1852.

Bruce, H. C. *Twenty-Nine Years a Slave, Twenty-Nine Years a Free Man: Recollections of H. C. Bruce.* York, Pa.: Anstadt & Sons, 1895.

Chamerovzow, L. A., ed. *Slave Life in Georgia: A Narrative of the Life, Sufferings, and Escape of John Brown, a Fugitive Slave, Now in England.* London: n.p., 1855.

Clarke, Lewis. "Leaves from a Slave's Journal of Life." *The Anti-Slavery Standard.* October 20, 1842.

———. *Narrative of the Sufferings of Lewis Clarke, During a Captivity of More Than Twenty-Five Years, Among the Algerines of Kentucky, One of the So-Called Christian States of North America. Dictated by Himself.* Boston: David H. Ela, 1845.

Douglass, Frederick. *My Bondage and My Freedom.* New York: Miller, Orton & Mulligan, 1855.

Eakin, Sue. *Solomon Northup's* Twelve Years a Slave *and Plantation Life in the Antebellum South.* Lafayette: Center for Louisiana Studies, University of Louisiana at Lafayette, 2007.

Ernest, John, ed. *Narrative of the Life of Henry Box Brown, Written by Himself.* Chapel Hill: University of North Carolina Press, 2008.

Grimes, William. *Life of William Grimes, the Runaway Slave, Brought Down to the Present Time. Written by Himself.* New Haven, Conn.: The Author, 1855.

Jacobs, Harriet A. *Incidents in the Life of a Slave Girl Written by Herself.* Edited by Jean Fagan Yellin. Cambridge: Harvard University Press, 2000.

Mellon, James, ed. *Bullwhip Days: The Slaves Remember.* New York: Weidenfeld & Nicolson, 1988.

Narratives of the Sufferings of Lewis and Milton Clarke, Sons of a Soldier of the Revolution, during a Captivity of More Than Twenty Years among the Slaveholders of Kentucky, One of the So Called Christian States of North America. Dictated by Themselves. Boston: Bela Marsh, 1846.

BIBLIOGRAPHY

Paine, Lewis W. *Six Years in a Georgia Prison: Narrative of Lewis W. Paine*. Boston: Bela Marsh, 1852.

Perdue, Charles L., Jr., Thomas E. Barden, and Robert K. Phillips, eds. *Weevils in the Wheat: Interviews with Virginia Ex-Slaves*. Charlottesville: University Press of Virginia, 1976.

Rawick, George P., ed. *The American Slave: A Composite Autobiography*. 19 vols. Westport, Conn.: Greenwood Publishing Company, 1972.

——. *The American Slave: A Composite Autobiography, Supplement, Series 1*. 12 vols. Westport, Conn.: Greenwood Press, 1977.

——. *The American Slave: A Composite Autobiography, Supplement, Series 2*. 10 vols. Westport, Conn.: Greenwood Press, 1979.

Slavery in the United States: A Narrative of the Life and Adventures of Charles Ball. New York: John S. Taylor, 1837.

Smith, Harry. *Fifty Years of Slavery in the United States of America*. Grand Rapids: West Michigan Printing Co., 1891.

Smith, James L. *Autobiography of James L. Smith, Including, Also, Reminiscences of Slave Life, Recollections of the War, Education of Freedmen, Causes of the Exodus, Etc*. Norwich, Conn.: Press of the Bulletin Company, 1881.

Sollors, Werner, ed. *The Interesting Narrative of the Life of Olaudah Equiano, or Gustavus Vassa, the African, Written by Himself*. New York: Norton, 2001.

Stroyer, Jacob. *Sketches of My Life in the South. Part I*. Salem, Mass.: Salem Press, 1879.

Yetman, Norman R., ed. *Life under the "Peculiar Institution": Selections from the Slave Narrative Collection*. New York: Holt, Rinehart and Winston Inc., 1970.

Travelers' Accounts

Bremer, Fredrika. *The Homes of the New World; Impressions of America*. Vol. 2. Translated by Mary Howitt. 1853. Reprint. New York: Negro Universities Press, 1968.

Buckingham, J. S. *The Slave States of America*. Vol. 2. 1842. Reprint. New York: Negro Universities Press, 1968.

Falconbridge, Alexander. *An Account of the Slave Trade on the Coast of Africa*. London: J. Phillips, 1788.

Kemble, Frances Anne. *Journal of a Residence on a Georgian Plantation in 1838–1839*. Edited by John A. Scott. New York: Alfred A. Knopf, 1961.

Lyell, Charles. *Second Visit to North America*. Vol. 1. 3rd ed. London: John Murray, 1855.

——. *A Second Visit to the United States of North America*. Vol. 1. New York: Harper & Brothers, 1849.

Marcus [Joseph J. Blunt]. *An Examination of the Expediency and Constitutionality of Prohibiting Slavery in the State of Missouri*. New York: C. Wiley, 1819.

Martineau, Harriet. *Society in America*. Vol. 2. London: Saunders and Otley, 1837. Reprint. New York: AMS Press, 1966.

BIBLIOGRAPHY

Olmsted, Frederick Law. *Journey in the Seaboard Slave States, with Remarks on Their Economy.* New York: Dix & Edwards, 1856.

Pearson, Elizabeth Ware, ed. *Letters from Port Royal, 1862–1868.* New York: Arno Press and the New York Times, 1969.

Pulszky, Francis, and Theresa Pulszky. *White, Red, Black: Sketches of American Society in the United States During the Visit of Their Guests.* Vol. 2. New York: Redfield, 1853.

Royall, Anne Newport. *Letters from Alabama, 1817–1822.* Edited by Lucille Griffith. Tuscaloosa: University of Alabama Press, 1969.

Russell, William Howard. *My Diary North and South.* Edited by Fletcher Pratt. New York: Harper & Brothers, 1954.

Thomson, William. *A Tradesman's Travels in the United States and Canada, in the Years 1840, 41, & 42.* Edinburgh: Oliver & Boyd, 1842.

von Briesen, Martha, ed. *The Letters of Elijah Fletcher.* Charlottesville: University Press of Virginia, 1965.

Diaries, Journals, Essays, and Books

Anderson, John Q., ed. *Brokenburn: The Journal of Kate Stone, 1861–1868.* Baton Rouge: Louisiana State University Press, 1972.

Betts, Edwin Morris, ed. *Thomas Jefferson's Farm Book with Commentary and Relevant Extracts from Other Writings.* Princeton: Princeton University Press, 1953.

Breeden, James O., ed. *Advice among Masters: The Ideal in Slave Management in the Old South.* Westport, Conn.: Greenwood Press, 1980.

Cartwright, S. A. "Slavery in the Light of Ethnology." In *Cotton is King, and Pro-Slavery Arguments Comprising the Writings of Hammond, Harper, Christy, Stringfellow, Hodge, Bledsoe, and Cartwright, on This Important Subject,* edited by E. N. Elliott, 690–728. 1860. Reprint. New York: Negro Universities Press, 1969.

Cobb, Thomas R. R. *An Inquiry into the Law of Negro Slavery in the United States of America. To Which is Prefixed, an Historical Sketch of Slavery.* Vol. 1. Savannah: W. Thorne Williams, 1858.

Collins, Robert. *Essay on the Treatment and Management of Slaves. Written for the Seventh Annual Fair of the Southern Central Agricultural Society.* 2nd ed. Boston: Eastburn's Press, 1853.

Easterby, J. H., ed. *The South Carolina Rice Plantation as Revealed in the Papers of Robert F. W. Allston.* Chicago: University of Chicago Press, 1945.

Farish, Hunter Dickinson, ed. *Journal and Letters of Philip Vickers Fithian, 1773–1774: A Plantation Tutor of the Old Dominion.* Charlottesville, Va.: Dominion Books, 1957.

Faust, Drew Gilpin, ed. *The Ideology of Slavery: Proslavery Thought in the Antebellum South, 1830–1860.* Baton Rouge: Louisiana State University Press, 1981.

Hundley, D. R. *Social Relations in Our Southern States*. New York: Henry B. Price, 1860. Reprint. New York: Arno Press, 1973.

Jones, Charles C. *The Religious Instruction of the Negroes. In the United States*. Savannah: Thomas Purse, 1842.

Leland, John, and L.F. Greene. *The Writings of the Late Elder John Leland: Including Some Events in His Life*. New York: G. W. Wood, 1845.

Lerner, Gerda, ed. *Black Women in White America: A Documentary History*. New York: Pantheon, 1972.

Moore, John Hammond, ed. *A Plantation Mistress on the Eve of the Civil War: The Diary of Keziah Goodwyn Hopkins Brevard, 1860–1861*. Columbia: University of South Carolina Press, 1993.

Racine, Philip N., ed. *Piedmont Farmer: The Journals of David Golightly Harris, 1855–1870*. Knoxville: University of Tennessee Press, 1990.

Saxon, Elizabeth Lyle. *A Southern Woman's War Time Reminiscences*. Memphis: Pilcher Printing Co., 1905.

Woodward, C. Vann, ed. *Mary Chesnut's Civil War*. New Haven: Yale University Press, 1981.

Sermons and Abolitionist Literature

Beecher, Charles. *The God of the Bible Against Slavery*. New York: American Anti-Slavery Society, 1855.

Garnet, Henry Highland. "An Address to the Slaves of the United States." 1843. http://www.blackpast.org/.

Hosmer, William. *Slavery and the Church*. Auburn: William J. Moses, 1853. Reprint. Freeport, N.Y.: Books for Libraries Press, 1970.

Marsh, Rev. William H. *God's Law Supreme: A Sermon, Aiming to Point Out the Duty of a Christian People in Relation to the Fugitive Slave Law: Delivered at Village Corners, Woodstock, Conn., on the Day of the Annual Thanksgiving, Nov. 28, 1850; and Subsequently Repeated, by Request, in Southbridge, Mass*. Worcester, Mass.: Henry J. Howland, n.d.

Mather, Cotton. *Tremenda. The Dreadful Sound with Which the Wicked Are to Be Thunderstruck. In a Sermon Delivered Unto a Great Assembly, in Which Was Present, a Miserable African, Just Going to Be Executed for a Most Inhumane and Uncommon Murder. At Boston, May 25th, 1721. To Which is Added, a Conference Between a Minister and the Prisoner, on the Day Before His Execution*. Boston: B. Green, 1721.

Walker, David. *Walker's Appeal, in Four Articles; Together with a Preamble, to the Coloured Citizens of the World, But in Particular, and Very Expressly, to Those of the United States of America, Written in Boston, State of Massachusetts, September 28, 1829*. 3rd ed. Boston: David Walker, 1830.

BIBLIOGRAPHY

Young, Joshua. *God Greater Than Man: A Sermon Preached June 11th, After the Rendition of Anthony Burns.* Burlington: Samuel B. Nichols, 1854.

Newspapers

Baton Rouge Gazette
Daily Gazette & Comet (Baton Rouge)
The Liberator (Boston)
North Carolina Watchman (Salisbury)
The North Carolinian (Fayetteville)
Raleigh Minerva
Raleigh Star, and North Carolina Gazette
The Star, and North-Carolina State Gazette (Raleigh)

Census Records

Compendium of the Enumeration of the Inhabitants and Statistics of the United States. Washington: T. Allen, 1841.

DeBow, J. D. B. *The Seventh Census of the United States: 1850.* Washington: R. Armstrong, 1853.

Historical Census Browser. University of Virginia. Geospatial and Statistical Data Center. 2004. http://mapserver.lib.virginia.edu/.

Kennedy, Joseph C. G. *Agriculture of the United States in 1860; Compiled from the Original Returns of the Eighth Census, Under the Direction of the Secretary of the Interior.* Vol. 2 Agriculture. Washington: Government Printing Office, 1864.

U.S. Bureau of the Census. Population Schedule. Eighth Census. 1860.

———. Slave Schedule. Seventh Census. 1850.

SECONDARY SOURCES

Abrahams, Roger D. *Singing the Master: The Emergence of African American Culture in the Plantation South.* New York: Penguin, 1993.

Abruzzo, Margaret. *Polemical Pain: Slavery, Cruelty, and the Rise of Humanitarianism.* Baltimore: Johns Hopkins University Press, 2011.

Anderson, Elijah. *Code of the Street: Decency, Violence, and the Moral Life of the Inner City.* New York: Norton, 1999.

"At hate crimes rally, some will decry black-on-black violence." *USA Today,* November 16, 2007.

Ayers, Edward L. *Vengeance and Justice: Crime and Punishment in the 19th-Century American South.* New York: Oxford University Press, 1984.

BIBLIOGRAPHY

Baptist, Edward E. "The Absent Subject: African American Masculinity and Forced Migration to the Antebellum Plantation Frontier." In *Southern Manhood: Perspectives on Masculinity in the Old South,* edited by Craig Thompson Friend and Lorri Glover, 136–173. Athens: University of Georgia Press, 2004.

———. "Accidental Ethnography in an Antebellum Southern Newspaper: Snell's Homecoming Festival." *Journal of American History* 84 (March 1998): 1355–1383.

———. *Creating an Old South: Middle Florida's Plantation Frontier Before the Civil War.* Chapel Hill: University of North Carolina Press, 2002.

———. "'Cuffy,' 'Fancy Maids,' and 'One-Eyed Men': Rape, Commodification, and the Domestic Slave Trade in the United States." *American Historical Review* 106 (December 2001): 1619–1650.

———. "'My Mind Is to Drown You and Leave You Behind': 'Omie Wise,' Intimate Violence, and Masculinity." In *Over the Threshold: Intimate Violence in Early America,* edited by Christine Daniels and Michael V. Kennedy, 94–110. New York: Routledge, 1999.

———. "'Stol' and Fetched Here': Enslaved Migration, Ex-slave Narratives, and Vernacular History." In *New Studies in the History of American Slavery,* edited by Edward E. Baptist and Stephanie M. H. Camp, 243–274. Athens: University of Georgia Press, 2006.

Bardaglio, Peter W. *Reconstructing the Household: Families, Sex, and the Law in the Nineteenth-Century South.* Chapel Hill: University of North Carolina Press, 1995.

Bassett, John Spencer. *Slavery in the State of North Carolina.* Baltimore: Johns Hopkins Press, 1899.

———. *The Southern Plantation Overseer as Revealed in His Letters.* Northampton, Mass.: Smith College, 1925.

Berlin, Ira. *Many Thousands Gone: The First Two Centuries of Slavery in North America.* Cambridge: Belknap Press of Harvard University Press, 1998.

Berlin, Ira, and Philip D. Morgan, eds., *Cultivation and Culture: Labor and the Shaping of Slave Life in the Americas.* Charlottesville: University Press of Virginia, 1993.

———. *The Slaves' Economy: Independent Production by Slaves in the Americas.* London: Frank Cass, 1991.

Bernier, Celeste-Marie. "'Emblems of Barbarism': Black Masculinity and Representations of Toussaint L'Ouverture in Frederick Douglass's Unpublished Manuscripts." *American Nineteenth Century History* 4 (Fall 2003): 97–120.

Berry, Daina Ramey. *"Swing the Sickle for the Harvest Is Ripe": Gender and Slavery in Antebellum Georgia.* Urbana: University of Illinois Press, 2007.

Berry, Mary Frances. "*The Slave Community:* A Review of Reviews." In *Revisiting Blassingame's* The Slave Community: *The Scholars Respond,* edited by Al-Tony Gilmore, 3–16. Westport, Conn.: Greenwood Press, 1978.

Bing, Robert L. "Politicizing Black-on-Black Crime: A Critique of Terminological Preference." In *Black on Black Crime: Facing Facts—Challenging Fictions,* edited by P. Ray Kedia, Bristol, Ind.: Wyndham Hall Press, 1994.

BIBLIOGRAPHY

Black, Daniel P. "The Black Male Concept of Manhood as Portrayed in Selected Slave and Free Narratives (1794–1863)." Ph.D. diss., Temple University, 1993.

Black, Kelli M. "Creating Infanticide: A Comparative Study of Early Modern British Servant and Antebellum American Slave Women." M.A. thesis, San Diego State University, 2003.

Blackhawk, Ned. *Violence over the Land: Indians and Empires in the Early American West.* Cambridge: Harvard University Press, 2006.

Blassingame, John W. *The Slave Community: Plantation Life in the Antebellum South.* Rev. ed. New York: Oxford University Press, 1979.

Boster, Dea H. *African American Slavery and Disability: Bodies, Property, and Power in the Antebellum South, 1800–1860.* New York: Routledge, 2013.

Boyer, Richard. "Honor among Plebeians." In *The Faces of Honor: Sex, Shame, and Violence in Colonial Latin America,* edited by Lyman L. Johnson and Sonya Lipsett-Rivera, 152–178. Albuquerque: University of New Mexico Press, 1998.

———. "Respect and Identity: Horizontal and Vertical Reference Points in Speech Acts." *Americas* 54 (April 1998): 491–509.

Brewer, J. Mason. *American Negro Folklore.* Chicago: Quadrangle Books, 1968.

Brown, Claude. *Manchild in the Promised Land.* New York: Macmillan, 1965.

Brown, Kathleen M. "'Strength of the Lion ... Arms Like Polished Iron': Embodying Black Masculinity in an Age of Slavery and Propertied Manhood." In *New Men: Manliness in Early America,* edited by Thomas A. Foster, 172–192. New York: New York University Press, 2011.

Brown, Steven E. "Sexuality and the Slave Community." *Phylon* (First Quarter [Spring] 1981): 1–10.

Bruce, Dickson D., Jr. *Violence and Culture in the Antebellum South.* Austin: University of Texas Press, 1979.

Bynum, Victoria E. *Unruly Women: The Politics of Social and Sexual Control in the Old South.* Chapel Hill: University of North Carolina Press, 1992.

Camp, Stephanie M. H. *Closer to Freedom: Enslaved Women and Everyday Resistance in the Plantation South.* Chapel Hill: University of North Carolina Press, 2004.

———. "'I Could Not Stay There': Enslaved Women, Truancy and the Geography of Everyday Forms of Resistance in the Antebellum Plantation South." *Slavery & Abolition* 23 (December 2002): 1–20.

Campbell, James. "'The victim of prejudice and hasty consideration': The Slave Trial System in Richmond, Virginia, 1830–61." *Slavery & Abolition* 26 (April 2005): 71–91.

Campbell, John. "As 'A Kind of Freeman'? Slaves' Market-Related Activities in the South Carolina Upcountry, 1800–1860." In *The Slaves' Economy: Independent Production by Slaves in the Americas,* edited by Ira Berlin and Philip D. Morgan, 131–169. London: Frank Cass, 1991.

BIBLIOGRAPHY

Cash, W. J. *The Mind of the South*. New York: Alfred A. Knopf, 1941. Reprint. New York: Vintage, 1991.

Clarke, James W. "Black-on-Black Violence." *Society* 33 (July–August 1996): 46–50.

———. *The Lineaments of Wrath: Race, Violent Crime, and American Culture*. New Brunswick, N.J.: Transaction Publishers, 1998.

Clinton, Catherine. "'Southern Dishonor': Flesh, Blood, Race, and Bondage." In *In Joy and in Sorrow: Women, Family, and Marriage in the Victorian South, 1830–1900*, edited by Carol Bleser, 52–68. New York: Oxford University Press, 1991.

Coleman, J. Winston. *Slavery Times in Kentucky*. Chapel Hill: University of North Carolina Press, 1940.

Collier, Aldore. "What's Behind the Black-on-Black Violence at Movie Theaters." *Ebony* 46 (October 1991): 98, 100, 102.

Coulter, E. Merton. "Four Slave Trials in Elbert County, Georgia." *Georgia Historical Quarterly* 41 (Fall 1957): 237–246.

Crouch, Barry A. "A Spirit of Lawlessness: White Violence; Texas Blacks, 1865–1868." *Journal of Social History* 18 (Winter 1984): 217–232.

Crowther, Edward R. "Mississippi Baptists, Slavery, and Secession, 1806–1861." *Journal of Mississippi History* 56 (May 1994): 129–148.

Cullen, Jim. "'I's a Man Now': Gender and African American Men." In *Divided Houses: Gender and the Civil War*, edited by Catherine Clinton and Nina Silber, 76–91. New York: Oxford University Press, 1992.

Currie, J. T. "From Slavery to Freedom in Mississippi's Legal System." *Journal of Negro History* 65 (Spring 1980): 112–125.

Denham, James M., and Randolph Roth. "Why Was Antebellum Florida Murderous? A Quantitative Analysis of Homicide in Florida, 1821–1861." *Florida Historical Quarterly* 86 (Fall 2007): 216–239.

Desch Obi, T. J. *Fighting for Honor: The History of African Martial Art Traditions in the Atlantic World*. Columbia: University of South Carolina Press, 2008.

Dew, Charles B. "Disciplining Slave Ironworkers in the Antebellum South: Coercion, Conciliation, and Accommodation." *American Historical Review* 79 (April 1974): 393–418.

Deyle, Steven. *Carry Me Back: The Domestic Slave Trade in American Life*. New York: Oxford University Press, 2005.

Dollard, John. *Caste and Class in a Southern Town*. 3rd ed. Garden City, N.Y.: Doubleday, 1957.

Dunaway, Wilma A. *The African-American Family in Slavery and Emancipation*. New York: Cambridge University Press, 2003.

Edwards, John C. "Slave Justice in Four Middle Georgia Counties." *Georgia Historical Quarterly* 57 (Summer 1973): 265–273.

BIBLIOGRAPHY

Edwards, Laura F. *Gendered Strife and Confusion: The Political Culture of Reconstruction*. Urbana: University of Illinois Press, 1997.

———. "Law, Domestic Violence, and the Limits of Patriarchal Authority in the Antebellum South." *Journal of Southern History* 65 (November 1999): 733–770.

———. "Sexual Violence, Gender, Reconstruction, and the Extension of Patriarchy in Granville County, North Carolina." *North Carolina Historical Review* 68 (July 1991): 237–260.

Egerton, Douglas R. *Gabriel's Rebellion: The Virginia Slave Conspiracies of 1800 and 1802*. Chapel Hill: University of North Carolina Press, 1993.

Elder, Robert. "Southern Saints and Sacred Honor: Evangelicalism, Honor, Community, and the Self in South Carolina and Georgia, 1784–1860." Ph.D. diss., Emory University, 2011.

———. "A Twice Sacred Circle: Women, Evangelicalism, and Honor in the Deep South, 1784–1860." *Journal of Southern History* 78 (August 2012): 579–614.

Elkins, Stanley M. *Slavery: A Problem in American Institutional and Intellectual Life*. 3rd ed. Chicago: University of Chicago Press, 1976.

Eltis, David. *The Rise of African Slavery in the Americas*. Cambridge: Cambridge University Press, 2000.

Escott, Paul D., et al. *Major Problems in the History of the American South*. Vol. 1. 2nd ed. New York: Houghton Mifflin, 1999.

Essah, Patience. "Slavery and Freedom in the First State: The History of Blacks in Delaware from the Colonial Period to 1865." Ph.D. diss., UCLA, 1985.

Essig, James David. "A Very Wintry Season: Virginia Baptists and Slavery, 1785–1797." *Virginia Magazine of History and Biography* 87 (April 1980): 170–185.

Faust, Drew Gilpin. *James Henry Hammond and the Old South: A Design for Mastery*. Baton Rouge: Louisiana State University Press, 1982.

Fett, Sharla. *Working Cures: Healing, Health, and Power on Southern Slave Plantations*. Chapel Hill: University of North Carolina Press, 2002.

Fischer, Kirsten. "'False, Feigned, and Scandalous Words': Sexual Slander and Racial Ideology among Whites in Colonial North Carolina." In *The Devil's Lane: Sex and Race in the Early South*, edited by Catherine Clinton and Michele Gillespie, 139–153. New York: Oxford University Press, 1997.

———. *Suspect Relations: Sex, Race, and Resistance in Colonial North Carolina*. Ithaca: Cornell University Press, 2002.

Flanders, Ralph Betts. *Plantation Slavery in Georgia*. Chapel Hill: University of North Carolina Press, 1933. Reprint. Cos Cob, Conn.: John E. Edwards, 1967.

Flanigan, Daniel J. *The Criminal Law of Slavery and Freedom 1800–1868*. New York: Garland Publishing, Inc., 1987.

Fogel, Robert William, and Stanley L. Engerman. *Time on the Cross: The Economics of American Negro Slavery*. 1974. Reprint. New York: W. W. Norton & Company, 1995.

BIBLIOGRAPHY

Forret, Jeff. "Before Angola: Enslaved Prisoners in the Louisiana State Penitentiary." *Louisiana History* 54 (Spring 2013): 133–171.

———. "Conflict and the 'Slave Community': Violence among Slaves in Upcountry South Carolina." *Journal of Southern History* 74 (August 2008): 551–588.

———. *Race Relations at the Margins: Slaves and Poor Whites in the Antebellum Southern Countryside*. Baton Rouge: Louisiana State University Press, 2006.

———. "Slave–Poor White Violence in the Antebellum Carolinas." *North Carolina Historical Review* 81 (April 2004): 139–167.

———. *Slavery in the United States*. New York: Facts on File, 2012.

———. "Slaves, Poor Whites, and the Underground Economy of the Rural Carolinas." *Journal of Southern History* 70 (November 2004): 783–824.

———. "Slaves, Sex and Sin: Adultery, Forced Separation and Baptist Church Discipline in Middle Georgia." *Slavery & Abolition* 33 (September 2012): 337–358.

Fountain, Daniel L. *Slavery, Civil War, and Salvation: African American Slaves and Christianity, 1830–1870*. Baton Rouge: Louisiana State University Press, 2010.

Fox-Genovese, Elizabeth. *Within the Plantation Household: Black and White Women of the Old South*. Chapel Hill: University of North Carolina Press, 1988.

Franklin, John Hope. *The Militant South, 1800–1861*. Cambridge: Harvard University Press, 1956.

Fraser, Rebecca J. "Negotiating Their Manhood: Masculinity amongst the Enslaved in the Upper South, 1830–1861." In *Black and White Masculinity in the American South, 1800–2000*, edited by Lydia Plath and Sergio Lussana, 76–94. Newcastle upon Tyne, U.K.: Cambridge Scholars Publishing, 2009.

———. *Courtship and Love among the Enslaved in North Carolina*. Jackson: University Press of Mississippi, 2007.

Freud, Sigmund. *Civilization and Its Discontents*. Translated by James Strachey. New York: Norton, 1962.

Frey, Sylvia R., and Betty Wood. *Come Shouting to Zion: African American Protestantism in the American South and British Caribbean to 1830*. Chapel Hill: University of North Carolina Press, 1998.

Friedman, Jean E. *The Enclosed Garden: Women and Community in the Evangelical South*. Chapel Hill: University of North Carolina Press, 1985.

Friedman, Lawrence M. *A History of American Law*. 2nd ed. New York: Touchstone, 1985.

Friend, Craig Thompson, and Lorri Glover, eds. *Southern Manhood: Perspectives on Masculinity in the Old South*. Athens: University of Georgia Press, 2004.

Gamber, Wendy. "Tarnished Labor: The Home, the Market, and the Boardinghouse in Antebellum America." *Journal of the Early Republic* 22 (Summer 2002): 177–204.

Genovese, Eugene D. *Roll, Jordan, Roll: The World the Slaves Made*. 1974. Reprint. New York: Vintage, 1976.

Gettleman, Marvin E. "The Maryland Penitentiary in the Age of Tocqueville, 1828–1842." *Maryland Historical Magazine* 56 (September 1961): 269–290.

Gilmore, Al-Tony. *Revisiting Blassingame's* The Slave Community: *The Scholars Respond*. Westport, Conn.: Greenwood Press, 1978.

Gleick, Elizabeth. "Stand and Deliver: The Reverend Jesse Jackson targets schools in his new crusade to combat the violence that blacks are doing to themselves." *People*, April 11, 1994, 97–100.

Glover, Lorri. *Southern Sons: Becoming Men in the New Nation*. Baltimore: Johns Hopkins University Press, 2007.

Glymph, Thaviola. *Out of the House of Bondage: The Transformation of the Plantation Household*. New York: Cambridge University Press, 2008.

Goleman, Michael J. "To Become Men: Resistance, Revolt, and Masculinity in Antebellum Rural Slave Communities." M.A. thesis, Mississippi State University, 2006.

Gomez, Michael A. *Exchanging Our Country Marks: The Transformation of African Identities in the Colonial and Antebellum South*. Chapel Hill: University of North Carolina Press, 1998.

Gorn, Elliott J. "'Gouge and Bite, Pull Hair and Scratch': The Social Significance of Fighting in the Southern Backcountry." *American Historical Review* 90 (February 1985): 18–43.

Graham, Sandra Lauderdale. "Honor among Slaves." In *The Faces of Honor: Sex, Shame, and Violence in Colonial Latin America,* edited by Lyman L. Johnson and Sonya Lipsett-Rivera, 201–228. Albuquerque: University of New Mexico Press, 1998.

Gray White, Deborah. *Ar'n't I a Woman?: Female Slaves in the Plantation South*. Rev. ed. New York: Norton, 1999.

Greenberg, Kenneth S. *Honor & Slavery: Lies, Duels, Noses, Masks, Dressing as a Woman, Gifts, Strangers, Humanitarianism, Death, Slave Rebellions, the Proslavery Argument, Baseball, Hunting, and Gambling in the Old South*. Princeton: Princeton University Press, 1996.

———. "The Nose, the Lie, and the Duel in the Antebellum South." *American Historical Review* 95 (February 1990): 57–74.

Griffin, Rebecca. "Courtship Contests and the Meaning of Conflict in the Folklore of Slaves." *Journal of Southern History* 71 (November 2005): 769–802.

———. "'Goin' Back Over There to See That Girl': Competing Social Spaces in the Lives of the Enslaved in Antebellum North Carolina." *Slavery & Abolition* 25 (April 2004): 94–113.

Grivno, Max L. *Gleanings of Freedom: Free and Slave Labor along the Mason-Dixon Line, 1790–1860*. Urbana: University of Illinois Press, 2011.

Gross, Ariela J. *Double Character: Slavery and Mastery in the Antebellum Southern Courtroom*. Princeton: Princeton University Press, 2000.

Gudmestad, Robert H. *A Troublesome Commerce: The Transformation of the Interstate Slave Trade*. Baton Rouge: Louisiana State University Press, 2003.

BIBLIOGRAPHY

Gutman, Herbert G. *The Black Family in Slavery and Freedom, 1750–1925.* New York: Pantheon Books, 1976.

Hackney, Sheldon. "Southern Violence." *American Historical Review* 74 (February 1969): 906–925.

Hadden, Sally E. *Slave Patrols: Law and Violence in Virginia and the Carolinas.* Cambridge: Harvard University Press, 2001.

Hahn, Steven. *A Nation under Our Feet: Black Political Struggles in the Rural South, from Slavery to the Great Migration.* Cambridge: Belknap Press of Harvard University Press, 2003.

Harper, C. W. "Black Aristocrats: Domestic Servants on the Antebellum Plantation." *Phylon* 46 (June 1985): 123–135.

———. "House Servants and Field Hands: Fragmentation in the Antebellum Slave Community." *North Carolina Historical Review* 55 (January 1978): 42–59.

Harris, J. William. *The Hanging of Thomas Jeremiah: A Free Black Man's Encounter with Liberty.* New Haven: Yale University Press, 2009.

Hemphill, Katie M. "'Driven to the Commission of This Crime': Women and Infanticide in Baltimore, 1835–1860." *Journal of the Early Republic* 32 (Fall 2012): 437–461.

Henderson, William. "The Slave Court System in Spartanburg County." *Proceedings of the South Carolina Historical Association* (1976): 24–38.

Heyrman, Christine Leigh. *Southern Cross: The Beginnings of the Bible Belt.* Chapel Hill: University of North Carolina Press, 1998.

Hilliard, Kathleen Mary. "Spending in Black and White: Race, Slavery, and Consumer Values in the Antebellum South." Ph.D. diss., University of South Carolina, 2006.

Hindus, Michael Stephen. *Prison and Plantation: Crime, Justice, and Authority in Massachusetts and South Carolina, 1767–1878.* Chapel Hill: University of North Carolina Press, 1980.

Hine, Darlene Clark, and Earnestine Jenkins, eds. *A Question of Manhood: A Reader in U.S. Black Men's History and Masculinity.* Vol. 1. Bloomington: Indiana University Press, 1999.

Horton, James Oliver, and Lois E. Horton. "Violence, Protest, and Identity: Black Manhood in Antebellum America." In *A Question of Manhood: A Reader in U.S. Black Men's History and Masculinity,* vol. 1, edited by Darlene Clark Hine and Earnestine Jenkins. Bloomington: Indiana University Press, 1999.

Hudson, Larry E., Jr. "'All That Cash': Work and Status in the Slave Quarters." In *Working Toward Freedom: Slave Society and Domestic Economy in the American South,* edited by Larry E. Hudson Jr., 77–94. Rochester: University of Rochester Press, 1994.

———. *To Have and to Hold: Slave Work and Family Life in Antebellum South Carolina.* Athens: University of Georgia Press, 1997.

Iliffe, John. *Honour in African History.* New York: Cambridge University Press, 2005.

Johnson, Guion Griffis. *Ante-bellum North Carolina: A Social History.* Chapel Hill: University of North Carolina Press, 1937.

Johnson, Lyman L. "Dangerous Words, Provocative Gestures, and Violent Acts: The Disputed Hierarchies of Plebeian Life in Colonial Buenos Aires." In *The Faces of Honor: Sex, Shame, and Violence in Colonial Latin America,* edited by Lyman L. Johnson and Sonya Lipsett-Rivera, 127–151. Albuquerque: University of New Mexico Press, 1998.

Johnson, Lyman L., and Sonya Lipsett-Rivera, eds. *The Faces of Honor: Sex, Shame, and Violence in Colonial Latin America.* Albuquerque: University of New Mexico Press, 1998.

Johnson, Michael P. "Runaway Slaves and the Slave Communities in South Carolina, 1799 to 1830." *William & Mary Quarterly* 3rd ser., 38 (July 1981): 418–441.

———. "Smothered Slave Infants: Were Slave Mothers at Fault?" *Journal of Southern History* 47 (November 1981): 493–520.

———. "Work, Culture, and the Slave Community: Slave Occupations in the Cotton Belt in 1860." *Labor History* 27 (Summer 1986): 325–355.

Johnson, Walter. "Clerks All! Or, Slaves with Cash." *Journal of the Early Republic* 26 (Winter 2006): 641–651.

———. "On Agency." *Journal of Social History* 37 (Fall 2003): 113–124.

———. *Soul by Soul: Life Inside the Antebellum Slave Market.* Cambridge: Harvard University Press, 1999.

Jordan, Winthrop D. *Tumult and Silence at Second Creek: An Inquiry into a Civil War Slave Conspiracy.* Baton Rouge: Louisiana State University Press, 1993.

———. *White over Black: American Attitudes toward the Negro, 1550–1812.* Chapel Hill: University of North Carolina Press, 1968.

Joyner, Charles. *Down by the Riverside: A South Carolina Slave Community.* Urbana: University of Illinois Press, 1984.

Kay, Marvin L. Michael, and Lorin Lee Cary. "'The Planters Suffer Little or Nothing': North Carolina Compensations for Executed Slaves, 1748–1772." *Science and Society* 40 (Fall 1976): 288–306.

Kaye, Anthony E. *Joining Places: Slave Neighborhoods in the Old South.* Chapel Hill: University of North Carolina Press, 2007.

———. "Neighbourhoods and Solidarity in the Natchez District of Mississippi: Rethinking the Antebellum Slave Community." *Slavery & Abolition* 23 (April 2002): 1–24.

King, Wilma. "'Mad' Enough to Kill: Enslaved Women, Murder, and Southern Courts." *Journal of African American History* 92 (Winter 2007): 37–56.

———. *Stolen Childhood: Slave Youth in Nineteenth-Century America.* Bloomington: Indiana University Press, 1995.

Klein, Herbert S. *African Slavery in Latin America and the Caribbean.* New York: Oxford University Press, 1986.

Kolchin, Peter. *American Slavery, 1619–1877.* New York: Hill and Wang, 1993.

———. "Reevaluating the Antebellum Slave Community: A Comparative Perspective." *Journal of American History* 70 (December 1983): 579–601.

———. *Unfree Labor: American Slavery and Russian Serfdom*. Cambridge: Belknap Press of Harvard University Press, 1987.

Labinjoh, Justin. "The Sexual Life of the Oppressed: An Examination of the Family Life of Ante-Bellum Slaves." *Phylon* 35, no. 4 (1974): 375–397.

Lachance, Paul. "Use and Misuse of the Slave Community Paradigm." *Canadian Review of American Studies* 17 (Winter 1986): 449–458.

Landers, Jane. "'In Consideration of Her Enormous Crime': Rape and Infanticide in Spanish St. Augustine." In *The Devil's Lane: Sex and Race in the Early South*, edited by Catherine Clinton and Michele Gillespie, 205–217. New York: Oxford University Press, 1997.

Lane, Roger. *Murder in America: A History*. Columbus: Ohio State University Press, 1997.

Lee, Jean Butenhoff. "The Problem of Slave Community in the Eighteenth-Century Chesapeake." *William & Mary Quarterly* 3rd ser., 43 (July 1986): 333–361.

Levine, Lawrence W. *Black Culture and Black Consciousness: Afro-American Folk Thought from Slavery to Freedom*. New York: Oxford University Press, 1977.

Lichtenstein, Alex. "'That Disposition To Theft, With Which They Have Been Branded': Moral Economy, Slave Management, and the Law." *Journal of Social History* 21 (Spring 1988): 413–440.

Lightner, David L. *Slavery and the Commerce Power: How the Struggle Against the Interstate Slave Trade Led to the Civil War*. New Haven: Yale University Press, 2006.

Lincoln, C. Eric. *Coming through the Fire: Surviving Race and Place in America*. Durham: Duke University Press, 1996.

Lindman, Janet Moore. "Acting the Manly Christian: White Evangelical Masculinity in Revolutionary Virginia." *William & Mary Quarterly* 3rd ser., 57 (April 2000): 393–416.

Lipscomb, Terry W., and Theresa Jacobs. "The Magistrates and Freeholders Court." *South Carolina Historical Magazine* 77 (January 1976): 62–65.

Lipsett-Rivera, Sonya. "*De Obra Y Palabra:* Patterns of Insults in Mexico, 1750–1856." *Americas* 54 (April 1998): 511–539.

Lussana, Sergio. "'Band of Brothers: Enslaved African-American Masculinity in the Antebellum United States." M.A. thesis, University of Warwick, 2006.

———. "To See Who Was Best on the Plantation: Enslaved Fighting Contests and Masculinity in the Antebellum Plantation South." *Journal of Southern History* 76 (November 2010): 901–922.

Malone, Ann Patton. *Sweet Chariot: Slave Family and Household Structure in Nineteenth-Century Louisiana*. Chapel Hill: University of North Carolina Press, 1992.

Martin, Jonathan D. *Divided Mastery: Slave Hiring in the American South*. Cambridge: Harvard University Press, 2004.

BIBLIOGRAPHY

McCurry, Stephanie. *Masters of Small Worlds: Yeoman Households, Gender Relations, and the Political Culture of the Antebellum South Carolina Low Country.* New York: Oxford University Press, 1995.

McDonnell, Lawrence T. "Money Knows No Master: Market Relations and the American Slave Community." In *Developing Dixie: Modernization in a Traditional Society*, edited by Winfred B. Moore Jr., Joseph F. Tripp, and Lyon G. Tyler Jr., 31–44. Westport, Conn.: Greenwood Press, 1988.

McDougle, Ivan E. *Slavery in Kentucky, 1792–1865.* 1918. Reprint. Westport, Conn.: Negro Universities Press, 1970.

McLaurin, Melton A. *Celia, a Slave.* Athens: University of Georgia Press, 1991. Reprint. New York: Perennial, 2002.

McNair, Glenn M. "Justice Bound: Aframericans, Crime, and Criminal Justice in Georgia, 1751–1865." Ph.D. diss., Emory University, 2001.

———. "Slave Women, Capital Crime, and Criminal Justice in Georgia." *Georgia Historical Quarterly* 93 (Summer 2009): 135–158.

McNair, Glenn Maurice. "The Trials of Slaves in Baldwin County, Georgia, 1812–1838." M.A. thesis, Georgia College and State University, 1996.

McPherson, Robert G. "Georgia Slave Trials, 1837–1849." *American Journal of Legal History* 4 (July 1960): 257–284.

———. "Georgia Slave Trials, 1837–1849." *American Journal of Legal History* 4 (October 1960): 364–377.

McWhiney, Grady. *Cracker Culture: Celtic Ways in the Old South.* Tuscaloosa: University of Alabama Press, 1988.

Megginson, W. J. *African American Life in South Carolina's Upper Piedmont, 1780–1900.* Columbia: University of South Carolina Press, 2006.

Millward, Jessica. "'As Cool as I Now Am': Identity, Abortion and Infanticide in the Slave South." M.A. thesis, UCLA, 1997.

Monkkonen, Eric H. *Murder in New York City.* Berkeley: University of California Press, 2001.

Moogk, Peter N. "'Thieving Buggers' and 'Stupid Sluts': Insults and Popular Culture in New France." *William & Mary Quarterly* 3rd ser., 36 (October 1979): 524–547.

Morgan, Jennifer L. *Laboring Women: Reproduction and Gender in New World Slavery.* Philadelphia: University of Pennsylvania Press, 2004.

Morgan, Philip D. "The Ownership of Property by Slaves in the Mid-Nineteenth-Century Low Country." *Journal of Southern History* 49 (August 1983): 399–420.

———. *Slave Counterpoint: Black Culture in the Eighteenth-Century Chesapeake and Lowcountry.* Chapel Hill: University of North Carolina Press, 1998.

———. "Work and Culture: The Task System and the World of Lowcountry Blacks, 1700 to 1880." *William & Mary Quarterly* 3rd ser., 39 (October 1982): 563–599.

Morris, Christopher. "The Articulation of Two Worlds: The Master-Slave Relationship Reconsidered." *Journal of American History* 85 (December 1998): 982–1007.

———. *Becoming Southern: The Evolution of a Way of Life, Warren County and Vicksburg, Mississippi, 1770–1860*. New York: Oxford University Press, 1995.

———. "Within the Slave Cabin: Violence in Mississippi Slave Families." In *Over the Threshold: Intimate Violence in Early America*, edited by Christine Daniels and Michael V. Kennedy, 268–285. New York: Routledge, 1999.

Morris, Thomas D. "'As If the Injury Was Effected by the Natural Elements of Air, or Fire': Slave Wrongs and the Liability of Masters." *Law & Society Review* 16, no. 4 (1982): 569–600.

———. "Slaves and the Rules of Evidence in Criminal Trials." In *Slavery and the Law*, edited by Paul Finkelman, 209–239. Madison, Wis.: Madison House, 1997.

———. *Southern Slavery and the Law, 1619–1860*. Chapel Hill: University of North Carolina Press, 1996.

Nash, A. E. Kier. "The Texas Supreme Court and Trial Rights of Blacks, 1845–1860." *Journal of American History* 58 (December 1971): 622–642.

Nash, Gary B. *Forging Freedom: The Formation of Philadelphia's Black Community, 1720–1840*. Cambridge: Harvard University Press, 1988.

Neely, Caroline Elizabeth. "'Dat's One Chile of Mine You Ain't Never Gonna Sell': Gynecological Resistance Within the Plantation Community." M.A. thesis, Virginia Polytechnic Institute and State University, 2000.

Norton, Mary Beth. "Gender and Defamation in Seventeenth-Century Maryland." *William & Mary Quarterly* 3rd ser., 44 (January 1987): 3–39.

Norton, Mary Beth, Herbert G. Gutman, and Ira Berlin. "The Afro-American Family in the Age of Revolution." In *Slavery and Freedom in the Age of the American Revolution*, edited by Ira Berlin and Ronald Hoffman, 175–191. Charlottesville: University Press of Virginia, 1983.

Oakes, James. *The Ruling Race: A History of American Slaveholders*. 1982. Reprint. New York: W. W. Norton & Company, 1998.

Olwell, Robert. *Masters, Slaves, & Subjects: The Culture of Power in the South Carolina Low Country, 1740–1790*. Ithaca: Cornell University Press, 1998.

Owens, Leslie Howard. "Blacks in *The Slave Community*." In *Revisiting Blassingame's The Slave Community: The Scholars Respond*, edited by Al-Tony Gilmore, 61–69. Westport, Conn.: Greenwood Press, 1978.

———. *This Species of Property: Slave Life and Culture in the Old South*. New York: Oxford University Press, 1976.

Painter, Nell Irvin. *Southern History across the Color Line*. Chapel Hill: University of North Carolina Press, 2002.

Parent, Anthony S., Jr. *Foul Means: The Formation of a Slave Society in Virginia, 1660–1740*. Chapel Hill: University of North Carolina Press, 2003.

Pargas, Damian Alan. *The Quarters and the Fields: Slave Families in the Non-Cotton South*. Gainesville: University Press of Florida, 2010.

Patrick-Stamp, Leslie. "Numbers That Are Not New: African Americans in the Country's First Prison, 1790–1835." *Pennsylvania Magazine of History and Biography* 119 (January–April 1995): 95–128.

Paterson, David E. "Slavery, Slaves, and Cash in a Georgia Village, 1825–1865." *Journal of Southern History* 75 (November 2009): 879–930.

Patterson, Caleb Perry. *The Negro in Tennessee, 1790–1865*. 1922. Reprint. New York: Negro Universities Press, 1968.

Patterson, Orlando. *Slavery and Social Death: A Comparative Study*. Cambridge: Harvard University Press, 1982.

———. "Whatever Happened to the Horrors of Slavery?" Presentation at the Rice Center for Cultural Studies, Moral Sensibilities in Cultural and Historical Context Session No. 11. January 19, 1989.

Penningroth, Dylan C. *The Claims of Kinfolk: African American Property and Community in the Nineteenth-Century South*. Chapel Hill: University of North Carolina Press, 2003.

———. "My People, My People: The Dynamics of Community in Southern Slavery." In *New Studies in the History of American Slavery*, edited by Edward E. Baptist and Stephanie M. H. Camp, 166–176. Athens: University of Georgia Press, 2006.

Peristiany, J. G., ed. *Honour and Shame: The Values of Mediterranean Society*. Chicago: University of Chicago Press, 1966.

Peristiany, J. G., and Julian Pitt-Rivers. "Introduction." In *Honor and Grace in Anthropology*, edited by J. G. Peristiany and Julian Pitt-Rivers. New York: Cambridge University Press, 1992.

Perrin, Liese M. "Resisting Reproduction: Reconsidering Slave Contraception in the Old South." *Journal of American Studies* 35 (August 2001): 255–274.

Phillips, Ulrich B. "Slave Crime in Virginia." *American Historical Review* 20 (January 1915): 336–340.

Phillips, Ulrich Bonnell. *American Negro Slavery: A Survey of the Supply, Employment and Control of Negro Labor as Determined by the Plantation Régime*. New York: Peter Smith, 1952.

Pitt-Rivers, Julian. "Postscript: The Place of Grace in Anthropology." In *Honor and Grace in Anthropology*, edited by J. G. Peristiany and Julian Pitt-Rivers, 215–246. New York: Cambridge University Press, 1992.

Potter, Claire. Review of *The Lineaments of Wrath: Race, Violent Crime, and American Culture*, by James W. Clarke. *Journal of American History* 86 (June 1999): 324–325.

Proctor, Nicolas W. *Bathed in Blood: Hunting and Mastery in the Old South*. Charlottesville: University Press of Virginia, 2002.

Putzi, Jennifer. *Identifying Marks: Race, Gender, and the Marked Body in Nineteenth-Century America*. Athens: University of Georgia Press, 2006.

BIBLIOGRAPHY

Raboteau, Albert J. *Slave Religion: The "Invisible Institution" in the Antebellum South.* New York: Oxford University Press, 1978.

Rawick, George P. *From Sundown to Sunup: The Making of the Black Community.* Westport, Conn.: Greenwood Publishing Company, 1972.

Rediker, Marcus. *The Slave Ship: A Human History.* New York: Viking, 2007.

Reese, Renford. *American Paradox: Young Black Men.* Durham: Carolina Academic Press, 2004.

Reidy, Joseph P. "Obligation and Right: Patterns of Labor, Subsistence, and Exchange in the Cotton Belt of Georgia, 1790–1860." In *Cultivation and Culture: Labor and the Shaping of Slave Life in the Americas,* edited by Ira Berlin and Philip D. Morgan, 138–154. Charlottesville: University Press of Virginia, 1993.

Reisinger, Scott R. "Let Justice Be Done to Slavery: The White Virginia Baptist Clergy and the Slaves, 1840–1865," *Virginia Baptist Register* 33 (1994): 1665–1685.

Rice, Jim. "'This Province, So Meanly and Thinly Inhabited': Punishing Maryland's Criminals, 1681–1850." *Journal of the Early Republic* 19 (Spring 1999): 15–42.

Richter, William L. "Slavery in Baton Rouge, 1820–1860." *Louisiana History* 10 (Spring 1969): 125–145.

Roth, Randolph. *American Homicide.* Cambridge: Belknap Press of Harvard University Press, 2009.

Roth, Sarah N. "'The Blade Was in My Own Breast': Slave Infanticide in 1850s Fiction." *American Nineteenth Century History* 8 (June 2007): 169–185.

———. "'How a Slave was Made a Man': Negotiating Black Violence and Masculinity in Antebellum Slave Narratives." *Slavery & Abolition* 28 (August 2007): 255–275.

Rothman, Joshua D. *Notorious in the Neighborhood: Sex and Families across the Color Line in Virginia, 1787–1861.* Chapel Hill: University of North Carolina Press, 2003.

Sale, Maggie Montesinos. *The Slumbering Volcano: American Slave Ship Revolts and the Production of Rebellious Masculinity.* Durham: Duke University Press, 1997.

Sampson, Robert J., and Lydia Bean. "Cultural Mechanisms and Killing Fields: A Revised Theory of Community-Level Racial Inequality." In *The Many Colors of Crime: Inequalities of Race, Ethnicity, and Crime in America,* edited by Ruth D. Peterson, Lauren J. Krivo, and John Hagan, 8–36. New York: New York University Press, 2006.

Sampson, Robert J., and William Julius Wilson. "Toward a Theory of Race, Crime, and Urban Inequality." In *Crime and Inequality,* edited by John Hagan and Ruth D. Peterson, 37–54. Stanford: Stanford University Press, 1995.

Saunders, Robert M. "Crime and Punishment in Early National America: Richmond, Virginia, 1784–1820." *Virginia Magazine of History and Biography* 86 (January 1978): 33–44.

Savitt, Todd L. *Medicine and Slavery: The Diseases and Health Care of Blacks in Antebellum Virginia.* 1978. Reprint. Urbana: University of Illinois Press, 2002.

Schafer, Judith Kelleher. "Slaves and Crime: New Orleans, 1846–1862." In *Local Matters: Race, Crime, and Justice in the Nineteenth-Century South,* edited by Christopher Waldrep and Donald G. Nieman, 53–91. Athens: University of Georgia Press, 2001.

Schermerhorn, Calvin. *Money over Mastery, Family over Freedom: Slavery in the Antebellum Upper South.* Baltimore: Johns Hopkins University Press, 2011.

Schlotterbeck, John T. "The Internal Economy of Slavery in Rural Piedmont Virginia." In *The Slaves' Economy: Independent Production by Slaves in the Americas,* edited by Ira Berlin and Philip D. Morgan, 170–181. London: Frank Cass, 1991.

Schwalm, Leslie A. *A Hard Fight for We: Women's Transition from Slavery to Freedom in South Carolina.* Urbana: University of Illinois Press, 1997.

Schwartz, Marie Jenkins. *Born in Bondage: Growing Up Enslaved in the Antebellum South.* Cambridge: Harvard University Press, 2000.

Schwarz, Philip J. *Slave Laws in Virginia.* Athens: University of Georgia Press, 2010.

———. "The Transportation of Slaves from Virginia, 1801–1865," *Slavery & Abolition* 7 (December 1986): 215–240.

———. *Twice Condemned: Slaves and the Criminal Laws of Virginia, 1705–1865.* Baton Rouge: Louisiana State University Press, 1988.

Schweninger, Loren. "The Underside of Slavery: The Internal Economy, Self-Hire, and Quasi-Freedom in Virginia, 1780–1865." *Slavery & Abolition* 12 (September 1991): 1–22.

———. "Slave Independence and Enterprise in South Carolina, 1780–1865." *South Carolina Historical Magazine* 93 (April 1992): 101–125.

———. "Slavery and Southern Violence: County Court Petitions and the South's Peculiar Institution." *Journal of Negro History* 85 (Winter–Spring 2000): 33–35.

Scully, Randolph. *Religion and the Making of Nat Turner's Virginia: Baptist Community and Conflict, 1740–1840.* Charlottesville: University of Virginia Press, 2008.

Sellers, James Benson. *Slavery in Alabama.* Tuscaloosa: University of Alabama Press, 1950.

Sellin, J. Thorsten. *Slavery and the Penal System.* New York: Elsevier, 1976.

Shingleton, Royce Gordon. "The Trial and Punishment of Slaves in Baldwin County, Georgia, 1812–1826." *Southern Humanities Review* 8 (Winter 1974): 67–73.

Shore, Laurence. "The Poverty of Tragedy in Historical Writing on Southern Slavery." *South Atlantic Quarterly* 85 (Spring 1986): 147–164.

Silkenat, David. *Moments of Despair: Suicide, Divorce, and Debt in Civil War Era North Carolina.* Chapel Hill: University of North Carolina Press, 2011.

Smallwood, Stephanie E. *Saltwater Slavery: A Middle Passage from Africa to American Diaspora.* Cambridge: Harvard University Press, 2007.

Smith, Merril D. "'Unnatural Mothers': Infanticide, Motherhood, and Class in the Mid-Atlantic, 1730–1830." In *Over the Threshold: Intimate Violence in Early America,* edited by Christine Daniels and Michael V. Kennedy, 173–184. New York: Routledge, 1999.

Smith, T. Lynn, and Homer L. Hitt, "The Composition of the Population of Louisiana State Penitentiary, 1859, 1860, and 1861." *Southwestern Social Science Quarterly* 20 (March 1940): 361–374.

Snyder, Terri L. "Suicide, Slavery, and Memory in North America," *Journal of American History* 97 (June 2010): 39–62.

Sparks, Randy J. *On Jordan's Stormy Banks: Evangelicalism in Mississippi, 1773–1876.* Athens: University of Georgia Press, 1994.

———. "Religion in Amite County, Mississippi, 1800–1861." In *Masters & Slaves in the House of the Lord: Race and Religion in the American South 1740–1870*, edited by John B. Boles, 58–80. Lexington: University Press of Kentucky, 1988.

Stampp, Kenneth M. *The Peculiar Institution: Slavery in the Ante-Bellum South.* New York: Alfred A. Knopf, 1956.

Stevenson, Brenda E. "Distress and Discord in Virginia Slave Families, 1830–1860." In *In Joy and in Sorrow: Women, Family, and Marriage in the Victorian South, 1830–1900*, edited by Carol Bleser, 103–124. New York: Oxford University Press, 1991.

———. "Gender Convention, Ideals, and Identity among Antebellum Virginia Slave Women." In *More Than Chattel: Black Women and Slavery in the Americas*, edited by David Barry Gaspar and Darlene Clark Hine, 169–190. Bloomington: Indiana University Press, 1996.

———. *Life in Black and White: Family and Community in the Slave South.* New York: Oxford University Press, 1996.

Stowe, Steven M. *Intimacy and Power in the Old South: Ritual in the Lives of the Planters.* Baltimore: Johns Hopkins University Press, 1987.

Stretesky, Paul. Review of *The Lineaments of Wrath: Race, Violent Crime, and American Culture*, by James W. Clarke. *American Political Science Review* 93 (December 1999): 970–971.

Stuckey, Sterling. *Slave Culture: Nationalist Theory and the Foundations of Black America.* New York: Oxford University Press, 1987.

Sydnor, Charles Sackett. *Slavery in Mississippi.* New York: D. Appleton-Century Company, 1933.

Tate, Thad W. *The Negro in Eighteenth-Century Williamsburg.* Williamsburg, Va.: The Colonial Williamsburg Foundation, 1965.

Taylor, Joe Gray. *Negro Slavery in Louisiana.* Baton Rouge: Louisiana Historical Association, 1963.

Taylor, Orville W. *Negro Slavery in Arkansas.* Durham: Duke University Press, 1958.

Taylor, William B. *Drinking, Homicide, and Rebellion in Colonial Mexican Villages.* Stanford: Stanford University Press, 1979.

Trussel, James, and Richard Steckel. "The Age of Slaves at Menarche and Their First Birth." *Journal of Interdisciplinary History* 8 (Winter 1978): 477–505.

Turner, Roger D. "Black on Black Violence: Moving towards Realistic Explanations and

Solutions." In *Black on Black Crime: Facing Facts—Challenging Fictions,* edited by P. Ray Kedia, 1–24. Bristol, Ind.: Wyndham Hall Press, 1994.

Van Deburg, William L. *The Slave Drivers: Black Agricultural Labor Supervisors in the Antebellum South.* Westport, Conn.: Greenwood Press, 1979.

Vandal, Gilles. "Black Violence in Post–Civil War Louisiana." *Journal of Interdisciplinary History* 25 (Summer 1994): 45–64.

———. "'Bloody Caddo': White Violence against Blacks in a Louisiana Parish, 1865–1876." *Journal of Social History* 25 (Winter 1991): 373–388.

———. "Regulating Louisiana's Rural Areas: The Function of Parish Jails, 1840–1885." *Louisiana History* 42 (Winter 2001): 59–92.

Wahl, Jenny Bourne. *The Bondsman's Burden: An Economic Analysis of the Common Law of Southern Slavery.* Cambridge: Cambridge University Press, 1998.

Walker, Clarence E. *Deromanticizing Black History: Critical Essays and Reappraisals.* Knoxville: University of Tennessee Press, 1991.

Walsh, Lorena Seebach. *From Calabar to Carter's Grove: The History of a Virginia Slave Community.* Charlottesville: University Press of Virginia, 1997.

Walvin, James. "Slaves, Free Time and the Question of Leisure." *Slavery & Abolition* 16 (April 1995): 1–13.

Wayne, Michael. *Death of an Overseer: Reopening a Murder Investigation from the Plantation South.* New York: Oxford University Press, 2001.

Webber, Thomas L. *Deep Like the Rivers: Education in the Slave Quarter Community, 1831–1865.* New York: Norton, 1978.

Weisenburger, Steven. *Modern Medea: A Family Story of Slavery and Child-Murder from the Old South.* New York: Hill and Wang, 1999.

West, Emily. *Chains of Love: Slave Couples in Antebellum South Carolina.* Urbana: University of Illinois Press, 2004.

———. "The Debate on the Strength of Slave Families: South Carolina and the Importance of Cross-Plantation Marriages." *Journal of American Studies* 33 (August 1999): 221–241.

———. "Masters and Marriages, Profits and Paternalism: Slave Owners' Perspectives on Cross-Plantation Unions in Antebellum South Carolina." *Slavery & Abolition* 21 (April 2000): 56–72.

———. "Surviving Separation: Cross-Plantation Marriages and the Slave Trade in Antebellum South Carolina." *Journal of Family History* 24 (April 1999): 212–231.

———. "Tensions, Tempers, and Temptations: Marital Discord among Slaves in Antebellum South Carolina." *American Nineteenth Century History* 5 (Summer 2004): 1–18.

West, Stephen A. "From Yeoman to Redneck in Upstate South Carolina, 1850–1915." Ph.D. diss., Columbia University, 1998.

White, Jack E. "Endangered Species." *Time,* March 1, 1999.

———. "When Brother Kills Brother." *Time,* September 16, 1985.

BIBLIOGRAPHY

White, Shane, and Graham White. *Stylin': African American Expressive Culture from Its Beginnings to the Zoot Suit.* Ithaca: Cornell University Press, 1998.

Wiggins, David K. "Good Times On the Old Plantation: Popular Recreations of the Black Slave in Ante Bellum South, 1810-1860." *Journal of Sport History* 4 (Fall 1977): 260-284.

——. "The Play of Slave Children in the Plantation Communities of the Old South, 1820-1860." *Journal of Sport History* 7 (Summer 1980): 21-39.

Williams, Heather Andrea. "'Commenced to Think Like a Man': Literacy and Manhood in African American Civil War Regiments." In *Southern Manhood: Perspectives on Masculinity in the Old South,* edited by Craig Thompson Friend and Lorri Glover, 196-219. Athens: University of Georgia Press, 2004.

Willis, John C. "Behind 'Their Black Masks': Slave Honor in Antebellum Virginia." M.A. thesis, University of Virginia, 1987.

——. "From the Dictates of Pride to the Paths of Righteousness: Slave Honor and Christianity in Antebellum Virginia." In *The Edge of the South: Life in Nineteenth-Century Virginia,* edited by Edward L. Ayers and John C. Willis, 37-55. Charlottesville: University Press of Virginia, 1991.

Wills, Gregory A. *Democratic Religion: Freedom, Authority, and Church Discipline in the Baptist South, 1785-1900.* New York: Oxford University Press, 1997.

Wilson, Amos N. *Black-on-Black Violence: The Psychodynamics of Black Self-Annihilation in Service of White Domination.* New York: Afrikan World Infosystems, 1990.

Wilson, David. "Colouring the City: 'Black-on-Black Violence' and Liberal Discourse." *Journal of Economic & Social Geography* 92, no. 3 (2001): 261-278.

——. *Inventing Black-on-Black Violence: Discourse, Space, and Representation.* Syracuse: Syracuse University Press, 2005.

Wolff, Cynthia Griffin. "'Masculinity' in *Uncle Tom's Cabin,*" *American Quarterly* 47 (December 1995): 595-618.

Wolfgang, Marvin E. *Patterns in Criminal Homicide.* 1958. Reprint. Montclair, N.J.: Patterson Smith, 1975.

Wolfgang, Marvin E., and Franco Ferracuti. *The Subculture of Violence: Towards an Integrated Theory in Criminology.* New York: Tavistock, 1967.

Wood, Betty. "'For Their Satisfaction or Redress': African Americans and Church Discipline in the Early South." In *The Devil's Lane: Sex and Race in the Early South,* edited by Catherine Clinton and Michele Gillespie, 109-123. New York: Oxford University Press, 1997.

——. "Prisons, Workhouses, and the Control of Slave Labour in Low Country Georgia, 1763-1815." *Slavery & Abolition* 8 (December 1987): 247-271.

——. "'White Society' and the 'Informal' Slave Economies of Lowcountry Georgia, c. 1763-1830." *Slavery & Abolition* 11 (December 1990): 313-331.

——. *Women's Work, Men's Work: The Informal Slave Economies of Lowcountry Georgia.* Athens: University of Georgia Press, 1995.

BIBLIOGRAPHY

Wood, Peter H. *Black Majority: Negroes in Colonial South Carolina from 1670 through the Stono Rebellion.* 1974. Reprint. New York: Norton, 1975.

Wurtzburg, Susan, and Thurston H. G. Hahn III. *Hard Labor: History and Archaeology at the Old Louisiana State Penitentiary, Baton Rouge, Louisiana.* Fort Worth: General Services Administration, 1991.

Wyatt-Brown, Bertram. "The Mask of Obedience: Male Slave Psychology in the Old South." *American Historical Review* 93 (December 1988): 1228–1252.

———. *The Shaping of Southern Culture: Honor, Grace, and War, 1760s–1880s.* Chapel Hill: University of North Carolina Press, 2001.

———. *Southern Honor: Ethics and Behavior in the Old South.* New York: Oxford University Press, 1982.

Yanuck, Julius. "The Garner Fugitive Slave Case." *Mississippi Valley Historical Review* 40 (June 1953): 47–66.

Yarborough, Richard. "Race, Violence, and Manhood: The Masculine Idea in Frederick Douglass's 'The Heroic Slave.'" In *Haunted Bodies: Gender and Southern Texts,* edited by Anne Goodwyn Jones and Susan V. Donaldson, 159–184. Charlottesville: University Press of Virginia, 1997.

INDEX

abolitionists, 465–466n15
abortion, 365, 373
abroad marriage, 246–247, 249, 252, 255, 275
abuse of spouse. *See* domestic abuse
accidental deaths, 80
Achebe, Chinua, 294
actio-noxalis, 100–101, 102, 103
Adams-Onís Treaty, 137
adultery, 46, 96, 234, 243, 244, 252–259, 271, 273, 282–283, 284–285
Africa, 3, 18, 21, 22, 28, 31, 32, 64, 203, 221, 263, 290, 294, 302, 319, 324, 326, 335, 394
age, 38; of consent, 352–353; and control of emotions, 164; as factor in commutations of sentence, 328, 339, 378, 379, 380; generational divide, 37, 241, 330, 362–363; and laws against rape, 355; of slaves in penitentiary, 138, 139, 379; as source of jealousy, 251; to start work, 168
agency, 3, 7, 8, 164–165
aggression, displaced, 357, 383
alcohol. *See* drinking; liquor
alibis, 283–284
American Freedmen's Inquiry Commission, 335
Amistad (ship), 293
Anderson, Elijah, 393
Angolans, 31, 294
appeals, 150–151
Arnoult v. Deschapelles, 101
arson, 243, 302, 327
Article 180 (1838), 98
Article 181 (1838), 100, 101, 425n56
Asante, 302, 324, 335
Ayers, Edward L., 60, 295, 390, 391

Ball, Charles, 227, 263, 268
Bambara, 30
banking, slave, 224–225, 230–231
banks, 212, 230–231
Baptist, Edward E., 45, 292
Barbour, James, 159–160

bastardy, 376. *See also* births, illegitimate
beheading, 125
Beloved (Morrison), 483n85
benefit of clergy, 64, 122, 327
Berlin, Ira, 167
Berry, Daina Ramey, 187
Beti, 324
betrayal. *See* disloyalty, among slaves
Biafrans, 31
Bibb, Henry, 4, 60, 313
births, illegitimate, 260, 334, 376, 378, 380, 381
biting, 310, 311, 326
Black, Kelli M., 369, 370
black community, 385, 394. *See also* slave community
"black-on-black violence," 26–27, 390–391, 392, 395; conservative view, 385; cultural explanations for, 385–386, 393; liberal view, 385–386; as social construction, 385–386, 394; structural explanations for, 393
Blackhawk, Ned, 7
Blassingame, John W., 2, 3, 4, 290, 291
boasts, 222, 255, 297, 300–301, 312, 336
bondmen: ability to travel, 214, 244, 246–247; as church leaders, 93–94; claim female slaves, 248–250, 254, 275; compensation for, 144; condemned to public works, 146; conflicts during courtship, 236, 237, 239; conflicts over clothing, 206–207; conflicts over food, 207–208; conflicts over other consumer goods, 208, 265–266; conflicts at work, 170–171; defend bondwomen, 287, 304, 342–343; and family conflicts, 261–266, 273, 275, 276–279, 287; as murderers, 55, 56, 138, 148–149; rejected by bondwomen, 275–276; seek reunion with bondwomen, 276–277; sexually assault bondwomen, 344, 346–348, 350–356; terminate marital unions, 276; in Virginia penitentiary, 138–141

INDEX

bondwomen: ability to travel, 214; attack bondmen, 337–338, 345, 346; and child rearing, 358–362; compensation for, 144; complain to master about violent husband, 268–269; condemned to public works, 146; conflicts at work, 169; conflicts during courtship, 239, 240; conflicts over clothing, 203–206; conflicts with other bondwomen, 84, 236, 239–240, 332, 338, 339, 340, 382; during Middle Passage, 203; expectations for bondmen, 265–266; fail to report domestic abuse, 269; gender roles of, 264–265, 299; as healers or midwives, 365; and honor, 332, 333, 336, 340, 342, 343, 346, 377, 380, 382, 383; inform whites of conflict, 79; and lying, 308; as murderers, 54–55, 56, 138, 148–149, 152, 337; as peacemakers, 75; plot to kill slave driver, 179; and pregnancy, 365–367; punishment of, 84–85, 125, 338–340; refuse to reconcile with estranged husbands, 277–279; reliance on enslaved men, 75; reputation for fighting, 84; significance attached to dancing, 304; as subjects of lies, 308–309; and temporary insanity, 162–163; terminate marital unions, 275; valuations, 134; and violence, 332, 337–338, 340, 344, 346; and violence against infants and children, 356, 363–383; and violence in defense of family, 251–252, 258–259, 309; in Virginia penitentiary, 138–141; and work, 366, 369
Bowen, James, 30
boxing, 166, 167, 186–187, 291
branding, 64, 109, 110, 121, 122–123, 126, 127, 151, 325–328, 329
Bremer, Fredrika, 325
Brevard, Keziah, 74, 169, 176, 268
bribes, 78
Brome (ship), 30
Brooke, Robert, 351
Brown, Henry "Box," 211, 214, 246, 274, 291
Brown, John (slave), 214
Brown, Kathleen M., 319
Brown, William Wells, 23
Bruce, H. C., 380
Buckingham, James Silk, 215, 222

burning to death, 126, 127, 361
Butterworth, William, 30
Bynum, Victoria E., 332, 344
Byrd, William, 260

Camp, Stephanie M. H., 19, 342, 372
Campbell, James A., 144
Campbell, John, 212
candy pull, 384
Carter, Landon, 260
Cartwright, Samuel A., 296
cash, 175, 181, 200, 208–210, 212, 213, 216, 217, 219, 220, 221, 222, 224, 227–228, 231, 235, 307, 389
castration, 324
Celtic culture, 405n2
chains, 86
challenges, 296, 297, 300
character, 160–162, 338, 378, 379, 380
Charleston District, S.C., 80, 107, 117, 147, 156, 158, 234, 266
Charriba, 30
Chicago, Ill., 387
child abuse, 261–262, 332, 333
child murder. *See* infanticide
children: attack parents, 362; disciplining, 333, 356–358, 360–363; fighting among, 168, 185–186, 311, 359–360; at mealtime, 359–360; as victims of violence, 356, 357, 358; as witnesses to violence, 356; work of, 358
Christianity, 33
Christmas, 77, 82, 86, 175, 189, 191, 194, 195, 219, 301, 304, 342
church records, 16–17, 35–36, 46
churches: condemn adultery among slaves, 253; condemn leisurely pursuits, 197–198; and enslaved manhood, 316, 319; growth of evangelical, 87–88, 89–90; and honor, 317–319, 334; and property disputes among slaves, 220–221; receiving enslaved members, 88; role in economic matters, 230–231, 233; role in slave discipline, 71, 87, 90–97, 108, 361, 362; segregation within, 88–89; and slave marriages, 270–271, 273–274; and slave membership, 95; and slave violence, 318–319, 336–337;

INDEX

and slaves' sexual offenses, 356; as social service institutions, 88; and white violence, 316–318
Cincinnati, Ohio, 387
civil law, 18, 72, 97–105, 108, 109, 110
civil rights movement, 386
Civil War, 293
Clarke, James W., 386, 387, 390, 391, 392
Clarke, Lewis, 214, 290, 293, 374
clergyable offenses. *See* benefit of clergy
clothing, 203–207, 213, 217, 219, 265, 276. *See also* coats; hats; stripping to fight
coats, 287, 311, 312
Cobb, Thomas R. R., 152
Code Noir, 125
code of the street, 393
Cole, Stephanie, 268
colored committees, 91–94, 319, 323, 356
colored conferences. *See* colored committees
common law, 102–105, 107, 116, 355
compensation: amount of, 131–132, 133–134, 352, 353; avoided through branding, 327; for convicted slaves, 110, 111, 121, 129, 130–134, 135, 141, 144, 155–156, 158, 340; for deceased slaves, in service to the state, 184; designed to prevent evasion of the law, 130; exceptions to policies, 133; sources of revenue for, 130; unavailable in Georgia, 133. *See also* valuations
confessions: admissibility of, 151–155; involuntary, 155; partial, 154–155; voluntary, 152–154
confinement, 86
conjurors, slave, 5, 64, 66, 87, 176, 239, 255, 298
consent, 344, 347, 351–352, 382; age of, 352–353
conservatives, 385
conspiracy to murder. *See* murder plot
conviction rates, 118–120, 121
corn shuckings, 161, 164, 187–188, 189, 198, 208, 303, 304
co-sleeping, 369
court records, 9–12, 14, 15–16, 19, 36, 53, 97, 336
Courts of Magistrates and Freeholders (South Carolina), 113

Courts of Oyer and Terminer (Virginia), 113, 129, 351; invite gubernatorial intervention, 159, 351, 352
courtship, 236, 237, 238–243, 291
craftsmen, slave, 5
Creole (ship), 293
creolization, 32, 43
criminal law, 97, 109–165
cross-plantation marriage. *See* abroad marriage
curses, 296, 300, 301

dancing, 197–198, 204, 209, 240–241, 251, 291, 297, 304, 342–343. *See also* frolics
dares. *See* challenges
death of master, 54
death penalty, 160
debts: among slaves, 203, 224–231; mediated by churches, 230–231, 233; and violence, 226–230
decapitation, 125
Desch Obi, T. J., 294
Deyle, Steven, 370
discrimination, racial, 393
disloyalty, among slaves, 38, 39, 40, 41, 66, 78, 181–183, 199
disorderly houses, 198
distribution of wealth. *See* inequality, economic
divorce, 272–274, 276
dogs, 85, 153, 181, 182–183, 341
domestic abuse, 237, 259–271; of children, 261–262, 332, 333, 357–358; as compensation for male powerlessness, 261; encouraged by plantation management decisions, 269–270; upon enslaved husbands, 264; upon enslaved wives, 259–260, 262–266, 269–270, 273; to establish parental supremacy, 261; and gender roles, 264–266; justified by men, 262; and masters' responses, 266–270; post–Civil War, 389; and power dynamics in enslaved households, 263–264; and separations, 275–277; tolerated in nineteenth century, 268; witnessed by children, 260–261
domestic servants, 4, 5, 168–169
domestic slave trade, 8, 18, 21, 23, 33–35, 214, 236, 241, 289, 343, 374–375, 377

INDEX

domesticity, 264–265
Douglass, Frederick, 243, 292–293, 325
drinking, 42, 46, 49, 60, 86, 96, 104, 151, 162, 187–192, 195, 196, 197, 198, 200, 217–218, 291, 303, 384; and passion, 163, 179, 188
drivers, slave, 4–5, 39, 74–75, 169; resistance to, 178–179; sexual assaults committed by, 348–349; slaves' resentment of, 177–178
drowning, 67, 381
Du Bois, W. E. B., 387
Dudley, Edward B., 162
duels, 313, 314–315, 317, 331
dysfunction, 385

ear biting, 310, 311
ear cropping, 125, 126, 241, 324, 340
East St. Louis, Ill., 387
Eastern Lunatic Asylum, 249
eating, 359–360
education, 391, 393
Edwards, Laura F., 332
Eglet (ship), 30
Elder, Robert, 317
Elkins, Stanley M., 2, 289, 290, 291
Eltis, David, 31
emancipation, 387, 388
emotions, 80–81, 199, 213, 236, 237, 292, 370, 382. *See also* passion
Equiano, Olaudah, 21, 30
ethnic differences, 28, 29, 30, 43
evidence, standard of, 281
Ewing v. Thompson, 102, 103
execution, 127, 128–129, 130, 133, 137, 138, 141, 148, 151, 153, 159. *See also* hanging
eye gouging, 292, 310, 311

factories, 170, 175
Falconbridge, Alexander, 29, 30–31, 203
family, black: allegedly dysfunctional, 385; economics of, 233–235; historiography of, 237–238, 259; slave, 6, 18, 19, 20, 23, 33, 36, 42, 292; and violence, 236, 237, 239–242, 245–246, 248–252, 253–279, 285–286, 298, 389, 390
Fante, 30
fatherhood, 266, 393
feigning illness, 169

femininity, enslaved, 19, 204, 332, 333, 382, 383
Ferracuti, Franco, 390, 391, 392
fiddlers, 191, 197, 209
field slaves, 4, 168–169
fighting: African styles of, 294, 310, 313; arranged by master, 167, 186, 187, 198, 310, 311, 313; to attract bondwomen, 185–186; by children, 185–186; foot, 294; as offense in church records, 46–47, 96, 316–318; refusal to engage in, 293; southern styles of, 293, 311; as sport, 167, 185–186, 187, 190; stick, 294, 313. *See also* violence
filicide, 365. *See also* infanticide
Fink, Mike, 300
Fischer, Kirsten, 370
Fitzhugh, George, 238
Fitzpatrick, Benjamin, 132
Flanigan, Daniel J., 52, 324
flotation test, 368
Floyd, John, 160
food, 207–208, 216, 218, 220–221, 223, 299, 307. *See also* eating
foot races, 186, 291
forgery, 109
fornication, 46, 96
Fox-Genovese, Elizabeth, 245, 254, 259, 263
Fraser, Rebecca, 16
Frazier, E. Franklin, 387
free blacks, 20, 127, 137, 157, 170, 194, 196, 206, 207, 211–212, 229, 254, 257, 307, 341, 343, 345, 352; in penitentiary, 141
Freedmen's Bureau, 259, 387, 389, 392
freedom, as reward, 41
frequency, of violence. *See* prevalence, of violence
Freud, Sigmund, 292
frolics, 161, 187, 190, 191–193, 198, 209, 240–241
frontier, 405n2
Funj, 324

Gabriel conspiracy, 23, 41, 135, 326
Gaillardet v. Demaries, 98
gambling, 18, 49, 291, 389; among enslaved men, 193–197; condemned by churches, 197; on slave fights, 186–187, 198

INDEX

Garner, Margaret, 372, 377–378, 483n85
Garnet, Henry Highland, 291
gender: 19; roles, 234, 263, 264–266, 285, 342
Genovese, Eugene D., 18, 22, 23, 34, 42, 47, 60, 168, 211, 252, 290, 349, 375, 406n3
ghosts, 346, 384–385. *See also* supernatural
gifts, 265–266
Giles, William B., 382
giving the lie, 287, 305–309, 334
Glover, Lorri, 289
Gold Coast, 30
governors' papers, 10
Gray White, Deborah, 19, 237, 240, 340, 356
Greenberg, Kenneth, 305
guns, 67–69, 72, 79, 104–105, 112, 118, 153, 173, 179, 182, 185, 207, 217, 255, 277, 296–297, 301, 314, 315, 331, 338, 343, 388, 390, 392, 393, 418n62
Gutman, Herbert G., 237, 290

Hahn, Steven, 74
Hammond, James Henry, 22, 82, 132, 253, 272
hanging, 85, 110, 111, 121, 125, 126, 127–128, 130, 134, 135, 136, 338, 340. *See also* execution
hard labor, as punishment, 50, 110, 144–146, 339, 340; in Louisiana, 146, 148–149, 171; in Virginia, 146, 381
Harlem, 390
Harris, William, 355
hats, 196–197, 206–207, 232, 233, 315
hauntings, 384–385
Hayne, Robert Y., 159
head butting, 178, 294, 310, 311, 313
healers, slave, 5
Hilliard, Kathleen, 202, 210, 215
Hindus, Michael Stephen, 349
Hine, Darlene Clark, 292
hired slaves: as assassins, 175–176; earn money, 201; work for other slaves, 174–176, 196; work for whites, 170–172, 174, 176, 195, 198
Historic Natchez Foundation, 13
homicide, 9–10; degrees of, 115–116, 136, 137, 160; during Reconstruction, 387; involving bondwomen, 337; involving slaves belonging to different owners, 52–53, 72, 110; involving slaves belonging to same owner, 54, 65, 107, 110–111, 112, 115, 170, 337; modern statistics, 386; rates of, 43–46, 49, 337, 386, 387–389, 392, 413–414n27; by region in Virginia, 61–63; slave-slave, as a legal offense, 115
honor, 19, 20, 21, 36, 42, 72, 287, 310, 311, 316, 328, 329–330, 389–390, 391, 405n2; and accusations of theft, 215, 216; in Africa, 294, 302, 312, 335; bondmen defend bondwomen's, 342–343; and bondwomen, 332, 333, 336, 340, 342, 343, 346, 377, 380, 382, 383; and church, 317–319, 334; codes of southern whites and blacks similar, 295, 304, 312, 313, 330; economic, 230; and enslaved men, 288–289, 292, 297, 304, 315; and family, 285, 304; historiography of, 288, 293–294; horizontal, 288, 330; and lying, 305–309; sexual, 333, 334, 343, 344, 346–347, 356, 378, 380, 382, 383; vertical, 288; and violence, 288, 289, 292, 294, 295–296, 297, 302, 305, 312, 313, 314, 330, 334, 336, 342, 346–347; white notions of, 288, 289, 333–334, 335; and white women, 333–334, 378, 380, 382
house raising, 187
Hudson, Larry E., Jr., 209
humiliation. *See* shaming punishments
humor, 315–316. *See also* southwestern humor
Hundley, Daniel R., 66, 196, 249
hunting, 207
hydrostatic test, 368

Ibrahima, Abd-al-Rahman, 290
identity, African American, 32, 38, 43, 244; enslaved female, 335–336, 342–343, 375, 382. *See also* femininity, enslaved; masculinity, enslaved
Igbo, 22, 29, 294, 324
Iliffe, John, 21, 319, 335
imprisonment, 86, 110, 125, 158
incarceration. *See* imprisonment
incest, 270–271, 459–460n84
industrial slaves, 201, 212
inequality, economic, 202, 203, 209–210, 235, 385, 393

INDEX

infanticide, 20, 23, 52, 53, 56, 67, 110, 111, 134, 137, 138, 141, 152, 156, 163, 333, 337, 338, 339, 356, 363–383, 481n67, 483n85; motivations for, 370–381; punishments for, 381–382; as resistance, 372–375, 483n86; and white women, 375–376
infidelity. *See* adultery
inner city, 385, 393
insults, 164, 177, 294, 297, 301–305, 312, 313, 333, 340, 342, 343. *See also* giving the lie
Irish, 43, 44, 387
irons, 126, 325, 329
Islam, 319
Italians, 387

Jackson, Jesse, 386
Jacobs, Harriet, 344
jail. *See* penitentiary
jealousy, 246, 247, 249, 250–251, 254, 284, 285; among bondwomen, 251–252, 253, 340
Jefferson, Thomas, 51, 86–87, 120, 135
Jenkins, Earnestine, 292
Jezebel, 334, 342, 344, 350, 352, 376, 381
Johnson, Joseph, 109
Johnson, Michael P., 5, 168, 369
Johnson, Walter, 7, 8, 208
Jollofes, 30
Jones, Charles Colcock, 43, 60, 74, 169, 202, 211, 213, 240, 253, 270, 341, 358, 364, 376
Jourdan v. Patton, 99
jurors, 114–115; questionable, 151
jury trials, 113–115

Kaye, Anthony E., 6, 7, 52
Kemble, Fanny, 176, 244
keys, 161, 200, 201, 213, 273
kidnapping, 29, 373
King, Wilma, 311, 345, 456–457
Kolchin, Peter, 3, 5, 7, 247
Kuba, 302

Lady Mary (ship), 30
land ownership, 391
language, 46, 161, 172, 202, 267, 271, 293, 296, 297–298, 300–309, 333, 336, 340–342. *See also* boasts; challenges; curses; giving the lie; insults; threats

lashes. *See* whipping
Latin America, 288
leg wrapping, 294
leisure, 19, 36, 46, 167, 168, 185–198
Leland, John, 271–272, 273
liability, civil, for slave violence, 98–105
liberals, 385
Lichtenstein, Alex, 211
liquor, 188–189, 198, 232, 275, 301. *See also* drinking
locks, 213
logrolling, 187, 306
Louisiana, as civil law state, 98–102, 103
Louisiana Civil Code (1838), 98, 100
Louisiana Purchase, 86
loyalty. *See* disloyalty, among slaves
Lumpkin, Joseph Henry, 38, 111, 281
lung test, 368
Lussana, Sergio, 187
Lyell, Charles, 43, 213
lying, 46, 96, 152, 220, 235, 305, 333, 340, 341–342, 361. *See also* giving the lie

Maille v. Blas, 99, 102
manhood, 254, 261, 262, 263, 288, 289, 291–293, 296, 300–301, 302, 304, 311, 312, 314, 316, 318, 320, 326, 329–330, 331, 390, 391, 392, 393
mania a potu, 162
manslaughter, 116, 120–122, 123, 125, 137, 147, 148, 149, 151, 158, 164, 282, 283, 285, 327, 328, 373
marriage, 4, 8, 236, 237, 238, 241, 243, 250, 252, 269–270, 280, 285, 290, 376; and evangelical churches, 270–271, 273–274; involuntary termination of, 274; and reconciliation, 276–278; voluntary termination of, 272–274, 275–276. *See also* abroad marriage; divorce
Martineau, Harriet, 22, 251
masculinity: in Africa, 290, 294; enslaved, 19, 68, 290–293, 294, 296, 297, 301, 312, 318–321, 329–330, 331, 332, 343; postwar, 391; white, 317–318, 354
masters: appeal court decisions, 150–164; arrange fights among slaves, 167, 186–187, 198, 310, 311, 313; belief in slaves' loyalty,

184; blamed for failing to prevent slave crimes, 132–133; charged with killing slaves, 117–118; criticize slaves' parenting, 357–358; curb slaves' violence, 71, 80, 186; dependence upon slaves, 71; and domestic abuse, 266–270; hostility toward violence among slaves, 72–74; liability for slaves' misconduct, 98–105; order slave crimes, 101, 104–105, 117–118, 133, 185; order slaves to capture other slaves, 180–184; order slaves to punish other slaves, 179–180; petition for compensation, 105–107; presence deters conflict, 79–80, punish slaves, 82–87, 336; reactions to slave-slave homicides, 110–113; reluctance to use court system, 111–112, 130

Mather, Cotton, 33
McDonnell, Lawrence T., 201
McNair, Glenn M., 18, 42, 44, 68, 120, 127, 349
Merrick, E. T., 102
Miami, Fla., 387
Middle Passage, 18, 21, 29–31, 32, 203, 244, 264, 294
miscarriages, 365–366, 368
mobility, 214, 244, 246–247, 309, 337, 340
money. *See* cash
Monkkonen, Eric H., 44
monogamy, 244, 278
monomania, 162, 282
Morehead, Charles S., 158
Morgan, Jennifer L., 372
Morgan, Philip D., 50, 167, 201
Morris, Christopher, 6, 7, 237
Morris, Thomas D., 98
Morrison, Toni, 483n85
mothers, 220, 336; alleged negligence, 368–369; exhausted, 369; object to child's choice of spouse, 241–242; and parental discipline, 356, 358, 360–361. *See also* infanticide; smothering
Moynihan, Daniel Patrick, 237
Moynihan Report, 237, 386
multiple victims, 55
murder. *See* homicide; murder plot; murder-suicide
murder plot, 54–55

murder-suicide, 24–25, 371
music, 197
mutilation, as punishment, 125–126, 133, 324. *See also* branding; ear cropping; shaming punishments

Nash, A. E. Kier, 150
Natchez, Miss., 14, 66, 67, 170, 210, 265, 300
The Negro Family: The Case for National Action (Moynihan), 237
neighborhoods, slave, 6, 33, 52–53, 214, 221, 226, 408n16
neonaticide, 365. *See also* infanticide
New Orleans, La., 14, 35, 61, 64, 69, 76, 99–100, 116, 119, 120, 126, 137, 149, 171, 172, 210, 227, 254, 331
New York City, 44, 387
North, the, 387, 392
Northup, Solomon, 216, 240, 244, 272
numeracy, 210
nurseries, 358

occupations: as factor in valuations, 134; as source of division, 4–5, 168–169, 340, 407n9
Okonkwo, 294
Olmsted, Frederick Law, 213, 373
Olwell, Robert, 47
ostracism, 35, 78, 183, 221, 329
"outlandish" slaves, 32
overturned convictions, 151

Painter, Nell Irvin, 237
pardons, 157–158, 162, 164, 339, 345, 381
parents: and discipline of children, 333, 356–358, 360–363, 382; modern, 393; objections during courtship, 241–242, 287; other slaves acting as, 360, 362
parricide, 126
passion, 163–164, 202, 238, 263, 281, 283, 285, 292, 308, 343, 354, 389
paternalism, 73–74, 152, 357–358
patrol, 315
Patterson, Orlando, 288
pedophilia, 354, 355
penitentiary: in Arkansas, 148; in Louisiana, 17, 146, 148–150, 158, 171; in Maryland, 148; in Virginia, 109, 138–144, 148

INDEX

Penningroth, Dylan C., 6, 7, 26, 175, 201, 202, 225, 226, 389
personal responsibility, 385
petitions, 17, 105–107, 336; based on age, 338; based on character of the convicted, 160–162, 284, 285, 338, 353–354; on behalf of enslaved cuckolds, 284–285; for commutations of sentence, 157–159, 284, 351, 371; for compensation, 155–157; and passion, 163–164; pleading temporary insanity, 162–163; to remedy legal error, 159–160
pets, 36–37
Philadelphia, Pa., 44, 387, 392
Phillips, Ulrich B., 51–52
physicians, 73, 162, 353, 367–368, 377
Piedmont Virginia, 15, 16, 61, 62, 63, 220
Pitt-Rivers, Julian, 333
playing the dozens, 303. *See also* insults
poisoning, 39, 40, 41, 54, 55, 64–66, 87, 114, 120, 125, 127, 134, 176, 179, 208, 215, 266, 298, 337–338, 341, 342, 366, 375
"Poke-easy," 293
policing, 391, 393
Polk, James Knox, 369
polygamy, 244
poor whites, 188, 192, 198, 211, 212, 292, 310, 311, 312, 313, 330, 344, 375–376; postwar, 392
popularity, 37
postpartum depression, 371
preachers, slave, 5, 319–323
pregnancy, 365–367, 369, 370, 372, 377
premarital sex, 335
prevalence, of violence, 41–52, 60, 69–70
pride, 343; in goods, 202, 205; in work, 173–174, 198
prison. *See* penitentiary
privacy, lack of, 212, 240, 300, 370
procedural fairness, 150–151
promiscuity, 243, 244, 253
property, 19, 20, 36, 42; insecurity of, 212–213, 216; and lying, 307; ownership of, 201, 202, 203, 226; slaves' conflicts over, 203–211; stolen and displayed, 219. *See also* theft
public works, labor on. *See* hard labor, as punishment

puerperal mania, 371
punishments, by master, 82–87, 336. *See also* shaming punishments

Race and Slavery Petitions Project, 17
racism, 385
railroads, 170, 171, 172, 196
rape, 20, 293, 324, 343, 344–356, 377, 382; and church disciplinary committees, 356; criminalization of, 355–356; of free women of color, 352; and the law, 349–352, 354–356; and slave drivers, 348–349; of underage girls, 352–355
Reagan, Ronald, 385
Reconstruction, 387–389, 391, 392, 394; in Louisiana, 387, 389; in Texas, 387, 388, 389
Redeemer governments, 392
Rediker, Marcus, 37
religion, 33
remorse, 80
reputation. *See* honor
resistance to slavery, 372
revolts, 41
Richmond, Va., 14, 34, 45, 60, 61, 62, 109, 116, 120, 122, 135, 136, 138, 139, 140, 141, 142, 144, 156, 159, 161, 170, 175, 210, 222, 233, 254, 276, 296, 325, 340, 364, 367, 368, 379, 381, 401, 403, 404
Roth, Randolph, 43, 46, 49, 50, 51, 56
rough-and-tumble brawls, 292, 310, 311, 312, 313, 392, 470n51
Royall, Anne Newport, 60
Ruffin, Thomas, 45, 152, 280, 288
runaways, 5, 6, 40, 81–82, 86, 118, 153, 155, 216; tracked by other slaves, 180–183

Sabbath, 60, 186, 190, 193, 201, 223
sale and transportation, 50, 109, 110, 111, 129, 135–138, 144, 147, 148, 156, 159, 160, 161, 163, 340, 344, 351, 352, 353, 371, 381, 382; of convicted bondwomen, 339, 346; economics of, 141–143; foreign countries' objections to, 137–138; shortage of recipient nations, 146
Sambo, 2–3, 289
satisfaction: and church, 317, 318; and honor, 313, 314

INDEX

Saxon, Elizabeth Lyle, 381
scars, 311
Schafer, Judith Kelleher, 60
Schwarz, Philip J., 18, 50, 52, 55, 56, 64, 66, 118, 127, 144, 324
Schweninger, Loren, 17
scratching, 311, 336
Seaborn and Jim v. State, 115
Seabrook, Whitemarsh B., 147
seconds, 313, 314
self-defense, 118, 154, 158, 264, 317, 345, 346, 390
self-sabotage, 20–21, 325
Senegambians, 31
separations: involuntary, 274; publicized, 276; voluntary, 272–274, 275–276
sex ratios, 3, 260
shackles. *See* irons
shame, 21, 260, 289, 329, 334, 335, 375–378, 380–381, 382
shaming punishments, 324–329. *See also* branding; castration
size, physical, 37–38
skilled slaves, 201
skin color, 5
slave community, 1, 3, 4, 5, 6, 7, 9, 20, 22, 25, 26, 33, 34, 47, 50, 52, 70, 72, 77, 107, 165, 167, 168, 170, 187, 202, 203, 208, 214, 221, 224, 226, 235, 236, 245, 247, 292, 329, 330, 333, 343, 345, 362, 380, 394, 395, 408n16
slave economy, 6, 167, 175, 227, 291; historiography of, 201–202, 208; as source of division, 202, 203, 231–235, 265
slave traders, 148; state dealings with, 141–143
slaves: aware of masters' disdain for fighting, 74; as consumers, 232–233; defend the master's interests, 184–185; help apprehend runaways, 180–183; inform whites of slaves' conflicts, 78–79, 112, 116; as market commodities, 73, 121, 245; punish slaves by master's order, 179–180; reactions to violence, 80–82, 166; reluctance to involve whites in conflicts, 77–78, 221, 233, 269; repay debts, 225–226; resist punishing other slaves, 180; resolve own disagreements, 72, 74–76, 107

Smith, William, 308
smothering, 369–370, 371, 373. *See also* infanticide
smuggling, 138
snitching, 77–78, 180, 219
"Snopesian crime," 302
solitary confinement, 159
southwestern humor, 300. *See also* humor
Spanish Florida, 137, 138
Spanish Louisiana, 179, 217
Stampp, Kenneth M., 41
State v. Dick, 115
State v. Samuel, 280
status, 4, 340
stealing. *See* theft
Sterling v. Luckett, 100
Stevenson, Brenda E., 6, 7, 237, 245, 252, 259
stocks, 86, 113, 117
strangulation. *See* suffocation
stripping to fight, 311–312
sublimation of instinct, 292
suffocation, 67, 366, 368, 370. *See also* smothering
stillbirths, 365, 367–368
subculture of violence theory, 390–393
sudden infant death syndrome (SIDS), 369
suicide, 20, 21–24, 163, 266, 267, 371, 380, 483n86
Sunday. *See* Sabbath
supernatural, 22, 221, 384
swearing, 167

taxes, 130–131
technicalities, legal, 150–151
Telfair, Alexander, 83
temporary insanity, 162–163
testimony, legal, of spouses, 279–281
Thacher, Joseph, 104
theft, 18, 46, 48, 96, 105, 175, 185, 200, 201, 203, 204, 210, 211–224, 265, 302, 305, 323, 328; denounced by slaves, 214, 216; detected by slaves, 221; encouraged by masters, 220; enslaved victims inform whites, 218–219; and masculinity, 291; as motive for violence, 215–218; punished by slaves, 221–222; to repay debts, 225

threats, 166, 182, 228, 232, 244, 250, 266, 278, 282, 283, 297, 298, 306, 312, 319, 336, 342, 347, 361
Tidewater Virginia, 61, 62, 63, 363
timing, of slave-slave homicides: by decade, 57–58; by month, 58–60; by year, 57–58
title, to slaves, 158
tobacco, 59
tools, 172
towns, 60–61
transatlantic slave trade, 21, 22, 29–31, 33, 37, 294
troughs, 359–360
truants, 169
trust. *See* disloyalty, among slaves
Turner, Nat, 293, 320–321, 322
Tyler, John, 352, 382

underclass, 385
unemployment, 393
urban slaves, 5, 14

valuations, 133–135, 145, 157, 353
values, 385–386, 390, 393
Vandal, Gilles, 387, 389
venereal disease, 256
violence: black against white, 38–39, 40, 47, 48, 49, 54, 70; and bondwomen, 332, 337–338, 340; as category of analysis, 7, 8, 19, 25; and church discipline, 316–319, 336–337; as consequence of infidelity, 236, 242, 253–259; cross-plantation, 9; and debts, 226–230; to defend enslaved women, 236, 245–246, 247, 248–251; during courtship, 236, 239–241, 242, 243, 248; to enforce claims to property, 203, 204–211, 213, 215, 222–224; and family, 236, 239–242, 245–246, 248–252, 253–259, 259–279, 285–286, 298; historiography of, 1–2; and honor, 288, 289, 292, 294, 295–296, 297, 302, 305, 312, 313, 314, 330, 331, 334; and leisure, 167, 168, 185–198; masters' punishment of, 74; to prevent theft, 216; as revenge, 77; and slave economy, 231–235; as source of division among slaves, 76–77; white against black, 49–50; and work, 167–179
"Virginia style," 311

Walker, David, 291
Ware, Charles Preston, 169, 204, 209
Ware, Harriet, 340, 341
weapons, 18, 63–69, 301, 309, 330–331, 338; as indicative of intent, 116–117
West, Emily, 16, 237, 246, 247
West, Stephen A., 392
West Indies, 137
Weston, P. C., 84
whipping, 64, 72, 80, 83, 85, 86, 109, 110, 112, 117, 118, 121–122, 123–125, 126, 127, 133, 137, 146, 147, 149, 151, 153, 159, 180, 218, 219, 231, 253, 269, 289, 325, 328, 329, 336, 357, 364, 373; by slave driver, 177–178
William (a slave) v. the State, 116
"Williams Negroes," 138
Willis, John C., 288, 295
Wills, Gregory A., 316, 318
wills, 203
Wilson, David, 385
Wise, Henry A., 141, 144, 156, 354, 382
Wolfgang, Marvin E., 390, 391, 392
Wood, Betty, 16
words. *See* language
work, 4–5, 19, 36, 167, 168–179; as cause of disputes, 172–175; distinctions among slaves based on, 174, 176–179; missed due to injury, 73; pride in, 173–174, 198; as setting for disputes, 169–170, 307
wrestling, 167, 186, 187, 291, 294, 296, 310, 311, 313, 392
Wright v. Weatherly, 102, 103
Wyatt-Brown, Bertram, 5, 6, 288

Yoruba, 335

www.ingramcontent.com/pod-product-compliance
Lightning Source LLC
Chambersburg PA
CBHW021414300426
44114CB00010B/484